A Companion to Public History

BLACKWELL COMPANIONS TO WORLD HISTORY

This series provides sophisticated and authoritative overviews of the scholarship that has shaped our current understanding of the world's past. Each volume comprises between 25 and 40 essays written by individual scholars within their area of specialization. The aim of each contribution is to synthesize the current state of scholarship from a variety of historical perspectives and to provide a statement on where the field is heading. The essays are written in a clear, provocative, and lively manner, designed for an international audience of scholars, students, and general readers.

The *Blackwell Companions to World History* is a cornerstone of the overarching *Companions to History* series, covering British, American, and European History

A COMPANION
TO PUBLIC HISTORY

Edited By

David Dean

WILEY Blackwell

Registered Office
John Wiley & Sons, Inc., 111 River Street, Hoboken, NJ 07030, USA
John Wiley & Sons Ltd, The Atrium, Southern Gate, Chichester, West Sussex, PO19 8SQ, UK

Editorial Office
350 Main Street, Malden, MA 02148-5020, USA

For details of our global editorial offices, customer services, and more information about Wiley products, visit us at www.wiley.com.

Wiley also publishes its books in a variety of electronic formats and by print-on-demand. Some content that appears in standard print versions of this book may not be available in other formats.

Library of Congress Cataloging-in-Publication Data
Names: Dean, D. M. (David M.), editor.
Title: A companion to public history / edited by David Dean.
Description: 1 edition. | Hoboken, NJ : Wiley, 2018. |
  Includes bibliographical references and index. |
Identifiers: LCCN 2017041634 (print) | LCCN 2017049813 (ebook) |
  ISBN 9781118508916 (pdf) | ISBN 9781118508923 (epub) |
  ISBN 9781118508947 (cloth)
Subjects: LCSH: Public history.
Classification: LCC D16.163 (ebook) | LCC D16.163 .C65 2018 (print) | DDC 900–dc23
LC record available at https://lccn.loc.gov/2017041634

Cover Image: © Photo Amsterdam Museum, Monique Vermeulen, Orphanage cabinets
Cover Design: Wiley

Set in 10/12pt Galliard by SPi Global, Pondicherry, India

Printed in Great Britain by TJ International Ltd, Padstow, Cornwall

10 9 8 7 6 5 4 3 2 1

For all my public history students: past, present, and future

Contents

List of Illustrations

Notes on Contributors

George H.O. Abungu is a former Associate Professor of Heritage Studies at the University of Mauritius. He is the founder of Okello Abungu Heritage Consultants, Nairobi, and from 1999 to 2002 was Director-General of the National Museums of Kenya. He has served as Vice-President and Executive Committee member of the International Council of Museums. In 2012, George was made a Knight of the French Ordre des Arts et des Lettres.

Vanessa Agnew researches and teaches on the cultural history of music, travel, reenactment, the history of science, genocide, and exile and refugee studies in the Department of Anglophone Studies, University of Duisburg-Essen, Germany. Her *Enlightenment Orpheus: The Power of Music in Other Worlds* (Oxford UP, 2008) won the Oscar Kenshur Prize for Eighteenth-Century Studies and the American Musicological Society's Lewis Lockwood Award. She co-edited *Settler and Creole Reenactment* (with Jonathan Lamb, Palgrave, 2010), special issues of *Rethinking History* 11 (2007) and *Criticism* 46 (2004), and book series *Historical Reenactment* (Palgrave) and *Music in Society and Culture* (Boydell and Brewer). She is working on a book project, *Right to Arrive,* which applies reenactment theory to Kant's rights of the stranger in order to reframe discussions around hospitality, the mediating role of culture, and the current refugee crisis.

Ana Lucia Araujo is a cultural historian and a Professor of History at the historically black Howard University in Washington, D.C. Her work explores the history and the memory of the Atlantic slave trade and slavery and their social and cultural legacies. She is particularly interested in the public memory, heritage, and visual culture of slavery. Over the last years, she authored the books *Brazil Through French Eyes: A Nineteenth-Century Artist in the Tropics* (2015), *Shadows of the Slave Past: Memory, Heritage and Slavery* (2014), *Public Memory of Slavery: Victims and Perpetrators in the South Atlantic* (2010), and *Romantisme tropical: l'aventure illustrée d'un peintre français au Brésil* (2008). She also edited a number of books: *African Heritage and Memories of Slavery in Brazil and the South Atlantic World* (2015), *Politics of Memory: Making Slavery Visible in the Public Space* (2012), *Paths of the Atlantic Slave Trade: Interactions, Identities* (2011), and *Living History: Encountering the Memory of the Heirs of Slavery* (2009). Her newest book is titled *Reparations for Slavery and the Slave Trade: A Transnational and Comparative History* (2017).

Michael Belgrave is a historian and foundation member of Massey University's Albany campus in Auckland, New Zealand. He was previously research manager of the Waitangi Tribunal and has continued to maintain a strong interest in Treaty of Waitangi research and settlements, providing substantial research reports into a wide number of the Waitangi Tribunal's district inquiries. More recently, he has been heavily involved in negotiating the historical aspects of treaty settlements with a number of iwi (Māori tribes). He has published widely on treaty and Māori history, including being lead editor of *Waitangi Revisited: Perspectives on the Treaty of Waitangi* (Oxford University Press). His *Historical Frictions: Maori Claims and Reinvented Histories* explores the way that generation after generation Māori claims have been articulated in the courts and in settlements relying on historical narratives which have changed significantly to reflect different times. His most recent book, *Dancing with the King* (Auckland University Press), a history of peace-making following the Waikato War of 1863–1864 won the 2018 Ernest Scott Prize. He has been an advisor to a number of government departments as well as to numerous iwi.

Hamad M. Bin Seray is Associate Professor in the Department of History and Archaeology, Faculty of Humanities and Social Sciences at the United Arabic Emirates University. He took his undergraduate degree in history at UAEU and his MA and PhD at the University of Manchester. He is the author of more than seventy-six publications including over twenty articles in refereed journals and eighteen books. These include *Aramaic in the Gulf, The Arabian Gulf in Syriac Sources, Non-Arabic Races in Pre-Islamic Makkah and their Religious, Commercial and Social Roles,* and *Civil Relations between the Arabian Gulf Region and the Indian Subcontinent and South East Asia from the 3rd Century BC to the 7th Century AD.*

Helin Burkay is a Post-Doctoral Fellow at the Rachel Carson Center for Environment and Society at the Ludwig-Maximilians-Universität München in Munich, Germany. She holds a PhD in Sociology from Carleton University and a BA in Political Science from Bogazici University. Her research is on the cultural politics of development, land, and food in the Middle East. She is currently working on two projects, one on the ethnic culinary heritage and politics of memory in Turkey and the other on the ethics of environmental research.

Thomas Cauvin is Assistant Professor of History at Colorado State University in the United States and teaches Public History, Museum Studies, and Digital History. Born in France, Cauvin received his PhD (open-access online) at the European University Institute in Italy, where he focused on the comparative study of museums and memories in Ireland and Northern Ireland (2012). President of the *International Federation for Public History,* his research focuses on public history, museums, memories, and the public uses of the past. He has published the first single-authored textbook on Public History in North America and several articles – in English, French, Italian, and Spanish – on the rise and internationalization of public history. As a public historian, he has worked with local communities for the creation of traveling exhibits, online crowd-sourcing projects, and historic preservation of French heritage in Louisiana.

Chia-Li Chen is Professor and Head of the Graduate Institute of Museum Studies at the Taipei National University of the Arts. She received her PhD in Museum Studies at the University of Leicester. She is the author of *Museums and Cultural Identities* (VDM Verlag) and *From Margin to Representation* (National Taiwan University Press) and has published several English papers in journals and books such as *Re-presenting Disability, Displaced*

Heritage and *Museum Revolutions*. Her research interests focus on three main areas: museums and contemporary social issues, especially the engagement and representation of the disabled and minority groups; museum, traumatic memories and human rights education; and the application of music in literature museums.

Indira Chowdhury is Founder-Director of the Centre for Public History at the Srishti Institute of Art, Design, and Technology, Bengaluru, India. Formerly professor of English at Jadavpur University, Kolkata, she is also the founder of Archival Resources for Contemporary History (ARCH), Bengaluru, now known as ARCH@Srishti. She has a PhD in history from the School of Oriental and African Studies, London, and her book *The Frail Hero and Virile History* won the Tagore prize in 2001. In 2010, she published *A Masterful Spirit: Homi Bhabha 1909–1966*. She was awarded the New India Fellowship to work on her book that has been recently published and titled *Growing the Tree of Science: Homi Bhabha and the Tata Institute of Fundamental Research* (OUP: 2016). She was President of the Oral History Association of India (2013–2016) and President of the International Oral History Association (2014–2016).

Catherine Clinton holds the Denman Chair of American History at the University of Texas–San Antonio and Professor Emerita at Queen's University Belfast. Her first book, *The Plantation Mistress: Woman's World in the Old South*, appeared in 1982, and her *Harriet Tubman: The Road to Freedom* was named as one of the best nonfiction books of 2004 by the *Christian Science Monitor* and the *Chicago Tribune*. *Stepdaughters of History: Southern Women and the American Civil War*, the published version of her Fleming Lectures delivered in 2012, was published by Louisiana State University Press in 2016. She has also published award-winning books for children, including *I, Too, Sing America* and *Hold the Flag High*. In 2016, she served as president of the Southern Historical Association. She serves on scholarly advisory councils for *Civil War History*, *Ford's Theatre*, and *Civil War Times*, and is a member of the Screen Writer's Guild. She was an advisor for Steven Spielberg's *Lincoln* (2012), following publication of *Mrs. Lincoln: A Life (2009)*. In 2015, Clinton participated in a round table at the Smithsonian Institution with US treasurer Rosie Rios and Secretary of the Treasury Jacob Lew, to discuss the prospect of honoring a woman on US currency; in April 2016, the US Treasury announced Harriet Tubman would appear on the front of the newly redesigned $20 bill.

Rebecca Conard is Professor of History Emeritus at Middle Tennessee State University and former Director of the MTSU Public History Program. She holds a PhD from the University of California–Santa Barbara and an MA from U.C.L.A. Her research into the history of public history has led to one book, *Benjamin Shambaugh and the Intellectual Foundations of Public History* (2002), and several shorter works, including the Winter 2006 issue of the *Public Historian* devoted to reflective practice. As a public history practitioner, she has co-founded two historical research firms and worked extensively with national, state, and local-level agencies and organizations. Long active in the National Council on Public History, she has served on the board, on various committees, and as vice president/president from 2001 to 2003.

Annemarie de Wildt is a historian and curator at the Amsterdam Museum (previously Amsterdam Historical Museum). She has curated many exhibitions on topics that focus on daily life, urban conflicts and culture, migration, and identity. Her exhibition projects include prostitution, Amsterdam songs, sailors' tattoos, the passion for football, animals in the city, neighborhood shops, graffiti, and the love-hate relationship between Amsterdam and the House of Orange. Her exhibitions are characterized by a hybrid variety of objects, often a mix of "high" and "low" culture and with a strong role for human stories. She has given many lectures and workshops in the Netherlands and abroad. Annemarie de Wildt is a keen blogger and has published various books/catalogs and many articles and blogs on the practice and dilemmas of curating and (contemporary) collecting.

Jerome de Groot is Senior Lecturer in the School of Arts, Languages, and Cultures at the University of Manchester. He researches on the representation of history in contemporary popular film, television, drama, and games, and on English literature between 1640 and 1660. His publications include *Remaking History: The Past in Contemporary Historical Fictions* (2015), *The Historical Novel* (2009), *Consuming History: Historians and Heritage in Contemporary Popular Culture* (2008, revised ed. 2016), and *Royalist Identities* (2004).

David Dean is Professor in the Department of History at Carleton University in Ontario, Canada, where he is also Co-Director of the Carleton Centre for Public History. He has published widely in the fields of public history and early modern British history, including *Law-Making and Society in Late Elizabethan England* (1996, 2002) and the co-edited collection *History, Memory, Performance* (2015). He edited *Museums as Sites for Historical Understanding, Peace, and Social Justice: Views from Canada*, a special issue of *Peace and Conflict: Journal of Peace Psychology* (2013). He was Company Historian to Canada's National Art Centre's English Theatre Company between 2008 and 2012 and is a Fellow of the Royal Historical Society. He is a member of the steering committee of the International Federation for Public History and co-editor of the new journal, *International Public History*.

Sandra H. Dudley is a social and material anthropologist and Head of the School of Museum Studies, University of Leicester. Intersecting anthropology, museum studies, and material culture studies, her work is focused in refugee and museum settings in Southeast and South Asia (Burma [Myanmar], Thailand, and India) and the United Kingdom. She has particular interests in forced migration and displacement, objects and collections, and ontology. Her publications include *Displaced Things: Optimistic Encounters in Burma, Museums and Beyond* (2018) and *Materialising Exile: Material Culture and Embodied Experience among Karenni Refugees in Thailand* (2010). She has edited and co-edited many books including *Museum Objects. Experiencing the Properties of Things* (2012), *Narrating Objects, Collecting Stories* (2012), *The Thing about Museums: Objects and Experience, Representation and Contestation* (2011), and *Museum Materialities: Objects, Engagements, Interpretations* (2010). She is Joint Chief Editor of Berghahn's international annual journal in museum studies, *Museum Worlds: Advances in Research*.

Jenny Edkins is Professor of International Politics at Aberystwyth University, Wales, United Kingdom. She is author of *Face Politics* (Routledge, 2015), *Missing: Persons and Politics* (Cornell, 2011), *Trauma and the Memory of Politics* (Cambridge, 2003), and *Whose Hunger? Concepts of Famine, Practices of Aid* (Minnesota, 2000). She is currently completing a monograph for Manchester University Press entitled *Change & the politics of uncertainty*. She is Co-Director of Performance and Politics International (PPi), a post-disciplinary grouping of scholars from arts and social science departments in

Aberystwyth established to explore the interface between aesthetic politics and political aesthetics and the complex relationship between performance and politics. She co-edits the Routledge book series *Interventions*, which has published over 100 cutting-edge critical volumes since 2009, and the textbook *Global Politics: A New Introduction*, now going into its third edition. She is on the organizing team of the Gregynog Ideas Lab, a summer school inaugurated in 2012 as an open meeting space for graduate students and early career faculty working on critical, post-structural, postcolonial, feminist, and psychoanalytic approaches to international politics.

Natasha Erlank completed her doctorate at the University of Cambridge and taught at the University of Cape Town and Rhodes University before moving to the Department of Historical Studies at the University of Johannesburg. She works principally on Southern Africa in the early twentieth century, and her research interests include gender history, the history of Christianity, and public history. Among her many publications is the co-edited *One Hundred Years of the ANC: Debating Liberation Histories Today* (2012) and the special issue of the journal *African Studies* (2015) on commemorating Sophiatown. Her article, "From Main Reef to Albertina Sisulu Road: The Signposted Heroine and the Politics of Memory," *The Public Historian* vol. 39, no. 2 won the National Council on Public History's G. Wesley Johnson Award for 2018.

Tanya Evans teaches Australian history and public history in the Department of Modern History at Macquarie University in Sydney, Australia. She specializes in the history of the family, poverty, and sexuality. She is passionate about researching ordinary people and places in the past and incorporating ordinary people and places in the process of her research and the construction of historical knowledge. Her three books so far have been about the history of "illegitimacy," poverty, and philanthropy. *Fractured Families: Life on the Margins in Colonial New South Wales* (New South, 2015) was a history of Australia's oldest surviving charity, The Benevolent Society, which was written in collaboration with family historians. She pitches her work at a variety of audiences because her research is targeted at disrupting people's assumptions about the history of the family. New South Press published *Swimming with the Spit:100 Years of the Spit Amateur Swimming Club* in October 2016. This is a community history of her local swimming club. She is currently writing a history of motherhood in Australia while continuing to research the different ways in which family history is practiced in Australia, England, and Canada.

Alix R. Green is Lecturer in History at the University of Essex. She read history at the University of Cambridge, and spent ten years in policy research and government relations before gaining her doctorate at the University of Hertfordshire. She brings her experience outside higher education to her current work on contemporary political history and the uses of history in public life. Her book, *History, Policy and Public Purpose: Historians and Historical Thinking in Government*, was published by Palgrave Macmillan in 2016. She is the founding convenor of the Public History Seminar at the Institute of Historical Research, London, and a Fellow of the Royal Historical Society. She is currently serving as the Society's Honorary Director of Communications and as a juror on its Public History Prize committee.

Richard Handler is a cultural anthropologist who has written on nationalism and the politics of culture, museums and the representation of history, anthropology and literature, and the history of Boasian anthropology. He is the coauthor, with Eric Gable, of *The New History in an Old Museum: Creating the Past at Colonial Williamsburg*

(Duke University Press, 1997). He is currently Professor of Anthropology and Director of the Program in Global Studies at the University of Virginia.

Te Herekiekie Herewini is Manager of the Karanga Aotearoa Repatriation Programme (KARP) based at Te Papa, Wellington, New Zealand. His role includes working alongside the Repatriation Advisory Panel, a group of Māori elders and cultural experts, as well as strategic planning, initiating the formal request to repatriate, and negotiating the return of the Māori and Moriori remains. Te Herekiekie is also a PhD candidate (part-time) at the University of Victoria in Wellington. Since KARP was established in 2003, it has repatriated over 419 Māori and Moriori ancestral remains from international institutions.

Steven High is Professor of History at Concordia University, Montreal, Canada, and co-founder of the Centre for Oral History and Digital Storytelling. Between 2005 and 2012, he led the Montreal Life Stories project, a large collaborative research project that saw 500 survivors of mass violence interviewed and their stories integrated into a wide range of public outcomes. He is the (co-)author of nine books, including (with Ted Little and Ry Thi Duong) *Remembering Mass Violence: Oral History, New Media and Performance*; *Oral History at the Crossroads: Sharing Life Stories of Displacement and Survival*; *Beyond Testimony and Trauma: Oral History in the Aftermath of Mass Violence*; and (with Ted Little and Liz Miller) *Going Public: The Art of Participatory Practice*.

Gulnara Ibraeva is an owner and principal investigator of the private research & consultancy firm, PIL, based in Bishkek, Kyrgyzstan. She is the author of numerous reports, manuals, and papers. Among those are *Extended Migration Profile: Kyrgyzstan 2010–2015* (2015), *Critical Discourse Analysis of a Media Case of Violence against Female Migrants from Kyrgyzstan* (in the book *Gender in Modern Central Asia*, LIT Vienna, 2015), *Gender and Migration* (2013), with Elias M., Elmhirst R. *Understanding Gendered Innovation Processes in Forest Landscapes: Case Studies from Indonesia and Kyrgyz Republic* (2017). She is the author of the books *Marriage Strategies in Kyrgyzstan: Generations of Fathers and Children* (2006), *Media and Languages in Kyrgyzstan* (2002), and, with Svetlana Kulikova, *The Historical Development and Current Situation of the Mass Media of Kyrgyzstan* (2001).

Hilda Kean is former Dean and Director of Public History at Ruskin College, Oxford, establishing the first MA in Public History in Britain. A Visiting Professor at the University of Greenwich and Senior Research Fellow at University College, London, her many books include *Animal Rights. Social and Political Change in Britain since 1800* (1998, 2000); *London Stories: Personal Lives, Public Histories* (2004); *Public History and Heritage Today. People and Their Pasts* (with Paul Ashton 2009, 2012); *The Public History Reader* (with Paul Martin 2013); *The Great Cat and Dog Massacre. The Real Story of World War Two's Unknown Tragedy* (2017, 2018). She is editing the *Routledge Companion to Animal-Human History* with Philip Howell in 2018. Her website is http://hildakean.com.

Seth M. Markle is an Associate Professor of History and International Studies at Trinity College in Hartford, Connecticut. His research focuses on the histories of cultural and political exchange between Africa and the African Diaspora. After graduating from Tufts University (BA, Africana Studies/English) in 2000, he continued working as a youth organizer in Boston before studying at New York University (PhD, History). Since 2003, he has worked in various hip-hop communities in Dar es Salaam (Tanzania),

Nairobi (Kenya), and Hartford, CT (United States) via research, journalism, radio broadcasting, arts education programming, youth development, event planning, and photograph and video documentation. Seth's *A Motorcycle on Hell's Run: Tanzania, Black Power and the Uncertain Future of Pan-Africanism, 1964–1974* was published by Michigan State University Press in 2017. Currently, he is working on two separate multi-modal research projects about the history of hip-hop in Tanzania and Hartford, respectively. His journalistic work on music and politics has been featured in *Pop'Africana* Magazine, worldhiphopmarket.com, CounterPunch.com, All.Africa.com, *Pambazuka News*, and Africanhiphp.com.

Hebe Mattos and **Martha Abreu** are Professors of History at *University Federal Fluminense* (UFF) in Rio de Janeiro, Brazil. They are authors of several books, research films, and academic articles and were pioneers in the studies of post-abolition in the country. They are coauthors and co-editors of articles and books about memory of slavery and the cultural history of post-abolition in Brazil, among them, "Jongo, Recalling History" in the hybrid e-book *Cangoma Calling: Spirits and Rhythms of Freedom in Brazilian Jongo Slavery Songs* (2013). They are also co-directors of *Present Pasts*, a series of four documentary films about the memory of slavery among the descendants of the last generation of African enslaved workers in Brazil (2012), based on the oral history archive they coordinated at Oral History and Image Lab of UFF (LABHOI). The films are also available online: *A Present Past – Afro-Brazilian Memories in Rio de Janeiro* (2011); *Verses and Cudgels – Stick Playing in the Afro-Brazilian Culture of the Paraíba Valley* (with Matthias Assunção, 2009); *Jongos, Calangos and Folias – Black Music, Memory and Poetry* (2007); and *Memory of Captivity* (with Guilherme Fernandez and Isabel Castro, 2005). The films circulate through characters, places, dances, challenges, and common expressions. Together, the different points of view on the history of the descendants of the last enslaved Africans add up, allowing a broader and more complex view of each of the addressed topics.

Jeremiah McCall is a teacher and historian who specializes in the effective uses of video games and other interactive technologies in history education, and the ways that the ancient world is represented in modern media. He has written extensively on these subjects, and his book, *Gaming the Past* (Routledge 2012), is the first program that focuses on training classroom teachers in the use of historical video games. Jeremiah teaches at Cincinnati Country Day School.

John Moses is a member of the Upper Mohawk and Delaware bands of the Six Nations of the Grand River Territory near Brantford, Ontario. He is a PhD candidate in cultural mediations at the Institute for Comparative Studies in Literature, Art, and Culture at Carleton University, Ottawa, Ontario, and a federal public servant with the Department of Canadian Heritage and Portfolio in Gatineau, Québec.

Serge Noiret is the History Information Specialist (PhD) at the European University Institute, Florence, Italy. His current research focuses on (digital) public history and digital humanities. He has published widely on contemporary Italian and European history and politics, public history, and digital history, including the special issue of *Memoria e Ricerca* on public history: *Pratiche nazionali e identità globale* (2011). With Mark Tebeau, he is editing the *Handbook of Digital Public History* (De Gruyter, 2019). He has taught at EUI, the University of Urbino, and the University of Naples; is a member of several Europe-based organizations concerned with digital history and digital humanities and is a member of the scientific board of the *Conseil Scientifique of the Réseau National des Maisons des Sciences de l'Homme* in Paris. From 2012 to 2017 he was President of the International Federation for Public History, and since 2016, President of the Italian Association for Public History.

James Opp is Professor of History at Carleton University, Ottawa. His current research projects include tracing the history of photographic archives in prairie Canada, exploring photographer Yousuf Karsh's commercial work in the 1950s, and tracking down obscure corporate archives of photographs. With John C. Walsh he is the co-editor of *Placing Memory and Remembering Place in Canada* (UBC Press, 2010) and *Home, Work, and Play: Situating Canadian Social History*, 3rd Ed. (Oxford University Press, 2015). He coproduced (with Anthony Whitehead) the *Rideau Timescapes App*, a free iOS app that delivers more than 700 digitized historical photographs to visitors of the Rideau Canal, a UNESCO World Heritage site in eastern Ontario. This project was awarded the Canadian Historical Association's Public History Prize in 2013.

Elizabeth Paradis, since graduating from Carleton University, Ottawa, with a master's degree in Public History, has worked as a documentalist, oral historian, filmmaker, and researcher on numerous historical and interdisciplinary projects in various institutional and professional public history settings. Her MA degree addressed the relationship between the past, history, and performance in historical reality television, and she has had the opportunity to explore First Nations, Quebecois, Environmental, and Canadian twentieth-century history, as well as theories of performance and gender. Most recently, Elizabeth has focused on copyediting, particularly for sociological publications, in addition to her work as an editorial assistant for this volume. When she is not soaking up all the joy she can from her young family, she looks forward to finding new ways to immerse herself in reflexive public history projects and fascinating editing work.

Lisa Peschel is a lecturer in the Department of Theatre, Film and Television at the University of York, England. She has been researching theatrical performance in the Terezín/Theresienstadt ghetto since 1998. Her articles on survivor testimony and scripts written in the ghetto have appeared in journals such as *Theatre Survey, Theatre Topics*, and *Holocaust and Genocide Studies* and in Czech, German, and Israeli publications. She has been invited to lecture and conduct performance workshops at institutions in the United States and Europe including Oxford University, University College London, and Dartmouth College. Her anthology *Performing Captivity, Performing Escape: Cabarets and Plays from the Terezín/Theresienstadt Ghetto* was published in 2014 (Czech- and German-language edition 2008) and her edited volume with Patrick Duggan, *Performing (for) Survival: Theatre, Crisis, Extremity*, in 2016. Awards include a Fulbright grant in the Czech Republic and fellowships at the US Holocaust Memorial Museum, the Center for Jewish Studies at Harvard University, and the Jewish Museum in Prague. She is currently a co-investigator on the £1.8 million project "Performing the Jewish Archive" funded by the UK Arts and Humanities Research Council.

John H. Sprinkle, Jr., a graduate of the University of Delaware, holds a PhD in American history from the College of William and Mary. After a decade as a private sector historic preservation consultant, he joined the National Park Service in 1998 where he has served in the National Historic Landmark program, the Federal Preservation Institute, and, currently, in the agency's Park History program. The views and conclusions in his chapter are those of the author and should not be interpreted as representing the opinions or policies of the National Park Service or the United States Government. Mr. Sprinkle is the author of *Crafting Preservation Criteria: The National Register of Historic Places and American Historic Preservation*. His next book will focus on the intersection of the land conservation and historic preservation movements.

Carolyn Steedman is Emeritus Professor of History at the University of Warwick. *Poetry for Historians*, which she has been wanting to write for twenty years, will be out with Manchester University Press in spring 2018. The book is not a collection of poems for historians, but about poetry and history writing as cultural activities and forms of making in the modern world.

Patrick Morales Thomas is an Anthropologist at the National University of Colombia. He holds a doctorate in Social Anthropology and Ethnology from the Ecole des Hautes Etudes en Sciences Sociales in Paris. His areas of work have focused on the analysis of processes of re-indigenization in Colombia, the development of public policies related to intangible cultural heritage, and historical memory of the armed conflict in ethnic communities. He is currently the coordinator of Team Approach Ethnic National Center for Historical Memory in Bogotá, Colombia.

Amy M. Tyson received her PhD in American Studies from the University of Minnesota, where she first became interested in labor and performance at living history museums – the subject of her book *The Wages of History: Emotional Labor on Public History's Front Lines* (Amherst: University of Massachusetts Press, 2013). She is Associate Professor of History at DePaul University in Chicago, where she teaches courses in public history, oral history, local and community history, popular culture, and modern US history. Her research interests center on nineteenth- and twentieth-century US social and cultural history, with a particular interest in how that history is interpreted and distilled for the larger public through museums, plays, art, music, and pageantry.

John C. Walsh is a Historian at Carleton University in Ottawa, Canada, where he is also the Co-Director of the Carleton Centre for Public History. He researches, teaches, and supervises graduate students in the fields of Canadian social and cultural history, public history, and memory studies. Along with James Opp, he is the co-editor of *Placing Memory and Remembering Place in Canada* (UBC Press, 2010). Walsh is currently working on a commemorative public art installation and documentary film for the Lost Stories Project (www.loststories.ca)

Kirsten Wehner is a curator, designer, and anthropologist whose practice explores how spaces and experiences can be shaped to foster cultural understanding, creative engagement, and appreciation and care for the non-human world. From 2011 to 2016, Kirsten was Head Curator, People and the Environment, at the National Museum of Australia (www.nma.gov.au/pate), and from 2004 to 2011 was Senior Curator and then Content Director for the Museum's gallery development program. Her curatorial experience encompasses more than thirty exhibitions, digital platforms, and interpretive programs exploring diverse aspects of Australian environmental history. She holds a PhD in visual and cultural anthropology from New York University and in 2018 will complete an MA in Narrative Environments at Central Saint Martins, University of the Arts, London. Kirsten's publications include the co-edited/authored volumes *Curating the Future: Museums, Communities and Climate Change* (2017, Routledge) and *Landmarks: A History of Australia in 33 Places* (2013, NMA Press). She is a member of the Australia-

Pacific Observatory of Humanities for the Environment (www.hfe-observatories.org) and was a 2015–2016 Fellow at the Rachel Carson Center for Environment and Society, Ludwig-Maximilians Universität, Munich, Germany.

Tim Winter is Research Professor at the Alfred Deakin Institute, Deakin University, Melbourne. He is the former President of the *Association of Critical Heritage Studies* and holds an ARC Future Fellowship on the Silk Roads of the twenty-first century. He has been a Scholar at the University of Cambridge, The Getty, and Asia Research Institute, Singapore, and published widely on heritage, development, urban conservation, and the international politics of heritage. His recent books include *The Routledge Handbook of Heritage in Asia* and *Shanghai Expo: An International Forum on the Future of Cities.* He is currently working on books on heritage diplomacy in relation to Belt and Road and twentieth-century conflict in Asia (warinasia.com).

Joanna Wojdon is Associate Professor at the Department of Methodology of Teaching History and Civic Education, Institute of History, University of Wrocław, Poland, a Fulbright alumna, a board member of the International Society for History Didactics, and Managing Editor of its Yearbook *International Journal of Research on History Didactics, History Education, and History Culture.* She has developed the first MA program in public history in Poland, offered at the University of Wrocław since 2014, and since 2018 also in English. Other areas of her scholarly interests include using information technology in history education (*E-teaching History*, Cambridge Scholars 2016), history and edutainment (*ISHD Yearbook*, 2015), political and propaganda influence on education, especially in Poland under communism (*Textbooks as Propaganda; Poland under Communist Rule 1944-1989*, Routledge 2017), and the history of the Polish Americans after World War II (*White and Red Umbrella: The Polish American Congress in the Cold War Era 1944–1988*, Helena History Press 2015.

Linda Young is a historian by discipline and was once a curator by trade. She taught aspects of Museum Studies and Cultural Heritage Studies for more than twenty-five years, for the last twelve years at Deakin University in Melbourne. Her book, *House Museums in the United Kingdom and the United States: A History* (Rowman & Littlefield, 2017), traces a variety of foundational motivations that throw new light on historic houses as a species of museum, and casts them as enabling an alleged personal, domestic dimension into the construction of national identities.

Acknowledgments

The *Companion to Public History* took shape through many conversations with Elizabeth Paradis, whose work as research assistant, second reader, and *confidant* shaped the book in important ways. Emily Cuggy copyedited the manuscript, Cameron Duder compiled the index, and Tascha Morrison managed the illustrations. I benefited enormously from having the opportunity to speak about the project at conferences organized by the National Council on Public History and the International Federation for Public History. Far too many people assisted in various ways to list them all, but I must mention Victoria Campbell, Mattea Chadwick, Calum Dean, Bruce Elliot, Gabrielle Etcheverry, Jennifer Evans, Erica Fagen, Tammy Gordon, Shawn Graham, Esmee Heil, Paul Litt, Meghan Lundrigan, Candice McCavitt, Jean-Pierre Morin, Del Muise, Michihiro Okamoto, James Opp, Jeff Sahadeo, Nadja Roby, Janet Siltanen, and John Walsh. During the final stages of the book I benefited from working with members of the International Federation for Public History, particularly Thomas Cauvin, Andreas Etges, Chantal Kestleloot, Anita Lucchesi, Catalina Muñoz, and Serge Noiret. Of course, whatever success the *Companion* has is down to the contributors, and I hope they are pleased with the final outcome; it was a pleasure working with you all. Thanks also to Tessa Harvey, who invited me to edit the *Companion*, and to Haze Humbert, Janani Govindankutty, Vimali Joseph, Aravind Kannankara, Sindhuja Kumar and Maddie Koufogazos, who saw it through production. As always, Janet Siltanen offered invaluable insights, advice, and support. I have been privileged to facilitate seminars and supervise graduate students associated with Carleton University's MA in Public History since 2002. It is to all of you that the *Companion to Public History* is dedicated with thanks and appreciation.

Introduction

DAVID DEAN

The *Companion to Public History* is a conversation about history in the public realm, the place of the past in the present, and how present-day concerns shape the ways in which we engage with and represent the past. History, after all, is everywhere. It is in our homes and in our streets. It is in our theaters, cinemas, and bookshops; it is on our television screens, our stamps, and coins. It is accessible with just a couple of clicks on our computers or taps on our mobile devices. We visit museums and historic sites to learn about the past, to be entertained by it, perhaps even to participate in re-creations of it. We read, speak, and perform the past in our everyday lives. We seek it out when we travel. We imagine ourselves in the past through sight, smell, taste, sound, and touch. We collect it and can be persuaded to buy something, believe something, or accept something because it has been used to convince us. We argue about the past, we use it when it suits us, and we are challenged by it.

As a student and then academic specializing in early modern (fifteenth to eighteenth century) British history, first in New Zealand and then in Britain, I sometimes found myself working on history projects that had very little to do with my specific field. They did, however, always involve using my skills as a historian to produce new histories in different ways, often in collaboration with others. I thought of this as doing history beyond the university, and if I called it anything I used the term *activist history*. Coming to Canada in the mid-1990s, I discovered that this had a name in North America: *public history*. By the early 2000s, now a history professor at Carleton University in Ottawa, public history became my second and then primary field of research, teaching, and graduate supervision. I helped establish a graduate program and then an interdisciplinary research center in public history and in subsequent years found myself performing roles such as a historical consultant with English Theatre at Canada's National Arts Centre and collaborator with the Ottawa-based Workers' History Museum. My research and teaching in public history grew to encompass theater and film, storytelling, and performance.

A Companion to Public History, First Edition. Edited by David Dean.
© 2018 John Wiley & Sons Ltd. Published 2018 by John Wiley & Sons Ltd.

My "going public" has coincided with the growth of the field of public history internationally.[1] The world's leading public history organization, the National Council on Public History (NCPH), formed in 1979, has now been joined by the International Federation for Public History/Fédération internationale pour l'histoire publique (IFPH-FIHP) founded in 2009.[2] Professional historical associations are appearing everywhere: the Canadian Historical Association's Public History Working Group was created in 2006, and both the German Historical Association's Committee for Applied History/Public History and Brazil's Rede Brasileira de História Pública in 2012. Inaugural meetings of public historians in Italy and Russia took place in 2017. Teaching public history has become an international phenomenon. The first graduate program in public history was established at the University of California at Santa Barbara in 1976; there are now scores of graduate and undergraduate programs across the United States and in Australia, Britain, Canada, China, France, Germany, India, Italy, the Netherlands, and Poland according to the NCPH's latest tally (Cauvin 2016; NCPH 2016). 2018 will see the appearance of the first international journal (IFPH-FIHP's *International Public History*) as well as the first Chinese journal of public history.

Public history has truly come of age, both for myself personally and for others across the globe, and this makes the appearance of the *Companion* very timely. Before describing how I've structured the book and its individual chapters, it is important to address some fundamental questions. What is public history? What is the relationship between public history and popular history? Or public history and public memory? How does public history differ from other forms of history and what unique contributions has it made to the discipline? Why and how did it become a global phenomenon and what implications does this have for the field?

What is public history?

Public history deals with the ways in which the past is created and presented in the public arena as history. To talk about "history" and "the past" is to talk about things that are not exactly the same thing, although we tend to use the terms interchangeably. The past is something that happened. It is no longer fully accessible to us. It is gone forever. History, on the other hand, is what we in the present *make* of those fragments that have survived of the past, and our making of that past takes many forms. To put it another way, the past is the content, both the object and the subject of our enquiry, while history is the process by which we deliver that content, hoping to make sense of it and, crucially for public history, share it with others.

Public historians are active in both the making and analysis of historical representations. Public history is about the ways in which the public engages with the past and about how the past is represented to the public. It is about the histories that the public creates, it is about preserving the past in the present for the future, and it is about how the past is used in contemporary society and its audiences.

Often seen as an applied approach to understanding and representing the past, and therefore as a slightly poorer cousin to the forms of scholarship required of historians working in the academic mainstream, public history as taught in colleges and universities often involves practical projects, field work, and internships. Students participate in the bread-and-butter activities of historians working outside of the academy in places such as museums, archives, historic sites, or the heritage departments of municipal, regional, and national governments. Such historians research the past but rather than produce an academic monograph or article, they write official histories and policy reports, curate exhibits, prepare guidebooks and training manuals, design websites and archive online resources, or help make decisions about heritage designation, archival preservation, and commemorative acts. Students thus learn how to initiate, create, and produce new forms of historical representation. They also learn how to work collaboratively rather than individually, with community partners, and in an interdisciplinary way. These are all experiences that they would usually not get in the traditional academic history classroom. Nevertheless, it is all too easy to overstate the differences between historians working in the academy and those working in public history institutions. Given that all historians conduct research, write, and represent the past, as individuals or as part of a team to varying degrees, a definition of public history that rests primarily on where they happen to be employed (or not) is an impoverished one.

A richer definition comes with a recognition that the key difference between mainstream academic history and public history lies with the public themselves: with the significance of audience. All historians, of course, would be pleased if their work reached the general public, but for those producing articles in academic journals, presenting papers at the conferences of learned societies, and writing monographs, their audience tends to be specialists or students. If the public ignores this work, it really does not matter; academic historians just move onto their next project. Even if a book captures the attention and interest of the public and becomes a best seller or the basis of a screenplay for a feature film, the author's research agenda was not shaped by the public but by their own singular interest and the requirements of the academy.

By contrast, the public has a major role to play in shaping the work of public historians. For those working in public history institutions, the past they research and represent is determined not only by their own interests but by what they perceive, or how the institution in which they work perceives, to be of value to the public. The anticipated needs of the visitor to a historic house or the player of a historically-grounded video game shape the product that the historian creates. Even public historians working in the academy find their work shaped by those with whom they are collaborating. Public historians write for audiences, choosing ways of communicating to suit particular needs. A sixty-word exhibit panel has to work equally well for visitors with no prior knowledge and those with some; a policy briefing has to be succinct, precise, and to the point without losing historical relevance. Should audiences fail to be engaged by the work of a public historian, this might have a profound effect on the individual's, institution's, or corporation's future planning, budget, and resources. There is then a high degree of accountability *to* the public and agency *by* the public with regard to both content and forms of representation in public history that distinguishes it from historical practice in the larger discipline.

Those in the field tend to talk of *the* public, but given the diversity and complexity of the audiences of public history, I would argue that it is more useful to think about *publics*. To demonstrate how thinking about the audiences of public history in the plural rather than in the singular can be helpful, we can turn to the example of the new Canada History Hall in the Canadian Museum of History in Ottawa-Gatineau, Canada. Telling the story of Canada from the arrival of the First Peoples through to the present is a considerable challenge. What histories should be represented? To help make that decision, the Museum thought carefully about visitors and identified six potential audience groups: sightseers, families, museum enthusiasts, history seekers, educational groups, and tour groups. Each were seen as having particular reasons for visiting the museum and varied, if sometimes overlapping, interests (Morrison and LeBlanc 2016).

Speaking of *publics* rather than *the* public compels us to be more nuanced in our analyses of historical representations and also when we come to talk about agency in public history. Public history as practiced, say, in museums and historic sites is controlled and regulated, not to mention framed, by professionals, by sponsors, by advisory boards, by management, and by various stakeholders with invested interests. For this reason, these forms of public history can be fairly described as top-down public history, however much attention is paid to the audiences of the historical representations they create. There is, however, also what we might call bottom-up public history, where individuals, families, or groups create history for themselves. This would include the collector who shares knowledge at an antique fair or a cook trying to re-create a dish from a handed-down book of recipes. It could be three generations of a family exchanging stories and sharing memories while they pore over a family photograph album. People might get together to reenact a famous battle, organize a festival, or commission a mural to celebrate a past event or person.[3]

Public history is not only about the history that publics receive and consume; it is also about the history that publics make. On occasion, public history from the bottom up was a response to perceived inadequacies of the history created by top-down public history. It is not coincidental that the formalization and growth of the field took place between the 1970s and the early 2000s at a time when in the larger discipline privileging political and constitutional history was being challenged by the new social history, women's history, black history, LGBTTQ history, cultural history, the history of the everyday, and postmodern history, to name only some of the exciting shifts of those decades. Many public historians were participants in or were influenced by these new approaches: museum exhibits began to offer visitors new stories, and academic books recovered hidden, forgotten, marginalized pasts. Offering supplementary or alternative narratives has been a feature especially of community-focused public histories. Such activist history tests and challenges traditionally accepted stories and in the process reveals and asserts the importance of new histories. Many were associated with movements variously described as radical history, people's history, feminist history, and history from below (Benson 1981; Cauvin 2016; Kean, Martin and Morgan 2000; Samuel 1994, 1998; Santhiago, 2016).

Associated with these shifting concerns were new approaches to researching the past. Methodologies and approaches such as oral history, microhistory, visual history, and the history of the body became especially important in the new social history (Burke 1992). Oral history and storytelling, testimony, witnessing, and remembering became important concerns leading to innovative approaches and practices (Portelli 1990, 1997). Another key shift came in the concept of the archive, moving beyond the formal archive to consider the value of, for example, the letters, papers, and diaries of non-elites or the objects of everyday life. Indeed, the notion of the archive was broadened to include spaces like living rooms and artifacts like family photo albums (Burton 2003). Many of the historians involved in these new ways of thinking about history might not have identified themselves as public historians, but many did so, were working in the field, or were activist historians working with individuals, networks, organizations, and communities outside the academy.

If the "new history" was not the particular achievement of public historians, the representation of those histories in the public arena can certainly be attributed to them. Those working in museums began to develop exhibits with a social history focus, interpreters at living history sites began telling more stories about marginalized people and addressing the inequalities of everyday life, and heritage plaques appeared commemorating a greater range and diversity of past lives and events. Moreover, it was in the field of public history that the implications of the new history became especially visible and led to more nuanced approaches incorporating not only new methodologies but also new theoretical insights.

Recognizing that publics create their own personal and individual, familial, group, community, regional, or national histories led to a reaching out to include the subjects of historical research in the production and representation of the past, a process described as "shared authority" (Frisch, 1990; High 2009, 2014). Encouraging consultation, collaboration, and diversity does not diminish the value of professional historical training, but it brings into the open questions of power, legitimacy, and privilege, and this has been uniquely part of the practice of public history. Public historians working in these contexts facilitate as much as they produce historical knowledge.

Public historians were also more concerned than their mainstream counterparts with contested histories. Historians have always debated different interpretations of the past, but when official narratives, supplementary narratives, and alternative narratives are competing for space and attention in the public arena, the stakes are higher than historiographical controversies within the discipline. It was public historians who were caught up in the "history wars" where museums, textbooks, monuments and memorials, heritage sites, and even banknotes were among the many sites of public history that became vigorously contested spaces, and continue to be so. This brought the relationship between history and memory into sharp relief not only as a theoretical and methodological problem but also as a political one with profound implications for the present.

Public historians have been at the forefront of discussions about the politics of memory, about how societies and individuals remember, about heritage and preservation, and about commemoration. Public historians are memory brokers.[4] It is not surprising then that they have been particularly sensitive to the work of cultural geographers, social scientists, and social theorists in their work. "Realms of memory" (Nora 1996), "imagined communities" (Anderson 1983), "the practice of everyday life" (de Certeau 1984; de Certeau et. al. 1998), and "collective memory" (Halbwachs 1925) are only some of the insights from other disciplines that have become common vocabulary in public history. Readers will encounter many more theoretical insights in the pages of this book.

Tasked with representing history that generates emotional responses from publics has also led public historians to take a leading role in thinking about affective history and sensory history. Affective history, which focuses on feelings and their embodiment in practice, and sensory history, which pays attention to sound, sight, smell, taste, and touch, have become more central to public history than any other field in the discipline, in part because of public history practice. Living history interpretation, engaging the senses and emotions in museum exhibits or history on film or stage, adopting persona in museums, historical reality television shows, or historical simulation games have led to new insights.

Responsive to the "affective turn," public historians have also been at the forefront of the "performative turn" in the humanities. Starting from the position that all human activities are performed as embodied representations whether we think of the practices of everyday life or the more formal framings as in theater, music, film, and dance, performance and performativity have become valuable ways of thinking about public history. Embodying history through performance embraces forms of representation that predate the field's formalization and institutionalization. Performance and performativity have always been part of how publics engage with the past.

The compass of the *Companion*

I wanted to take the opportunity of the *Companion* series to celebrate public history's diversity and complexity rather than offer a comprehensive introductory overview or a "how to" handbook or manual. There are already some excellent books that fulfill these roles (Almeda and Roval 2011; Cauvin 2016; de Groot 2009, 2016); Sayer 2015); and two appeared (Lyon, Nix, and Shrum 2017; Gardner and Hamilton 2017) after this book went to press.[5] By contrast, the *Companion* invites readers to explore the field by engaging with a wide range of approaches, practices, perspectives, and experiences.

The *Companion* speaks to public history internationally, transnationally, and to its interdisciplinary nature. The authors are currently working in eighteen different countries, although their work is much more international and transnational than this suggests, and I hope readers will appreciate reading chapters in which global voices and experiences come through strongly. The majority of the contributors identify themselves as public historians, but in these pages the reader will also find chapters exploring public history topics and arguments written by anthropologists, political scientists and sociologists, archivists and curators, and by those working in fields as diverse as archaeology, cultural studies, geography, memory studies, and museology. There are chapters from public historians working in academia (schools, colleges, and universities) and from those who practice their craft as professionals employed in archives, museums, historic sites, and national parks, or who work as private consultants, policy advisors, and community activists.

Several contributors are well-established names in the field of public history. Some are considered to be founders of the field in their respective countries; they and others have served as directors and coordinators of public history programs or played leading roles in public history institutions. Many contributors are mid-career, here taking stock of the field they have helped shape over the past decade or sharing the results of projects that have enriched our understanding of what public history is and how it can be transformative. There are also chapters that offer perspectives from those relatively new to the field.

The book begins with a prologue addressing the cover image from the Amsterdam Museum, and it ends with an epilogue discussing Tanzanian graffiti. The thirty-four chapters in between these bookends are gathered into seven parts whose titles encourage us to think of the field of public history in a dynamic way: identifying, situating, doing, using, preserving, performing, and contesting. Gathering particular chapters under certain headings is, of course, a somewhat arbitrary and even clumsy endeavor. Many chapters could have worked equally well in a different part of the book, although there are good reasons for clustering them in the ways the reader will encounter.

Part 1: Identifying public history

The book begins with four chapters that together constitute an excellent discussion of the field of public history following on from the remarks offered in the Introduction. What defines the field? Where has it come from? How has it evolved over time? What are the theoretical and methodological contributions that made public history distinctive from other fields of history? This section will introduce readers to the nature of the field and its development across the globe.

Rebecca Conard re-invigorates discussions about origins by exploring the growth of public history as a field of academic study, replacing the dichotomy of the public history/academic history model of the field's emergence with a more dynamic story of individuals, organizations, and pedagogical change. Hilda Kean asks not "*what* is public history?" but "*where* is public history?" By taking us beyond the museum, the archive, and the heritage building to everyday encounters with the past and by putting the public first and foremost, Kean encourages a more dynamic understanding of this rapidly growing and constantly evolving field. Jerome de Groot examines how different publics across the globe experienced and responded to the renowned historical film, *Russian Ark*. In doing so he offers new possibilities for understanding public history through analyzing global consumption of localized historical representations. The first part of the book closes with Alix Green's exploration of the reasons why, even in the era of "evidence-based" policy making, historians have too often found themselves on the outside looking in. Green dares us to contemplate a much deeper role for public history and public historians globally.

Part 2: Situating public history

The second part of the book explores the wheres of public history through sites of public engagement with the past and with history: museums, archives, digital media, pop culture, and place. These sites feature prominently in public history teaching programs, and these are the places where shared authority, agency, memory, contestation, performance, affect, emotions, memory, and heritage have been especially visible.

Kirsten Wehner gives us an insider's view of the ways in which the National Museum of Australia curates the past for the different publics that come through its doors. Carolyn Steedman takes us through a personal journey through the archives, engaging both with the theory and practice of archives and archiving. Serge Noiret offers a succinct overview of the rapidly changing world of digital public history, arguing that it has been responsible for breaking down national boundaries, empowering people everywhere to critically engage in making public history. Catherine Clinton has written history in a variety of ways from the scholarly monograph to film documentary and the graphic novel. Her graphic novel, *Booth*, is the primary focus of her thought-provoking interview by Elizabeth Paradis. John Walsh ends this part of the book with a chapter tracing the importance of space and place, showing how capital cities function as sites of memory and history. Focusing on Ottawa, Canada's national capital, he reveals the vital relationship between state formation, historical geography, and public history.

Part 3: Doing public history

Putting public history into practice is the focus of the next cluster of chapters, where authors write about very different experiences in doing public history. Indira Chowdhury's undergraduate students drew on a wide repertoire of historian's craft – oral history, performance, and storytelling – to address the "afterlives" of people and events in Bangalore's past. Steven High shows how storytelling has shifted agency away from researcher-driven agendas to working with communities in ways that empower them to tell their own stories in their own ways, encouraging collaborative and participatory forms of history-making.

Tanya Evans investigates one of the most popular forms of engagement with the past, family history and genealogy. She argues that as public historians continue their work with family historians, there is the potential to radicalize the field by embracing diversity.

Historical agency is a theme also taken up by Sandra Dudley, who leads us through the argument that objects also have agency, and proposes that a more useful way of thinking about objects is to think of their "potentiality." She opens up new ways of thinking about the effects objects have on publics in places like museums. This part of the book closes with Gulnara Ibraeva's account of how people do public history in public places, by taking readers through the complex history of a monument park in Bistek, Kyrgyzstan, where people construct their own memories of time and space alongside competing official narratives.

Part 4: Using public history

Making use of the past in policy making, politics, addressing past inequalities and injustices, and making arguments for change in the present is the focus of the next five chapters. Michael Belgrave shows how historical evidence, historical knowledge, and the particular skills associated with the discipline contributed to New Zealand's Waitangi Tribunal. The next chapter reprints the Canadian Truth and Reconciliation Report's discussion of reconciliation with a commentary by Patrick Morales Thomas, who raises important questions about the role of history and memory in the quest for transitional justice especially with indigenous peoples in settler, colonial, and post-colonial societies. The repatriation of objects and human remains from museums and cultural institutions to communities of origin is another issue where public history is used to correct past wrongs, injustices, and illegal activities and here is the focus of a chapter that takes the form of a conversation between George Abungu, Te Herekiekie Herewini, John Moses, and Richard Sandler facilitated by the editor.

Natasha Erlank's chapter reveals the power of the past to transform. She tells the story of Sophiatown in South Africa, where public historians played an important role in recovering, archiving, and representing the history of a fractured community. Ana Lucia Araujo explores sites associated with the Atlantic slave trade in West Africa, Brazil, and the United States. She identifies their role in the development of tourism and in promoting economic development, illustrating how public history can be used, sometimes successfully and often not, especially when the histories being told are challenging and uncomfortable.

Part 5: Preserving public history

Preserving the intangible and tangible past is on the agenda of many public history projects. What should be preserved, and why? How should it be preserved? We open with Tim Winter's careful exposition of the interaction between heritage, preservation, and globalization, calling for greater openness and receptiveness to local experience, collective knowledge, and alternative methodologies and practices. The case for preservation is often tied to national identity, where particular sites are deemed to be of "national importance." Hamad Bin Seray provides us with a visual and textual argument putting a strong case forward for the preservation of Al-Jazeera al-Hamra in the United Arab Emirates, a site of significance because of its location, its history, and its material heritage.

From these international contexts, we shift direction with John H. Sprinkle, Jr.'s, chapter, which takes us from the early years of the United States National Park Service, one of the most important public history institutions in the world, through to today. One theme that emerges is the tension between the need to conserve and preserve the landscapes and sites of the past while also ensuring they attract and engage visitors whose very presence risks compromising the preservation project. Linda Young discusses the changing world of house museums, where those celebrating elite lives are now joined by those of ordinary people and where interpreters celebrate the everyday as much as the exceptional. James Opp takes us into the world where individuals engage with the past on visual terms, constructing new narratives and creating new memory archives through the opportunities offered by digital photography.

Part 6: Performing public history

Australian historian Greg Dening once wrote "History – the past transformed into words or paint or play – is always a performance" (2002: 1). How we navigate the distance between past and present using embodied performance is the focus of five chapters that embrace the notion that we open up new possibilities for historical understanding by using all of our senses, through acting and composing, dancing and singing, storytelling, and play. We begin with Amy Tyson's overview of the concepts and practices of reenactment and what these performances tell us about the shaping of historical memory. Vanessa Agnew uses the conceit of the reenactment journey through the countryside to show how Paleolithic reenactment is a response to current environmental and social anxieties.

A remarkable story of survival and recovery is told by Lisa Peschel, whose project, *Performing the Jewish Archive*, seeks to discover, recover, and re-stage cabarets, plays, and other artistic works from the Terezin ghetto. Hebe Mattos and Martha Abreu reveal findings from their project, *Memory of Slavery*, which uncovers the role of *jongo* performances, now officially recognized as part of Brazil's intangible heritage, in preserving counter-narratives about slave history. The final chapter turns from public memories recovered and relived through corporeal performance, to the world of historical simulation games. Jeremiah McCall provides many insights into historical gaming arguing that it has become a vitally important place where publics participate in the past.

Part 7: Contesting public history

Contested and conflicting pasts and their representation are appropriately the focus of the final part of the book given how often these issues have come up in previous chapters. Thomas Cauvin offers many insights into the role of public historians in the making of histories, and he argues from his work on Northern Ireland that as participants they can play a role in conflict resolution. Jenny Edkins discusses a range of methodologies, theories, and approaches to the relationship between history and memory, particularly focusing on trauma and introduces readers to the concept of trauma time. Chia-Li Chen analyzes competing stories of memory and identity at two museum/memorial sites in Taiwan, showing how stakeholders can play both a positive and a negative role but that there is always room for dialogue and healing while acknowledging traumatic histories.

Joanna Wojdon shifts our attention to education curricula and textbooks. Drawing on her work in Poland and other European countries, she finds synergy between historical education and public history, positives as well as challenges. We end with Helin Burkay's chapter on contested pasts and food production. Constructing narratives of naturalism, harmony, and authenticity, Turkish olive producers suppressed historical discrimination against the Greek community while also appropriating their history. Burkay shows how food heritage speaks to the politics of identity, problematizing claims to heritage and authenticity that are core issues in the field of public history.

Beginnings and endings

I have chosen to bookend the thirty-four chapters described above with a prologue and an epilogue each of which offers a commentary with images which say much about what public history is and why it plays such a vital part in our lives.

Prologue: In June 2014, sipping mint tea with Janet Siltanen in the wonderful courtyard of the Amsterdam Museum, we watched as visitors and locals alike reached out to touch and were touched by the orphan schoolchildren's lockers re-purposed as exhibit cupboards. The space, and how publics were both drawn to it and used it, sharing old stories and discovering new ones, in a museum that has never failed to enthrall me with the way its exhibits and programming educate and entertain, celebrate and challenge, shake complacency and deepen understanding, captured all that is public history for me. Curator Annemarie de Wildt joined us that afternoon, and we begin with her discussion of this wonderful space and the photograph gracing the cover of this book.

Epilogue: In July 2016, I attended the very stimulating 3rd International Public History Conference at the Universidad de los Andes in Bogotá, Colombia. There, thanks to the encouragement of Avehi Menon and accompanied by Tim Compeau, I took time out for the Bogotá Graffiti Tour (http://bogotagraffiti.com/). Our guide, Jay, took us deep into a world I'd not taken much notice of before, and what I learned that day has changed the way I encounter and think about everyday public history. Jay had mentioned in passing that Dar es Salaam, Tanzania, was another place where graffiti artists stake claims to be public historians. We end with Seth Markle's brief history of graffiti in Tanzania and his engagement with the work of graffiti artist Mejah Mbuya.

The *Companion to Public History* is a conversation about public history. It began between myself and those who helped conceptualize the project. It grew to include the many people I approached to contribute to the volume, whether they could accept or not, and it deepened, broadened, and took unexpected turns as drafts arrived, were commented on, revised, and discussed further. Some joined in at conferences, notably those of the NCPH and the IFPH-FIHP, where I had the opportunity to speak about the project; others became part of it through helping with assessing and reviewing, translating and editing, copyediting and managing. As the epilogue and prologue make clear, the book has also been shaped by my lived experience of public history, by my everyday encounters with the past.

Ultimately, of course, there are multiple conversations taking place between the authors within the pages of the book and between the authors and you, the reader. It is my fervent hope that you will find the conversation a companionable one and, like all good conversations, that it is just the beginning of many more.[6]

Looking ahead

The contributors of this book come from many places, disciplines and professions, backgrounds and experiences, but what they share is a passion for understanding how publics engage with the past. Public history is, at its core, all about representations of the past, the process in making those representations, and the ways in which participants and audiences initiate, create, are affected by, influence, and contribute to the shaping of historical consciousness, meaning, and understanding through those representations.

It already seems clear that the interactive capabilities of the Internet will change forever how publics engage with the past. Individuals and groups are not only making private histories public, they are also reclaiming and reshaping the public histories they encounter by liking, re-posting, and commenting as well as offering histories of their own making through social media platforms and/or opportunities created through crowd-sourcing. It also seems likely that as public history becomes more and more international and transnational, then non-white, non-colonial, and non-English-language cultural and historical experiences will reshape the field in fundamental ways. Inclusivity has always been an issue in the field, especially for formalized, institutionalized public history. Alternative histories and diverse voices have only recently begun to find spaces within public history sites, institutions, and academic programs. This too is changing the field in exciting and fundamental ways.

Thinking more globally, to date public history has been served by a literature that is overwhelmingly American, European, and European settler-state focused. As it becomes more multicultural and multilingual, and as it comes to embrace the full diversity of human experience, the field will be transformed. I hope that the *Companion* will in the near future be complemented by work that will encourage a further de-centering of what is one of the most exciting fields in the Humanities.

David Dean
Ottawa, August 2017

Notes

1   I borrow this from the title of an important early collection of essays reflecting on historians working in the public realm (Dalley and Phillips 2001).
2   In 2010, IFPH-IFHP became a permanent standing internal committee of the world's most important organization of historians, the Comité international des sciences historique/International Committee of Historical Sciences (CISH/ICHS) in recognition of its significance within the discipline.
3   The many sites where publics engage with the past is evident from three national surveys in the United States (Rosenzweig and Thelen 2000), Australia (Ashton and Hamilton 2010), and Canada (Conrad et al. 2013). The surveys also sought to uncover levels of trustworthiness. They also reveal the priorities of the public historians designing the surveys and so serve as a useful barometer of the field.
4   I owe this phrasing to my colleague John Walsh.
5   In addition, there has been a steady stream of books focusing exclusively or largely on public history in particular national contexts: in the United States (Gardner 1999), Britain (Kean, Martin, and Morgan 2000), New Zealand (Dalley and Phillips 2001), Canada (Neatby and Hodgkins 2012), and Brazil (Mauad, de Almeida, and Santhiago 2016). Kean and Ashton 2009 and Kean and Martin 2013 offer broader geographies.
6   I would like to thank Calum Dean, Erica Fagen, Tammy Gordon, Jean-Pierre Morin, Elizabeth Paradis, Janet Siltanen, and John Walsh for their comments on this introduction.

Prologue: Orphan Cupboards Full of Histories

Annemarie de Wildt

Visitors to the courtyard of the Amsterdam Museum are always intrigued by the rows of lockers next to the terrace. They are one of the traces of the Burgerweeshuis – the Civic Orphanage, one of the oldest and best known children's homes in the Netherlands. Today, the rooms in which children once ate and slept contain museum displays. Tens of thousands of children grew up in the orphanage between 1580 and 1960. From the age of 11, boys and girls were strictly divided: the girls played in the big courtyard, the boys in the smaller one, which is now the museum terrace. The orphanage was exclusively for children of fairly well-to-do burghers (poorters). Both boys and girls received a good education and professional training. The girls stayed inside and learned sewing, needlework, and housekeeping. Boys started work outside the orphanage when they were 12, perhaps at the Dutch East India Company shipyard, or apprenticed to a carpenter or smith. The governors of the orphanage selected suitable apprenticeships, usually based on the father's profession. When the boys returned in the evening, they put their tools in these lockers.

In the twentieth century, the lockers lost their original function, and some were turned into rabbit hutches. In 1960, the last orphans left, and the buildings were transformed into the Amsterdam Historical Museum (since 2010, the Amsterdam Museum). Some lockers were used for small presentations, but most served as storage. Around 2004, the educational department suggested opening up more of the lockers as show boxes to present the results of projects with schools and various groups in Amsterdam. Designer Erna Tielen made the color scheme for the background.

The cubby holes, or "orphan cupboards" as they are usually called, have housed a great variety of small-scale exhibitions. Sometimes they contained displays connected to the exhibition in the larger museum. For instance, during the exhibition about Amsterdam East, when the museum launched its first storytelling platform, the youngsters from that neighborhood filled the cupboards with their stories. When the museum presented the work of the famous nineteenth-century painter George Hendrik Breitner, they were full of

A Companion to Public History, First Edition. Edited by David Dean.
© 2018 John Wiley & Sons Ltd. Published 2018 by John Wiley & Sons Ltd.

poems. After looking at the paintings, groups of adult migrants who were learning Dutch chose words and turned them into poems that were then exhibited in the cupboards.

The orphan cupboards are literally and figuratively without thresholds. During daytime, anyone can walk into the courtyard and look at them. Especially for groups that are not experienced museum visitors, this is a great advantage. Together with a foundation for the promotion of social participation, we worked with a group of migrant women, who created artwork on the theme of "home." Often the presentations in the lockers were the outcome of a larger project, such as the "education past and present" project with mothers and fathers with Moroccan roots. They met four times in the museum and talked about (changes in) education by means of paintings and objects from the museum collection. All of them were photographed in front of the work that had struck them most. These photos, together with a letter each parent had written on "My hopes for the future of my child(ren)," were exhibited in the courtyard. As always, the opening of the exhibition was a festive event with family and neighbors in attendance.

In general, the orphan cupboards have been a great way to work intensely with one group or school. We often work with artists to encourage new forms of expression. Amsterdam Tracks, for example, was made together with Artists&Co and the ISH Institute, a street dance collective. The young ISH dancers investigated their roots, interviewed family members, and looked for related objects that they could display in the cupboards. During the opening, they performed in the museum courtyard dances that were inspired by this quest into their roots. The presentations were often quite moving, for instance, the one made by children from an asylum center, or the "water in Amsterdam" project we did with a school of mostly Islamic children. One of the girls, who, like most of her female classmates, was wearing a headscarf, had made a drawing showing her hair all around her. On the blue painted paper, she had written "Under water my hair floats."

Orphan cupboard projects are a way of inviting new groups to the museum. In 2013, on the occasion of the 150th anniversary of the abolition of slavery in Suriname, the Amsterdam Museum set up a photo studio in the Oosterpark where the yearly Keti Koti ("break the chains") festival is held. We photographed around 200 people. A large group of museum colleagues and volunteers asked them what their festive Surinamese costumes meant to them, and the photos and stories offered in response were published on a special website. The next year the photos and some traditional folded headscarves were exhibited in the lockers, again with a party.

The cupboards are one of the various platforms the Amsterdam Museum uses for its public history projects. As the last people who spent their childhood in the orphanage are still alive, we launched an oral history project. Many former inhabitants of the Civic Orphanage shared their stories, which can be read and heard on our community website, Hart (Heart) Amsterdam Museum. Some of these stories were also used for the current (semi-permanent) exhibition in the orphan cupboards: the story of the Civic Orphanage. So if you find yourself in Amsterdam, have a coffee on our terrace and, afterward, wander past the cupboards and peek into the past of these buildings and the stories they have to tell.

Courtyard and Orphanage Cabinets, Amsterdam Museum.
Photo: Amsterdam Museum.

PART I

Identifying Public History

Complicating Origin Stories: The Making of Public History into an Academic Field in the United States[1]

REBECCA CONARD

What's in a name?

In the inaugural issue of *The Public Historian*, the late Robert Kelley, who coined the term "public history," offered a brief account of "Its Origins, Nature, and Prospects" (1978). Actually, he skirted the matter of origins, as if this were obvious, and opened with a straightforward definition of public history as "the employment of historians and the historical method outside academia" (Kelley 1978: 16). The phrase "and the historical method" soon disappeared from what became the fallback definition of public history in the United States, but Kelley had a more complex idea in mind when he and Wesley Johnson conceived the idea of a graduate program in Public Historical Studies at UC Santa Barbara (UCSB). In venues "outside academia," public historians would "work in the decision-making process as *historians* [emphasis his], bringing their particular method of analysis and explanation to bear upon points at issue, just as public administrators, economists … and other professionals have brought their expertise into policy making." As a corollary, public history would "have the result of greatly expanding professional employment for historians," which was a real concern in the 1970s, when the academic job market for history PhDs contracted (Kelley 1978: 20).

Forty years later, Wesley Johnson, reflecting on the early history of the National Council on Public History, expanded on the nature of the new academic field that he and Kelley conceptualized. Their vision – which might be described as one-third public intellectual, one-third public policy specialist, and one-third community historian or oral historian – was born from their particular experiences as historians. As a graduate student at Harvard and then Columbia, Johnson had studied under luminaries such as William Yandell Elliott and Zbigniew Brzezinski, brilliant scholars who served as advisers to presidents and high government officials. Quite understandably, they became role models for him. The idea that one could become a public intellectual was reinforced during the 18 months he spent in Paris conducting research in French archives for his

A Companion to Public History, First Edition. Edited by David Dean.
© 2018 John Wiley & Sons Ltd. Published 2018 by John Wiley & Sons Ltd.

dissertation. There, the daily press exposed him to "the many people ... who wrote for *Le Monde* and ... various magazines and newspapers who were public intellectuals. Maybe they were technically a historian, a political scientist, an economist, a gadfly who was bright. 'Public intellectual' was in view, and that's what I had in my life" (Johnson 2015, interview: 12). After joining the UCSB faculty in 1972, Johnson secured a large grant from the National Endowment for the Humanities (NEH) for a community and oral history project with the City of Phoenix, Arizona. This project, he states, "was very fortuitous because that's where my public history career started." Robert Kelley's route to public history was quite different. After publishing *Gold Versus Grain: The Hydraulic Mining Controversy in California's Sacramento Valley* (1959), Kelley found that he was in demand as an expert witness in water litigation cases. After awhile, "he then began teaching some of his students about how history, historian[s], could be helpful to the law in litigation as expert witnesses ... and so Bob got the idea ... [for] some kind of program in public history" (Johnson 2015, interview: 17–18).

This tripartite vision was the foundation for the UCSB program that began training master's and doctoral students in fall 1976. The invited participants who assembled in Montecito, California, for the First National Symposium on Public History in 1979 also reflected this vision. Fully half of them held academic positions but also were involved in some activity to reach wider, nonacademic audiences. The other half represented an impressive array of doctorate-holding historians who worked in the business and corporate world, in federal or state agencies, for historical organizations, for professional organizations, for philanthropic foundations, or as consultants. A few managed large oral history projects. Many held administrative positions with considerable responsibility and authority (First National Symposium on Public History 1979: 73–81).

Missing from this assembly were the leaders of four well-established professional organizations that represented an even wider world of historical enterprise: the American Association (now Alliance) of Museums, founded in 1906 (AAM), the Society of American Archivists (SAA, 1936), the American Association for State and Local History (AASLH, 1940), and the National Trust for Historic Preservation (NTHP, 1949). Nor were they invited to a follow-up meeting in Washington, DC, where a steering committee laid plans to form the National Council on Public History. Johnson (2015, interview: 44) explains that "we were very insistent ... on creating something new," meaning a new field of history, firmly based in the methods of historical research and analysis, and not just promoting alternative careers for historians who could not find academic positions. Even so, it was an omission that soon revealed a deep divide between academicians and the world of historical practice in nonacademic settings. On the one hand, many academic historians dismissed public history as a fad or a fool's errand. On the other, professional organizations were already involved in graduate-level training for professional work in museums, archives, government agencies, and other organizations engaged in history-based activities. As a result, the upstart public history movement was greeted with irritation, even hostility, among academics and professional practitioners alike.[2]

This essay aims to complicate the origin story, although it does not purport to be "the" history of public history, which would require a more sweeping inquiry. Among other things, I ignore the long tradition of historians who have served as public intellectuals as well as the historians who entered government service. Nor do I address the legions of amateur historians who have participated in the processes of history making since time immemorial. Rather, the aim is a more complete understanding of public history as an academic field, albeit one for which a clear definition is still elusive. Thus, this essay sketches the role of professional organizations in shaping graduate training. It also addresses a competing concept of public history as people's history, which challenged the notion that public history was simply nonacademic history. As a corollary, I consider the ways in which scholars working in new social history – and other disciplines – helped shape public history into an academic field. The ultimate goal is a better understanding of why public history, which was variously contested and dismissed in the crucial period of the mid-1970s to mid-1980s, nonetheless had the power to coalesce a disparate aggregation of historians into a movement that could sustain a new scholarly journal, a new professional association, and, ultimately, a new academic field.

The early landscape of professional training

Historians were key players in founding three of the four professional associations named above – SAA, AASLH, and NTHP – and continued to play leadership roles for many decades. Although historians were not involved in AAM's founding, eventually they joined the fold and assumed leadership positions in that organization, too. Importantly, because advanced degrees were considered essential, or at least desirable, for managing larger archives, museums, and historical organizations, professional associations monitored, nurtured, and then sought to order graduate training for professional practice.

Professional training for museum work came first. Between 1910 and 1940, several museums initiated in-house training programs and apprenticeships, and a few universities began to offer courses in museum methods. These early course offerings and programs were allied with the disciplines of natural history, art, and art history, reflecting the way museums professionalized along disciplinary lines (Coleman 1939; Teather 1991).[3] Even though the vast majority of museums in the United States were (and still are) history museums, training programs did not begin to address the needs of history museums until the late 1940s. From 1949 into the 1950s, the National Park Service (NPS) ran in-service training course in museum methods, both curatorial and interpretive, for its growing inventory of history and natural history museums (*NCHSB Quarterly Report* March 1950; Lewis October 1941). In 1948, the New York State Historical Association (NYSHA) began offering summer seminars on American social history and folk culture for museum interpretation and the restoration of historic buildings (*NCHSB Quarterly Report* March 1949). As museum-training programs proliferated, AAM took stock and in 1965 published a 30-page booklet on *Museum Training Courses in the United States and Canada*. At that time, only the Winterthur program at the University of Delaware and the Cooperstown Graduate Program in Museum Studies at the State University of New York, Oneonta, offered museum training that specifically addressed the needs of historic house museums and historic sites.

The SAA began to lay the groundwork for professional education immediately after it organized in 1936. A committee established to examine the training of archivists recommended an approach that privileged history. Having borrowed archival theory from European sources, American historian-archivists also sought to model training programs after European practices, with administrators and managers "recruited from the level of training required for the degree of doctor of philosophy in American history." But librarians also exerted influence in the professionalization process, which the committee back-handedly acknowledged by recommending training for a second class of archivists – those who wanted to prepare for jobs in business or local archives – at a level "equal to that of the Master's degree in the social sciences, with a support in library technique" (Bemis 1939: 157–159).

During the next three decades, archival education emerged with one foot planted in history and the other in librarianship. The early landscape included a mix of short courses, summer institutes, and graduate programs. The latter included a collaborative program between the National Archives and American University, which began in 1939, and another collaborative undertaking, launched in 1952, between the Colorado State Archives and the University of Denver's School of Librarianship and Department of History. In a slightly different vein, Philip Mason, Director of the Labor History Archives at Wayne State University, teamed up with the History Department in the early 1960s to create an archival administration specialization for the master's degree (Jones 1968). By the late 1960s, four universities were offering graduate programs in archival administration, while ten others were offering short courses or summer institutes.[4]

Professional training for work in historic preservation has a shorter history. In 1949, American University, in cooperation with the NPS and Colonial Williamsburg (CW), began offering an intensive summer Institute in the Preservation and Interpretation of Historic Sites and Buildings. It was hailed as "the only special course now being offered in this country" (*NCHSB Quarterly Report* March 1949; December 1949; December 1950). In 1962, when historical architect Charles Peterson retired from the NPS – after directing the Historic American Building Survey for nearly 30 years – he took his expertise to Columbia University. There, he worked with the School of Architecture to develop the first graduate program in historic preservation, anchored in architectural design, not history (Peterson 1982, interview: 20–22).

By the early 1960s, graduate education for professional work in institutions that preserved, managed, and interpreted history had begun to gain traction. Interdisciplinary and collaborative ventures characterized the advance guard. The most ambitious initiative was the Seminar in Historical Administration, which warrants special attention because it involved three of the four professional associations, and it persists to the present day.

The seminar in historical administration

Shortly after New Year's Day in 1957, historian Edward P. Alexander, then vice president and director of interpretation at CW, sat down and drafted a proposal for an eight-week "historical preservation seminar," which he shared with a few staff members and close academic colleagues, including historian Richard McCormick of Rutgers University. "We were all a little worried in the historical agency field," he later recalled, "because so many poorly trained people were going into historical society and museum work." While waiting for replies to his letters, he had lunch with Richard Howland, president of the NTHP, to discuss "setting up this Seminar on a cooperative basis." Anxious to secure the approval if not cooperation of leading universities, because he envisioned a dozen or so hand-selected doctoral students taking this seminar, Alexander also met personally with Wesley Frank Craven of Princeton and Oscar Handlin of Harvard (Alexander memoranda 1957, 11 January and 4 February; Alexander 1985 interview: 131–137).

As a result of these early discussions, Alexander revised the "historical preservation seminar" into a more formal proposal for a "historical interpretation seminar." He invited the AASLH to join as a third co-sponsor and solicited the cooperation of prominent scholars at "foremost" universities as a strategy for attracting "high-quality" graduate students. Citing the "magnitude of the movement to 'bring history to life' ... [at] state and local historical societies, the national historical parks, and the scores of restorations and 'outdoor museums' that are now interpreting our nation's history," Alexander's revised draft proposal noted that, "there exist no formal programs for training the personnel required to staff these enterprises" (Alexander Memorandum 1957, 6 May; Alexander 1957, Training Interpreters of America's Heritage). Backing up his assertion was a 1956 report by the AASLH Committee on Attracting Competent Personnel, which called for "training college people in the work of historical agencies as a means of meeting the increasing demand." If historical institutions were to "retain their integrity," the proposal intoned, "they must rest on a solid foundation of authenticity," and it was up to historians, both scholars and practitioners, "to assure an adequate supply of personnel equipped with both sound scholarly training and an understanding of the problems, techniques, and potentialities of presenting history through other media than the book and the lecture" (AASLH 1956, "Attracting Competent Personnel in the Field of Local History").

For a variety of reasons, the planned launch was delayed until summer 1959. This gave Alexander, Howland, and McCormick time to work on content and logistics with William Murtagh, Howland's assistant at the NTHP who was tapped to serve as seminar coordinator. During this period, the seminar focus shifted again; by September 1958, the planners were calling it a "seminar for historical administrators" (Colonial Williamsburg 1958, Revised Minutes March 13, Minutes September 4). The inaugural six-week seminar took place at CW from June to July 1959, with 17 graduate students from several prestigious universities. Coursework addressed the philosophy of historical interpretation; evaluation and analysis of historic resources for restoration and reconstruction; planning and development of interpretive programs; interacting with the public; and the basic components of administration: management, finance, public relations, and membership. Participants spent mornings in classroom sessions and devoted afternoons to "laboratory work" at CW or nearby historic sites. Faculty members, primarily professionals from the NTHP, AASLH, CW, and several historic sites and historical organizations, represented state-of-the-art historic site preservation, interpretation, and administration as of the mid-1950s (Colonial Williamsburg 1959, Tentative Schedule and Press Release; 1959 *Colonial Williamsburg News*).

In 1960, AASLH joined CW and the NTHP as a financial partner and co-sponsor. The timing was important for AASLH, which had grown rapidly in the late 1950s and was beginning to assert authority in the disorderly world of state and local historical agencies. As a case in point, in 1956 president Christopher Crittenden called for long-range planning and the development of new initiatives. Raising the standards for preserving and producing local history and creating professional jobs for college graduates emerged as high priorities of the council, which consisted largely of men who held graduate degrees in history. It is worth noting, then, that the AASLH council voted to become a Seminar in Historical Administration (SHA) co-sponsor as part of its policy "to recruit new talent to this field" (AASLH Annual Report 1960).

In 1962, the American Association of Museums joined as the fourth financial partner and co-sponsor, and the seminar title settled into the "Seminar for Historical Administration." A circa 1980 status check of SHA's effectiveness tallied a total of 388 graduates through 1979, with 245 of them deemed to be in professional positions in "the field" (Colonial Williamsburg circa 1980). The figures revealed a success rate of more than 60%. However, in about 1975, the SHA stopped recruiting graduate students because more universities were starting museum studies programs and, in Alexander's words, there were "plenty of well-trained young students coming into the field" (1985, interview: 135). Thus, the SHA switched to training young professionals, which, in turn, boosted its success rate. Even so, by this time, the SHA had established a reputation as a prestigious program. Today, well past its golden anniversary, the SHA continues to provide professional training for the administration of public history institutions.[5]

The AASLH education program, 1967 – circa 1985

Co-sponsoring the SHA was just AASLH's first foray into professional education. In 1961, the AASLH council, well satisfied with the SHA model, discussed the feasibility of establishing a second summer program but concluded that the demand was not yet sufficient (AASLH 1961, Minutes 29 August). Four years later, a way forward opened when Congress passed the National Foundation on the Arts and the Humanities Act of 1965, which has been called "the most ambitious piece of cultural legislation in American history" (Zainaldin 2013: 30). The act marked the advent of federal funding to support research, education, preservation, and public programs in the humanities and cultural arts. AASLH was quick to see the fit, and in 1967 received two grants from the new agency charged with disbursing federal grants in the humanities: the NEH. One grant funded a statistical profile of American historical societies, and a second, larger grant underwrote two, two-week regional seminars for historical administrators and a one-week institute on historical publications (AASLH Annual Report 1967). AASLH received two more NEH grants in 1968, which enabled it to finish its analysis of more than 3,000 historical societies, offer a second institute on historical publications, a third regional seminar on historical administration, and, in cooperation with the NPS, two new seminars: "Historical Museum Exhibit Design Techniques" and "Administration of Historical Properties." With additional NEH funding in 1969 and 1970, AASLH began to build a professional education program that soon dwarfed the SHA at CW, although AASLH continued to co-sponsor it. But, whereas the SHA recruited graduate students, at least until the mid-1970s, AASLH seminars targeted directors of small historical organizations and new professional staff members at larger institutions. By the end of 1970, NEH funding had enabled AASLH "to provide professional training to nearly 300 people actively engaged in historical agency work" (AASLH Annual Reports 1967, 1968, 1970).

For the next decade, federal grants enabled AASLH to expand the range of seminar topics and extend benefits to all members. In 1970, for instance, AASLH began to transcribe and edit selected seminar presentations for publication as technical leaflets or bulletins. In 1972, two-day workshops were added, designed to bring volunteers and paid staff members together to work on more effective programming and interpretation. Beginning in 1977, NEH also supported the development of independent study courses for professionals who could not take time from work to pursue college coursework. NEH also supported the AASLH Bicentennial State History (Book) Series, an ambitious multiyear project to publish scholarly but "well-written" brief histories of all 50 states, and the *American Issues Forum* (1976), a series of essays published in the bicentennial year, each written by a "distinguished American historian." AASLH also tapped federal funding available under the National Museum Act (1966), administered by the Smithsonian Institution, to support specialized seminars for managers and administrators of larger organizations, consultant services to small museums, and the creation of audiovisual training materials. Grants from the National Endowment for the Arts and the National Historical Publications and Records Commission helped AASLH expand its publications program. With funding through the Department of the Interior, AASLH collaborated with the NPS to research and prepare reports on potential National Historic

Landmarks. The steady flow of federal funds was not the only thing driving AASLH's growth and momentum during the 1970s – which grew from about 3,500 members in 1970 to nearly 7,000 in 1980 – but by 1975 federal funding supplied more than half of the organization's annual million-dollar budget, and the staff had swelled to a peak of 32 full-time employees (AASLH Annual Reports, 1971–1980).

During president Ronald Reagan's administration (1981–1989), severe budget cuts began to undermine AASLH's educational program. Consequently, AASLH began transitioning to self-supporting seminars and workshops and stepped up its efforts to secure grants from private philanthropic sources. Although AASLH continued to seek, and receive, substantial grants from NEH and other federal sources, which kept the education program strong through 1984, federal funding dropped by more than one-third in 1985. Coupled with other financial losses that hit in 1985, AASLH was forced to trim its staff from 30 to 23 and adopt other belt-tightening measures (AASLH Annual Reports 1981, 1982, 1983, 1986). Nevertheless, between 1967 and the early 1980s, federal grants enabled AASLH to build a comprehensive professional training program designed to raise the standards of practice and the level of professionalism at historical organizations across the nation.

Merging practice and scholarship

A few historians who pioneered careers in historical practice outside academia also sought ways, and perhaps felt an obligation, to incorporate professional education into graduate degree programs. Not only could institutions of higher learning provide more stability, but they were necessary in order to forge the link between scholarship and practice. Two of these pioneers deserve special mention: Edward P. Alexander and Frederick Rath. Their careers suggest the professional and interpersonal dynamics that were in play from the 1930s through the 1970s as practicing historians outside academia sought ways to influence graduate education in American universities.

Edward Alexander spent nearly his entire career in historical administration, and from the beginning he sought to infuse practice with scholarship. In large part, this was because he received his PhD from Columbia University, where he studied under Dixon Ryan Fox, a leader in the emerging field of social history. Fox is best known for co-editing the 13-volume *History of American Life* series (1928–1943) with Arthur Schlesinger, another prominent social historian, and for serving as president of NYSHA from 1929 until his death in 1945. When historian Julian Boyd resigned as the director of NYSHA in 1934, Alexander was just finishing at Columbia. Fox persuaded Alexander to take Boyd's place. That easily, in the depths of the Great Depression, Alexander's career was launched. He stayed at NYSHA until 1942, during which time he oversaw development of the Farmer's Museum at Cooperstown, then became director of the prestigious Wisconsin State Historical Society. His tenure at Wisconsin was short, however, because in 1945 CW began pursuing him to direct a new division of education. John D. Rockefeller III, CW's benefactor, "thought enough had been done with architecture and authenticity … and he wanted to see more historical interpretation" in the restored colonial village (Alexander 1985, interview: 3–8). From 1946 until 1972, Alexander built education and interpretive programs that were based in scholarly research, admired by many but, with the advent of "new" social history, increasingly criticized by others because CW adhered to the conventions of segregation in the South and marginalized the history of free and enslaved African Americans in colonial Virginia. Even so,

Alexander's stature as a historical administrator made him an influential figure in professional organizations. In addition to initiating the Seminar in Historical Administration, he was a co-founder and one-time president of AASLH, reorganized the American Association of Museums during his presidency of that organization (1957–1960), and helped organize the Virginia Historic Landmarks Commission in 1966. When Alexander retired from CW in 1972, he took his vast experience to the University of Delaware where, as the first Director of Museum Studies, he melded existing training programs in curating material culture and managing historic gardens into an interdisciplinary graduate certificate program in museum studies (Alexander 1981, interview: 41–42). In subsequent years, AASLH published his *Museums in Motion* (1979) and *Museum Masters* (1983), books that became classics in the field.

Frederick Rath, Jr. (ABD, Brown University) also spent his career forging practice and scholarship. He was among the many historians who found employment with the NPS during the 1930s, when federal work-relief spending enabled the NPS to establish a commanding presence in historic preservation and the interpretation of historic sites and house museums. Rath proved his credentials working on a number of high-profile NPS projects, so much so that NPS Chief Historian Ronald Lee tapped him to coordinate the work of the National Council for Historic Sites and Buildings, formed in 1947 under the auspices of the NPS as part of a larger public-private effort to mobilize a nationwide historic preservation movement. After Congress passed legislation in 1949 authorizing the creation of the NTHP (modeled after the British National Trust), Lee paved the way for Rath to become the NTHP's first executive director. In these back-to-back positions, Rath and Lee played key roles in transferring NPS professional standards for historic preservation, developed during the 1930s and 1940s, to the NTHP, which was to serve as the conduit for promulgating those standards to a nationwide network of preservation activists (National Council for Historic Sites and Buildings circa 1948; Rath 1988). At least that was the broad vision. Influential members of the NTHP, however, were not as wedded to history and research-based interpretation at historic sites.

While Rath was directing the NTHP, he established a fortuitous relationship with folklorist Louis Jones, director of the New York State Historical Association. In 1948, Jones began organizing summer seminars on the restoration and interpretation of historic buildings, which took place at NYSHA's headquarters in Cooperstown, and he sought assistance from the National Council on Historic Sites and Buildings (*NCHSB Quarterly Report* March 1949). Then, in 1952, Rath and Jones both began serving terms on the AASLH Council, which deepened their professional working relationship. As Rath tells the story, in 1954, shortly after he and his wife, Ann, returned from attending the third summer school on English Architecture, Art and Social History at Attingham Park, co-sponsored by the British National Trust and the Shropshire County Council, he bumped into Jones. The two struck up a conversation about the Cooperstown and Attingham Park summer programs. Before they parted, they "agreed … that we would go to our respective boards and ask from each $1,000, so that we could put together what turned out to be [the] first Historic House-keeping course," designed for curators and administrators of house museums. Rath subsequently left the NTHP to assist Jones in developing NYSHA's summer programs into the Cooperstown Graduate Program in Museum Studies, launched in 1964 and jointly administered by NYSHA and the State University of New York at Oneonta. The Cooperstown program initially focused on history museum administration and American folk culture so as not to cross into the territory of the Winterthur Program at Delaware, which was curatorial in focus. Jones and Rath approached Oneonta, a small campus in the state system, as a partner institution because they "felt we could do it our way. And at that stage we didn't want academicians telling us what our field was. ... [B]y this time, the middle '60s, we were professionals, and we didn't want the head of the history department telling us ... how to do it." Rath stayed at Cooperstown until 1972, at which time he assumed the position of Deputy Commissioner for Historic Preservation with the New York State Office of Parks, Recreation, and Historic Preservation. In that post, he completed the circle by hiring "dozens" of Cooperstown graduates to fill positions at New York State historic sites: "they [we]re part of the new professional corps" (Rath 1982, interview: 45–72, 86–90; Rath 1975; Rath 1987; Rath 1996).

By 1970, the landscape of professional education for careers in history was dotted with a variety of programs. During the 1970s, the landscape became busier and more varied. Growth in the early 1970s can be attributed to gradually increasing awareness among universities that there were opportunities for professional education in the humanities. Growth in the latter 1970s can, in part, be attributed to UCSB's bold assertion that public history was a new field of academic study. This assertion, coming from a respected research university launching a new graduate degree program with backing from two prestigious funders, NEH and the Rockefeller Foundation, conferred a measure of respectability on professional education. For the first time, not every PhD in history was expected to seek an academic job. Perhaps more important, professional careers in history did not necessarily require a doctorate.

Two surveys of colleges and universities offering some form of public history education – a 1978 survey conducted by the National Coordinating Committee for the Promotion of History (NCCPH) and a 1979 survey published under the auspices of *The Public Historian* – revealed more clearly the magnitude of what became known as the public history movement. The 1978 NCC survey, which canvassed more than 1,800 departments of history, identified 48 departments as being engaged in "curriculum change," meaning that the information submitted "described a new course of study, whether as part of an already established program or as an entirely new degree" (Jones 1979). The 1979 survey captured more detailed information on 35 graduate programs and another 10 colleges and universities with undergraduate offerings. The titles of these programs – applied history, preservation studies, historical editing and publishing, historic resources management, historic preservation, historic preservation and historic site archaeology, folk studies and historic preservation, archival administration, archival studies and information management, library science and history, archival management and historical editing, archival and records management administration, museum studies, museology, museum and preservation studies, historical administration, historical services, history and political science, history and law, and business, industrial, and technological history – indicate not only the various professional career paths that were being gathered under the umbrella of public history as the decade closed, but also the extent to which universities were crossing disciplinary boundaries to make degree programs more responsive to the job market (Anonymous, Public History in the Academy 1979b).

The tremendous growth in degree programs, which continued until the mid-1980s, came during the 1970's job crisis. AASLH, which also functioned as a sort of clearinghouse for job placement in historical agencies, noted, in 1973, that an "unfortunate employment situation ... coexists with the present surge in professional training." That year brought a record number of job inquiries, 223, many of them "from people whose vocational goal is teaching rather than historical society work, but many others ... from

highly motivated young people with good seminar and college training." In the following year, AASLH "aided institutions" in hiring employees for more than 100 positions,
but the number of job inquiries rose to 375. Job prospects continued to decline through
1977, when approximately 1,100 individuals sent inquiries to AASLH seeking positions
in a job market that remained essentially static. The disparity was amplified by a lack of
preparation among job seekers, many of whom had "trained for academic careers and
[were] without training or experience for agency work" (AASLH Annual Reports 1973,
1974, 1977). Beginning in 1978, when the public history movement really got under
way, the job market began to improve, but only slightly. A 1982 survey of state historical
agencies revealed a mixed picture as state legislatures grappled with an unstable economy
(Richmond and George). In this climate, employers benefited from an increasing number of job seekers who were equipped with college degrees but, in the estimation of
established professional organizations, lacked meaningful experience.

Forging public history into an academic field

Declaring public history to be a new academic field was one thing. Making it so was
quite another. There still are many who question whether public history even rises to
that status, or whether it is best viewed as a different "approach" to doing history.
Nevertheless, if one accepts public history as a legitimate field of academic study, two
parallel currents had the effect of shaping it. One is the promulgation of standards for
graduate education, which came from professional associations. The other is a bundle of
concepts and ideas that emerged from the intellectual community.

As academic degree programs began to multiply, the professional associations representing avenues of historical practice moved to establish standards for the content and
quality of graduate education. In 1973, the American Association of Museums created a
Museum Studies Curriculum Committee. This led to the development of "Minimum
Standards for Professional Museum Training Programs," published in 1978. AAM
standards called for two-year graduate programs "based on a relevant academic discipline," offered "in concert with one or more accredited museums," directed by a faculty
member possessing "substantial museum work experience," and requiring students to
serve a supervised internship (AAM 1978, 1983). Following AAM's lead, AASLH created a committee to establish standards for programs training graduate students for work
in historical agencies. Chaired by former AASLH director William Alderson, this committee decried "the proliferation of a great many college courses and 'programs' that
claim to provide preparation for people who will go to work in historical agencies."
More to the point, courses too often were "taught by people who are not experienced in
the field ... [and] without reference to or involvement of quality historical agencies"
(Bigelow 1979, pers. comm., October 4; Alderson 1980, pers. comm., January 14).
Reporting in mid-1980, the committee submitted recommendations similar to those
adopted by AAM, except that history was specified as the most relevant academic discipline and the internship component carried a lengthy list of "principles." The committee
also recommended that AASLH develop and publish a list of programs that met its
standards, although the organization did not take that step (AASLH 1980).[6]

The SAA, mindful of its professional border with library science, took a more studied
approach to developing guidelines. In the mid-1960s, a multifaceted discussion about
archival education developed among archivists and librarians, which led SAA to establish
a Committee on Education and Training. After several years of data gathering and a lot

of talking, the committee convened a special meeting of teachers of archival courses, which produced "Minimum Curricular Guidelines for Archival Training Programs."[7] The proposed guidelines were announced to the membership in the June 1973 issue of the *SAA Newsletter*, but formal adoption did not immediately follow. Instead, American and Canadian archivists continued to discuss, at conferences and in the pages of their respective journals, the need for, merits of, and best approach to setting guidelines. Incrementally, SAA issued guidelines in 1978 and 1988 before finally adopting comprehensive guidelines in 2002 (Peterson et al. 1977; SAA 1988; SAA website).

Guidelines for historic preservation education also developed a bit later, and they came not from the NTHP but from an allied association: the National Council for Preservation Education (NCPE). Formed in 1980, NCPE was, and is, a coalition of educational institutions that offer historic preservation education at the undergraduate and graduate levels. Unlike AAM, AASLH, and SAA, which draw their leadership primarily from practitioners in the field, NCPE's leadership, then and now, is composed of faculty associated with academic programs. Thus, NCPE approached the problem of setting guidelines differently, and, in some ways, with more authority. Essentially, a score of academics, representing the historic preservation education programs in existence in the early 1980s, set curriculum standards as a qualification for membership. NCPE (1984) also issued tenure and promotion guidelines for preservation educators. By the mid-1980s, NCPE's charter members had set the bar for developing, and improving, historic preservation education in the United States.

Regardless of the effort each of these associations put into developing standards for graduate education, the common bond was that all of them advocated parity between scholarship and essential skill sets for practice, and provided blueprints for curriculum change. Professional associations thus gave direction to the movement for curriculum change revealed in NCCPH's 1978 survey. The culminating effect drove a wedge into the traditional curricula of academic institutions.

While professional associations wrestled with curriculum matters, historians of a more philosophical bent pondered the meaning of "public" and "history" combined. In 1981, Ronald Grele, then director of the Center for Oral History Research at Columbia University, challenged academics and practitioners alike to think more deeply about the potential of public history:

> By its name, public history implies a major redefinition of the role of the historian. It promises us a society in which a broad public participates in the construction of its own history. The name conjures up images of a new group of historical workers interpreting the past of heretofore ignored classes of people. It seems to answer the question of whose public? whose history? with a democratic declaration of a faith in members of the public at large to become their own historians and to advance their knowledge of themselves *(Grele 1981: 48)*.

Grele's challenge harkened back to questions about the purpose of history raised by a previous generation of historians in the early decades of the twentieth century. His essay also called attention to a new generation of social historians, influenced by the civil rights, anti-war, and feminist movements at home and the History Workshop established by Raphael Samuel at Ruskin College in Oxford, who took a fresh perspective on the relevance question. In the pages of *Radical History Review*, founded in 1975, "new left" or "radical" historians championed public history as "people's history." This definition appealed to a segment of those who gravitated to public history, and the recent trend to associate public history with social activism speaks to its enduring magnetism. But in the 1970s and 1980s, new social history, which was not confined to the United States, inspired paths of inquiry that drilled into the role of history and historians in contemporary society. As a result, public history began to acquire a more legitimate claim to field status among academicians.

The intertwined growth of new social history and oral history fed one path of inquiry into the relationship between memory and history: how people remember the past as opposed to how historians methodically attempt to reconstruct the past. A related path of inquiry wandered into the mists of how people popularize and traditionalize the past through commemoration, performance, and other forms of representation. Much of the resulting literature was not aimed specifically at public history, but in juxtaposing the processes of history making among the populace with those schooled in the research and analytic methods of history, these streams of scholarship led to insights that public history educators used to shape the academic field. One of them is the concept of "shared authority" in the production of history, which Michael Frisch (1990) initially applied to the process of creating oral history. Scholarly inquiry into memory-history and heritage-history also raised questions about power relationships: who determines what becomes codified as history? What is the interplay between "agency" and "authority" in history making? "Shared authority" and "historical agency" are now key concepts in the discourse of public history. Both are based on the premise that history in the public realm is produced through complex, dynamic processes, far different from the stereotype of the lone historian hunched behind a desk overflowing with books and paper. Public historians also began to understand audiences not as passive receptacles but as quirky users or consumers of history who exercise agency idiosyncratically. The professional literature associated with museum practice opened eyes, but Roy Rosenzweig and David Thelen drove the point home in *Presence of the Past: Popular Uses of American History in Everyday Life* (1998), a staple in the core literature of public history.

Much of the scholarship that influences public history education has come from historians. But the environment of public history practice is interdisciplinary. Historic preservation, for instance, has been greatly influenced by the scholarly tributaries of cultural landscape studies, place studies, and historical archaeology. In many ways, this interdisciplinary stream of scholarship has helped to put history and culture back into historic preservation. And, of course, the professional literature on the specific principles and methods of archival management, museum management, historical administration, cultural resources management, historical editing, and other areas of practice is vital to public history education. From the professional literature also comes the model of reflective practice, a set of observed behaviors that exemplify the ways in which professionals in general integrate knowledge and experience in navigating real-world situations (Schön 1983).

Summing up

The spate of public history programs established from the mid-1970s to the mid-1980s proved to be only the first wave. There have been periodic pulses of growth since then. The current pulse, perhaps the strongest yet, seems to reflect widespread academic acceptance of public history as a field, with a corresponding tendency to shoehorn public history into the traditional understanding of a field as an area of academic study defined by a body of historiography. Indeed, public history is now energized by a rich body of intellectual thought, but it would be quite unfortunate if critical academic discourse were to overwhelm or, worse yet, become detached from the equally critical element of professional development for practice.

For this reason, it is worth considering how the audacious act of pronouncing the creation of a new field of history led to its actualization. Surely the early establishment of a journal bearing the name "public historian" offered a new kind of professional identity, one that linked history to something other than teaching. Just as surely, establishing a new professional association created a forum for exchanging ideas and experiences. But neither of these steps, important as they were, could force an academic field to materialize. The 1978 and 1979 surveys demonstrated the variety of ways in which educational institutions were experimenting with curriculum change during the initial wave. At the same time that academic departments were reaching out to meld scholarship with practice, professional associations were setting guidelines and standards for graduate education. Not only did these guidelines provide direction for curriculum change; importantly, they advocated parity between scholarly content knowledge and the theory, principles, and best practices associated with professional development. Finally, new intellectual currents, many of them tied to new social history, produced critical ideas that have been immensely useful for integrating scholarship and practice.

To present the making of public history into an academic field in this way, so neatly, implies that there is discernible order in public history education. Nothing could be further from the truth. Programs grow organically, drawing on existing faculty strengths and taking advantage of opportunities to partner with nearby institutions to assist with professional development. No program can do everything; thus, within the field of public history, programs develop specialties. If public history was hard to define in the beginning, the evolution of public history education may have clouded rather than clarified meaning. Public history, in many ways, is the big-tent field of history. Still, there is general agreement that public history is where scholarship and practice for real-world needs meet. On equal terms.

Notes

1 My thanks to Gerald George, Wesley Johnson, Barbara Howe, and Patricia Mooney-Melvin for valuable feedback on the initial draft of this essay.

2 Johnson talks about the backlash from academics in his oral history interview, but few published sources document the storm that brewed over public history for a few years. For good insight, see Gerald George, 1986, "The American Association for State and Local History: The Public Historian's Home?" in Barbara J. Howe and Emory L. Kemp, eds., pp. 251–263, *Public History: An Introduction* (Malabar, FL: Krieger Publishing Co.)

3 A notable exception was the path-breaking library school at Hampton Institute, established in 1925, which worked closely with the Hampton Museum to provide professional training for African American women; see Ashley N. Bouknight, Black Museology: Reevaluating African American Material Culture. PhD dissertation, Middle Tennessee State University, 2016.

4 The four universities offering graduate archival courses in schools of liberal arts and sciences were American University, University of Denver, Wayne State University, and North Carolina State University. Universities whose library departments or schools offered short courses and summer institutes included University of Texas, University of Washington, Columbia University, University of Illinois, Syracuse University, University of Oregon, Emory University, University of Wisconsin, Drexel Institute of Technology, and University of Chicago.

5 Since 2004, the SHA has been administered by Indiana University-Purdue University at Indianapolis. For more on the history of the SHA, see Dennis A. O'Toole, "The Seminar for Historical Administration: Déjà vu All Over Again," *History News* 59 (Winter 2004): 21–25.

6 Reflecting on the authoritative stance that AASLH took, it chose to call its recommendations "standards" rather than "guidelines." See "Standards for Historical Agency Training Programs," *History News* 36 (July 1981). The committee files contain an interesting mix of correspondence from program directors who found fault with the standards and others who were eager for the programs to be approved. Records of the American Association for State and Local History, Box 66.

7 The work of the SAA Committee on Education and Training can be followed through correspondence in the papers of successive SAA presidents, located in SAA Records, Subgroup 200/01, especially the Records of Presidents Everett O. Alldredge (1963–64), Clifford J. Shipton (1967–68), Houston G. Jones (1968–69), Charles E. Lee (1971–72), Wilfred I. Smith (1972–73), and F. Gerald Ham (1973–74), SAA Records, University of Wisconsin–Milwaukee.

CHAPTER TWO

Where Is Public History?

Hilda Kean

Introduction

I have taken a decision to start with the question "where" rather than the more conventional "what" to initiate a discussion on the nature of public history. "What" implies a definitive and static response: an article written with this title some 15 years ago seems already outdated in its somewhat timeless and prescriptive analysis (Liddington 2002). However, in a collection such as this, some broad settings of parameters are inevitable. The National Council on Public History offers a summary, namely, "public history describes the many and diverse ways that history is put to work in the world" (National Council on Public History, "What is public history," n.d.). This provides an answer of sorts to those seeking a definition, but it does not take the inquisitive reader further in thinking critically about the ways in which people engage with the past and the processes by which this can become accessible and relevant to contemporary life. "Where," I suggest, offers a more expansive journey through a range of ideas. Moreover, "where" implies place in a broad sense rather than a definition more appropriate for a textual dictionary-style approach. While the written word in such formats can provide definitions to close down debate, in different genres it may also open up frameworks as I hope to illustrate here starting with the discussion of two popular poems: Brecht's *Questions from a Worker Who Reads* and Auden's *Musée des Beaux Arts*. I choose these examples because they raise important questions about the processes by which the past is seen and then constructed into different sorts of histories. (They have also been popular ways into public history that I have often employed with my students.)

A Companion to Public History, First Edition. Edited by David Dean.
© 2018 John Wiley & Sons Ltd. Published 2018 by John Wiley & Sons Ltd.

Questions from a worker who reads ...

Fragen eines lesenden Arbeiters written by Bertolt Brecht in 1935 has been translated in various ways, for example, *Questions from a Worker Who Reads* (Willett and Manheim 1976), *A Worker Reads History* (Hays 1947), or *A Worker's Questions While Reading* (Samuel 1975). The poem is mostly styled in the voice of a worker reading a conventional history book mainly about warfare from ancient history such as Babylon or Thebes up to the expeditions of Philip of Spain, or Frederick the Great in the Seven Years War. It has been employed and reproduced in various contexts. It served as the frontispiece, for example, of *Village Life and Labour,* a collection edited by Raphael Samuel (1975). This was the first volume in a series projected by the History Workshop established by Samuel initially at Ruskin College, where he taught history for some 30 years, valuing the life experiences of the mature students, working women and men, whom he had taught (Kean 2010). He encouraged students to conduct their own research on topics of their choice combining archival or oral material with personal experience. Thirteen of these "unofficial" histories predated – and to some extent led into – the Routledge series and were published in pamphlet form between 1970 and 1973. They included *The Journeymen Coopers of East London* by Bob Gilding (1971), with an elegiac preface recounting his visit to the now derelict site of his former workplace on the London Docks:

> Reaching the end of the back road, I came to the stairs leading down into East Vault ... on my way up again I saw a tattered booklet on the stairs. I saw that it was the 1968 Half Annual Report of the National Trade Union of Coopers. My own name was printed on the front page, 'R.W.Gilding, London Branch President ... In place of the old blank windowed warehouses, they are building a yachting marina and a luxury hotel. (iii–iv)

The Routledge series (like the *History Workshop Journal* established in 1976) was intended to take this way of thinking further, albeit not using the term "public history," which was not current at that time. As the editorial in the first issue of the journal explained, "serious" history had fairly recently become a subject reserved for the specialist. To this was counterposed a collaborative approach encouraging accessibility: "We hope that the journal will reach many historians who work on their own, often in their spare time, without acknowledgement because they are outside institutions, and we hope in turn that they will write for us" (Editorial Collective 1976: 3). In a similar spirit, *Village Life and Labour* attempted "to encourage working men and women to write their own history instead of allowing it to be lost, or learning it second or third hand; to become producers rather than consumers; and to bring their own experience and understanding to bear on the record of the past" (Samuel 1975: xiii). The essays included those on the lives of harvesters in the nineteenth century or of the oral testimony of former workers who had toiled in the long closed stone quarries at Headington in Oxford. The inclusion of the Brecht poem here is firmly within the context of the heyday of British social history in the 1960s and 1970s when the idea of "history from below" was powerful. There was an emphasis, particularly in key works by E.P. Thompson (1963) or Sheila Rowbotham (1973), on the value of histories of working people that were alternatives to the status quo. The poem is included in the *Village Life and Labour* collection to be read as a challenge to the idea that history is only that of the leaders. This emphasis on history from below was linked to a time of radical trade union and political movements (Green 2013; Kalela 2011). Histories focused on working-class people's own interests may well still be valid, but the decline in trade union organization and education has led some to think about creating histories in more individualized ways. While the Brechtian worker may have read history questioning class omissions, as a human without such an identity other ways of processing the past may be developed. Thus, Paul Martin, who has published widely on working-class lives, now offers a more expansive (yet individualized) view of public history. Experiences of the past in everyday life, he argues:

> speak to a personalized, experiential or autodidactic knowledge that informs the individual on history's role in shaping their present. It is public history also because in its recognition it empowers the individual in their sense of its ownership and as contributors to what history is and how it is made. (2013: 2)

However, the poem raises more issues than those I have alluded to here. The poem is not simply about an alternative subject matter of history – harvesters or quarrymen – rather, it is an interrogation of the *existing* subject matter of history. It includes answers *and* questions, for example: "Was it kings who hauled the craggy blocks of stone?" or "Imperial Rome/Is full of arcs of triumph. Who reared them up?" In the 27 lines of the poem, there are 14 questions that demand answers: "Who," "Where," "Was there," and "In which?" Often a statement is made and then subject to scrutiny, for example, "Frederick the Great triumphed in the Seven Years War/Who triumphed with him?" The standard explanations are given before being questioned: the material being read is scrutinized. The book here is not being read to answer previously constructed questions; the subject matter itself gives rise to questions by the very stance (and omission) of the printed material. In this poetic narrative structure, answers cannot exist without the questions. Alternative readings are revealed by what is not said, at least in words, for example: "And Babylon, so many times destroyed/Who built the city up each time?" Despite the experiences of those without a literate voice not appearing in the standard histories, nevertheless they have been marked in the landscape. The source of the answers are included in the seven gates of Thebes, the rock slabs, the Chinese wall, the triumphal arches. Their material existence permits other histories to be written. This material culture, while crucial, is itself insufficient to provide different perspectives; it is the questions that the reader asks that create new possibilities. The poem is not about a worker (*Arbeiter*) who is a reader in the sense of being literate, but one who is actively reading (*lesenden*). The printed material only gives one sort of information (*In den Buchern*): the written word, books, are incapable of providing answers. Material culture – and imaginative questioning – provides different ways of thinking about the past even when a text appears to deny existence. The landscape may contain traces of a past, but it is in the present that they are being conceptualized for new times. That is, the process of creating meaning is key; it is not a given. There is not a simple "what." Privileging process implies activity and creativity rather than a given that is simply disseminated by professionally trained historians to readers or consumers. An emphasis on process creates a focus on how meaning is itself made rather than on the qualification of the person who is doing this.

Traces in the landscape

This idea, of course, does not only exist in poetic form. I want to consider two indicative examples of small traces in the landscape to illustrate how they permit the construction of different histories. The first refers to nearly 500 prisoner-of-war camps on the British

Figure 2.1 *Corso Vittorio.* Photo: Hilda Kean.

mainland in the 1940s (Edwards 2005). Most of the buildings of these camps have long been eradicated. This included the Moota, camp 103 in a remote part of northern England in Cumbria, which in 1942 held Italian and then German prisoners from 1944 to 1946 while they awaited repatriation. (Edwards 2005). (After the war, tens of thousands of men displaced from mainland Europe, including Poles, Latvians, and Estonians also sojourned here.) Here the buildings had been destroyed, including the chapel exuberantly decorated in poster paints by an unnamed German prisoner of war, an artist in peace time (Edwards). But still extant are two words written in once wet concrete: *Corso Vittorio* (Figure 2.1). This trace is an integral part of the modern garden center, and staff are happy to point out the words to interested visitors. *Corso Vittorio* is a reminder of the number of avenues named in Italy after Victor Emmanuel II, the first king after unification in 1861. The wording made in the concrete was a direct reference to home in another country. Because these traces (and other ephemera) exist, local historians could write about this hitherto unknown past and also mount a new exhibition in 2005 to commemorate the 60th anniversary of the end of the Second World War entitled "Cockermouth at War."

The second example refers to names and words scratched in 1845 on the Croick Church windows in a remote part of northeastern Scotland, over 20 miles from Dornoch (Figure 2.2). In May 1845, some 90 people were summarily removed from their homes of hundreds of years in Glencalvie and obliged, like thousands of others, to emigrate abroad to make way for sheep as part of the Highland Clearances (Craig 1990). The homeless families rested overnight in the churchyard: it seems that they would have thought it sacrilegious to take refuge inside. The scratches include individual names or statements such as "Glen Calvie people was in the churchyard here May 24th 1845." Much has been written about the Highland Clearances, and in recent years interest has been reawakened in the framework of the growth of Scottish nationalism. These small traces form part of this past brought into the present. They remain resonant because of their physical location – outside a building, a church – in an inclement and still very remote part of the Highlands (The Clearances n.d.). They are affective as they are almost hidden. In stark contrast is the highly visible statue of the Duke of Sutherland, who initiated many such evictions, that dominates the environs of nearby Golspie. It has created much controversy including imaginative initiatives by artists seeking to create different representations of the statue, including its imagined deportation to Sydney, Australia, mimicking the journey of evicted families (Gibson 1996; MacTotem 1998). In due course, "The Emigrants" statue, depicting a family group as a highly visible counterpoint to the Duke, was unveiled in July 2007 by the then first minister Alex Salmond, noting

Figure 2.2 Scratched words on Croick Church. Photo: Hilda Kean.

"The Scottish Parliament has rightly apologised for the highland clearances, acknowledging our debt to those who left these shores. But apologies, statues and memorials are not enough. We need to engage with our history and learn from it" (Highland Clearances memorial 2007). An identical statue to the one in Helmsdale had recently been unveiled by the Red River near Winnipeg, a city founded by some of those who left the Strath of Kildonan for Canada. The paltry scratched words express a reminder of a different sort: that their physical presence still remains evokes a narrative of durability.

While I have chosen the examples above deliberately, nevertheless I suggest that a starting point of a poem and a searching for a location of history-making outside the "conventions and coldness of the research seminar room" (Samuel 1991: 11) can help raise questions about the form of historical creation and engagement not necessarily found within set definitions that shut down debate.

Musée des Beaux Arts and Bruegel's "Landscape with the Fall of Icarus"

In my next example, W. H. Auden's famous poem *Musée des Beaux Arts* with its implicit reference to various paintings such as "The Massacre of the Innocents" by Pieter Bruegel the Elder in the Brussels gallery also takes the reader beyond the written word, this time to the visual (Mendelson 1977 (1938)). While the poem has conventionally been analyzed as being about humanity's capacity for ignoring difficult events – including the build-up to the Second World War when the poem was written – it can also be understood differently, particularly when analyzed in conjunction with Bruegel's "Landscape with the Fall of Icarus."[1] The painting partly relies on the viewer reading the title and also knowing the Greek myth of Icarus.[2] In his poem, Auden focuses on the ploughman "who may/Have heard the splash, the forsaken cry/But for him it was not an important failure," and whose back is seen at the center of the image and "the expensive delicate ship [that] sailed calmly on." But looking at the painting simply as an image (without reading the title or knowing Greek mythology) has produced different emphases when I have discussed this with students as a possible starting point for creating different histories. Some notice the shepherd gazing upwards; some concentrate on the type of agricultural implement; others the horse or the sheep; and some look at the ships in the context of exploration or trade. All, of course, are valid ways of seeing and thinking about the painting.

While the poem emphasizes the commonplace ignoring of suffering, it is also about the choice of focuses in life. For my history students, taking the poem together with the painting has also been about the choices that historians inevitably make in choosing subjects for the writing of history. As Finnish historian Jorma Kalela has recently reminded us, the rationale of historical research is to call the reader's attention "to one's selection and arrangement of particular past matters in order to demonstrate their present relevance" (2012: 50).

In this example, "where" has again suggested the existence of frameworks being constructed beyond the archive or text in the poetic and the painterly. Certainly much has been fashioned recently in public space not by historians (of any sort), but by artists. A good example are the forms of commemorating the bicentenary of the abolition of slavery on British soil in 2007. Funding was given to museums, most notably the International Slavery Museum in Liverpool that opened in August 2007, and received its one millionth visitor within three years. This complemented the new galleries on slavery in the Museum of Docklands in London, and the British Empire and Commonwealth Museum (now gone into liquidation) in Bristol, the third major slave trading port. The Liverpool museum declares itself to be "the only museum of its kind to look at aspects of historical and contemporary slavery as well as being an international hub for resources on human rights issues" (About the International Slavery Museum n.d.). The content and approach are innovative, but the form of this engagement with the past, a museum, is one of a much earlier period. Museums and art galleries had started to be important at a time of nation formation, particularly in Europe during the late eighteenth and early nineteenth century. Such institutions were often set apart physically from the everyday. Steps, classical architecture, and gardens as seen at the British Museum or National Gallery, for example, were features that ensured that the visitor engaged with (and was educated by) civilizing aspects away from the quotidian (Kean 2000; Duncan 1995). People come to know the meaning of a nation (or locality) "partly through the objects and artefacts which have been made to stand for and symbolize its essential values" (Hall 2005: 25). This form, however, is highly traditional albeit one adopted for nations seeking to create particular new identities, for example, in New Zealand. The new museum Te Papa in Wellington was created both to privilege a neglected Māori past and to signify a new way of thinking about New Zealand as two linked communities of Pakeha and Māori (Dalley and Phillips 2001).

Artists remembering slavery in the Lancaster and London landscape

Public art work in the form of human representational sculptures has been prominent in European culture from the nineteenth century (Michalski 1998; Read 1983). More recently, new, nonrepresentational forms have been increasingly deployed to reflect on the past and create new understandings. Concurrent with the establishment of the International Slavery Museum were various local initiatives. These included the work *Captured Africans*, sculpted by Kevin Dalton-Johnson using stone, steel, and acrylic and located outside the former customs house on St. George's Quay in Lancaster, once the fourth largest slave port in England (Rice 2003).While the work clearly acts as a memorial, it is also identifiable and attracts attention as a work of art. As artist Lubaina Himid suggests, "A monument needs to move, to move on, to help the people who engage with it to move on, it needs to be able to change with … the political climate and the visual debates of the day" (Rice 2010: 43). The location was intended, Dalton-Johnson argues, to make the slave trade and its history central to the stories the city told about itself. Alan Rice, an advisor to the Slave Trade Arts Memorial Project (STAMP), has elaborated: "Exhibiting the slave trade in a public space away from its usual relegation to an often tired museum gallery enables its full historical and contemporary implications to be teased out" (2010: 49).

Another work on a similar theme is *The Gilt of Cain*, a site-specific work in Fen Court, London, near the Lloyds building (Figure 2.3). This city garden is the site of a churchyard of the former St. Gabriel's Fenchurch Street, now in the parish of St. Edmund the King and St. Mary Woolnoth. The latter church had strong connections to the abolition movement. John Newton, the former slave trader, and subsequently anti-slavery campaigner, was rector from 1780 to 1807. The work combines material of the Scottish sculptor Michael Visocchi with the poetry of Lemn Sissay. Visually, the sculpture consists of variously sized cylindrical columns, resembling sugarcane – or possibly human figures. Alongside this is a structure representing a pulpit – or an auctioneer's platform. This is explicitly ambiguous. As Visocchi has explained, "the idea was that I could somehow use these sugar cane shapes so that they could be read on the site as figures, as anthropomorphic forms – and therefore could they not then surround a pulpit as a congregation?" (Rice 2010: 18). An additional layer of meaning is created by the words inscribed both on the figures and pulpit (and written in full on a nearby plaque.) The ambiguity in Gilt/ Guilt and Cain/Cane is developed particularly in the language of the city trader such as "ask price" or "closed position" written on the figures. Around two sides of the pulpit/ auctioneer's stand is the verse: "Cash flow runs deep but spirit deeper/You ask Am I my brother's keeper? / I answer by nature/by spirit by rightful laws/My name, my brother, Wilberforce."

The work was initiated by Black British Heritage, an organization chaired by Ken Martindale, who was involved in community politics, including the organization of Notting Hill Carnival for many years. Historian was not one of the many identities that

Figure 2.3 *Gilt of Cain*. Photo: Hilda Kean.

Martindale adopted. The statue of William Beckford, Britain's first millionaire and twice Lord Mayor of London and owner of over a thousand African slaves on his Jamaican plantation, still stands in the Guildhall, the former center of power in the City of London with a wording elaborating his defense of political freedom – though not the source of his wealth (Siblon 2012). It has attracted critical scholarly attention not least because it renders invisible the connection between philanthropy and slavery interests (Dresser 2007). However, while this formal statue of Beckford has a privileged place in the Guildhall, this location places it apart from a landscape of the City through which thousands of people move every day. Such movement was important for Visocchi: "My main attempt was to allow the sculpture to engage with the flow of the pedestrians and allow people to walk amongst it and to become part of it" (Rice 2010: 19). Arguably the nature of the Visocchi/Sissay work in contemporary form and public location in a place for both sitting and walking through – especially as a shortcut to the commuter stations of Fenchurch Street and London Bridge – engages with a potentially wider audience than a museum, particularly through the striking imagery that invites questioning.

Stumbling across the past in Germany

This idea of "coming across" a discredited part of a nation's past has been used to good effect by the artist Gunter Demnig particularly in Germany, as well as in Austria, Hungary, the Netherlands, Belgium, the Czech Republic, Norway, and Ukraine. His work both highlights and individualizes the victims of Nazi oppression. Echoing some of the ideas of psycho-geographers, coming upon unexpected details from the past in contemporary wanderings, over 43,500 stumble blocks (*Stolpersteine*), small bronze plaques on small concrete blocks, can be found embedded in pavements (Figure 2.4). Initiated by Demnig in 1997, by the end of 2013 they were present in more than one thousand locations. They are of a standard form and include brief details of the individual names of people who had lived nearby with dates of birth and of either deportation or murder at the hands of the Nazis (Stumbling Stones – Stolpersteine 2011). While the work is an artistic representation, it was made possible through the research of historians (including family historians) and, of course, the very existence of those who had died but lived in a

Figure 2.4   *Stolpersteine* (Stumbling Stones), Vienna. Photo: Hilda Kean.

particular locality. Since the blocks are within the pavement and not normally indicated on nearby walls, it is inevitable that pedestrians walk upon such memorials in a way they would be unlikely to walk on, say, a gravestone within a church, without making a conscious choice to do so. In this case, the pedestrian, if the ground beneath their feet is noticed as they stumble, may choose whether to stop and read the name or whether to pass on. As indicated in the image here, since the stumble stones are indeed part of quotidian life, they may also attract rubbish and cigarette butts. It has been suggested that the very walking over "keep[s] the memories alive by inadvertently rubbing the rust off the metal and bringing back the shine." Moreover, to read the inscriptions one needs to bend over, "which may be interpreted as bowing to the victims in tribute" (Scheffer 2008).

Although previously the German artist Jochen Gerz had also used small stones with engravings to memorialize those who had been murdered by the Nazis, that project was somewhat different in the process of execution and reception. With the assistance of German Jewish communities and his students, a list was compiled of the names of the 2,146 Jewish cemeteries extant in the country before the Second World War. These names were individually engraved on the same number of paving stones that were removed from the square in front of the seat of the Saarbrucken provincial government. Initially this was carried out in secret (and illegally) with the stones being removed at night and replaced with engraved ones (Young 2002). Significantly, they were placed with the inscriptions adjacent to the ground and were thus invisible. In due course, the provincial parliament gave approval, and the square was renamed "The Square of the Invisible Monument" (Platz des unsichtbaren Mahnmals).The pedestrian is obliged to walk over the stones to gain access to the building, they do not just stumble on a discrete example (2146 Stones – Monument against Racism 1993). Further, they are unaware of the specific inscription over which they are walking. Such a construction obviously plays with the idea of not knowing (but still remembering), whereas the Demnig project is, in some ways, more didactic and confrontational, making forgotten aspects of the past visible and clearly present in the contemporary landscape.

Artistic comment on murder through slavery or the Holocaust is, of course, about significant issues in the life of a nation. These are not, obviously, books, museums, or television programs presented by trained historians but reminders of the past deliberately created amid everyday landscapes. Those who encounter such works (and perhaps think about this engagement) are not "workers" who "read"; but nor are they necessarily like the "ploughman" turning away. They are physically present and have an opportunity to engage with the past represented before them.

Political pasts and artistic representation in contemporary life

These are not the only aspects of the past that artists have used to create contemporary meaning. Public and accessible histories have been created of less dramatic moments too. Thus, on the platforms of London's busy underground station, Charing Cross, which is routinely used both by Londoners and by visitors to nearby Trafalgar Square, are a series of woodcuts created by David Gentleman. His contemporary artwork became widely known through his poster designs for the Stop the War Coalition's demonstrations against the Iraq war, particularly "Bliar." This earlier work, like the slavery and anti-Nazi works discussed above, is site specific. The images do not portray the life of Queen Eleanor, in whose honor the cross at Charing was first erected to commemorate her death in 1290, but rather the activities of the medieval craftsmen and women who created this well-known landmark.[3]

Perhaps the most famous contemporary British artist to focus on historical political events in accessible form is Turner prizewinner Jeremy Deller. His reenactment of the "Battle of Orgreave," a key moment in the 1984–1985 miners' strike in which hundreds of miners were physically attacked and arrested by the police, and subject to hostile and falsified media coverage, preceded any political commemoration of an "anniversary" of the event (Bailey and Popple 2011; Deller 1999). The staged reenactment mimicked the practice of English Civil War reenactors such as the Sealed Knot and, employing former miners and police, enabled a revisiting on a personal level for participants of what had become an iconic moment in political history. Although some of his work that is critical of the political status quo (such as his "English Magic" show for the Venice Biennale in 2013) is shown within art galleries, much of his work has continued to employ forms of popular history-making outside such institutions.[4] Thus, Procession in Manchester in 2009 celebrated the past, present, and future of the city with a parade including floats such as "The last of the industrial revolution" recalling the former mills, a hearse bearing floral tributes to closed northern clubs such as the Hacienda, or banners remembering the Peterloo massacre (Jeremy Deller's Procession 2009). Many of the banners were created by Ed Hall, former convenor for London Bridge, the London-wide shop stewards movement of the 1980s, with whom Deller often collaborates. Now a prolific banner maker for contemporary unions and campaigns, Hall employs motifs from the past to comment on the present. His commissions have included those for former pits in the Durham coalfields where the Durham miners' gala provides an opportunity for people to demonstrate their allegiance to a past history of the area even when, as Mellor and Stephenson (2005) have noted, some of the pits now being memorialized closed as long ago as the 1930s.[5] The issues that Deller and Hall raise in their practice have resonance within debates in contemporary art theory – but they also have relevance for public historians.

Social knowledge on the internet

The parades that Deller and Hall encourage with people moving through the landscape to remember and (re)create their own histories combine the new (politics and history as art practice) with the old (banners with slogans and visual images) to create particular historical identities, in similar ways to those employed by Chartists or Suffrage feminists (Kean 2005). By way of contrast, one of the newest forms of history-making might be found not in the public landscapes of the City of London, the streets of German cities, or the Croick Church or Moota garden center, but in the public fora of the Internet. This has been used by state bodies such as the BBC to create specific national histories such as the People's War website which was launched in June 2003 and ran for three years, receiving some 47,000 written contributions. In this newest of forms there was, as Lucy Noakes has put it, a coming together of different concerns: "Cultural memory of the Second World War operates hegemonically, incorporating elements of subordinate [sic] memory which can be made to fit: with the dominant and marginalising or silencing more oppositional, challenging narratives of the war" (2009: 138). Other official bodies such as the perspicacious archival project co-directed by Daniel Cohen at George Mason University to collect "digital sources from everyday projects" in the wake of the bombing of the New York Twin Towers on September 11, 2001, were outstandingly successful in collecting more than 150,000 items from thousands of individual contributors that were then transferred to the Library of Congress (Cohen 2005: 215–216). However, the Internet, through the collecting of material and the sharing and exchanging of ideas, is also a form of knowledge creation, in the way that Raphael Samuel describes history as a social form of knowledge: "the work of a thousand different hands" (Samuel 1994: 8). Knowledgeable enthusiasts have used this form of publishing and dissemination to reach wide audiences. A straightforward example is the authoritative website of Peter Higginbotham, formerly employed in computer services at the University of Oxford, which since 2000 has provided comprehensive information on workhouses including details of the locations and buildings as well as links to other material. It is now a key source for family and local historians (The Workhouse n.d.). But perhaps some of the most interesting historical work at present is that which adopts crowdsourcing techniques in different ways. As I have argued elsewhere, the exchange of information on family and local history websites helps create social knowledge. People engage with their own generated materials rather than simply being audiences (Kean 2011). However, Internet exchange and debate can create historical knowledge even when this is not the explicit intention of participants. Thus, Paul Martin, for example, has persuasively argued that the compilation of obscure 1960s beat, psychedelic, and pop records onto recordable compact discs (CDR) can be defined as public history practice. The enthusiasts who do this and disseminate this to other enthusiasts are, he elaborates, creating historical musical social knowledge. In so doing, they are also problematizing the music industry's official narrative (Martin 2011). Similarly, the Autosport's "Motorcycle Racing Nostalgia" forum (n.d.) is ostensibly not a history site. Known users include former famous bike racers, while others are keen enthusiasts. Some who contribute hide their identities. A key feature of this community is what you know and also how. Thus information can be offered through "being there" as a rider or spectator, and by looking at old programs, newspaper cuttings, or photographs. Some of the threads of conversation may discuss old racing grounds with contributors posting images or discussing the merits (or lack thereof) of the two-stroke engine. There are often competitions of sorts, sometimes called WWW (Who? Where? When?) This may involve guessing who the helmeted rider is in an obscure photograph, perhaps accomplished through situating the response in a broader context of knowledge formation: "that circuit was discontinued then," or "that type of bike was manufactured later." Apart from the past of racing and the motorcycle industry, a broader context can be created. A good example is the links to the photographs posted by Paul Gander of a European cycling holiday from a 1953 family album. The visitors to this site may have been interested in the particular bikes, but 11 million had visited it before the owner decided to sell reproductions of the photos (Gander 2011). For those inclined to dismiss such discussions as trivial and not worthy of the epithet of "history," it should be noted that this also mimics the practice of academic scholars, for example, through discussion sites like H-net. To take but one example, on H-net Public History in July 2013, one discussion centered around the make of the car that Marinetti envisaged in his Futurist manifesto. While one contributor mused on whether this was a car at all, another described a Blitzen Benz that broke the land speed record at Brooklands in 1909 that had debuted at the Frankfurt speed trials. The Australian academic who had initiated the question duly accepted this explanation. Certainly the Vienna Technical Museum has welcomed interest from bike enthusiasts in its collection of professional photos of the Salzburg circuit of the old Austrian grand prix, permitting their use by the nostalgia forum.

Conclusion

Some readers of this chapter may not accept some of the examples discussed here as forms of public history. While some may be concerned to create rigid definitions of historical practice, I would prefer to use the metaphors adopted by Paul Ashton and Paula Hamilton (2010) or Martha Sear (2013) when thinking through how to define public history in books on Australian practice. Ashton and Hamilton have suggested that history in the broadest sense might be thought of as a house with many rooms, inhabited by various practitioners such as the makers of films, community historians, or museum workers, some of whom inhabited more than one room while "many make occasional visits to other parts of the house" (2010: 8). Martha Sear has developed this metaphor suggesting that "perhaps if we thought of history as ecological, not architectural, we might take a different view ... Maybe then we'd see it connected to other forms of history-making... as part of a dynamic system where every diverse and distinctive element contributes to the vigour and health of the whole" (2013: 213). Such a dynamic, rather than static, approach may also help us see, as Brecht's worker exemplified, the value of asking questions of apparently accepted subject matter as a way of taking forward debate – and the creation of new histories.[6]

Notes

1   See an image of the painting at http://www.artchive.com/viewer/z.html. Matisse also created an Icarus image during the Second World War, seen as a comment on his despair of the Nazi invasion of France.
2   The myth tells the story of Icarus, who escaped imprisonment in Crete with the assistance of his father who fashioned for him feathered wings bound with wax. Icarus failed to obey his father's instructions and flew too near the sun, where the wax melted and he drowned.
3   The current cross dates from 1863; the original version from the 1290s was destroyed in 1647. Artists' work on the underground system is not unique. Eduardo Paolozzi, for example, designed the mosaics at Tottenham Court Road station. However, the Gentleman example is a specific reference to working lives of ordinary people in the capital.
4   The controversial video critical of the institutions of the City of London and royalty, particularly the slaughter of a protected bird by Prince Harry, can be seen at http://www.theguardian. com/artanddesign/video/2013/may/29/venice-biennale-jeremy-deller-english-magic-video.
5   The banners themselves have become part of the remembered past. Thus, the Houghton Lodge banner depicts former miners and their families parading at an earlier Durham gala with an earlier banner.
6   Thanks to Russell Burrows, Anna Davin, Gloria Edwards, Ken Jones, Paul Martin, and Farhana Sheikh for information or helpful comments on an earlier draft.

CHAPTER THREE

Consuming Public History:
Russian Ark

JEROME DE GROOT

Much work in public and popular history has tended to focus on Anglophone and Eurocentric traditions, texts, practices, historiographies, and institutions. This is mainly due to the fact that the organizations that study, resource, and facilitate public history – universities, learned societies, professional bodies, types of heritage sites – have historically tended to be in the West, particularly in the United States, United Kingdom, and Australia. The International Federation for Public History (IFPH) was launched in 2010 after the National Council on Public History (NCPH) "taskforce" on internationalization had illustrated the need for such a body, given the increasing amount of work being done in the field outside the United States.[1] The investigation of the public and popular manifestation of history globally is therefore a pressing and new field of inquiry, encompassing discussion in a variety of disciplinary contexts. Understanding the international and national contexts of popular historical output is key to comprehending how and why it contributes to the historical imaginary. However, finding common ground for an investigation of popular history *across* national cultures is difficult. Work is generally confined to one particular national context or site. Hence, our understanding of "public" and "history" in this subdiscipline tends to rely upon particular notions of either. Public history might be characterized as driven by Western, Anglophone academic models, its historiography that of a particular set of practices, and its sense of the "public" very much predicated upon a participatory democratic model. Increasingly this is changing, or being challenged, by work in China, Russia, South America, and around Europe.

Furthermore, outside of the museum and heritage site sector, scant attention has been paid to the experience of the user, reader, viewer, or participant in public history.[2] How viewers of costume drama or historical television respond to and engage with fictions of the past is something of a mystery. What, then, of public history around the world (at a local level), or of more global participation in public history? How do audiences engage with historical texts produced in different cultures, and what might this tell us about

A Companion to Public History, First Edition. Edited by David Dean.
© 2018 John Wiley & Sons Ltd. Published 2018 by John Wiley & Sons Ltd.

public history more generally? How can historical products enable us to think about the ways that the past is conceptualized domestically and internationally? Most importantly, what should scholars understand about the "use" of history around the world by "amateurs": users, readers, viewers, participants, and consumers?

This chapter cannot address in totality these key questions, although it is important to raise them. However, it suggests a few ways forward and, particularly, models that might allow a new set of ways of addressing publics and their histories. As a case study, the chapter takes the film *Russian Ark* (dir. Sokurov 2002), a bravado account of Russian and European history based in/on the Hermitage Museum in St. Petersburg. The chapter considers the film itself, with its meditations upon art, history, national identity, and tourism (as well as the formal qualities of rendering the past, most obviously evidenced in its single 96-minute tracking shot). It also looks at the film's reception around the world, from reviews to audience reactions. The chapter examines the varying ways that a public historical text might be made to mean in varying contexts thinking about national history, global identity, and the celebrity of the arthouse film. This allows the chapter to meditate upon the nature of public history in an increasingly globalized media system, and to look at varying models for how and why audiences seek to consume the past, be it "their" past or that of "others." The film's strange status allows us to see how the histories of other countries are dreamed by those who watch fictions about them.

The film

Darkness. Indistinct but disturbing noises. A man's deep voice begins: "I open my eyes and I see nothing. I only remember that there was an accident. Everyone ran for safety as best they could. I just can't remember what happened to me" (*Russian Ark* 2002). Other sounds begin to intrude and then images of gorgeously dressed women and men in uniform. The narrator-speaker sees them: "How strange … where am I? Judging by their clothes, this must be the 1800s." The camera begins to move, following the participants as they wander around outside and music plays. The narrator-speaker continues to reflect upon what is happening as if it is some kind of performance: "Can it be? Has all this been staged for me? … What kind of play is this?" The film hence begins in an extremely self-conscious way, articulating its own staginess and locating understanding of events in dramaturgical sensibility. The narrator-speaker is figured as the audience, located in the same space of observation as the "actual" viewer. It becomes clearer that the camera is intended to be the point of view of the unnamed narrator-speaker, and he wonders why no one sees him: "Can it be that I'm invisible or have I simply gone unnoticed?" His marginalization is key to the idea the film fosters of eavesdropping, accidently stumbling onto events. The only person who "recognizes" the narrator-speaker is a man dressed in black who interrogates him (his gender is assumed) about where and when they are, and which language they are speaking.[3] They begin to wander the rooms of the Hermitage. Each room contains a situation from Russian history, although the rooms are not visited in chronological order. They finally emerge into the final royal ball held by Tsar Nicholas II in 1913.

The opening sequence of *Russian Ark* reflects upon the time-machine quality of the museum, placing objects that allow for a historical engagement within the now.[4] Opening this way also figures the subsequent movement through Russian history and European art as part of a nightmare, or at best a strange dream. It is a confusing and complex opening that introduces some of the key aesthetic, ethical, and historiographical concerns of the film. The beginning of the film expresses a certain terror, confusion, anxiety, and the vague certainty of a traumatic event ("there was an accident"). The narrator-speaker does not participate, but rather watches, at times literally from outside looking in. Events – such as they are – take place outside of his agency. However, the first-person point-of-view framing ensures that the narrative appears to be being "experienced" directly rather than, as in most film, participated in by the characters. The investment of the audience in what is happening is therefore brokered by the framing device, at once distanced while being very much sensorially involved. The affinity of the "actual" audience with the speaking voice situates those watching diegetically "in" the film while also distancing them from the unfolding action. Therefore, this film from the beginning reflects upon the "use" and experience of watching it, and frames various questions about the status of the viewer and the ethics of watching history unfold, of consuming a richly decorated past.

The film was shot in one entire take and travels through 33 rooms of the Hermitage. It was filmed digitally on a Sony HDW-F900 by Tilman Büttner, a relatively famous Steadicam operator. Büttner could only do one take given the physical demands of carrying the 35-kilogram camera (Ross 2002). The shoot involved 1,300 extras and 186 actors, plus a crew of around 46 (including 10 relating to the camera and recording). It was filmed in one day on December 23 due to the popularity of the museum as a tourist destination, and the take had a window of only four hours because Sokurov wanted to use natural light. Although the film's form suggests a keen authenticity associated with the driving narrative linearity of the action, Sokurov cleaned it up a lot in postproduction. In particular, he tinkered with the coloring, and reframed much of the film. The sound – all the music, narration, and dialogue – was added in postproduction. These various production elements are important for two reasons. First, because they contribute to the muscular, pioneering mythos of the making of the film, and second because consideration of the material elements of film production is key in current scholarship. A sense of the production context of a cultural text is central to understanding how and why it is being made (Bordwell and Thompson 2003). For a film that is so self-conscious about its artistry and wroughtness, the collaborative quality of the production is key to its meditation upon the ways in which narrative is constructed. Through their absence, the viewer becomes aware of filmic techniques that are generally unseen (while evidently seen): editing, music, acting, camera movement, and multiple takes. The continual tracking of the camera makes the film simultaneously wrought and naturalistic. It also comments clearly on the way in which film narrative – and realism – is constructed through the techniques of editing, acting, and movement. Bravura tracking shots have often been used in historical film to conceptualize the historicity of a certain participant, and to critique narrative models of the "flow" of history (Bordwell 2002). For instance, the famous three-minute club sequence in *Goodfellas* (dir. Scorsese 1990) works with the film's use of freeze-frame to reflect upon witnessing, storytelling, and how memory works, as well as on how historical film might narratively articulate these things through the tropes of realism.[5] Scorsese also uses a long, spiraling tracking shot in his adaptation of Edith Wharton's *The Age of Innocence* (1993). The camera sweeps around a party in the 1870s. Through a combination of authorial voiceover and camera movement, the film reflects as if through the eyes of the character Newland Archer upon the guests at the dance and the art on the walls. However, the camera also moves around this character, establishing a kind of narrative distance from him while seeming to express, through the voiceover, an understanding of his actions and character. Hence, it establishes a kind of authorial disconnect and a type of irony that reflects Wharton's own technique and makes the film more novelistic. As with the *Goodfellas* moment, it is a highly wrought but equally complex authentic moment that reflects upon the aesthetics of realist representation and, particularly, of narration. Finally, Joe Wright's *Atonement* (2007) has a five-minute sequence on Dunkirk beach tracking around various situations and moving from participant to participant. Horses are shot, men groan and die, a small male choir sings. There are explosions, multiple vehicles, and a large cast is choreographed. Similarly to the two Scorcese scenes, Wright's tracking shot is at times from the point of view of a character but also veers away from this figure and considers him. There is a crucial distancing from the protagonist, something not found in Sokurov's tracking shot, where the association of the view is constantly with the narrator-speaker. Wright's film has a clear concern with myth-making and narrative, reflected in this sequence. *Atonement*'s narrative turns on a lie, and the "atonement" is the idealistic fictionalizing of events that, in the film's final moments, the audience discovers are the ones they have been watching. The tracking shot therefore reflects upon the tropes of linearity, realism, and authenticity when representing the past. It reminds the audience of the progressive nature of film, its seemingly ineluctable linearity. While purporting to be extremely realistic (insofar as it moves with the characters in an unedited way, much more akin to "real" experience), the tracking shot is so baroquely excessive in comparison to contemporary fast-edited film that its deployment is often considered radically old-fashioned.

Sokurov's decision to shoot in one take is therefore important to the film's aesthetics, and, hence, its historiographical engagement. The film presents Russian history as a set of moments accessed sequentially (the linearity of the tracking shot) but out of chronological time. At one moment the European wanders from an Italian gallery in the time of Catherine the Great to a room full of tourists with guides. They are diegetically existing simultaneously, as the European wanders from room to room. The film therefore reflects upon the mimetic representation of the past attempted by most historical film. It also presents time as a disconnected set of events. When governed by a narrative template, "time" and "events" become "history": a discourse constructed to tell some kind of story, to articulate some form of truth, but, ultimately, as the narrator-speaker argues at the opening, as fictional as a play. He notes, pointedly, "I hope it is not a tragedy," surely echoing Marx's famous injunction, via Hegel, about history as tragedy and then farce made in *The 18ᵗʰ Brumaire of Louis Napoleon*. The European also mentions that "Russia is like a theatre," and he sees the performance of politics and power in the palace as a dramatic charade. There is a brief scene in slow motion, and a long discussion of painterly naturalism.

The formal innovation of the film forces the viewer to think about visual pleasure (and art), temporality, and space. By constricting the normality of the cinematic frame, Sokurov manipulates the audience into thinking about the ways in which narrative and time are wrought and constructed for us as linear, progressive, teleological phenomena. He reflects upon the relationship of cinematic time to history, both created as pageants to oppress and control the audience. He is hardly the first Russian director to do this – Sergei Eisenstein theorized the political applications of montage and editing in the 1920s – but in this instance he maps the way that the camera captures and relates time and space to a complex sense of the historical imagination. The first scene that is encountered in *Russian Ark*, involving Peter the Great, includes the prominent clicking and then striking of a clock to ensure that the question of time and linearity are uppermost in the diegesis. The second scene – like the final ball, discussed below – includes shots of musicians that linger on the sheet music in front of them, emphasizing the relationship of multidimensional artistic production and experience to formalized time schemes and subsequent linear narrative. The film itself is experienced formally as a multidimensional piece of music, a sequence of events in time working with one another like a clock, intersecting and interlocking.

There is little linearity in the script and, again, this is a challenge to directionality. The dialogue between the European and two modern dwellers of St. Petersburg (an actor and a medical doctor) is fractured and seems at times to ignore the rules of dialogue or grammatical interchange. Therefore, the ways of developing relationships and articulating character in film are generally challenged. The scene suggests that an idea of a dialogue with the past is a chimera, something desired but impossible (similarly, the European and the narrator-speaker demonstrate the inability of participating in events from "history"). Scenes also challenge chronology, as "actors" from multiple time zones move around one another. The action also goes outside the palace, and into its walls. The protagonists meet a man during the siege of Leningrad making his own coffin. At this point the narrator-speaker (whose knowledge has been vast, for a confused participant, and strange) discusses Russian history during the twentieth century, from the 1917 Revolution to World War Two and into the contemporary moment. This wide sweep of discussion and conceptualization shows the European "out of time." He does not understand, cannot conceive of, the million people who died in the siege of Leningrad. The film thus meditates upon the modes and moments of Russian history, thinking about periodization and historical caricature.

One of the key elements of the film is its meditation upon the transporting nature of art. Art materially exists in the present but looks back to its moment of creation; it is at once record and affective instance. The European calls some figures in a work "Eternal People." Yet there are also several discussions of beauty, something seemingly transhistorical but surely historically contingent. The European tells a modern character off for not understanding an El Greco painting of the Apostles because he "hasn't read the Scriptures." The "modern" figure does not have a theological appreciation of the beauty of the image. Appreciation of what beauty might be is dependent on historical situation, and the scene thus also reflects upon post-Enlightenment "modernity." Similarly, art is something solid that exists in space and time, imagination and reality. The European sees Antonio Canova's *Three Graces* and reflects upon the creation of something "real" from solid material: "What feel for the material," he exclaims. As with conceptualizing architecture as "frozen music," sculpture might be seen as an art that is materially expressed in three dimensions. In the following scene, a blind woman feels the sculpture, her sensory encounter with the solidity of the art through touch as well as sight (the European also smells several works). Art has multiple affective qualities, and a consideration of the response to it is complex. The European discusses art with the blind woman and they look at several pictures. He also dances with a lonely woman whose encounter with a painting allows her to express a particular self-sufficient subjectivity: "this painting and I have a secret." Several times the camera pans to a picture for some time and moves around, "looking" at the art and somehow experiencing it. Is this palimpsest version of art "real" in any way? Around the protagonists and the paintings, historical actors rush around and discuss gossip or matters of state.

The metaphor of the ark in the title suggests the Hermitage floating on the sea or river that is history, somehow transporting from beyond the deluge strange things to populate the world anew. Its conscious echo of biblical determinism and apocalypse provokes a debate about the value of art and of conservation, and the relationship of works from the past to identity in the present. Ковчег has a secondary meaning of "reliquary" in Russian, so the film furthermore suggests that the Hermitage and its collections have an aspect of the relic about them. This would figure the tourist as a pilgrim, seeking an encounter with the transcendent (and unhistorical). The ark is both a memorial and a living thing, something that has iterative power in the now due to its age and its contribution to something ineffable in the present. Art is also something that, collected, contributes to a sense of national identity. Major art collections are part of a nation's cultural heritage, so on the one hand they allow for a self-presentation, whereas on the other they package an easy sense of national identity to be fetishized, desired, and controlled by tourists. The film presents the dream of art, a sense that the movement through the Hermitage is both nightmare and uncanny dream. Similarly, the contribution to Russian national identity of the Hermitage is problematized. The viewer is a tourist, gawking at the artworks that make up the cultural remains of an empire; comprehending Russia through art painted elsewhere, or understanding Russian history via a palace built to house tsars.

Andrew Higson's (2003) influential work on costume drama shows how scholarship generally situates such film as politically conservative, linear, and indicative of a particular type of national identity. *Russian Ark* might be seen to undertake this kind of work. It is narratively linear, fascinated with property, things, houses, ownership, and inheritance. It seeks to construct a lineage, a genealogy of sorts, while also reflecting upon the way that this straight-line, explanatory construction is fundamentally part of what heritage culture – in the shape of museums – contributes to the imagined community of nation. *Russian Ark* seems to reflect this linearity. Its final scene is a beautiful costume ball, staging the last moment of Tsarist extravagance before the various revolutions that famously involved the storming of the Hermitage, then the Winter Palace, in 1917 (shot influentially by Eisenstein in 1927's *October*). There is a certain melancholy in watching the end of empire staged here. History overtook the figures represented. Their beautiful movement is nostalgic insofar as it looks back with some mourning, but the film is not sentimental here. The ball scene emphasizes movement and splendor. The camera lingers on the extravagantly dressed guests as they begin to dance. It moves with them, and for some seven minutes follows the dancers, shifting between couples.

The dance is a spectacle – many people watch it – and something done for its own pleasure. The dance offers another formalized way of negotiating space and time. It gives the participants pleasure and they applaud the musicians, who have created, through their own interpretation of linear text on a page (their music stands are lingered on), something that lives in three dimensions. It is beautiful geometry, within the ordered space of the ballroom. However, in contrast to the clean lines of text, music, wall, and window, the scene restores the human body to the dance to the music of time. It is a strange, peculiar scene that seems to associate bodily dynamism with a kind of historicity.

For all its formal, linear direction, the film seems to cleave at this point and through to something more rhizomatic. Paintings and art relate to one another as a nexus. The Hermitage is a vast hive of meaning and beauty, with the route taken through it generally random. The route is sometimes through back corridors, or gardens: this is not a march of history, but a meander around. Art allows for this sense of intertextuality and connectivity outside of a precisely tooled progression of events. The various self-reflective aesthetic and formal effects – tracking shot, script, even the intertextual references to art and other films – have forced the audience to reflect upon their own engagement with filmed (and written) history, their own aesthetic and ethical encounter with the past. The tracking shot is not a progression, but a stately set of movements tending toward a direction (but not a linear movement). It suggests a historiographical sensibility that eschews rationality for emotion and an affective "truth" in the aesthetic encounter.

Reviews and responses

Apart from its meditation upon historicity, observing, and art, the film is important for scholars of public history because of the way it has been produced as a global historical product. This is in great part due to the reviews and responses that situate the piece culturally. Pierre Bourdieu argues that the value of a work of art is something constructed by its "symbolic production":

> The sociology of art and literature has to take as its object not only the material production but also the symbolic production of the work, i.e. the production of the value of the work, or, which amounts to the same thing, of belief in the value of the work. It therefore has to consider as contributing to production not only the direct producers of the work in its materiality (artist, writer, etc) but also the producers of the meaning and value of the work – critics, publishers, gallery directors and the whole set of agents whose combined efforts produce consumers capable of knowing and recognizing the work of art as such, in particular teachers (but also families, etc.). (1993: 37)

For Bourdieu, the contribution of those who help create a film's cultural worth is part of the production of the text. They help construct the "meaning *and* value" of the work, and unpicking their contribution is key. This has become increasingly complicated in a multicultural, transcultural, globalized, homogenized, international, and, importantly, online cultural landscape. How a text is given meaning and value through the intervention of a multiplicity of users is increasingly seen as key to understanding the matrix of cultural production.[6] The following section of the article considers the ways in which *Russian Ark* was received and constructed by various groups as a means of considering how it performs culturally and, most importantly, how its engagement with history and representation of the past is understood. There is a unique archive of response to the film that provides a great deal of important information about the ways audiences comprehend and understand it (or are instructed in how to consider it). Engaging with this archive raises a number of methodological and epistemological problems that demonstrate the complexity of working on public history in the contemporary moment.

The Internet Movie Database (IMDB) lists 121 external reviews that are generally newspapers, magazines, or blogs with some cultural weight. The list is mainly alphabetized but with a set of "key" publications at the top (*Guardian, Village Voice, Washington Post*, and *The New York Times*). This listing takes in reviews in English, Portuguese, French, Spanish, Dutch, German, Turkish, Hebrew, Romanian, and Italian. It thus presents an extremely globalized sense of the cultural production of the text. Rotten Tomatoes and Metacritic also collect reviews. While Metacritic tends to be more United States based, responses on Rotten Tomatoes come not just from across the United States, but also from countries such as Uruguay, the United Kingdom, and Australia. Of all these reviews, only one (discussed below) is in Russian. This may be due to linguistic challenges, but it also demonstrates something about the interface between Anglophone critical traditions and those of other, possibly more problematically configured cultures.

There are very few responses listed, for instance, outside of what we might define as the West, suggesting that the discourses that Bourdieu (1993) illustrates contributing to cultural production apply mainly within a particular Western, post-Enlightenment (or maybe postmodern) epistemology of intellectual engagement, public sphere, and cultural-capitalist production.[7] The transition or translation into this sphere of a film shot in Russia, in Russian, celebrating Russian history and its art collections, figures a crucial importing, as the critical responses demonstrate.

The complexity of Western critical response to the film demonstrates its sophisticated texture and ambiguities. Peter Bradshaw, writing in *The Guardian*, recognizes the key contribution that the film's formal work makes to a challenge to standard ideas of temporality: "Why abandon the grammar of cinema? The edit is what gives the film-maker the ability, in Tarkovsky's phrase, to sculpt time – and space too (2003). He argues that Sokurov's work is a meditation on national identity, establishing the Hermitage in post-Soviet Russia as a fulcrum for imagining the then and the now (and the relationship between the two). Philip French in *The Observer* is more critical, noting the worrying linearity of the film: "What *Russian Ark* resembles is a historical pageant, a *son et lumière* show without three-dimensional characters, and rather narrowly focused" (2003). This idea of the "pageant" of the past is sustained by the film's central "tracking" aspect interpreted as historiographical metaphor here. The eminent critic Roger Ebert's review is worth quoting at length because of some of the problematic lacunae it highlights (and attempts to fill). Ebert points out the way that the film presents "the grand sweep of Russian history":

> I found myself in a reverie of thoughts and images, and sometimes, as my mind drifted to the barbarity of Stalin and the tragic destiny of Russia, the scenes of dancing became poignant and ironic. It is not simply what Sokurov shows about Russian history, but what he does not show – doesn't need to show, because it shadows all our thoughts of that country. (2003)

The film in this reading prompts a set of responses in the viewer, drawing images from their memory. The viewer dreams the Russian past, imposing a reading onto a representation rather than engaging with the film itself. It provides a site for the viewer to imagine a version of Russia. Ebert points out the film's reluctance to provide history post-Revolution (the "contemporary" scenes are not "history"), and the eloquent absence therefore of twentieth-century events and horrors. The film creates irony through what is not represented, a seeming echo of something unseen. Yet Ebert also suggests that the viewer comes to the film with a set of previously created caricatures about Russian history (barbarity, tragedy) that *Russian Ark* itself strives to answer by ignoring. Russian national identity, constructed by the non-Russian viewer, is focused solely on violence, discord, and trauma. Russian history, on Ebert's reading, is continually inflected by the events of the past century. Russia in the historical imaginary is constantly the site of tragedy and pathos. For Ebert, the dancing of the aristocrats is poignant as they are metonyms for the people of the country (and of Europe, potentially), innocently dancing while events overtake them. Writing in *The New York Times*, though, Stephen Holden is more critical of these dancers. Rather than having any "lingering nostalgia for the pre-revolutionary era of czars and serfs," he argues, Sokurov is more concerned with "the historical blindness of an entitled elite blissfully oblivious to the fact that it is standing in quicksand that is about to give" (2002). These two critics disagree, therefore, on the conclusions of the film and hence its historiographical stance. Ebert sees a historical poignancy and tragedy in the innocence of those who cannot see the future; Holden considers this lack of sight culpable and something the film condemns.

Ebert argues further that the form contributes a formal dreamlike aspect: "the effect of the unbroken flow of images ... is uncanny" (2003). The contribution of the film's form to its meaning is something highlighted by nearly every critical response to the text. Jake Wilson, reviewing in Australia, argues that the form creates its own challenging hauntology:

> a productive tension between continuity (in 'real' space and time) and discontinuity (in its fictional shifts between epochs) suggesting the simultaneous presence and absence of the past, while the same theme emerges through the many enigmatic references to artworks and historical events, which serve as challenges to the audience's own fallible cultural memory. (n.d.)

Wilson's argument is that the movement of the camera and the film counterpoint one another and allow for a complex historiographical engagement which is felt, crucially, by the audience. Similarly, Noel Megahey argues that "it celebrates this summation of the duality of the Russian nature – a past that can't be denied, a present that is striving to redefine itself – it explores the dichotomy between its Asian nature and its desire to be European" (2003). Sometimes, though, the concentration on the materiality of the text is part of negative reviews suggesting that the form is too prevalent. It prevents "die Schönheit und Größe der russischen Kultur zu präsentieren" ("showcasing the beauty and grandeur of Russian culture") (Maiwald 2003).

Despite the diversity of responses, only one of the critical reviews that IMDB lists is in Russian. This review points out that the film, already played in at least 20 countries around the world, was only screened in St. Petersburg and Moscow once; suggesting that Sokurov's audience was not domestic in any way. This is an extremely hostile review, suggesting that Sokurov is something roughly translated as a "Russian missionary of culture," manipulating a faddish Western interest in heritage and history (Barabash 2003).[8] Some Russian response to the film has highlighted its problematic conservatism.[9] It is important to recall this relatively sour suggestion of inverted cultural imperialism when considering the global situatedness of the film. *Russian Ark* might be seen as much as a tourist destination as the Hermitage itself, presenting a version of history that is a cliché for export rather than contributing to a genuine conversation about the value of historical and aesthetic production to national discussions.

In general, then, the international critical responses are celebratory and engaged. They demonstrate the complexity of the film's take on Russian national identity and on historical representation, and introduce key moments or precursors (Andrei Tarkovsky, André Bazin, Mike Figgis, and Max Ophuls are all mentioned) into the discussion. They admire the technical feat and variously attempt to read the form of the film into its content and narrative. They also highlight the film as a global product, something that despite its very domestic specificity – a set of versions of Russian history, very precisely situated in a Russian location – it somehow speaks to an international audience. Indeed, Megahey suggests as such (in terms that echo those used by Ebert) when he writes: "Some of the best moments in the film operate on an instinctual and emotional level, where you aren't expected to keep up with the cultural, historical and political references" (2003). The affect is as key as the intellectual engagement undertaken in this reading. The specificity of the historical and political locutions is sometimes unimportant.

However, the reviews generally provide a wealth of information about how the film is constructed as an arthouse masterpiece with gravitas and something to add to the history of cinema; an intervention and a historiographical wonder that is both educative and a delightful experience. The brief cameo of Russian responses, though, demonstrates the continuing problem of writing about film from different cultures.

Away from the "official" reviews, in the various online communities that sustain film consumption throughout the world, there is a proliferation of responses to the film. These range from the semiofficial to more offhand commentary. These online reviews enable us to understand further the way that a text has worked in the public imagination. Semiofficial responses are generally found on websites that either mimic older forms of reviewing or seek to enfranchise the user-participant. Online review accumulator sites such as Rotten Tomatoes, IMDB, and Metacritic, and retail sites such as Amazon enable "amateur" users to post reviews. Less formalized types of responses are recorded in social media sites and microblogging services. It is also important to recall that most of the responses are to the film as consumed in a variety of situations: some in the cinema, but most at home either on DVD, streaming video, or broadcast television. As Laurent Jullier and Jean-Marc Leveratto argue, the "diversification of the modes of film consumption has been accompanied by an unprecedented evolution of film discussion as a means of comparing opinions, exchanging information, and sharing knowledge" (2012: 147). There is a swathe of information, and this presents a methodological problem. How to mine these responses, and how to characterize and use them as a way of understanding the reception of the film? What work is being done in constructing and imagining the past? How to approach these responses, which are only a percentage of all existing responses?

The range of user responses demonstrates the increasing investment that audiences and viewers place on responding to films. They reveal a new epistemology insofar as the user assumes a certain authority and understands that they contribute to the comprehension of the film by articulating their views. The user reviews are also a shorthand way of seeing how a text has been received, and how this reception might contrast with more mainstream indicators of value. For instance, there are 170 reviews of *Russian Ark* on the American Amazon.com (plus 33 on Amazon.co.uk, 12 on Amazon.fr, and 16 on Amazon.de). Comparably, the film that won the 2002 Best Foreign Picture Oscar, *No Man's Land* (dir. Tanovic 2001) has slightly fewer reviews in the United States but comparable numbers in Europe. *Chicago*, winner of the 2002 Best Picture Oscar, has 1,444 reviews on Amazon.com.

The user-reviews contribute to the online crowdsourced reputation of the film. Review accumulator sites pull reviews from "real" critics and also host user or audience reviews. They give star ratings, which add to a general score. Importantly, sites like the Internet Movie Database ask users to rate a movie, so *Russian Ark*'s headline information is that it has an average rating of 7.3 out of 10 from 10,528 users. This raw data contributes to a film's reputation and gravitas online. If you Google "Russian Ark," the IMDB entry is the second hit (after Wikipedia), and the user rating status is part of the result given. Google results highlight the film's "score" from accumulator sites and compare them (89% from Rotten Tomatoes, 86% from Metacritic). Accumulator sites contrast the critic with the user, establishing a hierarchy of response. However, the audience is still on a continuum with the professional, rather than somehow lower. They are part of the way that the text is constructed in the online domain, participating as Bourdieu's "producers of the meaning and value of the work" (1993). Hence, the audience is to a certain extent enfranchised by this participation in the valuation, accruing cultural capital through their engagement with the film but also challenging the hierarchy of authority surrounding the production.

Russian Ark has around 150 user responses on Rotten Tomatoes, 164 on IMDB, and about 40 on Metacritic (not all in English – there are some Spanish, Italian, French, and Portuguese postings). IMDB also has discussion boards relating to the film, with at present around 80 strands of up to 30 postings (ranging from discussions of plot to questions about the film's music). While many of the review-responses are relatively brief, some are extended to two or three paragraphs. IMDB, because of its reputation as a cinephile website, has much longer user reviews with participants seeking to undertake cultural work rather than the briefer interventions made on Rotten Tomatoes.

In general, the user reviews are positive, and celebrate the technical accomplishments of the film. Users cite the film's "pure originality and concentration" and their pleasure: "an absolute delight" (Rotten Tomatoes, original post by AlexanderD 2012; original post by Hi H 2008). Key terms are repeated: sweeping, pageant, memorial, impressive, unique. The costumes are regularly praised, as is the beauty of the *mis-en-scène*. For a film that is in many ways uber- or meta-authentic, many respondents point to a surreal quality in the dreamlike narrative. Many user-reviewers describe the experience of watching the film as a "history lesson" or being on a museum tour: "A brilliant and entertaining look at Russian history" (Rotten Tomatoes, original post by verycreativename n.d.). The member of the audience becomes in some ways a pupil, in others an interested tourist: "The viewer moves throughout history to bring alive the story of a building which continues to be of fundamental importance to the Russian people" (Rotten Tomatoes, original post by John B 2012). This flatness of response, though, is characteristic. Russia and Russian history become in the reviews somewhat monolithic, and there is little engagement with the detail of the text or its historiography. The model is the pageant of history, occurring in front of the interested observer, but with little critical engagement.

Yet, of most interest might be the negative responses. They allow an insight into the expectations of many film viewers. Key seems to be a lack of plot or narrative in the film, a sense that expedience, purpose, and direction are necessary. Some responses claim that the bravura technical accomplishment of the film mean that it is only really for the cinephile and movie buff; somehow its precision and difficulty ensure that it can only be appreciated by someone who is more "expert" than the common viewer. This again demonstrates a presumed hierarchy among audiences. The Russian history sometimes backfires: "We left baffled, having learned little or nothing of the Russian history or culture that we had set out to acquire" (Metacritic, original post by Keri 2003). This latter response is richly suggestive of the agency of the viewer and their purpose in engaging with a historical text. Again, many reviewers reacted to the perceived dryness of the film in communicating the past: "if you want a dose of history, visit a museum or historical site in person. But skip the film" (IMDB, original post by gruenig 2003); "the museum looks fantastic in the movie and it encouraged me to visit it sometime but as a movie, I don't find it interesting at all" (IMDB, original post by Thomas Lun 2003). Many of these negative responses argue that the form and narrative structure of the film get in the way of appreciating the art or, similarly, does not add anything. The disjunction between the historical and artistic content is what provokes disquiet, that is, the filmicness of the text.

What is fascinating about the user responses in these various forums is the lack of critical engagement with the history that is being presented. If it is mentioned at all, the film's history is presented in a very flat way, that is, it is accepted relatively uncritically. Hence, the reviews demonstrate a range of sophisticated response to the form of the film, but do not find a way of relating that to the content (which is surely one of the key points that is being made). The closest the reviews get to a critique is to highlight how the history shown is generally that of the nobility. Historiograpically, then, the reviews seem to suggest an engagement with a film that is clearly fictional and highly wrought – so much so that it is difficult to mention anything *other* than its form when discussing it – yet a lack of appreciation of the complexity of historical representation or narrative that the film seems to offer. History, in these responses, is presented by the film almost in a documentary style, as a set of lessons and factual reenactments. Given the film's self-conscious artistry, and its self-reflective representation of art and artifice, this suggests that, if these interested, active, intelligent, inquisitive viewers are generally happy to accept relatively uncritically what they are "told" by film, then it might well be the case that most other historical film would provoke such a passive response.[10]

Amazon user reviews are slightly more complex as a genre. They, too, assign a star rating and accumulate the ratings among the reviews posted. They are also rated according to how "helpful" they might be to a user, so the reviews themselves become part of a discourse of usefulness. When reading reviews, they are ranked automatically by this "helpful" index. On the one hand, the Amazon reviews seem to enfranchise the user, giving them a voice in the transactional retail process and ensuring a resistance to the cultural gatekeepers who would seek to make taste. On the other, Amazon reviewers contribute their thoughts free to a corporation that then uses their intellectual property to market and sell product. Amazon review culture has become a niche comic genre, with elaborate reviews given to mundane objects (for example, there are around 650 satirical reviews of the BIC for Her range of ballpoint pens). In mocking the review genre, users demonstrate that it has become a prevalent mode of engaging with product. The tone of the online review is brief, often breathless, and somewhat credulous. A language of evaluation has been evolved by the user groups. Furthermore, these reviews are part of Amazon's branding, a way of suggesting interaction and customer enfranchisement. The "value" of something is crowdsourced, and this seemingly democratic model creates a sense of interactivity. The customer has power here, and might make an intervention (Dobrescu, Luca, and Motta 2012).

Offhand commentary is generally found in shorter-form social networks and microblogs. Twitter, for instance, reveals immediate responses to the film: "Correct. RT @StephensSimon: Sokurov's **RUSSIAN ARK**. Simply astonishing" (Twitter, original post by @Poppy_Corbett 2013). However, it has also become facetious shorthand for long and ponderous production, seen most recently when users repeatedly compared the Opening Ceremony of the Sochi Olympics to the film: "Not sure why Russians didn't just show the film Russian Ark to celebrate history and culture" (Twitter, original post by @progressiveman 2014). This latter response is more interesting than it first looks, suggesting a perception that the Olympic opening ceremony and the film had something in common about presenting an onward and progressive march of Russian nationalist history. Even more anonymously, the *Russian Ark*'s page on Facebook is "automatically generated based on what Facebook users are interested in, and not affiliated with or endorsed by anyone associated with the topic" (n.d.). The page has content pulled from Wikipedia and related page links; 11,750 people "like" the topic.

Conclusion

There is a wealth of information relating to the way that this film is understood in the public domain, how it contributes to the historical imaginary, and the work that it is understood to do. In order to understand how popular texts function, and how the discussion around them contributes, in Bourdieu's words, to the "meaning and value" of the piece, it is necessary to survey a wide range of data and to engage with an archive that is still growing and expanding. It involves a shift in methodology to looking at user experience, and an understanding of the new epistemological possibilities opened up by the Internet, particularly relating to international understanding of national pasts. The consumption of the past as product is something that is still little understood, but this swathe of material allows for a new, more complex appreciation to be reached. The historiographical account of these responses is yet to be written, but it will be an important part of work on the relationship between the global and the local historical imaginaries.

Data-mining massive collections of information such as these archives of responses has begun to be undertaken by historians and literary scholars.[11] They give a different, shifting perspective on texts and events. In the present case, the critical and audience reactions to this ambiguous and strange film reflect the ways in which it has been situated internationally: as a primer on Russian history, as a way of understanding the relationship between Russia and Europe, and as a meditation upon the value and work of art. They demonstrate the film's ability to reflect upon how the past is represented. They also show how the historiographical stance of the film might be largely unseen, or unremarked upon.

This chapter began with an address to wider, global definitions of "public" and "history," and to the work that both might be expected to do. In many ways, *Russian Ark* addresses this, asking how a text, a piece of art, might instill or imbue a kind of historical understanding. It also challenges, or meditates upon, multiple ways of thinking about history and the relationship to the past. However, the film also presents a challenge. It is unique, and as such means that creating a taxonomy or methodology using this example is probably impossible. It is also a text that provides a warning for those in the West eager to embrace historical product from other cultures. The self-consciousness of *Russian Ark* demonstrates its understanding as a film of how it might function in the popular global historical mainstream, and how it might enter into critical debate. It serves as an opportunity and as a warning to those who would study texts in their international, global, or glocal contexts and make suggestions about how the historical imaginary is resourced and supported.

Notes

1 See the formal Special Issue international interventions of the *Public Historian* since 2010, for instance, Holger Hoock, "Professional Practices of Public History in Britain," *The Public Historian*, 32: 3 (2010), pp. 7–24. See also the work of the IFPH: http://www.publichistoryint. org/wordpress/.

2 A notable exception is Clare Monk, *Heritage Film Audiences: Period Films and Contemporary Audiences in the UK* (Edinburgh: Edinburgh University Press, 2011). On museum audiences, see Eilean Hooper-Greenhill, *Museums and their Visitors* (London and New York: Routledge, 1994).

3 The "European" is based on the Marquis of Custine, a diplomat who wrote about his experiences in Russia during the 1830s.

4   See, for instance, *The Museum Time-Machine: Putting Cultures on Display* ed. Robert Lumley (London & New York: Routledge, 1988).

5   This is imitated in the opening of P. Thomas Anderson's 1997 *Boogie Nights*, a three-minute Steadicam shot that enters a club following a character. Scorcese (see also *Casino*, 1997), Anderson (*The Master*, 2013, and *There Will Be Blood*, 2007), and Wright (*Pride & Prejudice*, 2005), all discussed here, use the tracking shot very self-consciously in their historical work. See Kevin B. Lee's video essay "Steadicam progress – the career of Paul Thomas Anderson in five shots," and the scientific study he cites about how Anderson's shots in *TWBB* literally – physiologically – produce multiple viewpoints, *Sight & Sound*, January 9, 2014, at http://www.bfi.org.uk/news-opinion/sight-sound-magazine/features/video-steadicam-progress-career-paul-thomas-anderson-five.

6   The work of Henry Jenkins on fan culture is key here: Henry Jenkins, *Fans, Bloggers and Gamers: Exploring Participatory Culture* (New York: New York University Press, 2006) and *Convergence Culture: Where Old and New Media Collide* (New York: New York University Press, 2006).

7   For further discussion on this, see work on national cinemas around the world, and for models of cultural colonialism particularly Toby Miller, Nitin Govil, John McMurria, and Richard Maxwell, *Global Hollywood* (London: BFI Publishing, 2001) and same authors plus Tina Wang, *Global Hollywood 2* (London: BFI Publishing, 2005).

8   The Russian text is this: "Русские миссионеры от культуры, похоже, на Западе опять входят в моду." Translations compared through GoogleTranslate and ParalinkOnline. The use of translation tools in accessing these reviews raises another epistemological quandary about considering the "consumption" of the past in popular culture. It enables a wider sense of response, but at the same time is dependent on a new type of technology that renders flat and uninflected versions of reviews.

9   Andrei Zorin, for instance, Professor of Russian History at Oxford: "a rather traditional (and conservative) vision of Russia as an only legitimate heir to the centuries of European culture." E-mail to author, April 13, 2013. This response is characteristic of those expressed by Russian historians and cultural scholars.

10 As a coda to this, compare the user responses to *La Retour du Martin Guerre* (1982), which might be considered a key film for constructing a historiographical sensibility. Very few engage with the film's discourse of storytelling, authenticity, ethics, and historical truth, http://www.imdb.com/title/tt0084589/reviews?start=10.

11 See, for instance, the work of Daniel J. Cohen, "From Babel to Knowledge: Data-Mining Large Digital Collections," *D-Lib Magazine*, March 2006, at http://www.dlib.org/dlib/march06/cohen/03cohen.html.

CHAPTER FOUR

Historians on the Inside: Thinking with History in Policy

ALIX R. GREEN

"History matters" has been a rallying call in recent years, as historians have argued for the value of historical perspective in the making of policy. The "case for history" has been made in persuasive ways (Macmillan 2009; Tosh 2008), but less attention has been given to *how* historians could influence the world of political decision making, given the very different imperatives that shape academe and government. Historians have, of course, always been active in political affairs. The early social histories of the Webbs, the Hammonds, and Tawney aimed to provide the evidential basis for social and economic progress (Vernon 2004). Historians engaged in both propaganda and public education during the First World War, and have served inside government as specialists (Tosh 2014). In the latter decades of the century, health, education, and welfare have, notably, drawn the attention of historians, who have taken platforms outside the profession in attempts to influence policy (Berridge and Strong 1991; Porter 1986; Thane 2009). This rich and varied work is part of a lineage of politically oriented historiography that has been woven into the discipline since its nineteenth-century beginnings.

Some issues have prompted not just historians, but policymakers, think tanks, and the media to turn to the past. For example, comparisons between 2008 and historical economic crises – particularly the crash of 1929 – were prominent in the public discourse of the time, and treated as significant material for informing policy, not least by the then British prime minister (and history PhD), Gordon Brown (2010). More recently, attitudes in Germany – both politically and at community level – toward accepting refugees from Syria have been interpreted in light of the Nazi past and the expulsions and forced migrations that followed the end of the Second World War. In early 2017, the past informed very different responses to President Trump's use of an executive order to suspend the resettlement of refugees in the United States and entry to the country by citizens of seven Muslim-majority countries: a betrayal of America's historical promise as the 'land of opportunity', or resonant of prior attempts to apply discrimination in immigration policy?

A Companion to Public History, First Edition. Edited by David Dean.
© 2018 John Wiley & Sons Ltd. Published 2018 by John Wiley & Sons Ltd.

The very readiness with which history is invoked in the media and in political discourse has sharpened professional historians' sense of the ways in which politicians ignore, distort, misconstrue, and misrepresent the past. The case for bringing history into policymaking often rests on the premise that historical perspectives offer insights that would improve the quality of political judgments. Policy problems that seem new rarely are, nor are the "radical" or "innovative" solutions proposed to address them. Taking the long view expands our understanding of a country, issue, or individual. Carefully inspecting the historical analogies invoked in policy debate should help avert injudicious and precipitous decisions (Neustadt and May 1986).

This is important work, but the present chapter takes a different approach. The aim here is to explore the potential roles of historians and historical expertise inside policy-making. As historians, we cannot expect policymakers to use such expertise well unless we give serious attention to *how* history could work effectively with the processes of policy formulation and within the structures, realities, and constraints of the political system. Similarly, we cannot advocate greater prominence for historical sensibility in the scholarship of policy formulation unless we are willing to engage more consistently and purposefully with relevant fields, both within and beyond the humanities. These are both complex tasks, and they require us to rethink our mental models, not only of the policy process but also of historical practice.

A history gap?

History has struggled to position itself as a discipline that has distinctive and relevant contributions to make to public policy. In Britain, the interventions of notable individuals and of collective endeavors such as the *History and Policy* network have enhanced the appreciation of historical insights among policymakers, yet historical expertise is not routinely sought as part of the policy process. It should be noted that there are specific areas of policy where historians' claims to evidential primacy are uncontested. In former colonies of white settlement, the independent successor states have, in recent decades, instituted enquiries and tribunals to address the grievances of aboriginal populations for the many forms of aggression, discrimination, and injustice they experienced, often perpetrated well into the twentieth century (Hickey 2006; Milloy 2013). The Waitangi Tribunal in New Zealand – established as a permanent commission in 1975 to consider breaches of the 1840 Treaty of Waitangi guaranteeing Māori ownership of lands and other properties – has created a sector employing more historians than any other (Dalley 2009: 80–81).

Such work is important – morally, socially, and politically. Clearly focused on historical research, the tribunal does not, however, readily provide historians with a case for the value of history in policymaking more broadly. Fields such as economics have pressed their claims to supply the rigorous basis for informed policy decisions, behavioral psychology the evidence for effective realization of policy goals. Political scientists, sociologists, and anthropologists, among others, have concerned themselves with defining the policymaking process and understanding the institutional systems and cultures that shape, reinterpret, and divert it. History is implicit in many aspects of political scholarship, yet as a distinctive discipline it is conspicuous in its absence. The case study, for example, requires careful contextualization to be meaningful; examining policy choices means asking how the issue emerged and was conceptualized by political actors; understanding how policy formulation and implementation happens calls for attention to institutional cultures and practices that have historical dimensions. That such efforts call on methodological insights from another discipline is rarely explored (Wood 2014).

Rationalist models that divide the policymaking process into stages, from problem definition to evaluation, are an obvious target for historians and other humanists as practitioners of an "ecological approach to human affairs" (Gaddis 2002: 62). We can criticize the "largely ahistorical theories, models and projections" (Szreter 2011: 219) of more influential disciplines – and the failure of policymakers to learn from history – but surely cannot stop there if we hope for more historically informed approaches. Often overlooked by historians are developments within other fields that offer the opportunity for productive dialogue. Political scientists have, for example, been subjecting rationalist models of policymaking to revision and challenge for some time, emphasizing that they have a deterministic dynamic that cannot accommodate contingency: agents have no meaningful choice when faced with "rational" and "irrational" options (Hay 2002). Description and narrative are being recognized as offering ways to capture vital considerations, such as culture and context, which cannot easily be integrated into prescriptive and mechanistic approaches (Kerr and Kettell 2006; Kiser 1996; Weiss and Bucuvalas 1980).

Historians tend to relish the debunking of myths, the disruption of neat narratives, and the destabilization of certainties. A notable target has been political conceptions of the "family in crisis," which have been on the political agenda in the UK since the 1970s, with apparent symptoms including family breakdown and absent fathers, the preference for welfare over work, poor discipline and juvenile delinquency, and neglect of the elderly (Thane 2011). We can mobilize historical insight to expose such conceptions as ideologically conditioned assumptions rather than informed analyses; by extension, we can *also* use those skills and sensibilities to build cogent arguments showing that powerful beliefs about how policymaking works or what constitutes "useful evidence" are just that: beliefs. They are not stable or inevitable realities, nor self-evident truths, but have a historical existence with which we can engage. An essential connection between history and politics was envisaged in the nineteenth century, subjects "which belong to each other," as J. R. Seeley, the first Cambridge Regius Professor of History, put it. Historians not only understood their function in terms of furnishing "the empirical validation of experience" for practical politics, but also had their currency and credentials for the task widely acknowledged (Seeley 1895; Bell 2009: 211; Burrow 1983; Wormell 1980). Understanding more recent beliefs about evidence and policy as historical phenomena is an important task in itself, but it also frees our intellectual imaginations to conceive of other, future, contexts in which different beliefs are possible.

Attending to policy advice in historical perspective suggests two interlinked themes that help us understand the absence of history as a discipline in political thinking: the privatization of politics and the emergence of a "quantitative imperative" in evidence for policymaking (Green 2014). The privatization of politics over the course of the twentieth century can be understood as a bottom-up claiming of political space by emancipated citizens constructing "their own personal manifestos of complaints, causes, and commitments" (Hilton et al. 2013: 1). A top-down alternative may emphasize an ideological shift beginning with the Thatcher administrations that deprivileged professional judgment and made individuals, and their preferences and choices, the reference point for political arrangements (Hood 1995; Skelcher 2000). Wherever we place the agency, policy advice became contestable (Bevir and Rhodes 2010). The emergence of influential political actors outside government – think tanks, NGOs, advocacy groups, trade associations, lobbying agencies, and so on – created new forms of expertise that mobilized knowledge with political acumen.

Governments also sought more politically attuned forms of advice. The specialists brought into state service as "irregular" officials during the Second World War – including economists, engineers, geographers, and computer scientists – were invoked in support of technocratic principles in the debates from the late 1950s about administrative reform. Yet the Churchillian dictum of experts "on tap but not on top" was not destabilized, nor did government become more permeable to the specialist outsider. Rather, a more complex policy environment emerged, in which advice acquired a political edge. During Harold Wilson's first premiership (1964–1970), the appointment of ministerial Special Advisers (SpAds) became established practice in Britain (Blick 2004), a role that has become even more prominent in Canada, Australia, and New Zealand (Eichbaum and Shaw 2010). SpAds have come under particular scrutiny, perhaps because they seem to encapsulate a more divisive, factional form of politics, in which partisan advantage takes precedence over public accountability, and spin over substance (Committee on Standards in Public Life 2003; Public Administration Select Committee 2001).

My concern here is not, however, with these lines of argument, often based on the financial cost of the "spadocracy" and errors of judgment on the part of individuals; nor is the criticism always justified. More important is what the role reveals about influential forms of expertise in government. The Special Adviser is the definitive personal-political role. SpAds technically serve the administration as a whole, but they are usually appointed due to a close connection with their respective ministers. The SpAd, alongside the think tank and the lobbyist, is part of a pluralized, privatized, and politicized policy environment to which the academic is an outsider. Specialist knowledge has no automatic primacy in political decision making; any evidential claim or policy proposal represents one perspective among many; its influence is necessarily contingent. Multiple routes to shape a policy agenda make the environment hard to navigate for those without the new political expertise.

Governments consider many factors when making decisions: how unified the administration is, the economic climate, the electoral cycle, what is happening in broader contexts, and so on (Bennett 2013). The likely reaction of the electorate (particularly those who tend to vote, such as older people), interest groups, and the media is also a consideration. One of the striking features of Tony Blair's incoming New Labour government in 1997 was how it prioritized operating effectively in this environment – cultivating relations with the press, for example, or introducing mechanisms for people to input into public services – alongside a rhetorical emphasis on "evidence-based policymaking." There is an apparent tension here; what happens when evidence conflicts with political imperatives, public opinion, or collective interests?

The appeal to "evidence" is itself a highly political maneuver. For the Blair administrations, evidence-based policymaking was part of a pitch to establish Labour's credentials as a party of government: efficient, pragmatic, inclined to modernize, and suspicious of ideological agendas (Wells 2007). The party's manifesto pledge, "what counts is what works," like many apparently self-evident "truths," conceals layers of difficulty and dispute. So, we can never know enough from research to remove doubt; we do not live in an ideal space in which knowledge "translates" directly into policy; there will always be political judgments to be made in a democratic system, for example, on ethical grounds; implementation is complex and can defy universal prescriptions from the center (Cox 2013; Lipsky 1983; Mulgan 2005). Methodological critiques have been made; no form of evidence speaks for itself and "changes in tense – from 'worked' to 'work' to 'will work' – are not just a matter of grammatical detail" (Cartwright and Hardie 2012: ix).

In this chapter, however, the important task is to unpack the implications of "evidence-based policymaking" for the role of expertise of various forms in policymaking, and for history as expertise in particular. Evidence-based policymaking does accord space to some forms of specialist knowledge: for example, medical expertise on alcohol and drug harmfulness or the efficacy of new treatments; or social research on educational standards and the impact of welfare provision. But it does not necessarily give these forms of knowledge primacy in political decision making; rather, evidence-based policymaking draws them into the political arena. As Hill reminds us, "there is a 'politics' of analysis," which ensures that there is no neutral evidence base for policy choice, nor can communities of expertise claim to be disinterested in the process of evidence selection and use (Hill 1993: 18–19).

Hierarchies of method are created in the pursuit of clarity, yet here both "hierarchy" and "clarity" are fundamentally misleading and unstable in the complex contexts in which public policy must be made and implemented. In the context of the UK National Health Service, for example, the standard guide for assessing evidence places Randomised Control Trials (RCTs) and Systematic Reviews at the top (level 1), with expert opinion at the bottom (level 4). Methods are cast as self-contained, rankable entities, rather than as potentially complementary approaches to understanding the same phenomenon (Bulmer et al. 2007; Kelly et al. 2010). While the policymaker may claim "what counts is what works," the medical researcher may actually be offering something much more tightly defined: "what works here." The "cultural competence" of a program tested in one location for application elsewhere, or with a different target population, may be limited (Cartwright and Hardie 2012). The preference for quantitative forms of evidence is also marked. Numbers appear definitive and authoritative, even though researchers may add careful caveats, for example, about causation, correlation, and extrapolation. Engaging a plurality of methods to explore different dimensions of the same problem is one response, but pluralism tends to be implicitly circumscribed and relevance to policy assumed not to extend beyond the social sciences.

In this context, humanities scholars are particularly disadvantaged. Our distinctive offerings bring to the surface and explore in human terms the caveats of other research methods. We ask the questions about values, habits, and beliefs with which reductive approaches are not concerned. These insights "mess up" the apparent clarity of numbers and destabilize claims for generalizability. They call for careful attention to, among other things, the assumptions that underlie the formulation of a policy, to the contexts in which it might be implemented, to the language in which it is presented, and to the audiences on whose response success may depend. For historians, the political "short-termism" and the lack of institutional memory in government have, rightly, been particular concerns. These perspectives are vital, but how can they be made to matter in a policy environment where influence is dispersed and narrow interpretations of evidence prevail?

History has tended to be marginalized in policy discourse as lacking both relevance to contemporary issues and the apparent objectivity of numbers. The status of history is further complicated by the problem of the past; for politicians keen to emphasize modernizing credentials or to establish a reputation for efficacy and resolve, history is a burden. New Labour's pitch relied on setting a "year zero" for not just the party, but for the country: "Can Britain escape from its past?" asked Peter Mandelson and Roger Liddle the year before Labour won a landslide general election victory (1996: 8). How can

we address this difficult, indeed, demoralizing, situation? Recognizing that we are confronted by something more fundamental than a "history gap" – which can be "bridged"
by making historical research more accessible to political scientists and policymakers, or
by judicious interventions into public debates – is an important step. Indeed, academe
and policy are often conceived in such terms: two cultures separated by a "relevance" or
"rigour-relevance" gap (Fincham and Clark 2009; Nightingale and Scott 2007).

The affinity of history and policy

The metaphor of "bridging the gap" is revealing. Bridges allow access to and commerce
between domains otherwise divided. Bridge building is an attractive metaphor to reach
for, as each side can commit to dialogue while retaining territorial integrity – a central
concern for the founders of the *History and Policy* network (Szreter 2011). We should
be willing, however, to consider the constraints that this model places on our thinking,
and on the ability of history to influence policy in fundamental ways, as opposed to providing informative background material. Advocacy for history is not enough. How can
we frame the proposition for history in policy so that these qualities of mind articulate
with policymaking, rather than just speak to policy issues?

   We can start by recognizing that it is an advantage for history, among the humanities,
that historical thinking is embedded in the ways political scientists and policymakers
make sense of the work of government. Influential recent work in political science has
taken a resolutely historical turn, defending history's "approach to meaning in which the
state appears as a differentiated cultural practice composed of contingent and shifting
beliefs and actions" (Bevir and Rhodes 2010: 79). In the political sphere itself, historical
reasoning and explanation are everywhere, evident in discussions on constitutional
reform and education, immigration, and foreign policy. Indeed, "what decisions do *not*
flow to some extent from assumptions about what the past appears to teach? History is
useful, and utilized. It pervades the decision-making process of individuals and groups"
(Graham 1983: 8). Historical modes of thought are prevalent in, even essential to, political scholarship and practical politics, but they are not exercised within the disciplinary
framework of history; it is "historian free" history (Berridge 2008).

   Is there, however, an opportunity to claim an integrated – rather than anecdotal – role
for history in policy? If history matters for policy thinking, how can historians, and their
disciplinary conventions, approaches, and insights matter too? How can these be made
to count as a valuable form of expertise inside the policymaking process? It is important
here to emphasize the fundamental difference between integrating history as expertise
into policymaking and sharing the results of historical scholarship with policy audiences.
The latter is about creating bridges and transferring knowledge, but retaining territorial
sovereignty. By contrast, the former deemphasizes intellectual authority; the focus is,
instead, on the practice of historianship and how it can "discipline" historical modes of
thought within government.

   There is a further step we can take in reframing the proposition for history in policy,
one that is important if it is to be persuasive. That is, to bring out the deeper affinities of
history and policy. So, the historian is almost certainly right to observe, "it's more complicated than that," but it is in handling complexity that history comes into its own.
Policy is multidimensional, messy, uncertain, ambiguous, shifting, and contested because
so too are the human beliefs, commitments, decisions, and interactions at the core of the

exercise of power. There may be rational aspects to it, but they are rational only insofar as *people* are pursuing what they, or others, define as "rational" approaches. Policymakers are equipped, as we all are, with necessarily imperfect information and must operate within constraints that are necessarily imperfectly understood (Simon 1972). There is no "view from nowhere" (Bevir and Rhodes 2010: 74–75; Nagel 1986).

History as a discipline is animated by, rather than confronted with, the context-dependent, contingent, subjective, and often conflicting nature of human perspective. Historians are "more comfortable with becoming" than those in other fields, as John R. Gillis puts it – that is, they can embrace instability, unpredictability, and inconclusiveness (2009: 172–173). Inconsistencies are not anomalies to be eliminated or controlled, but rather are opportunities for further exploration and richer understanding. History's embrace of the subjective and the reflexive can be viewed as an analytical strength for policymaking, rather than conceded as a weakness relative to other disciplines. Historians are well equipped to unpick and inspect the historically conditioned assumptions and notions that are part of a policymaker's "world of ideas" and used, often unconsciously, to reach important decisions and judgments (Bobrow 2006: 573). These notions draw on attitudes and beliefs; for example, about the reach of the state or the legitimacy of preemptive war; they have an essential "valuative" dimension that cannot be examined using quantitative techniques. Indeed, all fields of policy – including science, medicine, and technical areas such as energy, the environment, or defense – involve "valuative matters" (Jacobs 2012): for example, dignity at the end of life, fairness in the distribution of wealth or payment of taxes, the legitimacy of state surveillance of citizens or the ethics of indeterminate custodial sentences.

The case for affinities between history and policy may not, however, be welcome, nor working in government appeal to more than a limited number of historians. To become a "historian on the inside" might bring an uncomfortable sense of complicity, for those working to redress the dominance of a historical tradition that marginalized the many and for those concerned that the political system tends to do the same (Gavin 2007). It is hard to believe, however, that society would benefit from a principled withdrawal of historians from engagement with policymakers. And, indeed, do we not have here a further opportunity to recast what may seem a hindrance to history in policy as a distinctive strength?

History shares with policymaking a fundamental concern with human action and agency in context(s). Regardless of their intellectual preferences and political convictions, power is a ubiquitous concern for historians, and we are attentive to evidential traces of the relationships within which it is exercised (Clark 2011). Can we use these qualities to become "constructive sceptics" and "'punch our weight' with integrity" in the corridors of power (Cox 2013: 142)? Can we apply to policy the same critical sensibility that is central to our academic work: a "duty of discontent" that does not accept the claims, conceptualizations, or categorizations of historical actors or of scholars (including ourselves) without due attention?

One way to understand the role of constructive skepticism in policymaking is to see the latter as a learning process: a socially embedded practice involving iteration and reiteration, in which "the principal condition both of and for current decisions is previous policy" (Freeman 2006: 373). Constructive skepticism allows the historian to apply some pressure to conceptions of previous policy and current dilemmas, to inspect assumptions about target groups and possible interventions, in the context of a collective endeavor. Discontent can play a vital role, but it cannot be an end in itself if the historian is to play a productive and routine part in policymaking: "if we refuse to acknowledge any role other than criticism – if we are willing only to level down and never to build, [or] explain ... – we are evading a responsibility only we can fulfil" (Collins and Evans 2007: 140).

Seeing policy as a learning process also allows us to recognize a further affinity with history. In the description of policy learning as "an act of imagination, invention, and persuasion as much as (or as well as) comprehension, deduction, assimilation" (Freeman 2006: 382), we can recognize the complex orchestration of historical interpretation. This point of affinity – in the *process* of making meaning – is an important one for how we present the proposition for history in policy. We are talking here not about knowledge of the past in the sense of having access to a repository of potentially illuminating perspectives or an archive of analogies, although historians can offer that too. Policymaking as a reflexive, iterative learning process, which is framed and shaped by interpretations of the past, suggests the importance of the more self-conscious, enquiring approach characteristic of disciplinary history. It means *thinking with history in policy*, rather than bringing historical perspectives to the notice of policymakers.

We must recognize here the centrality of collaboration, rather than competition, between different specialisms, using "collective puzzling" to address complex policy problems (Hoppe 2011; Winship 2006). The temptation to "assert the importance of one's own discipline to the making of '"better" policy" may be "almost irresistible" (Kraemer 2004). We need, however, to be alert to "explanatory imperialism" (Jacobs 2012: 213) and actively cultivate a sense of the *complementarity* of different forms of knowledge within the policy learning context. Historians, no less than economists, political scientists, and others, will surely need to be advocates not just for the merits of their own disciplines, but for a genuinely rich ecosystem of expert advice.

Shared concerns and broad approaches have produced significant intellectual cross-fertilization between the humanities and the social sciences, including the field of social science history (Jordanova, forthcoming). Nevertheless, we tend to operate largely within the confines of our own disciplinary communities. Few scholars will become equally adept in the methods of multiple disciplines, but as active participants within an ecosystem of policy advice we should at least aim for a working familiarity with relevant adjoining specialisms and a sense of how complementary insights can be developed.

Working with a focus on complementarity in addressing policy problems calls not only on an appreciation of other disciplines' claims to knowledge, but also on a particular kind of *self*-awareness. Self-awareness here implies an understanding of the distinctive aspects of historianship along with an ability to identify and articulate how historical thinking relates to, informs, and interlocks with other forms of knowledge to create an ecosystem of expertise. Other forms of knowledge would include disciplines, such as economics or sociology; professions, notably public servants in different roles; but also what could be called the political expertise of advisers and think tanks.

For those historians engaged in the policy advice ecosystem, having a grasp of how the approaches, inclinations, and insights of history align with policymaking as a process – or set of processes, loops, debates, and negotiations – is surely of value. The alternative is to rely on establishing the relevance to policy of history as content, necessarily on a case-by-case basis. This shift in emphasis from "content" to "process," that is, from history as a product (whether historical perspectives or the more problematic "lessons") to history as a distinctive way of thinking is central to history in policy.

For policymakers, the shift draws historical thinking into policy in a productive way, one that works with the inherent complexities and ambiguities of political decision making. The historian's contribution becomes more "usable" than admonishments for "bad history" or the insight that what seems novel has a much longer past. History as content is also problematic as it raises the issue of differing interpretations. Historians disagree, which provides a vital dynamic to the discipline. Differences of interpretation make the notion of "good history" intellectually suspect; a single account of a past event, however compelling its credentials, necessarily excludes others, and can only serve as a kind of counterpoint or backdrop to present considerations. Scholarly differences also present a significant practical challenge for policymakers. It is difficult for either side to identify a means to bring history as "content" into an influential role in policy development.

The limitations of history as content are illustrated well in the then British prime minister Tony Blair's address as recipient of the US Congressional Gold Medal in 2003, just after the invasion of Iraq. In a phrase that has become for historians the definitive expression of political contempt for the past, he said: "there has never been a time ... when, except in the most general sense, a study of history provides so little instruction for our present day" (Blair 2003; Colley 2003; Littler and Naidoo 2004). History as "instruction" has little traction on the policymaker, unless there is an inclination to seek it. Indeed, Blair had been uninterested in the consensus of expert opinions sought four months before the invasion: that intercommunal resentments were prevalent and independent organized forces (potential allies) absent, and hence that the invading coalition could not rely on an Iraqi welcome (Macmillan 2009).

Even those policymakers inclined to value historical perspective may find the "instruction" of historians difficult to receive and assimilate, and historians themselves are unlikely to be equipped to answer the "so what?" question that their evidence prompts. Shifting our emphasis away from the provision of knowledge to the integration of expertise should help to resolve this impasse; the need to make judgments, reach decisions, and realize strategic goals means that the policymaker is "specifically concerned with processes, the bread and butter of historians" (Trask 1978: 223). From the latter's perspective, this means attaching a new sense of value to *historianship*: the disciplined analytical labor – the process – of "doing history." Historical perspective is a valuable resource, but it is inherently limited in its influence on policy in two ways: it is applied to a particular issue or cluster of issues in the present (for example, through analogies or taking a "long view"), and it is likely to be "viewed as a preface, organizationally, and an afterthought conceptually to real policy work" (Stearns 1982: 9).

By contrast, history as process offers a way of thinking through problems, opening up issues, putting pressure on assumptions, and asking different kinds of questions (Berridge 2000) as part of "collective puzzling." Historians will always draw on the resources of the past – and I come next to doing exactly that – but we can be bolder in the claims we make for the distinctive and important purchase of our ways of working on contemporary political issues.

The "history office" and other models

Before developing the idea of collaborative, multi-perspectival policymaking further, it is worth looking at the resources of our own professional pasts. Both policymakers and historians in the United Kingdom have noted the absence of historical insights and institutional memory in government and made proposals to remedy it. While the two sides have, unsurprisingly, had different views as to the importance of history to "good" policymaking, the proposals reveal some interesting commonalities. They have tended to affirm the historian's status as a specialist and to emphasize the provision of perspective and context; so, history offers "enlightenment" and a reliable record rather than implications or advice.

The Historical Section in the postwar British Treasury is the obvious place to start. The experiment in what was termed "funding experience" began in 1957, and the Treasury Historical Section (THS) was formally established in 1965. An official history program had been established in 1908, focusing on naval and military history and, indeed, the THS emerged from just such work during the Second World War (Pilling and Hamilton 2011). The Section should also be understood, however, in the context of Britain's "technocratic moment" (Edgerton 2005: 187–188). The "amateurism" of the policymaking class, so the narrative went, left the civil service unable to meet the demands of modern, interventionist government. The introduction of professional, technical, and managerial skills would rationalize the system and help arrest national "decline" (Balogh 1959; Fabian Society 1964). In this context, the Treasury's objective should be – in the words of under-secretary Peter Vinter – to use the "special expertise of the historians in the most productive way." "Funding experience" would help ensure decisions were made with efficiency and economy. The Treasury historians were involved in the drafting of historical memoranda – "a quick and accurate conspectus of all that has gone before" – and the compilation of chronological frameworks and historical narratives, to be appended to "seeded files," consisting of the most important documents relating to a particular policy situation, such as "minutes of chief meetings, decisive analyses, correspondence and memoranda, and submissions to ministers" (Beck 2006b: 155, 12, 62).

The "funding experience" initiative had a number of senior champions at the Treasury, including, it is interesting to note, Sir Richard Clarke, father of the future Labour minister Charles Clarke, who was to comment: "I don't mind there being some medievalists around for ornamental purposes, but there is no reason for the state to pay for them" (Woodward and Smithers 2003). The Section never managed, however, to integrate historical work into the core business of the Treasury, and was finally closed in 1976. Officials found little time to read the lengthy (often multivolume) memoranda, let alone use them as working tools; senior staff criticized historians for offering "value judgements" rather than contenting themselves with narrative. The historians expressed frustration with their marginal status and with the lack of interest and response from officials. The challenges of the "History Office," far removed from the corridors of power and producing "largely unread institutional histories" have not been confined to the United Kingdom (Graham 1983: 13).

The "gulf" separating the THS from its "consumers" is a problem that resonates with present-day, university-based historians (Beck 2006b: 140). *History and Policy* recently proposed in its evidence to a Select Committee inquiry on civil service skills, that "sustained bridge building" between government departments and "policy-minded historians" was required (Delap et al. 2014). Historians have become increasingly concerned about the abuse, distortion, and neglect of history; it is surely no coincidence that the network was set up in 2002 during Blair's premiership. *History and Policy* now offers a portfolio of activities: coordinating seminars, running interactive workshops, and responding to consultations, as well as its longer-standing project commissioning and making available an extensive library of policy papers. This is vital work, but the gulf remains; if we want to see history as an influential form of expertise in policymaking, then we need to consider other, complementary, ways to pursue that aim. Whether the "History Office" is in a school of humanities, a university policy institute, a think tank, or a government department, a model in which historians are remote from the "business" of policymaking and focused on the provision of historical perspective seems unlikely to succeed.

So what are the alternatives? A pilot "hindsight project" to enrich existing foresight work in government is one proposal, highlighting history's "ability to unpack assumptions, myths and the lost contexts" (Higgitt and Wilsdon 2013: 84). Pilot projects are part of proving the concept; connecting hindsight and foresight – a pitch that has already been made in theoretical terms – could be a valuable way to establish the credibility of historical thinking in policy (Staley 2006). Projects are, however, bounded entities; the "hindsight" label potentially creates a temporary "History Office," and even a successful scheme could be set aside at its conclusion without any consideration given to ongoing arrangements.

The high-profile government chief scientific adviser, supported by a network of departmental advisers, is a model which has proved appealing, and one that can also draw on a more successful precedent than the "History Office" (Cooper and Anderson 2012; History and Policy). Rohan Butler (1917–1996) was an Oxford historian who served in the Ministry of Information and then the Foreign Office during the Second World War. In 1962, he completed an official history of the Abadan Crisis of 1951–1954 as part of the "funding experience" initiative. His work "fed into, guided, and influenced ongoing discussions and reviews within Whitehall by juxtaposing the lessons of history, contemporary realities, and possible new directions for both foreign policy and methods," an appraisal that invites favorable comparison with the THS (Beck 2006a: 545). Butler went on to act as historical adviser to foreign secretaries of different political hues for the remarkable span of 19 years.

The call for historical advisers is a form of advocacy for history, highlighting the need for historical perspective to inform policymaking and the lack of institutional memory in government departments. How such advisers would operate remains largely unexplored. The senior level of a chief historical adviser (CHA) may ensure a hearing with ministers and, indeed, with academic historians, placing the CHA in the role of broker or "boundary spanner." Brokers can be influential in that they mediate between contexts and constituencies, carrying and interpreting messages, and negotiating the terms of collaboration (Freeman 2006). They are, however, "marginal natives," their status always uncertain and unstable (Berridge 2000: 378; Hammersley and Atkinson 1995). Accountability is divided, raising questions of trust and integrity, and calling on significant skill to balance assimilation and separation (Williams 2012). Further, becoming isolated on one's professional terrain – consulted only on matters with a clear connection to history – remains an issue for the CHA, particularly if historical advice is not embedded within the policymaking activities of the wider department.

Butler offers a promising exemplar, suggesting that historians can discharge their responsibilities to both Clio and client effectively, and without intellectual and professional compromise (Rothman 2003). We should acknowledge, however, that both political and academic cultures have changed since Butler's time at the Foreign Office. As explored above, narrow definitions of relevance and value, and instrumental understandings of the relationship between "evidence" and "policy" now prevail. The "What

Works Network" exemplifies the simplistic, linear model of knowledge transfer, with its approach defined under the headings of "generate," "transmit," and "adopt" (What Works Network 2014).

How influential either the historical adviser or "histories" can be on the politicization of policy advice is questionable. Nor does the "fugal exchange between public service and university scholarship" performed by Butler (Oresko 1996) attune with today's academic careers, where scholarly productivity is a priority for recruitment, and the impact of confidential outputs cannot easily be evaluated as part of research quality assessment (in the United Kingdom, currently the Research Excellence Framework). The CHA model is far from unproblematic; we should be wary of reaching for it as the self-evident solution to a lack of historical advice in government.

Historians in the mix

Any proposal to address the narrow instrumentalism of current policy discourse by bringing in historical advice runs the risk of making claims for "what works" not too dissimilar from those on which its own critique is based. Nonetheless, ideas have to be put forward and debated if we are not to repeat cycles in which policymakers and historians express concern at the gap dividing them and call for more effective dialogue, only for little to change in their relationship. The discussion that follows is not prescriptive in intent, but aims to refresh the conversation about the role of history in policy as a vital dimension of public life.

Common to the "History Office" and CHA models is the specialist status claimed by the historian. Specialisms define themselves by fields of expertise (Brint 1990) – along with associated attributes such as credentials – so it should not be so surprising that specialists may find their domains of operation demarcated along similar lines. Can historians work as experts without that expertise excluding them from engagement with the general "business" of policymaking?

Our assumptions about the nature of our expertise matter here; how the problem is defined inevitably shapes the solutions that are considered. If we hold "expertise" to lie primarily in content knowledge, or observe that it is displayed in the insights that emerge from historical study, then the problem is one of transfer or translation: how do we as historians ensure that our insights reach and inform policymakers? It would be sensible in this context to find ways to improve the channels of communication and ensure that research is made accessible to policy, and thereby increase its influence. But can reframing the problem help us formulate other, complementary models?

Influence, like power, is "neither a substantive entity, nor an institution, nor even a possession, but rather an attribute of the relationships within which it is exercised" (Clark 2011: 131). This points us to some significant issues for history in policy to confront. Expertise may be "inherently interactional" but it is at the same time "inescapably ideological, implicated in the evolving hierarchies of value that legitimate particular ways of knowing as 'expert'" (Carr 2010: 17). Expertise is, indeed, often perceived as a possession; over the course of a career in academe, it is the capital we accumulate and in which we trade. The pitch for history, or for any discipline, has in turn tended to rest on the claim to specialist knowledge and the distinctive value of that knowledge to policymaking.

The authority of the expert is problematic, however, when it comes to collaborations outside academe, something public history has been alive to for some time. An imbalance of power arises if status within the project is defined by expertise; if one party possesses it, the other becomes the beneficiary, and a linear knowledge-transfer mechanism is set up. Perhaps we have been too invested in the notion that historical expertise is something we own (and policymakers lack), preventing us from forming the kind of collaborations that have developed with curators, archivists, and broadcasters, for example. Thinking of expertise in terms of how it potentially relates to people, structures, and activities inside government may help us get past this obstacle, but I do not underestimate the scale of the challenge. If policy influence is relational, how do historians as experts establish their value and credibility in the first place? In what currencies or languages are relations with policymakers, advisers, and other specialists negotiated and differences resolved?

Three implications of the discussion so far need to be taken into account. The first is that contemporary policy issues are multidimensional, requiring processes of learning and "collective puzzling" that involve an array of perspectives and approaches. Second, "experts" tend to be confined to tasks defined by their specialism, which undermines their ability to bring distinctive insights and thinking styles to bear on wider policy practice. Third, that being "on the inside" matters: being not just located inside government, but integrated into the "business" of the department.

These three implications suggest that we need a model that mixes or blends the expertise of different people to allow them to collaborate effectively, and one that can fit within government structures and ways of working. Again, there is a historical precedent on which we can draw. Although never fully realized, a recommendation of the Fulton report of 1968 – which examined the "structure, recruitment and management, including training, of the Home Civil Service" – points us to a further property of the mixed policy unit: dynamism (Civil Service Commission and Baron Fulton of Fulmer 1968). Membership of the unit was designed to be temporary, with civil servants and "outsiders" on secondment and fixed-term contracts expected to move on or back to their former areas of employment after a period of service.

The "policy-planning unit," as it was termed in the report, can no more be lifted from its historical context than can Butler's role as historical adviser. It was a product of its time, when the state was extending its reach, and planning was regarded as essential for an efficient modern government. Aspects of the recommendation now seem dated, as indeed they are – that the unit should be staffed by "comparatively young men and women," for example – as does the confidence in, and the language of, "planning" itself. Yet the core idea remains persuasive, that a mix of specialisms, and of "outsiders" and "insiders," is needed to respond to policy issues, and that movement in and out of the unit would help bring into policymaking imagination, drive, and connectivity to new thinking in a variety of fields.

The dynamic character of the policy unit seems particularly important when thinking about the role of academic disciplines. Misunderstanding, if not mistrust, between university-based historians and those working in government, business, the military, and other organizational settings has been an issue in North America, reinforced by different associations, conferences, and journals. Public history in the United States developed as field by training and credentialing students as specialist practitioners, explicitly prepared for "a *public* rather than an *academic* career" (Kelley 1978: 19). The notion of history as one discipline, many professions, conveys parity of esteem in compelling terms (Banner 2012), but we do need to consider the effect of subdivisions within a discipline on the vitality of the whole. Demarcating a new specialist domain can generate a wave of intellectual energy, but does it also apply a label to such work that then makes transitions between specialisms more difficult? This is a particular concern where not only field but institutional boundaries are involved.

The historian on the inside appointed on a permanent basis becomes an institutional historian. Retaining the mindset of constructive skepticism and avoiding the marginalization of the "History Office" model would be a challenge. By contrast, a "portfolio" academic career offers a promising, if not unproblematic, prospect. So, historians may work primarily in higher education, but be able to move between settings, and have such experiences recognized through promotion and other forms of reward. Secondment into the policy unit offers the opportunity to apply, test, and develop historical thinking in an interdisciplinary and interprofessional context at the heart of political decision making. On return to the classroom, their students can gain a richer sense of the value of historianship and the traction of history on present-day issues. New avenues for scholarly work could also be opened up, enriching our understanding of government and offering insights into the ethical, theoretical, and methodological dimensions of history as a discipline. Some MA students studying at particular universities can certainly access such insights already (for example, the Institute of Contemporary British History, King's College London, is connected to *History and Policy*). Yet this remains a minority activity available to a small minority of relatively specialized postgraduate students. The potential for portfolio historians reaching a wider population of general history students remains to be realized.

The benefit for government of an integrated and dynamic model of history in policy would be access to fresh perspectives from across a discipline, but also, over time, to a wider network of alumni historians with direct experience of practical policymaking. The key, I suggest, is that the insider or outsider status of a historian does not solidify, but that the two frames of reference inform each other. Greater exchange between academe and policymaking should bring new and productive dimensions to roles in both settings and help build a broader community of policy enquiry, rather than just better bridges between separate domains.

Becoming an insider, at least on a temporary basis, involves more than a shift in location. The government department and the mixed policy team offer very different contexts, habits, practices, and constraints from university equivalents. It is worth focusing here not on the operational adaptations the historian would make – secondments will always involve a degree of acculturation – but instead on what could be termed "mindset." A common theme in literature on academic involvement in policy is "speaking truth to power" (Hoppe 1999; Palmowski and Readman 2011; Sassower 2014). This language has an immediate appeal for the constituencies that use it, but it conceals attitudes and assumptions that should be examined critically.

Both "truth" and "power" are too monolithic to be acceptable. Historians now handle the term "truth" with a due sense of provisionality, at least in our scholarly work, but the truth/power discourse affirms an authority and an entitlement that are far from provisional. Of course, historians *are* likely to have a richer and more intellectually sophisticated understanding of the past than policymakers. The issue is not the expertise itself but, again, the relational contexts in which it is understood and exercised. "Power" here is also problematic, invoking an illusory world of omnipotent elites (Brint 1990). The authority to speak claimed by the historian may be intellectual, but there is an implicit *moral* charge to the truth/power discourse (indeed, this is suggested by the Quaker origins of the phrase). The discourse creates, rather than merely reflects, a fundamental opposition between academe and policy that makes collaboration problematic (a bridge too far?).

The term "authority" gets us to the core of the mindset problem, one that public history has been confronting for some time. Public history projects can affirm identity and agency in communities, but they also *con*firm the authority and the social utility of the historian as professional (Sherman 1995). So, activities designed around co-production can, at the same time, draw attention to the difference between the authority of the historian and that of the participants. In the UK, public engagement by historians has been nourished primarily by social history. The History Workshop impulse to democratize ownership of the past and to reveal histories and historical voices that had been concealed, silenced, or marginalized by elite narratives has had an enduring influence. The commitment to history against the gradient of power has ensured that the authority of the historian has been confronted and problematized. Public history of this lineage has opened up new forms of academic practice as well as creating frameworks for communities to make their own histories through co-production and co-curation (Ashton and Kean 2009; Boon 2011).

However productive this lineage has been for histories from below, it has had serious implications for the relationship between history and policy. A desire to correct the balance of power can render elites as anonymous and faceless as subaltern actors once were (Clark 2011). The "making" of history has not been shared with policymakers as it has with communities of various kinds, but remains instead squarely within the historian's domain. The moral charge of "speaking truth to power" can acquire an unacknowledged edge that entitles the historian to instruct, correct, even admonish the policymaker, rather than to explore, share, and collaborate. The impulses from historians to shape the public understanding of the past and to influence policymaking may come from the same desire to prove our authority and social utility (Stevens 2010). Yet the latter is caught up with other inclinations, values, and beliefs that have not been fully disentangled and debated. It has proved more comfortable for historians to retain the authority and the privilege of the external critic, commentator, or instructor rather than to give serious attention to how co-production might apply to and within policy contexts. This endeavor concerns the discipline of history as a whole – it speaks to fundamental questions of who we are as historians and why and for whom we practice our craft. Public history has, however, a central role to play, if the field can recognize the importance and relevance of its central concerns to policy engagement, and vice versa.

PART II

Situating Public History

CHAPTER FIVE

Nation, Difference, Experience: Negotiating Exhibitions at the National Museum of Australia

KIRSTEN WEHNER

Since the National Museum of Australia was first proposed in modern form in the 1970s, it has often been understood, by at least some of its stakeholders, staff, and commentators, as a key site of nation making. That is, the museum has been seen as a place that constructs historical representations, such as collections, exhibitions, architectures, and texts, that render evident to itself the "imagined community" of the nation (Anderson 2006). The institution is understood from this perspective to take cultural effect through inviting, or persuading, visitors to understand themselves as citizens constituting and responsible for the national community and its ideals. It also enables them to acquire skills, such as knowledge of their country's past, considered critical to full participation in civic and political life (Bennett 1995; 1996; Miller 1993).

At the same time, exactly how the museum should understand and position itself in relation to "the nation" has been invariably a matter of debate, contest, and negotiation (Anderson and Reeves 1994). Successive cohorts of museum producers have grappled with, and with each other, over what version of national history the institution should endorse, how to respond to critical understanding of the nation as a tool of social power, and, in particular, how to reconcile the nation's integrating and boundary-making processes with Australia's cultural diversity. Running through these debates, one significant thread, most consistently articulated by curatorial staff, has gone beyond questions about how the museum should construct national history to argue more radically that the concept of the nation is inherently inadequate to the task of framing the institution's cultural mission.

This chapter considers the National Museum's evolving relationship to the nation, focusing particularly on two recent permanent gallery projects: *Journeys* and *Landmarks*.[1] These mark, I suggest here, something of a shift in the institution's conception of national history. I begin my discussion in this chapter by sketching the museum's genesis and evolution, noting particularly how groups of planners and producers established a range of possible understandings of the institution's relationship to the nation. I then

A Companion to Public History, First Edition. Edited by David Dean.
© 2018 John Wiley & Sons Ltd. Published 2018 by John Wiley & Sons Ltd.

consider how, in 2003, these possibilities were reconfigured as the museum's governing council initiated and then endorsed the findings of a review that reported the institution's exhibitions as failing to tell a cogent, coherent, or inspiring "story of Australia." *Journeys* and *Landmarks* were developed in response to this finding, and their curatorial teams were consequently obliged to recognize the council's call for the museum to develop a more integrated, celebratory national narrative. At the same time, the curators were determined to sustain, and indeed further develop, the museum's established commitment to representing Australia's cultural diversity.

Drawing on my experience as senior curator and, from 2005, content director, for *Journeys* and *Landmarks*, I explore in this chapter how the museum's gallery development curators responded to these tensions by moving away from the frame of "the nation" and "national history" to focus instead on Australian history as a web of diverse, located historical experiences. The curators understood Australian society as inherently fluid and plural, best conceptualized as a field of cultural-ecological "difference." They envisaged the museum as developing Australians' capacities to understand themselves as constituted through and acting within this field, and argued that *Journeys* and *Landmarks* should consequently center on "experience" as the realm in and through which cultural-ecological difference was produced and re-produced.

In this chapter, I consider how this curatorial philosophy shaped three key aspects of the galleries' interpretive scope and style, reflecting particularly on how these choices contested tropes of the nation. First, I discuss *Journeys'* and *Landmark's* representational frames, exploring how the curators prioritized the "local" as the space-time in which experience emerges and difference is produced and takes effect. Second, I consider the curators' interest in depicting lives as particular rather than emblematic of broader historical structures, exploring how the teams chose display techniques understood to activate object capacities to express the trajectories, complexities, and agencies of specific individuals or groups. Third, I attend to the curators' efforts to create the galleries as open-ended narrative arenas that would invite visitors to collaborate in processes of meaning making, enabling them to perform their own "difference" in relation to represented others.

Significant recent scholarship has elucidated how museums the world over are now centrally engaged with negotiating divergent, competing, and often incompatible constructions of national histories and identities. Much of this research has importantly traced how museums' representational practices participate in broader public cultural discourses. It has often focused on the ways in which museums contribute to the "politics of recognition" through valorizing or eliding the interests and perspectives of particular social constituencies in national histories, thus authorizing (or not) those groups' power to shape their societies (McLean 2005: 1).[2] One trajectory within this field has concentrated, more ethnographically, on the institutional practices through which museums produce national representations such as exhibitions. This work has developed an understanding of museums as locations in which producers negotiate multiple understandings of the nation, as these are expressed in media, ranging from governmental policies to marketing strategies to collecting traditions.[3]

This chapter draws on and extends this work through exploring how the National Museum of Australia's response to "the nation" can only be understood, in the context of the production of the *Journeys* and *Landmarks* galleries, in terms of curatorial critique of and attempts to move beyond this frame. This is to suggest that, in seeking to understand how contemporary museums can be considered sites of nation making, it is important to start with exploring the museum as a distinct institutional location, rather than assuming, a priori, that it is engaged in representing the nation. This approach also enables exploration of how museum processes of engaging the nation are shaped as much by curatorial responses to questions, including nonrepresentational questions, relating to material culture and museological practice as they are through interactions with broader public cultural discourses of national identity. For, as I elucidate below, the *Journeys* and *Landmarks* curators' repudiation of the frame of the nation and their turn to experience emerged as their theoretical critique of the totalizing implications of "national history" came into conversation with their developing understanding of how the museum's collections recorded, expressed, and produced cultural life. This shift was also catalyzed through the curators' consideration of how exhibitionary environments could distinctively embody, perform, and invite visitor enactment of cultural difference.

Constructing the museum

The National Museum of Australia was established in 1980, mandated to, as the relevant legislation puts it, collect, research, and interpret material relating to Australian history, including the "natural history of Australia" and the "interaction of man with the Australian environment" (Museum of Australia Act 1980). The Commonwealth government's Committee of Inquiry, which initially framed the institution, envisaged it as breaking with the disciplinary boundaries according to which museums defined themselves as institutions of natural history, anthropology, or history (Commonwealth of Australia 1975). The museum was duly established as focusing on three interrelated themes seen to encompass the entire sweep of Australian history. Today, these are described as: People and the environment, Aboriginal and Torres Strait Islander cultures and histories, and Australian society and history since 1788.

The Committee of Inquiry was wary of framing the museum as "national" and, indeed, reflecting its interest in the then emerging field of human ecology, called for the institution's scope to be defined geographically rather than politically or culturally. The committee argued that a "continent, rather than a nation, is the ideal focus for a museum [because] the natural boundaries are more permanent and powerful than man-made boundaries" (Commonwealth of Australia 1975: 71). Indeed, the committee saw even these "natural boundaries" as fluid and permeable, arguing, for example, that "the museum should portray, when appropriate, European and Asian and American influences on Australia's human and natural history" (73). The committee recommended that the new institution be called the "Museum of Australia," resisting the inclusion of the words "national" and "Australian" in its name because they believed these would lend the institution to being used as a platform for parochial declarations of Australian identity.[4]

Despite this early framing, museum planners soon began imagining the institution as focused on the nation-state and, more specifically (and instrumentally), as a technology designed to instantiate in the Australian public a sense of national identity.[5] Indeed, as Australia's established social norms and political structures were challenged from the 1970s by new constituencies, such as increasingly influential ethnic communities and feminist, Indigenous, and environmental movements, museum planners began to consistently frame the institution as tasked with creating a new version of Australian history and identity. This version reinforced the frame of the nation but also acknowledged the diversity of experience within its unfolding and asserted its inclusion of cultural plurality.

Thus, the Interim Council, reporting in 1983 on the first major planning exercise for the museum, called for the institution to provide visitors with a "factual and accurate account of our developing nationhood" that would "stimulate national pride and a greater sense of Australian identity" (Commonwealth of Australia 1983: 2, 51). This treatment of national history was to include, on the one hand, the "explorers, bushrangers, aviators, sporting figures and other popular heroes," emblematic of the usual cast of characters in orthodox national histories centered on the forging of a masculinist, Anglo-Australian identity through war, labor, sport, and the pioneer's struggle to dominate "the bush" (Dale 1997). It was also, however, reflecting the tenets of social history, to address "the everyday life – work and leisure – of people in both city and country," as well as less celebratory aspects of the nation's past such as "poverty, depression, strikes, loneliness, racism, natural disasters, disease and flies" (Commonwealth of Australia 1983: 40). The museum was to emphasize the "diverse cultures of the Australian community," particularly ethnic diversity as it has arisen through migration, as well as recognize the "pluralistic philosophies and practices that were evolving to promote the worth of diversity." This was to demonstrate how "within two centuries Australia has become one of the world's significant multicultural societies" (Commonwealth of Australia 1983: 69, 40).[6]

As the museum's internal intellectual and organizational culture developed from the late 1980s, this vision for the institution as narrating the evolution of a cohesive national community inclusive of, and indeed distinguished by its inclusion of, sociocultural difference, was increasingly contested from within the organization. Curatorial staff in particular were influenced by increasing interest in Australian academic historiography in critique, de-construction, and self-reflexivity (Turner 1993), and argued that the museum needed to do more than simply represent the nation as including cultural diversity. Curators insisted that the institution had to engage with the ways in which different groups within Australian society occupied distinct social positions and consequently experienced historical trajectories and produced historical narratives that varied from and were potentially incommensurate with any singular national story. Embracing the "new museology's" call for a turn away from objects and toward information, ideas, stories, and questions (Stam 2005),[7] this vision for the museum was often expressed in terms of the institution representing diverse voices, opinions, and perspectives in and on Australian national history.

In 2001, the National Museum opened its primary exhibitions and public programs facility on Acton Peninsula, near the center of Canberra, Australia's capital city (Figure 5.1). As the institution's five opening permanent exhibitions were developed, some museum producers re-asserted its articulation to the nation, with government stakeholders' interest in the institution as a technology for forging national identity converging with multinational interpretive design companies insisting that the institution needed to distinguish itself as a destination brand by claiming national history and identity as its content territory. At the same time, Australian public culture was increasingly characterized by highly politicized debates over the significance for national self-understanding of histories of British-Australian settler violence against Indigenous Australians, as well as the growing cultural plurality of Australian society. Museum staff responded to these discourses by seeking to reconcile a national frame with their commitment to a representational practice that was inclusive of cultural plurality and also refused any simple statement about Australian identity. Indeed, many staff aimed to problematize the concept of the nation as inherently exclusionary of subaltern social interests. As the then director Dawn Casey put it, the museum was a "consciously nation-building exercise"

Figure 5.1   National Museum of Australia, 2005. Photo: George Serras.

that needed to "bring the community together ... to take pride and comfort in a cultural identity that is a mosaic, a compelling picture made up of different parts" (2001: 7). The museum also needed, Casey argued, to be a "forum," a place that would "speak with many voices, listen and respond to all, and promote debate and discussion about questions of diversity and identity" (6).

Reflecting this vision, the museum's five opening exhibitions presented a complex narrative web that represented many different kinds of Australians and varieties of Australian experience, while also showing how different people might hold different views of the past, thus revealing the contingent nature of historical truth (Trinca and Wehner 2006). The *Nation: Symbols of Australia* gallery explored how representations of "being Australian" were socially and historically produced, often playfully and ironically deconstructing well-known icons of Australian national identity by juxtaposing different interpretations. *Horizons* traced the peopling of Australia, contesting established national narratives of, for example, the development of an open, pluralistic society by discussing migrant experiences of discrimination and exclusion. *Tangled Destinies* brought European-Australian responses to Australian environments into conversation with Indigenous understandings, constructing settler efforts to "domesticate" as the first faltering steps in learning how to live with the continent in a nondestructive way. *Eternity* and the *Gallery of First Australians*, while embracing less contingent and reflexive historical narratives, also contested celebratory Anglo-Australian narratives of national history and identity. *Eternity* presented highly personalized stories of diverse individuals, articulated to themes of emotion, which asserted that the stories of everyday Australians were as nationally significant as those of more well-known people. *First Australians* demonstrated the diversity of Indigenous Australians and the fluidity of contemporary Indigenous identity, resisting its construction as a stable "other" to white Australian identity. Moreover, the gallery narrated how, for Indigenous Australians, the past since colonization was characterized by dispossession, injustice, and survival, rather than any advent into Australian civilization.[8]

Critique and response

As soon as the museum opened its doors at Acton Peninsula, its embrace of a critical historiography, and particularly its complex rhetorical position in relation to the nation, catapulted it to the center of Australia's history wars (Macintyre and Clark 2003). Conservative commentators insisted publicly that the museum's exhibitions showed left-wing bias; that displays denigrated those who had historically occupied positions of authority in Australian society – particularly Euro-Australian men who had achieved eminence as, for example, explorers, politicians, and businessmen – and depicted Australian history as essentially a tale of injustice, oppression, and exploitation. As journalist Miranda Devine (2001) expressed: "the underlying message of the National Museum of Australia ... is one of sneering ridicule for white Australia. It's as if all non-Aboriginal Australia is a joke."[9] The museum's council, its ministerial-appointed governing body, responded by appointing a four-person panel, headed by sociologist John Carroll, to review the institution's exhibitions and programs. When the panel reported in 2003, the council endorsed its findings.

The *Review of the National Museum of Australia*, or the Carroll Review as it became known colloquially, opened with a broad statement about the "extraordinary achievement" of the museum. It repudiated claims that the institution displayed a systematic political bias, and acknowledged that the museum should address cultural diversity and the "mosaic of everyday life," as well as presenting "darker historical episodes" in ways that "opened the possibility of collective self-accounting" (Commonwealth of Australia 2003: 12–14). The review also, however, conclusively rejected the museum's embrace of an interpretive pluralism and its reflexive, multi-voiced historiography, and called for the institution to concentrate instead on developing a coherent historical narrative that described the unfolding of the nation. The Museum, the Review argued, should "tell the story of Australia," and

> Present the primary themes and narratives of Australia since the arrival of the British, through the building of the nation to the country's place in the contemporary world. This includes evoking national character traits; detailing exemplary individual, group and institutional achievements; and charting the singular qualities of the nation (Commonwealth of Australia 2003: 13).

The review's vision for the museum was grounded in its sense that a stable Australian identity existed to be represented. The panel rejected the argument made, for example, by eminent historian Graeme Davison in his review submission, that the "imagined community we call the nation is by its very nature plural and in flux" (Davison 2001). It insisted rather that there is "more consensus than plurality at the core of the national collective consciousness" (Commonwealth of Australia 2003: 9). Moreover, the panel argued that this identity was grounded in an overwhelmingly positive tale of collective achievement – the unfolding in Australia of the Western civilizing tradition (McCarthy 2004: 20). Thus, the review imagined the museum representing the story of Australia as "the establishment of a notably stable, efficiently managed, prosperous democracy, with very low levels of institutional corruption, with relatively low social inequality and a largely inclusive ethos, which has integrated immigrant peoples from hundreds of other places with reasonable success" (Commonwealth of Australia 2003: 9).

The museum responded to the Carroll Review with a wide-reaching program of collection development and gallery refurbishment, including the redevelopment of the

Nation and *Horizons* galleries as two new permanent exhibitions. These eventually opened as *Australian Journeys: Connections with the world* (now *Journeys: Australia's connections with the world*), in 2009, and *Landmarks: People and Places across Australia*, in 2011. As the curatorial team, then led by senior curator Mathew Trinca, formed to progress these projects in 2004, they were faced with the challenge of acknowledging council's endorsement of the review's call for the museum to produce an integrated, broadly celebratory national history that included, but was not challenged by, cultural difference. At the same time, the curators were committed to continuing to build the museum's sensitivity and capacity to respond to Australia's cultural plurality. Indeed, the team aimed to improve upon the institution's existing interpretive practices in this regard.

The Museum's 2001 exhibitions had asserted an encyclopedic representation of Australia's cultural plurality, but by the time the review panel handed down its report, the curators were already discovering that this claim was impossible to realize. The museum's exhibitions tended to produce visitor experiences of exclusion from national narratives, as much as inclusion, drawing attention to who was missing from the exhibitions as well as who was featured (Trinca and Wehner 2006). The museum's reliance on multiple voices to represent a differentiated community also tended, problematically, to abstract difference from the precise historical conditions in which it had been produced and experienced. Different perspectives on the past began to appear as simply markers of a contemporary national imaginary, rather than as expressive of actual lived experiences and the relations of power through which they had been shaped.[10] Moreover, it was evident that visitors, beyond the members of the Carroll Review panel, often failed to respond as expected to the deconstructionist tenor of many of the museum's displays. In *Nation*, for example, visitors often missed the framework of national symbols altogether, failing to gather ironical or critical interpretive intent, and reading installations as descriptive of historical conditions or indeed national identities rather than expressive of certain understandings and constructions of them.[11] For the gallery development curators, this suggested that the museum needed to move beyond ironical statements that revealed the constructed nature of "the nation" to develop new normative frameworks for conceptualizing Australian society.

Reconceptualizing the past

The curatorial team responded to these tensions by refocusing on the museum's relevance for and responsibility toward its public. The curators argued that the institution's core role was to build Australians' capacities to understand and respond to contemporary social and environmental challenges, such as Indigenous disadvantage, social dislocation, and ecological devastation (Janes 2009).[12] As I noted in my introduction to this chapter, the curators conceptualized Australian society as inherently and inescapably plural and fluid. They argued that many of their country's contemporary challenges had arisen because Australians, or, more precisely, socially and economically powerful Anglo-Australians, had responded negatively to social and environmental variability, experiencing it as threatening and problematic, and seeking to control it and either obliterate it or use it as a technology of oppression. Indigenous disadvantage, for example, developed as Anglo-Australians constructed Aboriginal Australians as inherently inferior, thus rationalizing and enabling processes of racial discrimination. Ecological devastation emerged as European settlers perceived local environments as nonproductive landscapes ripe for "improvement" through the introduction of, for example, imported species.

Developing this analysis, the curators proposed that the museum should understand Australian society and environment as an ever-changing field of formations of cultural-ecological difference, in which people's identities and social positions and therefore their attitudes and actions were constituted through ongoing interactions and inter-relationships with others (human and nonhuman).[13] The museum's role was to help Australians understand themselves as produced through and within this field of difference, to experience it productively and positively, and to develop their capacities to act within it in ways that developed a more equitable, just, and sustainable Australia. The curators conceptualized this role as encompassing three dimensions. First, the museum needed to develop Australians' grasp of their country's diversity and indeed to cement an idea of Australia as inherently diverse. Second, it needed to build Australians' analytical understanding of how variability had been historically produced, thus humanizing those constructed in hegemonic discourses as "other," and contesting the essentialization of "otherness" that is integral to oppressive social technologies, while also generally building capacities to conceptualize variability. And third, the museum needed to encourage Australians, including those constructed culturally as "the norm," to see themselves as participants within, rather than observers of, the web of similarities and divergences that constituted the inescapable grounds of social life. The curators proposed that the museum should develop Australians' capacity to experience engagements with those who were in some way different from them as significant in – indeed desirable and necessary for, and even bringing pleasure to – the production of the self.

The concept of the nation, the curators argued, was incompatible with this vision for the museum's public role. By definition, they suggested, the nation was an abstract, totalizing idea that valorized an ideal community in which everybody was, or would eventually become, essentially the same: sharing a common culture and language, inhabiting the same relationship to a homogenized land, and occupying as citizens an identical relationship to the state (Anderson 2006). Moreover, the concept tended to position "community" beyond the realm of actual lives and relationships, as something to be aspired to and joined by those willing or able to embody certain appearances, attitudes, and behaviors. Nationalist discourses naturalized these characteristics as expressing an essential national genius, thus obscuring how particular national formations expressed the interests of certain (elite) social groups and worked to exclude from civic life those who failed to conform to dominant constructions of national identity. In concert with a broader and well-established scholarly critique of "the nation" as a tool of hegemonic social power, the curators argued that the concept was fundamentally inadequate as a framework for building Australians' skills in understanding, embracing, and negotiating cultural-ecological difference as a defining and ongoing characteristic of social life.

Objects and visitors

The gallery development curators' turn away from "the nation" and "national history" as the museum's primary representational referents developed in conjunction with their deepening engagements with the institution's collections, and indeed was driven as much by their material investigations as by their embrace of critical cultural theory. By the early 2000s, the National Museum had developed a collecting philosophy centered on what Martha Sear and I have elsewhere called "secular relics" (Wehner and Sear 2010). Rather than endeavoring to establish typologies, development sequences, or examples of cultural excellence, museum curators typically sought to acquire objects with a detailed provenance describing how an object illuminates the life history of a person or group. The museum had developed a strong democratic bias, collecting material relating to diverse "everyday" people as much as more celebrated or notorious cultural "heroes," and valuing objects that were seen to embody a good "story," that is, a story that linked with a well-documented and preferably dramatic individual biography that spoke to significant social trajectories (Hansen 2005a; Wehner 2012).

Responding to this institutional trajectory, the gallery development curators argued that the museum's collections described the Australian past as a web of diverse, interlinked lives, human and nonhuman, that had in some way engaged and intersected with and with each other in specific local circumstances within the fluidly bounded and internally differentiated Australian continent. The curators proposed that the museum's objects recorded and indeed embodied and had participated in shaping people's (and non-people's) experience, the daily unfolding of their lives within particular cultural-material conditions. Moreover, the collections, the curators argued, revealed the realm of lived experience as the space-time in which cultural-ecological difference was produced, as people's habits, convictions, and ambitions were enacted within the context of broader structures and flows that included, but also exceeded, those cohering around the nation-state. For the curators, if the museum wanted to help visitors live well with difference, it needed to help visitors apprehend, investigate, and engage others at the level of lived experience. This could be achieved, they argued, through activating and engaging audiences with objects' embodiments of experience.[14]

As the gallery development process progressed, the curators' interest in engaging visitors with lived experience as a path to building understanding of difference was further consolidated through their thinking about what kinds of interpretive approaches would produce the most engaging exhibition experiences. The curators argued that exhibitions addressing national history were usually, and perhaps inevitably, exclusionary. Visitors were placed in the position of finding themselves within the national narrative, through, for example, locating representations of ethnic categories with which they identified. If visitors did not find resonant identity markers, they experienced a sense of alienation from the national community. The museum curators argued that, in contrast, centering *Journeys* and *Landmarks* on the unfolding of people's lives, especially if displays captured some of the experiential and emotional complexity and nuance of those lives, would provide visitors with multiple points of connection with others, as these might emerge through, for example, shared experiences of kinds of places, sensations of loss, and common interests.[15] For the curators, the realm of located experience was simply more meaningful for visitors because it constituted the space-time in which they lived their lives, while the nation inevitably remained abstract, distanced, and in many ways oppressive.

Localizing history

The *Journeys* and *Landmarks* exhibition brief, written with the Museum's council as a primary audience, proposed that the galleries address "Australian history" or, more precisely, "central or key themes in Australian history" (National Museum of Australia 2004: 1). This framing acknowledged and addressed the review's calls for the museum to focus on the "story of Australia" and its "primary narratives and themes," while also opening up space for the curators to move the galleries away from any description of a singular national history or definition of national identity or character. Drawing on a model of ethnographic history that resonated with their sense of the collections as recording and expressing the qualities of unfolding lives,[16] the curators proposed that *Journeys* and *Landmarks* explore "key themes in Australian history" through detailing "particular experiences in their place or location." This approach was envisaged as enabling the galleries to "acknowledge the diversity of people's experiences" and "promote care and precision in representing the past," while also maintaining a sense of "historical continuities between experiences in different times and places" (National Museum of Australia 2004: 4).

Journeys and *Landmarks* thus developed as addressing an Australian history and engaging with discourses about what constituted "central" or "key" themes in that history, but through the frame of the local as the space-time of situated experience. *Journeys* was conceptualized as a trans-local history of Australia that traced the passages of people, and objects, to and from the Australian continent, exploring how these journeys established connections between places in Australia and overseas.[17] *Landmarks* was envisaged as a place-based history of Australia since European colonization that would trace how ten trajectories in Australian life had unfolded in particular locations as groups of people engaged local ecologies, technologies, and each other in efforts to build communities.[18] In a sense, the galleries were conceptualized as a "pigeon pair," with *Journeys* looking outward from the continent to examine Australian lives in a global context, and *Landmarks* turning inward to consider how the particular social and ecological conditions of the continent had produced distinctive lifeways.

In developing each gallery's interpretive structure, the curators began with lists of themes that were, in many ways, deeply conventional, reflecting existing concepts of the major trajectories in Australian, indeed national, history. *Journeys* was envisaged as beginning with the first European imaginings of the southern continent, then tracing successive voyages of European discovery; convict settlement; free settler arrivals stimulated by the nineteenth-century pastoral expansion and gold rushes; journeys associated with political federation of the Australian colonies and the nation's participation in the world wars; postwar immigration schemes; and more contemporary sporting, leisure, political, and artistic exchanges. *Landmarks* was similarly framed as commencing with the first European settlements on the continent and its exploration and mapping; the growth of pastoralism; development of democratic movements; agricultural expansion; developments in science and education; the rise of manufacturing, mining, and finance industries; and the character of urban life.

The curators understood these themes, however, as neither delineating the unfolding of a narrative of national development nor as primary interpretive structures that needed to be summarized or explicated in the galleries. Instead, the curators saw the themes as constituting primarily a conceptual tool that could help guide the selection of more particular stories, ensuring good coverage of the sweep of Australian history and intersection with stakeholder expectations about key themes, while not necessarily defining or structuring visitor engagement with the galleries. As the exhibitions took form, curatorial choices about display techniques placed interpretive emphasis on individual, group, or place lives, resisting the articulation of these stories as examples of broader historical trajectories. Thematic perspectives appeared as subordinate historical context for people's stories, and, in *Landmarks*, as a linking mechanism drawing local narratives into relationship with each other.[19]

Journeys thus begins with an interpretive panel introducing the gallery's focus on how the passages of "migrants, traders and travellers ... connect Australia with the world" (Figure 5.2). It notes the ancient and continuing pattern of arrivals and departures to the continent and invites visitors to consider how the journeys of people and their objects connect places in Australia with places overseas. The gallery, as it winds along a narrow, elevated mezzanine, then presents 45 exhibits, each comprising of a three- or four-sided display case holding groups of objects with associated textual, visual, multimedia, and touch elements. Each exhibit focuses directly on describing an individual's, or group's, experience, evoking how the objects on display participated in and reveal that life/lives. Although these exhibits are arranged in a very rough chronology, there are no interpretive panels articulating individual exhibits to broader historical themes, such as "postwar migration" or "voyages of discovery," that could be understood as stages in the unfolding of a national narrative. Indeed, the positioning of the exhibits within the gallery space, and the use of display furniture that allows visitors to see through their glass sides, creates the impression that the exhibits are somehow loosely tethered, almost floating and shifting in relation to each other.

Landmarks, at twice the size of *Journeys,* more strongly deploys the gallery's themes as a structuring mechanism, though here too the themes are subordinated interpretively to more local framings. *Landmarks* is introduced with interpretive text that describes the gallery as a place-based history exploring how "people have engaged with landscapes, flora, fauna and technologies to develop distinctive Australian communities." Visitors then move through ten modules, each addressing a theme such as "Colonial Foundations," "Expanding the Economy," and "Urban Life." Each module encompasses three or four "place" exhibits, each of which focuses in detail, through the relevant thematic lens, on the unfolding history

Figure 5.2 Entrance to the *Journeys* gallery, National Museum of Australia, 2009. Photo: Jason McCarthy.

of a particular location and how people, landscapes, plants, animals, and technologies have interacted over time to produce that place. The Colonial Foundations module, for example, comprises exhibits exploring Sydney, Hobart, Melbourne, and Adelaide, four of the first British settlements on the continent (Figure 5.3). A rather modest interpretive panel introduces each module, describing the relevant theme and noting the featured places, but design choices such as graphic treatments and lighting ensure that the individual place exhibits are signified as the focus for visitor attention. As in *Journeys*, *Landmarks'* thematic modules are arranged somewhat chronologically, at least in the early parts of the gallery, but circulation routes are multiple, and visitors can choose their own path through the displays.

For the curators, *Journeys* and *Landmarks* were envisaged as, through their very framing, contesting the frame of the nation as adequate to an understanding of and engagement with Australian life. Each *Journeys'* exhibit emphasizes the movements of people to and, importantly, from the continent, with these flows sometimes occurring multiple times in the same life. As such, the gallery problematizes nationalist discourses that focus on the privilege of joining the nation and construct the populating of the continent as a process of national becoming. Exhibits suggest instead that people have not just joined Australia, but also abandoned it and indeed that casual visits to the continent might, even if they are totally unconnected with the production of the nation-state, also be seen as significant in shaping Australian society. Moreover, the gallery draws attention to how journeys to and from Australia create enduring connections between places in Australia and places overseas, revealing how Australians may feel that they belong simultaneously to both Australia and other countries and consequently contesting nationalist ideas about the necessity of exclusive patriotic attachment. *Landmarks*

Figure 5.3 View into the *Landmarks* gallery, National Museum of Australia, 2011. Showing the Colonial Foundations module running along the mezzanine and visitors exploring part of the Sydney and Hobart exhibits in the foreground. Photo: George Serras.

similarly contests the frame of the nation, asserting not the fluidity and permeability of national boundaries, but rather focusing in on how lives are made, in terms of their imperatives and conditions, in subnational places. *Landmarks* asserts that people act not in terms of "building a nation," but rather in the interests of building their own lives and communities in specific places.

Moreover, both *Journeys* and *Landmarks* contest national narratives that valorize certain individuals and events as more significant than others in Australian history. In developing the galleries, the curators sought to recognize and encompass the demographic diversity of Australian society and the ecological diversity of the continent, while ensuring that the galleries did not claim to be encyclopedically representative of that diversity. Stories of well-known individuals and events are presented in similar manner to those more obscure. Thus, in *Journeys*, the exhibit featuring Captain James Cook's voyages of discovery along the east coast of Australia, an iconic story in conservative European-Australian imaginings of national becoming, is nestled next to similarly sized and treated exhibits on Torres Strait Islander journeys around the north of Australia, Macassan arrivals in search of *trepang* (sea cucumber), and convict stories of loss and connection with loved ones left behind in England. In *Landmarks*, place exhibits include the stories of politicians and pastoralists building towns and settling the inland, but equally feature Indigenous peoples defending their country from colonization and nonhuman species such as grasses, termites, and kangaroos shaping human lives. In a sense, both galleries aim to open up the cast of players seen to participate in life in Australia, moving beyond assertions about national contribution to validate diverse kinds of lives and ambitions and to recognize that these are not generally articulated toward nation making.

Representing experience

In resisting "the nation" as a frame for *Journeys* and *Landmarks*, the curators aimed to develop Australians' capacities to engage productively with "difference," including understanding how people were culturally different, how that difference has been produced historically, and also humanizing this difference so that visitors may understand how and why people became categorized as different. Responding to this ambition, the curators resisted articulating the stories of individual lives and local histories as examples, or indeed exemplars, of broader historical trajectories or categories. Rather, they focused on revealing individual lives and local histories in as much specific detail as possible, evoking the qualities of each person's and place's life-world and narrating their biographies to emphasize the complexity of agency and experience in the unfolding of each life and place. Engaging visitors with difference relied on a model of deep, detailed interpretation of particular experiences.

Journeys and *Landmarks* are consequently both object rich, featuring dense assemblages of artifacts. These are selected and displayed to suggest the particular material and cultural character of each person's or place's life, without asserting any kind of mimesis or reconstruction. Interpretive text and images focus on describing the particularities of each biography, detailing how objects on display were made and used, constructed from materials from a place or shaped by the natural forces of a place, and narrating stories in which people's relationships with the objects reveal their experience and understanding of their lives. Objects are positioned within displays to invite visitors to articulate their bodies to them and imagine how it must have been for represented others to wear a particular piece of clothing, work on the goldfields with a cradle and pan, or build a house from homemade concrete bricks. Interpretive text, sometimes quite overtly, encourages visitors to examine displayed objects in a detailed, interactive mode, and many exhibits include audiovisual installations or tactile and interactive elements that invite exploration of the sensory and kinesthetic qualities of represented lives.

In *Journeys*, for example, this approach is developed through each exhibit centering on a prominently positioned and lit "key" object – an artifact that has figured significantly in a person's or group's life – associated with further groups of objects that evoke threads of the trans-local histories of the collections. Visitors are invited to move around each display, encountering different groupings of objects that draw out various aspects of a person's life experience. The Carmelo Mirabelli exhibit, for example, centers on a camera purchased by Mirabelli when he migrated to Australia and used over many subsequent years to document his life (Figure 5.4). Different parts of the display draw the camera into relationship with objects such as the bicycle Mirabelli rode long distances while working as an itinerant laborer; the apron he redesigned, drawing on Sicilian traditions, to enable him to become a renowned fruit-picker; and an Italian wine bottle gifted to him by a friend joining him in Australia from Sicily. Around the base of the exhibit, visitors can follow a set of photographs that Mirabelli took and sent to his mother in Italy, enabling her to share remotely in his experiences of working in the Queensland cane fields, spending weekends experimenting with trick photography with his friends, and buying his own home.

Conscious of museological traditions in which migrants are essentialized as either incomers adding value – often in the form of cultural leavening –to an already established national body or as beneficiaries of national largesse,[20] the *Journeys* curators aimed to present Mirabelli as a distinctive individual who, although a postwar Italian

Figure 5.4   Carmello Mirabelli exhibit, *Journeys* gallery, 2009. National Museum of Australia. Photo: Lannon Harley.

migrant, could not in any way be understood as archetypal. Exhibit narratives present Mirabelli's life not as defined by his journey to Australia, but rather give equal weight to his life in Italy before his emigration and in Australia after his arrival and indeed focus on his continued sense of connection with both Sicily and places in Australia throughout his life. Graphic elements, such as the exhibit's multipage flipbook, explore how displayed objects evoke threads of experience within Mirabelli's life, providing information about broader social conditions that adds context to his life's events, but equally draw out the complexity of his emotional responses. Rather than Mirabelli emerging as a postwar migrant who is defined by an experience of loss, longing, and separation – or alternatively hope, rescue, and thankfulness – narrative text, first-person quotes from letters and reminiscences, archival images, and images of object details combine to explore how Mirabelli's life developed as an active response to historical conditions and, as in any human life, incorporated a wide range of sensations and responses. The curators aimed to present Mirabelli as a living, complex individual in whose life visitors might find resonances with their own experience, while also revealing how the particular events of Mirabelli's life had produced him as someone "different."[21]

Performing difference

In developing *Journeys* and *Landmarks*, the curators aimed to represent Australian cultural-ecological difference in a way that engaged audiences with exploring how and why people and places were produced as different through their life events and the conditions and structures within which they unfolded. As I've presaged above, the curators also aimed to move beyond concepts of exhibitions as representational spaces, to explore how *Journeys* and *Landmarks* could be constructed as environments in which visitors experienced themselves as participants within a "field of difference" and indeed practiced social processes of engaging with others across difference. Developing this interest, the curators conceptualized *Journeys* and *Landmarks* as performative spaces in which visitors should be understood not as passive recipients of information, but rather as active participants in the process of making meanings from displayed materials. The curators envisaged visitors as, in a sense, performing their own difference through their interactions with the exhibits as they responded to display elements in terms of their own interests and histories and considered how represented others connected with or diverged from their own experiences.[22]

Responding to this ambition, the gallery development curators, in collaboration with the exhibition designers, sought to create *Journeys* and *Landmarks* as relatively open interpretive environments. In both galleries, visitors are invited to forge their own circulation routes, taking their own path to link up exhibits in particular ways, often crossing their own tracks or circling back to reengage with material they may have already encountered. *Journeys*' reliance on three- or four-sided display cases encourages visitors to move around exhibits to view them from different angles, with different members of a visiting group often engaging with each other from different sides of a case. In *Landmarks*, visitors move through a series of more enclosed spaces, comprising display cases grouped around a central "open display" plinth, so that they need to move around within the space to investigate how the different elements interconnect. In many instances, visitors can also see through or across exhibits to others, thus creating multiple opportunities for visitors to think about the relationships between displays and the diverse lives and places they evoke.

Within exhibits, the curators aimed to develop an expansive interpretive approach that provided visitors with sufficient information to make sense of the display but did not over-determine its meaning. Interpretive text and images are at the front of each display case, positioned below viewers' line of sight, thus inviting visitors to articulate primarily to the exhibited objects and creating space for their imaginative and affective responses in advance of their turn to explanatory information. Exhibit labels describe how people made and used the objects on display, adding in broader historical context where necessary, but the "museum voice" does not seek to explain what an object means, nor define why the curators feel an object is significant. The tone is particular and open-ended, inviting visitors to understand how an object relates to a person's life, but also to develop their own imaginative responses to its meaning and significance.

Journeys and *Landmarks* were designed to produce in visitors a sense of being embedded in a field of others. Both galleries refrain from offering vantage points where visitors can stand back from the gallery as a whole, or from particular exhibits, to make an authoritative overview. Rather, visitors are encircled by exhibits and asked to move their bodies and their gazes around to engage with different elements of displays, bringing them into relationship with each other through their own movements. The *Landmarks* gallery's Land of Opportunity module, for example, includes an exhibit exploring Sunshine, now a semi-industrial suburb of Melbourne, Victoria, and, at one time, a center of Australian manufacturing (Figure 5.5). A large stripper-harvester (a piece of agricultural machinery) manufactured at Sunshine in 1911 anchors the exhibit. As visitors move around this object, they encounter, on one side, displays evoking the vision and ambition of H. V. McKay, the businessman who founded the Sunshine Harvester Works, built it into a highly profitable enterprise, and constructed a company town to house his loyal workers. On the other side of the harvester, displays focus on the Sunshine factory workers, their lives and conditions, and their role in precipitating Australia's first legislated minimum wage case. As they explore this exhibit, visitors move around the

Figure 5.5 Sunshine exhibit, *Landmarks* gallery, National Museum of Australia, 2011. Photo: Jason McCarthy.

harvester, physically as well as imaginatively engaging with the different experiences of the people who made the distinctive Sunshine community and, potentially at least, considering how their own experiences are similar to or different from these varying positions. To the rear of the harvester, the object articulates to the Extending the Farmlands module, with exhibits narrating the machine's role in the lives of the Sutton family, who used it on their farm until the 1950s, thus further extending visitors' sense of the dimensions of difference that circulate around and through this object.

Conclusion

The National Museum of Australia is, by definition, a national museum, in the sense of being funded through the Australian Commonwealth (federal) government and thereby mandated to address the entirety of the Australian public and, arguably, to represent Australia to the world. The museum's relationship to the nation-state, and particularly its role in constructing and promulgating narratives that valorize the cohesion and character of the national community, has remained, however, far from settled. Indeed, I argue that this relationship is best understood as a central arena through which museum producers and stakeholders negotiate the institution's role and activities. Understanding the museum's role in producing or contesting national narratives consequently relies upon a detailed exploration of institutional processes, only some of which center on questions about the representation of different social groups.

This chapter has mapped out some of the dimensions of the National Museum's response to "the nation," focusing particularly on how the curatorial team developing the *Journeys* and *Landmarks* galleries between 2004 and 2011 reshaped entrenched, if complex, institutional traditions of representing Australia's cultural diversity to respond to the demands of a critical, conservative review of the museum's exhibitions and programs. As I have described here, the museum's gallery development curators advanced an understanding of Australian society as a "field of cultural-ecological difference," elaborating this concept in relation to cultural critique of the concept of the nation, institutional collecting philosophies, and an understanding of exhibitions as spaces of collaborative meaning making. Reflecting this approach, the curators framed *Journeys* and *Landmarks* as webs of local histories, creating exhibits that produced deep, nuanced treatments of individual, group, or place biographies and that adopted an open interpretive style that invited visitors to engage imaginatively, emotionally, and analytically with represented others – in other words, to perform their own difference within the exhibition space.

Since *Journeys* and *Landmarks* opened in, 2009 and 2011, respectively, the museum has not undertaken research that might establish how visitors are actually experiencing the galleries. Indeed, it is quite challenging to think about what kinds of research methodology might access visitors' subjective interconnections with the lives they encounter in the exhibits. Anecdotal evidence, mostly collected through curators lurking among the displays, suggests that many visitors are engaging in the mode of interactive looking, listening, touching, moving, and talking that the curators envisaged, and conversations with visitors suggest that some, at least, are exploring how and why their own experiences connect or diverge from others' experiences. At the same time, some visitors, and indeed occasionally external commentators, express disappointment at the galleries' lack of a clearly articulated narrative of national becoming, or alternatively their lack of detailing of national government structures that have constrained processes of becoming and belonging. For the museum, questions about how to manage the "nation" remain an ongoing challenge, and opportunity, for participating in the shaping of Australia's cultural fabric.[23]

Notes

1   At the National Museum of Australia, a "permanent gallery" is a large-scale exhibition designed to remain in operation, with ongoing refreshment of stories and changeover of objects, for 10 to 15 years. The museum, in 2016, presents five permanent galleries. These exhibitions account for the bulk of the institution's visitation and are the foundation of ongoing educational programs and docent tours. Further information about the museum's permanent galleries is available at http://www.nma.gov.au/whats-on/exhibitions/now_showing#Permanent_galleries.

2   Edited collections and monographs in this area include Aronsson and Elgenius (2014), Boswell and Evans (1999), Erskine-Loftus et al. (2016), Fladmark (2000), Gore (2002), Kaplan (1994), Karp and Lavine (1991), Karp, Kreamer and Lavine (1992), Kavanagh (1999), Knell et al. (2011), Levitt (2015), Macdonald (2003), MacDonald and Fyfe (1996), McIntyre and Wehner (2001), Simpson (2001), and Walsh (1992).

3   Key studies include Harrison (1993), Handler and Gable (1997), Macdonald (2002), Mason (2007), and Shannon (2014). The author's doctoral dissertation (Wehner 2007) provides an ethnography of the development of the National Museum of Australia, focusing on the period from 1997 to 2001.

4   Professor John Mulvaney, personal communication, 16 April 1998.

5   In 1992, the Museum of Australia was re-legislated as the National Museum of Australia. This shift reinforced the institution's articulation to the nation-state, though it was probably also driven, in part, by branding issues. The public often confused (and still do) the Museum of Australia, and indeed the National Museum, with the Australian Museum, a natural history and anthropology museum located in Sydney and funded by the New South Wales state government.

6   See Zubrzycki (1992) for an elaboration of this proposal by a key member of the Interim Council. Bennett (1995) provides a cogent critique of the Interim Council's incorporation of over 40,000 years of Aboriginal life on the Australian continent within a linear narrative of the development of "multicultural Australia." Message (2009) discusses the National Museum's history in relationship to the development and transformation of multiculturalism in Australia.

7   Key texts contributing to the idea of the "new museology" include Vergo (1989), Weil (1990), and Ames (1992). See Kreps (2003) and Witcomb (2003) for discussions of the development of the new museology and its relationship to critical museological practice that attends to questions of power and representation.

8   See Wehner (2007) for an extended description of the museum's permanent exhibitions opened in 2001.

9   See Windschuttle (2001) and Shanahan (2001) as further examples of critical reaction. For discussion of this debate, and the ensuing review of the museum's exhibitions and programs, see Anderson (2002), Attwood and Foster (2003), Macintyre and Clark (2003), McCarthy (2004), Dean and Rider (2005), Hansen (2005b), and Trinca and Wehner (2006).

10 This response was influenced by critical assessments of multicultural discourses as assimilationist technologies. Authors such as Hage (2000) and Gunew (2004) argue that representations asserting cultural plurality as a national characteristic confine expressions of difference to those that do not challenge existing social, economic, and political structures of power. Ethnic traditions in food, for example, may be tolerated and indeed valorized, while political traditions are excluded. Multiculturalism, these authors argue, essentializes cultural differences, commoditizing them for consumption and use by a cosmopolitan elite as markers of taste.

11 See Butler (2007) for an extended discussion of the representational challenges of using irony in exhibitions.

12 The curators tended to focus on Australians as the museum's core public. International visitors were generally understood as a secondary audience.

13 "Difference" is a foundational concept of Western poststructuralist philosophy and an extended discussion of the curators' use of this term in relation to this tradition is beyond the scope of this chapter. For the curators, "difference" was a significant idea because it asserted that identity did not preexist but was rather produced through culturally situated interactions and interrelationships. Consequently, the concept emphasized that people's cultural variability could not be separated from their position within a society (see Gunew 2004; Hage 2000). See Mason (2008) for a useful introduction to the relationship between cultural theories such as poststructuralism and museum studies.

14 See Dudley (2010; 2012) for essays exploring the nature of objects as recording, embodying, and expressing lived experience.

15 See Message and Healy (2004) for a discussion of the museum's interest in the "active and emotional engagement of the visitor with material and stories on display" in the exhibition galleries opened in 2001. These authors note the significance of this "affective" interpretive focus in the museum's efforts to distinguish itself as a "new" kind of museum.

16 As Thomas (2001) describes, ethnographic history in Australia emerged from the late 1970s through the work of historians Greg Dening, Rhys Isaac, Donna Merwick, Inga Clendinning, and Paul Carter. These scholars, inspired by anthropologist Clifford Geertz's interest in "thick description," sought to understand the cultural nuances and complexities of historical situations and events, particularly in circumstances of cross-cultural engagement. They also emphasized the multiplicity of historical perspectives and narratives.

17 See Oakman (2010) for a discussion of *Journeys* in relation to developing scholarly traditions in transnational history, and particularly its capacity within the Australian context to disrupt the frame of the nation-state.

18 See Wehner (2017) for a brief discussion of *Landmarks* in relation to the National Museum's participation in broader Australian scholarly traditions in cultural geography, place studies, and environmental history. See Oakman, Sear, and Wehner (2013) for a book version of the *Landmarks* gallery content.

19 As Oakman (2010) elucidates, the curators' interest in shifting historiographical focus from long-term processes to expressions of human agency, from the general to the particular and from large to small, reflected developments in subaltern studies emerging through the 1990s and early 2000s (Chaturvedi 2012; Ludden 2002).

20 See Kirshenblatt-Gimblett (1998), McShane (2001), Message (2006), and Witcomb (2006; 2009) for discussions of museological representations of migration and cultural diversity, particularly in the Australian context.

21 Although discussion of curatorial process of developing the *Landmarks* and *Journeys* exhibits is beyond the scope of this chapter, it is worth noting that *Journeys*' and *Landmarks*' interpretive approach was strongly shaped by curatorial engagement and collaborative research with represented individuals, families, and communities. This practice resonated with critical museology's interest in shifting exhibit development away from questions of representing cultural plurality or providing community "access" to museum spaces to focus instead on practices of cultural authorship that emerge through exchanges between museums and communities (Kreps 2003; Witcomb 2009).

22 This conceptualization of exhibitions resonates with a number of strands of museological thinking. These include Clifford's (1997) elaboration of museums as "contact zones" (see also Schorch 2013), constructivist learning theory's emphasis on the interpretive frameworks that visitors bring to and apply within exhibitions (Hooper-Greenhill 2000), and the concept, developed at the Pitt Rivers Museum, Oxford, of the "relational museum" as a "trans-cultural artefact" produced through "relations between the museum and its source community" (see https://www.prm.ox.ac.uk/RelationalMuseum.html).

23 My sincere thanks to the Rachel Carson Center for Environment and Society, Munich, Germany, for enabling me to prepare this chapter through a 2015-16 Carson fellowship and to the National Museum of Australia for enabling my sojourn in Munich. The National Museum also generously provided images for this chapter. I am deeply indebted to my curatorial colleagues, and in particular Martha Sear, Daniel Oakman, George Main, Jennifer Wilson, and Mathew Trinca, with whom I shared the adventure of developing *Journeys* and *Landmarks*. Their creativity, cleverness, and collegiality inspire, inform, and are discussed in this chapter, but the views expressed here are my own and do not necessarily represent those of the National Museum of Australia or my colleagues.

CHAPTER SIX

Archive Fever, Ghostly Histories

CAROLYN STEEDMAN

This title – the first part of it a title I was given to write to – evokes Jacques Derrida's great contemplation of archives and archivization of 1995. Here, "Archive Fever" evokes *Archive Fever*, the English-language version of his meditation (Derrida 1995a; 1995b; 1996). The French "Mal d'archive" denotes a different thing from archive fever. A cumbersome though literal translation would have given us *pains, ills, badness, harm, trouble, wrongs, sickness*, even *evil*, of the archive. The translation of "mal" as "fever" also locates a (metaphorical) high temperature in an individual (only a singular human body can be fevered, though many may suffer fever at the same time), not in the space and place of an archive. The febrile, agitated search for some kind of origin, for the beginning of something or other, is inadvertently personalized in translation from French to English. The sickness that is Western culture's obsessive search for beginnings, for some discernible point of origin for its own self, was certainly one of Derrida's preoccupations throughout his long writing career (Derrida 1976). But in *Mal d'archive* he made it very clear that it was the archive itself that was bad (Derrida 1995b). There are archives themselves, which are selected, collected, and cataloged material fragments of past events; and there is also the political horror of the twentieth century out of which history and other narratives of the past are produced. These last are named as "archives du mal," that is, as archives of evil and evil archives. They are the statistical and documentary record of warfare and civil strife, of massacre, murder, and genocide; they are the secret, but only half hidden, manipulations of private citizens by states and governments. If Derrida ever provided a working definition of the term "archive," he did it in the loose-leaf "Prière d'insérer" (Derrida 1995b). This does not appear in the American version (1996). In this addendum, he brooded on the revisionist histories written out of this evil archive; the history, historiography, and sociology of the Holocaust hover over this little piece of paper. So I have never known – is one meant to know, in the first place? – whether it is the archive, or whether it is formal, modern, academic history writing, that Derrida is talking about, in all versions of *Archive Fever*. Certainly, something like academic history is what he has in his sights for most of the book, which offers a sustained contemplation of a work of history: Yosef Yerushalmi's account of Freud as a kind of historian, who produced a kind of historical story to understand his contemporary context: early twentieth-century anti-Semitism in western and central Europe (Yerushalmi 1991).

Much to the point of this chapter, and probably to any discussion of public history and the archive, is the state's involvement in the making and management of archives: there is an old historical story about the institution of archives as an embodiment of state power and as measure of state involvement in the lives of its citizens and subjects (Le Goff 1992; Müller 2010) to which Derrida made reference. Derrida originally wrote "Mal d'archive" (entitled "The Concept of the Archive" while it was being composed) for an event at which, as he put it, "an archive was taking place." In the summer of 1994, the Freuds' home in exile in Maresfield Gardens, north London, was inaugurated as The Freud Museum. This is how archives happen, said Derrida; they come to dwell permanently in a place. There is an institutional passage "from private to public" when a house becomes a museum (Derrida 1995a: 10). He emphasized museum over archive, for in strict point of definition The Freud Museum is not an archive. Its most famous artifact is Freud's analytic couch, which followed the family from Vienna to London in 1938. Of course, the couch itself is an archive, of psychoanalytic practice and many memories, dreams, and forgettings, but only in metaphorical usage. Or in the sense established by Antoinette Burton, who has taught us to read homes and the domestic lives lived in them as forms of historical evidence. In *Dwelling in the Archive* (2003), she questions the "traditional" archive by using Indian women's novels, memoirs, and histories as narratives that subvert conventional accounts of colonial modernity. She argues that we can use their accounts of "home" as a source for rewriting history.

In 1994, Derrida was in a house that had once been a home. It may not be clear exactly *what* became an archive on that inaugural day; but it must have been this setting, this north London street, this substantial 1920s bourgeois villa that provided the beginning for his lecture. There is always trouble in getting started on any piece of writing, quite apart from the "mal," the sickness, of all beginnings and the search for them. Derrida did write his lecture before he delivered it; but the lecture (in published form, article, or book, French or English) is strange indeed in its refusal to get going. It will not (never will) begin its discussion of beginnings. So we could say that it starts (rather than begins) with a house other than The Freud House in which Derrida was standing. In the opening stretches, Derrida spoke about the *arkhe*, the origin or source of things. In his exegesis, it is a kind of place where things (all things or entities, including power) begin. Power is bound up with, *is*, the authority of the idea that things did once begin; that there are, in fact, starting points. He moved on to the Greek city-state, its administration and management effected by means of the legal documents that inscribed it in the first place. These originary, original, authoritative documents were stored in an *arkheion*, which was the residence of the city's superior magistrates. Here, an *archon* presided over various meetings and legal proceedings. Over a long period (BCE), the *archons* lost much of their authority, becoming mere judicial officers with the mere (though still significant) power to conduct preliminary inquiries in cases to be brought before a jury. After the mid-fifth century BCE, *archons* were no longer empowered to give their own judgments (Lanni 2006). But this was not the history that Derrida told in July 1994: what interested him, what allowed him to make a kind of start, was the idea of a magistrate utilizing the power of the documents stored in his domicile. The documents, containing stories of what had already happened in and about the law, were archived in his home.

Public and domestic, inside and outside, privacy and the social world, law and legal systems and their documentation, are terms we need for understanding modern public history, as both a system of knowledge and as a social practice. As a public historian, or as someone doing public history, what is your relationship to the archive? Do you suffer

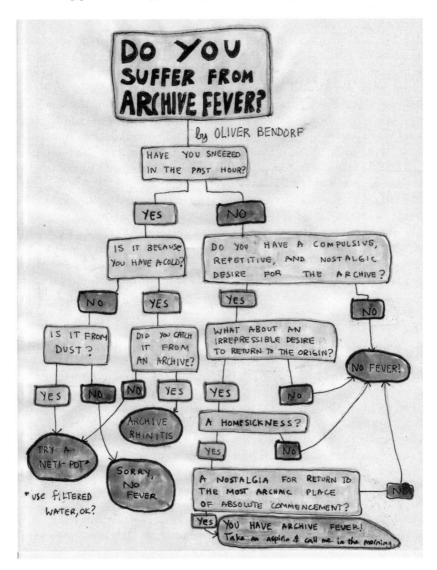

Figure 6.1 Oliver Bendorf, "Do You Suffer from Archive Fever?" There's something irreducibly comic to the English English-language reader about the idea of 'archive fever.' In English English 'fever' is an archaism: only modern babies have fevers, medically speaking. The ridiculous image of a historian suffering from a fever in or about or thinking about an archive was the foundation of *Dust* (Steedman, 2001); the comic potential of the term certainly isn't lost on Oliver Bendorf. Source: http://archivesmonth.blogspot.ca/2013/10/do-you-suffer-from-archive-fever.html

from archive fever (Figure 6.1)? Is your fever of a different kind from that experienced by, say, a local trainee solicitor sent to search the land records in the county record office, in order to better effect the purchase of a piece of property for a client? Or the fever of a doctoral student entering data extracted from poor law settlement examinations into the Excel document stored on their computer? Who is it that conducts the fetishistic, impossible search for origins, in the calm space of an English county record office search room? Is archive fever an illness suffered by "professional" searchers (academic, university historians) alone, or can anyone get it? The elaboration of archive fever, its detailed and developing etiology, and the "archival turn" taken by the Western academy over the last ten years, may all serve to exclude the dead and gone who were actually named and listed by the state, whose names end up in archives, as well as those who seek them and their stories out, for personal, family, or community reasons (Burton 2005; Bashforth 2012; Eskildsen 2008; Eskildsen 2013; Manoff 2004).

Let us be as specific and brief as Derrida was in our account of the time, space, and circumstances to which these questions are addressed. This chapter is about UK (specifically English and Welsh) public archives: county and borough (local) record offices. Included in this category is the national Public Record Office (PRO), renamed The National Archives (TNA) in 2003. Most UK historians (family, local, business, public, and academic) are referring to these places when they talk about visiting archives. This is a relatively new vocabulary: 30 years ago, you talked about "going to the record office" or "getting to my sources," not "going to the archives." They are public repositories in that they hold records of national and local government and administration; and in that they are funded out of both national and local tax revenues. This is why people like me, users of these spaces and places, become quite agitated when required to pay for a personal subscription to an Internet database provider. Ancestry.co.uk, for example, provides (among other materials) baptism, marriage, and burial details extracted from the parish records held in county record offices. "They're *our* records!" you cry. "I don't see why I should pay to look at them!" But, of course, looking at or consulting them (which you could do for free if you took the train to one of the county towns in which they are stored) is not what you are paying for. Payment is for the transcription and digitization of original records, and for the search facility. Local public record offices do not charge for entry, but they do charge for photocopying, photography, or for any digitization they might undertake on your behalf.

Access to the physical space and the search facilities (card and online catalogs, hand lists) is free; but it is probably not a right. A comparison between England and France is often made in this regard. A Declaration of Archival Rights was made by the National Convention in France's early revolutionary era, in June 1794. This proclaimed the right of all citizens to free access to all archives belonging to the nation. The point is not that this right was short-lived, but that it was established in the first place. The Archives Nationales had been inaugurated in 1790, and a further state decree, also of 1794, made it mandatory to centralize all pre-1789 archives seized during the early years of the Revolution (Le Goff 1997). These dates and details are important components of French national identity as it has been written historically, and are symbolic of the memorial heritage of the national community. They are in themselves *lieux de memoire* (Milligan 2005;Pomian 1992).

They ordered these things differently in England and Wales. A Public Records Act came into force in 1838 (1 & 2 Vict. c.94) for the safe preservation of "the public records" (Great Britain 1837-38 V.653). Public records were in effect legal documents originating in the central high courts and in parliament. The PRO began to accept papers and documents from governmental departments in the 1840s, but there were no formal or legal requirements for an office of state to transfer its records. By 1840 there were rules and regulations governing the use of the PRO, but these were determined as matters of office administration, not as individual right of access (Great Britain 1840 XXIX, 597). Right of access was not stated in law, and entry was not free until 1852, and then only for "scholarly purposes." Lawyers – the PRO's majority of users – continued to pay for access. Up until the mid-twentieth century all legislation was for the safekeeping, restoration, preservation, storing, filing, and cataloging of pieces of parchment and paper, not for the people who might want to consult them. The "admission of such persons as ought to be admitted to the use of Records, Calendars, Catalogues and Indexes" mentioned in the 1838 Act was an administrative and office procedure, not an interpellation of users and searchers. This admissions regime was in force for a long time, but in January 2005 the Freedom of Information Act (47 Eliz II c.37) was applied to TNA and replaced the 1838 Act and all successive Public Records Acts (47 Eliz. II c.36). This late twentieth-century legislation *does* interpellate users – readers, citizens – as well as the records themselves (Levine 1986; Shepherd 2009), for the 2000 Act created a "right of access" to information held by public authorities.

County and borough record offices, the sites in which so much family and local history has been found and made and enacted over the last half century, are also repositories for local government records. Some counties made provisions for the preservation of their legal records as early as the seventeenth century. Proceedings of the county court of quarter sessions had to be kept for reference purposes; but arrangements varied widely across the country, and nowhere was there provision for public access to them. The earliest modern county record office was established for Bedfordshire and Luton in 1913 on the initiative of a local history society and a local notable who served on the county council (Shepherd 2009). County and borough record offices, established as public facilities with search rooms and catalogs, developed throughout the interwar years. Local record offices operate by law, though the legislation that governs them is permissive, not mandatory: "A local authority may do all such things as appear to it necessary or expedient for enabling adequate use to be made of records under its control" (10 & 11 Eliz. II c.52). Counties and boroughs and metropolitan authorities are obliged to preserve their records, but not to make them available to the public (though all do). Their foundational collections are administrative and legal: parish records, containing the lost narratives of so many lives, are there because the parish was a fundamental unit of civil and ecclesiastical government for more than a thousand years. Local record offices contain much more than parish records and quarter sessions rolls and constabulary enrolment registers; over the last half-century, county and borough archivists have accepted many personal, family, and business records for preservation.

If you could measure the activity called "doing history" by the yard, and if you accepted that family, local, and academic searchers, researchers for local legal firms, and those doing the legwork that underpins television costume drama, are all active in the role of "historian," then local record offices are the sites in which most historical activity takes place. In 2010–2011, 5% of the United Kingdom's adult population visited a local record office, 60% of whom were researching family history (Public Services Quality Group 2011; The National Archives n.d.). But some of those were virtual visits, made online, and the anecdotal evidence from across the country is that the search rooms of local record offices are quieter places than they were five years ago. Family historians and genealogists can now conduct much of their research at home (Gender, Theory and the Archive: A Symposium 2013).

Are visitors to archives, including virtual visitors, in danger of contracting archive fever? As material places, archives are prosaic and everyday, and for the main part cater wonderfully and accommodatingly to their clientele. Most local record offices are supported out of a local authority's leisure, heritage, and culture budget, and most archivists enact this relationship of civil society in their dealings with the public. They are in the business of accommodating all sorts of people in their search for their own heritage. No more than the PhD candidate sitting next to them in the search room are family and community historians suffering from a compulsive desire to return to a place of absolute commencement. They are looking for their granny, or for an entry in an 1898 school logbook that may mention a great-grandfather. They might be looking for all the children who attended a village school in the 1890s for a community project on, say, childhood in Warwickshire in the second half of the nineteenth century. Like the PhD student using records from the same parish for an account of child labor and apprenticeship in the mid-eighteenth century, both types of historian are using the tiny fragments of past time to fill in the spaces of a historical story that they have already started to construct or tell. A historical story like the experience of women during the Second World War (which is why you might want to know about your granny), or a story of plebeian life and labor in eighteenth-century England (which is why you're collecting statistics on apprenticeship) has sent all these historians to the search room in the first place. And what they all do, if they are lucky enough to find anything, is perform, narrate, write, or tell the history they make, *after the archive* (Steedman 2011).

Making history, after the archive

All historians write or tell themselves in the guise of some narrative about the past. Like every other historian who has narrated what they found in a local record office or other kind of repository, I shall now attempt to draw general and theoretical propositions from a particular historical story about "doing history": my own experience in the archive. The story I tell now is about the time I spent with one of the dead, from early nineteenth-century England. Joseph Woolley was a stocking maker (a stockinger, or framework knitter) who kept diaries and account books during the era of Luddism: the great machine-breaking crisis of early nineteenth-century England (Binfield 2004; Steedman 2013; Thomis 1972; Weir 1998). You can follow the Luddite Rebellion day by day, on an exemplary public history website (Luddite Bicentenary n.d.). Where are we now, 200 years on? On the 11th of November 1813/2013, when I first sat down to write this chapter, we were in the West Riding of Yorkshire, with military men and barristers and attorneys sending in their claims to the War Office and the Home Office for expenses incurred in the apprehending, charging, and prosecution of General Ludd's followers. The newsmen were busy as well, reporting on compensation claims by Sheffield manufacturers for the destruction of their machines over the summer months. And there was still a market for stories of Luddism back in its county of origin, Nottinghamshire. In August, local newspapers reported the suicide of a "respectable" Nottingham framework knitter at Pentrich, in the north of the county: on Tuesday 27th July 1813, the body of stocking maker William Hall was found hanging in a stable near town. It was said that he had suffered from depression for some time; he had left home the day before, slipping out unbeknownst to the wife and seven children that he left behind (Derby Mercury 1813). But Luddism had moved north, onwards and upcountry from Nottinghamshire, away from the stocking trade, to other ruined textile industries, in this period of war, blockade, harvest failure, and general food shortage; of revolution and counterrevolutionary action by the British state (Bohstedt 2010; Thompson 1963; Wells 1988).

Figure 6.2 "The Leader of the Luddites." British Museum.

I do not think that Joseph Woolley, the diarist of Clifton, looked much like the cross-dressing rebel depicted in this print from 1812 (Figure 6.2). This beautiful and stirring image connects Luddism, machine breaking, and protest against the downturn in the textile trades, to the theater of eighteenth-century food riots described by E. P. Thompson (1971), and anticipates, for example, the Rebecca Riots against grain prices in the early 1840s (Rees, 2011). For a man to dress in women's clothes and, accompanied by "real women," take direct action against tolls, tithes, and high food prices, made many points, not least about the connection of state policy to the everyday life of households in times of economic crisis. But Joseph Woolley probably looked much more like the young man in the 1805 image used on the cover of *An Everyday Life of the English Working Class* (Steedman 2013). I spent seven long years with Joseph Woolley while working on *An Everyday Life,* after I first encountered him in Nottinghamshire Archives, the county record office. For me, *this* is how he looked, or how he figures in my mind's eye: this image of the young knitter at his frame, eyes turned away from the infinite sky. He was about 30 years old when his first surviving diary opens, so the stockinger in the print is of the right age to be him (Figure 6.3).

Figure 6.3   "Stockingmaker." Print from the Book of Trades, or Library of the Useful Arts, 1805.
Picture Collection, The New York Public Library, Astor, Lenox and Tilden Foundations.

I "found" Woolley in an archive. Found is in inverted commas because I want to
demonstrate that I am well aware of the problematic social history mission of "rescuing" historical subjects: from oblivion; from silence; from what E. P. Thompson calls
"the enormous condescension of posterity" (1968: 13; Steedman 2001). The idea of
"rescue" does not imply an equal relationship between historian and historical subject;
rather it implies a moral superiority on the part of the person doing the rescuing. And
as Cath Feely (2013) has recently remarked, how do we know they want to be rescued?
Or rescued in the way the historian sees fit? She describes the objections of one the
descendants of a character (or historical subject) depicted in Channel 4's *The Mill*
(2013). *The Mill* was, as she says, an extraordinary experiment in one kind of public
history, using archival material to script a period drama. The records of Quarry Bank
Mill, Cheshire, were used to tell the story of the indentured child and adolescent
laborers that management obtained via the Poor Law system. But though it claimed to
be faithfully based on extant records, the script turned the story of one apprentice,
Esther Price, into something that never actually happened. Her appearance in the local
magistrates' court on a charge of assault was translated into a version in which she was

sexually assaulted by a mill overseer. One of the overseer's descendants responded to Channel 4, pointing out that there was no evidence whatsoever that the overseer had ever behaved in the way depicted, or of the court proceedings enacted on the screen: "My g-g-grandfather Charles Crout was the overseer in the tv programme 'The Mill'. There is no evidence that he was… abusive in any way to the workers. This was all just fabricated for tv viewing" (Brandis 2013).

I was in Nottinghamshire Archives, in the last stages of writing *Labours Lost* (2009). I had returned to check a page number, or a document reference – having to go back to check something you should have noted first time around is what I tell PhD students to avoid at all costs. Waiting for my documents to arrive in the search room, I did something I do encourage students to do: have a look through the card catalog at the "Diaries" section. You never know what you might find. I found the diaries of a framework knitter from the very same village as the magistrate whose justicing notebooks I was waiting for. At first I searched them for references to Sir Gervase Clifton Bart, JP, but was soon caught up in Woolley's account of labor and love, and the law's impact on everyday life and feeling, between about 1800 and 1815. I knew immediately what my next project would be. Woolley's is a unique account; but it was deposited in Nottinghamshire Archives when academic interest in working-class life provoked by Thompson's *Making* (1963) was on the wane, under the regime of post-structuralism and the cultural turn (Feldman and Lawrence 2011). The Woolley volumes are known to local historians and to historians of the hosiery and knitwear manufacture, but as one of them remarks, there is not an awful lot in them about the stocking manufacture (Amos n.d.). And they are a little indelicate; among many other things, Woolley wrote about the sexual lives of his friends and neighbors in graphic detail. The diaries contain many accounts of drunken nights out, pub-yard fights, and alehouse trashing – not really what serious twentieth-century labor historians of the Luddite era were looking for in their working-class subjects. His 100,000 words are spread over six volumes of *Old Moore's Almanack*. The almanacs had blank sheets for writing inserted between calendars, predictions, and "curious" detail. This was probably done by a local printer or bookseller unpicking the originals and sewing them up again to sell as diaries. The journal that Woolley kept on the blank pages most likely originated in the monetary accounts that it was wise for anyone working in a putting-out system to maintain. I suspect that some of his interest in the sexual shenanigans of Clifton village originated in the life-cycle events (births, legitimate and illegitimate; marriages and deaths) that his father, who was parish clerk, was obliged to record in the parish books. Joseph was probably helping his father by keeping notes which would later be formally written up. I worked on Woolley's diaries for what must have been six years, but I only once held the original volumes in my hands, sitting at a table right under the duty archivist's watchful eye. This was in 2012, right at the end of the project. The volumes are very frail; Nottinghamshire Archives provided a photocopy for the use of researchers. In 2007 I paid for a photocopy of a photocopy, and worked on the diaries at home. I have not been very much *in the archive* with Joseph Woolley. Scarcely at all.

I believe I know quite a lot about archives, or rather, about English local record offices. They are an important source for most of what I know about the social organization, management, and policing of communities in the past. For example, it was a county archivist who first explained to me the difference between the hundred and the wapentake as units of county government and administration. I learned about the parish, as a unit of civil and ecclesiastical government, in a record office. A parish was the place where everyone lived up until the twentieth century. Everything I know about *how the*

whole damn thing worked came from archivists. In the self-satisfied arrogance that I tried
to describe in *Dust* (2001), those places, those record offices, belonged to me; they were
the academic historian's special place; her home. I am aware of the problems attached to
the label "professional historian," so from now on I am in role as an academic, or university-based historian (Jensen 2012). In a historical change of some importance, and of
which I entirely approve, record offices are not my place anymore. In the 1960s, a majority of provincial record office users were academic historians; they now constitute a
usergroup of less than 10% (The National Archives n.d.). The archive is not my smug-
historian's place anymore; it is everyone's place. But that is not the reason for working
on Joseph Woolley's diaries in my house: I could not afford to stay in a hotel, however
flea-bitten, for the days, months, years I spent with him.

On turns and turnings

The archival turn has been just one of many taken by Western historical studies over the
last quarter century (Jobs and Lüdtke 2010). It provokes new questions about historians' responsibilities to their subjects; to the dead and gone they discover and write about.
These are questions that were not asked – that were not conceptualized – 20 years ago.
Who owns history? And what is it that you own, if you do? Who has the right to speak
for the dead? For particular categories of the dead? (21st International Congress 2010).
Questions like these are asked out of ethical consideration of the historian as writer, in
relationship to their historical subjects. Global history calls for an even newer ethic of
historical reconstruction and imagination. Academic historians have been asked to exercise their moral responsibilities by moving beyond local and national stories, toward
global universalism. We should, it is said, undertake an empirical, universal history,
encompassing the history of the universe itself. An ecumenical, transnational history is
extolled as the moral duty of the historical profession (of academic, university-based
historians) (Christian 2010; Haggis 2012). At the same time, new protocols of imagining and writing have emerged from Holocaust history and sociology, forcing the question: "Who can claim the moral ground to consider the meaning... of the lives and
deaths of others?" (Cohen 2010: 43). The ethical turn suggests that our responsibilities
are greatest toward those that we imagine into being. To write about some person or
group of people in the past, you have to imagine them first: dress them in certain ways,
provide the setting and landscape of their life, in your own head; but it is in writing that
you become morally responsible for your imagined figures, for your writing will communicate an idea, story, or theory of them to some kind of public.

   This was the new historiographical regime under which I wrote Joseph Woolley (and
Sir Gervase Clifton Bart) into being. I focused on the stocking maker; on his way of seeing, on the way he framed his own experience in writing. His experience included the
activities of Gervase Clifton, administering summary justice (and other kinds of justice
too) from his country house, which stood close by the village in which Woolley worked
his knitting frame. Both men wrote, but produced very different kinds of writing: the
stocking maker's 100,000 words are counterposed to the brief, formal, and incomplete
records of magisterial business that Clifton kept from 1770 until his death in 1815. Their
writing coincides for six years between 1800 and 1815. I used the magistrate's notebooks to contextualize what the working man had to say about everyday life in early
nineteenth-century Nottinghamshire. It was the extraordinary conjunction of two sets
of records, produced by two men from opposite ends of the social spectrum (sometimes

about the same incidents) that allowed me to ask questions about the meaning of law in working-class communities; about gender; about the category of "experience" itself; and of course, about Luddism, here in its county of origin. At the peak of the Nottinghamshire crisis in January 1812, twenty-nine stocking frames were destroyed during one night in Clifton village. The magistrate was not at home. The stocking maker's diary for 1812 (if he kept one) has not survived. So on the face of it, there was no way in which the magistrate's or the stockinger's writing could be used to measure ordinary life against the experience of violence and rebellion. In the data I had, nobody looked out of the window at political terror; neither man bore witness to History rushing past in the street. Nothing in their writing, for it does not exist for 1812, flashes up in a moment of danger (Benjamin 1977; 1992). What to do – how to proceed in research and analytic terms – when the ordinary, or the everyday, has no opposite in the extraordinary of the great public and political world? That was the nagging question that shaped the years I spent with Joseph Woolley. Those questions were my own archive fever. They would not let me go; they preoccupied me. They were not to do with trying to find an origin, or beginning (for what? For Luddism? The English working class? Everyday life at the turn of the nineteenth century?). I could not conduct a feverish, anxious search for origins that I believe to be epistemologically impossible. If fever it was, it was about what to do; how to think about Joseph Woolley and his context; how to exercise my responsibilities toward him. And – if fever it was – I had this fever in my own house, at my desk, in front of my word processor (and in my dreams), not in the archive.

Joseph Woolley's diaries are important; they ought to be made known to historians working on sexuality, violence, and the everyday life of the English working class. But I had trouble with him right from the start. I was not sure I liked him very much. I knew I had no right to be bored by his interminable narratives of drunken nights out and alehouse trashing; but bored I was. On first reading, I thought him a bit of a misogynist, even though I knew I had no right to be offended by that, either. I was always grateful, right from the start, that he did not come with a story of suffering as his passport to the historical record (Auslander 2010): I did not have to feel the awkward, superior, subordinating impulse of sympathy that has been a feature of my relationship with all the abject child-laborers, child-murdering maidservants in the condemned cell, and paupers pleading for relief before a magistrate about whom I've written in recent years. I did not have to (or want to) rescue this "poor stockinger... from the enormous condescension of posterity" (Thompson 1963: 13). When I finally understood that I did not have to write him out of my superiority as a historian, as his rescuer, I began to like him a lot more.

And then I transcribed. I copied out, in my own writing, Joseph Woolley's words. I slowed my reading to the pace at which he had put them on the page. Transcription makes you read in a different way: for spaces and absences, erasures and repetitions, for intended ironies, literary allusions, and jokes. You discard your earlier presumptions and assumptions; a man is revealed as no misogynist at all, but as a writer who empathized with the difficulties of many women's lives, who noticed violent and deeply unhappy sexual relationships and recorded them, and who wrote about women as if they were the same kind of creature as men. Someone read or imagined through the window of transcription becomes a writer.

Still, I never could have looked forward to an evening at the pub with Joseph Woolley. Nor he me, for that matter. I wrote about this, a kind of imagined scene in an 1801 alehouse, in a last-minute preface to the book, and sent the manuscript off to the publisher.

The readers' reports suggested that I had seriously misrepresented Joseph Woolley. In discussing him as a single man, it appeared that I had written him as a sad and lonely voyeur of other people's pleasure. I had discussed his remaining unmarried by reference to the birth order of the Woolley siblings, the death of his half-brother which made him the eldest boy, the longevity of his parents and their dependence on him, the great changes that took place in stocking manufacture during these years, the particularity of tenantry on Sir Gervase's lands, and to the sexual conventions of the time. I had quoted the demographers and historians who tell us that about four in ten late eighteenth-century English people fell into the category "never married" (slightly more women than men), but it is still a calculation that shows Woolley to be not unusual among his peers. I had described how deeply affected he was by the pregnancy of his dead brother's wife. His reaction to sister-in-law Rose Woolley's affair with the one-eyed, melancholic seducer, returned soldier Sam Boyer and the birth of her bastard daughter (with Joe's brother not cold in his grave) troubled him very much. I had put what Joe wrote in some kind of context; I had said that as for his own sexual life, it lay concealed deep beneath the words he put on the page. Joseph Woolley wrote what he wanted to write and omitted what he did not care to display. But to my readers, I had written about a man who lacked the trappings of masculine success. I had described his many detailed accounts of pub-yard fights, and pointed out that though he never once, textually speaking, raised his own fists, that did not mean that he did not spend his Saturday nights out on the randan (out on a binge), just like his companions. That he too may have lived the raucous romantic life of Clifton, and never mentioned it. But he had been read, through my words, as a not-properly-plebeian framework knitter, of the sort that would have given E. P. Thompson pause for thought. In short (though not the anonymous reader's words), I had an attitude problem with Joseph Woolley.

I believed I had been found out: found out in all my doubts and anxieties over my right to write about Joseph Woolley in the first place ("who has the right to speak for the dead?"), doubts about time and money spent on an obscure working-class Englishman in the perspective of global history, doubts about whether he mattered enough for a whole book. Found out as in exposed, my feelings and motives uncovered, revealed to view. I found a solution (which was only a solution in writing) among the more recently dead than him: my father. I thought about not looking forward to meeting Woolley in the Clifton pub, circa 1801, and realized why: it would have been far too much like meeting my father for a drink in a South London pub, in 1967 I think it was. Home from university for Christmas, my friends and I were entertained by my father, an old charmer with an authentic working-class background, and his fund of stories about Up North. Many years later the stories would turn out to have been about leaving (leaving the North, other women besides my mother, a child along the way, and us: the pathetic family of his middle years). But the stories were "so papered over with secrets that even their shape was uncertain" (Ashbery 1994). They still are not known; will never be known. Then, at the end of his tale, high on audience appreciation, my father cracked a joke, one you would now call politically incorrect, that silenced us all. And I – in shame and embarrassment, protective of him, defensive – retorted silently but defiantly to my friends: "Yeah. Well. You want working-class? That's what you get." The added embarrassment of being down at the pub with Joseph Woolley in October 1801 would have been the unmerciful teasing of his friends, and that some woman, for a laugh, would have emptied a hat full of piss over my head (Steedman 2013). (The hat incident is one of many in which he describes women and men having a laugh in this way.) I understood then that my assumption in reading and accounting for Joseph Woolley's stories had been that like my father, he will keep his secrets. Most of us around the 1967 pub table were students of history, being schooled in a Thompsonian account of the English working class. Had we known about Joseph Woolley, we would probably have wanted him to be a different kind of working man from the one he actually was. He lived in Nottinghamshire, at the epicenter of the 1811–1813 crisis, but never mentions Ludd. We could not have imagined him thronging the pages of Thompson's *Making*, turning experience of labor relations in the stocking trade and the relationships of everyday life into class consciousness. We could not have employed him to fill out the contours of "the radical artisan" (Eley 2005: 162). If you want to account for Joseph Woolley, you have to write against many accreted historical assumptions about men like him.

These memories and new imaginings of Joseph Woolley all happened outside the archive. My father and he were both in the pub, both of them working-class men who were not as working-class men were meant by their historians to be. I had to think again about what I knew already about history writing. I had to repeat to myself what I already knew but had forgotten, about the impossibility out of which all modern Western history is written, whether it measures an event of 40 years past, or 200. History writing must include Afterward. This is the knowledge shared by writer and reader, of what happened after the events described. The historian may struggle to abandon the days, weeks, years, between the "then" they write, and the "now" of their writing. They struggle with the impossible task of writing without "what happened afterward" because they know that the "aftermath," "repercussions," "result," and "later developments" were not known to the protagonists of the story they are constructing. This is why what you write as a historian never is, and cannot be, what *was* there, what *it was like*, once upon a time (Rancière 1994: 63).

This is the treachery of history writing. It is not the same as French writer Annie Ernaux's (1993) declaration that all who write about their own (family, class, community) have already betrayed them. Or, perhaps, Ernaux's stricture does apply to all those who write about class in the past: in their deep identification with their historical subjects, many *engagé* scholarship historians of the mid-twentieth-century (like me) were forced to contemplate the betrayal involved in writing about the working-class dead and gone. That is why Joseph Woolley and my father are together in the pub. They are not ghosts; they are the dead: the dead imagined and figured and written *outside the archive*. Or if they are ghosts, they are of the type investigated by US sociologist Avery Gordon. The ghost represents "something to be done," in the present or in the time of writing history. Gordon says that this "something to be done is not a return to the past but a reckoning with its repression in the present, a reckoning with that which we have lost, but never had" (Gordon 2008: 183). Gordon's ghosts, her account of how the past operates in the present, is much more useful for historians wanting to understand what kind of thing (way of thinking; form of writing) History is, than is the idea of Archive Fever. The past works in the present in innumerable individual imaginations, and in stories told about those imaginings. The ghost appears. It may appear or happen in some kind of archive; but the archive is not the unique site of its appearance. The ghost – the haunting of the present by the past – appears because of another, further manifestation, which is History itself. Gordon says that history is "a ghostly ... totality that articulates and disarticulates itself and the subjects who inhabit it" (2008: 184). "History" here is both "the past" *and* the various kinds of story that gets written or told about the past. It is there; and it is also made (imagined and written) by many kinds of historian. Gordon's

History is also understood as "a wavering yet determinate social structure." We inhabit it, and it inhabits us. History, unlike the other major retrieval enterprise of sociology, is "never available as a final solution for the difficulties haunting creates for the living." History is always "a site of struggle between the living and the ghostly," for the living, in or out of the archive, can only ever partially "grasp the source of the ghost's power." Gordon appears sanguine about this. She does not diagnose or pathologize our attempts as archive fever. And it happens (the ghost happens and we try to understand the meaning of its happening) everywhere: inside and outside the archive; wherever we happen to be when we are "doing history."

Before writing *Mal d'Archive*, Derrida also contemplated ghosts. The specter in *Spectres of Marx* (1994) is something that is not there; it is not real, but it still intrudes into whatever present is here and now and real. This ghost speaks to us, interrogates us. If we manage to exorcize it, we should at the same time grant it "hospitable memory," says Derrida, "out of a concern for *justice*" (1994: 175). Out of all the forms of history available – all the retrieval enterprises of the modern world – public history is best placed to speak to the ghost, work out what it means, articulate the haunting of the present by the past wherever the apparition appears: inside or outside the archive. Ghostly power is much more fruitful a concept than is archive fever – which was never much to do with archives in the first place.

CHAPTER SEVEN

Digital Public History

SERGE NOIRET

Digital history, or history in the digital era?

Digital history has transformed the kinds of sources used by historians, and the tools for accessing, storing, and managing them, without having thoroughly discussed their critical use. Particularly in academic environments, the use of digital tools, of coding languages, metadata, software, and databases is transforming the relation between historians and digital sources. At an international level, the impact of the "digital turn" generated numerous epistemological and methodological questions within a profession already facing general uncertainty and anxiety about the future of traditional historiography, and confronted with new digital forms for narrating the past. Digital history rewrites and reinterprets the history profession through the mastery of new digital practices (Clavert and Noiret 2013). Changes to the historian's professional practices – there has even been talk of a new historicism (Fickers 2012) – are such that the impact of digital history on traditional forms of narrating the past must be examined for different historical periods (Hartog 2015). In light of the public availability of these technologies – many tools are in the public domain – we must ask ourselves if we should not seriously review the very relationship we (historians and the public) currently hold with individual and collective memory, and with history as a science dealing with the past (Joutard 2013).

Not everyone agrees with French sociologist Michel Wieviorka (2013), who speaks of a "digital imperative" in today's social sciences; nor is there total acceptance of American historian Anthony Grafton's (2014) position that history as a discipline will be digital, or will not exist at all, in a very near future. Indeed, the experience of historians working to master (and even create) digital technology would have led to the creation of silos and caused dismay among colleagues grappling with the digital turn. There are real challenges associated with managing digital technologies that are increasingly public, widely available, and because of this, successfully being used outside the profession (Noiret 2012), by whom Carl Becker (1932) called "Mr. Everyman." In 2002, Rolando Minuti

A Companion to Public History, First Edition. Edited by David Dean.
© 2018 John Wiley & Sons Ltd. Published 2018 by John Wiley & Sons Ltd.

wrote of the "uncertainties of a mutation"; Daniel J. Cohen and Roy Rosenzweig warned of the "promises and perils of Digital History" in their 2005 digital history manual; while, even in 2013, the Catalan scholar Anaclet Pons wrote a book titled *Digital Disorder*, making reference to the babel created by messy and difficult-to-master digital sources previously described by Borges (1971); in French, Milad Doueihi (2011b; 2013; 2015) accentuates the necessity for rethinking the impact of the digital on humanities disciplines because of new methods now available to look at cultural objects.

Other approaches to digital history are neither optimistic nor pessimistic, but instead reflect the focus of those who wish to understand these technological transformations from a critical positivist standpoint – Cohen and Rosenzweig (2005) spoke of a "tech-norealism" – that is certainly interested in the role and impact of digital technologies without being subsumed by them. In her book *History in the Digital Age*, Toni Weller (2012) argues that not all historians who use digital sources are "digital historians." She highlights the unhealthy impact the digital revolution can have if applied to the preexisting practices of historians working within their professional tradition.[1] Echoing Weller, the results of a significant American study of the application of information technology to historiography emphasize that "the underlying research methods of many historians remain fairly recognizable even with the introduction of new tools and technologies, but the day-to-day research practices of all historians have changed fundamentally" (Rutner and Schonfeld 2012).

More "digital history" than "digital humanities"

We should value the particularities of digital history as a discipline and the digital practices of the historian: the search for different sources and the diverse narratives prepared for the Web. If it is true that digital humanities offer practices and methodologies that are common to the humanistic sciences (Schreibman, Siemens, and Unsworth 2004), it is also true that these practices and concepts are better developed within a single discipline. This happens specifically for digital history, which aims also to visually represent the past and to construct narratives that are not solely or essentially based on texts (Natale et al. 2015). Digital history, then, is about a proper epistemological dimension, one specific to historians. Historians need to answer queries about the past, use digital sources, and create narratives and contents that must be available to others and continually monitored. Digital humanities are providing methods and tools to all humanists, but historians use tools in the digital realm that are sometimes different from those needed by other digital humanists confronted with literary and linguistic computing, text analysis, text encoding, and annotation. For Stephen Robertson, director of the Center for History and New Media at George Mason, digital history is indeed different from literary studies and might be considered as a separate discipline. His reflections influenced the 20th anniversary celebrations of the center, held in the autumn of 2014, which highlighted the importance of digital media forging a renewed history profession, a reflection inherited by his predecessors (Cohen and Rosenzweig 2011; Roy Rosenzweig Center for History and New Media 2014). Robertson emphasized two points: "First, the collection, presentation, and dissemination of material online is a more central part of digital history ... Second, in regards to digital analysis, digital history has seen more work in the area of digital mapping than has digital literary studies, where text mining and topic modeling are the predominant practices" (Robertson 2014).

Sharon M. Leon's *User-Centered Digital History (n.d.)* is about being able to translate the past into history, to help audiences visualize the past, and to communicate with an identified audience like she did when retrieving and curating for the Web the histories and memories of national monuments on the National Mall in Washington (Roy Rosenzweig Center for History and New Media n.d.). Reaching audiences through the digital is an essential skill for public historians, who must ask themselves "why do history if it is not for the public?"

Almost all of the well-known challenges of the historian's work, from establishing a research hypothesis to finding, accessing, and managing written documents and other multimedia sources; to grounding a narrative and, especially, communicating research results as narrative; and finally, to the teaching of history, are today partially or completely mediated by a computer screen and though the Worldwide Web. Digital history as a specific field within the trans-discipline of digital humanities, however, does not consist solely of the use of new digital tools to facilitate old practices. One must also take into account what Patrick Manning (2015) calls the building of a world-historical archive of data. Peter Haber (2011) has referred to this as a general process of "datification" of the past: "big data" management is about enormous amounts of digital data being made available as sources allowing for interdisciplinary data mining of stored documents (Mayer-Schönberger and Cukier 2013).[2] Statistical calculations, geolocalization, programs that analyze pixels in images, the building of historical maps, text editing enhancement and curation, and so on, are all about digital history and involves developing close links between technologies that are able to alter the very parameters of research itself. In the wake of the digital era, historians now work in a context that makes it possible to formulate new epistemological questions in their analysis of the past, and to receive new answers, something that has been underlined strongly by David Armitage and Jo Guldi in *The History Manifesto* (2014). Asking themselves what the historian's role is in today's society, Armitage and Guldi actively face the challenge of the digital turn that transformed the way historians work with archives, produce knowledge about the past, and communicate such knowledge. When the authors talk about "big digital data," they do not even scratch the surface of this digital revolution. They offer examples of how historians can transform their methods when applying them to enormous corpora of digital documents. Jo Guldi looks at how to deal today with big data and the management – through new digital techniques – of what she calls "dark archives," or invisible archives that governments do not want us to discover until they are "declassified," or, without their permission, made available through Wikileaks. For example, the Old Bailey digital project in the United Kingdom fosters long termism (or *longue durée*) as opposed to what the *The History Manifesto* heavily criticizes, short termism from a research perspective based on small archival corpora.[3] The authors of the *Manifesto* look at new tools and techniques capable of intelligently exploiting digital primary sources. They used Franco Moretti's "distant reading" text-mining capacities when engaging with big data, a very different approach from close reading of single primary sources, which leads instead to forms of short termism in historical research (Guldi and Armitage 2014). Distant reading of sources allows researchers to answer "big questions."

Both ways of looking at documentation and sources are needed when doing digital history, but only a small number of historians master the tools that are needed to provide answers to emerging scientific questions. Even fewer create original programs – as Guldi did with Paper Machines[4] – that enable new forms of analysis and new ways of treating and interacting with data according to hypotheses enabled by digital analysis (Cohen et al. 2008).

Many historians today are more properly *historians using digital tools* rather than *digital historians* or digital humanists. But history itself (sources and historiography) and the memory of the past have, in fact, become digital, irrespective of the ways in which historians, either individually or as an organized professional group, are linked to the digital turn, the digital humanities, and with digital (public) history. Despite the frequent lack of an institutionalized framework for digital humanities (such as the one in England, for example [Terras et al. 2013]), a positive acceptance of technology has had beneficial and extensive consequences for the historical profession. However, the public diffusion and wide circulation of the past and individual memory on the Net, what could be called digital *public* history,[5] mediated or not by digital public historians, often lacks historical consciousness, internal and external criticism of sources, and contextualization. For example, many digital archives now offer access to digitized historical photographs; but these pictures are harvested in the Web without any kind of open linked data from their original archival context. So we use and quote photographs often ignoring the very story lying behind single images, which happens systematically within social media archives of images like Instagram or Tumblr. Photos are lost in social media and on websites without their original caption or metadata curation, and when they are retrieved in gigantic photo archives, they become useless as far as historical research and public history are concerned. The lack of digital curation challenges the professional historian's role in the digital world.[6]

Web 2.0 and crowdsourcing

The scope of the changes in the historian's activities through digital technology is of such magnitude that we must investigate the impact of digital history on traditional forms of narrating the past. Digital narratives dealing with either collective or individual memory or historiography may change the perception of timescale and the very relationship between different historical periods and their declination in our present, a process described by François Hartog (2015) using the concept of "presentism." Asking questions about the public presence of the past allows us to deal with these crucial issues.

There are many problems to consider when we refer to digital public history practices. From the perspective of the presence of the past and of history in society, the Internet has eroded the distinction that once existed between academic research and Mr. Everyman's public handling of the past, by allowing anybody to upload memories and historical documentation on the Web. The online communication of autobiographical narratives about the past to a large number of people on the Net has become a widespread universal activity, like the abuse of selfies in social media: in 2006, *Times Magazine* published a cover dedicated to "You" as person of the year, "because you [we] control the information age."

With the emergence of a new Web 2.0 participative Web era around the year 2004, forms of historical narration became accessible to whoever used the Net. In addition, new modes for writing on the Web, such as blogs, enabled interaction between authors and readers not only in terms of critical interventions or suggestions for enriching and engaging with arguments, but also with the direct and immediate addition of documentary sources. Readers can engage interactively with the authors of historical narratives since the Web 2.0 technically enables participatory activity for everybody (Cohen and

Rosenzweig 2011). Digital public history is about organizing the relationship between Internet technologies and history via social media and Web projects. It has contributed in this way to making "high culture" accessible to different publics and, in the best cases, already filtered by professional and public historians, or through shared authority practices in a participatory fashion and engaging with specific communities or with the public at large (Noiret 2014a).

With the arrival of Web 2.0, history and the study of memory are no longer the sole prerogative of the academic community: through participatory and direct forms of writing, anyone can become involved in the past on the Web. Tapping into community knowledge through public participation (what is generally referred to as crowdsourcing) using diverse forms of participatory labor and knowledge on multiple topics enables the integrated management of digital content by whoever has the opportunity, some basic technological know-how, and adequate knowledge of past events. In this second phase, the Web fosters a live and shared public history, practiced interactively by everyone and no longer limited to the activity of academic historians who often use the Web to upload, in open access, their traditional publications in closed formats such as PDF files. For example, menus from nineteenth-century New York restaurants can be entered directly into a database maintained by the New York Public Library,[7] or, thanks to the Europeana 1914–1918 crowdsourcing project, First World War commemoration is becoming a popular way to collect individual and family documents and memories not publicly accessible until then.[8]

These forms of crowdsourcing – such as the collective management and collection of important digital sources – constitute explicit interactive practice of digital public history in the participatory Web era we are currently experiencing.[9] Melissa Terras (2010), with the Transcribe Bentham project, one of the first crowdsourced activities developed on the Web and which is now seen as an archetype of interactive public activity in the humanities, defined crowdsourcing as a community effort that requires a scientific focus to evaluate each contribution. This public knowledge and labor requirement for completing public history projects is occurring in a variety of fields and topics in the digital humanities, and with great public interest and participation.

On the other hand, archives such as those of Mark Twain, Edgar Allan Poe, and the Herman Melville library in the United States[10]; the Swiss *Rousseau Online* project[11]; or the *Dictionnaire Montesquieu* developed with the participation of international specialists[12]; and, more recently, the international digital encyclopedia of World War One,[13] derive from the technical and scientific work of editorial committees that do not make use of the kinds of external support and crowdsourcing procedures we described earlier that are typical of Web 2.0 and, when dealing with the past, of digital public history practices. These latter projects are instead academic digital history projects, not digital public history ones, either because of the way in which they were designed, their intended audience, or the absence of the public as direct facilitators of the projects themselves. Sometimes, digital public history projects ask the public to complete the content of the site by adding their own stories and documents. This is the case with the Bracero History Archive Project in the United States, which "collects and makes available the oral histories and artifacts pertaining to the Bracero program, a guest worker initiative that spanned the years 1942–1964," attracting millions of Mexican agricultural workers. Today, the Bracero History Archive continues to collect the stories of the Bracero program, and anyone can contribute.[14] More recently, Denise Meringolo's Baltimore Uprising 2015 Archive Project looks at the local population and asks for contributions in order to differentiate the sources explaining and documenting the Freddie Gray uprising: "Preserve the Baltimore Uprising is a digital repository that seeks to preserve and make accessible original content that was captured and created by individual community members, grassroots organizations, and witnesses to the protests that followed the death of Freddie Gray on April 19, 2015 ... Too often, history is shaped by official accounts" (Preserve the Baltimore Uprising n.d.). This kind of digital public history project is also about political militancy and civil rights defense. It collects different kinds of sources, from written accounts to photos, videos, oral recordings, produced recordings, and e-mails. It is a scientific contribution by outstanding public historians as part of the American civil society movement, well summarized these last years in the United States by the Twitter hashtag #BlackLivesMatter.

Digital public history, as we have just seen, is largely about the collective creation of invented digital archives. Open public history cultural projects attract the curiosity of those who regard the Web as a space that encourages new collective collaboration practices thanks to which everyone can add their own piece of knowledge. As already mentioned, the curation of a whole body of text by a significant writer such as Jeremy Bentham would not be possible without the interactive Web 2.0 and the direct participation of an otherwise silent public in the development of cultural projects. Providing personal documents to complement multimedia archives is seen in projects such as Preserve the Baltimore Uprising; The September 11 Digital Archive,[15] the invented digital public archive which is entirely overseen today by the Library of Congress in Washington; the Parallel Archive,[16] dedicated to the history of totalitarian Communist regimes in Eastern Europe before 1989; or, more recently, the *Grande Collecte*, undertaken by Europeana, the European Digital Library, in November 2013 on the occasion of the centenary of the First World War, in order to digitize sources and first-person accounts. These are initiatives that can only be carried out through the active presence of a skilled public that possesses both knowledge and documents, and, above all, the existence of easy-to-manage technologies that enable connecting digital public history projects with their publics.

The PhotosNormandie project, a photographic archive uploaded to Flickr, of the June 6, 1944 D-Day and the Battle of Normandy, has been one of the first initiatives that considered drawing on public knowledge with the use of Web 2.0 technologies. Launched in January 2007, PhotosNormandie is not about providing one's own documents to an invented archive through crowdsourcing as with the September 11 Digital Archive, but rather it is about capturing unexpressed knowledge of an unknown and specialized audience interested in D-Day, and knowing about places shown in photographs shot in Normandy during the summer of 1944. As a digital public history project, PhotosNormandie sought comments for the pictures and suggested enriching and/or changing existing captions of the over 3,000 photos of the landing and the Battle of Normandy which would enable these images to be "redocumented" as primary sources (Peccatte and Le Querrec n.d.). The public history aspect of this knowledge comes through the shared authority activity between a group of specialists adding new descriptive metadata to the pictures and the curators of the project. The Flickr archive has found locally, thanks to the scientific collaboration of local experts, unexpected and rigorous means of public validation and curation of photographs.

However, a past that becomes public certainly creates the danger of seeing academic specialists, who know about critical historical methods and historical knowledge, as no longer relevant in the digital turn. On the other hand, there is also the danger of seeing the complexity of heuristic research diminishing in front of a widely known digital selection of documents without any innovative value for "high scientific research." Finally, as Peter Lagrou (2013) commented, the digitization highways and big data available for some topics could determine the kinds of archival research that can be made and, as a consequence, the kinds of research topics that can be chosen: nobody has enough time anymore – nor the financial support – to go for long research trips and stay in archives. In addition, the absence of a thorough knowledge of the Web by academic historians could have the thankless consequence of decreasing the professional capacity to sort through individual discourses about the past online. Thus, we would be surrounded by forms of narrating the past developed with neither the necessary critical attention nor the professional filter historians could offer to validate everyone's history and memories on the Web.

Family memories made up of materials and primary sources discovered at home and completed with online content can be easily shared on the Web. New "genealogists" – one of the most important activities online (De Groot 2016) – can thus write their own histories without providing narrative context or the necessary historiographical depth. The past is no longer something distant and historicized, but it is felt in the continuous present. In order to ensure the impartiality required for managing the past, undertaking document collection, for filtering, mediating and bringing the community and different publics together online, and for directing new knowledges about the past through the resources provided by digital technologies, a new generation of historians, whom we could call digital public historians, must transform themselves into professional intermediaries capable of providing a scientific framework for collecting documents and for critically managing new "invented" archives that have been uploaded to the Internet thanks to individual contributions and crowdsourcing procedures. Digital public historians share their authority with a public of "crowdsourcers" in the same way that Michael Frisch (1990) envisioned ways of applying best oral history practices to collecting memories.

Mediating between individual and collective memories

In 1998, just five years after the birth of the Worldwide Web and a few months after the spread of its use in universities around the world in 1996, American historians Roy Rosenzweig and David Thelen were asking themselves about the presence of the past in American society. The most significant and eloquent findings of their research still shed light for us today on history's modes of communication and sources of the past on the Net (and beyond). The authors indicated that the American public had a clear preference for a history without intermediaries and, more precisely, for an appreciation of the past *without the mediation of academic historians*. The American public – as well as the Australian and Canadian publics, as discovered through similar research on the public presence of the past and forms of history in their respective countries (Ashton and Hamilton 2010; Conrad et al. 2013) – preferred to discover their own pasts through public history cultural institutions like museums and historical parks, and to find out about days past through direct experience with its traces without mediation by professional historians (Meringolo 2012; Owens 2014).

This kind of direct encounter with the past in local communities today also takes place on the Web, since digital public history activities on Web 2.0 sites favor face-to-face encounters with history and its sources. These become interpretable by the general public in museums, exhibitions, and physical sites of memory not only through the mediation of public historians but also through the Net itself, which interacts directly with the public. Rosenzweig and Thelen's (1998) analysis of how the mediation of the knowledge about history had to be managed in the United States demonstrated what would happen with the advent of Web 2.0 and with interactive digital platforms. In their surprising research findings, the authors discovered that the public preferred to act for itself, recount its "own" history, and, in general, preferred to search for their family history through genealogy without examining the "big picture" (De Groot 2016). Already in 1998, Rosenzweig and Thelen sensed the narcissistic potentials of the Web more than the urge for popular participation in the construction of collective memory and historical discourses through digital technology – a history centered on individual and community experience, often unmediated, that sought to project the local onto the global (Cauvin and Noiret 2017).

Rosenzweig's (1998) later reflections on the fact that anyone could become a historian thanks to the Web most certainly arose from this study. This idea that everyone was uploading their own view of the past online was already a hypothesis confirmed in an Italian study which monitored the Italian History Web between 2001 and 2003 (Criscione et al. 2004).

Pierre Nora (2011) wrote about the same phenomenon in France in some reflections that followed the publication of his series of books on *les lieux de mémoire*.[17] Although discussions in France did not refer to mediation by "public historians," Nora pressed for historians to get into the field, engage with the public, and transform themselves into mediators of collective memories. Their role was not to choose which memories would be active in the present, nor to dictate how to manage these memories; instead, it was the present public and collective consciousness that would determine the selection of sites of memory, and the historian's duty to jump in and contextualize them: "L'effet du travail des historiens sur la mémoire française est … de lui redonner vie, et même de l'arracher à la mort si l'on ose le dire, de refabriquer pour les hommes d'aujourd'hui une mémoire habitable et à la mesure de l'avenir qu'ils ont à dessiner" (Nora 2011: 446–447). We are facing a first crisis of the history of the present time (what French are calling *l'Histoire du Temps Présent*) whose agenda seems now to be dictated by commemorations and national memories.

In any case, digital public history, understood as a new modality of presenting history and creating digital narratives with and for the public, is still not overly disseminated in the same way in all countries and continents (Danniau 2013; Noiret 2009). And, a public historian's professional role is to act as an intermediary between the activities of the general public with the past and with memory on the Web (Noiret 2015). Roy Rosenzweig, who, in contrast to Pierre Nora, was already dealing with the Web at the end of the 1990s, invented the field of digital public history in this way. The kind of professional mediation that Rosenzweig strived for was channeled into digital public history. This has enabled interaction with popular cultural history, highlighting its needs, writing chapters on a "useful" history and promoting aspects of the past in the present and the public use of history (De Groot 2016; Noiret 2014b; Samuel 1998). Nora (2011) differs from this view only because he still does not think of the Web as an enabling factor in the promotion of physical sites of memory, nor as a carrier itself of virtual sites of memory requiring interpretation.[18] It should be noted that the profession of public historian is not recognized in France; Henry Rousso (1984; 2011), as a historian of the present, for example, has said that he was not professionally prepared to be a "*historien public*" (Nora 2011), and mentioned "applied history" as being the job of "miracle-workers." However, "public historian" is precisely the professional figure that Nora and Rousso describe, even though in their own thinking this figure continues to be a traditional historian working in the public sphere, and possessing good communications skills.

The history and memory that are circulated online, partially narrated and interpreted by anyone, facilitate the uncritical and decontextualized reproduction of individual and collective memory, that is, each individual's "blind" horizon. This abstract localism is not able to read the complexity of historical processes in their totality, nor is it able to insert these into the larger contexts called for by Nora. More drastically, Phillippe Joutard (2013), a historian of the nexus between history and memory, thinks that the spontaneous forms of narrating the past online are simply forms of memory that have nothing to do with the epistemology of history. Joutard does not invoke the significance of Web-based mediations on memory and therefore does not recognize a professional role for digital public historians in addressing the lack of historical consciousness in individual and collective memories.[19] Peter Lagrou (2013) openly criticizes the role of historians who remain complacent in the face of the dominant cultural hegemony, arguing that academic historians abandoned their critical and social role in the *polis*, having been seduced instead by the contingent cultural necessities of power or old national liturgies, or distracted by the study of globalization.

A public historian must mediate with the public presence of the past on the Web through first-person contributions to the narrative of the past in virtual space. Creating digital public history that is capable of critically confronting and mediating the relentless display of private memories – and of embalmed collective memories – is indeed a professional role that should be taken up by public historians. Educators and public historians have the duty to critically interpret falsely "objectifying narratives": above all, these virtual narratives, and the more insidious viral narratives, promote alternative collective memories to "official" history and invent new "national legends." This is what occurs in Metapedia, a European parody of Wikipedia, with its nationalistic, racist, and revisionist narratives, and its intention to shape European academic language in an effort to recuperate what Metapedia calls "real" pasts and "lost" collective national memories (Metapedia Mission Statement n.d.).

Between 2001 and 2003, an analysis was carried out of the Italian web and its historical content. The purpose of this research was to investigate attempts at spreading revisionist histories, Holocaust denials, or alternative invented collective memories (Criscione et al. 2004). At that time, the existence online of an alternative to academic history was already extensive. Like the current trend of people wanting to talk about themselves and creating new sources, such as oral narratives or diaries,[20] these phenomena go beyond a digital exhibitionism promoted by global social media. This exuberant online presence of everyone's past responds, through digital mediation, to our globalized society's profound need to connect individual, family, collective, and community memories with a local, regional, or national past (Garde-Hansen, Hoskins, and Reading 2009; Hughes 2012; Marshall 2011).

While oral history interviews comprising a body of individual accounts relating to a research topic are coherent and have a well-defined structure constructed by the interviewer, memories on the Web are often isolated, fragmentary, and lack thematic direction. These memories do not benefit from the historian's critical and interpretive abilities (Hamilton and Shopes 2008; Lucchesi 2014).

In relation to the new forms of cultural mediation, media scholar José van Dijck (2007) observes how, from its inception, digital technology intervenes in our personal memory beginning with the change in the relationship between the author and their personal documents and memories. In effect, digital programs made them feel obliged to classify, catalog, select, and contextualize their records of their past, with the additional motive of sharing these records with others (van Dijck 2007). The innovative and interactive attention that the digital implies for the physical traces of our individual past has enabled the emergence of novel forms of interaction between the Web and individual and collective memories, which has created new digital sources for public history and new contexts in which public historians analyze and communicate them.

International digital public history: Local, global, glocal

Public history benefited enormously from the impact of digital technology on traditional activities involving nonacademic audiences. For this, we can say that digital history today, in the absence of academic historians, and especially digital public history, involves the work and mediation of *digital public historians* (without that name) who deal with the past, together with media and communication specialists. Moreover, in this discipline – which comes out of the forms of validation and languages traditionally dealt with in academic laboratories (various forms of writing, diversification of media and sources, appearance of new digital sources, and new communication processes used to write about the past) – the impact of digital technology has not abolished local history practices or divided them from those now available online. The practices, professionalism, languages, and the intended audience of public history largely benefited from the connection to the Web, and fostered new communication forms directed to different audiences. The transition to the digital era only incorporated other dimensions for further refining the task of public history itself: interpreting the past of specific communities and sharing this history and collective memory with all the mediums and media at our disposal.[21] More than in other disciplines, Web and digital technology have strengthened established professional practices in the field of public history and direct interactions with the public, opening them up to other audiences with new tools for communicating and disseminating the very contents of the past in the digital era.

Digital humanities knowledge, digital history and its potential, are integral parts of new training needed in public history programs where they exist, especially in Anglo-Saxon countries.[22] Digital history teaching activities are complementary forms of training for the management of primary sources or the interpretation of objects in museums and exhibitions, a field in full development thanks to the digital and which requires the professional authority of digital public historians. The digital turn and the Internet first generated, and later fulfilled, the pressing social need to promote identities, local cultures, and collective memories, as well as to promote these at a global level. In this way, digital public history frequently also fosters *glocal* knowledge. Globalization phenomena reach local identities, which would not otherwise have access to a global public through traditional historical narratives. Thanks to digital public history and the versatility of the Web and digital tools that facilitate the global promotion of local pasts, public history has reached different types of publics at the international level.

In her keynote lecture at the 2nd Brazilian Public History Conference in September 2014, Linda Shopes said that digital history – added to social history and the presence of a targeted audience – is now central to oral history practices. Digital techniques returned "orality" to oral history. A digital dimension has integrated online histories to website projects, opened up public history internationally by extending traditional oral history projects, and enhanced the capacity to share interviews into audio/video formats globally and through open access. These practices enable communities to interact in their own language. A deeper understanding of local cultures differentiates international digital public history from digital history and, even more, from digital humanities activities; the latter all too often being confined to the English language (Shopes 2016).

By way of the Web, individuals, communities, and work groups can create spaces of history/memory and give them life in tune with specific communities, promote them at a global level, and link dispersed members of their own communities internationally with a potentially universal audience (Miccoli 2013a; 2013b).Today, the Web is used to fill the role of the once physical community now missing in the field, or to collect the memories and testimonies of communities that are dispersed in time and space.[23] In effect, digital technology helps overcome spatial-temporal barriers in order to unite similar audiences and publics, which favors the transnational, the global, and the comparison between different – yet, nevertheless, similar – local realities (Wirtz 2012). Public historians could use the potential of digital public history to collect memories and sources from these communities. Alon Confino (2012), for example, tried to reconstruct the pre-1948 invisible Palestinian past of Tantura, Dor, in today's Israel. Confino studied cadastral maps, aerial photography, and photographs of Palestinians recorded prior to May 22–23, 1948. But could user-generated content from social media and crowd-sourcing activities on the Web help in discovering original Palestinian diaspora documents? Re-enacting 1948 Palestinian memories should be possible thanks to digital public history practices (Confino 2012).

On the other hand, one of the major benefits of digital public history may come from its capacity for communicating, describing, interpreting, and showing local historical experiences as global experiments with the use of similar methods applied to different local communities. Digital public history assumes as its methodological purpose that local history, an intimate and close dimension that interests people everywhere, can be part of the reflection on the processes of globalization and of a comparison of the local at the planetary level.

Through a comparison of the public and global dimensions of a local case, digital public history facilitates refining some universal concepts of world history, such as, for example, genocide, crimes against humanity, or even dictatorship (International Coalition of Sites of Conscience n.d.). Local experiences and memories are transferred to other local communities in other continents. In creating new interpretive and narrative spaces through digital public history's new practices at the global level, the *glocal* – a neologism derived from globalization (Robertson 1995) – clarifies the spatiotemporal dimension of *international public history*.

Indeed, the breaking of spatiotemporal and local/global barriers in the interpretation of the past characterizes digital public history, which permits refining the memories of collectivities and individuals across the world. Such is the case with the testimonies of Sri Lankan mothers, who, with support from social networks and with the publication of digital oral history archives, have had international reach (Herstories n.d.). This digital project generated the creation of an exhibit in Toronto in 2014, during which visitors were able to express their views. Their comments, which were published on the virtual exhibit on the website, stress the universal value of the Sri Lankan project. Consider, also, how the Yad Vashem (n.d.) website can reunite Holocaust victims and their memories in the places where their relatives currently reside.

The national community in the United States came together around the first large digital public history project worldwide, The September 11 Digital Archive. This large digital archive was opened to testimonies from everyone and offers the memories, history of, and sources on the event beyond its interpretation. Furthermore – and this aspect has innovative significance in terms of digital archives – The September 11 Digital Archive website reflects on how the attacks on the Twin Towers were directly or indirectly experienced live, or deferred at the international level, promoting the local within the dimension of a global experience shared by the public worldwide (Sparrow 2006). The National September 11 Memorial and Museum, the museum of the memory of the attacks, promotes interaction by supporting a tour and inviting other testimonies to contribute to the museum's sources online through social media, benefiting teaching and research, and giving value to its contents at the global level. The possibility of reading translations of the site's content in various languages highlights the global attention it has received, whereas content in other US museum websites and digital history tours is usually provided only in English. The 9/11 Museum Audio Guide is an iPhone app – also available in several languages – that completes the narrative with diverse accounts of what occurred on September 11, 2001, in Lower Manhattan and with interactive modes in physical itineraries that maximize the visitor experience (Cocciolo 2014).There is a constant growth in the use of digital applications for smartphones designed primarily for providing virtual historical tours through the geolocalization of the visitor in urban locations.[24]

Recomposing dispersed or diminished diasporic communities with a common history at the global level or reconstructing memory pathways with digital technology enriches the experiences of public history in "analogue" historical museums at every level. In this way, physical exhibits and tours promote, integrate, and make themselves visible in the digital environment. With the help of digital communication technologies, these broaden the scope of realities and knowledge transfers, co-participation in memories, and interpretive historical narratives about objects and physical sites.[25]

The interaction with the past and its publics is disseminated by means of the World Wide Web and social networks. The diary of Susan Horner, written between 1861 and 1862 during an eight-month trip to Florence and conserved in the British Institute's archive of the city, lives around the world on our smartphones thanks to an app that offers cultural tours of the city through the eyes of this young middle-class Victorian lady interested in Italy's *Risorgimento*.[26] Here, we are witnessing the clear effect of transposing the past onto our present.

The motley world of open access (free access to knowledge through digital technology), supported through social media and cellphone apps, has enabled the public sharing of history around the world and revived it in the present. Reaching diverse worldwide audiences and sharing the experiences of the past has never been this easy or so widely accessible. The creation of a free and open encyclopedia like Wikipedia and, later, the collection of documents in all formats made available globally through Wikimedia, had put in motion, starting in 2001, the various possibilities of a participatory process to the creation of digital public history content. Today, the scientific authority provided by public historians in museums, archives, and libraries, extended online with multimedia tours, has notably enriched the museum, archive, and library experiences, inspiring interaction and garnering direct participation from the public.

So we may conclude by saying that digital public history practices enable the Canadian public to be touched by the oral testimonies and photographs of Sri Lankan mothers; and at the same time, the Sri Lankan public, after decades of civil war, is made aware of Canadian interest in their histories through a digital public history project like Herstories, a website that universalizes the history of a long civil war by transforming it into a glocal episode in the history of humanity.

Notes

1   Such caution on the impact of new technologies can be found in Italy in E. Grandi, D. Paci, and E. Ruiz, 2012, "Digital History: La storia nell'era dell'accesso," *Diacronie,* no. 10. The same sense of caution appears in an essay published in a special issue of the historical journal *BMGN* (see G. Zaagsma, 2013, "On Digital History," *BMGN – Low Countries Historical Review,* vol. 128, no. 4). Meanwhile, D. J. Staley speaks of the possibility of visualizing history through the computer as another tool to add to writing, which has dominated the discipline for centuries (see *Computers, Visualization, and History: How New Technology Will Transform Our Understanding of the Past.* Armonk: M. E. Sharpe, 2013).

2   See also D. Boyd and K. Crawford, 2012, "Critical Questions for Big Data," *Information, Communication & Society,* vol. 15, no. 5, pp. 662–679; and K. Crawford, 2013, "Think Again: Big Data: Why the rise of machines isn't all it's cracked up to be" *Foreign Policy,* May 10, 2013. Lastly, an example of the datification of History can be found in the essay by J. Van Eijnatten, T. Pieters, and J. Verheul, 2013, "Big Data for Global History: The Transformative Promise of Digital Humanities" *BMGN – Low Countries Historical Review,* vol. 128, no. 4, pp. 55–77.

3   Visit *The Proceedings of the Old Bailey, London's central criminal court, 1674–1913,* at www. oldbaileyonline. org.

4   Armitage and Guldi write that "Applying Paper Machines to text corpora allows scholars to accumulate hypotheses about *longue-durée* patterns in the influence of ideas, individuals, and professional cohorts," (2014: 91). Guldi applied her software to global land reforms corpora from the twentieth century (see www.joguldi.com/vita).

5   On digital public history, see M. J. Galgano, J. C Arndt, and R. M. Hyser, 2013, *Doing History: Research and Writing in the Digital Age* (Boston: Wadsworth/Cengage Learning); and the ad hoc chapter in T. Cauvin, 2016, *Public History: A Textbook of Practice,* pp. 174–187 (London: Routledge); and S. Noiret and M. Tebeau, forthcoming 2019, *Handbook of Digital Public History* (Munich: De Gruyter).

6   But, of course, alternative contexts are built around photos that are widely available on websites worldwide. The digital historians should use an alternative external criticism of the document, such as what I did with violent pictures of the second intifada in Palestine in 2002, circulating images with captions in all languages worldwide (see "Visioni della brutalità nelle fotografie di rete," in *La cultura fotografica in Italia oggi. A 20 anni dalla fondazione di AFT. Rivista di Storia e Fotografia,* ed. S. Lusini (a cura di), pp. 88–106 (Prato, Archivio Fotografico Toscano-Comune di Prato, 2007).

7   *What's on the Menu?* is available online at: http://menus.nypl.org/).

8   This huge crowdsourcing activity has been organized in France from 2013–2014, and has enriched the Europeana project commemorating the Great War: *Europeana, 1914–18.* See http://www.europeana1914-1918.eu/en.

9   A more in depth definition of "invented archives" can be found in Roy Rosenzweig. «The Road to Xanadu. Public and Private Pathways on the History Web» in Daniel J. Cohen and Roy Rosenzweig. *Clio Wired [...], op. cit.,* pp. 203–235 (available online at: http://chnm. gmu.edu/essays-on-history-new-media/essays/?essayid=9).

10   See the Mark Twain Project Online (http://www.marktwainproject.org); the Edgar Allan Poe Society of Baltimore (http://www.eapoe.org/); and Melville Marginalia Online (http://melvillesmarginalia.org).

11   *Rousseau Online* can be visited at http://www.rousseauonline.ch/about.php.

12   *Le dictionnaire Montesquieu* is available online at http://dictionnaire-montesquieu.ens-lyon.fr/fr/accueil/.

13   Visit http://www.1914-1918-online.net/.

14   Visit http://braceroarchive.org/contribution.

15   *September 11 Digital Archive* is available http://911digitalarchive.org.

16   Parallel Archive is available at http://www.parallelarchive.org. Also see É. Deák, "Study, Store and Share Unpublished Primary Sources: The example of the Parallel Archive," in *Contemporary History in the Digital Age*, eds. F. Clavert and S. Noiret, pp. 83–94 (Brussels: Peter Lang, 2013).

17   When asked about the significance of the *lieux de mémoire*, Pierre Nora (2011) emphasized the need for historians to provide meaning and life to the traces of the nation's collective memory *in the present*.

18   Nora deliberately writes on the physical and nonphysical sites of memory that historians interpret.

19   Joutard, in contrast, does not highlight how the presence of historians on the Internet can promote a leap in the quality in the interpretation of uncritical individual memories (Philippe Joutard, op. cit.). For a more in-depth understanding of his thinking, see the author's *Histoires et mémoires: conflits et alliances*. Paris: La Découverte, 2013.

20   José van Dijck (2007) stresses the significance of personal diaries ("writing the self") found in Internet blogs – new forms of writing used for communicating the intimate, individual memory through the digital.

21   Think, for example of the Omeka content management system, which made museum tours and interactive displays accessible online through the management of multimedia collections (available online at http://omeka.org), or Movio in Italy, an "open source kit for creating online virtual displays," created by Telecom Italia and the ICCU (Istituto Centrale per il Catalogo Unico delle biblioteche italiane) (available online at http://www.movio.beniculturali.it).

22   Only in September 2015 was the first Masters in Public History created in France at the University of Paris-East-Créteil, and, in Italy, at the University of Modena and Reggio Emilia.

23   After having lost the American Civil War, thousands of former Confederates moved to Brazil in 1866 with a view to maintaining the system of slavery for the cultivation of cotton. Slavery in Brazil was abolished in 1888. Today the community of Confederate descendants is reestablishing connections with the southern states in the United States. See Esposito 2015.

24   See *Curatescape* (available online at http://curatescape.org). Curatescape involves a series of smartphone apps that create a virtual and public urban history narrative. Developed by Mark Tebeau in the United States for the city of Cleveland (and now for many other cities), it was a trailblazer in the new element of individual access to the virtual content of digital public history.

25   For the 500th anniversary of Machiavelli's *Principe*, the public benefited from digital public history activities available through a smartphone app and connected to Machiavelli's physical places of memory. See the *San Casciano Smart Place. I Fantasmi del Principe*, a project created between 2012 and 2014 by the *Communication Strategies Lab* and Luca Toschi at the University of Firenze (http://www.csl.unifi.it/progetti/san-casciano-smart-place/).

26   Susan's Horner Florence, iPhone application, available at https://itunes.apple.com/us/app/susan-horners-florence/id787766904?mt=8. It is based on the *Horner Collection* of the British Institute of Florence.

Chapter Eight

Popularizing the Past through Graphic Novels: An Interview with Catherine Clinton, Author of *Booth*

Elizabeth Paradis and Catherine Clinton

How we present the past to the public, as much as the kinds of narratives we are able to tell, is shaped by the formats we choose when *doing* history. What we have gleaned about the past from archives, repertoires, and memory is compressed, expanded, simplified, emphasized, or marginalized – altered in innumerable ways by the craft and practice of academic and public historians. The beauty of history is in the interplay of art and science: the gaps in our factual knowledge invite historical imagination, disruptions in chronology, and even anachronisms, when they are required to help convey a specific and authentic historical message. Some forms of public history, such as the graphic novel, naturally lend themselves to well-researched, yet entertaining and creative explorations of the past.

Compared to traditional academic historical narratives, page and word limitations and challenges associated with assigning and creating effective and authentic dialogue – based on historical research, but often without the assistance of historical quotes and citations – necessarily restrict the extent and depth of the historical knowledge about any particular past that can be communicated by graphic novels. With their combinations of imagery, dialogue, and narrative text, graphic novels do, however, offer significant opportunities to present multiple viewpoints and alternative narratives of the past, and to express complex historical details and insights (material, as well as social and political) concisely and poignantly. Moreover, their advantages for enlivening history and disseminating it to new publics are undeniable. Graphic novels relate narratives with immediacy and intimacy, and, despite what some may assume, can do so without trivializing the past (Smith 1987, p. 90). As Stephen Tabachnich (2009: 2) argues in his introduction to *Teaching the Graphic Novel*, graphic novels can convey nonfictional narratives "with the depth and subtlety that we have come to expect of traditional novels and extended nonfictional texts." It is not surprising, then, that this form of public history has been gaining legitimacy even among academic historians.

A Companion to Public History, First Edition. Edited by David Dean.
© 2018 John Wiley & Sons Ltd. Published 2018 by John Wiley & Sons Ltd.

Typically, graphic novels are collaborative efforts – a story's narrative structure, mis-en-scène, and dialogue are carefully balanced and negotiated among its contributors (author, illustrator, and editor) to ensure that the final product conveys the right balance of emotional and factual authenticity to ensure both its popularity and effectiveness as history. In graphic novels about the past, these collaborations are deepened as historical research is shared to contextualize the storyline as well as the linguistic and visual aspects of the narrative.

The process of *doing* history as a graphic novel is dynamic. While the historical narrative is shaped by the form of its telling, so too is the historian or public history practitioner's engagement with the past. The freedom to fictionalize, to seek and convey unexplored histories, or to address controversial, traumatic, complicated, and hazy pasts encourages creative analysis of historical data and a broader search for (and use of) relevant historical sources. *Maus* (1980–91), Art Spiegelman's Pulitzer Prize–winning graphic novel about his father's experiences of the Holocaust, in which humans are represented as animals, arguably set the stage for modern graphic novels to be accepted as a means of relating powerful and difficult narratives about the past. Although artists and academics are increasingly turning to this popular art form to bring dramatic and compelling histories to younger and nonacademic audiences, the graphic novel remains an underused and underexplored avenue of public history.

One historian who has tackled the genre is Catherine Clinton, PhD, Denman Endowed Professor of American History at the University of Texas at San Antonio, and 2016 president of the Southern Historical Association. In addition to her career teaching and researching at universities internationally, she has used her expertise to bring the histories of the American South, American Women (Mary Todd Lincoln, and Harriet Tubman, among others), and the Civil War to audiences outside of academia. Clinton has written historical fiction novels for children and has been involved in a number of public history projects, acting as a consultant on documentary films and on Steven Spielberg's feature film *Lincoln* (2012). Each of these experiences has enabled Clinton to share her work with a broader public, and her graphic novel, *Booth* (2010), responds particularly to a need her students expressed for more accessible forms of history attuned to their generations' interests beyond traditional academic writing.

Booth, published in 2010 and illustrated by graphic novel artist Tanitoc, tells the story of John Wilkes Booth, leading up to his assassination of President Lincoln. Drawing on her extensive knowledge and research about Booth and his famous American stage family, Clinton portrays the failed actor as both a charismatic womanizer and a troubled young man who willingly became increasingly entangled with Confederate rebels plotting against Lincoln. She focuses on Booth's relationships – enriched by her interplay of historical imagination, alteration, and fact – to humanize this otherwise vilified historical figure and offer her readers possible explanations for his murderous act. The deliberate foregrounding of the emotional in *Booth*, such as the conflict between Booth and his brothers, which acts as a device for exploring divisions within the country during the Civil War, perfectly illustrates how intrinsically dramatic and ambiguous pasts lend themselves to the graphic novel format. Not only can graphic novels provide a creative space for educated speculation about the past, but they can also be used to convey nuanced historical understanding.

The following is an excerpt from an interview I conducted via e-mail with Catherine Clinton in August 2015.

Perceptions of public history: Process and experiences

EP: Why is it important for you, as an academic, to write/do popular history?
CC: From a very early age I became interested in the notion of a wider audience for my work, and while I was at a place like Harvard for my undergraduate work and then on to Princeton for the doctorate, I saw it working fairly effectively for academics to seek out broader audiences, when they chose this kind of audience. But the effort would have to be an individual one that would fit a person's interests and attitudes ... Some scholars had no interest at all beyond the campus – or the ivy-covered cloister ... but I very much saw the impact of televised dramas about the past, films about the past, and general awareness of the impact of history on present-day issues.

EP: What do you mean by impact (dissemination of information or changing public attitudes about the past and about history?)
CC: How can we not be struck that a very vivid and impassioned debate about the Confederate flag and its place in public spaces is a matter of heated debate in 2015? How can we not see that the interpretation of slavery's past and its legacy for black and white Americans is of primary importance? History lives and breathes and resonates, and those of us who do history cannot retreat to the past, but must face forward and let our readers, listeners, and viewers engage with the way in which historical issues shape our ideas for today and paths for the future. I am committed to facing forward rather than backward ... even as a historian.

EP: As academic historians have increasingly come to accept the importance of affect, imagination, and reflexivity in the creation of histories (written and otherwise), have you had more opportunities to engage in public history projects that require you to mix facts with fiction?
CC: When I worked on scripts for commercial television – none of which have been produced as of yet ... I was encouraged to use my imagination – within the boundaries of historical possibilities. It's only natural that embellishment and fictionalization creep in ... But I would always remind my producers that I was *not* hired strictly for my imagination but for my historical sensibilities and being able to draw on actual, verifiable characters and incidents ... The old "based on a true story" brand.

So I would refrain from including fictive material in any work I published unless it was clearly a fictional work – for example, the fact with fiction for two of my children's picture books (which are clearly designated as fiction), and my graphic novel, which is just that, a novel.

EP: Do you think these popular forms of history, like your comic, are gaining legitimacy in academia? Why?
CC: Absolutely – I just did a review of a Civil War graphic novel (Ari Kelman and Jonathan Fetter-Vorm's graphic novel, *Battle Lines of the Civil War*), which was quite powerful – and I think we need to reach out and get HISTORY into all the formats we can. The nooks and crannies of the present need to be filled up with the imaginative and exciting details of the past, which do continue to fascinate.

I'm a big fan of fictionalized films and television. I remember being engaged by Michael Mann's version of *The Last of the Mohicans* ... Which was an embellishment of historical fiction – but Daniel Day Lewis is naturally a favorite of mine, as he was a completely amazing embodiment in his screen portrait in *Lincoln*.

Who can doubt the power of a film like *Glory*, which never fails to impress me. I am a big fan of the director, Ed Zwick, who did mainstage plays at Harvard, while I did experimental dramas in the little theater … but he was certainly destined for great things, and he has created some of my favorite war scenes in films: *Legends of the Fall, Courage Under Fire,* and the aforementioned *Glory.*

I also welcome good television series based on historical periods: who knows how many fans of the frontier came out of *Dr. Quinn Medicine Woman* – not to mention female interest in becoming doctors? But today, for example, I am a very big fan of the television series *The Americans,* which deals with the Reagan 80s. One of my colleagues at Queen's University Belfast was able to get her students engaged with the historical concept of entailment by having them study episodes of *Downton Abbey*! By any means necessary, I say. I confess things like "Drunken History" entertain me because it's based on the premise that you understand events being satirized, although I can also see that that's *not* as often the case as I would like.

EP: I read that you were concerned about using your real name for Booth because of the attitudes some academics have about public history projects. What do you think has changed to make public histories more acceptable in themselves and as teaching tools?
CC: When I first decided to tackle the genre of the graphic novel – well over a decade ago – I think that historians were not as aware as they are today that social media, comics, and Internet streaming are here to stay. Today's scholars have to learn to embrace the technology or it will pass us by. Some that might have derided my interest in reaching out to those who did not want to read heavily-footnoted, thick-as-a-doorstop books might now see that we have to get kids hooked on history, however we can.

Engaging an audience with a good story is our purpose, and to educate our audience to appreciate the importance of investigating the past, and incorporating whatever past they find into our sense of who we are as a nation, and where we might be going as a people – this is a worthy quest.

EP: How have your experiences with making various popular histories (children's books, a comic, as a historical consultant for films) been similar and/or different from each other? Which have been most collaborative? Which have involved the most public engagement and/ or "felt" most like public history?
CC: Writing in another format – a children's book or a graphic novel – is not really demonstrating "public history," but plying my trade as a writer outside of the academy. But I do think using my historical talents to help with other – broader – dissemination of historical ideas could be properly credited as "public history." So working on documentaries (which I've done often), and consulting on museum exhibitions, which can be very fun and engaging … as well as contributing to a project such as Spielberg's *Lincoln,* gives me a very positive feeling about allowing my research to reach a wider audience.

I believe my input on a screenplay or a film results in my work, my individual insights showing up on a widescreen – and therefore they're reaching an audience of millions, rather than the scores classroom by classroom, or the hundreds reading my books … So there is a reason for trying to branch out.

EP: How have your public projects affected your academic practice and/or your perception of what it means to "do history?"
CC: "To do history" means we engage more with the past, and to confront how we need to tailor our goals and expectations, to break out beyond ivy-covered walls. And that often means to speak directly and simply – so in many ways learning to write for television, or learning to write for children, means we simplify and demystify much of our historical practice.

EP: Has your approach to academic writing changed at all because of your experiences with public history (simplifying, etc.), or do you see your academic career and your public history career as entirely separate?

CC: I do see these careers as intermingled – but perhaps sometimes tangled … as I would like to think that my writing is part of a craft, and my craft is important to me …. but my guild is important to me as well. As you can just go and be a writer, but to be "trained as an historian" meant something, and there were standards and methods and a litmus of evidence and format required, much of which I still very much respect.

Yet also when I first started out and wanted to write about women's lives in the past, and be engaged with their stories … I was told this wasn't "real history," and it was a long hard slog to try to incorporate this aspect of the past into the guarded "guild" of history. I remember when my first book was selected by the History Book Club – one of the few and one of the first to deal with women's history, it seemed a very hard won victory. This was in the 1980s … which is shocking and sad, as so much great women's history had come before, but then again a true flood of great work has come after.

So from my earliest days as an historian, I decided that academic writing was in some ways a fairly narrow, twisted, and at times a deceptive path. I would joke with graduate school friends that I wanted to see my books in grocery store aisles … particularly Piggly-Wiggly in the South. I have not yet realized that dream, but finding a copy of *Harriet Tubman: The Road To Freedom* (which was about my twentieth book) was a big thrill.

EP: Do you feel that your authorship/voice should be made visible to the audience regardless of the format of your history, and if so, why?

CC: I think that all we really have is our own voice – and our own vision, and it's important to try to get that across with every piece of work we produce. I don't think it's as much a matter of ego, as it is trying to recreate a fresh understanding of the past through your own eyes.

EP: I guess what I was trying to ask here was whether you think it's important for the audience to be aware of your role as the author and of how your work shapes the past that you're representing (for them to be reminded that they're looking through your eyes and that history is not just fact, but is crafted)?

CC: I always explain to my students that the past is always there waiting for us to explore – and history is just one aspect of that past, even if it is a conventional wisdom. One person's conventional wisdom can be another person's heresy … when I first began my work on Harriet Tubman, there were many skeptical of her worthiness … and I was seriously dismayed to see how much ignorance about her abounded. And now here she is a candidate for appearing on American currency, whether it's the ten dollar bill or twenty dollar bill, it's still amazing that within a relatively short period of time American culture has come to recognize her greatness, and has lifted her from the children's shelf as a folk figure into the pantheon of American heroes where she belongs. To encourage this transformation, I needed historical context and the tools of academic writing to position Tubman within the framework of American exceptionalism, in all the nuances of this phrase, to represent her as a liberator and patriot, and all that she represents, in her best and fullest interpretation.

Graphic novels: presenting the past and "doing" history

EP: Why is it important for the public to engage with the past through graphic novels?

CC: A picture really can be worth a thousand words – and most particularly the images of a graphic novel can convey emotion, and reaching out from the page to touch the reader is an incredibly important aspect of this literature. To be touched then allows us to seek out more engagement with the past. If you see a movie about the past, and are intrigued, then you might read a book. If you read a book, then you might want to read a diary or some letters, or go visit an historic site. And so the chain of being hooked on history encircles and charms.

EP: Who is the audience for your historical graphic novel and how does your awareness of your audience (age, gender, etc.) influence your narrative choices?
CC: I really hoped my graphic novel would be embraced by early readers straight through to adults – really accessible and broad.

But I did not make narrative choices based on this interest in a wider audience; however, it is necessary to make sure to try to have realistic characters who represent human qualities. You cannot paint only flawless heroes and wicked villains and other stereotypes, but you must include mixed or even contradictory qualities, those dynamic qualities make people human and, in the end, more fascinating.

EP: You used short introductions to your chapters to inform your readers about general historical facts. Was this something that, as an academic, you felt was necessary, and/or was this a response to the challenges of writing history in graphic novel format?
CC: Since so much of my story was fictionalized I thought it was essential to frame the fiction with authentic and exacting details at the start of the tale – so to begin with a dose of analysis, a dab of insight, before we trample off into Booth's inner dialogue and his romping through history. I certainly played fast and loose with his motives, with his reactions and romances, but he was a natural born romantic himself, ripe for exploitation – with his manhunt diary and other artifacts.

EP: What are the advantages of presenting history in a graphic novel?
CC: It's important to try and reach an audience of young people who might think of history as only dead and, deadlier, boring – trying to invest the past with characters and drama and images can engage those who have low expectations. The power of images can bring characters to life ... And bring the past to life as well.

The format of the graphic novel can motivate many students who have problems with reading for comprehension, by reaching them on other levels. Indeed, some educators have called graphic novels books for non-readers ... but it's important not to lose this group, and if we can hook them with graphic novels, then they might grow into readers.

EP: How do you think the public relates to the past differently in this medium?
CC: I have every reason to believe that the graphic novel does particularly well at probing into the adolescent consciousness ... minds more open to feelings and better able to put their creativity to use.

EP: Would you agree with the argument (I believe it was Art Spiegelman who said it) that the mis-en-page and language of comics (versus manuscripts) more closely mimics the way humans think, and that this makes them a more accessible, intimate, and immediate format for relaying a narrative.
CC: It can very much be a matter of scale – the way the visual format allows us to reduce and open up simultaneously. Thus things leap off the page ... And the pace allows for more complexity, offering multiple interpretations. The writer is reduced to emotional bare bones – and the reader therefore gets to find a human scale, allowing infinitesimal small pleasures of humanity to evolve with this form.

EP: How did you experience the challenge of having to "put words into other people's mouths?" (dialogue bubbles, etc.)

CC: It was really quite fun, like the internal conversations in our head that we never get to write down … I felt as restricted by the limitations of dialogue as I do in everyday life … "Oh, I wish I had said" and regretting having only "staircase wit" (all the clever things you think of on the way out …). But I also had to think of representing both men and women, blacks and whites, and trying to be true to the period, true to my story, true to the moment so as not to practice retro dialogue … it's a great juggle, but also great to juggle.

Booth

EP: Why did you choose the graphic novel format to tell your history of Booth?

CC: Because I wanted to write about this epic era and this larger-than-life character in a way that I thought had not yet been explored by the many hundreds of books on the assassination. I knew about the 150th anniversary coming up, and hoped it would be a way of commemorating and not really celebrating, but showing the complex shades and dimensions that led to this historical moment, when a 26-year-old could really change the course of history.

EP: Did the story of Booth give you more leeway to "fill in the gaps" in the historical record? Can you say something about your choices, for example, how you decided which truths to tell and which aspects of the past to alter?

CC: There is so much we don't know about Booth – he was mysterious and yet he also gave us some autobiographical material that shows his flair for drama. He definitely had a need to be larger than life. He had so many complex relationships with a variety of women – and this made me extremely intrigued. So I decided to try to imagine an actor driven by family demons and insecurities into a world of make-believe – once he conquered that world, he wanted the larger stage of espionage, danger, and scandal.

He was really consumed by his demons, and drove himself over the brink as his conspiracy to cause another uprising against the government, to reinvigorate the Rebel Cause, was madness.

We know a lot about Booth and his background, yet there are still some missing links that were challenging to contemplate – he was a young man deeply scarred by his background who hungrily sought power. His tragic rise and fall makes a nearly Shakespearean tale that fascinated me from long before I became a scholar.

EP: Aside from your fascination with the drama of Booth's life, were there any other reasons you chose to create your narrative this way? Were you thinking about the desires of your audience or about larger historical issues that could be represented by Booth's personal drama? How did you make decisions about what historical facts to include, change, or eliminate – did your "academic side" fight for details against your "writer side" that pushed for drama?

CC: I worked with a very creative and talented editor, Tanya MacKinnon, who was very exacting about motivations – and was relentless … trying to shape the book into arcs, which had dramatic integrity and political sensibility – not at the expense of authenticity, but at times, accuracy was damned.

At one point she asked me to stop writing and devise an emotional biography for each of my characters, with her list of questions (here reduced to a third): "Does he respect his father? Did he like his mother more? What did he feel like when his father beat him? His mother? Was his mother emotionally available? Did he know his grandparents? Did he like an uncle? When did he first understand what class his family was? What did he feel when he understood class? When did he decide what he wanted to be when he grew up? Is that what he's doing now? If not, why not? Did he want to be better than his parents? How? Is he a planner or a procrastinator? When did he take his first drink? Get drunk? Who was there? What's his favorite pub? Why? Would he pay for sex? Would he spend his savings on clothes or a horse? What does money mean to him? Does he have a lot or a little? Does he save or spend? Does he read the newspaper daily? Does he understand politics? Does he like to debate? Tell tall tales? Is he an exhibitionist or an introvert? Does he have many friends or few? To whom would he tell his most important secret? How did he feel when his dog died? Has he had a gay dream? Was he frightened or titillated? How did he treat the family's domestics? Did he play an instrument? What song does he whistle when he's alone?"

So "what song does he whistle when he's alone" to me is a real example of the kind of details you must push for in any kind of historical writing … questions that I fear are not uppermost in the concerns of authors of historical monographs. Increasingly, I think biographers are becoming savvy, and I am a member of the Biographers International Organization, which is less than a decade old, and the writers in this group do seem to grasp the need to work in a public history rather than academic mode.

Good history will try to excavate such details, but in the graphic novel we *fabricate* them.

As I commented in a recent review of Ari Kelman and Jonathan Fetter-Vorm's graphic novel, *Battle Lines of the Civil War,* by the war's opening battle, in one of the earliest chapters, they are fabricating the death of the first soldier to die in the Civil War, telling their story in their own powerful manner, with the little boat sailing to shore, with a spike in a soldier's chest … totally invented, but equally – totally effective.

EP: Could you explain your motives in making these choices (selecting, compressing, reducing, emphasizing, or inventing)? Were they shaped by the demands of the graphic novel format? Would you have told the same narrative in a traditional book or another medium of public history?
CC: I don't think I would've been as free to tell my own individual version with so much creative license, unless I was in this seemingly unrestricted format, the graphic novel. At the same time the graphic novel presents so many choices … so many demands … that my words had to be carefully picked, as if I were composing a haiku.

So I was forced into knowing my characters so that their words could come out of my mouth and onto the page, in an almost cryptic fashion. I could only have told such a story in a work of historical fiction – like the graphic novel. This could've been a movie script as well – but I would've felt it was dishonest as a documentary – too much exaggeration … Too much speculation … Too much invention.

EP: You announced to your readers that Booth is thoroughly researched historical fiction. Do you still feel that the public needs to be alerted to the mix of fact and fiction present in a historical graphic novel, or do you think that audiences are now more aware of these negotiations in all forms of history (academic and public)?
CC: I think that there is so much mis-education on this matter – many of my readers/ commentators on Amazon would refer to my earlier thoroughly researched books of academic biography as a "novel." It's as if modern readers are abandoning genre for taste. Readers blur the line between fiction and history – in a somewhat distorted view. So I think that academics and book critics are in need of alerts and explanation – but the general readers are very rarely aware of any such negotiation.

They are looking for a good story and hoping that what you present is somewhat true … "Based on a true story" still has allure. But there seems to be less and less appreciation of accuracy, and an acceptance of blurred lines and crossing fine lines, the chasm between fact and fiction.

EP: How did your research process in making Booth differ from that of your academic publications?
CC: I had to keep close track of all the visual elements available to offer to the artist – he was from another country and completely unfamiliar with Lincoln – detailed copies of my materials. Otherwise my methods are almost always the same for all research projects.

EP: Did the visual elements of the comic, which often have to address everyday details (such as the kind of label on a tin of food), force you to look beyond your normal historical sources? If so, did this process bring you closer to the past you were narrating?
CC: I have always been very attached to visual elements of the past and had an interest in illustrations, photography. I am also very hooked on historical sites, and prefer a face-to-face tour rather than any virtual experience – although it's not often possible, but I do try. It was very easy for me to provide over a hundred examples of nineteenth-century decor, style, dress, and so on. This was something that came in handy, of course, when I worked with the designer, Joanna Johnston, who did the amazing costumes for a cast of hundreds in *Lincoln*.

EP: Many public history projects are highly collaborative. With Booth, the writing was completed prior to Tanitoc's illustrations. How much collaboration was there about the mis-en-page or other rhetorical visual elements of the comic, or about the narrative?
CC: Tanitoc is a respected and esteemed artist, and at the time of our collaboration, was the head of the International Bande Dessinée Society. I was totally trusting of his judgment, and so impressed by what he brought to this project through color and visual élan. The book had a distinct palette and style that I found impressive and engaging – so to me I could not really correct anything but an anachronism or error.

Looking forward

EP: What type of public history do you want to attempt next?
CC: First and foremost, I will be the President of the Southern Historical Association in 2016, and want my organization to be more responsive to the current issues that involve so many members of our society – trying to get an annual discussion of "Southern History in the Headlines." Plus I am sure many of the debates over monuments and public commemorations of the Civil War, including issues of the Confederate flag, will engage me in the coming year, if not perpetually, as we struggle with this legacy in twenty-first century America.

I am also hoping to work on a series of workshops to train discussion leaders who will organize public forums to talk about narratives of war for audiences of veterans and their families. I hope to use literature, autobiographies, documentaries, film – and yes, graphic novels – and other media to engage a wide audience with an appreciation of new studies of war – through a program sponsored by the National Endowment for the Humanities.

This proposed project fits in nicely with my new book project on the care and treatment of Union soldiers during the American Civil War who were diagnosed as "insane," as I explore case files from my database inmates at St. Elizabeth's Hospital in wartime Washington, D.C.

One of my colleagues suggested the title "Crazy for the Civil War," but it's too heartbreaking and serious a story for this kind of humor. I began the project looking at suicide, which became too personally and professionally challenging – and so I broadened my scholarly perspective and evidence base to look at larger issues of war's impact on mental health for those were sent to asylums.

Even though I think it might be too harrowing a topic for another graphic novel, we all have Spiegelman's *Maus* as an exemplar. I am especially touched by J.P. Stassen's *Deogratias: A Tale of Rwanda*, as one of the books that shows us how impossible topics are sometimes made possible through an accessible format and an empathetic portrait.

Graphic novels are yet another way for the past to be represented, performed, and popularized for the public. As they gain acceptance, the hope is that they will be used to creatively explore complex and authentic (but not necessarily factually accurate) pasts through the reflexive collaboration of historians and graphic artists, who will relate these narratives to those uninterested in traditional historical writing.

CHAPTER NINE

Becoming a Center: Public History, Assembly, and State Formation in Canada's Capital City, 1880–1939

John C. Walsh

In 1904, the landscape architect Frederick Todd, a disciple of Frederick Law Olmsted, delivered his first report of recommendations to the Ottawa Improvement Commission (OIC). The OIC was the first of a series of major planning initiatives that unfolded in Canada's capital city through the first half of the twentieth century, as federal political leaders wished to cultivate a more explicitly ceremonial, aesthetically inspiring, and thus politically useful landscape in the city's core. Todd understood well the desires of his patrons. At the very start of his report, he commented:

> [n]ot only is Ottawa sure to become the centre of a large and populous district, but the fact that it is the Capital of an immense country whose future greatness is only beginning to unfold, renders it necessary that it shall also be the centre of those things which are an index of man's highest intellectual attainments, and that it be a city which will reflect the character of the nation, and the dignity, stability, and good taste of its citizens. (Todd 1904: 2)

While his own concerns were mostly with the region's parks and parkways, Todd saw the value in a route that would better facilitate travel between Parliament Hill, site of the legislature and its prime minister, and Rideau Hall, the residence of the governor general, the British royal representative and ceremonial head of the Canadian state.

Close to a hundred years later, the National Capital Commission (NCC), a regulatory agency that grew out of the OIC and its successors, proudly unveiled the "Confederation Boulevard" on June 30, 2000.[1] It was in many respects a conclusion to the planning efforts started by Todd in 1904 and shared a nearly identical sensibility about the importance of this local planning project for the interests of the nation. At its opening ceremony, prime minister Jean Chretien made the route's purpose clear: "Confederation Boulevard will let all Canadians celebrate our rich heritage every day of the year" (Bell 2000: C7). As shown in Figure 9.1, it is a route connecting several different roadways and bridges. The Confederation Boulevard is a by-product of decades of work in this respect, as it

A Companion to Public History, First Edition. Edited by David Dean.
© 2018 John Wiley & Sons Ltd. Published 2018 by John Wiley & Sons Ltd.

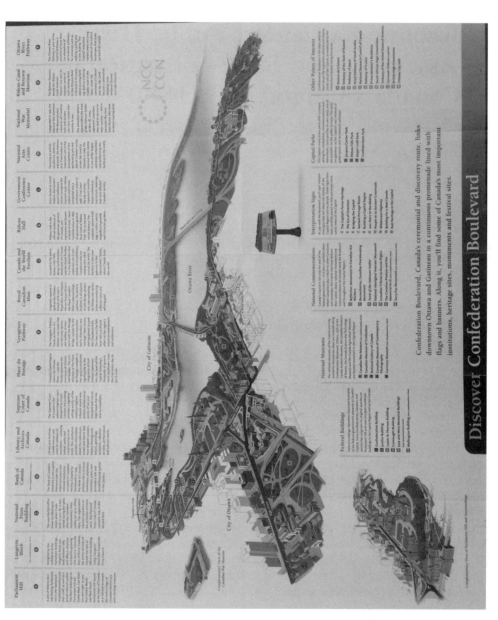

Figure 9.1 National Capital Commission, "Discover Confederation Boulevard." Source: Carleton University Library.

seeks to provide a historical and geographical narrative about not only Ottawa as a capital city, but also, revealingly, provides a map to some of the most well-known spaces of public history in the city:

> Confederation Boulevard is the Capital's ceremonial and discovery route, which encircles the downtown areas of Ottawa and Gatineau. It is the route that foreign dignitaries and the Royal Family take for processions and state visits. And it is a route that reflects Canada, as it connects many sites and symbols of national significance – institutions like Parliament and the Supreme Court of Canada, as well as museums, heritage sites, embassies, monuments, parks, pathways and beautiful natural landscapes. (National Capital Commission n.d.)

As a name and rhetoric, "Confederation Boulevard" is a fiction, a (hi)story that requires explanation on websites and in brochures because it does not exist in the everyday speech acts of people who live in Ottawa. Much confusion would result if a visitor asked a local resident for directions to Confederation Boulevard, despite the fact that this route appears on maps and in print.[2] For as much as the NCC hopes residents of Ottawa will explore this route themselves, its invention was and remains primarily for people from away: it is a tourist destination and a "heritagescape" (Garden 2006; Gillot, Maffi, and Trémon 2013).[3]

There is an important body of scholarly literature, much of it informed by memory studies, which would call our attention to the contested politics of this heritagescape. This literature identifies the historical and contemporary debates, struggles, and sometimes violent confrontations that have unfolded in capitals with respect to the rising of monuments, the installation of murals, and the opening of new museum exhibits.[4] In these studies, we see the politics of public history as it involves its various stakeholders, including political leaders who seize on these moments as a way to reassert their authority, especially when it has been challenged. Some of the most fascinating work done in this respect demonstrates that it is sometimes public historians working for the state who become targets for the ire of the stakeholders, including those for whom they work (Dean 2009).

Relatedly, there is an important body of scholarship that would focus explicitly on heritagescapes as produced space (Lefebvre 1991 [1974]). Since the early to mid-1990s, a spatial turn in the humanities and social sciences has intersected with a memory turn in geography and planning studies. The result is a sophisticated, exciting, and sometimes contentious body of literature that considers the dialects among space, place, and memory.[5] If we understand place as "spaces which people have made meaningful," as Tim Cresswell (2004: 7) suggests, the inscription of memories in, on, and through space is one of the ways in which "place" is constructed and reconstructed across time. Within the heritagescapes of capital cities, such as that offered by Confederation Boulevard, this process is complicated by the fact that the "place" being constructed is an abstracted and simplified ideal of the nation-state. By design, "the local" in capital cities has historically been dis-placed by the heritagescaping of the nation (Gordon 2015; Savage 2009).

This approach to the politics of public history offers much to how we could think about Confederation Boulevard. An important set of studies would identify how it normalizes a settler history and collective memory about Canada, especially its ties to the British (and more subtly French) imperial project, while marginalizing and forgetting Indigenous histories and memories. Others might emphasize the militarism that dominates so much of the route, especially at the War Museum, the National War Monument, and the Peacekeeping Memorial. One could also anticipate approaches that call our attention to the ways in which Confederation Boulevard, as an NCC project, has inflicted physical and emotional harm on peoples and places for whom Ottawa is home.[6]

This is very important work, and more remains to be done, but I want to suggest a different, complementary way of approaching public history in capital cities like Ottawa, one that looks more closely at work done behind the scenes of heritagescapes like Confederation Boulevard. This approach goes back to Frederick Todd's prescient observations about Ottawa when he remarked, "that it shall also be the centre of those things which are an index of man's highest intellectual attainments." When he said this in 1904, Ottawa was very much becoming a "centre" within which a national archive and a national museum were already collecting and indexing, and thus "assembling," a public history of Canada. Importantly, both institutions were also becoming bureaucratized within the larger formation of the Canadian federal civil service. In doing so, these organizations emerged as important spaces for the forging of public history as a profession in Canada. Through their practices of assembly and bureaucratization, furthermore, both the national archive and national museum were also active contributors to the history of modern Canadian state formation in the late nineteenth and early twentieth centuries.

In what follows, therefore, I am going to retell the stories of the emergence of the archive and museum in Ottawa at the turn of the twentieth century, focusing specifically and selectively on the entwined themes of assembly and bureaucratization. The stories I tell about the former will be somewhat familiar to students of public history, especially when discussing the collecting of documentary and material cultural heritage. The stories I tell about the latter, especially about such things as annual reporting and labor, are perhaps less familiar. Yet it is by telling these two sets of stories alongside one another that I hope to show a different kind of politics of public history that is somewhat unique to capital cities but also, we shall see, fundamental to the history of the profession and its practices.[7]

Assembly and bureaucracy in the nineteenth century

Before coalescing in specific government departments devoted to public-history-related activities in the twentieth century, researching and representing the past for an imagined "public" was done by a wide range of nineteenth-century actors who produced historical narratives in service of their other professional tasks. In Canada, no group was more important at the federal level than surveyors and natural scientists attached to the Geological Survey of Canada (GSC). Created in 1842, GSC agents were deployed across the country to explore, identify, and capture natural resources, especially minerals like coal and iron ore. They worked in teams, including guides, axemen, paddlers, and often other scientists or surveyors whose work complemented that of the geologists. When a government-funded GSC museum opened in Montreal in 1856, the focus on geology was pronounced, although some natural scientific specimens as well as random ethnographic artifacts were also acquired in the course of the field expeditions. After 1877, when the GSC mandate expanded to include more emphasis on natural history, natural scientists of the GSC looked more closely at the botany of Canada, seeking to identify what species currently existed, which ones thrived, and which other species might also do the same. Both sets of work teams were charged with identifying fields for colonization, and also with documenting emerging social and cultural landscapes of both settler and Indigenous peoples that they encountered in their travels, and from whom they derived much needed local knowledges (Dowling 1900; Grek-Martin 2007; Waiser 1989). In the course of their work, these surveyors and scientists collected reams of Indigenous, settler, and ecological heritage through both stories and material culture that they bundled into their reporting.[8] As the GSC's mandate expanded across the nineteenth century, its museum also diversified somewhat, although it was, until the early twentieth century, dominated by its geological collection.

These collection efforts relied not just upon those in the employ of the GSC. By the end of the nineteenth century, Indian agents and Royal Canadian Mounted Police (RCMP) had also begun to become important agents of acquisition of Indigenous material culture, and some of their confiscations found their way into museum and other departmental storages located in the capital. Important, too, were contributions made by both professional and amateur settler archaeologists and ethnographers, the former concentrated in universities and the latter in the burgeoning culture of associational life so important to middle-class formation in Canada (as elsewhere) in the second half of the nineteenth century. After it was formed in 1883, the Royal Society of Canada, a federal national academy of academics, artists, and scientists, played an instrumental role in fostering the assistance of researchers and collectors outside of the GSC to contribute materials specifically for the museum.

The GSC museum was Canada's first national museum (although its name did not officially change to the National Museum of Canada until 1927) and its first high-profile institution of heritage assembly. Its profile owed much to the energy and effectiveness of William Logan, who directed the GSC until his retirement in 1869. Logan was rather brilliant at situating the GSC's work within both the politics of modern state formation and nationalism, as well as forming important relationships with geologists and scientific societies throughout the North Atlantic world (Shipley 2007; Zeller 1987). This came to a head in Logan's award-winning work on the Canada displays at the 1851 Great Exhibition at London's Crystal Palace. Deploying an effective combination of maps, narrative, and material specimens collected by the GSC, Logan made the Province of Canada exhibit a must-see for visitors, as both the British and Canadian press heralded its aesthetics and its message of a "modern" Canada-in-the-making. The 1851 exhibition, and others that soon followed, set a pattern of display and communication for not only other directors of the GSC but also many of its scientists, including John Macoun, a botanist and natural historian appointed in 1881 who was a key figure in the museum's history in the late nineteenth and early twentieth centuries (Waiser 1989).

For all of the GSC's recognized political and economic importance, it would be kind to describe the museum's early days in Canada's capital as ramshackle; until a new building designed to be a museum was constructed in the first decade of the twentieth century (it is today the Canadian Museum of Nature) and opened in 1911, the museum was beset with all sorts of problems and limitations related to its institutional home in Ottawa (a converted hotel located blocks from Parliament Hill). In fact, there was controversy when the museum and the GSC were relocated from Montreal to Ottawa in 1881, in part because Montreal was still the commercial hub of Canada, and the museum was always intended to showcase natural resources for domestic and foreign investors as much as it was for public education. Still, both before and after the 1881 move, the work of collecting, indexing, and displaying never stopped. As one of its agents boasted in 1893: "Suffice it to say that the verdict not only of Canadians who are justly proud of their natural collection at Ottawa, but visitors from other countries have time and again been struck with the REMARKABLE COMPACTNESS, UTILITY, and perfect classification of the Museum" (The National Museum 1893: 11).[9]

In the nineteenth century, the "public" for whom this historical material was intended ebbed and flowed with the ways in which the material was communicated. At various international and domestic exhibitions, in public lectures, and through the production of material intended for schools and universities, the GSC had a tradition of popularizing its work with a wide audience. The museum was somewhat different in that, while anyone could visit it in Ottawa, its chief public seemed to be legislators, "visitors from other countries," and a commercial class of investors and capitalists from Canada, the United States, and Great Britain, that the federal government and GSC hoped to entice to Canada's major resource industries. From its start in 1856 as a government-funded public museum, it was one that saw its public in much the same kind of utilitarian instrumentalism that, as Suzanne Zeller (1996) explains, defined the scientific knowledge it produced.[10] And like all museums, for the fraction of the collections that the public could see on display, there was countless more warehoused in every spare inch of the old building. Indeed, the repeated calls for a new, fireproof building were always predicated on the immense scope of the collection, its ever-growing character, and the fact that its vulnerability to fire or flood posed a great threat to both the economic future and cultural heritage concerns of the state.

While the GSC museum was the most important center for material heritage assembly in late nineteenth-century Ottawa, assembly of documentary heritage owed most to the Historical Archives Branch of the Department of Agriculture, created in 1871.[11] The Historical Archives devoted itself to collecting the documentary heritage of colonial-era (i.e., pre-1867) Canadian history, especially documents associated with military, political, and commercial leaders and associated "great" events from that past. Much as surveyors and field scientists traversed Canada for material culture that made its way to the National Museum, archive staff traveled all over the country to identify and acquire the scattered remnants held in personal, public, and commercial hands. The Archives director, Douglas Brymner, did much of the international travel that expanded in the early 1880s, as he and his chief deputy, Joseph-Étienne-Eugène Marmette, traveled to London, Paris, Rome, and eventually Washington to manufacture handwritten copies of a wide range of imperial documents that were then sent back to Ottawa. In the course of this work, staff forged important relationships across Canada with private collectors and historical societies where important collections then resided. Much as GSC scientists did with colleagues in the United States and Europe, Brymner and Marmette nurtured professional relationships with their counterparts (especially in Britain and France) from whom they sought to learn best practices for records management. Alas, much of what they learned in this respect was not applied until the early 1900s, after Brymner's death.

The Historical Archives had its own William Logan–like figure in the person of Douglas Brymner, the first Dominion Archivist appointed in 1872, a position he held for the next 30 years until his death in 1902. Brymner was a journalist at the time of his appointment, and his "expertise," unlike that of Logan, who had an international reputation as a geologist, was mostly in his enthusiasm and energy for collection rather than actual records management.[12] His annual reports to the legislature are replete with the details of his and others' journeys to acquire (or copy) documents and bring them back home to his poorly equipped and understaffed offices in the basement of East Block on Parliament Hill (Brymner 1884; 1887; 1898). Brymner, as Matthew Dyce explains, was collecting documents faster than they could be organized, as the impulse was to centralize all these materials first and worry about what to do with them second: "A question never even presented for debate was where the documents should be kept – Ottawa was the unquestioned centre and it followed as a given that organization and order could only be achieved once the documents arrived there" (2014: 67). Indeed, as late as 1897, Brymner conceded in his annual report that "[u]ntil preparations, now in progress, are completed for the reception of the documents, access cannot easily be obtained to them, they being piled on the floors of the rooms in which they are stored" (1898: vii). While documents associated with Canada's colonial past were filling up the Historical Archives, there was still no plan in place for assembling the documents produced by the federal government and its various agencies. By the close of the nineteenth century, this gap in the documentary heritage reached an acute stage. As Joseph Pope, a powerful civil servant in Ottawa from 1878 to 1921, warned the Secretary of State in 1897, "[t]he basements and attics of the Departments are now crammed with documents of various kinds. There is a limit to their capacity however, and that limit must nearly be reached" (Atherton 1979: 39).

Pope's comments point to one of the effects of the Historical Archives' first generation of assembly; the "public" for whom Brymner was working was decidedly limited. To be sure, a wide range of people, even with limited time and resources, could see some of the acquired materials through Brymner's published annual reports, which always included typeset copies of many of the records that the archives had acquired over the previous year. Yet Brymner's archive was intended mostly for historically curious members of the legislature for whom he worked, and for the emerging class of academic historians and public intellectuals who were creating for themselves an exclusive and exclusionary professional space from which to narrate the story of Canada (Dyce 2014; Kingsford 1886).[13] Brymner hoped his archive would have a great effect on a larger Canadian public, but that effect would be more indirect, found more in the new historical narratives to be written from the records rather than the records themselves.

Both the GSC museum and the Historical Archives Branch were thoroughly bureaucratized in this era. Both hired staffs, established hierarchies, organized and regulated office work, and practiced the routines of accounting and record keeping ("the file") that Max Weber identified as hallmarks of a "modern" bureaucracy (1978 [1968]). For example, as Matthew Dyce (2014) has uncovered, Brymner went so far as to direct one of the branch's bookbinders to observe and report upon the work habits of a female clerk, Miss Braden, whom Brymner thought might be unreliable. The reporting sent back to Brymner described everything Braden did – noting, for example, her arrival for work on May 4, 1897 at 8:30, cutting out dress patterns to 9:30, going upstairs at 10:00, taking books apart at 10:30, reading the *Ottawa Citizen* at 11:00, and so on. This surveillance continued for four months, and Brymner cited it to others in the service. This kind of surveillance was becoming a fact of the federal civil service by the late 1890s, as more women and a greater range of men were hired to do work within the differentiated offices of the bureaucracy. Like all of this office work, it was carefully documented and preserved in files.

Performances of bureaucratic professionalism also occurred in more publicly visible ways, especially in the rigorous annual reporting that was submitted to the legislature and then normally printed for public consultation. Much of the reports are full of a kind of statistical banality that looks decidedly dull, uninteresting, and routine, just as it was supposed to appear to the audience for whom these reports were written. For example, we learn in the 1886 Annual Report of the GSC museum that "the number of letters written is 270, many of which partake of the nature of 'reports'" (Selwyn 1887: 47A). Shortly after in that same report appears an exhaustive, detailed inventory of every item added to the museum's collections as well as its donors (not only the agents of the GSC, as expected, but also agents from other government departments and also private citizens). And almost every year, the museum director would explicitly call for a new, improved building pointing to the detailed, statistical data in the annual reports as evidence of the need and worthiness for that request.

While similar in form and intent, the annual reports submitted by Douglas Brymner sought to provide more explicit explanation and justification for the expenses associated with the Historical Archives Branch. Brymner went into great detail about which documents had been identified, copied if necessary, and collected, and also what histories were being recovered from these documents and thus returned to Canada's collective historical consciousness. For example, in his annual report for 1891, Brymner discussed the copying and collection of British Colonial Office records related to the early history of settler colonization in the British colony of Upper Canada (ca.1791–ca.1841). About the significance of this acquisition, he concluded: "An inspection of the correspondence and other documents will, however, show that immediately after the division of the Province [of Quebec into Upper Canada and Lower Canada], the system was in full vigour, and was attended with prejudicial consequences to the settlement of the country" (Brymner 1892: xi). It was little coincidence that Brymner would go into such deep detail and interpretation about these colonial efforts at colonization, for in 1891 the federal government, in conjunction with railway companies, was undergoing a massive effort to introduce white settlement into the Canadian West and to resettle Indigenous populations onto reserves. Going well beyond describing the documents assembled in Ottawa, therefore, Brymner's annual reports also offered interpretations of their larger historical meaning and the importance of those meanings to the then-present. While Brymner and the Historical Archives Branch faced different institutional challenges than the GSC museum in terms of needing to justify its existence, both sets of these annual reports demonstrated the public historical work of collection and indexing, but framing that work as important to the political project of state building while doing so in a modern, rational, bureaucratic manner.

Continuity and transitions in the early twentieth century

In the early twentieth century, a new group of learned "experts" began to do the assembly work of cultural historical materials in the GSC museum. The first of these were ethnographers, anthropologists, and archaeologists such as Edward Sapir, Diamond Jenness, Harlan Ingersoll Smith, and Marius Barbeau. Sapir was recruited in 1909–1910 to establish a new division of anthropology within the GSC and within the museum, immediately followed by Barbeau and Smith. These scholars set out to "salvage" both material and intangible heritage before, they assumed, it was lost to the profound structural and cultural changes of industrial and urban modernity (Nurse 1997). Their influence within the museum was palatable as the heavy emphasis on geology and botany in museum displays was tempered somewhat with increasing space devoted to the cultural heritage of Canada, much of it dedicated to Indigenous peoples and older white rural settlements in French Canada. The assembly work done by these scholars relied heavily on professional and personal social networks, although rarely that of Indigenous peoples, even though so much of the collection was focused on their cultures. More extensively and systematically than their nineteenth-century predecessors, this new generation of experts reframed the assembly of cultural and social historical material as social scientific methods of data collection and management.

Susan Roy (2010) offers an invaluable example of this in her detailed study of Harlan Ingersoll Smith, who served as the head archaeologist at the museum from 1911 to 1937. In addition to collecting reams of material culture, Smith also created a detailed database that was intended to aid further research and assembly work for generations. As Roy explains, Smith's "goal was to create a national archive that would house a comprehensive and permanent record of the location of found artefacts, ancient village sites, burial places, shell heaps, and pictographs, along with information about how to gain access to the sites, including contact names and map references" (2010: 90). To assemble this archive, Smith drew from an extensive array of settlers, some of whom worked for other branches of the government (such as Indian agents and RCMP officers), fellow archaeologists and ethnologists inside and outside the academy, and even representatives from the Canadian National Railway. This kind of office work was an amalgam of social scientific research methods and modern bureaucracy, one that privileged a certain kind of acquired expertise. This was all work done on paper, housed in filing cabinets, and thoroughly unspectacular. It was work designed to make the assembly of Indigenous material culture, like all bureaucratic work, routine and reproducible.

While work behind the scenes at the museum built upon but also expanded from its nineteenth-century antecedent, the more visible face of public history work was also undergoing change in the early 1900s. Most important was how these new experts displayed a commitment to public education that expanded from that demonstrated in the nineteenth century. This included Harlan Ingersoll Smith, who described the museum's approach to education and its understanding of its "public" in revealing terms: "The impressions of childhood are so easily made that every possible effort is made to attract the children. It is hoped that even greater attractions may be offered to working people and children as public opinion develops and the Museum gains in facilities…. It is really the people unable to travel, or perhaps to buy books and pictures, who need the services of the institution more than any other class" (1913: 33). While the nineteenth-century museum had used exhibitions and school materials to reach a broader public, Smith's invocation of "working people and children" reflects the heightened role for the museum itself to function as a pedagogical space and exert the "civilizing impulse" that Tony Bennett (1995; 2013) explains is a hallmark of public museums. It was also no coincidence that Smith said this at a point in Ottawa's local history where its working-class population was especially large viz-à-viz its professional middle-class population (which included people like Smith) as the city's lumber industry and manufacturing dominated the region's economy. And it is revealing, too, that Smith was addressing a local population in Ottawa despite the fact that his was a national institution traditionally associated with the ambitions of nation building, colonization, and internationally recognized knowledge creation. While that did not change, at least initially, it did become more expansive in the ensuing decades.

Throughout the interwar years (1919–1939), the museum became more committed to using the practices of assembly to cultivate a "public" both locally in Ottawa and across the country. A key figure in this was Marius Barbeau. Among all of Barbeau's extensive professional accomplishments during his time with the museum (he was employed there from 1911 to 1945, but was intimately involved with the museum right until his death in 1969) was his commitment to make the collections more visible and useful.[14] Barbeau made the museum's collection more readily accessible to scholars (including undergraduate university students), he was a tireless public speaker who could address schoolchildren with as much comfort as he could a fund-raising dinner at the city's prestigious Chateau Laurier hotel, and he and other members of his staff took to national radio (Canadian Broadcasting Corporation) airwaves to produce weekly programs that introduced people to the museum's holdings and taught lessons about the broader cultural significance they held. Elaine Keillor (2004) also explains how, in the 1920s and 1930s, Barbeau recruited Canadian classical musicians to come to the museum, explore the folk music collection he had produced (and even encouraged them to add to the collection themselves), and then offer public performances from selections. Some of this performance was done in Ottawa, but even more was done across the country and internationally. Barbeau and others developed new social and institutional networks that still privileged the museum as a center of assembly, but also sought to connect this assembly work to the cultural lives of a wide range of Canadians.

As the museum reached out to a wider public in the first decades of the twentieth century, internally there were some new divisions of labor in the museum that replaced the nineteenth-century model in which the scientist-collector was also expected to catalog, conserve, and prepare displays. As early as 1913, one of these new experts, the archaeologist Harlan Ingersoll Smith, identified the changes afoot as follows: "It is recognized that one of the great needs of the museum today is more mechanical and clerical help to release the higher paid specialist from much of the work which could just as well be done by others and so enable him to devote his entire time to his special work" (1913: 29). A similar division of labor had already been affected in the archive where, from the late 1870s, a wide range of "clerks" had been hired to copy original historical material and to put this material into a classificatory order that more senior actors, in particular Douglas Brymner, had instituted. In 1903, the National Archives had their mandate expanded to include the selection and preservation of current federal government records, and this resulted in an important expansion in the organization's resources, as it became an independent, stand-alone institution. Yet, as Terry Cook (2005) explains, there was little change in how the archive actually functioned, as it was not until the 1950s when there was a systemic professionalization of the National Archives and the number of trained archival "experts" grew both in their number and in their influence in how the institution operated. Both in Ottawa's museum and in the archive, these divisions of labor created different levels of visibility of the public historical work being done, and the associated new hierarchies of authority and institutional power that accompanied them are a part of the history of public history that remains, for now, little studied and woefully underappreciated.

Conclusion

Capital cities are privileged sites for public history. Heritagescapes like Ottawa's Confederation Boulevard, Washington's National Mall, and Canberra's Parliamentary Triangle are destinations for domestic and international tourists, the scenes of annual celebrations and commemorative ceremonies, and also, importantly, sites where individuals and groups travel to protest and challenge the political status quo. Yet, in less dramatic spaces in capital cities, within office buildings, processing facilities, and warehouses, one can find a wide range of public historical work being done in the service of the state.[15] I have suggested here that we think about all this "invisible" work as assembly, as the accumulation of materials, knowledge, bodies, and memories (Müller 2015). The flows of these things both into and back out from the capital and its heritage institutions not only affirmed and normalized the political and cultural authority of the national archive and national museum, but also a broader Canadian federal state in formation. Assembly work in these networks also took on an explicitly bureaucratic dimension, one that sought to make heritage assembly visible to the public (via annual reports, for example) but which also strove to legitimize itself to the legislature as effective, economical, and valuable. This is what Frederick Todd observed when in 1904 he described Ottawa as becoming a "centre" and "a city which will reflect the character of the nation, and the dignity, stability, and good taste of its citizens." And while he did not specify it, public history was very much involved in all of this geopolitical change.

Thinking of public history in the context of the federal civil service is perhaps less dramatic and spectacular than putting public historians on the front lines of great societal debates and conflicts, and yet it points to a significant and overlooked dimension of public history as a profession as well as a field of study. Within the historically emerging and evolving assembly work of public history in capital cities lies a rich tapestry of work and workspaces that might challenge some of our assumptions about "what" public history means and "who" is in fact a public historian. The "historian," for example, is a rather historically recent participant in Ottawa's heritagescape, for it was journalists, scientists, ethnographers, and archaeologists who did the bulk of knowledge work in the period (ca.1870–ca.1939) explored here. In this respect, there is a strong parallel with the pattern identified by Denise Meringolo (2012) in her groundbreaking work on the history of public history's professionalization in the United States. Furthermore, the division of labor that emerged in Ottawa's national archive and later in the national museum introduced new job titles (such as "clerks") and job descriptions that created hierarchies, first around skill and experience, and later between academically trained "researchers" and professionally trained "technicians." What historically was the impact of these divisions for the ways in which heritage assembly and display work unfolded? How did other elements such as gender and race complicate class- and skill-based hierarchies within these institutions? Which work has historically been valued as "public history," and has that changed over time?

These questions point to the necessity of rethinking some of our assumptions about the politics of public history both as a contemporary phenomenon as well as a historical formation. Public history is bound up not only in the politics of nationalism and nation building, but also in the more difficult-to-see struggles over state formation. To locate these politics, we need to shift our scholarly gaze away from the geographies of heritagescapes and look more carefully at the quotidian spaces of offices, processing centers, and warehouses, and at the bodies and personalities that have historically worked in and through them. That is a legacy for the profession whose significance still needs more attention academically and more awareness for contemporary practices.

Notes

1   The NCC is a federal government agency responsible for a massive urban and rural territory on both sides of the provincial border of Ontario and Quebec above and alongside municipal governments in Ottawa and Gatineau as well as those of the two provinces. Its history of expropriation of private property, especially the razing of an entire working-class neighborhood, LeBreton Flats, and some of its failed experiments in commemoration, have made it a flashpoint for local debate and dissent.

2   As such, it is a near-perfect example of the importance of print capitalism to the formation of the "imagined community" of the nation in Benedict Anderson's (2006) sense of the term. Indeed, while only some Ottawa residents would know where "Confederation Boulevard" exists, both they and Canadian tourists would assume immediately that it was somewhere near Parliament Hill, the single most iconic geopolitical avatar of the Canadian national political imaginary.

3   By "heritagescape," I refer to the ways in which specific commemorative and public historical sites are networked with one another to form a larger whole. Like all landscapes, a heritagescape is a social, cultural, and material construction that changes over time. The making and remaking of these is sometimes referred to as "heritagescaping."

4   See, for example, the range of interdisciplinary case studies offered in Lisa Knauer and Daniel Walkowitz, eds., *Memory and the Impact of Political Transformations in Public Spaces* (Durham, NC: Duke University Press, 2004); and Uta Staiger, Henriette Steiner, and Andrew Webber, eds., *Memory Culture and the Contemporary City* (Palgrave Macmillan, 2009).

5   This is given more extensive discussion in James Opp and John C. Walsh, "Introduction: Local Acts of Placing and Remembering," in Opp and Walsh, eds., *Placing Memory and Remembering Place in Canada* (UBC Press, 2010), 3–21. Some important contributions to the literature and its debates include Stephen Legg, "Contesting and Surviving Memory: Space, Nation, and Nostalgia in *Les Lieux de Mémoire*," *Environment and Planning D* 23, 4 (2005): 481–504; "Collective memory and the politics of urban space," special theme issue of *GeoJournal* 73, 3 (2008); Doreen Massey, "Places and their Pasts," *History Workshop Journal* 39 (1995): 182–192; David Harvey, "From Space to Place and Back Again," in *Justice, Nature, and the Geography of Difference* (Oxford: Blackwell, 1996).

6   Scholars have already begun to tell these kinds of stories about Ottawa's Confederation Route, including Carol Payne and Jeffrey Thomas, "Aboriginal Interventions into the Photographic Archives: A Dialogue between Carol Payne and Jeffrey Thomas," *Visual Resources* 18 (2002): 109–125; Tonya Davidson, "A Scout's Life: English-Canadian Nostalgia, Colonialism, and Aboriginality in Ottawa," *Journal of Canadian Studies* 48, 3 (2014): 108–132; Paul Gough, "'Invicta Pax' Monuments, Memorials and Peace: An analysis of the Canadian Peacekeeping Monument, Ottawa," *International Journal of Heritage Studies*, 8, 3 (2002): 201–223; Roger M. Picton, "Rubble and ruin: Walter Benjamin, post-war urban renewal and the residue of everyday life on LeBreton Flats, Ottawa, Canada (1944–1970)," *Urban History* 42, 01 (2015): 130–156.

7   This essay seeks to contribute to a mode of thinking about the history of public history that is given more fuller treatment in Denise D. Meringolo, *Museums, Monuments, and National Parks: Toward a New Genealogy of Public History* (Amherst, Massachusetts: University of Massachusetts Press, 2012).

8   There are important parallels in this respect with work done for the Fisheries Museum, which was created in 1884 as part of the Department of Marine and Fisheries until it was unceremoniously shuttered in 1918. Its assembly work was both ecological and cultural, although less concerned with heritage than that of the National Museum. For an outstanding treatment of this museum's history, see William Knight, "Modelling Authority at the Canadian Fisheries Museum, 1884-1918," PhD Thesis (Carleton University, 2014).

9   This editorial was largely a call for a new building as it championed the museum's accomplishments and warned, repeatedly, it could all disappear from fire without a proper home for the collection.

10   Zeller argues that most if not all branches of Victorian science, regardless of where it was practiced, adopted this stance.

11   The history of the National Archive has benefited from a vibrant scholarly literature, much of it in the journal *Archivaria*. See, for example, Jay Atherton, "The Origins of the Public Archives Centre," *Archivaria* 8 (1979): 35–59; Ian Wilson, "'A Noble Dream': The Origins of the Public Archives of Canada," *Archivaria* 15 (1982–83): 16–35; Laura Millar, "Discharging our Debt: The Evolution of the Total Archives Concept in English Canada," *Archivaria* 46 (1998): 103–146.

12   Brymner was succeeded by another journalist, Arthur Doughty, who also held the position for 30 years (1904–1935) and, in many ways, built upon the institutional foundation established in the late nineteenth century.

13   Engineer, civil servant, and also author of a multi-volume history of Canada (published between 1887 and 1898), William Kingsford lamented the general ignorance in Canada that the Historical Archives Branch even existed, urged other scholars to consult the records, and praised Brymner's work in newspaper editorials that were then republished in a modified form in *Canadian Archaeology: An Essay* (1886).

14   This is a recurring theme in several of the essays in Lynda Jessup, Andrew Nurse, and Gordon E. Smith, eds., *Around and About Marius Barbeau: Modelling Twentieth-Century Culture* (Gatineau, Quebec: Canadian Museum of Civilization Mercury Series, 2008).

15   This includes historical research done to inform policymaking and implementation, about which we still know too little but which is another important dimension of public historical work in capital cities.

PART III

Doing Public History

CHAPTER TEN

Looking the Tiger in the Eye: Oral History, Heritage Sites, and Public Culture

INDIRA CHOWDHURY

The Bangalore Fort holds great significance for Bangalore city and the history of Mysore state. It began as a mud fort built by Kempe Gowda I in 1537, and later was reinforced and strengthened with stone by Hyder Ali, who became the ruler of Mysore in 1761. During the Third Anglo-Mysore War in 1791, the fort was captured by Lord Cornwallis. Only a small part of the fort remains today, with only one gate permitting visitor access – the Mysore Gate and two bastions. More importantly, there is very little public involvement with the sites associated with the fort. Most tourists and visitors complete their visit to the Bangalore Fort in under ten minutes, while local residents take it for granted. In 2012, the Srishti School of Art, Design, and Technology's Centre for Public History completed a project at the fort that endeavored to revive public interest in, and engagement with, this historic site. The project was designed as a public history intervention with the purpose of exploring how to re-engage local audiences with events that happened long ago at a heritage site that is preserved and protected today by the Archaeological Survey of India (ASI). The project also aimed at presenting a critical perspective of the past, turning away from the popular, anachronistic presentation of Tipu Sultan as one of the earliest "nationalists." The project investigated forms of pedagogy that integrated archival research and collective memory to present a compelling historical narrative about Tipu Sultan's time at the Bangalore Fort.

The problem we set out to address through this project focused on how to offer visitors an experience of this historical site through storytelling. It was also important to create a historical narrative that introduced audiences to the historian's craft – where do historians find their facts, how do we interpret the landscape and the material culture at the site, and how do we distinguish stories and legends from historical facts? As we were also concerned about enhancing the appeal of the site to local residents, we attempted to incorporate their stories through oral history interviews. We harmonized historical methodology with elements of visual communication design to make the narrative more attractive. This chapter will take a critical look at the project in order to reflect on the

A Companion to Public History, First Edition. Edited by David Dean.
© 2018 John Wiley & Sons Ltd. Published 2018 by John Wiley & Sons Ltd.

new questions that emerged. What kind of engagement can we design to make a heritage site meaningful to its audiences? How can public history make the historian's craft transparent to lay audiences? Are there ways in which public historians can render "heritage" spaces protected and preserved by government agencies more inclusive? With these objectives in mind, we experimented with form and attempted to explore what happens when we juxtapose past and present by comparing the lives of the site's historical inhabitants with the lives of present-day residents of the locality; and through this exercise try and understand what meaning the site still holds for them.

Context and background[1]

This public history project was undertaken as a student project at the Srishti School of Art, Design and Technology with 11 undergraduate students for a full semester (August–October 2012). The Centre for Public History (CPH), which began in 2011, is uniquely located within the Srishti Institute of Art, Design and Technology in Bangalore. The first center of its kind in India, CPH attempts through its courses and projects to fill the lacuna that exists between historical research and its communication to a wider audience. The location of CPH within an institution of design enables us to work closely with designers and visual communicators, creating new understanding of how historical knowledge may be presented in unconventional ways, and enhancing and transforming audience experience. CPH has been exploring different forms of interpretation of archival material that move beyond the textual and into the realm of performance and audio-visual communication. The Bangalore Fort project, called "The Tiger Comes to Town," was envisaged as a course for undergraduate design students. Aware of the fact that historical subjects rarely appeal to young undergraduates who do not belong to the humanities, the poster advertising the project provocatively asked: "Think you can bring a 260 year old tiger back to life?" Designed, conceptualized, and taught by Aliyeh Rizvi and Indira Chowdhury, the project combined archival research with visits to the fort and other related sites such as the Summer Palace in Bangalore; the Dariya Daulat Bagh at Srirangapatna, the palace in Tipu's capital city near Mysore which was built in 1784; and the fort at Srirangapatna where Tipu fell in 1799. These historical fieldwork visits took students out of the archives and into the landscape where the last Anglo-Mysore War of 1799 was fought. Students were also trained in oral history and interviewed local residents around the Bangalore Fort about what the fort meant to them. Oral historian, curator, and journalist Rama Lakshmi designed a walk around the fort and trained students in creating narratives out of archival and oral history material (Figure 10.1).

The story of the fall of fort in 1791 was dramatized and scripted by Meera Sankar and performed by students through shadow puppetry adapted from a local artisanal and storytelling tradition. Common in Karnataka and the adjacent state of Andhra Pradesh, the local performative tradition of shadow puppetry uses puppets made of translucent leather painted with vegetable dyes (Blackburn 1996). Inspired by this tradition, Nikita Jain, a young faculty member and former student of Srishti, helped the project adapt this tradition by using laser-cut cardboard figures with perforations that cast filigreed shadows on the screen. A curated audioscape from interviews conducted by students was created by Meera Sankar and played in the guard room of the fort. The logo for the project used on T-shirts and other collaterals was adapted from calligraphy from Tipu Sultan's time by Chitradip Pramanik. Students were also asked to create a booklet about the project, and they worked with the visual language of Tipu's times with Sonalee

Figure 10.1 Rama Lakshmi with students at the Fort discussing the docent walk, October 2012. Photo: Indira Chowdhury.

Mandke, Faculty in Visual Communication Design. Supervised by Ramesh Kalkur, they also sketched at the fort and at Lalbagh, Bangalore (what used to be known as the Cypress and Rose Garden), which Tipu and his father, Hyder Ali, had created with help from the Thigala community, which moved to Bangalore from nearby Tamil Nadu. Students thus became acquainted with the visual culture of the eighteenth century.

Another important part of the project pedagogy was an introduction to the landscape of the past and relating that to the present-day landscape. This exercise was undertaken by artist and curator Suresh Jayaram, who took the students on a walk around the market area (the *pete*), which is the old fort area of Bangalore. This multifaceted pedagogy shaped the outcomes of the project: a curated walk, a shadow puppet theater about a local historical event, and a booklet that presented the documentation of the project. Thus, through performances and visual representations, the project addressed three of the CPH's key concerns: in what ways can we adapt historical material and local traditions to create distinctive visual forms of representation? how can we include local voices from the present when telling the story of a heritage site that belongs to a much earlier period? and more generally, what can historical inquiry take from the disciplines associated with art, craft, and design, such as visual communication, craft, and performance?[2]

One of the key concerns for such public history interventions are permissions and funding. Our project coincided with the 150-year celebration of the ASI, which was founded in 1861 by the government of British India, with Sir Alexander Cunningham as its first director general. Dr Gautam Sengupta, who was director general during 2010–2013, took a great interest in our project and sanctioned funds for it. In the wake of the funds made available by the ASI, permission to use the fort for our program was not difficult to procure. But our relationship did not mature into a collaborative one; this was mainly because of the large-scale projects that the ASI undertook that year. The commemorative celebrations held by the ASI were rather different from ours in scale, focus, and content. The ASI projects were very large projects that focused on surveys, conservation, and preservation. Our project by contrast was a small experimental one that tried to use different modes of narrative to generate and sustain public interest in a heritage site. Within our project there was active collaboration between designers, historians, artists, and museum and theater professionals. Our collaboration did not include the ASI, which was the funder and a major stakeholder in the project. The ASI, which views itself as the main authority for the preservation and interpretation of heritage sites, did not view us as their equals but perceived us as "service providers." However, we did manage to impact their understanding of what was important about the fort, and in some ways our project paved the way for the recognition of the knowledge and creative interventions that a nonspecialist group was capable of.

The aim of our project was to focus on local history and to bring alive for an urban audience the story of the fall of the fort. A more general aim was to evoke the life and times of the "Tiger of Mysore" as Tipu Sultan, the eighteenth-century ruler of Mysore was called. The tiger was a symbol adopted by Tipu; his throne, armor, and weapons, as well as coins, flags, and the uniform of his soldiers, were all embellished with the tiger motif. Deeply interested in technology, Tipu is known to have used iron-cased rockets in wars against the British. During his reign, he sent ambassadors to the court of Louis XVI and diplomatic missions to the Ottoman Empire and the Sultanate of Oman. Tipu also allied with the French against the British; not only was his army trained by the French, but he had also, in 1797, participated in a Jacobin Club headed by Francois Ripaud. The club had declared him to be "Citizen Tipoo" and the members had sworn "hatred to all Kings, except Tippoo Sultaun, the Victorious, the Ally of the French Republic," pledging "War against all Tyrants, and love towards your Country and that of Citizen Tippoo."[3]

After his death in the Fourth Anglo-Mysore War, the British found a mechanical automaton that was made for Tipu: a painted wooden tiger in the act of mauling a British soldier. Bellows attached inside make the tiger growl while the soldier gives out a helpless mewl. This automaton also hides a small pipe organ inside it. Tipu's Tiger was brought to London as part of the official looting which followed Tipu's death during the Fourth Anglo-Mysore War (1798–1799). First displayed at the East India Company's Museum in 1808, it was moved to the South Kensington Museum, at present the V & A. It reminded its first audiences of the "historical events that had brought it from Mysore to London." The Tiger also embodied "moral judgements and colonial justification" (Davis 1999: 184).

Art historian Susan Stronge's (2009) detailed study of Tipu's Tiger shows how the Tiger became the basis of nineteenth-century perceptions about Tipu's fanatic hatred of the British. By contrast, the replica of Tipu's Tiger that is displayed inside Raunaq-e-Jahan, or the Summer Palace, in Bangalore is tiny and toylike, lacking the impact of the original. What the displays at the Summer Palace emphasize instead are the rockets built by Hyder Ali and Tipu Sultan, invoking superior technological expertise. As a part of the project's outreach activities, we organized two public lectures that focused on technology during Tipu's reign. Eminent aerospace scientist Roddam Narasimhan spoke on "Tipu's Rockets, the 'Iron Duke' and modern rocketry," and Professor Sharada Srinivasan, well-known scholar of archaeometallurgy, spoke on "Wootz and the Damascus Blade: Metallurgy in the 18th Century." Both talks, held at public venues, focused on the prehistory of modern technology in India.

Today, Tipu is evoked politically in several contexts, from the proposed naming of Bangalore's airport as the Tipu Sultan International Airport in 2012 (rejected after a storm of public debates), to the naming of a new university after Tipu in 2013. Such controversies remind us that the Tiger of Mysore is not yet forgotten. A legend in his times, Tipu was feared as much as he was admired. Not surprisingly, a cluster of myths grew around him – stories that are repeated even today. Despite Tipu's legendary status, we found that most visitors to Bangalore Fort would hardly pause to reflect on this particular site of Tipu's resistance to the British. The fort fell to British forces in 1791 and shortly afterward, Tipu lost the Third Anglo-Mysore War in 1792. Tipu signed the Treaty of Seringapatnam (now Sringapatna), under which he ceded territory while Lord Cornwallis took hostage two of his young sons.

Our study of the fort also included several visits to Tipu's Summer Palace, which once lay within the fort walls. Although connected by the same historical narrative, Tipu's palace and Tipu's fort are now physically separated by a hospital that was built during the colonial period. Standing in a busy market place, the Bangalore Fort is a reminder of a past that sharply differs from the present. Focusing on the eighteenth century, the architecture and iconography of the fort and the military history of the battles fought at the site, the students engaged with the social meanings of legends and stories in order to experiment with how to make historical narratives compelling enough so that our public history intervention could present multiple narratives that conveyed the complexities of the eighteenth century, and the significance that past events have for the present.

Except for the marble plaque that commemorates the "British Assault that was delivered on March 21, 1791," there is little else at Bangalore Fort today to remind visitors of the battle that was fought there. The commemorative plaque installed by the British is on the outer wall facing one of the busiest streets. In front of that same wall there are fruit and vegetable sellers who sit on the pavement below the plaque, oblivious of its significance. It is not unusual for most visitors to miss the plaque and thus miss the connection with the Third Anglo-Mysore War. The fall of the fort was only one among a series of events that ended the war. The documentation booklet that the students produced at the end of the project included two paintings by British artist Robert Homes: "The death of Colonel Moorehouse [sic] at the storming of the Pettah Gate of 7 March 1791," and "The reception of the Mysorean Hostage Princes by Marquis Cornwallis, 25 February 1792."[4] Both these eighteenth-century "documentary" paintings and the battle and court scenes in the mural on the walls of the Dariya Daulat Bagh Palace became objects of reflection for the students, bringing together the importance of understanding historical contexts and ideological frameworks.[5]

One of the things that our project explored was what Tipu meant to the people who lived near the fort. Was he still perceived as a hero, or was he generally forgotten, invoked only by politicians and special-interest groups? Our project attempted to map legends and historical events onto the contemporary heritage site of the Bangalore Fort in order to understand their relationship to each other. In India, very few heritage sites are brought alive through historical narratives. Our goal was to restore human history to a heritage site so that visitors could relate to the place differently. In order to do this, we needed to understand the different ways that local history intermingled with circulated legends. Students undertook archival research and read secondary material in order to

Figure 10.2   Students interact with local residents during the Fort walk, October 2012. Photo: Indira Chowdhury.

build their understanding of the area. They also explored through oral history interviews how the stories of local communities could be used to revive interest in an archaeological site. However, as we shall see, the unexpected outcomes of the interviews made us rethink the relationship between the ordinary lives of present-day inhabitants of the locality and the heroic dimensions of Tipu's life. In its final iteration, our project deployed three modes of orality: a guided walk by students, an audiovisual shadow puppetry show inside the fort, and an audioscape of oral history interviews with some of the local residents played at the guard room of the fort. The intended audience for these oral interventions was imagined to be a mix of local residents of all age groups and school-children, but we found that each mode attracted a particular kind of audience. The walk was attended by schoolchildren and local residents; the shadow theater, though targeted at children, drew adults and local residents; and the audioscape, targeted at the local residents, appealed more to a literate, educated audience who were not from the neighborhood (Figure 10.2).

Project design and public history pedagogy

The project stimulated new thinking about the nature of public history as a discipline. As Constance Schultz has pointed out: "[T]he goals and practices of public history are often interdisciplinary in their scope and require cooperation in collegial enterprise for their implementation" (1999: 24). In the United States and Canada, public history emerged as a discipline that aimed to locate history beyond academia alone. It initially focused on preparing students for work in archives, museums, and heritage sites, and by the first decade of the twenty-first century many places in the United States and Canada embraced interdisciplinarity and performance and design projects, thus moving away from the limitations of public history's earlier purpose. As Dean, Meerzon, and Prince have pointed out in their pioneering volume *History, Memory, Performance* (2015), scholarly practices can be transformed at the intersection of history and performance in ways that bring fresh insights into the ways in which history and the theater engage with the past. Echoing these concerns, the CPH deployed the tools of visual communication design, video, and digital media in order to bring the past alive in different ways for different audiences. The CPH's unique location within a design institute enabled this process.

We found ourselves redefining the nature of enquiry that public history sets up for itself. Public history for us was not merely interdisciplinary, but also a hybrid discipline that combined historical enquiry with other modes of knowing the past: through visual forms, through performance traditions, and through communication tools. The content of public history moved beyond texts and documents to include art, design, and culture. The pedagogical challenges that we faced working with design students who did not have a background in history motivated us to find ways of representing the past from documents, paintings, and material culture, giving them narrative and visual form. We began by exposing students to popular history by going on a walk led by Arun Pai of Bangalore Walks, an enterprise that combines history and tourism. Pai walked the group of students in and around the City Market area, telling stories about the British attack on Tipu's Fort in 1791. This was followed by a period of reading available biographies of Tipu Sultan as well as critical texts on the eighteenth and nineteenth centuries that presented different conceptual frameworks with which to understand the past. Such an exercise also enabled students to critically understand the dynamics of popular history which is deployed by enterprises such as Bangalore Walks.

Edward Said's concept of Orientalism opened up ways of understanding imperial ideology, and Sanjay Subrahmanyam's concept of the "early modern" alerted us to indigenous developments that were not necessarily European impositions. These readings served two purposes. On the one hand, they called into question the students' own notions of modernity, which they had not until then seen as related to eighteenth-century India. On the other, they drew out the links between Tipu Sultan, the French Revolution, and the American Revolution, and made clear the reasons why Tipu was demonized in popular discourses of eighteenth- and nineteenth-century British Empire.[6] Students were also introduced to different versions of Tipu's life.[7] This was followed by a period of archival research at the State Archives and the Mythic Society Library, where students sought out contemporary accounts of the Anglo-Mysore Wars, biographies of Tipu Sultan, and articles from the *Mysore Gazetteer*. One of the contemporary texts that fascinated students was a translated version of Tipu Sultan's dream diary. The diary, written in Persian in Tipu Sultan's own hand, contains descriptions of 37 dreams that were recorded between April 1786 and January 1899. Found by Colonel Kirkpatrick in Tipu's palace, the diary was presented to the Court of Directors of the East India Company in 1800 by Alexander Beatson on behalf of the Governor-General Marquess Wellesley. Tipu's dream diary, as we shall see, became an important part of our project's shadow puppetry show, showing audiences the kind of historical resources that were available from Tipu's times. Students were also trained to conduct life story interviews with people who lived or worked in the fort area about their understanding of their locality and also what the fort and Tipu meant to them. Their interviews raised more complicated questions about not just the relationship between history and legend, but also about ways of viewing place, especially when many residents were not "native" to the area but had migrated from other parts of India. What, then, was the sense of place that these interviews presented? What occupied center stage – the hustle of city life or the remembered village? What were the ways in which people laid claim to history? Although students began their interviews with the idea of excavating legends about Tipu Sultan, their interviews yielded a plethora of local legends, some connected and others unconnected to the legendary Tiger of Mysore. Oral history broadened the focus of the project and enhanced its interpretative scope, reminding us that any public history project would have to deal with not only the past in the present but also with different perceptions of the past.

In the next phase of the project, students worked in groups to create narratives for a Fort Walk that would present multiple dimensions of the life of Tipu Sultan. Through the stories they narrated in the course of this walk students could take their audiences beyond the four walls of the fort and into the terrain that Tipu roamed and the times to which he belonged. The fort became a site of memory and a location to rehearse the many dimensions of his life. This part of the project raised an interesting aspect of public history: how do we communicate controversial elements? Most of our students were reluctant to discuss the cruel acts of this eighteenth-century ruler, perhaps because most had grown up unconsciously absorbing the anachronistic and nationalist stories of Tipu Sultan's patriotism and how he had challenged the British. They were also reluctant to express negative views about Tipu, who is seen as a representative of Muslims – a minority community in India. We overcame this reluctance by appealing not to their sense of the past, but to their understanding of contemporary controversial political figures, inviting them to imagine how they would be represented 300 years hence. A discussion around present-day politics in India, pointing out how politicians often play with the credibility of their audiences and leave numerous unanswered questions about the origins of communal riots, enabled students to think about how they would present the contentious and provocative aspects of a ruler they wanted to uncritically admire. The students were trained to create a script of the walk-through selections from their archival research by Rama Lakshmi, an oral historian and freelance museum consultant who herself was trained at the Smithsonian. The guided tours normally offered at Tipu's Summer Palace and at the fort at Srirangapatnam where he was killed are focused on historical events and on the palace architecture. Our project aimed to create a narrative that went beyond these conventional interpretations and offered instead a narrative based on past and present experience, and on historical reflexivity.

Our walk was crafted to speak about the experience of life within the fort during the siege that took place more than 200 years ago. The walk also included insights into how we interpret historical sources, how we look at material culture, and how we understand the specificity of the architecture of the fort and identify where it was damaged and rebuilt. The walk sought to inspire audiences to pay attention to the fort and its architecture. Unfortunately, the ASI no longer allows visitors to view the dungeons. The dungeons nonetheless remained part of the story as students walked groups of 10–15 people around the fort. They recounted how Captain David Baird was imprisoned in Tipu's dungeons at Srirangapatna from 1780 to 1785; later it was Captain Baird, who, as major general, led the siege of Srirangapatna in 1799. If the Fort Walk focused on Tipu and his times, the shadow puppet show focused on a specific event: the fall of the fort in 1791. It is here that the students interpreted a larger dimension of local history. In their walks around the fort, they had come across the Dargah of Bahadur Khan, who was the *killedar* (Keeper) of the fort when it fell to the British. Bahadur Khan had died defending the fort and was much admired for his bravery. As noted by contemporary British soldiers:

> Wherever gallantry is recorded, Bahadur Khan, *killedar* of Bangalore, will hold a conspicuous place among the heroes of our times. True to his trust, he resigned it with life, after receiving almost as many wounds as were inflicted on Caesar in the Capitol. (Mackenzie 1793)

After the battle, Charles, Second Earl of Cornwallis, wanted to return the body of Bahadur Khan to Tipu. Tipu is said to have responded to Cornwallis that a soldier must be buried at the spot where he fell. Finally, the British buried Bahadur Khan near where he died. At this spot now stands the Dargah Hazrath Mir Bahadur Shah Al-Maroof Syed Pacha Shaheed. The students had visited this *dargah* in the middle of the busy marketplace just off Avenue Road. Over time, the burial spot had become a *dargah*, or a shrine, where people pray. Bahadur Khan, we discovered, had been transformed from soldier to saint. Bahadur Khan the soldier featured in the shadow play about the fall of the fort in 1791 (Figure 10.3).

When students presented their work at the fort, we had three specific outcomes: (1) an audioscape of oral histories playing at the guard room soon after one entered the fort, (2) a curated storytelling walk around the fort that included local legends and historical understandings of Tipu and his times, leading to (3) a small improvised theater in an alcove of the fort where a story about the siege of the fort was enacted with shadow puppets. The entire show engaged with different time frames. The oral histories focused on the relationship between past and present, often looking at the past within the present;

Figure 10.3   The shadow puppets depicting the attack on the Bangalore Fort in 1791, October 2012. Photo: Indira Chowdhury.

the Fort Walk focused on Tipu's life and times, demonstrating how the past lived on in the present; and the shadow play drew on a single event, the siege on the fort, and juxtaposed it with a few of Tipu's dreams in animation. This constant interplay of past and present created the basis of our pedagogy. What makes public history different from conventional genres of historical engagement is that the public historian builds on the basis of multiple sources of historical knowledge. As Thomas Cauvin has pointed out, public history asks for a "reassessment of the traditional role for the historian as well as their relations with a multitude of actors involved in the production of historical narratives" (Cauvin 2016 : 2).

The mixed pedagogy that combined archival research, oral history, visual communication, drama, and narratology pushed us to reflect on the nature of public history and the designing of learning modules. We realized that public history pedagogy should engage with different forms of communication in order to succeed. Making the "Tiger of Mysore" interesting to our audience and bringing the fort alive in contemporary imagination required us to address several interlinked areas: archival research, oral history, and visual communication design.

History, oral history, and storytelling

We began with the question: what part do local histories play in defining collective identity in an urban environment? What is the context by which local communities engage with their past and with the history of the place they now occupy? Since many of the local residents are migrants, how do they relate to a place that has become part of their lives only recently? In contrast, how do residents who have lived here for a longer period of time relate to the historical dimensions of place? What are their experiences of it? How can their memories and experiences be explored to create new, contemporary relationships with heritage sites and build a sense of shared history? Most often archaeological sites are perceived as remnants of a spectacular and significant past, thus fostering no connection with present-day landscapes that have been reshaped by the forces of history. Moreover, these sites are divorced from latter-day human history and, as a result, there is very little understanding of the relationship between the archaeological site and human habitation around it. The students in this project attempted to understand how legends survive migration and other forms of socioeconomic disruption. Drawing together different sources and traditions of knowledge, the project used oral histories to interpret the history of the site and the meaning it still holds for those who live in its vicinity.[8]

The oral histories told us more about the present and the ways in which people perceive the past. For example, Sayed Ahjaz, who lives and works near the fort, freely intermingled legend and history in his interview with Anukriti Arora. Sayed Ahjaz's interview demonstrates how earlier cycles of change are perceived by those who witness change in their own times. Ahjaz spoke of the work on the Bangalore's *Namma Metro* which would forever change the landscape that was familiar to him.

> **SA**: This *dargah* belongs to the time of Hazrat Tipu Sultan Rehmadlale. It is four hundred years old. At that time it was a cemetery, and the area behind it belonged to Hazrat Tipu Sultan Rehmadlale. There were farriers here and Tipu's horses would get shod there.
>
> The fort that he has in Bangalore is historical. Nobody can make another fort like that ever. Now, the work of Metro construction is going on there and when the Metro is built then the fort will not be visible anymore and they will not be able to keep it open.

Ahjaz also recounted a miracle story about the building of the fort. He spoke about the mysterious saint Tawakkal Mastan Aulia, who came from Iran with his brothers, Tipu Mastan and Manek Mastan. Tawakkal appeared as a laborer during Hyder Ali's (Tipu's father) attempt to transform the original mud fort into a stone fort. This story was repeated by Imtiaz Ahmed, the *khidmatdar* of the Tawakkal Mastan Dargah, not far from the fort in his interview with Nikita Jain:

> **IA**: We are from Bangalore city. There is a place named Cotton Pete – this is a place where we live. It is in O.T.C [Old Taluk Catcherry] Road and here is the Dargarh of the great Tawakkal Mastan Saharwardi Ahmedullale and here I am, his servant. When Astan-E- Hazrat Tawakkal Mastan Shah Saharwadi came here, he was working at the Fort of Tipu Sultan which is near the market, as a laborer. He used to just touch the stones and the stones would automatically arrange themselves. He used to work like this and after work, like everyone used to go for wages but Baba never used to take his wages. He only used to take a bite of an apple and then leave the place … Haidar Ali was very anxious to know that who is this person who never takes the wages. What is this about? So he asked one of his soldiers to follow him.
>
> The soldier noticed that when it is *Iftari*, meaning *roza* time, he takes a bite of an apple, eats it and then go and sits at a crossing and at that point his body breaks into three pieces. The two soldiers who saw this went back to Haidar Ali and said that someone had murdered Mastan Baba. Haidar Ali was saddened. But the next morning, Mastan Baba came back to work. Then Haidar Ali asked him, "Are you a *wali* of Allah?" Then Mastan Baba replied, "Yes, I am." Thus everyone came to know that Mastan Baba is an *Aulia* [a friend of Allah, a saint]."

Tawakkal Mastan's Dargah is not far from the fort. Indeed, Tipu was said to be named after Tipu Mastan, the elder brother of Tawakkal Mastan, whose *dargah* is in Arcot. The stories about Tawakkal Mastan alerted us to the live connections that the fort has to the surrounding area. A related legend is connected to the Karaga festival of the Thigala community that is celebrated every year. The Thigalas, a horticultural community, were brought by Hyder Ali to Bangalore during the creation of Lal Bagh in Mysore and the Rose and Cypress garden in Bangalore by Hyder Ali and Tipu. The Karaga is a Hindu festival and always involves a celebratory visit to the Tawakkal Mastan Dargah to honor the relationship Tawakkal Mastan had to the Thigalas. While such stories of shared appeal of a Sufi saint across communities are not uncommon in India, coming across them in oral history interviews alerted us to the importance to seeing the fort as part of a larger landscape of shared stories.

There were also several controversies surrounding Tipu's religious policy, such as the ruthless massacre of Mangalorean Christians, and his intolerance toward his British prisoners, who were all converted. But he was also perceived as a friend to several Hindu temples and *mathas,* and several of his ministers, including his *Dewan,* Krishnacharya Purnaiya, were Hindus. He also corresponded with the *Shankaracharya* of Sringeri *Matha,* sending the *matha* cash and gifts when it was attacked by marauding horsemen in 1791. While such details did not surface in the oral history interviews, what did become clear was that the reasoning interviewees drew upon often came from very practical traditional knowledge. Alasingari Bhatta has for several decades been the priest at the Kote Anjanaiya Swamy in Kalasipalyam, a temple across the fort. Old and weak in health, he is no longer able to carry out his duties as before. While the priesthood is hereditary, globalization has placed new constraints on the role, and he cannot expect any immediate help from his son in carrying out temple duties as his son is a temple priest in the United States. His interview with Spandana Sridhar demonstrates the ways in which local communities bring a specific understanding to a historical character who lived in a warrior society, one very different from their own:

> **SS**: Now this fort and palace was built by Hyder Ali and existed during Tipu Sultan's rule. Tipu is a Muslim ruler – why do you think he never harmed any of the temples that were so close to his fort and in fact, within the fort itself?
> **AB**: Now he was born in Devanahalli, in Devanahalli there were lots of Hindu artisans. Lots of his close advisors were Hindus. Also Tipu would travel a lot, he would stay at one place for more than a few days, so while traveling he would often take shelter in temples, all over Mysore and Bangalore. Chikkadevaraja Wodeyar built the temple, later Hyder Ali built this fort. So the temple already existed.

Alsingari Bhatta articulated his interpretation of religious tolerance in eighteenth-century Bangalore by evoking the close bonds of community in the area where Tipu grew up, a place that the Hindu artisanal community shared with Muslim families.

These narratives were included as audio excerpts that played in the guardroom during the second iteration of the project on December 22 and 23, 2012. Although this audioscape drew in a curious audience, the local community was more interested in the walk and the shadow puppetry. This alerted us to the fact that we had inadvertently created two competing forms of orality: the shadow puppetry with its strong visual element which was about the heroic Tiger of Mysore, and an audioscape about people whose everyday struggles made them no less heroic but whose stories were already familiar to the audience who visited. The context of heroic resistance invoked by the shadow play seemed to place constraints on a more complex and inclusive interpretation.[9]

The challenges of practicing public history

We began with the Bangalore Fort and Tipu's times but soon found ourselves moving beyond the fort into local history and exploring forms of local knowledge. Our multidisciplinary approach made us look at the deep relationship that exists in India between different forms of orality and how oral history itself is shaped by other oral narratives. Our explorations blurred the boundaries that are often set up between different disciplines, changing the ways in which we think about history. For all participants involved in the project, doing public history was about a practical and critical engagement with the past. The challenges we faced were therefore methodological, interpretative, and representational.

One of the challenges we faced while getting students to interview members of the local community was that after their primary research, they perceived themselves to be more knowledgeable about Tipu and the fort than their interviewees, who were often of humble origin. Initially, the concept of a "shared authority" seemed difficult to include within the interpretative framework (Frisch 1990).However, students soon realized that the purpose of oral history was not to gather information but to engage with their interviewees in order to understand what the site and the events from 200 years ago meant to the local community. Interactions with the local community were fraught with other difficulties: (1) our students come from all over India and are not able to speak or understand the local language, Kannada; (2) since the fort area is mainly surrounded by the city market, most interviewees were busy with their shops and could not find time for extended interview sessions; and (3) there were also class and community issues, as most of our students belonged to the English-speaking upper classes and also to the Hindu community. Oral histories were conducted with people who spoke Hindi, the national language, or with the help of translators.

There were also challenges of representation. As students worked on the script of the shadow play, they wanted to exercise creative choices when framing the story of the fort. Thus, in their first iteration, the narrative flowed seamlessly from the events during the siege of the fort to the events described in Tipu's dream diary, making it appear as if there was continuity between the events of 1791 and Tipu's dreams. While this approach enhanced the dramatic elements, we decided that one of the purposes of a public history project was to make the audience aware of different kinds of historical evidence. Tipu's dreams are varied; they are about battle strategies, about visitations by mystic saints, and sometimes about miraculous events. But above all they seem record his preoccupation with the British, whom he regarded as his main adversary. After much discussion of creative license and the purpose of the project, we found that there was no justification for "fictionalizing" the dreams. We decided to separate the presentation of the story of fort from the dramatized presentation of Tipu's dreams. The two narratives were presented on separate screens and, although they did speak to each other, they were not represented as seamlessly flowing into each other. The narrative incorporated a traditional storyteller or *sutradhar*. In the dramatization of the fall of the fort, it was the voice of the *sutradhar* that distinguished between the events at the fort and Tipu's dreams. The process producing this historical narrative alerted us to the specific needs of public history projects that must engage with audiences from diverse backgrounds. While dramatization might hold the audience's attention and can be an effective tool of intervention, public history offered an opportunity to raise audience awareness about historical sources and their interpretation.

One of the most difficult moments in the project presented itself when students struggled to find a language in which to represent the more controversial aspects of Tipu Sultan's life, including the forced conversion of Hindus and Christians to Islam, and his generous donations to Hindu temples and monasteries. This problem of finding a language in which to talk about historical paradoxes was overcome through a comparison with present-day controversial figures and ways in which they might be represented in history written in the future.

Addressing these tricky questions convinced us that public history pedagogy has to address the "after lives" of historical figures that often appear like specters in the present. These specters need to be addressed, named, and elucidated upon; not treated as academic problems that are confined to the ivory tower of academic history. In a postcolonial context, it was particularly important for historical presentations to be approached with an awareness of the interpretative models that have been used in the past. This project convinced us that in order to engage our audiences with new forms of historical understanding, we needed to engage with the mundane, the exotic, and the controversial. The Tiger, we concluded, had to be looked in the eye.

The practice of public history has always reminded us about the importance of sustaining multiple dialogues: between politics and history, between memory and history, between personal and political experience, and between past and present. This truth came home to us sharply as we were just about to end the project. On November 22, 2012, workers digging at a Metro Rail site excavated a cannon and a cannonball that belonged to the Tipu Sultan era. A second cannon was discovered a few days later. The site of these discoveries was the City Market Metro Station that was being constructed between Tipu Sultan's Summer Palace and the Bangalore Fort. The act of ushering in a modern system of transportation thus serendipitously revealed weapons from Tipu's time, the twelve-foot long cannons almost reclaiming the territory that once belonged to the Tiger of Mysore. The past was not only real but also very much alive, and called for public historians to engage it in dialogue.

Notes

1   I would like to thank all the students who participated in the project and acknowledge the contribution of Aliyeh Rizvi, whose enthusiasm for Tipu Sultan directed our proposal to ASI.
2   In hindsight, the definition of historical enquiry that we worked with was similar to Hayden White's explication of the "practical past" – a concept he develops from the work of philosopher Michael Oakshott. White calls upon historians to engage with the "practical past" that reveals itself in creative works. See White (2014).
3   See this website on the relationship between Tipu Sultan and the Scots: http://www.tigerandthistle.net/tipu315.htm
4   I am deeply grateful to Susan Stronge of the V & A, London, for enabling our students to work with images of Tipu-related artifacts there and to the National Army Museum, London, for giving students permission to use some of the Tipu-related paintings from their collection. I thank Aarthi Ajit and Waseem Shaikh for work on the final documentation brochure.
5   Janaki Nair has demonstrated how after Tipu's death the British actively sought to re-narrate Tipu's story by critiquing the murals on the walls of Dariya Daulat Bagh palace where Tipu had recorded his successful battles against the British. See Nair (2011).
6   Readings were drawn from different sources: Said (1994); Brittlebank (1997); Habib (2001a); Subrahmanyam (2001); Nair (2005); Chatterjee (2012).
7   Details of Tipus life were drawn from different representations: Hasan (1951); Forrest (1970); Habib (2001b).
8   Compare for example, Cenker and Thys-Senocak (2008).
9   Compare Frisch and Pitcaithley (1990).

CHAPTER ELEVEN

Storytelling, Bertolt Brecht, and the Illusions of Disciplinary History

STEVEN HIGH

"But I am a survivor and today I am 22 years old. And I am no longer alone. I have a new family. I am the mother of this family, and I have 16 children – girls and boys. Some of my children are older than me. You may ask yourself, 'how is this possible?' This family grew because of the genocide, because of our need for family. We were the survivors. This is my adopted family, the family who adopted me. My family is made up of orphans, of students at my school who are also trying to fight loneliness. Together we make groups and choose a father and a mother. When you are chosen as a mother you can't refuse, even if you are shy. I was once shy, but over time I have learned how to be a mother, to take care of my children."

– Leontine Uwababyeyi, age 22 (Mapping Memories, 2011)

Leontine Uwababyeyi composed her digital story, entitled "My Two Families," as part of Mapping Memories, a participatory media project that brought together seven young people with refugee experience. Facilitated by feminist filmmaker Liz Miller and working in partnership with the Canadian Council for Refugees, the group met four hours a week over three months at Concordia University's Centre for Oral History and Digital Storytelling. A survivor of the Rwandan genocide now living in Montreal, Quebec, Leontine was only eight years old when the slaughter began, and "everything changed" (Miller 2013). As true of other group members, Leontine was taking her story public for the first time. In scripting her story, she had a number of decisions to make. What aspect of her story did she want to share with others? How much of her story should she tell? Who did she want to reach? What was the point? Peer support was an integral part of the storytelling process, as the young people shared their some-times difficult stories with one another over food that they prepared together (Mapping Memories 2011).

While these digital stories are now available online, the group's immediate goal was to develop a collaboratively produced memoryscape bus tour of the city. A bus tour, you might ask? We have all probably experienced the tedium of tourist buses where the

A Companion to Public History, First Edition. Edited by David Dean.
© 2018 John Wiley & Sons Ltd. Published 2018 by John Wiley & Sons Ltd.

guide's muffled voice directs our attention to one city landmark after another in a superficial mash-up of past and present. But this was no ordinary bus tour. The intention here was to transform the interior of the bus into an immersive storytelling space where stories are shared by means of prerecorded audio as well as in-person commentary as each young refugee introduced her or his story and answered questions. There was also music and impromptu dance, as the diverse multicultural crowd included many family members. Occasionally, the bus stopped and everyone got off to hear a place-based story anchored in the city itself. The tour ended in the Old Port area of Montreal, where we were invited to toss flowers into the St. Lawrence River in memory of those who lost their lives in the Rwandan genocide. This small act follows the commemorative practice of the city's Rwandan community, which organizes a similar ceremony at this site each year to mark the anniversary of the 1994 genocide.

Mapping Memories was part of the wider Montreal Life Stories project, a seven-year community–university research alliance that brought together dozens of researchers, artists, educators, human rights activists, survivors, and other community members to record the oral histories of 500 survivors of mass violence and to bring these stories into the public using new digital technologies and arts-based methods. Survivor communities were an integral part of the project, often directing these efforts and (co-)authoring the results. What is of particular relevance here is that the wider project enabled Montrealers to encounter Leontine's story in a variety of places. For example, 350 subway cars were "equipped" with QR-coded audio portraits that enabled commuters to download one of nine life stories, including Leontine's. Her poster read: "In our family, we say that it is better to live two times than to die two times." Leontine's story was incorporated into a curriculum module for grade eleven high-school students across Quebec, and into the year-long "We Are Here" exhibition at the Centre d'histoire de Montréal. She even toured her digital story to 20 area high schools, reaching thousands of other young people. These visits followed the conventions of the film screening, with the young storytellers introducing their digital story and answering questions afterward. Finally, the entire process was the subject of a short documentary film, produced by Liz Miller, as well as a series of scholarly books and articles authored by team members. This essay is now part of the wider cultural and scholarly production.

I began this chapter with Leontine Uwababyeyi's digital story, and the specific context of story creation and public diffusion, because it highlights some of the challenges and opportunities that we face as oral and public historians. The digital revolution and a resurgent interest in participatory approaches and personal storytelling are shaking things up. Once-distinct heritage institutions such as libraries, archives, and museums are becoming more alike and in some cases merging their functions. A new emphasis on "immaterial culture" in the museum and heritage preservation world has also pushed story and storytelling to the forefront. According to Laurier Turgeon, we are now living in a "new era of heritage" (2010: 23). The research environment within our universities is likewise changing, as humanities and social science disciplines go public in new and creative ways. One indication of the scale and scope of this transformation is the recent emergence of new subfields in public sociology, public geography, public archaeology, and the public humanities. These newcomers join more applied disciplines with a long history of participatory research and public engagement. Here too the lines have blurred, as disciplines cross-pollinate and new cross-disciplinary methodologies are taken up. The rise of digital storytelling, photo-voice, audio or sound walking, participatory mapping, and other arts-based methodologies have generated considerable interest within heritage institutions and the wider public history community. But in such a crowded field, it is becoming increasingly difficult to distinguish a "public history" project from other disciplinary or interdisciplinary engagements with the past. Is it useful then – or even appropriate – to think of Leontine Uwababyeyi's digital story and the interdisciplinary project that produced it as "public history"?

To some extent, there is nothing new about this ambiguity. Historically, the overlapping fields of oral and public history have had an ambiguous relationship to each other and a sometimes fraught relationship to the wider discipline of history. Paula Hamilton and Linda Shopes, for example, called oral and public history "uneasy bedfellows" as the "populist stance" of oral history proved "subversive" to disciplinary history, whereas public history developed a more "conventional" professional identity inside state history and heritage institutions (2008: xii). Unlike ethnography, which is at the disciplinary core of anthropology, oral history emerged on the margins of established disciplines. Its place within the university was therefore tenuous. Even today, most oral history projects are community based, and much of the field has been directed at the public archiving of marginalized or local voices. Public history, by contrast, is very much tied to state institutions and national practices of public remembering, commemoration, and memorialization. The nation-state thus supplants the individual or marginalized community as the primary unit of analysis. But this is changing, and the differences between oral and public histories are not what they used to be. The co-creation and co-diffusion of Leontine's story is thus part of a wider rethinking that is under way across the humanities and social sciences. One of the most compelling aspects about oral and public history is its capacity to "redefine and redistribute intellectual authority, so that this might be shared more broadly in historical research and communication rather than continuing to serve as an instrument of power and hierarchy" (Frisch 1990: xx).

Yet many have raised productive questions about "what is involved in the act of listening to and telling 'risky stories'" (Salverson 1996: 181). All stories, Kay Schaffer and Sidonie Smith remind us, "emerge in the midst of complex and uneven relationships of power, prompting certain questions about production: Who tells the stories and who doesn't? To whom are they told and under what circumstances?" (2004: 5). We also have to inquire into public receptivity for some kinds of stories over others. What stories resonate and why? Is sharing always the right thing to do? The wider politics of story sharing is therefore vitally important.

Historically, scientific research is deeply implicated in the "worst excesses of colonialism." As Linda Tuhiwai Smith cautions, the "word itself, 'research,' is probably one of the dirtiest words in the indigenous world's vocabulary" (2012: 1). Too often, researchers have failed to give back or otherwise contribute to the indigenous communities in which they worked. Oral and public historians continue to struggle with this poisonous legacy. Robin Brownlie and Roewen Crowe, for example, noted that a young Aboriginal woman living in a poor inner city neighborhood of Winnipeg, Manitoba, when approached to participate in an oral history project, replied: "So you want to hear our ghetto stories?" This comment sparked a great deal of political reflection, as Brownlie and Crowe considered the ways in which these "ghetto stories," once collected, "can lend authority or 'street cred' – to those who can appropriate them despite their own social distance from such experiences" (2013: 203). The subsequent circulation and retelling of these stories by outsiders is similarly fraught. The risk of appropriation or commodification is real. "Thoughtlessly soliciting autobiography may reproduce a form of cultural colonialism that is at the very least voyeuristic," warns Julie Salverson (1996: 182). Mocking the practice, bell hooks devastatingly writes:

> No need to heed your voice when I can talk about you better than you can speak about yourself. No need to hear your voice. Only tell me about your pain. I want to know your story. And then I will tell it back to you in a new way. Tell it back to you in such a way that it becomes my own. Re-writing you I rewrite myself anew. I am still author, authority. I am still coloniser, the speaking subject, and you are now at the centre of my tale. (1990: 345)

The rest of this chapter explores the possibility that storytelling is emerging as an ethical and political counterpoint to more conventional ways that history is understood and engaged with in historical writing and public history production. Surging interest in storytelling is an expression of profound ill-ease at the "foreign disciplinary gaze" that has treated *other* people as "data" to be mined (Miller 2011). In this context, storytelling represents an acknowledgment of local knowledge as well as a recognition of community-based agency, expertise, and authorship, as it forces scholars to engage with the intentionality and wider context of storytelling. More tellingly, perhaps, the storytelling turn in public history encourages wider collaborative alliances and participatory approaches to history making.

Fourth wall conventions

In thinking about these issues, the work of Bertolt Brecht in 1930s Germany has proved to be something of a revelation to me. In traditional theater, spectators are invited to identify and sympathize with those on stage. Brecht believed that the theatrical illusion of staged reality was a passive exercise that depoliticized audiences rather than activating them to be more critically engaged with the world around them. In mainstream theater, actors do not acknowledge that they are being watched, thus engendering the illusion that the play is real. In response, he sought to break the theatrical fourth wall – the invisible wall at the front of the stage that separates the actors from the audience – in order to raise awareness and create implicated, active audiences. Thus when an actor speaks directly to the audience, as the audience, and thus acknowledges its presence, s/he steps out of character, breaking the illusion of a separate reality.

After delving into performance studies as part of my work in the Montreal Life Stories project, I came to the conclusion that my chosen discipline of history has its own fourth wall conventions. Our writing is based on rigorous empiricism, and we constantly strive to put things in their historical context. The historical narratives that we write or otherwise produce are "inextricably bound" to our conclusions, and our "historical analysis derives much of its force from the upward or downward sweep of the plot" (Cronon 1992: 1348). The focus on the past, however, has often meant the active suppression of the present. We are taught to write in the third person and in the past tense, to maintain critical distance, and to focus on the past rather than the present. As in theater, these disciplinary conventions help to maintain a scholarly fourth wall between ourselves and our readers, and between the written past and the lived present. Historian Raphael Samuel, founder of the History Workshop movement in the United Kingdom, once wrote that disciplinary history is a "cunning collection of strategies which bolster the authority of the narrator and induce in the reader the willing suspension of disbelief. ... the evocative detail on which historians pride themselves is there for what Barthes satirically describes as a 'reality effect.' Verbatim quotations are introduced as a talisman of authenticity." (Samuel 1991: 91)

These critical reflections raise new questions about disciplinary norms and boundaries. Disciplinary historians do not speak of objectivity much anymore, but it continues to structure everything that we do. Our authority is still premised on the idea that impartiality comes with distance, or detachment. Writing in the third person thus renders the historian's own subjectivity invisible, as historical narrative is written from the perspective of "what literary theory would describe as an 'omniscient narrator'" (Portelli 1990: 57). Raphael Samuel went even further when he suggested that as a discipline, historians have a firm idea of "who is, and who is not a historian." There is, he argued, an "unspoken assumption that knowledge filters downward. At the apex there are the chosen few who pilot new techniques, uncover fresh sources of documentation, and formulate arresting hypotheses" (1994: 4). To be close to one's subject of research or part of the story is still to risk being viewed as biased or dismissed as "presentist," a pejorative term still used to describe a historian who projects the present into the past. Even today, the present is largely suppressed in historical writing. Critical distance is at the core of disciplinary authority and identity. "Within positivist strains of social science," writes historian Mary Jo Maynes, "life stories are reduced to the status of the anecdotal, adding color or personal interest but unreliable as a basis for generalization" (Maynes et al. 2008: 5).

Public history is not immune to this stance. Many public historians earned degrees in disciplinary history and have approached public historical interpretation with much the same professional detachment. This is changing, however, as public history programs and institutions are becoming more interdisciplinary. Here, I am reminded of the work of Cathy Stanton. In her prize-winning book on site interpretation in post-industrial Lowell, Massachusetts, Stanton found that the National Park Service located poor wages and working conditions safely in the distant past. Visitors could therefore be forgiven if they left feeling more thankful than ever that they did not live back then. In effect, the cultivation of a sense of pastness at the historic site served to reinforce an already strong belief in societal progress that renders invisible current workplace struggles in the United States and the world over. The availability of these former textile mills for historical interpretation and public visitation is further evidence of the persistent powerlessness of working people in the face of capital mobility and deindustrialization. As Stanton suggests, the site's exclusive focus on the past may come "at the expense of people still living in the present" (2006: xii). Arguably, it is only when we consider the relationship between past and present – and break the historian's fourth wall that separates them – that we succeed in implicating people politically in the here and now. This is a discomforting thought for disciplinary historians in particular, of which I am one, as it challenges much of what we do.

Yet the tension between past and present plays out in different ways in different countries. At the same time that public history was emerging as a field of historical inquiry in the United States in the 1970s, there emerged in France the field of "histoire du temps présent," or the "history of the present time" (Muller 2006). Historian François Bédarida led the way in carving out an institutional home within disciplinary history for those interested in productively exploring the space between history and memory. Robert Frank (1992), for example, has noted that historians of the recent past do not have the same distance from their subjects as do historians of earlier time periods. Others like Pierre Nora (1992) have noted that contemporary history was once considered impossible to do scientifically, as the historical archives were not available and people could not remain objective. This new subfield of academic research in France thus provided a space within disciplinary history where past and present could be considered together.

Oral history and public history promise a similar break from disciplinary fourth wall conventions. Oral history, for example, pulls the narrator into the historical narrative. This represents a decisive change, notes Alessandro Portelli: "[t]his is not just a grammatical shift from the third person to the first person, but a whole new narrative attitude" (1990: 57). At a minimum, this shift implies a "much deeper political and personal involvement" of the historical narrator. "Writing radical oral history," Portelli continues, "is not a matter of ideology, of subjective sides-taking, or of choosing one set of sources instead of another. It is, rather, inherent in the historian's presence in the story, in the assumption of responsibility which inscribes her or him in the account and reveals historiography as an autonomous act of narration" (1990: 41). Subjectivity is thus located not only in our narrators, but in ourselves as researchers and authors. Self-reflexivity is thus a necessary first step.

A similar shift can be seen in public history scholarship and practice. Museums and other public institutions have been forced to adjust to new political realities, and to collaborate with some so-called "source communities" in the curation of their material culture (Peers and Brown 2003). This shifting curatorial practice is most visible in the case of Indigenous peoples where a movement to "repatriate" materials acquired in the past has gained strength. Research ethics review in many white settler societies, including my own, is at its most vigilant when the research is directed toward first peoples. In Canada, for example, university researchers are now required to get incoming as well as outgoing ethics approval before they can conduct their fieldwork in Indigenous communities. More generally, activist public historians have sought to "break down the walls that separate people from their past and that divide those who study the past from those who have lived it" (Green 2000: 1). For historian James Green, remembering is a "conscious political act" (2000: 10).

While these efforts are still being described as "radical" or "progressive," participatory approaches and power-sharing arrangements are becoming much more common within public history practice. In recent years, public and oral historians have been urged to "share authority" with their interview partners and source communities. Historian Michael Frisch originated the term in 1990 to describe the shared authority of the oral history interview between the expert authority of the researcher and experiential authority of the interviewee. Since then, this idea has evolved into a wider and more profound sharing of authority over the entire history-making process (High 2014). Learning with rather than simply about represents a fundamental shift in knowledge production, and breaks the disciplinary illusion of the omniscient historical narrator or curator (White 1973). Similar challenges can be found in other disciplines. In *Pedagogy of the Oppressed*, for example, Brazilian Paulo Friere criticized the way that educators assigned students a passive role as "docile learners." In its place, Friere advocated a dialogical process where students became "co-investigators" with their teachers. Trust, he argued, is established by "true dialogue" (2009 [1970]: 91). The current emphasis on story and storytelling in scholarly and public discourse is part of this wider political questioning.

The place and meaning of stories

"To tell a story," writes Alessandro Portelli, "is to take arms against the threat of time, to resist time or to harness it. The telling of a story preserves the teller from oblivion; a story builds the identity of the teller and the legacy he will leave in time to come" (1981: 162). We exchange stories all the time: stories of origin or departure, childhood stories, coming-out stories, war stories, stories of survival or struggle, birthing stories, and stories of the land or our neighborhoods. Local or tacit knowledge is "embodied in life experiences and reproduced in everyday behaviour and speech" (Cruikshank 2005: 9). Telling stories is one way to become visible, either as an individual or as a group. It is also a way to "claim or negotiate group membership and to demonstrate that we are in fact worthy members of those groups" (Linde 1993: 3). Story sharing is often tied to wider processes of community building and political advocacy, as its affective power is considerable in "an age that celebrates stories and storytelling" (Greenspan 2013: 44-45). More troubling, perhaps, personal testimony also functions as an authenticating device for outside activists, educators, and researchers who can appropriate the experiences of others. "Recontextualizing knowledge," Cruikshank notes, "is not and never has been a neutral activity" (1998: 69).

Storytelling as everyday practice is most closely associated with premodern, rural, or indigenous communities where oral culture remains strong and most visible to others. Cruikshank, who has spent much of her life working with Indigenous people in Canada's northern Yukon Territory, notes that researchers need to know the cultural context in which these stories emerge if we hope to understand their intended meaning. We not only have to understand what the story *says*, but also what it *does*. Reflecting back on the stories that her female interview partners shared with her, Cruikshank wrote: "I learned to follow the complex plots and to understand that when women told me stories they were actually using them to explain some aspect of their lives to me" (1990: 15). Gradually, she "came to see oral traditions not as 'evidence' about the past but as a window on ways the past is culturally constituted and discussed" (14).

Places are made meaningful in the act of remembering. All human communities "develop their own occasions, rituals, archives and practices of remembering" (Smith and Watson 2010: 25). In Ulster, for example, Irish folklorist Henry Glassie quickly realized that he was "dealing with tales that were alive and throbbing with importance" (1995 [1985]: 33). Contemporary storytellers continued to "fill a crucial role in their community. They preserve its wisdom, settle its disputes, create its entertainment, speak its culture. Without them, local people would have no way to discover themselves, and their community would lie vulnerable to rot creeping from beyond" (Glassie 1995: 63). Families, however, remain central to intergenerational transmission. Anthropologist Christine Walley, for example, recalled that for her family "every place, every building, every piece of ground in Southeast Chicago seemed to hold a meaning or story," and it was "through these stories that we came to be tied to this place across generations" (2013: 22). We are literally surrounded by stories.

Once anchored in locality, these place-based stories serve as important prompts to remembering. In his epic oral history of Harlan County, Kentucky, Alessandro Portelli wrote that "you feel the nearness of the beginnings. The stories go back to a pristine wilderness, the first migrations and settlements, the Revolution, yet this is a living memory, entrusted to generations of storytellers" (2010: 13). Recalling the scars left by the labor struggles of the 1920s and 1930s, one of his interviewees, Gurney Norman, observed that "every stretch of road is marked with blood. There isn't a curve that doesn't have a story, and that's why I like to drive these roads, is to have the stories return to my own thinking" (2010: 229). The subsequent erasure of these everyday sites of remembering thus serves to cut the ties that bind past and present, setting us adrift. For geographer Doreen Massey, the identity of places "is very much bound up with the histories which are told of them, how these histories are told, and which turns out to be dominant" (1995: 185).

Recorded life stories, by contrast, do not exist in "nature" but are the "synthetic product of social science – but no less precious for that" (Portelli 1997: 4). Among other things, life history interviews offer us "unique glimpses into the lived interior" of other people and of wider group subjectivities (Thomson 1998: 26). There is a growing realization that a story can tell us more than the "empirical data" contained therein (James 2000: 122). After spending a lifetime interviewing Holocaust survivors, Greenspan observed that though "stories matter," they are "fragments that always point beyond themselves" (2013: 44-45). Many have turned to narrative analysis to uncover the underlying logics of people's stories. In his path-breaking book, *Dona Maria's Story*, for example, historian Daniel James examined Peronist Argentina through the narrated life of a local labor and political activist in the meatpacking town of Berriso: "Dona Maria was narrating, telling me a story about her life, reconstructing her past in a selective way that would both legitimize it to me and make sense of it to herself" (2000: 122) For James, "we have to learn to read these stories and the symbols and logic embedded in them if we are to attend to their deeper meaning and do justice to the complexity found in the lives and historical experiences of those who recount them" (124).

There is sometimes a great deal of tension when personal stories are elicited within public spaces. Historian William Westerman (1998), for example, found that Central American refugees living in the United States in the 1980s soon realized that North Americans would not listen to their overtly political critique of United States foreign policy in the region. However, these same audiences proved much more receptive to first-person testimony. While storytelling can be an effective vehicle for advocating political change, listeners shape what can and cannot be said. Oral history interviews work much the same way. But as Alistair Thomson cautions, our memories become "risky and painful if they do not conform within the public norms or versions of the past. We compose our memories so that they will fit with what is publicly acceptable, or, if we have been excluded from general public acceptance, we seek out particular publics which affirm our identities and the way we want to remember our lives" (1998: 300).

The presumption that audiences can be emotionally moved to act and remember is the driving force behind the large testimony projects of the past quarter century. Over one hundred thousand Jewish survivors of the Holocaust have been interviewed, and their stories archived. Thousands more survivors of mass violence have given their testimony to truth and reconciliation commissions in countries around the world, starting with South Africa. Other large-scale projects have recorded war veterans, pioneer settlers, immigrants, indigenous people, workers, and LGBT communities. These efforts to preserve the stories of often marginalized people have been criticized by some, as relatively few have so far accessed this enormous volume of material. There are also growing concerns about the ability to preserve oral stories initially recorded on reel-to-reel, u-matic tape, analog audio cassettes, mini-cassettes, beta-max, VHS, and a wide variety of digital formats. Who is listening, and will these interviews still be there in the morning? The next section explores some of the ways in which oral and public historians are re-animating these stories through new digital and arts-based techniques.

Storytelling and public history

So what then is the place of storytelling and stories within public history scholarship and practice? This is not an easy question to answer with any finality. We operate within a fast-changing digital environment where people regularly share with others on popular social media sites, in blogs, or in tweets. Mobile media is also changing how we interact with our immediate environment. New digital tools and phone applications are inviting people to play with and contribute to history in new and creative ways. There is particular interest in maps as an analytical tool to explore place-based stories, or displacement itself. In fact, the digital map is now considered to be a navigational platform that guides us through the overwhelming amount of online data. The Museum of London's Streetmuseum phone application, for example, layers archival images over present-day streetscapes. Cleveland Historical, for its part, produces a GPS-enabled map showing points of interest in the city. Other projects have elicited stories using new digital tools such as Omeka, developed by the Center for History and New Media at George Mason University, to create online memory banks where people can upload photographs, audio or video clips, text documents, or other relevant information.

All of these changes have had a dramatic impact on how we collect, share, and interpret recorded life stories. A growing number of researchers now organize their interviews using database software, allowing us to interact with the audio–video material directly and to find connections between individual recordings and identify wider patterns (High et al. 2012; Jessee et al. 2010). Likewise, the rise of the walking interview has led us to rethink the oral history transcript, still the primary analytical and search tool in the field. At the research center that I co-direct, for example, we have developed a new geo-transcription methodology that plots walking interviews on Google Maps, pinning speech objects that then permit us to use Google Street View to see the places that people are referencing. The resulting multimedia transcript is geo-stamped as well as time-stamped. There are, of course, many other ways that new technologies are transforming how we curate public history.

The past decade has seen the proliferation of digital spoken word archives, making a diverse range of historically significant digitized and born-digital recordings widely accessible to a much wider audience than traditional archives. The Archives of Lesbian Oral Testimony, for example, is a new open access archive of complete audio and video recorded interviews, something that is still quite rare in the field (Chenier 2014). Another notable example is the Prisons Memory Archive (2004) in Northern Ireland, which interprets the histories of the Maze and Long Kesh prisons through online archived interviews with the wives and children of political prisoners and guards as well as cleaning staff and teachers. It is a powerful example of place-based storytelling, as interviewees were recorded as they walked through the ruins of the Maze as it was being demolished. The project's interactive platform contains 175 interviews organized into keyword categories, or the walking interviews can be watched in their entirety. The religious or political affiliations of those being interviewed are never identified, forcing visitors to the online archive to listen to differing points of view. It is this effort to sidestep political and religious binaries that animates the project. All sides were scarred by "The Troubles" in Northern Ireland.

Many other public history projects are going beyond community affirmation in an effort to bridge persistent social, political, and economic divides. A good example of this activist stance is Joey Plaster's award-winning "Polk Street: Lives in Transition" project in San Francisco. Interested in gentrification and neighborhood change in the Tenderloin district, Plaster conducted 70 interviews with LGBT youth, the homeless, and area business people and home owners. As there had been a great deal of tension, and some conflict between these groups, Plaster organized "listening parties" and mediated neighborhood dialogues in a sustained effort to build connections. The Polk Street project also produced a traveling multimedia exhibition and a radio documentary aired on National Public Radio, available on Plaster's website (2010). The project, which started local and then reached wider national audiences, shares stories for political and societal change.

As always, ethics is of vital concern. What are our responsibilities to source communities as well as to the individuals who share their stories with us? Some fundamental questions about the inherent goodness of open public access are being raised by researchers working in partnership with Indigenous communities. In recent years, Indigenous people's efforts to regain some control over the use of their history and heritage have extended to the creation of community-based archival databases. Several Australian online heritage projects in particular have explored ways of creating community digital repositories that respect indigenous management systems and cultural protocols. These include the Traditional Knowledge Revival Pathways project in Northern Queensland, the Ara Irititja project in South Australia and, most importantly perhaps, the Mukurtu project at Tennant Creek in the Northern Territory (Denison et al. 2012). The Mukurtu Archive, for example, allows Warumungu people to determine the terms of access to and distribution of their cultural materials. Everything in the archive is annotated and linked to a set of cultural protocols, agreed to collaboratively. Richard Ganhuway Garrawurra described these kinds of knowledge centers as "breathing places" that keep Aboriginal cultures strong "for our children" (Gibson 2009).

In December 2010, Kimberly Christen and her Indigenous collaborators developed Mukurtu, a freely adaptable and open source digital archive and content management tool aimed at the specific needs of Aboriginal peoples. The cultural protocols, or coding, are specific to the Indigenous community. Each community can therefore adapt the software to reflect its "own cultural protocols and dynamic intellectual property needs" (Christen 2012: 2873). For Christen, indigenous "systems of knowledge production, circulation, and access do not resonate with liberal notions of autonomous subjects acting to attain universal knowledge within a generic public domain of ideas; to the contrary, they stretch the definition of 'public' and how it can be imagined" (2011: 189). She proposes the notion of "reciprocal curation," where archived materials are co-annotated based on local and scholarly knowledge (2011: 193).

Until recently, oral historians have been poorly positioned to harness the power of place in our research (Anderson 2004). Generally, place has been treated in a "superficial, euclidian, manner – a frame for research rather than an active part" (Riley and Harvey 2007: 348). The proliferation of mobile devices and new mobile methodologies is changing that. Guy Debord and the French Situationists of the 1950s have been a point of particular inspiration, as has Michel de Certeau, whose conception of walking has been characterized as a form of urban emancipation that, at its best, opens up democratic possibilities (de Certeau 1984). One emerging public history practice that takes full advantage of this democratic possibility is the in situ memory-based audio walk.

A good place to start is the work of Toby Butler. An oral and public historian at the University of East London, Butler has published extensively on his evolving memory-scape practice (2007, 2008b). In the audio walk entitled Drifting (2005), for example, he playfully let the Thames River select who would be interviewed by building a skiff and floating it downriver. Whenever it touched shore, Butler interviewed someone he encountered nearby. The resulting online memoryscape thus explores people's changing relationship to the great river. He followed this up with Dockers (2005) and Ports of Call (2008b), which tapped already archived oral history interviews in the area. Particularly insightful is the article Butler co-authored with sound artist Graeme Miller, on Miller's own Linked audio walk that returned the voices of London residents to the site where they had been uprooted to make way for a highway (Butler and Miller 2005). It represents oral and public history at its very best.

Most audio walks, in my experience, explore the human consequences of displacement and sudden transformative change. This is certainly true of the two Montreal-area audio walks that I co-developed. In the first, A Flower in the River, we invited the public to walk with the city's Rwandan community as it commemorates the 1994 genocide (High 2013, 2014). Walkers follow the route taken by the community each April, from the busy downtown streets of the city to the memorial clock tower on the shores of the St. Lawrence River in the Old Port area. Walkers are accompanied by six members of the Rwandan community, who each shares part of their life story. In the background, layered beneath these individual stories, are the sounds of the community itself, recorded during the annual commemoration. The challenge we faced here was to re-ground global and transnational stories in the city, making the walk an in situ experience.

In the second audio walk, Canal (2013), walkers encounter the past and present of a single locality. The Lachine Canal area has undergone dramatic changes, as mills and factories were closed and then demolished or converted into high-end condominiums. The adjoining working-class neighborhoods were devastated by deindustrialization, losing half of their population between 1961 and 1991. Our audio walk and booklet aimed to make visible some of these absences and divides, contributing to a wider discussion about the politics of urban change. To that end, the audio walk comprises interviews with people holding sometimes dramatically different perspectives; stories can divide as well as unite. We therefore hear from long-time residents who oppose the wholesale condo-ization of the canal area, as well as from some of the gentrifiers themselves. Our commitment to multi-vocality extended to the language of the Canal audio walk itself. While walkers can opt for either English or French narration, the voices of our interviewees remain a mash-up of the two. The resulting audio walk therefore challenges both the French-only policies of the Quebec government and the segregated bilingualism of the federal government in Canada where you are supposed to live comfortably on your own side of the linguistic fence. Montreal is a global city, and we constantly bump up against other languages in our daily lives.

One might argue, then, that memory-based audio walks are by nature Brechtian, as participants are not so much immersed in another world as they are confronted by two worlds experienced at once. In an urban context especially, the surrounding environment impinges on our listening in a multitude of ways. Sounds of construction or automobile traffic compete with the voices whispering in our ears, as does the physical need to negotiate oncoming pedestrians, or cross busy streets. The notion of augmented reality fails to communicate the resulting temporal and spatial frictions. An audio walk is not so much an immersive experience as it is a liminal or dissonant one. A number of other oral and public history practices are similarly positioned. There is tremendous political possibility when past and present uncomfortably rub up against one another (High 2014).

Conclusion

So, in the final analysis, what would a Brechtian approach to public history look like? As in theater, I think it has a lot to do with the incorporation of participatory approaches into our practice and to be fully engaged with the world around us. In an era of multimedia authorship and collaborative practice, oral and public historians have developed a variety of ways to implicate their present-day audiences and to work with them in the history-making process. This essay began with the digital story of Leontine Uwababyeyi, which speaks of what she experienced during the 1994 genocide and how it has shaped her life ever since. Digital storytelling is now a worldwide phenomenon, and is rightly hailed as a "signature pedagogy" in the humanities and social sciences (Benmayor 2008). The place and meaning of stories can thus be understood as both a living "practice of everyday life" and as a "framework for understanding historical and contemporary issues" (Cruikshank 2005: 60).

I would like to conclude with the words of Canadian sociologist Robert Storey, who has worked closely with injured workers struggling within an economic system that has maimed them and a workers' compensation system that often demeans them. In the Injured Workers History Project, a community–university research alliance, he learned that the sharing of stories of hardship and hurt has built solidarity and broken down the isolation that the system fosters. But for there to be hope that things can change, injured workers also needed to be exposed to stories of successful struggles in the more distant past. For Storey, "[r]adical theory in this moment is a theory that highlights links between private troubles and public issues" (Storey 2015: 81). He reasoned: "If injured workers could conquer their fears in the past, then they could do the same in the present" (58). Now, more than ever, oral and public historians have an important role to play in re-contextualizing this knowledge – but to do so, we must first break the fourth wall that keeps us detached from the present day. Public history belongs to all of us.

CHAPTER TWELVE

Genealogy and Family History

TANYA EVANS

Family history has become one of the most widely practiced forms of public history over the last 30 years. It links the past to the present in powerful ways as producers of the phenomenally popular global television series *Who Do You Think You Are?* have revealed. This program, of course, is a work of public and family history. A range of academic historians working in public history share my fascination with the recent growth of genealogy across the world. However, many also choose studiously to ignore its popularity. It is scholars in other disciplines, especially sociology, human and cultural geography, as well as information studies, who have dominated scholarly discussion on its practice and meanings (see Basu 2007; Kramer 2011; Nash 2002, 2015; Yakel 2004; and De Groot 2015). Over the last five years, I have written about the politics of family history in Australia on the basis of my research and interviews with family historians. My work is now focused on understanding the varied ways in which family history is practiced in different countries and what impact this has had on the development of historical consciousness around the world.

The growth of family history

Family historians were once sidelined by libraries and archives, but are now one of their largest client groups. At a workshop on family history held at Macquarie University, Sydney, in September 2014, Anne-Marie Swirtlich, director general of the National Library of Australia (NLA) told the audience that family historians are now a "significant user group of the National Library, representing 25% of visitors to the reading rooms and 12% of reference queries received." The NLA, like libraries and archives around the world, are providing a new suite of services for family historians. The growth of family history from the 1970s has revolutionized access to historical sources within archival institutions and on the Internet. When I started my career as an historian in late 1990s England, researching at the London Metropolitan Archives and The National Archives at Kew, I was intrigued by the ways in which academic and family historians were categorized

A Companion to Public History, First Edition. Edited by David Dean.
© 2018 John Wiley & Sons Ltd. Published 2018 by John Wiley & Sons Ltd.

as different, our needs and requirements dichotomized by the cultural institutions within which we worked on many of the same sources and where we shared space. When I moved to Australia from London in October 2008, I learned that family history was especially popular among individuals coming to terms with their convict pasts (Spurway 1989). Family history in Australia, and elsewhere, has become one of the strongest cultural industries over the past 30 years, but we have much to learn about the practice in different contexts.

Family history has captured people's imaginations at different times, in different nations. Before the twentieth century, historians have revealed how it was a practice largely associated with social aspiration. The Genealogical and Historical Society of Britain was established in 1850 and the British Society of Genealogists followed in 1911. Migrants who made their homes throughout the British Empire were among the keenest genealogists, congregating in formal societies as they settled in foreign lands (Kenneally 2014). In Australia, they established the Society of Australian Genealogists in 1938, the same year of the sesquicentenary of white settlement. Elsewhere in the Antipodes, the New Zealand Society of Genealogists came in 1967. In other settler nations, the Genealogical Society of South Africa was founded in 1964. In Canada, there remains no overarching national body of genealogists, but provincial and local organizations have flourished. The Ontario Genealogical Society was founded in 1961, while others followed in the wake of the Centennial of Confederation in 1967, such as the British Columbia Genealogical Society, which was founded in 1971.

In the United States, the Latter Day Saints' Genealogical Bureau was formed in 1888, and the first US national body, the National Genealogical Society, came together in 1903 (Little 2010). François Weil (2013) has charted the ways in which genealogy began as a "private quest for pedigree" among status-seeking settlers in colonial America until the late eighteenth century, becoming increasingly egalitarian and more widely practiced among the middle class and free African Americans from the antebellum era. From the 1860s to the mid-twentieth century, genealogy became an exclusionary practice infused by eugenic concerns and anxieties around race. In the mid-twentieth century, it was profoundly affected by the civil rights movement and multiculturalism, which broadened its practice among all social groups in many nations (Weil 2013).

The practice of family history underwent enormous growth and democratization across the world from the 1970s and became a global phenomenon following the publication of Alex Haley's *Roots: The Saga of an American Family* in the United States (1976). This reached hundreds of millions of people across the world in both book and television series format (De Groot 2009; Weil 2013). Its global success led to the establishment of the African American Family History Association in 1977.

Grassroots, local family history organizations were encouraged to join together nationally, and the United Kingdom–based Federation of Family History Societies provided an umbrella organization in 1974. There are now 180 societies linked to it around the world (De Groot 2015). Its Australian parallel followed four years later in 1978 (Federation of Family History Societies n.d.). These organizations, mainly run by volunteers, have all helped to develop an interest in both local and social history, but many members fret about their aging membership and how best to incorporate young people in order to guarantee their survival.

The Americans, Australians, and Canadians and their Pasts national surveys that gathered data on popular uses of the past have revealed the particular popularity of family history in white settler immigrant nations. Each survey revealed that the personal and familial remain people's "principal focus for connection with the past" (Ashton and Hamilton 2010: 135; Conrad et al. 2013; Rosenzweig and Thelan 1998). Many individuals began their family history as nations publicly celebrated key nation-making dates. In Australia, genealogy really took off as the country moved toward the bicentenary of white settlement in 1988. In Canada, genealogists were encouraged to begin their research by the Centennial of Confederation in 1967, which was "a seminal moment that encouraged various initiatives in community history that led seamlessly to an interest in family" (Muise 2011). There is clearly a link between national celebrations and intimate lives that deserves further research. The *Canadians and Their Pasts* survey revealed that 1 in 5 of the 3000 respondents had undertaken family history in some form in the past 12 months. The practice of family history differed for individuals of different ethnic and cultural groups but was particularly significant for immigrants (Conrad et al. 2013). In Canada, sociologist Ron Lambert's 1990s research based on a paper survey of 1348 members of a Canadian genealogical society revealed that family historians were motivated to begin research at particular moments in the life cycle. Muise (2011) continued Lambert's extensive national survey on genealogical communities in Canada, which involved large-scale surveys of genealogists. These have revealed that there are many more people practicing this vernacular community history than is often realized. Muise's respondents told him that family history was so important to them because it helped construct a sense of community belonging.

The impact of television on family history

This steady growth in family history at the local, national, and international levels preceded the transmission of the enormously popular television series *Who Do You Think You Are?* in the United Kingdom in 2004, but there is no doubt that the program, now broadcast globally, has encouraged many more individuals to research their family's history across the globe and to engage with the practice. The television program, a plethora of digital sources, and the increasing popularity of family history have had a significant impact on the services of archival offices and libraries across the world in recent years. Until recently, production companies based in different nations produced the programs locally, and versions have been broadcast in Britain, Australia, Canada, the Czech Republic, Denmark, Finland, France, Germany, Ireland, Israel, Norway, the Netherlands, Poland, Portugal, Russia, South Africa, Sweden, and the United States. Warner Brothers recently bought the worldwide rights to the program, and it remains to be seen how it alters as a result.

Following the first broadcast of *Who Do You Think You Are?* the numbers of visitors in some libraries and archives around the world increased, relevant websites were visited far more frequently than before, and there were more e-mailed requests for help. In early 2008, the Society of Australian Genealogists welcomed 77% more new members than for the same period in 2007. Many were family historians who had started family trees but abandoned them when the task became too complicated or tiresome. They now returned to their family trees re-energized by the program and embracing the possibilities promised by the technological revolution and enhanced software. The demand for Web-based services has been identified as the most significant impact of the program (Evans 2011, 2015; Yeats 2008). As Richard Evans suggests, this popular demand for archives and libraries to provide better services to family historians, and the associated need for increased state funding, have the potential "to make a significant contribution to the revival of public history in Australia" (2008: 82.1). Graeme Davison has also argued that the digitization of many historical sources has enabled more family historians to become active researchers, but he remains concerned (as many of us do) about the marketization of this process by companies like Ancestry.com (Davison 2009). For decades family historians have volunteered their labor and services for free, transcribing historical material to aid family historians in their research. Many are now horrified to discover that companies like Ancestry have the rights to this data, resulting from their labor, and charge genealogists to access it. As De Groot (2015) suggests, we need to think about the impact of Ancestry.com replacing the state as the gatekeeper to many researchers' historical knowledge. Has information about the past become a commodity in our neo-liberal age?

Motivations

We still have much more to learn about the motivations and output of family historians as well as the impact of the digitization of historical sources. The NLA survey that I opened this chapter with reveals that family history researchers are looking for much more than "who" they are; they also seek the answers to "what" and "why" questions and to understand more about the historical contexts of their ancestors. The NLA's research reveals that family historians are looking for historical understanding as well as knowledge.

By contrast, many family historians have been dismissed as "misty-eyed and syrupy" by professional and academic historians, and their findings and practices deemed irrelevant to the wider historical community (Keneally 2014). Some people have categorized genealogists as conservative, with a big and a small "c," for their supposedly nostalgic search for a golden age of the family. Noeline Kyle argues that genealogy provides families with a sense of identity in a period when many of them are undergoing transformation and disruption: it "was once a quest for social status and recognition, but in the 1990s [and beyond], as its base has broadened, it has become a search for identity" (1998: 81). Others have suggested that they search for their family trees to find "something solid in a shifting world" (Davison 2004: 83). Family history research therefore satisfies a need to search for roots in a postmodern and uncertain age. British historian Jerome De Groot suggests that "the increasing desire to delve into origins possibly betrays a contemporary anxiety about social atomisation and the fracturing of family structures." It is often a conservative reaction to change, and he argues that family history provides practitioners with a sense of security and identity, an "insight into self-hood" (2009: 79). Others have argued that the recording of the births, deaths, and marriages of ancestors provides individuals with "narrative machinery" (Brennan 2000: 48). For some, it is a means of providing a scaffold for the past, creating sturdy or precarious foundations for present circumstances and lives; people are now told that they need to understand their pasts in order to look forward to the future. Historical research conducted by individuals, often with little training, provides some practitioners with a sense of identity and enables them to historicize their understandings of the present. One practitioner explains her passion as follows: "In exploring our family tree we immerse ourselves in history and in the process we transform it and make it personal. This is *our* history ... part of *our* identity" (Docker 2001: 21; emphasis mine). Research has revealed how family history can have a powerful transformative impact on researchers.

Family historians as new social historians

I have argued elsewhere that family historians can be both new social historians and the protectors of privilege and prestige. In nineteenth-century Australia, elite settler families searched for and referred to British aristocratic lineage when making claim to new social positions in the colony. Members of these pioneer families self-consciously left historical evidence – print, pictorial, and material – in order to cement their legacies and their cultural and political power. Cultural repositories, museums, and galleries reinforced the process. At the turn of the twentieth century, descendants of early colonial elite families helped establish the Royal Australian Historical Society to make their mark on Australian history and the nation's memory (Doyle 2001; Evans 2015). Settlers in other nations made similar claims using the same methods, as Weil (2013) has demonstrated for the United States and others for elsewhere (see Martinez 2008 and Szonyi 2002).

By contrast, many family historians, working since the 1970s and researching their poor white and mixed racial ancestry, are determined to reveal the histories of society's marginalized, of the "ordinary" people in their past (Bashforth n.d.). Australian historian and archaeologist Nick Brodie tells us in his recent book that the "heroes and heroines of this story are everyday folk who helped people a continent and generate a nation. They are my kin, and I share their stories because their joys and struggles echo millions of others that have been forgotten" (2015: ix). As the British National Archives guide to genealogy expresses it, "Family history allows you to bring your ancestors back to life; by telling their stories you are giving a voice to Britain's forgotten sections of society" (Barratt 2004: xi). Family historians working on their poor white ancestors often style themselves as new social historians, the vanguard of the "history from below" movement, determined to reveal the histories of society's marginalized. De Groot (2015) enjoys watching this process of enfranchisement play out, but also frets about the conservative political implications of family history.

The legacies of the post-1970s expansion of mass higher education, the emergence of the new cultural and social history, and the democratization of history has left us knowing much more about the lives of black, mixed-race, poor, and traumatized men and women, who were often previously neglected by the historical record. Public history has been vital to the creation of this knowledge. It has also changed the way in which history is both produced and consumed. We can see how group lives, linked by historical experience, are the cornerstone of numerous public history projects like Find & Connect (2015), and how the digitization of sources has aided their construction. Family historians have been crucial to their success. Such projects have created a space for the articulation and representation of the life stories of traumatized individuals and helped them to trace their families. Public recognition of the suffering of the Stolen Generations, Forgotten Australians, returned soldiers, victims of forced adoptions or sexual abuse, and other troubled social groups, has focused on their neglect in the historical record. These projects show how knowledge of these people's histories is vital in acknowledging their suffering in the past and providing the possibility of reconciliation in the present. These forms of public family history, funded by the state, have important agendas of recognition and inclusion (Swain et al. 2012). This is the flip side to the conservative consequences of family history so often evoked by critics.

The Amateur/Professional divide

Recently, scholars, and public historians in particular, have troubled assumptions about family historians and the demarcation between academics and "amateur" family historians. There has long existed a tension between meanings of professionalism and amateurism in our understanding of family history and genealogy. There is much confusion about these terms, which is not helped by people who use them interchangeably (Foster 2014; Yakel 2004). Scholars have suggested that genealogists and professional historians parted ways in the late nineteenth century as the professionalization of the discipline of history took shape in the universities and was marked by the acquisition of academic degrees. The Royal Historical Society in England was founded in 1862, the English Historical Association in 1906, the American Historical Association in 1884, the Canadian Historical Association in 1922, and the Australian Historical Association coming much later in 1973. These organizations required members to possess university degrees to gain admission, and "amateur" family historians were shunned from their hallowed halls in the process (Weil 2013).

Many of us who work in the field of family history are familiar with the way that family historians continue to be derided, although academic disdain for genealogists remains hard to document because it is usually articulated orally and rarely in writing. Academics have been quick to distance themselves from genealogists in their desire to set themselves apart from and above those "amateur" family historians; from those who supposedly "wallow in self-indulgent nostalgia" (Bashforth n.d.). Australian historian Victoria Haskins has written thoughtfully about her engagement with family history on behalf of her grandmother in the late 1990s, as she took a break from a PhD, on the relationship between white Australian and Aboriginal women: "At the time, I viewed family history with a serious cringe factor, and felt that this despised pursuit was appropriate to my general uselessness as a 'real historian'" (Haskins 1998: 15). Professional historians who practiced family history used to do so on the sly, rarely drawing attention to their work. There were, however, always exceptions and in Australia these included Grace Karskens, Victoria Haskins, Maria Nugent, Babette Smith, Carol Liston, Perry McIntyre, Lucy Frost, and Cassandra Pybus (Evans 2011).

A recent trend troubling the boundary between academic and family history in America, England, and Australia is the flurry of historians publishing work based around their own family histories. This seems set to continue for some years yet. As De Groot (2015) suggests, family history troubles the binary between amateur and professional and is therefore something that public historians need to engage with.

In England, Alison Light's *Common People: The History of an English Family* was published in October 2014. It is a living, breathing history of how the Industrial Revolution made its impact on English lives. Light reveals her immensely evocative family history in four sections, which begin with each of her grandparents' stories. What follows is a "history of being paupers" that her grandmother never told. We read how her forebears coped, or did not, with fortune, fate, disease, and accidents, and how they never escaped the poverty that framed their lives. The book is her response to the death of her father and leads her to claim the workhouse as her ancestral home. Light allows us to make some sense of the intimate lives of the English poor over the past 200 years. Using family history, she successfully makes the micro, macro. In her notes, Light states that she hopes her book will "encourage others to write their family history as a public history" (2014: 255).

We can link her work on the migratory habits of nineteenth-century English families with that of historians working on their family histories elsewhere. Joseph Amato in the United States has traced seven generations of his family from Sicily, Prussia, Acadia, England, Ireland, New England, and the Midwest of the United States to reveal a broader history of America's poor, and its movement from farm and village to town and city in *Jacob's Well: A Case for Rethinking Family History* (2008). In Australia, Penny Russell (2014) is currently researching her Congregationalist family who migrated from the East End of London to Sydney. This trend is less developed among historians in Canada, but here labor historians have often relied on genealogy to piece together the histories they write. Novelists have also been heavily reliant on the techniques of family history for their own research (Caron 2006; Hodgins 1998; Munroe 1991, 1995, 1999).

Many of the above historians' nineteenth-century ancestors seemed frequently on the move across the globe, trying to "better themselves." Most, of course, failed in that endeavor. As these examples show, and there are many others I could list (as Light (2014) states on her first page, "everyone does family history nowadays"), we should reap the evidence accumulated by these researchers to understand more about the global transformations within which these lives were located.

Some people, mainly the well-to-do, have been doing family history for centuries, but it is time for all of us to recognize the political significance and consequences of others reclaiming their past in these ways. As Amato states, "individuals can now give themselves a history" (2008: 234). Public historians should encourage amateurs and professionals alike to take up Light's rallying cry on behalf of family historians, and scholars also need to acknowledge the value of family historians' labor as well as their important contributions to historical knowledge and consciousness.

Gender and family history

There is a powerful relationship between feminism and family history, which builds on the genealogy of women's engagement with alternative modes of making history. Bonnie Smith (1998) and Mary Spongberg (2002) have shown the many ways in which women's diverse contributions to history have been marginalized by male (and later, female) academics since the early nineteenth century. Women have always made significant contributions to family and local history, often outside of the academy (Thirsk 1996). Women also came to dominate public history, in all its varied forms, as it emerged as a sub-discipline in the twentieth century (West 1999).

Both Spongberg and Smith have revealed the ways in which the professionalization of history in the nineteenth century and the "birth of the seminar," undertaken in the wake of Leopold Von Ranke, split the practice of history into scientific/professional and unscientific/unprofessional approaches. This split was gendered, as women were excluded from the academy and shunned from the seminar room. Spongberg (2002) has shown the diverse ways in which women wrote history for centuries before the emergence of the Women's Liberation Movement in the 1960s, when we normally date the arrival of women's history in the white Western world. Women's liberationists from the 1960s produced a plethora of historical work revealing the lost histories of women, both "ordinary" and "extraordinary." As Spongberg suggests, this work was presented as pioneering and the centuries of female contributions to scholarship including family history, practiced outside of the academy, was left largely ignored. It is important for current scholars to revalue this work and not to ignore the significance of historical research being undertaken outside of the academy at all times. Feminist historians in particular should embrace the "amateurish" and the "other" pursuits of often-female family historians and recognize its political significance.

Women's contribution to their family history has often been material, visual, and oral rather than textual (Evans 2012). The historical profession has been slow to value these contributions to broader historical consciousness and knowledge, and it is really only in the last ten years or so that cultural history has forged a space for the analysis of objects and the ways in which they can be used to make history. While male lines of descent have been prioritized in Western European family history, women challenged these by producing their family history using material culture including clothes, quilts, art, and jewelry. They used these to challenge and renegotiate their power relationships within families and their local communities. Patriarchs and matriarchs often nurtured women, especially those who never married, as historians within their family before the twentieth century (Weil 2013). Women used material culture to record their history, and it was a culture within which they predominated. Feminist art historians Rozsika Parker and Griselda Pollock (1981) urge us to revalue this form of women's labor and its products, and to recognize women's varied contributions to making history. Current research by younger scholars is continuing their project (Cramer 2017; Parker and Pollock 1981).

The work of pre-twentieth-century family historians was often also linked to their contributions to local historical scholarship as they established their homes and communities. This was especially the case for those women who moved to nurture families and settle properties in distant lands, far from the homes of their birth and large family support networks. Local knowledge gave women power and authority within their new communities and friends they might rely upon in times of need (Lovell 2005; Stabile 2004). It is for this reason that family history is particularly strong within migrant, settler nations like Australia, Canada, South Africa, and New Zealand.

Family history has always been understood as a gendered practice, a pursuit dominated by women of a certain age. The increasingly close relationship between military and family history has begun to trouble these assumptions, and men are becoming more prominent as family historians as they trace the military paths of their ancestors, aided by the digitization of military records (Stanley 2014; Thompson 2013). Technological transformation has also brought different demographics into the family history fold (Davison 2009). Rootsweb and Genealogy.com, together with the global behemoth of Ancestry.com, are among the world's most visited Internet sites. Researchers need to concentrate on what meaning is being made of the research being undertaken using these portals. When I began my research on family history, I hypothesized that research conducted in the 1970s and 1980s might have been focused on how a family's lives slotted into national narratives. However, I discovered that family historians have always used their research to try to "know themselves," to search for their personal identity. Family history has allowed people to craft stories about their past in order to understand their lives in the present. Those lives can be traced through complex networks around the world, which enable us to trouble national historical narratives using the details of myriad intimate lives to do so.

The political uses of family history

I have argued for the radical political potential of family history if public historians work on the history of the family collaboratively and with members of diverse communities. My research explores some of the ways in which family history can empower researchers and how different categories of researchers might cooperate. I have undertaken collaborative research with genealogical communities in Australia, including the Society of Australian Genealogists and descendants of clients of The Benevolent Society (Australia's oldest surviving charity established in 1813), to show the ways in which Australian history has been transformed by the contributions of family historians. I have argued that previously marginal histories of Aboriginal, mixed-race, and "illegitimate" families have been discovered by thousands of their descendants who reveal a deliberately forgotten history. Brought together with pioneer narratives and other stories about the colonial past, family history thus challenges our understanding of Australian history (Evans 2015).

I have not worked on my own family tree, but the techniques of family history are key to my historical method. It is well known that practitioners of public history celebrate history as "a social form of knowledge" (Kean 2004; Samuel 1994: 8). Many hope that historical projects based on collaborative endeavors using the labor of those both inside and outside the academy will create "shared authority" (Frisch 1990; Rosenzweig n.d.; Swain, Sheedy, and O'Neill 2012). Most public historians have been influenced by Alistair Thomson and Michael Frisch's work on shared authority, and many aim to integrate this method into their research, while also acknowledging its limits and the complex power relations involved (Adair, Filene, and Koloski 2011).

When I worked on The Benevolent Society project, I argued that there were significant personal, intellectual, and political reasons for collaborating with family historians. I hoped that we could do more than allow family historians to merely participate in it. I was determined that a new history of the organization should be different from histories written by former staff members of the charity, which are mostly uncritical and celebratory, and that it should be communally produced. I believed that it was vital to incorporate the life stories of lone mothers into a history of The Benevolent Society in its 200th year because they have remained one of the largest client groups of the charity since its establishment. They continue to be among the most disadvantaged members of Australian society. Including the biographies of lone mothers and their children in a broader history of the organization gives these women's lives legitimacy which they lacked during their lifetimes. I also hoped that the contributions of family historians would have political purpose. The past is connected with the present in this research to demonstrate the reasons for the continued poverty of lone mothers today and to make an argument for contemporary policy change.

Our project began with a call out to family historians via local and national media who had undertaken research using the charity's archives. The Benevolent Society requires written permission to access their archives at the Mitchell Library, State Library of New South Wales, and library staff informed me that the largest numbers of users of The Benevolent Society archive are family historians. It became clear that thousands of descendants of women who gave birth at the Benevolent Asylum during the nineteenth century have searched for their "illegitimate" ancestors. Their histories reveal the legacy of social inequality for women, non-whites, and the poor.

All of the family historians I have collaborated with have found their research satisfying on both an intellectual and an emotional level. It is understood as an ongoing process, and it has undoubtedly changed their lives. They do not want their research to end, and they are not seeking the truth about their family's history. They might be driven by an emotional engagement with the past, the desire to learn more about their family's past in order to learn more about their present selves, but that is not the only concern of their inquiries. Their knowledge about the past has a significant transformative impact on their present lives. Emotions do not blind family historians to structural issues or broader social contexts, and many (if not all) family historians embrace the challenging nature of their discoveries. Researchers need to better understand family historians as historical subjects, and how their research has changed their lives. Scholars need to ask: how do family historians engage with the self when reconstructing the life stories of their ancestors, and what impact has that had upon their lives?

Sociologist Anne Marie Kramer used Mass Observation data from the University of Sussex to survey the motivations of genealogists in England and argues for the ways in which family histories were used to map connectedness, kinship, and create a resource for "identity-work" and "belonging in time" (Kramer 2011). Roots tourism as explored by Paul Basu (2007) encourages the Scottish, Irish, and other diasporas to travel the world, undertaking family research. These practices enable family historians who visit sites of migration to better understand their place within the globe and the ways in which their identities might transcend national and racial boundaries. Cultural geographer Catherine Nash suggests that family history can be used to make claim to "pure" ethnic positions but also to trouble national identities and "exclusive models of national belonging" (2015: 133). This does not mean we must remain blind to the exclusionary practices of genealogy, especially at historical moments when anxieties about race and eugenics have been particularly powerful (see Martinez 2008; Weil 2013).

Many family historians have moved beyond the archive and online resources to learn about their family history from other sources. DNA is allowing new connections, between people and space, to be made by researchers across the world. The company 23andMe allows individuals to bring their "ancestry to life through their DNA" and to "find relatives across continents or the street." In exchange for a sample of their saliva and US$99, customers are provided with details about their family history as well as their genetic makeup. Individuals are increasingly turning to science to "prove" their family history, and Ancestry.com is now cashing in on this market along with a host of other companies offering DNA searches. We might suggest that this turn to science has bulldozed over any claims that history might make to this production of knowledge, but Kenneally's research reveals that genetics is "not as determinative as we feared" and that cultural history continues to shape individuals more than we might assume (2014: 314).

Conclusion

An examination of the exponential growth and impact of family history around the world reveals the democratic possibilities of public history, the different constituencies involved with historical production and consumption, and the complex ways in which all of us make meaning of the past through our own family story. It is important for public historians and historians of the family to engage with family historians by disseminating their research and knowledge, and to collaborate with them on a variety of local, national, and transnational projects. Different historical constituencies, professional and amateur alike, have much to learn from each other, and we need to value our different contributions. Academic, public, and family historians need to be comfortable with uncertainty and ambiguity; but the further work we do together, the greater the potential to learn more about our subjects. Our knowledge, however, always remains provisional, conflicted, and in a constant state of flux. De Groot suggests that genealogy can be argued to be "a mournful and doomed attempt at constructing meaning …. Yet it is also something that is happening despite theory, and needs to be further understood before it can be coherently critiqued" (2015: 126). Researchers should heed his clarion cry.

CHAPTER THIRTEEN

The Power of Things: Agency and Potentiality in the Work of Historical Artifacts

SANDRA H. DUDLEY

MADAM – the artificer having never before mett with a drowned Watch, like an ignorant physician has been soe long about the cure that he hath made me very unquiet that your commands should be soe long deferred; however, I have sent your watch at last and envie the felicity of it, that it should be soe near your side, and soe often enjoy your Eye, and be consulted by you how your Time shall passe while you employ your hand in your excellent works. But have a care of it, for I put such a Spell into it that every Beating of the Ballance will tell you 'tis the pulse of my Heart which labours as much to serve you and more Trewly than the watch; for the watch I believe will sometimes lie, and sometimes be idle and unwilling to goe, having received so much injury by being drenched in that briny bath, that I dispair it should ever be a Trew Servant to you more. But as for me (unless you drown me too in my Teares) you may be confident that I shall never cease to be, Your most affectionate, humble servant,

"CHR. WREN."
(*Quennell and Quennell* 1920: 101–102)

With this delightful, undated, note to his future wife, Faith Coghill, Christopher Wren (1632–1723) returns the watch that she had asked him to have repaired after she had dropped it in some water. Wren is, of course, taking the opportunity to write a love letter to Faith, and gently to rib her a little too, perhaps, for having "drowned" and "drenched" the watch in the first place. In the process, he attributes characteristics to the watch that seem to personify it. He resents it for the physical closeness it will have to Faith and for the reliance she will place on it. Indeed, he writes of it as he might write of a true rival for her heart, not only expressing envy but also pointing out its faults: it will not be as true, as constant, as ardent, and committed as he (though, he adds, showing a kind of empathy and solidarity with the watch too, this is actually Faith's fault and he hopes she will not cause this to happen to – will not drown – him as well). What is more, Wren says there is something of *him* now intrinsically connected with the watch: its ticking is magically

A Companion to Public History, First Edition. Edited by David Dean.
© 2018 John Wiley & Sons Ltd. Published 2018 by John Wiley & Sons Ltd.

coupled with the pulsing of his heart. So although he distinguishes himself from and envies the repaired watch, in sending it back to Faith he also sends with it something of himself.

In his loving, softly teasing, message, the great seventeenth-century architect beauti-fully brings to the fore many of the issues with which this chapter is concerned. His letter provokes questions, long-established in social and cultural anthropology, about the role and value of objects in social relationships and especially in gift exchange (which I do not touch upon here); but more than this, it stirs reflection on the *active* nature of an object's role and effects and their connections to and impacts upon persons. That is to say, the watch is not simply an item of exchange that represents aspects of, or a particular moment in, the relationship between Faith and Christopher, and, more generally, watches used by women of a certain social class in seventeenth-century England. In its life with Faith and Christopher, some of its properties – material and contextual – had particular, active effects upon each of the two people involved with it, and upon their relationship with each other. Moreover, if it were on display in a museum today, some of its properties may have effects upon those who encounter it. Building on this, this chapter is especially concerned with what kinds of object properties and effects may be entailed in our engagements with things. The chapter is thus primarily focused on particular, key ele-ments in the so-called material and ontological 'turns' in the humanities and social sci-ences, and their relevance to the broad field of museum studies. They are especially germane, as I reflect at the end of the chapter, to interpretive and exhibition-making practices. Exploring the analytical and practical implications for these practices is not, however, the purpose here. Instead, this chapter attempts to offer a considered approach to the possibilities of things.

Objects, subjects, things

In this chapter, I mostly use the terms "object" and "thing" interchangeably. They are, however, not always so employed. Writers in realms such as that of developmental psy-chology, for example, tend to use the term "object" alone in their discussions of the material things with which people deal, interact, and form attachments (Santos and Hood 2009). Yet for many in the humanities and social sciences, "object" is a problem-atic word. In the context of critical and literary studies, for instance, in a now classic paper Brown (2001) draws a careful distinction between "thing" and "object." In his words:

> As they circulate through our lives, we look *through* objects (to see what they disclose about history, society, nature, or culture – above all, what they disclose about *us*), but we only catch a glimpse of things. We look through objects because there are codes by which our interpretive attention makes them meaningful, because there is a discourse of objectivity that allows us to use them as facts. A *thing*, in contrast, can hardly function as a window. We begin to confront the thingness of objects when they stop working for us: when the drill breaks, when the car stalls, when the windows get filthy, when their flow within the circuits of production and distribution, consumption and exhibition, has been arrested, however momentarily.
>
> (Brown 2001: 4, emphases original).

As Brown goes on to explain, for him "thing" and "object" essentially connote different sorts of relationships between persons and the thing/object in question.

Brown's distinction between "thing" and "object" is one attempt to move away from, when appropriate, the perpetual passivity that seems to be indicated by the word "object," not least because of its grammatical associations: the object is something that is the *recipient* of an action; it is done to rather than doing. Associatedly, it implies the simultaneous existence of a "subject" – usually a human one. The trouble with a perspective in which objects are inert and submissive to subjects, however, is that it tends to produce a restrictive anthropocentric view of both objects and the ways and worlds in which they operate. We see Faith's watch, for example, as just a watch, made up of its clock face, mechanism, and case: made by people, bought by Christopher and given to Faith, damaged by Faith, repaired at Christopher's behest, and then returned by him to her (Figure 13.1). We may imagine how the watch appeared to the human eyes that beheld it and how it felt in the different hands that cradled it. We are almost certainly interested too in such things as the materials from which it was made, the name of its maker, and the dates of its production and purchase by Wren. But we are much less likely, in this purview, to consider what might have happened *to* people or other objects when the watch crossed their path, to reflect on the *watch's* effects and what might be the active ramifications of changes in its form and action, or, even, to ask about the watch's point of view.

Various authors in different subject areas have sought to address how we approach, and even define, objects. Of late, there have been the stirrings of what we might term an ontological turn: a turn toward the objectness of objects and the nature of their existence,

Figure 13.1   Watch, Benjamin Hill (movement) c. 1650–1660. London. Victoria and Albert Museum.

and, in some cases at least, away from meaning and the construction of knowledge. Thus, in a particularly influential book, for example, Olsen (2010), an archaeologist, calls for a greater attention to the thingliness of things (especially the things we take for granted and do not even notice most of the time) and for less concern with social meanings. In contemporary continental philosophy, meanwhile, some of the materialist writers participant in the so-called "speculative turn" (Bryant, Srnicek, and Harman 2011), particularly those known as object-oriented ontologists or object-oriented metaphysicists, have taken a distinct approach to de-anthropocentrizing analyses of the material world. These authors vary in their individual perspectives, but in general they maintain that *all* worldly occupants – people, animals, houses, rocks, trees, cars, light bulbs, grains of sand, watches – should be treated as "objects," although different kinds of objects have different qualities. Moreover, they insist on the material and individual existence of these objects – which Harman defines as "unified entities with specific qualities that are autonomous from us and from each other" (2011: 22) – contrary to most philosophical traditions that have sought to abandon the notion (and problem) of objects. Harman sets out a useful summary of the ways in which this purging of objects has been attempted, including, for instance, arguing that an object is "*nothing more than*" what humans think it to be, or the sum of its effects,[1] or a fleeting manifestation of a continual trajectory of becoming,[2] or its gathered qualities[3] (Harman 2011: 22–23, emphasis original). Indeed, while I do not have space to discuss them here, these kinds of efforts to reduce or ignore objects *qua objects* populate university library shelves throughout the humanities and social sciences, and not only in philosophy. They also, as we will see, go well beyond mere matters of terminology. First, however, it is necessary to consider some of the ways in which the effects of objects have been considered.

Object agency

In recent years, some varying positions have been taken on the capacity of material things to bring about effects. In some areas of the debate, this capacity has been characterized as the "agency" of things. However, while the concept of agency is less problematic when applied to human subjects, it is considerably more contentious when applied to non-sentient objects. For some writers, it is an appropriate concept, at least if carefully defined so as to exclude intentionality (Dant 1999; Gell 1998; Gosden 2005). Thus, Gell, for example, allows that agents might be distinguished as either "primary" or "secondary," where the former are "intentional beings who are categorically" distinct "from 'mere' things or artefacts" and the latter, while they may be "secondary," are nonetheless agents (1998: 20).[4] To illustrate what he means by this, he uses the example of Pol Pot's army and the human destruction caused by their planting of land mines in Cambodia. From one perspective, the soldiers themselves are the agents: "they could have acted differently," while the mines, as Gell puts it, "*could not help* exploding once trodden on" (p. 20, emphasis original). And yet, as he argues, soldiers are not simply men: they are men with guns and mines – weapons that make men soldiers, and which, once fired or laid, enabled Pol Pot's soldiers to cause the terror that they did. The soldiers' "kind of agency," Gell writes, "would be unthinkable except in conjunction with the spatio-temporally extended capacity for violence" enabled by the mines (1998: 21). The mines, in Gell's terms, distributed the soldiers' personhoods (as other things do for you and I), enabling them to be at once in numerous locations and moments. So for Gell, things have agency, but ultimately it is the objectified social agency of their human maker or user: "I describe artefacts as 'social agents' not because I wish to promulgate a form of material-culture mysticism, but only in view of the fact that objectification in artefact-form is how social agency manifests and realizes itself, via the proliferation of fragments of 'intentional' agents in their secondary artefactual forms" (Gell 1998: 21).

Understanding this aspect of Gell's argument makes clear that his perspective does not attribute an inappropriate subjectivity to inert things. But his argument remains problematic and contentious for many, for a number of reasons that I do not have space to explore here.[5] One that is core to our present purposes, however, and to which I shall return, may be the very use of the word "agency" with reference to objects, however carefully the subsequent argument is drawn up. Meanwhile, the notion of agency (albeit defined in different and particular ways) is also core to other approaches. In actor-network theory, for example, all actants, be they human, animal, or object, have agency and effects, are embedded in relations, and can bring about transformations (e.g., Latour 2007; Law and Hassard 1999). In philosophy, in the variant forms of object-oriented ontology, all objects (human and nonhuman) are active and agentive (Bryant 2011; Harman 2002).

The notion that objects can be said to have some kind of agency is thus found in a range of academic approaches to the world. Nevertheless, for many the idea remains problematic, with agency properly attributable only to human subjects. Such critiques often come from a constructivist perspective in which the material world as we perceive it is in fact a creation of our contingent minds (Knell 2012). In this view, the conclusions that we draw as a result of our sensory engagement with the thing, the *representation* of the object that we create, is a construction formed from our piecing together of our percepts and influenced by our pre-existing knowledge and our own social, cultural, and historical situatedness. Importantly, that representation is not the object. Moreover, the sense data that contribute to it will differ when different properties of the object are, for whatever reason, predominant or hidden at the time of encounter, thus contributing to the construction of differing representations in different moments. I find it difficult to disagree with this constructivist approach, and while it is not universal, it is today the dominant view in museum studies and most humanities and social sciences.

But the creation of a contingent representation of an object that this constructivist approach emphasizes, is an *epistemological* process; it is concerned with seeking to know, and to characterize what we know about the object. Moreover, it is an approach that in its view of how we perceive and interpret objects is, in Bryant's terms, "epistemologically antirealist" (Bryant 2011: 23), because it implies that our representations of the world belong within the mental realm, are always socially, culturally, and historically contingent, and are not objectively accurate, uninterpreted representations of material reality. This seems fair enough. But – and it is a very big but – the epistemology of objects (how we *know* them) is not the same as their *ontology* (what they *are*). Most studies are legitimately and importantly preoccupied with the former – and with associated political and ethical questions of representation, power, accessibility, learning and so on – but occasionally they confuse ontological questions about objects with epistemological ones.

So, because Faith's and Christopher's mental representations of and associations with the watch are not the actual watch, for example, it does not follow either that the actual watch does not exist or that it has no effects on Faith and Christopher. Objects are not the things we come to know and represent: they are both more and different, as we do not access all their properties, and we interpret, in forming our representations, those properties that we do access: "all objects [including humans] translate one another,

[but] the objects that are translated are irreducible to their translations" (Bryant 2011: 18). Ontology equally cannot be reduced to epistemology: the latter tells us nothing about the being, identity, and effects of the existent object, but about the different (and also important) matter of how we form representations of things. This view is what Bryant terms ontological realism, and it is both a view that can coexist with epistemo- logical antirealism and one that I share. Constructivist approaches are invaluable in reminding us of the subjectivity with which, and the myriad influences upon which, and the ways in which we come to form, represent and communicate our perceptions, ideas, and arguments – how we see and understand the world, in other words. But this human- centric and skeptical focus can be augmented by, and certainly need not be in conflict with, an ontological one.[6] In the latter, we are interested not in how people come to know and interpret objects and the world, but in the existence and nature of objects and their effects upon one another (Bryant 2011) – what the world is. So while it may be true that different people interpret and respond to the world differently as a result of their cultural influences and experiences, and while we may argue that objects as people under- stand and represent them are not the same as their physical equivalents in the material world (matters of epistemology), unless we are to retreat into an entirely idealist position and argue that the material world does not physically exist, we still need an explanation both of what objects *are* and of the *material* (as well as social, cultural, and personal) effects that they can have (matters of ontology).

Put simply, I, other people, and my dog will all react differently to the large fir tree down the road from my house that one day suddenly appears not as its normal arboreal self but dressed up as the Gartree Giant (Figure 13.2); but none of our reactions would be what they were, were the tree/giant not so disguised – if the tree/giant did not have the material reality that it has. As Schwenger writes, "not only does our existence articu- late that of an object through the language of our perceptions, the object calls out that language from us, and with it our own sense of embodied experience" (2006: 3; see also Thrift 2008: 9). Faith must have felt great dismay when she dropped her watch, her lovely present from Christopher, in "its briny bath" and, on fishing it out, discovered that it would no longer run. The physical cessation of its mechanism by salt water was a material actuality that meant, of course, not only that she could no longer use the watch to tell the time but that she had spoiled something given as a token of love. This damage, and the fault or limitation the soaking brought to the watch, in turn impacted Christopher too. It not only caused Christopher to have the watch repaired, but also to produce the letter and to utilize the watch as a repository – agent, even, in Gell's use of the term – of his affection. One might argue at length, of course, that both Faith's and Christopher's ideas about the watch – of it as a watch in general, and of what it represents to them of each other and of their relationship – are socially, culturally, personally, and historically contingent constructions, and The Watch as it is represented in each of their minds is not the watch as it is as a physical, mute object. But – and this does not, I suggest, contradict such arguments; it is additional to them – the watch as a physical, mute object is neither without influence on the mental representations they form, nor without effect on subse- quent events and possible alterations in those representations. I will explore this – and why it is the watch, not just Faith in her clumsiness, that has effects – further below.

So in needing to account for the effects of material objects upon us, we can perhaps begin by agreeing with the speculative realists, among others, that we live in a world of objects, human and nonhuman, animate and inanimate, all of which can have effects. Moreover, I suggest that as a next step we accept that the attribution of agency, or even

Figure 13.2 The Gartree Giant, Burton Overy, Leicestershire. Photo: Angus Mackinnon.

active-ness, to objects is problematic. In part, this is because of the connotations of the terminology: most objects in the world are inanimate, and while they might be argued to have a form of *life* in a biographical, and in many cases also a social, sense (c.f. Appadurai 1986; Hoskins 1998; Kopytoff 1986), analytically they are not considered to have consciousness or intention, and as we have seen, for many consciousness and intention are necessary properties of agency.[7] In part too, there is the problem that agency as conceived in a Gellian formulation is still ultimately human agency, albeit distributed. Such a perspective remains anthropocentric and explains nothing about the influence of one inanimate object upon another in the absence of people's influence. Moreover, agency however constructed does not, it seems to me, allow sufficiently for temporality and historicity, or for uncertainty and unpredictability. Yes, landmines once laid may not cause death and injury until much later; but their *agency* in doing so – if that is how we choose to frame it – is already enacted, and there is a simple, unidirectional relation between the two events (laying and exploding). But what if one or more of the mines does not explode where it lies? Perhaps it never explodes at all and simply stays in the ground; perhaps it is picked up by a child and moved somewhere else, only to explode much later; perhaps it is not found for many decades, and is then defused and placed in a museum; or perhaps it simply lies there indefinitely, ultimately corroding, disintegrating, and polluting the earth … but in any of these events, does 'agency' in Gell's terms adequately explain the effects and periodicity of the mine? In my view, it does not – or at least, it does not do so without complex, additional qualifications and explanations (as we also found to be necessary in ensuring object 'agency' does not imply object intentionality).

How else, then, can we describe and analyze the qualities or characteristics of objects that produce certain effects and cause humans, animals, or inanimate things to respond in specific ways (for example, handled vessels filled with hot, caffeine-containing liquid produce quite different actions than do flat pieces of cloth)? Bryant writes of a "democracy of objects," in which people are not only "objects *among* the various types of objects that exist or populate the world" but in which each object has "their own specific powers and capacities" (2011: 20, emphasis original). In the human case, of course, these "powers and capacities" include consciousness and mind, and the formation of socially, culturally, and historically situated mental representations of other objects. This emphasis by Bryant and other object-oriented ontologists on the "powers and capacities" of the different objects within the world is important for its stress not only on what objects can do and on how they influence each other, but also for its prioritizing of the reality that objects *have* any effects at all. While it is true that in order for Faith's watch to have the function of a timepiece, it has been imbued with a set of social meanings which Faith and others have come to understand, it is also the case that without the watch's possession of a clock face and inner spring mechanism, both material properties of the object, it could not tell Faith the time. If, for example, its face were blank or its inside empty or rendered still by having been soaked in water, the effects of the watch would substantively change, as Faith unfortunately discovered. This apparently obvious point about the object's material properties and their effects has been surprisingly absent from much scholarship that pays attention to objects. Yet if, in our approaches to understanding and interpreting objects, we focus on their potencies and faculties, it becomes clear that things are far from passive. Moreover, if we approach everything in the world as an object, the distinction between objects and subjects fades away. That is, rather than taking a view in which (human) subjects act upon, perceive, and interpret objects, we instead see ourselves and everything else alike as objects with a range of properties, having effects and being affected as these objects variously and repeatedly engage with one another.

Object potentialities

Reflecting on Bryant's emphasis on objects' "powers and capacities" and on the effects of objects has led me to focus not on agency but on *potentiality* and *actuality* (Dudley 2014a). I will expand on this shortly, but first it is necessary to understand that potentialities and actualities, while not the same as, connect very closely with, the object's *properties* (c.f. Dudley 2012). "Properties" refer to all those characteristics (and their internal relations with each other) within the object (c.f. Merleau-Ponty 1962; Tilley 2004) that define the thing. These properties include both what might be called quantitative (for example height, weight, etc.) and qualitative (such as color, texture, shape, smell, sound) characteristics.[8] Moreover, properties not only define the object but also inform the sensory data that could be received and processed by a percipient. Most importantly, the sum of these properties encompasses not only those apparent in one, present moment but all those existent or potentially existent *throughout* the object's life, including during its creation, decay, and final destruction.

Drawing on an Aristotelian distinction, we can talk of an object's *potentialities* and *actualities*, where, simply put, a potentiality is a possibility in the object and an actuality is a result of that possibility being realized. For Aristotle, potentiality (*dunamis*) actually has two senses: the power of something to bring about a change or effect (e.g., the skill of the horologist), and what something has when it is the source of change in something else or itself (e.g., a pile of metal, glass, and other parts that together have the potentiality to become, once appropriately put together, a working watch).[9] Thus, the material transformation of a "drowned" watch into a functioning one, for example, actualizes the potentialities of both watchmaker and timepiece: the former's power to bring about a change, and the latter's capacity to tell the time (both of which are fully actualized in their successful coming together).

These sorts of changes are important aspects of objects' being (in an existential sense) and materiality. The metamorphosis of a lifeless collection of metal and glass into an effective watch originates in the materials' potentials to take on, together, another form, albeit through the skill of another. The potentiality of the horologist, however, lies in his skill to bring about effects upon or changes in *other* objects. Yet, this latter sense of potentiality is not, I suggest, restricted to humans alone. It also holds true when we reflect upon the properties of objects, including human beings, and their capacities to cause, precipitate, or stimulate particular responses or reactions in other objects. Object potentialities in that sense are only actualized, and the object properties concerned only externalized, when they do indeed bring about an effect of some kind which may, for example, be the production of sense data in the body of a human being and the associated mental construction of a representation of the object by the same human being (exemplified, perhaps, by Faith's undoubtedly strong attachment to her watch).

Alert readers may now be objecting that my claim that some of the object's potentialities are actualized in the perception of the object by a human being, conflicts with my earlier contention that how people come to know objects has nothing to do with what makes objects what they are. But there is no contradiction here. Talking of the "actualization" of certain object potentialities that produce a particular effect on another object – perhaps a person – is a way of describing what happens when the particular properties concerned are, even if only momentarily, in some way influential outside only the internal reality of the object itself. "Influential" might mean simply that a particular set of properties – say, largeness, grayness, wrinkliness, trumpeting, and the possession of a trunk – have been seen, heard, and haptically intuited by an observer; or it might also imply even greater effects, such as the coursing of adrenaline and its resultant biological consequences, and the eventual running away of the observer. The object's properties continue, however, to be interpreted by other objects: ontological realism does not deny epistemological non-realism. But neither is, or should, the opposite be true: the observer's constructed representations do not reflect the reality of the object. Yet, while Bryant is right to argue that there is often too much slippage between the questions of epistemology on the one hand and ontology on the other, in real, quotidian life outside the realm of philosophy, they are ultimately, hopelessly, entangled.

That capacity of objects to influence or act upon others, and to change or bring about change, then, I call *potentiality* rather than agency. Potentiality lacks any implications of intentionality or subjectivity (inadvertent or otherwise), and thus obviates the need for qualification (though we could describe intentionality, where it exists, as a particular potentiality in its own right). Potentiality describes object properties not yet or not presently actualized, and is thus something that is inherent to the object's being, whatever kind of object happens to be in question. Potentiality also conveys a very different sense than does agency of an object's capacities, implying multiple and indefinitely available possibilities still held in reserve for latent, perhaps as yet unknown, future use. Agency, on the other hand, in addition to its other problems suggests a more limited and more directed or specific set of powers.

Potentiality in public history and the museum

> Do curators ... perceive artefacts primarily as things of themselves, rather than as things beyond themselves? To put the question more generally, are artefacts regarded by curators as basic to the existence of museums, or is it the knowledge concerning artefacts which is basic, the artefacts being merely illustrative of that knowledge? (Gathercole 1989: 73)

In public history contexts, people are likely to come into contact with historic buildings and artifacts. Sometimes these places and things have little impact on visitors; sometimes their effects are very powerful even (or sometimes, especially) where things cannot be touched, picked up, or used, and even when nothing is known about their provenance or use. In part, this may be about a sense of authenticity. We know from recent scientific research, for example, how much more people value original objects over replicas, looking at them for longer and differently (Binnie 2013; see also Quian Quiroga, Dudley, and Binnie 2011). Yet, things can have potent effects even when their authenticity is unknown or unexplained.

The possibility of utilizing these kinds of potent influences of objects upon people, and the embodied and emotional responses they provoke, in educational activities and exhibition strategies has also been explored elsewhere (Golding 2010; Wehner and Sear 2010). If an object makes a significant impact on a visitor, this impact is in turn likely, for example, to render the visitor's subsequent response to contextual information empathic as well as cognitive, thus enabling a greater connection with, interest in, and later recollection of, its history. But, as I have previously argued, a powerful effect on a visitor of an object also has a value of its own: the very experience of being overwhelmed, delighted, or horrified by an artifact as a result of encountering its physical reality and without necessarily knowing anything whatsoever about it, is itself a powerful and occasionally life-changing event (c.f. Dudley 2012). It is in such moments that the object's potency lies primarily in its "power to fixate, rather than simply the capacity to edify or inform" (Clifford 1985: 244). How can we better understand and explain these effects, visceral and emotional reactions that are less about learning and the quality of interpretation and more about something powerful but harder to rationalize? Can the notion of potentiality help here? What does potentiality mean for our understanding of objects, of their effects on us, and of historicity and memory?

In the museum setting and elsewhere, then, visitors may sometimes, on viewing certain objects, have experiences powerful enough to stop them in their tracks. It is true that in the context of our daily life these kinds of encounters are, as Olsen phrases it, "the tip of the iceberg" compared to all the others wherein we notice things barely or not at all (2010: 74), but in public history or museum settings these unsettling, potent engagements with things need notice. For one thing, in such moments – and the powerful encounters in questions may indeed only last a moment – the viewer is aware of the discombobulating simultaneity of, in Brown's terms, the artifact's objecthood and thingness. Were I to have such an encounter with Faith's watch, for example, I would be aware of its objecthood as a watch but also of something about it – its thingness, its momentary refusal to obey the rules – that had caught me unawares, making me catch my breath as watches as objects do not usually do. But more than this, in that moment, however fleeting it may be, the object – the watch – appears fixed and particular. This is in notable contrast to the ways in which objects are characterized from a number of theoretical perspectives. Ingold, for example, develops a Heideggerian approach in which he sees an object as "a thing that has been thrown before the mind, in a form that can be apprehended. Life, however, is *in* the throwing and *in* the apprehension. It is the becoming of things perceived and ourselves as perceivers" (2010: 301, emphasis original). This processual, generative picture of the world does not seem to me, however, adequately to explain many of the encounters that occur between objects (considering people as objects too). Even if theoretically and/or actually material things are always in some state of flux, that is often not how they are encountered – and it seems essential that we recognize this if we want to understand the *experiences* of objects, be they watches, people, rivers, or cathedrals. So in any single interaction, in any one moment of awareness of something, an object appears to the other object engaging with it to have a certain set of properties, a certain essence, and certain effects, even if to a theorist it is actually mutable and processual. Moreover, how an object's properties appear to a particular percipient at any single moment is also dependent upon *which* of the object's properties are evident, or realized, at the time, because any object has more properties than are apparent and experienceable and/or utilizable in any specific instance.

Life-as-it-is-lived does not, then, entirely consist of continually flowing lines (to use Ingold's terminology), but does also have some stops and starts, moments of joy and amazement, instances of disorientation and disgust. Moreover, it is important to seek to understand not only the moments when we might be thrown off balance by something that catches us by surprise in a museum, but also how we look back on the past and the importance of objects to that process. It is not original to argue that objects carry the past forward into the present (c.f. Olsen 2010), but encounters with them, which potentialities are actualized in those encounters, and which memories are triggered, are, like all such engagements, transitory and fleeting. Moreover, after the encounters are over, if they and the objects concerned are remembered at all, they are remembered as fixed states and forms experienced only momentarily. Life, looked back on at least, is perhaps not so much in the throwing, as Ingold would have it, as in snatched moments (c.f. Ingold 2010: 301).

How then does this help us find ways to enable more people to have powerful and memorable experiences in public history settings? One interpretive approach may lie in helping visitors develop more empathic connections to the potentialities and actualities involved in historic objects and places and their narratives. For example, if we had Faith's watch to display, an objective of engaging visitors in the story of the love affair and the watch not only from Faith's and Christopher's points of view but *also* from the watch's perspective, would permit the revealing of the watch's as well as the couple's potentialities and effects. It would allow the viewer to grasp not only the effects of Christopher's action in giving Faith the watch and of Faith's subsequent clumsiness, but also of the watch as physical object with all its own potentialities. It is, for example, smooth and round, which means it has the possibility of being cupped in the palm and stroked in a certain way – a potentiality that is certainly actualized once it is given to Faith, partly because the shape, smoothness, and coolness of the watch make this pleasing to do, and partly because the pleasure is enhanced by it having been given by Christopher. Caressing the watch, for Faith, is a substitute for touching Christopher. The watch also has a working mechanism and clock face, which confer the potentiality of telling the time; again, often actualized in Faith's hands. And that working mechanism and its delicacy also have the possibility of going wrong – a potentiality that Faith discovers accidentally and which triggers not only Christopher's conveyance of the watch to a skilled horologist and the watch's subsequent repair, but also a charming love letter. Taking an interpretive stance such as that which emphasizes the importance of the object's, as well Faith's and Christopher's, perspective, potentiality, and efficacy, then, may reorient the stories we seek to offer to our audiences. It does not negate human effects, but it incorporates too the role played by the hitherto supposedly passive object.

But perhaps we need to be mindful too of the possibilities inherent in looking at artifacts even when one knows nothing about them (c.f. Dudley 2012, 2015). Even without or before knowing the story of Faith's watch, just gazing upon it could produce a powerful experience for some visitors – perhaps because of its watch-ness, or its worn smoothness, or its shape, or its serving as a reminder of another object (and possibly person), or for any other of a myriad of reasons. And even though sight is the only sense directly utilizable when the watch is displayed under glass, visually exploring details can allow the viewer to imagine what the object *feels* like, too: their haptic fancy, as it were, is tickled (c.f. Dudley 2014b: 306). Most importantly, the objects that normally appear so passive and quiet under gaze or glance alike, seem, in those moments when they stir, move, shock, or fascinate someone, to be gazing actively, even defiantly, back. In those transitory moments, the visitor is aware of the actualization of the object's potentiality to unsettle, discombobulate, and otherwise affect, and for a brief instant at least the artifact is no longer a torpid representation of something else, but *is itself*, provocative and unruly, refusing to submit quietly to the normal expectations of museum and visitor.

Faith's and Christopher's snatched moments are not just *represented* by Faith's watch; they are *in* Faith's watch. But such a historic artifact, like so many others, enables not only the telling of a powerful story from the past; it can also become part of the stories of those who gaze upon it today. As public historians and museum practitioners, we can enhance that possibility to the benefit of our visitors, whether we frame it in terms of potentiality, agency, or something else.

Notes

1 Harman's example in this instance is Latour's actor-network approach (e.g., Latour 2007).
2 Harman cites Bergson here. Currently influential in social anthropology, archaeology, and more broadly – including in museum and heritage studies – this approach is exemplified in the work of Tim Ingold (e.g., 2011).
3 The Scottish Enlightenment philosopher David Hume, as Harman points out, is the classic example of this approach.
4 Some writers have more recently sought to tease apart intentionality and agency in relation to some areas of human agency, too. So, for example, various authors in Harrison, Byrne, and Clarke 2013 are careful to distinguish where indigenous agency discernible in the formation of museum collections was intentional and where it was not.
5 For extended critical discussions of Gell's perspective, see, for example, Alves 2008, Bowden 2004, Layton 2003, and Morphy 2009.
6 I use "skeptical" in the philosophical sense, referring to this approach's Kantian implication that we can never know the world as it is, things as they are (c.f. Kant 2005 [1781]).
7 I use the word "analytically" here to make clear the context within and about which I am writing. This neither ignores nor negates particular worldviews which hold that objects, or certain objects at least, do have a form of consciousness and/or intention.

8   The division between quantitative and qualitative properties is form of separation that has a long history: John Locke described the former type as primary qualities (measurable, determinable with certainty, existent in the thing itself) and the latter as secondary qualities (properties of objects that result in particular sensations and effects in percipients) (Locke 1979 [1690]). Pye makes a similar division but articulates it differently, so that Locke's primary qualities are for him "properties" and the secondary qualities are "qualities" (2007 [1968]). He emphasizes that the former are "out there" whereas the latter are "in here: in our heads" (p. 47, emphasis original). I concur with Ingold, however, that this is a problematic distinction in its Cartesian "polarisation of mind and matter" (2011, p. 30). Ingold goes on to utilize the word "properties" rather than "qualities" in his own discussion, presumably to avoid the mentalist and subjectivist connotations of the latter term, and it is for this reason that I also prefer the former version.

9   My interpretation of actuality (*entelecheia* or *energeia*) as realized potentiality, however, arguably diverges from Aristotle, There is not space in this chapter to elaborate on either Aristotle's arguments or mine in relation to potentiality and actuality; suffice to say that his usage of actuality and explanation of how something moves from potentiality to actuality has been subject to considerable later debate (e.g., Coope 2009; Kosman 1969).

CHAPTER FOURTEEN

An Unfinished Story: Nation Building in Kyrgyzstan

Gulnara Ibraeva

In place of a preface

In the year 2000, 30 kilometers from Bishkek, in Chong Tash village, the Ata Beyit (Graveyard of the Fathers) memorial complex was officially opened (Figure 14.1). The complex, which occupies two hectares, initially consisted of a sculptural composition and museum in honor of the repressed of Stalin's Soviet Kirgiziya. The sculptural composition included the place where 138 persons shot during the repression were initially buried, and a memorial statue at the place they were reburied. The Ata Beyit museum displays documents and photographs on political developments in Kyrgyzstan in the 1920s and 1930s, and materials about those shot at Chong Tash.

The construction of the Ata Beyit memorial complex and the national historical monument did not end in 2000. An additional memorial complemented the sculptural composition with the tomb of the famous author Chingiz Aitmatov in 2008. This was followed by the tomb of the heroes of the April 2010 revolution and, finally, in 2016, another memorial complex, marking the centenary of the national liberation uprising of the Kyrgyz people against the colonial policy of the Russian Empire (Urkun[1]).

The architecture and design of all the sculptures at Ata Beyit have something in common. In essence, they are made from white-gray marble slabs in combination with stars of red granite, monumental figures hewn from stone and engravings, in the spirit of socialist realism. At the same time, they use ethnic and religious symbols: on the monolithic slab of marble at the site of the mass (re)burial of the repressed of 1938 there is a tunduk,[2] a modern national symbol; an arch in the Islamic architectural style and a granite wall listing the dead are at the center of the composition remembering the heroes of the April revolution; there is a white marble wall with an engraving of Aitmatov in basrelief and a bronze book on a granite pedestal at the burial site of the great writer; while three vertical arrows symbolizing uuks (sticks) from a yurt supporting a tunduk with

A Companion to Public History, First Edition. Edited by David Dean.

Figure 14.1 Monument to Soviet Repression (foreground) and Urkun Memorial (background), Ata Beyit National Memorial Complex, Chong Tash, Kyrgyztan. Photo: Nurlanov Ilgiz.

symmetrical bas-reliefs on both sides represent the Urkun victims. Each of the complexes has its own borders, and each one lies at its own level in the space.

As a result, Ata Beyit, initially conceived of as a museum to remember the victims of Stalin's repression, has taken on the status of a national historical memorial complex, dedicated to the history of the creation of Kyrgyz statehood.

A national tragedy?

"There are *lieux de mémoire*, sites of memory, because there are no longer *milieux de mémoire*, real environments of memory."

–Pierre Nora

In 2011, an article was published on the cogita.ru website by British political scientist Catherine Owen entitled "A Visit to Ata-Beyit: Dialogue with the Communist Past Closes in Kyrgyzstan." The author formulated the aim of her article as follows: "In this paper I take a trip to the Ata Beyit memorial complex and try to make sense of the history buried here, while at the same time making an attempt to critically analyse certain aspects of how the Kyrgyz nation and state are presented in one way or another by the memorial" (2011, n.p.)

One of the main theses of Owen's text is a critique of the authorities and society, who appear unable to "think critically about Soviet terror" and could not preserve the basic "meaning of the memorial": "reconciliation with the past." It was not by chance that the author gave such significance to thinking about the past, as she believes that

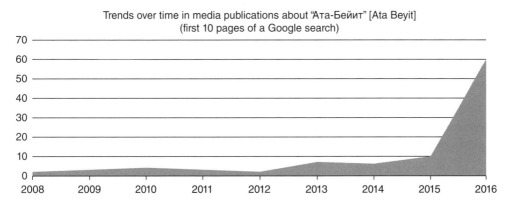

Figure 14.2   Trends over Time in Media Publications About Ata-Beyit (author generated).

democratization is an evolutionary and progressive process that is impossible in a post-totalitarian society "without critical engagement with the past." Owen adds that societies "which do not undergo this process are likely to reproduce the repressive tendencies of the old regime. In democratic societies the past – whatever it may be – is a living part of the present, whereas states which seek to ignore or modify their past are more likely to exhibit an increase in authoritarian ideologies" (2011, n.p.)

Attempting to answer the challenge of the British researcher motivated me to formulate my own burning questions: What is the role and place of Ata Beyit in the social consciousness and the development of Kyrgyzstan's society? How are the multiple transformations of the complex perceived in public opinion, especially among the country's academics and intellectuals? How has the initial meaning of the Ata Beyit complex been changed in its subsequent transformations?

A Google search reveals that until 2011 the number of even informational publications about the memorial was steady, and the number did not change significantly until 2016 (Figure 14.2).

However, even today public discourse is limited to dozens of event-related pieces of journalism about various activities that took place at the memorial, except for Regina Khelimskaya's documentary book *Secrets of Chong Tash* (1994) on the excavations and the opening of the memorial, and several historical biographical works about the history of Stalin's repression and the mass shooting at Chong Tash (Jakupova 1999; Kokaysl and Usmanov 2012). The theme of political repression and the repressive Soviet past has not been developed in the program statements and debates of political parties, nor of governing or opposition politicians. It is also not popular on social networks: individual posts considering past repression do not lead to broad discussions. The critical article by British researcher Owen (2011) received only one comment by a reader who wrote laconically: "A pity."

If you talk to most Kyrgyz, self-stereotypes are apparent: the Kyrgyz are a freedom-loving, rebellious, warlike people. At first glance, recent history appears to back up these self-characterizations: the Kyrgyz Republic is one of only two countries in the Commonwealth of Independent States to have lived through two revolutions in under two decades. Crowds are quite easily mobilized to protest against "harassment" by this or that official; to associate themselves in protest against other groups and communities, or against certain policies and governance practices; and to burst into revolutionary uprising.

But these masses are indifferent to the issues of the nation's past. This is even true of citizens who actively bestow upon themselves the title of "patriots" of the country, who are in favor of strengthening national traditions and culture. It is as if cultural memory is not included in the understanding of the nation's traditional culture.

A veil of silence also surrounds Ata Beyit in the national academic community. With a huge community of historians, political scientists, and sociologists, Kyrgyzstan was slow in the early 1990s to explore questions of political repression. There was also no surge of interest after the excavation and discovery of Ata Beyit stimulated real scientific discourse in this field, or at the times when the complex was given new meanings. In general, issues of political reprisals against prominent political and public figures of Soviet Kyrgyzstan have become a specialized field of only two researchers in the country since the turn of the millennium.[3] Thus, even 25 years after Kyrgyzstan gained its sovereignty, the history of political repression in the Soviet period remains sealed off from the academic community.

However, the veil of silence surrounding Stalin's (and Khrushchev's) repression is not unique when it comes to understanding Kyrgyz society's past. Kyrgyz intellectuals and academics are also silent about the 1916 revolt, the 1990 interethnic clashes, and other historical events.[4] Thus, the centenary of the *Urkun* Kyrgyz uprising in 1916 passed almost unnoticed in Kyrgyzstan. Historians and other social scientists held several conferences and seminars, where professionals argued and failed to reach a consensus on the number of victims of the *Urkun*[5] or about how to define the phenomenon itself.[6] However, the split did not take the form of widespread academic discussion, and officials from the presidential administration took preventive measures to control the agenda concerning the *Urkun*.[7] Thus, "a minefield of public deafness and dumbness"[8] and "civil inattention"[9] was formed around the *Urkun* centenary, as well as around the transformation of Ata Beyit.

In searching for the reasons for the public silence around Ata Beyit and other key events from the past of the country and people, a number of concepts are explored in this chapter: Yurchak's concept of "inside-outsideness," Ushakin's "spiral of silence" concept of aphasia, and Baudrillard's concept of the end of the silent majority.

In thinking about lack of interest in political issues among different social groups in the late socialist period, researcher Alexei Yurchak (2014) formulated the concept of "inside-outsideness" in relation to authoritative discourse. He distinguishes this state among late Soviet citizens from apolitical apathy, hypocrisy, and bigotry. "Inside-outsideness," according to Yurchak, is a "position that was at the same time inside and outside the rhetorical field of [reputable] discourse and did not constitute support for any government or opposition." Since the degree of interest in public policy in the Kyrgyz Republic periodically increases and involves large numbers of people, even extending to participation in revolutionary events, it is difficult to use the concept of inside-outsideness to explain the silence around the social reimagining of Ata Beyit.

The famous concept of the "spiral of silence" proposed by Elisabeth Noelle-Neumann (1996) explains silence as having a protective function: if a member of society feels that his or her views may lead to isolation from society, that person will refuse to speak about them. The premise of the "spiral of silence" mechanism is that "a person who has the strength not to lie but lacks the courage to tell the truth will stay silent" (42) Silence is presented in this case as a tragic weakness, a sign of spiritual failure, and damage to the fundamental human capacity for speech, subjectivity, and self-expression. In this context, the stereotypical language of the media replaces robust speech, while "chat" acts as a surrogate artificial replacement for missing, underdeveloped organs: mind, heart, and spirit. However, the level of "revelations and disclosures" and the information wars between politicians that take place in Kyrgyzstan's national press cannot be described as continuing fear and domination of a totalitarian consciousness. Some journalistic publications do critically reflect on the memorial as an object of memory. However, these publications have neither become a touchstone for broad public debate in search of truth and reconciliation with the past, nor have they given rise to political and administrative consequences. Therefore, to interpret the social silence in terms of a spiral of silence is entirely inadequate.

The explanatory concept proposed by Sergei Oushakine (2009), building on Roman Jakobson's (1990) concept of linguistic aphasia, posits that the creation of post-Soviet consciousness, with a characteristic culture of silence, is similar to the aphasia mechanism.[10] The reasons for silence, according to the author, are structural (not psychological): "the instability of the social system," lack of trust in the (de)formed social system, and "weak social identity." The aphasia mechanism is described by the author as follows: "In the resulting 'state of uncertainty' of the 1990s, one of the ways the new closedness manifested itself was as a condition of peculiar discursive paralysis. Fragmentation of a relatively uniform field of Soviet cultural production was not able to automatically erase the feeling of a symbolic community – both experience and language. Post-Soviet polyphonic style was largely unable to produce an effective nominal framework capable of not only identifying the existence of the gap, but also the nature of the relationship between Soviet and post-Soviet practices and identities" (Oushakine 2009: 23–24) It is proposed that the concept of aphasia may explain the mode of reproduction of the Soviet style in official post-Soviet festivals, and determine the language used to construct the media discourse around the events of 2005 and 2010 in Kyrgyzstan, that are called revolutions. Drawing parallels between the "discursive minimalism" of liminal groups in traditional societies on the one hand and silence in the context of changing social positions of groups on the other, Oushakine emphasizes the "normality" of silence – or discursive and subjective insufficiency – as a symptom of separation from the world of the past, a certain degree of suppression of habits formed in a previous stage of development.

The recent history of sovereign Kyrgyzstan, full of transitions and mimicry, is replete with examples of eclectic appeals to symbolism and the language of the historical past (both Soviet and pre-Soviet). Every new step begins with the unmasking of the previous one, the renunciation of yesterday's declarations, statutes, and subjectivity, and a search for new values. The resulting impotence leads to a cultural dead end and regression: the inability to find a new symbolic rationale to develop a democratic state led already under President Akaev, and to rationalize appeals by politicians to the "tribal democracy of the Kyrgyz," the heritage of epics, and the values of traditional society. The values of a secular state are giving way to the practice of an accelerating and totalitarian Islamization, only for the danger and alien nature of certain forms of Islam to be re-declared; celebration of the multicultural development of the country and a human rights-based society have been transformed into an assertion of the dominant rights of the titular ethnic group to "development" and "security." The reference point of national sovereignty has been replaced by a search for "big brother" patrons, but every so often the "brothers" turn out not to be "the right ones," and the search continues. In the context of social destabilization, intellectuals and politicians are unable to come to an adequate understanding of the changing cultural order, leading to a kind of discursive paralysis. Thus, the aphasia phenomenon can explain the lack of analysis and reflection in the Kyrgyz Republic about key historical events, including the story of Soviet political repression.

Social silence around Ata Beyit is seen in an even more radical way when applying the explanatory concepts of Jean Baudrillard (1983), who proclaimed "the end of the social and political" as "the only real problem of modernity," the symptoms of which are the "silence of the masses, the silence of the silent majority." The logic of the concept is that the subject of interpreting the past is gone:

> Withdrawn into their silence, [the masses] are no longer (a) subject (especially not to, or of, history), hence they can no longer be spoken for, articulated, represented, nor pass through the political 'mirror stage' and the cycle of imaginary identifications. They do not express themselves: they are surveyed. They do not reflect upon themselves, they are tested. The referendum (and the media are a constant referendum of directed questions and answers) has been substituted for the political referent." (Baudrillard 1983: 26–27)

Adopting Baudrillard's explanatory model gives rise to a series of arguments and counterarguments. On the one hand, the establishment of a memorial to political repression in the Soviet period at Ata Beyit while the monument to Dzerzhinsky in the center of Bishkek is well preserved, at the same time as a positive, nostalgic discourse is under way about the importance of Kyrgyzstan's Soviet past, runs parallel to questions about genocide of the Kyrgyz population in the pre-Soviet and early Soviet periods of history. This supports the idea that a historical subject is absent, and that historical reflection and evaluation of the masses is a statistical rather than a social category. On the other hand, it was fully specific will and subjectivity that led to the creation of Ata Beyit and to its transformation and the imparting to it of new meaning. Can one say that groups in power and individual politicians acted as subjects of will and only used the masses for manipulation? In order to determine the applicability of Baudrillard's concept, it is important to trace in detail the constructed memorial's subjects.

The subjects of the constructed memorial complex

The story of the disclosure of the secrets of the Chong Tash burial and the creation of its memorial has its own heroes. The key figure who spoke about the persecution and mass grave was Byubyura Kydyralieva, the daughter of a former guard at the Narodnyi Komissariat Vnutrennikh Del (NKVD) sanatorium in Chong Tash. Kydyralieva's father proved to be an unwitting witness to the shooting, and kept the terrible secret until his death. On his deathbed, he instructed his daughter to tell people about this tragedy at a time when speaking about it would not endanger her. Byubyura Kydyralieva waited another 50 years until a period of restructuring occurred and Kyrgyzstan became an independent state. In December 1990, she was able to meet KGB officer Bolot Abdrakhmanov and finally tell the story of Chong Tash (Baktybaev 2011).

KGB officers led by Colonel Bolot Abdrakhmanov conducted excavations at Chong Tash in the spring and summer of 1991, involving archaeologists and journalists. Over the next 16 years, the press periodically recounted the fate of the two key people without whom the memorial would not have been possible: Byubyura Kydyralieva and Bolot Abdrakhmanov. Both consider themselves unjustly wronged, forgotten by authorities who did not appreciate their contribution to the history of the people and the state.

In numerous media interviews, both point out that they not only discovered a mass grave, but also lifted the veil on the tragic "extermination" of the intellectual elite of Kyrgyz society. The ceremonial reburial of the remains of those executed took place on August 30, 1991 (Aitmatov 2013).

The Ata Beyit memorial complex to the victims of Stalin's repression was only opened at the initiative of the first president of the Kyrgyz Republic, Askar Akaev, in 2000, nine years after the remains of the repressed were reburied.[11] At the opening ceremony, President Akaev commented on the significance of the events: "Unlike others, we did not descend into nihilism with regard to history, both in the Soviet and the pre-Soviet periods of our history. We did not destroy monuments and did not try to erase people from our own history from memory for the sake of short-term political expediency. Historical amnesia is evil: the process of reassessing the past needs time, and should be done not by order from above, but by the people themselves." It is important to note that at the beginning of the 2000s, before even all the Baltic states had opened museums of the Soviet occupation, and when post-socialist countries had just started thinking about museums dedicated to totalitarianism and terror, the opening of a memorial to victims of the repression in the 1930s appeared bold and promising. But Akaev's promises to reevaluate history came to a dead end, frozen in the expectations of later events. One such event was the death of the famous author Chingiz Aitmatov in June 2008. The initiative to bury Aitmatov at Ata Beyit came from the second president of the Kyrgyz Republic, Kurmanbek Bakiev. The main argument offered was that his father Torokul Aitmatov, one of the first Communist Party Leaders in the Republic, was among the repressed shot in 1938 and buried in the cemetery. The writer's family did not particularly agree with the decision,[12] but none of the relatives or other persons contested the president's decision. The memorial complex at the writer's mausoleum was constructed five years later.

By that time, the Ata Beyit memorial complex had already been turned into a real cemetery. After the April revolution, at the initiative of the leaders of the Interim Government and in accordance with an Interim Government decree, 27 of the 87 people who died in the April events and received the status of Heroes of the Revolution were buried there. At the funeral ceremony, Almazbek Atambaev, in his role as Prime Minister of the Interim Government, imbued with pathos a new significance to the memorial as a place to remember those who gave their lives for the Kyrgyz state: "The 7th of April was a turning point in the history of Kyrgyzstan. And every year we begin to understand what a great deed it was. Our heroes knew they would die. They are like the 300 Spartans, who were protecting their state." The hurried decision to "museify the revolution" at the Ata Beyit memorial complex and the subsequent attempt to legally recognize the "April Heroes" as equal to the heroes of the Great Patriotic War and the Afghan War demonstrated the limitations to the authority of the Provisional Government, and their will to acquire the support of the masses.

Several public organizations and movements to defend the interests of the Heroes of the Revolution, including Aikol Ala-Too and Meken Sheytteri, actively lobbied for tangible and intangible benefits, and for perpetuation of the memory of living and dead members of the movement. For several years after the April 2010 events, Ata Beyit hosted symbolic meetings and self-identification of members of the organizations at memorial events. The graves of those buried at the "Aprillers" memorial have several times been the site of meetings with national political leaders and of reports about the long memory of the completed revolution. Thus, surviving Aprillers, and citizens expressing solidarity with them, have used the Ata Beyit space fairly effectively to reproduce their group identity and gain political dividends from the policy of remembering the fallen of 2010.

However, by the end of the sixth anniversary, Aikol Ala-Too and Meken Sheytteri, which originated as mass social movements and membership organizations, had noticeably lost their collective identities and the power to influence the country's political leadership. Internal organizational scandals and the diminution of resources due to further mobilization of members weakened the Aprillers and damaged their reputation. Even one of the main components of a collective memory – the desire to avenge victims – gradually lost its emotional power for the members of the groups: on hearing the criminal verdict on key figures in the legal case regarding the events of 2010, even the closest relatives of the dead from the White House stopped coming (Asinov 2016).

Who are our fathers?

From the beginning, the history of Ata Beyit was not completely transparent. On the contrary, it was full of mythologizations and forgeries, small and large falsehoods and omissions. Initially this related to the memorial to the victims of Stalin's repression. The first myth asserts that the "cream of the Kyrgyz intellingtsia" of the 1930s are buried at Ata Beyit. This has been said from the first days by Byubyura Kydyralieva, who told society about the burial, by officers of Kyrgyzstan's State Committee for National Security, and by journalists; however, based on the archive list of "repressed persons whose skeletal remains were discovered at Ata Beyit in June 1991" signed by V. P. Melnikov, the head of Kyrgyzstan's KGB, it can be seen that only 37 of the 137 identified dead were included, and only 24 of them were leading members of the party and Soviet bodies. Of those shot and buried, the place of work of 22 was recorded as "without defined employment," and for another two "no information" was given; 21 of the dead had the status of "worker" or "laborer," while another 18 were collective farm workers and ordinary workers on state farms.

The second myth is that Ata Beyit is the plaintive place of burial of those who can be called Fathers of the Nation – in other words, men. In fact, during excavations at the burial site in 1991, the remains of 138 persons were found (by a count of skulls), yet most documents record this number as 137. The remains of one person – the only woman – were not identified and are typically excluded from official counts. Due to the lack of proof of the woman's identity, the opinion arose that she was an "accidental victim, perhaps an involuntary witness."[13] It is not possible to establish how this supposition came about. No one was interested in the identity of the unknown woman either during the excavation or afterward, and the name of the memorial, which was proposed by the writer Chingiz Aitmatov, closed the "women's theme," it seems, forever. However, the name was and is no more than a metaphor; those buried varied widely in age: many were not more than 30, but there were elderly people over 70 and the average age was 47.[14] It is noteworthy that in traditional Kyrgyz culture the distinction between older men (elders), fathers, and young men is governed by a tight functional hierarchy (Ibraeva 2008).

A third myth is that those buried at Ata Beyit gave their lives in the name of Kyrgyz statehood and independence. In addition to members of Interhelpo[15] (the purpose of which was to support the USSR as a whole and not Soviet Kirgiziya in particular), several of the individuals to all appearances were not citizens of Soviet Kirgiziya. Two of them were even prosecuted for illegal crossing of the border, for smuggling, and for unlawful prospecting for gold. Of the 137 individuals, 44 were ethnic Kyrgyz (just over a third); 35 were Uighurs (more than a quarter); 11 were ethnic Germans; 16 were Russians, Belarussians, and Ukrainians; and there were also Czechs, Hungarians, Poles, Chinese, Koreans, Dungans, Jews, Tatars, and even Estonians and Kumyks. In all, persons representing 19 ethnic groups were buried there.

The fourth myth is that the remains at Ata Beyit are of repressed persons who were shot and thrown into a brick kiln on November 5–8, 1938, as evidenced by the preserved indictments of four of those buried, and by eyewitness Abykayev Kydyraliev, who worked as a guard at the NKVD dacha. Despite the assertion that the group of repressed persons whose remains are now buried at Ata Beyit were executed between November 5 and 8, 1938, there are some individuals whose deaths cannot be dated with certainty. Therefore, various sources indicate different dates for the execution of Bayaly Isakeev, Chairman of the Council of People's Commissars of the Kirghiz SSR. In the book *History of Kyrgyzstan through the Eyes of Witnesses* (2012), Kokaysl and Usmanov refer to an article in the newspaper *Pravda* that claimed he was shot on September 12, 1938, while an archival list of Kyrgyzstan's SCNS from 1991 records his shooting as occurring in the afternoon of November 5, 1938.

Controversies and doubts regarding the date of Bayali Isakeev's death are secondary, as there is also obvious falsification. For example, Umar Chodobaev appears in the list of the buried on the tombstone memorial (though not in its alphabetical place), but he does not appear in the state police's archive list of those buried in Ata Beyit. According to Khelimskaya's journalistic investigation, the reason for Chodobaev's inclusion in the list of those buried at Ata Beyit was that he was expelled from the Communist Party and executed at an unknown time at an unknown location: however, there is only circumstantial evidence for this based on the fact that his son illicitly added his father's name to the memorial after it was completed and that there has been indifference from politicians and managers (Khelimskaya 2011).

A fifth myth claims that victims of Stalin's political terror are buried at Ata Beyit. The notion that the repressed and buried at Ata Beyit were innocent victims who condemned totalitarianism may not reflect the entire dialectical complexity of political life in the 1930s. According to the testimony of a number of historians, some of those buried had been accused of ordering shootings of other people, and that they themselves were active participants in the Stalinist terror. Those mentioned most often include Khasan Dzhienbaev and Abdukadyr Abdraimov, who held the post of second secretary of the Central Committee of the Communist Party of Kirgiziya in succession and were part of the Kyrgyz "troika" (Orlov 2011).

A new wave of revelations and discoveries of "untruths" arose from the burial at Ata Beyit of those killed during the April 2010 events. Here, the main myth concerned whether or not they were in fact buried heroes and architects of a just, popular revolution. The press has repeatedly published incriminating information that some of the 87 who received the title of Heroes of the Revolution were not involved in the deadly storming of the White House, but were injured accidentally or under suspicious circumstances. Journalists quite transparently hinted at the possibility that those recognized could well turn out to include persons who looted and were injured in clashes with persons legitimately defending their property. Arguments of this kind are fueled by information from law enforcement agencies and the courts on the criminal convictions of some of the Heroes, particularly 15 of the 87.

Later, another myth was debunked with the revelation that the death of an Apriller buried at Ata Beyit had been hoaxed. It was found that the body buried at Ata Beyit under the name Maralbek Maksymbekov was, in fact, Duyshenbek Chalbaev. Maralbek was a labor migrant in Russia in good health, and Chalbaev's body was allegedly falsely identified by his son in order to receive a compensatory payment as a relative of a dead Apriller.

Finally, the latest myth is connected to the perpetuation of the memory of the victims of the *Urkun* at the centenary of this historic event. An independent commission mandated by a 2015 Presidential Decree to study the 1916 events and find the remains of *Urkun* victims was allocated three million soms of funding.[16] As a result, in the summer of 2016, an initiative group under the supervision of the head of the independent commission to study the 1916 events transported human remains discovered in the Chaar-Archa area of the Issyk-Kul region for reburial in the Ata Beyit memorial complex (Azhymatov 2016).[17] The authorities did not allow the burial to take place, arguing that "the remains must be analyzed first," and that the commission should hand them over for analysis. This was probably for a criminal DNA analysis, which cannot be performed in the country as it lacks the necessary equipment and other supplies (Nichiporova 2013). In turn, members of the independent commission insisted that they did not trust the government and the country's leaders and insisted that if such analysis were needed, it should happen at Ata Beyit itself. Therefore, in practice, both sides (the government officials forbidding the burial of the remains and the members of the commission) either revealed a terrible lack of awareness of what was communicated, or the whole dispute was a bluff and the question of DNA analysis was no more than a ruse.

If a memorial opens, does that mean it is needed by someone for something?

When interpreting the monumental and behavioral symbolism of the permanent construction at Ata Beyit over 11 years from the date of its opening, Owen said that "the *tunduk* over the grave of the victims of Soviet repression can be interpreted as a physical manifestation of the burial of the Soviet past under the new identity of Kyrgyzstan. The symbolism leaves no ambiguity, claiming the victims of the Chong Tash shooting as martyrs of modern Kyrgyzstan" (2011, n.p.).

Owen adds:

> Three days after the April 2010 massacre, more than 10,000 people gathered at the Ata Beyit funeral of 168 victims of the revolution: the coffins were wrapped in the red cloth of Kyrgyzstan's national flag. Strikingly, the ceremony was the scene of a demonstration of Kyrgyz statehood: soldiers silently stood on guard while a recording of the national anthem was played and while mullahs intoned funeral chants in Arabic. As noted by one observer, the use of only Kyrgyz language at the Ata Beyit funeral ceremony (except for the welcome, duplicated in Russian) contrasted sharply with the deliberate bilingualism of most official ceremonies, where the two languages are interspersed throughout the event. Speakers on the podium referred to the audience at the funeral ceremony either as relatives (*tuugandar*) or as brothers in faith (*musulmandar*). (2011, n.p.)

The intention of the authorities to use the memorial complex as an instrument for national state building is clear. For this instrumentalization, it is not important for whom the memorial unites and how; the important thing is that it portrays a titanic struggle for Kyrgyz statehood. In the discourse of the authorities, no ideological or values-based controversies arise between the different time components of the memorial. As Jypar Jeksheev, a public figure affiliated with the government, stated: "You cannot see the events that occurred in 1916, in the 1930s and in April 2010 as separate from each other … You should agree that they have one thing in common – the struggle of the Kyrgyz people, the political elite and patriotic young people, for the future of Kyrgyz statehood. Regardless of age, form of state, methods of struggle, content and essence, it consists of dramatic and heroic, and still far from complete, pages of our history, embodying the fight of the Kyrgyz people against violence and diktat" (2015).

The driving force behind the ongoing construction of the Ata Beyit memorial is not only political and concerned with nation building. Other factors, such as strengthening legitimacy and seeking (corrupt) financial resources, are no less important for the transformation of the role and history of Ata Beyit.

The key actors in the construction of the memorial complex include the country's presidents: Akaev, Bakiev, Otunbaeva, and Atambaev. The rule of Askar Akaev was distinguished by a love of symbolic events and excessive commemoration. At his initiative, an event took place celebrating the 3000th anniversary of the city of Osh (the southern capital of Kyrgyzstan). One thousand years of Manas were solemnly and internationally celebrated in 1995 by the building of a provisional "Manas village" in Bishkek, and renovation of the museum and *kumbez* of Manas in Talas.[18] At Akaev's initiative, the Year of Mountains was declared in 2002, and a series of themed events took place. The important symbolic events also included the opening in 2000 of the Ata Beyit memorial complex.

It is noteworthy that all the events listed coincided with years of presidential elections, and took place in the pre-election period or soon before it began. Was this coincidental? The desire of President Akaev to establish his authority as legitimate not only on rational grounds in accordance with legal decisions, but also to use "tradition" has already been described in the literature (Ibraeva 2008). But it seems that the issue is not only about the symbolic capital of the president and the "traditional" legitimization of his power.

Given the many revelations of corruption in the Akaev regime, the financial side of organizing memorials or celebrations is also important to consider. According to Government Decree 510 of November 24, 1995, for the celebration of the 1000th anniversary of the Manas epic, 67.9 million soms (more than US$6.2 million) was allocated for just one stage of the Manas-1000 Programme (actually, preparations for the celebration), as part of which the Manas aiyyly project, a wedge-shaped concrete structure, was allocated 13.7 million soms (about US$1.3 million). The Osh-3000 celebration cost the state treasury 199.2 million soms (about US$7.5 million).[19] Despite the fact that the cost of preparing for and celebrating many symbolic events and festivals is usually not advertised, it has become a negative tradition that after such events, criminal cases are initiated for misappropriation and embezzlement of very significant sums of public funds.[20]

President Almazbek Atambaev was an active initiator of Ata Beyit constructions, as well as other symbolic events and spaces. The extent to which this interest is connected with financial opportunities is an open question. It is only clear that the financial scale of every subsequent event becomes greater and greater. The memorial at Aitmatov's mausoleum at Ata Beyit, according to his sister, cost US$400,000 to construct; while according to media reports building the third memorial construction, to those who died in April 2010 – including the mausoleum, the memorial wall, and the tombstones – was estimated to cost 20.8 million soms (US$443,000). City services later calculated that in fact 26 million soms (more than US$553,000) was spent.[21] According to the Ministry of Finance, building the memorial to those who died during the 1916 events at Ata Beyit had by early August 2016 reached a cost of 135,374,000 soms.[22]

Is it possible that at a future date some visitors will find it convenient to "discover" the colonial discourse and the corresponding re-signifying of Ata Beyit? The history of architecture and monuments shows that the desire to embellish the historical memory is not unique to Ata Beyit or the recent history of Kyrgyzstan. Maurice Halbwachs asserts: "history is always a problematic and incomplete reconstruction of what no longer exists. Memory is a timeless phenomenon, experienced by connection with the eternal present. But history is a representation of the past. Because of its sensate and magical nature, memory coexists only with those details that suit it" (2005: 10). The authorities today have privatized the idea of memory of the victims of political repression or those struggling for Kyrgyz statehood and independence, in order to proclaim loudly that this was in the past. Because everyone understands that, if you put up a statue, it is a matter of the past. But, in fact, it is the present...

Notes

1   *Urkun*: Exodus. This refers to the flight of the Kyrgyz population from Russian imperial troops to China in 1916.

2   *Tunduk*: North, or the roof of the yurt (the trellis hole at the top of the yurt to let in light and air). From the outside, the *tunduk* is covered by *kiyiz*, mats made of felt. The *tunduk* can be easily opened and closed with a rope.

3   S. Ploskih and P. Degteryanko P., http://www.dissercat.com/content/reabilitatsiya-repressirovannykh-grazhdan-v-kyrgyzstane#ixzz4Gqrjrns.

4   Perhaps the exception is Eleri Bitikchi, who has written tirelessly in the last two years about the 1916 events, and the perception of contemporaries of this historic event. See http://kgcode.akipress.org/unews/un_post:7557, etc.

5   Supporters of one position believe that the Kyrgyz people have been victims of dramatic injustice: radicals count up to a million people. Supporters of this version of history say the scale of human loss means that *Urkun* can be classified as genocide of the Kyrgyz by the Russian imperial power. Following this logic, Russia, in the form of its contemporary political leaders, should admit the crime and repent. Supporters of a second position speak of 40 victims in total as a result of the Kyrgyz uprising and their escape to China, and highlight the number of victims among the Russian population also to clearly distinguish between the crimes of imperial Russia and the deeds of Soviet and post-Soviet Russia. Supporters of the third position do not consider it important to establish the number of human losses on either sides, considering them all to be victims of the colonial regime, and believe that such claims are designed to muddy the uprising in the interests of the colonial powers by highlighting that a peaceful defenseless population was exterminated in the uprising.

6   The debate was around whether the revolt was national liberation from the colonial yoke of the Russian Empire or a spontaneous rebellion by the people who had succumbed to the provocations of the Russian imperial administration, which in turn was looking for a pretext for mass extermination of the local population and further colonization of Semirechye.

7   The state authorities tried to keep the discussion of 1916 under control, by supporting "ideologically verified" meetings and seminars, but preventing an international academic conference on reevaluating the 1916 events in Bishkek, as well as by constructing local monuments also in an information vacuum, while adopting a presidential decree on the establishment of a new composition at the Ata Beyit memorial complex in memory of the victims of 1916 (Presidential

Decree "On the Centenary of the Tragic Events of 1916" of 2015). Conceived of as a wide-ranging discussion with the participation of academics from different countries, by the time it was held in May 2016, the "Rethinking the Uprising of 1916 in Central Asia" conference had lost a number of its organizers (the Manas Kyrgyz-Turkish University, the Kyrgyz National University, Arabaev University, and even several international organizations) and was held almost behind closed doors, without any informational support. The organizers of the conference spoke of intervention by the presidential administration and pressure being exerted to prevent a wide-ranging discussion.

8   Vladimir Maksimov, the editor of *Kontingent* magazine, also described the phenomenon of non-interference and compromise that engulfed the Soviet people at the time of the mass repression.

9   The term was introduced by British sociologist Anthony Giddens to refer to fixed cultural patterns of behavior in certain situations.

10 Translated from Greek, "aphasia" means the "inability to speak." Oushakine (2009) defines the phenomenon as follows: "By the post-Soviet aphasia I mean the symbolic production, in which the disintegrating capacity of the discursive field to maintain the adequacy of the relationship between the signifier and the signified is compensated for by a variety of symbolic substitutions and regression to forms of prior periods. Aphasia thus denotes the dual phenomenon, under which discursive losses are combined discursive compensations."

11 The disgraced ex-president currently lives in Russia, in Moscow, where his family ran to after his regime was overthrown in the 2005 revolution.

12 According to the writer's sister's statement, he expressed a wish to be buried not at Ata Beyit, but in the city cemetery … she said that it was unimaginable that the writer could find rest at Ata Beyit, among the victims of Stalin's repression (Alymbaev 2013).

13 Asanalieva N. Without the right to oblivion. Chong-Tash is knocking in the head. *Slovo Kyrgyzstana* newspaper. 2016, 27 January http://slovo.kg/?p=53304; Aitmatova R. 2013. White Pages of History: My Memories. www.literatura.kg/uploads/roza_ajtmatova_belyje_stranicy_istorii.pdf

14 Interestingly, when the heroes of the April events were buried at Ata Beyit, the speeches expressed grief for dead youth and even adolescents. However, the list of the buried reveals that most of the dead men were over 40 years old.

15 Interhelpo was an industrial cooperative from Czechoslovakia that volunteered to answer a call by Vladimir Lenin to build socialism on the territory of modern Kyrgyzstan. It primarily consisted of Czechs, Slovaks, and Hungarians. The Interhelpo Cooperative was created in 1923 in Zilina, Czechoslovakia. In 1924, a contract was concluded between the Soviet government and Interhelpo representatives for resettlement in Kyrgyzstan. On April 24, 1924, the first train arrived in Kyrgyzstan, with 13 carriages carrying people, and 14 carriages of equipment, including machines for carpenters and locksmiths, lathes, wheel-making equipment, tailoring and shoe shops, agricultural machines, some machines for tanneries, and a complete sawmill. In 1925, it was recognized as the best cooperative in the Soviet Union. Liquidated in 1943, many Interhelpo members were victims of repression, while others returned to Czechoslovakia or were killed at the front. Some of the Interhelpo members remained in Frunze (Bishkek).

16 Presidential Decrees "On the Centenary of the Tragic Events of 1916" and "On a Memorial for the Victims of the Tragic Events of 2016."

17 The publication reports a speech by Beknazarov, the Head of the Commission to Study the Events of 1916, where he stated that he knew places containing the remains of hundreds of victims of the *Urkun* and was ready to show them on demand. However, the remains were not publicly presented either before or after, and a ritual burial did not take place.

18 *Kumbez*: Burial place. Kumbez Manas is a burial place that has been assigned to be the place of ritual remembrance for the epic hero Manas. Although according to historical sources, Manas is a purely literary character who incorporated the features of various Kyrgyz warriors,

the vast majority of the population truly believe that the remains of Batyr Manas, the great military leader, unifier of the Kyrgyz clans and tribes, lie at this place.

19   Kasybekov A. This will be a great holiday. VB, September 18, 2000, http://members. vb.kg/2000/09/18/03.htm.

20   For example, 11 million soms were misappropriated during the construction of the hippo-drome at the Second World Games of nomads, Kabar News Agency, December 10, 2016, http://www.kabar.kg/law-and-order/full/87555; "The First World Nomad Games cost a total of 102 million soms," Israilova Zh., Knews News Agency http://knews.kg/2016/06/ vsemirnye-igry-kochevnikov-duh-predkov-ili-gromkaya-ambitsiya/; the second games cost a hundred times more: US$30.5 million. Kabar News Agency, October 10, 2016, http:// www.kabar.kg/rus/wng2016/full/112259.

21   http://kyrtag.kg/news/monument_zhertvam_aprelskoy_revolyutsii_ustanovlen_v_ memorialnom_komplekse_ata_beyit_/, http://www.for.kg/news-168633-ru.html.

22   http://www.kabar.kg/economics/full/110634. It is not clear from the announcement whether this is the full cost of construction, or just part of the total budget.

PART IV

Using Public History

CHAPTER FIFTEEN

Colonialism Revisited: Public History and New Zealand's Waitangi Tribunal

MICHAEL BELGRAVE

For three decades, historians, Māori claimants, and lawyers have gathered before the Waitangi Tribunal in New Zealand to review almost every facet of New Zealand's experience of colonization (Hayward and Wheen, 2004). Māori (with Moriori of the Chatham Islands) are the indigenous people of New Zealand, a tribally organized Polynesian society who share a common language. They make up around 15% of the country's population. Since 1985, the tribunal has been given a statutory responsibility to hear Māori claims that the Treaty of Waitangi, the 1840 treaty of secession on which claims of British sovereignty have been based, was breached at any time from the treaty signing to the present (Orange 1987). This is not quite academic history, even less popular history, but has become a highly specialized form of public history, which brings together indigenous memory (located in both written and oral histories), intense archival analysis, and legal advocacy (Belgrave 2014; Byrnes 2004; Phillipson 2004; Sorrenson 2014). All of this takes place in a highly charged political context, where the place of Māori in the contemporary world is the subject of widespread social and political debate. The questions to be answered are set by the Waitangi Tribunal's jurisdiction and by its legal setting. Claims are made by Māori that the "principles of the Treaty of Waitangi" have been breached by the Crown, and it is the responsibility of the tribunal to investigate these claims, and of historians to provide the evidence and argument for the tribunal's findings. Over more recent decades, an increasing number of these claims have been settled by negotiation. These settlements include the constitutional recognition of tribes, the transfer of capital and land, and the acknowledgment of wāhi tapū (sacred sites), all justified by a negotiated narrative which outlines the historical claims and the relationship between the Crown and the tribe since 1840, a list of treaty breaches acknowledged by the Crown, and an apology.

There are few international parallels. At times, the tribunal has been considered a forum for truth and reconciliation, with the telling of Māori narratives of grievance allowing communities to move on, to make a transition from "grievance mode" to

A Companion to Public History, First Edition. Edited by David Dean.
© 2018 John Wiley & Sons Ltd. Published 2018 by John Wiley & Sons Ltd.

"settlement mode" (Waitangi Tribunal n.d.). It has been a place where Crown officials have had to reconcile their decisions with those of living claimants, particularly in the hearing of fishing and environmental claims in the 1980s (Waitangi Tribunal 1988). But since 1985, the Waitangi Tribunal has been heavily involved in claims going well beyond living memory. While these are the subject of oral histories, the reliance on exploring historical evidence gives the Waitangi Tribunal a very different character from similar commissions. In the United States, between 1946 and 1978, the Indian Claims Commission created a national process of investigating how Native American land was alienated across the country (Rosenthal 1990; Sutton et al. 1985). While this did involve historical research, it was undertaken by or alongside anthropologists, coining the phrase ethnohistory. The Indian Claims Commission had a very narrow brief: to explore how Native Americans lost their lands, to assess a fair value for these lands, and to make recommendations for compensation. One of the distinctive features of the work of the Waitangi Tribunal has been the very limited role of anthropology.

The Waitangi Tribunal's brief is generally wider than that of commissions elsewhere, despite also having a national focus. Claimants can raise any concerns they have about the actions of the Crown, from 1840 to the present, and ask to have these tested against what are called the "principles of the Treaty of Waitangi." Claims have included the making of war and the confiscation of land which followed; the execution of individuals for supposed crimes; the taking of sometimes relatively tiny pieces of land for public works; and the mechanisms whereby individual tribes lost their land through a variety of different Crown purchasing regimes. Undermining tribes as collectives and imposing individualism provides an overarching constitutional grievance that has at times challenged the Crown's claims to sovereignty (Waitangi Tribunal 2014).

Historians have become central to this process, because New Zealand colonization generated mountains of paper. The Treaty of Waitangi recognized Māori customary rights to land, villages, forests, fisheries, and other property, and promised to protect Māori customary control over these resources. Coupled with Māori military power, this ensured that the alienation of Māori land required some legal instrument. Land had to be purchased, and there had to be evidence of the extinguishment of aboriginal title. This was also true for land purchased by the Crown between the 1840s and 1860s, land confiscated after the New Zealand wars of the early 1860s, and land sold or take for public works after title had been awarded a Crown title following a court investigation of customary interests after 1865 (Oliver 1991; Ward 1999). It was even true for land confiscated for alleged rebellion. From 1865 until the present, Māori land has been managed by a separate judicial title system, under the Native Land Court (from 1947, the Māori Land Court) (Boast 2013). Customary Māori land was given individualized titles by the court following an investigation of customary interests. Since the middle of the 1860s, Māori had been coming to court and explaining their customary relationship with the land through extensive genealogies and narratives of settlement conquest, intermarriage, and their relationship with the land and its resources. Many of these individual title claims generated hundreds of pages of transcribed evidence. Almost all of this has survived.

Unpacking this evidence, making sense of these historical processes, and explaining them in a contemporary judicial and political environment has created a very specific sort of history, and one that is completely dependent on a substantial number of specialized historians (Phillipson 2012). Over the last 25 years, at least, more historians have been involved in this treaty process than have taught New Zealand history or held permanent academic positions. Inevitably, these inquiries are long and detailed, with massive banks of written evidence, many weeks of hearings, and often many years separating the first hearing and the release of the final report. The test of these historical narratives rests almost entirely on documentary evidence. Claimants may not need to show an unbroken customary tie to their lands and resources, as required elsewhere, but they do need to show an unbroken archival trail from the past to the present.

New Zealand's fourth Labour government was in 1985 overcome by a fit of naïve enthusiasm when it passed an amendment to the Treaty of Waitangi Act 1975, giving the Waitangi Tribunal wide-ranging powers to review New Zealand's history of colonization. The Waitangi Tribunal had in the first 10 years of its operation not only earned the respect of government and the public, but also of Māori claimants, for its clear and forthright exposition of Māori perspectives on a significant range of contemporary issues. Claims heard before 1985 were primarily based on the environmental impact on Māori communities of government funding and of expensive, and ultimately unsuccessful, energy substitution schemes. The tribunal explained to non-Māori a way of life long since dismissed by non-Māori as disappearing, in language that was clear and convincing to Māori and non-Māori alike. This struck a chord not only with those environmentalists opposing such developments, but even with the government itself. Not only had the tribunal been a clear voice for Māori communities, but its recommendations (for its powers were limited to recommendation) were largely practical. They did not involve unwinding 150 years of colonization, nor did they in practice challenge the Crown's sovereignty during the 1980s and 1990s. They made it appear that Māori tribal needs could be relatively easily met and Māori political demands just as easily appeased. Moved by the success of these early tribunal reports, Minister of Justice Geoffrey Palmer expanded the tribunal's membership, gave it powers to undertake research, and extended its jurisdiction back to 1840, the year when New Zealand became a Crown colony on the basis of the Treaty of Waitangi. The treaty was signed on Queen Victoria's behalf by Lieutenant Governor William Hobson and 550 chiefs (some refused to sign), representing tribally based communities across the North and South Islands of New Zealand.

Māori have a long history of appealing to the Treaty of Waitangi as recognizing their rights as indigenous people. While written to transfer sovereignty from chiefs to the British Crown, the treaty guaranteed Māori chiefly authority, promised to protect Māori ownership of lands, forests, fisheries, and all other properties, and granted Māori rights as subjects of her Majesty Queen Victoria. The treaty captured the humanitarian mood of the 1830s and was designed by the Colonial Office and interpreted by its Church Missionary Society sponsors to protect Māori against an expected wave of British migrants encouraged to New Zealand by the utopian enthusiasm and commercial boosterism of Edward Gibbon Wakefield's New Zealand Company (Burns 1989; Olssen 1997; Orange 1987). Over the following decades, an increasing number of migrants overwhelmed a declining number of Māori and power shifted quickly and permanently into the hands of the white settlers. By 1900, the area of land owned by Māori rapidly declined, to around 10% of the country's total land area (Ward 1999). Māori were marginalized politically, economically, and culturally, although they did from 1867 have representation in Parliament and had adopted and adapted Christianity, literacy, and European farming methods and technology. The Treaty of Waitangi became a rallying point for Māori protest precisely because its promises came to have no legal status. An 1877 judicial decision declaring the treaty a "simple nullity" denied that the treaty was part of domestic law and as a result could not be tested by the courts (Williams 2011;

Wi Parata v. The Bishop of Wellington, 1877). According to the judgment, the treaty's obligations were real, but how these obligations were recognized was entirely the Crown's prerogative. This did not prevent Māori from appealing to rights under the treaty in court cases, petitions, and commissions of inquiry (Orange 1987). In these pleadings, the treaty provided a convenient narrative of loss for lands, fisheries, forests, and chiefly authority. The British and then New Zealand government still emphasized the treaty as a guarantee of Māori rights, but without the courts to say otherwise, the official treaty was little more than a defense of the legal processes used to denude Māori of their lands and tribal authority.

While appeals to the treaty had become an essential part of iwi (tribal) relationships with Parliament and the courts, a Māori consensus over the importance of the treaty was far from complete. In the 1920s, Apirana Ngata, the most significant Māori leader of the early twentieth century, downplayed its importance, primarily because he had little need for the courts as a parliamentarian and cabinet minister (Ngata 1963). Historians also had great difficulty in seeing the treaty as an honorable agreement aimed at protecting Māori rights (Beaglehole 1936; Wards 1968). They gave a much greater emphasis to the practical politics of settlement and were generally suspicious that the Colonial Office was simply sugaring the pill of imperial expansion. They had difficulty accepting that Māori could have understood the treaty's constitutional language and were doubtful that any agreement had been reached at all. The skepticism was carried into Ruth Ross's influential 1972 analysis of the language and translations of the treaty, and even in Claudia Orange's bestselling 1987 history of the Treaty of Waitangi. By the early 1980s, Māori were as likely to dismiss the treaty as a fraud as to revere it as a sacred covenant (Belgrave 2005; Harris 2004; Hill 2009). All of this changed in that decade, primarily because of the work of the Waitangi Tribunal.

The government had little understanding of the dramatic impact of extending the tribunal's jurisdiction back to 1840. Policy advisers saw only a limited number of historical claims to resolve, and Geoffrey Palmer, the Minister of Justice, ignored warnings from the historian, Alan Ward, who described the move as opening up a Pandora's box (Ward n.d., pers. comm.). Nobody in 1985 anticipated that 30 years later, these historical investigations would still be continuing or that the review of New Zealand's past which would take place would be so extensive or comprehensive.

Many claimants and their lawyers argued that they had been waiting 150 years for their grievances to be heard. This could not have been more wrong. For almost every major tribal claim (if there was a paper trail to explore the grievance), there was a history of court cases, petitioning, or commissions of inquiry. There were commissions on pre-1840 purchases, on Crown purchases, on the confiscation of Māori land during the wars of the 1860s, and on a whole series of grievances flowing from the decisions of the Native Land Court. New Zealand's European population may have subjected the colonial past to a process of forgetting, but in the 1980s both Māori and the Crown also chose to forget their long history of grievance, hearing, and settlement. All of the first series of major historical claims to be settled, Ōrākei, Ngāi Tahu and Tainui and Taranaki confiscation claims, had earlier been "settled" by "full and final" agreements, and all had been the subject of Royal Commissions in the past. What Māori did remember was that, in the past, compensation had been financial and paid in annual installments over decades. With no compensation for inflation through the 1960s and 1970s, these compensation figures were dramatically eroded (Waitangi Tribunal 1991). As the Waitangi Tribunal began its new inquiries into these grievances, Māori rejected compensation payments and demanded that for future settlements, if "land was taken: land must be returned."

Both Māori and the Crown also chose to forget the complexity of investigating historical evidence, the time taken by investigations, and the cost. Earlier commissions, such as those into confiscated Māori land from the 1860s and into pre-treaty European land claims, took several years without the input of professional historians (Myers et al. 1948; Sim et al. 1928). Both Māori and the government put their trust in the naïve belief that goodwill, postcolonial awareness, and the Waitangi Tribunal's bicultural procedures and its ability to rely on the Treaty of Waitangi would make their earlier settlements irrelevant. For some time, the tribunal had a Māori majority and adopted procedures which recognized Māori cultural practices. Enthusiasm and a sense of novelty pushed aside any appreciation from past experience for the complexities of investigation claims.

When the tribunal began exploring historical claims in the late 1980s, there was a growing academic literature on which it could draw, a literature unavailable for earlier inquires. However, historians taking part had to recognize that historical research for a claims process was both judicial and political, and its form would be different from that of academic history. Historical research would have to serve the tribunal's judicial function to investigate claims by Māori that they continued to be prejudiced by actions taken by the Crown from 1840 to the present. The test of the Crown's actions were the "principles of the Treaty of Waitangi." In 1975, Parliament had given the Waitangi Tribunal the jurisdiction to determine the principles of the treaty, a very new concept, rather than to refer directly to its text. This was largely because Ruth Ross (1972) had argued that the Māori and the English text of the treaty varied considerably, and it was impossible to reconcile the two (Belgrave 2005; Ross 1972). Although the Māori text had been signed by almost all of the Māori chiefs by putting their name or their marks to the treaty, it had been the English text that was at the center of debate about the treaty and had been appealed to in the courts since the 1840s. With such confusion, Parliament decided to allow the tribunal to establish principles through the examination of both texts.

By the time that the tribunal began investigating historical claims, it had already determined most of the principles of the Treaty of Waitangi which would inform its historical investigations. These principles included partnership, protection, and participation, and the right to develop resources according to available technology. These were very late-twentieth-century notions, but they had been developed by looking at how Māori would have understood the treaty as explained to them by Lieutenant William Hobson and his missionary translator and advocate, Reverend Henry Williams (Waitangi Tribunal 1987). In applying these principles prior to 1985, the tribunal was making contemporary judgments on contemporary policies, policies which coexisted with the Māori renaissance. But after 1985, the principles would be used to judge the actions of the Crown, at any time between 1840 and the present. Colonial officials could be judged by postcolonial standards, found wanting for their failure to implement principles which were only to be discovered a century later.

The risk of presentism in applying the principles of the treaty to the past has raised concerns from a number of historians, who have criticized the tribunal for expecting a nineteenth-century Crown to take Māori rights into account, while being intent on expanding the frontier of British capitalism (Byrnes 2006; Howe 2003; McAloon 2006; Oliver 2001; Phillipson 2004). However much the tribunal has attempted to justify its findings as reasonable in interpreting the actions of the Crown at any particular time, the extent to which it relies on a discussion of the Treaty of Waitangi driven by late twenti-eth-century sensibilities makes this difficult. It is not that contemporary criticisms of the government of the day, both by Māori and non-Māori, cannot be found: they form a common part of the historical evidence. If the tribunal treats these marginal perspectives as normative, it distorts their significance in past debates, making the past too much like the present. Over the last decade the tribunal has tightened its understanding of its capacity to criticize the actions of the Crown in the past, relying on the existence of evi-dence from the time that reasonable options were then available, which today could be seen as compatible with "treaty principles"(Phillipson 2004; Phillipson 2012; Waitangi Tribunal 2006).

A more serious problem, in practice, is the difficulty of assessing historical research within a forum that is fundamentally legal and political and in which non-historians, lawyers, and tribunal members make the ultimate decisions. Evidence is prepared by historians, who engage with archives and sometimes collect oral evidence, and then pre-sent historical arguments with the usual trappings of historical scholarship: footnotes, lists of archives, and detailed bibliographies. Even the archival material they use is pack-aged for the tribunal, initially in massive paper document banks sometimes running to tens of thousands of pages, but more recently in compact, but even more extensive, digital databases. Tribunal evidence has the look and feel of history. However, the ques-tions to be answered are determined by the tribunal's governing legislation, the Treaty of Waitangi Act 1975. The tribunal must investigate claims made by Māori against the Crown. The Crown is very specifically defined: it involves the executive and the legisla-ture, but not the judiciary; the Māori Land Court, which manages the alienation of the majority of Māori lands; and excludes local government. For a claim to be successful, the Crown must be found responsible; not colonization, not capitalism, and not racism. At the very time when historians were shifting their attention away from the state and toward broader social and economic forces in explaining imperialism and colonization, the tribunal put the focus back on the state (Byrnes 2004; Howe 2003). Not only was the state to provide the primary explanation for the impact of colonization on Māori, but it was to be the only explanation (Belgrave 2005).

From the middle of the 1980s, the tribunal was praised because its procedures recog-nized Māori cultural processes and hearings were held on marae (Māori meeting places), with evidence being heard in te reo Māori (the Māori language). However, the tribunal's methods of evaluating historical evidence have been far more conventional, and it has had considerable difficulty incorporating Māori cultural understandings of history into its deliberations. Paper archives have overwhelmed the oral history of the marae. Because aboriginal title was recognized in New Zealand – more because of Māori economic and military power than because the treaty dictated it – its alienation had to be achieved through some Crown-derived legal process (Hickford 2011; McHugh 2004). Even before 1840, Europeans claimed that they had purchased Māori land (Lee 1993; Moore et al. 1997; Myers et al. 1948). Many of these purchases were recognized by the Crown as extinguishing aboriginal title, and the land was claimed by the Crown, with some of it being awarded to the settler claimants. For most of the time between the 1840s and the 1860s, preemption prevailed, and title was extinguished by Crown purchasing. In the 1860s, a substantial amount of land was confiscated for supposed rebellion – although even some tribes who fought for the Crown lost land through confiscation. In the 1860s, the government created the Native Land Court, with powers to determine customary rights to land and to issue Crown-recognizable and transferable titles. The process was designed to give Māori property rights that were equal to those of Europeans, but more significantly to ensure that these tradable rights passed quickly into European hands. Then there were takings by the Public Works Act from 1876 and a tool box of smaller instruments for parting Māori owners from their land. These legal processes created paperwork, and it is to these files that the tribunal has turned its attention. Despite two major fires destroying a good percentage of Native Affairs records, the amount of archival material is prodigious. Nearly the entire record of the Native Land Court has also survived.

In the racially polarized debate over Māori rights of the 1970s and 1980s, claims to Māori sovereignty were more national than tribal, and the claims were always against the Pākehā (European non-Māori) rather than the Crown. The tribunal at the time believed that the holistic investigation of tribal claims against the Crown, both contemporary and historical, would lead to the recognition and reestablishment of tribes within the national economy. Māori tribes tended to be seen as discrete and autonomous sovereignties, with exclusive territories. Ranginui Walker (1992) describes pre-European New Zealand as divided into "forty-two distinct tribal groups." In reality, Māori rights to land were extremely complex, based on webs of intersecting, shared, and overlapping interests (Ballara 1998). This was not an egalitarian democracy, despite Europeans commonly describing it as "communistic." Māori society was hierarchal, but far from inflexible. The fluidity of Māori customary title allowed for adjustments in the mana (authority) of individual leaders, for groups to be formed and reformed as circumstances changed, and for alliances to be formed in response to larger threats.

European political and legal systems had great difficulty in recognizing mana, particularly given the high level of competition between rangatira (chiefs). The Crown accepted the responsibility, however reluctantly, to recognize Māori customary title, through purchase or Native Land Court investigation. Recognition was almost inevitably a precursor to extinguishment. This meant surveying blocks and acknowledging the customary interests of particular tribal communities. Imposing fixed boundaries and exclusive tenure inevitably cut across the customary rights of others. Warfare, gifts of land, and even marriage alliances were replaced by competition for Crown recognition, often fought through the courts as those who had been shut out sought to reassert their rights. Crown purchasing and the Native Land Court combined customary and colonizing agendas, and the Waitangi Tribunal inevitably inherited these roles while also attempting to address cumulative grievances against the Crown. Many of these grievances were as much about the Crown or the Court's failure to recognize mana as they were about extinguishing Māori interests through purchase or confiscation.

Once the tribunal began hearing historical claims, customary tensions re-emerged. The tribunal began with a series of inquiries which, tribe by tribe, attempted to recognize the mana and grievances of each. But right from the first hearing of its first historical inquiry, tensions between the tribe involved, Ngāi Tahu, and their northern neighbors over their customary interests threatened the investigation and continues to be a matter of litigation and tension between the two groups, over two decades after the tribunal's report (Belgrave 2005; Waitangi Tribunal 1991). The bone of contention was a sparsely populated territory, upset in the 1830s by military raids and reprisals, and there is insufficient historical evidence to resolve the issue. Each iwi must rely on their own tribal memory, bolstered by the slim smattering of primary source details which support their claim, ignoring or discounting the rest. Tribal memories and histories incorporate narratives which explain pre-contact use and conflicts over the land. After 1840, these histories incorporated the Crown, but still as part of the customary landscape. The Crown's relationship was not just with the iwi but with its neighbors and rivals. While the Crown remains the legislative target of the treaty process, interrelationships between claimant groups have taken up almost as much of the tribunal's time as the claims against the Crown (Waitangi Tribunal 2007).

There is a legal imperative for assuming that Māori customary rights are exclusive. The common law assumes, as does the treaty's promise of undisturbed *exclusive* possession, that aboriginal rights can only exist if they are exclusively held. However, such an assumption is clearly at odds with the nature of Māori custom, where interests are shared by different communities. This does not mean that there was not a sophisticated process of customary management of such rights. Rights based on genealogy are always complicated by the intricacies of marriage lines that run back over generations through different tribal communities in different places. It took the tribunal until its Te Urewera Report in 2009 to accept that customary interests were shared and that they were demonstrated through the different customary histories of claimants. The tribunal argued that it did not

> try to smooth these histories into a single historical narrative. Tribal histories embody the experience and understandings of different hapu [tribe] and iwi [larger tribal unit] as they have been passed down and retold over generations; they are not necessarily compatible with one another. (Waitangi Tribunal 2009)

Historians have become much more important to this process, despite a reluctance to become involved in what was seen as tribal history and therefore epistemologically distinct from academic history. Māori communities were uneasy about academic encroachments on tribal knowledge, and the issue remains a sensitive one. Historians had previously emphasized their role in telling the story of the Crown's relationship with the claimants, rather than in providing "traditional" histories.

Historians became necessary because of the role of the Native Land Court in the nineteenth century. Māori appearing before the Court presented their evidence as histories of association with the land, in hearings which sometime produced thousands of pages of transcription. Because the vast majority of these histories have survived, they can be explored historically and to do so requires professional skills. At first these court-based traditions were cherry-picked for narratives that supported contemporary claimant positions. Such approaches did little more than provide the deceit of independent professional support for tribal histories. More sophisticated ways of exploring these traditions have emerged; ways that do not attempt to make categorical decisions over which tradition should be preferred over others. These traditions, both in the oral and written form, are part of the living identity of tribal groups and the way that they imagine their communities, with traditions that are flexible enough to adjust to the times, but that still reinforce particular relationships between them and their lands and resources, and also with their neighbors. In the Urewera report, the tribunal acknowledged all these histories, recognized their mana and the mana of those who told them, and accepted that only rarely would they need to test one against the other (Waitangi Tribunal 2009). In some cases, there is irrefutable archival material to support one narrative over another, but this is far from common. In most cases, resolving the tensions between conflicting narratives is beyond the positivist historical methodologies being applied in these inquiries. Many of these traditions refer to the times which long proceed the coming of Europeans to

New Zealand. Historical and archaeological methods are simply insufficient to decide one against the other. The historian can only demonstrate different and similar relationships with the same lands and resources. Resolving these differences is a political rather than academic exercise. For most historical purposes, there is no need to do any more than recognize the complexity of these different historical identities. However, claimants are often re-litigating lost decisions from the past or making competing claims today to resources or cultural recognition. They are often reluctant to accept shared relationships, despite the tribunal and the treaty settlement process increasingly incorporating such compromises (Wheen and Hayward 2012).

Despite Māori enthusiasm for filing historical claims between 1987 and 1990, and the rising expectation that these claims would be heard and settled, the fourth Labour government developed no framework for settling the claims once the tribunal was done with them. From 1990, the government encouraged claimants to bypass the tribunal, on the assumption that many claims were self-evident and did not need extensive research and hearings. Despite welcoming negotiations (government has consistently preferred negotiations to tribunal enquiries), there was no process established. The Ngāti Whātua report on land in Auckland made very moderate recommendations; however, though it was released in 1987, it took four years to settle (Hill 2009; Kawharu 1989).

By the early 1990s, a new National Government, intent on radically extending the neoliberal experiments of its Labour predecessor, was uncertain as to how the Treaty of Waitangi and the tribunal fit into its agenda. Labour had bequeathed National a ponderous and politically contentious charabanc for investigating claims, but it had done little to show where it was heading. The only settlements it negotiated were forced upon it by the courts. It was left to National to devise a settlement policy, and it did so as part of the government's determination to contain state expenditure and further reduce so-called dependency on the state. The "fiscal envelope," as it was called, attempted to contain fiscal risk settlements by setting the ceiling for settlements at $NZ1 billion and creating a model to establish relativities between claims and between tribes for compensation (Gardiner 1996; Wheen and Hayward 2012). This settlement policy succeeded in uniting Māori against the government – a surprisingly rare event. Yet the framework for settling claims is largely intact two decades later. The ceiling may have risen somewhat, and some of the lines in the sand shifted, such as exclusion of the conservation estate in settlements, but an increasing number of settlements have been achieved within the framework.

The anger generated by the release of fiscal envelope policy soon dissipated, when two leading iwi negotiated settlements. These were made possible by strong personal relationships between Douglas Graham and tribal negotiators, Tipene O'Regan for Ngāi Tahu, and Robert Mahuta for Tainui (Graham 1997; New Zealand Institute of Advanced Legal Studies and McLay 1995). Graham was a senior minister in the National Government, able to sway an often reluctant cabinet. Tainui achieved their settlement with the Crown without any tribunal investigation, but for decades it had been impossible for the Crown to justify the invasion of the Waikato (the Tainui heartland) in 1863 and the vindictive confiscation of tribal land for settler towns and farms (Boast and Hill 2009; McCan 2001; O'Malley 2016). In contrast, Ngāi Tahu had been the first iwi to emerge through a full historical investigation, and also had a long history of investigation and partial settlement. The tribunal had found that the tribe had lost most of the South Island and had been reduced to tiny and uneconomic reserves as a result of a series of inequitable purchases between 1844 and 1864 (Waitangi Tribunal 1991). Even with a thorough and generally robust tribunal report, the Crown refused to accept the tribunal's historical findings as the basis for settlement. In what has become a standard negotiating position, a tribunal report has been considered an assistance in negotiating a settlement, but not authoritative.

The initial success of these two major negotiations, and of several Taranaki confiscation settlements that followed, deceived the government into believing that it had broken resistance to the "fiscal envelope" and established a viable framework for negotiation. When the Labour-led Government of Helen Clark took office in 1999, negotiations took on a low priority until 2007. The Office of Treaty Settlements (OTS), within the Ministry of Justice, began talking to groups that had the organizational structures and had achieved a Crown-recognized mandate to negotiate, irrespective of whether or not the tribunal had investigated their claims (Waitangi Tribunal 2007). Without strong ministerial leadership, OTS became bogged down. Negotiations, unlike the tribunal's hearings, took place behind closed doors. While the OTS talked with one group, all others affected were shut out, apprehensive toward but unable to influence the outcome. Māori groups were well aware that in such contested relationships with the Crown, those who went first often did best. Tribunal interventions on behalf of those shut out were cautious, tending to defer decisions, until a greater degree of certainty in the negotiations was apparent, but by this time it was often too late (Waitangi Tribunal 1993).

The distortions came to a head in 2006, with a proposed settlement with Ngāti Whātua Ōrākei. The tribe had already negotiated four limited settlements for its lands in Auckland over the previous three decades.[1] Like Tainui and Ngāi Tahu, the iwi had a strong organizational structure, and an increasing commercial presence in downtown Auckland. Ngāti Whātua's histories emphasized their hegemony over the Auckland isthmus and the North Shore, based on their seventeenth-century invasion under military leader Tuperiri. Yet many other tribes also had historical narratives that associated them with Tamaki. When these groups approached OTS, they were asked to provide information and reassured that it would be taken into account. When in May 2006, after four years of secret negotiation, a proposed settlement was released, it generally reflected Ngāti Whātua's historical narratives to the exclusion of the others. The Historical Account prepared to justify this acknowledgment of cultural exclusivity was riddled with historical errors. An urgent hearing of the Waitangi Tribunal exposed serious failings in how the settlement had been negotiated, and demonstrated how historical issues had been marginalized by the OTS's determination to settle (Waitangi Tribunal 2007). As negotiated history, the proposed settlement was compromised history.

Yet lessons were learned. The government accepted the necessity of negotiating with a broad range of claimants with common interests, despite their different histories, however difficult this appeared. Michael Cullen, the second most senior cabinet minister in the Labour-led Government, took responsibility for negotiations, and a large-scale multi-tribal agreement over the central North Island forest lands followed. OTS had come to appreciate, as had the Waitangi Tribunal sometime earlier, that dealing with the historical and the traditional past required an acceptance of both the contested nature of this past and the extent to which many iwi histories needed to be recognized and, if not reconciled, at least allowed to coexist. In little less than two years, a new and inclusive negotiating model for Tamaki was put in place, involving Ngāi Tai ki Tāmaki, Ngāti Maru, Ngāti Pāoa, Ngāti Tamaoho, Ngāti Tamaterā, Ngāti Te Ata, Ngāti Whanaunga, Ngāti Whātua o Kaipara, Ngāti Whātua Ōrākei, Te Ākitai Waiohua, Te Kawerau ā Maki,

Te Patukirikiri, and Te Rūnanga o Ngāti Whātua. The agreement demonstrated the extent to which competing Māori communities could cooperate to negotiate settlements, without riding roughshod the over the histories of others.

The new negotiating process dealt with customary history much more creatively than had the tribunal. Although recognizing a multiplicity of interests, the tribunal's district enquiry model, which looked at a large group of claims together, inevitably homogenized the experience of different Māori communities (Office of Treaty Settlements 2016). Negotiations, although under a pan iwi (tribal) umbrella, have been with individual iwi, allowing each Historical Account to reflect distinct histories and experiences. The settlement is recorded in a Deed of Settlement, and then confirmed by legislation. The deed outlines commercial and cultural redress, and provides historical narratives justifying the settlement. These narratives identify the negotiating iwi through their traditional history (the Background) and provide an agreed-upon Historical Account of their experience of the Crown from 1840 until 1982. The deed also includes a list of Crown Acknowledgements, the concessions on which the settlement is justified, and a Crown Apology. The Background is provided by the iwi, with little interference from the Crown, and tells their story. Potential conflict with neighbors and their conflicting histories is largely avoided by the stylistic device of not naming anyone other than tribal members and their hapū. Governors can be named, but officials and private citizens remain anonymous. Responsibility rests with the Crown and with the Crown alone.

The Historical Account is a narrative that relies almost entirely on written documentary evidence. The Crown Acknowledgments identify the wrongs admitted by the Crown. There are different levels of acknowledgment: first, the Crown may be prepared to acknowledge that the tribe has a grievance, but does not necessarily accept that this grievance is well founded; at another level, the Crown accepts that it has acted in bad faith; and finally, at the highest level, there is recognition of breaches of the Treaty of Waitangi and its principles. The apologies are drafted and presented by the Crown, but with consultation with the iwi. The Tainui apology was presented by the Queen herself, but iwi have very different views on the need for and style of their apologies. Apologies do not quite have the same status as in the Australian debate over the "stolen generations."[2] For some claimants, the apology is a solemn, important, and even religious aspect of reconciliation, while at the other extreme, many claimants regard the apology as unnecessary, or even hypocritical, recognizing that while the treaty settlement might be a step forward, it is not necessarily transformative of either the relationship between Māori and the Crown or of the communities involved.

These historical settlements are not negotiated by equals. There is considerable pressure for the iwi to reach settlements. They provide state recognition of customary identity, essential in influencing planning decisions in local government, for negotiating contracts to deliver health welfare and educational services, and for successful iwi participation in the contemporary economy. Some iwi's commercial operations have been particularly successful, and iwi are now major players in New Zealand fisheries and agriculture. The Crown's control over the style of the Historical Account is also a way of calming the language of grievance, reducing some of the passion of inherited memory, and of a long and painful history – as outlined in evidence to the tribunal and to some extent in tribunal reports – to a rather bald narrative of events. Statements of pain and trauma do appear, but are projected onto the claimants in the acknowledgments and apologies drafted by the Crown. Yet negotiation remains for some tribes a painful experience, one completed with misgivings.

The place of history in the negotiations has also changed dramatically as the process of settlement has gained momentum. Treaty settlements have always been presented as a response to historical grievances. The tribunal's role has been and remains to investigate these grievances, determine if they are well founded, and recommend ways to resolve them. Early recommendations of the tribunal were detailed and extensive, but have since around 1990 been largely limited to the recommendation to negotiate a settlement. But treaty settlements are more focused on the present than on the past. They have become part of a much larger process of transforming Māori tribal communities and their relationships with the Crown, creating modern tribal identities able to participate in the national and international economy, and able to assist in raising the social and economic well-being of their members. The settlement process has become more concerned with mana than grievance. The size and scope of the settlements are now only loosely linked to the claimants' unique experiences of colonization. Tribes in Tauranga have received moderate settlements, despite a history of war and confiscation, because the lands involved were limited, whereas Ngāti Porou, who were allied with the Crown and retained much of their land, have received considerably more (Boast and Hill 2009; Waitangi Tribunal 2004). Relativities recognize the size of a tribe's "original" area of land, estimated by the Crown, but are never made public. The Crown may acknowledge the complexities of shared and overlapping interests, but in compensation it only pays once for each acre. There are the "special factors," including claims involving war and land confiscation, which may increase the total financial compensation but have had little significant effect on the overall quantum of settlement and are generally decided before OTS, and the claimants assess the historical grievances through negotiating the Historical Account.

The Historical Account is no longer the most important place where claimants assert their customary interests over the landscape. Recognition of cultural associations to wāhi tapū and the return of some sites allow claimants to imprint their customary histories on the landscape, without relying entirely on the Background or Historical Account. The process of settlement has now been standardized to the extent that how much cash, land, and other resources are returned and the extent of cultural redress are mostly determined before negotiations over the Historical Account, Crown Acknowledgements, and Apology take place. Ngāti Toa, under the military leadership of Te Rauparaha, were one of the most powerful tribes in New Zealand in the 1830s and 1840s. Without a comprehensive tribunal report, they were offered an agreement in principle which listed the financial settlement and the lands to be returned in great detail, but simply announced that work on the Historical Account, Acknowledgements and Apology would begin once the agreement in principle was signed (Finlayson n.d.).

There is less need for the claimants and the Crown to contest historical issues, because they no longer have financial sums or customary recognition to attach to them. A process that was established to explore and resolve history has been successful by marginalizing the grievances as history. This process of marginalization began much earlier, when the tribunal and the Crown prioritized historical claims in the mid-1990s. As a result, the historical claims have become detached from contemporary issues. The tribunal's historical jurisdiction was extended in 1985, partly because of a belief by the tribunal that contemporary claims can only be understood in historical context. The bifurcation of the contemporary with the historical has created a process of historical investigation divorced from contemporary issues, while the contemporary demands of the negotiation process placed history in the margins. Before the Waitangi Tribunal, historical issues may be intensely debated, supported by extensive and detailed research, and with heated exchanges between claimants and lawyers. When it comes to negotiations, the same historical event may be dealt with in a paragraph, with a very small team of claimants, Crown, and claimant historians in less than an hour, with a text becoming increasingly formulaic as the number of settlements increases. The very absence of lawyers in some of these negotiations is a sign of how marginal the history itself has become.

The role of Crown historians has become much more significant in settlement, where OTS, the Crown's negotiating arm, uses historians to negotiate the Historical Accounts and to draft the Crown's Acknowledgements and Apologies. Here, the Crown historians are in a much stronger position than they were before the tribunal. While the accounts have to be negotiated and agreed upon, OTS dictates their style and vetoes material it considers inappropriate. In most cases, this veto is justified on academic grounds, because the evidence is insufficient to support the text. However, because the draft is designed to support the Crown's acknowledgments of breaches of the Treaty of Waitangi, and the Crown is ultimately the judge of its own conduct, claimants' historical grievances, as they understand them, are not comprehensively covered. An earlier finding by the Waitangi Tribunal carries little weight in these negotiations. While the Crown will generally accept the tribunal's reasoning, it does so through its own deliberations. However, for the most part, claimants and the Crown reach agreement on the major grievances that need to be addressed, and in the end accept the common narrative to describe these grievances.

When the tribunal began its investigations, historians hoped that the history that would emerge would transform New Zealand historiography, give Māori stronger voices in their own history, and help resolve tensions between Māori and non-Māori histories that had been emerging the since the 1970s (Sorrenson 2014; Ward 1993). By the beginning of the 1990s, following the release of the Ngāi Tahu report, there was strong support for the tribunal's innovative and rigorous work. Academics still had lingering suspicions about historians for hire – the universal criticisms leveled at the public historian. A decade later, a number of historians were increasingly uneasy at the extent to which tribunal history was driven by political rather than academic imperatives. Rather than looking innovative, the tribunal's history echoed a dated fatal impact approach to colonization, as did its focus on the state not as an instrument of colonization but as its cause (Byrnes 2004, 2006; Howe 2003; Oliver 2001, 2002). The specialist nature of both tribunal history and settlement history has significantly reduced its ability to influence broader historiography (Belgrave 2005, 2006). Until recently, those working in the field have little time to think globally or to be active in debates occurring outside the hearings or the negotiation meetings. Historians outside of the process cannot keep up with the huge volumes of evidence, the transcripts of cross-examination, or even the tribunal reports themselves, which each comprise of hundreds if not thousands of pages.

Some academics have worked for claimants or the tribunal, including Māori historians who have given evidence on behalf of their iwi. Yet for historians working on the new imperial history, outside of tribunal work, the vast storehouse of evidence and argument has influenced their work only marginally. Critical debates on the historical worth of the tribunal reports have concentrated only on early reports released prior to the mid-1990s. There has been no comprehensive academic review of the nature of the tribunal's historical findings or reports published since 1995. Very few of the tribunal's reports have been reviewed by the *New Zealand Journal of History*. Perhaps more significantly, Māori historians have increased in numbers, and while they have represented their iwi in hearings and negotiations, their historical focus has been quite different, more informed by personal and tribal imperatives than by the need to hear and resolve treaty claims (Harris 2004; Keenan 2009; Wanhalla 2009; Wanhalla 2013; Williams 2015). Yet the treaty process has also been significant in helping to legitimize historians within Māori communities and to help heal the widening rift between Māori and non-Māori historians' existing prior to 1985. The tribunal has also generated a massive fund of research, primary documentary material, and oral evidence, all of which is increasingly available digitally. Treaty history has not transformed New Zealand history, but as the work of the tribunal winds down and as settlements are completed, tribunal history will provide a massive resource for future historians. These historians will be unlikely to share the preconceptions and agendas underpinning tribunal history, tied as it is to the political needs of Māori tribal revival at a time of neoliberal reform and mediated by the specific legislative requirements of the Treaty of Waitangi Act and settlement negotiation. But at the same time, Māori history will emerge more confident, using the resources brought to light by this history in ways that remain to be seen.

Notes

1   The Ōrākei Block (Vesting and Use) Act 1978 led to the return of title to 29 acres of land and a $200,000 loan from the Māori Trustee. The Ōrākei Settlement Act 1991 returned small areas of land and paid the tribe $3 million, as recommended by the Waitangi Tribunal in its 1987 report. In 1993, the Surplus Auckland Railway Lands on-account transferred $4 million to Te Rūnanga o Ngāti Whātua and the Ngāti Whātua o Ōrākei Trust Board. Finally, in 1996, the iwi received $8 million as compensation over loss of access to housing at Ōrākei.

2   The term used to describe Aboriginal children forcibly removed from their families to boarding schools where they were to educated to be assimilated into White Australia. To apologize was a major political controversy until 2013, when the Federal Government of Australia issued a formal apology. See Human Rights and Equal Opportunity Commission, "Bringing Them Home: Report of the National Inquiry into the Separation of Aboriginal and Torres Strait Islander Children from Their Families," Canberra: Commonwealth of Australia, 1997.

Chapter Sixteen

Repatriation: A Conversation

George Abungu, Te Herekiekie Herewini, Richard Handler, and John Moses

Repatriation[1]

David: So let's begin with you Richard, given your reputation in the field of public history and your recent published work on the topic (Handler 2015), could you outline what you think are the main issues concerning cultural heritage, repatriation, and patrimony?

Richard: Sure, I'd be glad too. Of course, I don't consider myself to be an expert on this, and I look forward to hearing from the others who I'm sure know a lot more than I know, but I'll frame the discussion with four main issues as I see them, and I'm going to take as the prototypical or paradigmatic case that of the metropolitan museum that owns or contains objects that have been gathered from around the world in the last two or three centuries. There are different kinds of repatriation situations, but let's take this as a pretty common one, so I'm thinking of museums like the natural history museums in New York City or Chicago. I think the first thing to ask about any objects that could become subject for repatriation claims would be to ask the museum how those objects were acquired, how they came to be in that museum, what were the circumstances, who bought them, and especially who bought them from whom, and why did the seller have the right to sell them. There's a lot to say here, which I won't get into now other than to mention that there were a lot of objects acquired during colonial and imperial moments when there were people – anthropologists, missionaries, and so on – who wanted objects and who found it easy to find people who claimed they had the right to sell these objects to these collectors, but as we all know, oftentimes objects in their original social context were not alienable in the way things are in a cash market.

So that's my first point: you have to ask the museums how they acquired objects, and from whom, and did those people have the right to sell them. The second issue is are there people or groups who can claim to have created or owned those objects or claim that they should; in

A Companion to Public History, First Edition. Edited by David Dean.
© 2018 John Wiley & Sons Ltd. Published 2018 by John Wiley & Sons Ltd.

other words, that whatever the circumstances of acquisition by the museums, those museums do not have the right to own them. The third issue is that if there are spokespersons staking a claim for a museum object, we should ask what exactly do they want beyond making a claim on the object? Do they want the object returned to them or to their community or family or group, or do they want some kind of interpretive control? They may not want an object to be returned from the safe spaces in the museum, but they may want control over how it is shown, who gets to view it, how it is interpreted, and so on. And that then leads to what I thought would be the fourth issue, which is about how metropolitan museums that own these objects that are subject to repatriation claims can find ways to work with and cooperate with claimants. So museums can be receptive to these claims and help people in other communities figure out what they want to happen to these objects, how they want them to be curated or cared for as the case may be.

John: Well, to comment on what Richard has said from a Canadian perspective, and my viewpoints are those of a policy analyst working with the aboriginal affairs directorate of the federal department of Canadian Heritage. The repatriation of objects, whether we are talking about individual artifacts or entire collections, back to communities of origin or modern-day descendant populations, is just one of a number of possible outcomes as aboriginal governments or indigenous governments and Canadian federal governments get together to speak in terms of issues around cultural heritage and language. This is something that is very timely here in Canada given our new government with both a new approach both in respect to a renewed commitment to the United Nations Declaration of the Rights of Indigenous Peoples and the final recommendations of the Indian residential schools Truth and Reconciliation Commission that came out less than a year ago. There are a number of cultural heritage and languages related provisions within that document including in respect of collecting institutions like museums archives, libraries, and galleries, and so forth. All that is just to say that as a function of the legacy of residential schools experience in recent Canadian history, for many indigenous groups coming from Canada the priority is not so much the fate of tangible culture heritage but the fate of intangible cultural heritage, including especially language. So, I'll just leave it at that for now.

Te Herekiekie: Kia ora (Greetings) and thank you for this opportunity to be part of this conversation. Firstly, I would to acknowledge the movement we are part of, groups of communities and indigenous peoples who are seeking the return, repatriation, and restitution of our ancestral remains and cultural treasures housed in institutions around the world. In my view, this work began with the ancestors when they saw their treasures leaving their homelands, and I am part of that continuum in seeking their long awaited return.

I have worked in the Karanga Aotearoa Repatriation Programme at the Museum of New Zealand Te Papa Tongarewa (Te Papa) since October 2007. My understanding of repatriation issues comes from a Māori political perspective, where they are part of a broader movement to seek recognition of our indigenous treaty rights as protected within the Treaty of Waitangi signed in 1840 between Māori chiefs and the British Crown. Repatriation in my view comprises of several elements that need equal attention and consideration including political, cultural, spiritual, and the very practical application of resourcing. In respect to New Zealand, we have separated the repatriation of taonga (traditional Māori cultural items) from those of Māori and Moriori ancestral remains. The return of both are very important; however, the program I manage is specific to the return of our ancestral remains only, and therefore when we begin having conversations with overseas institutions that house our ancestors, the institution is clear about our intentions.

David: I wanted to ask about the 2002 Declaration of the Universal Museum[2] in which several of the major metropolitan museums argued that collecting happened in the nineteenth century when there were different sensibilities and values, that those objects have become part of the heritage of the countries that housed them, that their actions in collecting, preserving, and displaying these objects has fostered respect for other civilizations and saved objects which might otherwise not have survived, and finally that the objects held in the universal museum are for all the world's citizens and not just specific peoples or specific communities and specific nations. I know, George, on another occasion you pointed out that the museums involved were only North American and European museums and had other issues with the Declaration.

George: Yes, I have written on the Universal Museum controversy (Abungu, 2008). I thought there were two points about it. One is that there was a lot of fear on the part of the so-called big museums, and the other is that there was an attempt to entrench their privileged positions and ensure that nobody would question what they have and under what circumstances. And tied to this fear was this demand for repatriation from Greece and Turkey and many other parts of the world, and so they felt a need to fortify their position. And I think this was counterproductive, because essentially they were saying we are not going to be respectful of people's feelings and history, and for them the fact that this injustice was done in the past but it shouldn't affect the present because things are no longer done like that.

I should say I have never been a proponent of massive repatriation, but I have been a proponent of the need to recognize rights, the right to own, and the right to make a decision about use, and the need for museums to recognize these and negotiate with people claiming these rights. And so this begins by respecting the others and their needs. So that was my position at the time and since.

Richard: I take a radical position on a lot of this, which is that these museums can well afford to part with the stuff if it's the right thing to do or if other cultures have a claim to them. There is no such thing as world heritage, it changes according to world situations, artifacts can be returned, they can be lost, they can be destroyed, they can be forgotten, and world culture goes on. What you referred to, David, just sounds like museums protecting their turf. So I'm not sympathetic to that sort of thing. That doesn't mean I know what to do in any one particular case because often people who make claims for repatriating objects or control over those objects don't necessarily have good claims to make, but I wouldn't accept those kinds of blanket universalistic statements.

John: I'd have to note that I've worked on these matters around cultural heritage and patrimony within a Canadian setting for about 25 years now, and although I'm not especially familiar with that document, I would say it hasn't got much sway within the Canadian context anyways. Here in Canada we do not have any national or federal repatriation legislation that would be equivalent, for example, to NAGPRA (Native American Graves Repatriation Act) in the United States. Leading institutions at the national, provincial, and territorial levels do have their respective policy statements on repatriation processes, access to collections mechanisms, and that kind of thing more so than any of the kinds of international documents of the kind that are being described or might be out there. We are more governed by the 1995 policy statement on the inherent right of aboriginal self-government that recognizes an inherent right for aboriginal peoples in this country to make their own laws in respect of culture, heritage, and language, and by definition that includes the custody of artifacts and also certain national museum policy statements that have been forthcoming since the early 1990s. I'm thinking especially of the 1992 Canadian Museums Association joint task force report on museums and first peoples that recommended best practices to which the leading institutions in the country should conform in respect to their policies around repatriation and access to collections.

Richard: Let's start with what the local communities want, let's not start with grand abstract principles by powerful metropolitan institutions.

John: Yes, indeed, within the modern-day treaty process here in Canada, which by definition refers to comprehensive land claim agreements and aboriginal self-government agreements, each and every one of them – and there are more than 75 right now currently under negotiation – each one of them has a more or less detailed culture, heritage, and language chapter touching on issues such as museum artifacts and disposition. Above and beyond, as I said previously, in many circumstances as it turns out the disposition of artifacts and collections are not necessarily the cultural and heritage priority for indigenous peoples, and again this is a function of the legacy of the residential school system, so the more pervasive concern is in respect of techniques to retain and revitalize indigenous languages.

Te Herekiekie: I wish to state upfront, before 1840 some Māori chiefs participated in the trade of Toi moko or Māori preserved tattooed heads. Furthermore, as indicated above in 1840 the Treaty of Waitangi was signed between Māori chiefs and representatives of the British Crown, which broadly protected Māori property and cultural rights, made my ancestors British subjects, and allowed the British Crown to govern the country, which opened the door to settlement by other British subjects.

Through the colonization process, Māori communities from the 1860s became vulnerable to injustices such as land confiscations by the Crown. Alongside the loss of land, important Māori cultural items were taken, as well our ancestral remains. Te Papa's research reveals the extent of items collected, traded, and exchanged at the hands of newly established colonial museums in New Zealand, and those institutions in Australia, the United Kingdom, Europe, and the Americas. In my view, restitution is required for events that happened both pre and post 1840.

In New Zealand, much work was done by Māori from the 1970s to influence how our domestic museums viewed Māori artifacts, ancestral remains and engaged with the traditional owners of such treasures. Unfortunately, a small number of "museum professionals" within New Zealand continue to hold onto antiquated ideas as expressed by the universal museum model. Frankly, the idea of a universal museum that continues to hold, collect, and exhibit cultural and human remains removed unethically shows little progress has been made in international museology in respect to recognizing indigenous perspectives and rights. One of the aims of the universal museum should be to provide opportunities to learn about unethical collecting, how indigenous peoples view the loss, and to provide a template or model of how to best resolve these issues to the satisfaction of all parties concerned.

David: I was reading the United Nations Expert Mechanism on the Rights of Indigenous People from last summer (July 2015) in which they spoke about the importance of religious and cultural sites and providing access to, as well as the repatriation of, ceremonial objects and human remains. I wanted to invite us to speak a little more about indigenous knowledge and beliefs in relation to the repatriation process. On the one hand, it seems to me that a successful negotiation necessarily entails a respect for aboriginal and indigenous knowledge on the part of the metropolitan museum, yet I know of cases where this has to a degree been compromised by actions the institution has taken before returning an object. So, for example, I was reading about a case where a *toi moko* (Māori tattooed head) was being returned to New Zealand by a museum in Rouen but before returning they had decided to photograph it and create a 3-D rendering of it, which I understand is *tapu* (prohibited). So I wondered about such negotiations where a metropolitan museum is willing to return an object or human remains, which suggests a respect for the community of origin yet insists on carrying out an action that is disrespectful of indigenous culture simply in order to retain the object – in this case virtually – in their collection.

Te Herekiekie: To this day, I continued to be amazed, astonished, and somewhat rattled by ill-conceived comments by those holding Māori and Moriori ancestors in their institutions overseas. As a child I learned that Māori tradition provides a framework of the world that is comprised of both physical and spiritual elements. One of the important spiritual elements is tapu or the sacred. For me, as a Māori living today, I wish to offer respect and dignity to those tūpuna (ancestors) who are still awaiting to return to their homeland. This same respect has been implemented in Te Papa's Kōiwi Tangata Policy, which provides guidelines of how we care for our ancestral remains, according to Māori cultural tradition and also sound museum conservation practice. Although Te Papa views photographic images as an important element for registration purposes and research, our focus is not to put these images in the public domain, as essentially they are images of deceased ancestors. Overwhelmingly our research continues to reveal Toi moko in most situations are the heads of fighting chiefs and warriors protecting their communities from the enemy force. To add, I see them in the same light as New Zealand soldiers who died in World War One, who are commemorated for their valor and courage. The action of placing images of these ancestral heads in the public domain offers them little respect and dignity. To add, I appreciate that part of our work is to educate and inform other museums about the importance of repatriation; however, in saying that, not all people we meet welcome our perspective. But the need to educate, enlighten, and offer humanity to these same institutions continues.

George: You know, for the last six years I was vice-president of the International Council of Museums (ICOM) and a member of the Executive Council for six years; so for twelve years with ICOM I've been involved in these discussions, putting forward policies and so on and so I've seen quite a bit of arrogance on the part of museums. I think at issue is the differences between the way communities understand things that they value and the way museums value things. I think in this case definitely there was an objectification by the museum because once a human remains or whatever becomes part of the collection it becomes an object and for them it doesn't matter what others think. And so I think it is the refusal on the part of the museum to acknowledge that what they have objectified is not an object according to others but something that is human, it is an ancestor, or someone's human remains is the problem. And the way the museum has been constructed, of course, is where they have the power to decide what to do, and so you don't have the opportunity to freely discuss these things. So I've continued to argue that repatriation can't work without the museum changing the narrative and changing the thinking about what they see as collections. And so if during the negotiations, if they still treat some of these things – about which really they should have a different view than the way it's been used in the museum's collections – then when people claim human remains, the objects stop being objects; they become human.

I have seen this happen currently in southern Africa, where the South African and Namibian governments are trying to get back some of the victims of massacres whose remains were taken to German museums and elsewhere. They are saying, okay you may have kept them in bottles as specimens, you may have kept them in storage, but once we are demanding their return you need to change your thinking and understand that these are people, these are no longer objects, and so now you need to treat them with respect, and return them with respect, for example, by providing them with a casket or whatever. There is a lot to that, and I think the Western world has not come to terms with that; they are still thinking that what becomes a museum object remains a museum object. I think this is where we need to also start. You know there is no need to start digitizing what you've had for the last hundred years, perhaps obtained illegally, when the communities are now asking you not to do it. So I think this is absolutely unacceptable. And I think most communities have been patient now for a long time.

Of course, there are other objects that are negotiable, and I certainly don't think everything should be taken from museums. Opening up doors and dialogue and conversation can create really a good atmosphere, and I think in some cases we've seen how this has worked and museums and communities have cooperated, for example, where the museum has said alright, you are the owners, and so we ask for this to be on loan and acknowledge that you have the rights.

David: Can you give us an example where dialogue has been successful?

George: Yes, for example, in Kenya where among many communities you have grave posts, and these come with elaborate carvings and the more elaborate the carving the more important the person in the society, a chief, and elder, and so on. And they are put on the grave, they are called *kikangu*, and you can find them in east Africa, particularly in Kenya. And in the 1970s and 1980s, lots of these were stolen, and I have personally seen them in museums in Germany, the United States, and other places. And when they were taken they were seen as pieces of art, but for the people these were not works of art. In one case I know in one community, one of their chiefs had died in the 1980s, and his *kikangu* holding his spirit was taken away and ended up in the University of Illinois in the United States. And it so happened that two of the people who has studied this particular *kikangu* were working at the University and realized, and they contacted the museum and they were told, "Oh, it was stolen." So they knew it! So, to cut a long story short, it took a long time, it took even a visit from the Kenyan Minister of Culture to the United States, and finally it was brought back. And there were a lot of rituals as it was taken to the plane, like it was a human and it came back and there were lots of ceremonies and rituals. What struck me most was that the people said that since he was taken away we knew he was on a long journey, but they knew he would come back. And then they said that since he went away we had had a lot of problems – famine, drought, diseases – we've had a tough time, but now that he's back we know things are going to be okay. And for them it was personal, it was emotional, they were crying, and you know they had this satisfaction, they were so satisfied that this *kikangu* had returned back. So that was a long and bumpy negotiation, but it ended up being successful.

Now, in the case of another individual whose *kikangu* was in one of the universities in the United States, the university refused to return it, but after some political maneuvers and negotiations they agreed to return it directly to the community. And now we have an issue that many museums in the United States want to return the *kikangus* because it is no longer fashionable to have them and they feel better about returning them but now there are many questions such as who is responsible for bringing them, who is going to pay for that, who is going to welcome them, who is responsible for the negotiations, where should they go, and I'm told that there are some that have been held up for a year at the Denver airport so, you know, that is another problem. So, here are examples of successes and also of difficulties and what happens when repatriation happens without planning. These are very complex negotiations.

John: The former Canadian Museum of Civilization (now the Canadian Museum of History) has a policy where they do indeed record including through photographs or other digital media images of anything that is repatriated back to a community of origin. This is presented strictly in the context of being a security feature should at some point in the future the piece goes missing or gets damaged, so at least there is a high-level image of it for future generations, for identification purposes, and even perhaps for future replication purposes. I think most of the communities of origin that are receiving material back are satisfied with this as being an added security feature and nothing beyond that. There is other work going on around about what people are calling digital repatriation, and it is in that situation where major museums – whether we are talking at the national or regional levels – are trying to provide electronic access to indigenous communities through the museum's databases so that communities that might not previously have been able to have access to those objects in the collections can do so. But there are issues there in terms of access, especially in the northern and more remote communities in the Canadian landmass. Many indigenous communities simply don't have access to the necessary technology, they don't have the bandwidth capability, they're not online to the extent that they would be able to take advantage of such digitized databases even if they were available, so there had been criticism here in the Canadian context that this talk around digital repatriation is for want of a better term a dodge that enables these museums to ultimately retain possession of the objects themselves without actually returning to the communities of origin, so that has to be recognized as well.

Richard: I just wanted to comment that the discourse of the dominant institutions is always the same; they just can't let go of this narrative that there is some kind of universal history of human culture that it's their right to curate, and as John has just said these are often dodges. Now I'm certainly happy to look at instances where local communities and museums come to an agreement that's mutually beneficial, so, for example, a local community says, yeah, that's great you keep the objects and look after them for us and this might help us down the road, and that's great, that's good, but I just don't buy the discourse that there's a universal history that has to be preserved. I mean, think about your own family history. Supposing you had your mother's diary or some private piece of family history that maybe you wouldn't want to be known to other people, maybe you would want to destroy it and you wouldn't want it to be published. It's not a part of universal history – in fact, there *is* no universal history.

John: Indeed, if I can interject on that point, I know that speaking in terms of those Canadian collections with which I'm most familiar; quite aside from the artifact collections themselves there are the ethnographic field notes that were taken by the early researchers and that type of thing.

Richard: Yes. Right, right.

John: And often the astonishingly thing, by today's standards, is the intrusive nature of some of the questioning that went on at the community level. This is not something that would be acceptable today with modern-day standards of ethical guidelines for research, and so forth, with the notion of freely given prior and informed consent, and that those being interviewed have to sign off on before being interviewed. There is a lot of material in some of the early archival records of museums that remains extremely sensitive today, and again it's an example of information that they should not have been recording in the first place, but to the extent that they remain within museums today is another area of contention.

Richard: Yeah, that's right.

John: It automatically and ultimately gets back to the very basic issues of who speaks on whose behalf and who has the right relative to public interpretation and mediation of a culture, who is considered a reliable narrator as opposed to a well-informed witness, this kind of thing. Certainly here within Canada – and it's something we're seeing around the world, certainly in respect to global aboriginal and indigenous cultures – is the emergence of a new leadership class of indigenous scholars and academics who are grounded both in their indigenous traditional knowledge in terms of mastery of their indigenous languages, systems of governance, their entire worldview, and then, quite aside from that, they have the mainstream academic credentials as well. These people are really emerging in the forefront of the disciplines and indeed creating entirely new indigenous-based disciplines that 20 years ago, frankly, did not exist. So here within the Canadian setting we're starting to see the emergence of departments at Canadian universities, departments of indigenous governance, and so forth, different approaches to indigenous critical theory that were unknown 20 or 30 years ago which are now a new feature of the Canadian academic landscape and increasingly becoming part of the international academic landscape.

Richard: Which then raises an interesting question, which is that Western social science has always aspired to be universalistic … is there such a thing as local knowledge that wants to remain local or local knowledge that doesn't aspire to be universal, and if scholars from different places join the conversation we would expect the conversation to change, for example, ideas of what counts, or what counts as knowledge to be valued would change, but we might also find changing rules about what should be discussed or theorized.

David: I wonder if we could shift direction a little bit and talk about strategies of negotiation between various communities and groups and museums. I was listening to a lecture by Brian Rose, who is a professor at the University of Pennsylvania, where he spoke about negotiations with the Turkish government that eventually led to the return of gold objects from the university's museum to Turkey and, in return, the museum has received a steady flow of objects for temporary exhibits, and so on, but he also mentioned that authorities in Turkey have recently tried to convince Berlin museums to repatriate objects by threatening to withhold permission for German archaeological digs in Turkey.[3] So I wondered if you could comment on such a strategy or tell us of others that you know about. Another, for example, might be instances where museums in Greece or Egypt have deliberately created empty niches with signage drawing visitors' attention to the absence of the object that would or should be there and its current location in, say, the British Museum.

Richard: Well, they are fine with me. Look, the problem you have in the discussion of something like the Elgin marbles is that to what extent does the Greek government today represent the ancient Greek civilization, and so on. You always have those kinds of problems; or we might ask, is the Turkish government really all that better as an ethical entity than the Berlin museums. But putting that aside, again the metropolitan researchers and collectors simply think it's their God-given right to go anywhere and why shouldn't they have to bargain for access? They should learn to accept it when people say no. That they need to get used to that kind of idea seems kind of striking, and yet you know these people are not the lords of the earth they wish they were and yet they act as if they were.

George: Well, I understand these political moves because at some point you have to use every means possible to secure the return, and the tactics used by the Greeks and so on, and neither do I say they are always doing the right thing. I know and you'll remember that some, maybe ten years ago there was this problem between the Getty and Italy when one of the curators at the Getty was accused and sentenced in Italy for buying objects without securing the proper permissions. And the Getty tried to say it was not involved, it was just this one curator, and Italy took a very strong position that this was an issue between Italy and the Getty and also involved the government of the United States. And a lot of material was returned to Italy, so that is a case of a dispute between a country and an institution where the country put their foot down and said we don't want to see you in our country if this is how you are going to behave. So yes, that happens, and of course we all know about the case of the Elgin Marbles and the British Museum. You know I'd say that the problem has been where the museums have been inconsiderate in listening and putting these issues to discussion. For example, the British Museum, of course, has said there is nothing to discuss with the Greeks in the case of the Elgin Marbles, and when you shut the door on negotiations it becomes a real problem. And I think that sometimes that negotiations, even if they take years, do help release the tensions and to tell the other person that you are concerned and that you care and that you appreciate what they are trying to say, but when you say "no, we have completely no negotiation strategies and don't want to," well, that means you do not care and then you might have to use political clout to put pressure. So I understand, but I don't think every country wants to do that because there are other implications, so Germany might decide to counter with moves that affect Turkey economically or affect diplomatic relations, so really I think no country wants to go to that extent, and so when we really close those doors it becomes a problem. I think that is also where ICOM and its mechanisms for using international negotiators is so important, and I think there is a need to support that mediation process. It may not lead to repatriation, particularly of nonhuman objects, but it leads to opening up spaces for dialogue, and in dialogue anything is possible

John: Yes, and I think you know there is that body of international legal obligations under the auspices of UNESCO and ICOM so, for example, the International Convention to Prevent the Illicit Traffic of Cultural Properties that the government of Canada is party to as well as dozens of other countries around the world. Typically one would assume or at least one would hope that these are negotiated under much more collegial terms than what's been described here, but certainly in Canada, for example, apart from our participation in these UN conventions we do have bilateral arrangements in place with other individual countries in the world to facilitate various kinds of exchanges so that is another aspect as well. Also under the Canadian cultural properties export and import provisions there are mechanisms whereby the ministry has the authority to designate collecting facilities locally and in indigenous communities as accredited museum facilities that are approved to accept new repatriated artifacts. So Canada's national government is able to complete the repatriation of cultural artifacts from a foreign country back into Canadian territory, and then the minister once the object is back within Canadian borders has the authority further to have that indigenous artifact deposited in culturally appropriate indigenous communities in Canada, so that's something that exists as a possibility as well.

David: I wonder if we could move the conversation toward the even more contentious issue of metropolitan museums holding human remains.

Richard: Yes, you know again I don't have any patience with, well, let's take the example of the Kennewick man. It may be that you can't conclusively identify present-day people who really can claim to be the successors of the people whose remains were found, but it's a kind of technical problem and in terms of the political issue again I'm just not interested in accepting the narrative that science has the right or should prevail over the needs and rights of local communities. And I also don't believe that there's any one piece of evidence or object or skeleton that if we were to lose it we could never tell the complete human story. In fact, we can't tell the complete human story. Period. It's made up of a lot of fragments, so I would say let's give up the fragments, let's return them to the people who want them, and let's look for new kinds of evidence. Maybe we can tell some better stories.

Te Herekiekie: Te Papa is in a unique situation as it is underpinned by legislation that supports a bicultural museum, in a contemporary multi-ethnic New Zealand. In addition, as a museum it is also required to be a viable commercial enterprise, that educates and entertains New Zealanders and overseas visitors about Māori and New Zealand history, the natural environment, science, and to promote our national identity. To add, the Karanga Aotearoa Repatriation Programme is supported by high government policy that recognizes the importance of Māori communities, their cultural aspirations and traditions, and requires these elements to be active components in seeking the return of tūpuna (ancestors). As the repatriation manager at Te Papa, I've had the opportunity to visit a number of different institutions in Australia, Canada, United States, the United Kingdom, and Europe. My view is that there is a genuine desire by many institutions to return the ancestral remains they house. When we have an agreement in place to repatriate, we also begin the process of negotiating the formal handover ceremony. In countries such as Australia, Canada, and the United States, we delicately ask about the possibility of local indigenous representatives being part of the handover, as acknowledging the tangata whenua (first people of the land) is critical for us, and in most cases the museum will support this to happen. Once the ancestors arrive home, they are all welcomed onto our national marae (community space) at Te Papa by their living descendants, local iwi (tribal groups), and senior government officials, and placed in the wāhi tapu (sacred repository). Our aim is to return all ancestors to their places of origin around the country, to be embraced and welcomed home by their kith and kin, where they may have eternal rest. Through the repatriation process, Te Papa's role is one of facilitator, between Māori and international museums; secondly, it is also an administrator of government resourcing; thirdly, as an active negotiator and researcher; and lastly, as an innovative contemporary bicultural museum that actively engages with Māori cultural perspectives and aspirations. All the above is held together by the goodwill of strong leadership of Māori, Te Papa, and the New Zealand government. Since 2003, Te Papa's repatriation program has repatriated close to 420 Māori and Moriori ancestral remains; however, we still have 530 ancestors still awaiting their homecoming. "E kore e mutu te aroha mō rātou, e kore e warewaretia. Our love for them will never cease, and they will never be forgotten."

George: I think it's important not to forget that this process of illegal acquisition of cultural heritage and material culture and all that has its roots in the historical context of colonialism and domination and all that kind of thing. That has a serious effect on the current practice of illegal trafficking that continues to go on, particularly in places of conflict, for example, in West Africa in places like Mali, where they have developed partnerships not only in the trafficking of artifacts, but also in the trafficking of small arms and also of drugs, and so all three go together. And they end up in the north, and in museums and in collectors' hands with a view of ending up in museums. So I think that this is something that we should not divorce from the reality of the present, and when we are discussing issues of repatriation and the types of repatriation, we should also try to tie it to the present practices that have their roots in these old practices of domination and transfer of people's spiritual and emotional and other heritage. These things are connected. We also see that they are promoting a kind of disintegration of societal arrangements like loss of respect for elders and traditional management systems. In the long run, what we see as a museum problem may actually affect a lot of other things that we see coming up in discussion about the destruction of heritage sites and museum properties in some of these conflict areas. Because museums have proved their value, they have received attention and shown that some of these things that they call museum specimens are important and you can make a political statement out of them. So I think we should learn from this and try to connect all these things together, we should try to look at this issue from a much longer and a much wider perspective.

David: Well, I think that is a great point to end on. Thank you everyone for participating in this discussion, which I'm sure the readers of the book will find very thought provoking.

Notes

1   Due to technical problems only David, John, and Richard were able to discuss this issue live; Te Herekiekie added his comments to the transcript, while George joined the conversation through a subsequent telephone interview with David.

2   The *Declaration of the Importance and Value of Universal Museums* (2002), originally posted on the British Museum's website, was reprinted with commentaries by Peter-Klaus Schuster and George Abungu in ICOM's *Focus* 2004: https://committeeforculturalpolicy.org/wp-content/uploads/2013/06/CCP-WebLibrary-Museums-ICOM-Universal-Museums.pdf.

3   Brian Rose, "Who Owns Antiquity? Museums, Repatriation, and Armed Conflict," Laurence Eitner Lecture on Classical Arts and Culture, 4 October 2013: https://classics.stanford.edu/events/c-brian-rose-penn-who-owns-antiquity-museums-repatriation-and-armed-conflict-video.

CHAPTER SEVENTEEN

The Transformative Power of Memory: Notes on the Final Report of the Truth and Reconciliation Commission (TRC) of Canada in Light of the Colombian Experience

PATRICK MORALES THOMAS

Introduction

What are the blockages to reconciliation? The continuing poverty in our communities and the failure of our government to recognize that "Yes, we own the land."

This phrase spoken by Steven Point, Lieutenant-Governor of British Columbia, could just as easily be attributed to a member of the Nasa people of southwestern Colombia or any of the 102 Indigenous groups currently recognized as such in that country. As a country that has been marked by more than 50 years of war whose intensity (as the Honourable Constitutional Court of Colombia has observed) has disproportionately impacted ethnic regions and communities, Colombia has a different context and approach to the past than Canada. Questions about reconciliation, however, are similar in both countries: the TRC's conclusions to the report on the abuses experienced by Canada's First Peoples within an official educational policy framework in residential schools deeply resonate with recent perspectives on reconciliation in Colombia, spurred on by the final phase of negotiations between the Revolutionary Armed Forces of Colombia – People's Army (FARC-EP) guerrilla group and the state. Among the agreements reached between the two groups is the creation of a TRC in 2017.[1]

Colombia's approach to dealing with the past concerning the war has been innovative insofar as it has proposed a process of reconstructing historical memory in the midst of the conflict. Nine years of work have enabled official institutions working on the issue to posit the importance of memory as an avenue for reaching the truth and in this way restoring dignity to the victims of the armed conflict.[2] The voices of those who have directly suffered as a result of conflict have shared not only their traumas

A Companion to Public History, First Edition. Edited by David Dean.
© 2018 John Wiley & Sons Ltd. Published 2018 by John Wiley & Sons Ltd.

but also their experiences of resistance. This has enabled a national platform for accounts of the war that had previously been invisible to a large portion of the country. Victims are increasingly and powerfully understood as social agents in their own process of healing and redress. As in Canada, however, national society is still far from valuing the contribution of Indigenous knowledge with respect to reconciliation. This is because, on one hand, there has never been reciprocal respect between the two parties and, on the other, because the healing process, as it is understood in Indigenous traditions, is slow and complex. As indicated by the TRC through the testimony of Survivor Evelyn Brockwood, "We have to slow down, we are moving too fast, too fast ... there are still many tears to shed before we can speak of *reconciliation*" (What Have We Learned 2015: 120).

As indicated by the Commission in the introductory pages of the Report, reconciliation entails a process of strengthening Indigenous cultural traditions, a path that can only be taken by revitalizing the cultural practices of ancestral peoples. Engaging memory in Colombia, as described in the normative frameworks designed by Indigenous groups for guiding national reparations policy,[3] involves addressing the past within the terms of original Indigenous laws in order to strengthen their own legal traditions and the symbolic and social systems that were fragmented by the conflict.

For Indigenous Colombians, the war of the last 50 years is just one expression of a conflict that has existed for much longer. In the process of reconstructing the historical memory of the genocide of Indigenous Amazonians associated with the rubber boom during the first decades of the twentieth century,[4] Indigenous communities in the region teach us, as a society, about their sophisticated cultural practices for overcoming painful and dangerous memory. Healing the past means *burying the basket of pain* and *sweetening the word death* with the help of the coca, tobacco, and sweet cassava spirits. Only the *word of life, the word that dawns*, can produce a social state that is conducive to carrying out the rituals and sacred songs necessary for overcoming suffering and grief. The Commission's Report states that there can be multiple and diverse meanings to reconciliation from an Indigenous perspective. In northern Colombian Amazonia, reconciliation means *sweet word, the word that dawns*. But how willing are we to listen to them beyond the official apology issued during a few hours' visit to the region by representatives of the three governments responsible for the massacre?[5] The case of the genocide during the rubber boom demonstrates how far Colombia is from creating the conditions for a public dialogue that the Report identifies as being an indispensable foundation of the process of reconciliation. Healing is definitely a long process: it took one hundred years of tears for the Indigenous people of the Colombian Amazon to incorporate their memory of trauma into their cultural traditions and thereby make sense of a conflict that the national society is still reluctant to face. What can we learn from the *sweet word* of the Indigenous peoples of the Amazon? Without a doubt, their particular way of healing the relationship to their traumatic past can direct us to ways of rethinking relations between Indigenous peoples and national society, which in the Colombian case are profoundly marked by visions of deep-seated historical discrimination and the development of extractive policies in ancestral lands.

Healing the wounds of the past for Indigenous nations involves reestablishing balance, and to a certain extent, healing the relationships between different levels of their symbolic universe, which, of course, entails healing the relations with the non-Indigenous world, which we know to be an integral part of their traditional cosmogonies. For the Indigenous people of the Sierra Nevada of Santa Marta, who, like First Nations in Canada, were subjected to a policy of Indigenous residential schools over seven decades, the memory of this educational policy – marked by physical and symbolic violence – is part of a larger continuum of conflict and exploitation of traditional lands that began with the arrival of Europeans on the continent. Their view of reparations includes the possibility of recovering their ancestral lands that have been subjected to different forms of violence and, in this way, heal the extensive interconnected network of sacred sites that have been affected by the historical conflict. These sacred sites are not restricted to their ancestral lands. Humanity's balance depends on the interconnection between sacred sites located in cities as far away as Bogotá or in regions that extend all the way to the European continent. Their job as the "older brothers" of humanity is to care for and reestablish an ancient balance on which all our survival depends, including that of the non-Indigenous "younger brothers."

Even when the episode of the residential schools for Indigenous children from Sierra Nevada de Santa Marta is dealt with from a comprehensive view of violence against the region's Indigenous peoples, it is no less true that more recently, and at the request of the Indigenous leaders of affected communities, work on the historical memory of these painful events has begun. Unlike the initial approach, which has focused on audiovisual work by Indigenous people on the impacts of this era,[6] the work of reviewing written and oral histories on the subject has been taken up in recent months with the guidance of the Directorate of the Archives of the National Center for Historical Memory and the leadership of Indigenous researchers. Jealously safe-guarded by the community, the cleaning and cataloging of an archive dating from 1840 to 1982 has begun to generate a rich process of social appropriation of the past and a rereading of the events associated with the residential school policy using oral sources. This activity demonstrates the relevance of the TRC Report's recommendations regarding the need to build a solid documentation policy as an essential component of historical clarification, truth, and reconciliation.

However, elucidating events and contexts, and identifying and recognizing historical responsibilities, is just one step toward starting a much-needed public dialogue about reconciliation. The real challenge will perhaps be translating complex Indigenous cultural constructions to the national society about the past and healing in order to create what can be referred to as an intercultural pedagogy of respect and non-repetition.

There is no doubt that the Canadian TRC experience represents a highly relevant resource for the challenges that the future Colombian Truth Commission will pose, especially since they are about to establish the procedures and scope or ethnic participation in the Commission. The role that TRC commissioners have played in facilitating public dialogue between diverse and sometimes contrasting actors and visions constitutes one of the most valuable lessons for the Colombian case. At the same time, apart from the geographical distance and obviously different contexts, the similar historical experiences and productive proposals being put forth by ethnic groups for revisiting the past as a means of healing are surprising. This final point suggests the relevance of creating exchanges between Indigenous groups in Canada and Colombia as a way of enriching both countries' approaches to reconciliation on their long road toward creating respectful relations between national society and Indigenous peoples.

Excerpt from *what we have learned: Principles of truth and reconciliation*[7]

Reconciliation

To some people, "reconciliation" is the reestablishment of a conciliatory state. However, this is a state that many Aboriginal people assert never has existed between Aboriginal and non-Aboriginal people. To others, "reconciliation," in the context of Indian residential schools, is similar to dealing with a situation of family violence. It is about coming to terms with events of the past in a manner that overcomes conflict and establishes a respectful and healthy relationship among people, going forward. It is in the latter context that the Truth and Reconciliation Commission of Canada has approached the question of reconciliation.

To the Commission, "reconciliation" is about establishing and maintaining a mutually respectful relationship between Aboriginal and non-Aboriginal peoples in this country. In order for that to happen, there has to be awareness of the past, acknowledgement of the harm that has been inflicted, atonement for the causes, and action to change behaviour. We are not there yet. The relationship between Aboriginal and non-Aboriginal peoples is not a mutually respectful one. But, we believe we can get there, and we believe we can maintain it. Our ambition is to show how we can do that.

In 1996, the *Report of the Royal Commission on Aboriginal Peoples* urged Canadians to begin a national process of reconciliation that would have set the country on a bold new path, fundamentally changing the very foundations of Canada's relationship with Aboriginal peoples. Much of what the Royal Commission had to say has been ignored by government; a majority of its recommendations were never implemented. But the report and its findings opened people's eyes and changed the conversation about the reality for Aboriginal people in this country.

In 2015, as the Truth and Reconciliation Commission of Canada wraps up its work, the country has a rare second chance to seize a lost opportunity for reconciliation. We live in a twenty-first-century global world. At stake is Canada's place as a prosperous, just, and inclusive democracy within that global world. At the TRC's first National Event in Winnipeg, Manitoba, in 2010, residential school Survivor Alma Mann Scott said:

> The healing is happening – the reconciliation.... I feel that there's some hope for us not just as Canadians, but for the world, because I know I'm not the only one. I know that Anishinaabe people across Canada, First Nations, are not the only ones. My brothers and sisters in New Zealand, Australia, Ireland – there's different areas of the world where this type of stuff happened.... I don't see it happening in a year, but we can start making changes to laws and to education systems ... so that we can move forward.[1]

Reconciliation must support Aboriginal peoples as they heal from the destructive legacies of colonization that have wreaked such havoc in their lives. But it must do even more. Reconciliation must inspire Aboriginal and non-Aboriginal peoples to transform Canadian society so that our children and grandchildren can live together in dignity, peace, and prosperity on these lands we now share.

The urgent need for reconciliation runs deep in Canada. Expanding public dialogue and action on reconciliation beyond residential schools will be critical in the coming years. Although some progress has been made, significant barriers to reconciliation remain. The relationship between the federal government and Aboriginal peoples is deteriorating. Instead of moving toward reconciliation, there have been divisive conflicts over Aboriginal education, child welfare, and justice. The daily news has been filled with reports of controversial issues ranging from the call for a national inquiry on violence toward Aboriginal women and girls to the impact of the economic development of lands and resources on Treaties and Aboriginal title and rights.[2] The courts continue to hear Aboriginal rights cases, and new litigation has been filed by Survivors of day schools not covered under the Indian Residential Schools Settlement Agreement, as well as by victims of the "Sixties Scoop."[3] The promise of reconciliation, which seemed so imminent back in 2008 when the prime minister, on behalf of all Canadians, apologized to Survivors, has faded.

Too many Canadians know little or nothing about the deep historical roots of these conflicts. This lack of historical knowledge has serious consequences for First Nations, Inuit, and Métis peoples, and for Canada as a whole. In government circles, it makes for poor public policy decisions. In the public realm, it reinforces racist attitudes and fuels civic distrust between Aboriginal peoples and other Canadians.[4] Too many Canadians still do not know the history of Aboriginal peoples' contributions to Canada, or understand that by virtue of the historical and modern Treaties negotiated by our government, we are all Treaty people. History plays an important role in reconciliation; to build for the future, Canadians must look to, and learn from, the past.

As commissioners, we understood from the start that although reconciliation could not be achieved during the TRC's lifetime, the country could and must take ongoing positive and concrete steps forward. Although the Commission has been a catalyst for deepening our national awareness of the meaning and potential of reconciliation, it will take many heads, hands, and hearts, working together, at all levels of society to maintain momentum in the years ahead. It will also take sustained political will at all levels of government and concerted material resources.

The thousands of Survivors who publicly shared their residential school experiences at TRC events in every region of this country have launched a much-needed dialogue about what is necessary to heal themselves, their families, communities, and the nation. Canadians have much to benefit from listening to the voices, experiences, and wisdom of Survivors, Elders, and Traditional Knowledge Keepers – and much more to learn about reconciliation. Aboriginal peoples have an important contribution to make to reconciliation. Their knowledge systems, oral histories, laws, and connections to the land have vitally informed the reconciliation process to date, and are essential to its ongoing progress.

At a Traditional Knowledge Keepers Forum sponsored by the TRC, Anishinaabe Elder Mary Deleary spoke about the responsibility for reconciliation that both Aboriginal and non-Aboriginal people carry. She emphasized that the work of reconciliation must continue in ways that honour the ancestors, respect the land, and rebalance relationships. She said:

> I'm so filled with belief and hope because when I hear your voices at the table, I hear and know that the responsibilities that our ancestors carried ... are still being carried... even through all of the struggles, even through all of what has been disrupted ... we can still hear the voice of the land. We can hear the care and love for the children. We can hear about our law. We can hear about our stories, our governance, our feasts, [and] our medicines.... We have work to do. That work we are [already] doing as [Aboriginal] peoples. Our relatives who have come from across the water [non-Aboriginal people], you still have work to do on

your road.... The land is made up of the dust of our ancestors' bones. And so to reconcile with this land and everything that has happened, there is much work to be done ... in order to create balance.[5]

At the Victoria Regional Event in 2012, Survivor Archie Little said:

[For] me reconciliation is righting a wrong. And how do we do that? All these people in this room, a lot of non-Aboriginals, a lot of Aboriginals that probably didn't go to residential school; we need to work together.... My mother had a high standing in our cultural ways. We lost that. It was taken away.... And I think it's time for you non-Aboriginals... to go to your politicians and tell them that we have to take responsibility for what happened. We have to work together.[6]

The Reverend Stan McKay of the United Church, who is also a Survivor, believes that reconciliation can happen only when everyone accepts responsibility for healing in ways that foster respect. He said:

[There must be] a change in perspective about the way in which Aboriginal peoples would be engaged with Canadian society in the quest for reconciliation.... [We cannot] perpetuate the paternalistic concept that only Aboriginal peoples are in need of healing.... The perpetrators are wounded and marked by history in ways that are different from the victims, but both groups require healing.... How can a conversation about reconciliation take place if all involved do not adopt an attitude of humility and respect? ... We all have stories to tell and in order to grow in tolerance and understanding we must listen to the stories of others.[7]

Over the past five years, the Truth and Reconciliation Commission of Canada urged Canadians not to wait until its final report was issued before contributing to the reconciliation process. We have been encouraged to see that across the country, many people have been answering that call.

The youth of this country are taking up the challenge of reconciliation. Aboriginal and non-Aboriginal youth who attended TRC National Events made powerful statements about why reconciliation matters to them. At the Alberta National Event in Edmonton in March 2014, an Indigenous youth spoke on behalf of a national Indigenous and non-Indigenous collaboration known as the "4Rs Youth Movement." Jessica Bolduc said:

We have re-examined our thoughts and beliefs around colonialism, and have made a commitment to unpack our own baggage, and to enter into a new relationship with each other, using this momentum, to move our country forward, in light of the 150th anniversary of the Confederation of Canada in 2017.

At this point in time, we ask ourselves, "What does that anniversary mean for us, as Indigenous youth and non-Indigenous youth, and how do we arrive at that day with something we can celebrate together?"... Our hope is that, one day, we will live together, as recognized nations, within a country we can all be proud of.[8]

In 2013, at the British Columbia National Event in Vancouver, where over 5,000 elementary and secondary school students attended Education Day, several non-Aboriginal youth talked about what they had learned. Matthew Meneses said, "I'll never forget this day. This is the first day they ever told us about residential schools. If I were to see someone who's Aboriginal, I'd ask them if they can speak their language because

I think speaking their language is a pretty cool thing." Antonio Jordao said, "It makes me sad for those kids. They took them away from their homes – it was torture, it's not fair. They took them away from their homes. I don't agree with that. It's really wrong. That's one of the worst things that Canada did." Cassidy Morris said, "It's good that we're finally learning about what happened." Jacqulyn Byers told us, "I hope that events like this are able to bring closure to the horrible things that happened, and that a whole lot of people now recognize that the crime happened and that we need to make amends for it."[9]

At the same National Event, TRC Honorary Witness Patsy George paid tribute to the strength of Aboriginal women and their contributions to the reconciliation process despite the oppression and violence they have experienced. She said:

> Women have always been a beacon of hope for me. Mothers and grandmothers in the lives of our children, and in the survival of our communities, must be recognized and supported. The justified rage we all feel and share today must be turned into instruments of transformation of our hearts and our souls, clearing the ground for respect, love, honesty, humility, wisdom, and truth. We owe it to all those who suffered, and we owe it to the children of today and tomorrow. May this day and the days ahead bring us peace and justice.[10]

Aboriginal and non-Aboriginal Canadians from all walks of life spoke to us about the importance of reaching out to one another in ways that create hope for a better future. Whether one is First Nations, Inuit, Métis, a descendant of European settlers, a member of a minority group that suffered historical discrimination in Canada, or a new Canadian, we all inherit both the benefits and obligations of Canada. We are all Treaty people who share responsibility for taking action on reconciliation.

Without truth, justice, and healing, there can be no genuine reconciliation. Reconciliation is not about "closing a sad chapter of Canada's past," but about opening new healing pathways of reconciliation that are forged in truth and justice. We are mindful that knowing the truth about what happened in residential schools in and of itself does not necessarily lead to reconciliation. Yet, the importance of truth telling in its own right should not be underestimated; it restores the human dignity of victims of violence and calls governments and citizens to account. Without truth, justice is not served, healing cannot happen, and there can be no genuine reconciliation between Aboriginal and non-Aboriginal peoples in Canada. Speaking to us at the Traditional Knowledge Keepers Forum in June of 2014, Elder Dave Courchene posed a critical question: "When you talk about truth, whose truth are you talking about?"[11]

The Commission's answer to Elder Courchene's question is that by *truth*, we mean not only the truth revealed in government and church residential school documents, but also the truth of lived experiences as told to us by Survivors and others in their statements to this Commission. Together, these public testimonies constitute a new oral history record, one based on Indigenous legal traditions and the practice of witnessing.[12] As people gathered at various TRC National Events and Community Hearings, they shared experiences of truth telling and offered expressions of reconciliation.

Over the course of its work, the Commission inducted a growing circle of TRC Honorary Witnesses. Their role has been to bear official witness to the testimonies of Survivors and their families, former school staff and their descendants, government and church officials, and any others whose lives have been affected by the residential schools. Beyond the work of the TRC, the Honorary Witnesses have pledged their commitment to the ongoing work of reconciliation between Aboriginal and non-Aboriginal peoples. We also encouraged everyone who attended TRC National Events or Community Hearings to see themselves as witnesses, with an obligation to find ways of making reconciliation a concrete reality in their own lives, communities, schools, and workplaces.

As Elder Jim Dumont explained at the Traditional Knowledge Keepers Forum in June 2014, "in Ojibwe thinking, to speak the truth is to actually speak from the heart."[13] At the Community Hearing in Key First Nation, Saskatchewan, in 2012, Survivor Wilfred Whitehawk told us he was glad that he disclosed his abuse:

> I don't regret it because it taught me something. It taught me to talk about truth, about me, to be honest about who I am.... I am very proud of who I am today. It took me a long time, but I'm there. And what I have, my values and belief systems are mine and no one is going to impose theirs on me. And no one today is going to take advantage of me, man or woman, the government or the RCMP, because I have a voice today. I can speak for me and no one can take that away.[14]

Survivor and the child of Survivors Vitaline Elsie Jenner said, "I'm quite happy to be able to share my story.... I want the people of Canada to hear, to listen, for it is the truth.... I also want my grandchildren to learn, to learn from me that, yes, it did happen."[15]

Another descendant of Survivors, Daniel Elliot, told the Commission:

> I think all Canadians need to stop and take a look and not look away. Yeah, it's embarrassing, yeah, it's an ugly part of our history. We don't want to know about it. What I want to see from the Commission is to rewrite the history books so that other generations will understand and not go through the same thing that we're going through now, like it never happened.[16]

President of the Métis National Council Clement Chartier spoke to the Commission about the importance of truth to justice and reconciliation. At the Saskatchewan National Event, he said:

> The truth is important. So I'll try to address the truth and a bit of reconciliation as well. The truth is that the Métis Nation, represented by the Métis National Council, is not a party to the Indian Residential Schools Settlement Agreement.... And the truth is that the exclusion of the Métis Nation or the Métis as a people is reflected throughout this whole period not only in the Indian Residential Schools Settlement Agreement but in the apology made by Canada as well....
>
> We are, however, the products ... of the same assimilationist policy that the federal government foisted upon the Treaty Indian kids. So there ought to be some solution.... The Métis boarding schools, residential schools, are excluded. And we need to ensure that everyone was aware of that and hopefully some point down the road, you will help advocate and get, you know, the governments or whoever is responsible to accept responsibility and to move forward on a path to reconciliation, because reconciliation should be for all Aboriginal peoples and not only some Aboriginal peoples.[17]

At the British Columbia National Event, the former lieutenant-governor of British Columbia, the Honourable Steven Point, said:

> And so many of you have said today, so many of the witnesses that came forward said, "I cannot forgive. I'm not ready to forgive." And I wondered why. Reconciliation is

about hearing the truth, that's for sure. It's also about acknowledging that truth. Acknowledging that what you've said is true. Accepting responsibility for your pain and putting those children back in the place they would have been, had they not been taken from their homes....

What are the blockages to reconciliation? The continuing poverty in our communities and the failure of our government to recognize that, "Yes, we own the land." Stop the destruction of our territories and for God's sake, stop the deaths of so many of our women on highways across this country.... I'm going to continue to talk about reconciliation, but just as important, I'm going to foster healing in our own people, so that our children can avoid this pain, can avoid this destruction and finally take our rightful place in this "Our Canada."[18]

When former residential school staff attended public TRC events, some thought it was most important to hear directly from Survivors, even if their own perspectives and memories of the schools might differ from those of the Survivors. At a Community Hearing in Thunder Bay, Ontario, Merle Nisley, who worked at the Poplar Hill residential school in the early 1970s, said:

I think it would be valuable for people who have been involved in the schools to hear stories personally. And I also think it would be valuable, when it's appropriate ... [for] former students who are on the healing path to ... hear some of our stories, or to hear some of our perspectives. But I know that's a very difficult thing to do.... Certainly this is not the time to try to ask all those former students to sit and listen to the rationale of the former staff because there's just too much emotion there ... and there's too little trust ... you can't do things like that when there's low levels of trust. So I think really a very important thing is for former staff to hear the stories and to be courageous enough just to hear them.... Where wrongs were done, where abuses happened, where punishment was over the top, and wherever sexual abuse happened, somehow we need to courageously sit and talk about that, and apologize. I don't know how that will happen.[19]

Nisley's reflections highlight one of the difficulties the Commission faced in trying to create a space for respectful dialogue between former residential school students and staff. While, in most cases, this was possible, in other instances, Survivors and their family members found it very difficult to listen to former staff, particularly if they perceived the speaker to be an apologist for the schools.

At the TRC Victoria Regional Event, Brother Tom Cavanaugh, the district superior of the Oblates of Mary Immaculate for British Columbia and the Yukon, spoke about his time as a supervisor at the Christie residential school:

What I experienced over the six years I was at Christie residential school was a staff, Native and non-Native alike, working together to provide as much as possible, a safe loving environment for the children attending Christie school. Was it a perfect situation? No, it wasn't a perfect situation ... but again, there didn't seem to be, at that time, any other viable alternative in providing a good education for so many children who lived in relatively small and isolated communities.

Survivors and family members who were present in the audience spoke out, saying, "Truth, tell the truth." Brother Cavanaugh replied, "If you give me a chance, I will tell you the truth." When TRC Chair Justice Murray Sinclair intervened to ask the audience to allow Brother Cavanaugh to finish his statement, he was able to do so without further interruption. Visibly shaken, Cavanaugh then went on to acknowledge that children had also been abused in the schools, and he condemned such actions, expressing his sorrow and regret for this breach of trust:

> I can honestly say that our men are hurting too because of the abuse scandal and the rift that this has created between First Nations and church representatives. Many of our men who are still working with First Nations have attended various truth and reconciliation sessions as well as Returning to Spirit sessions, hoping to bring about healing for all concerned. The Oblates desire healing for the abused and for all touched by the past breach of trust. It is our hope that together we can continue to build a better society.[20]

Later that same day, Ina Seitcher, who attended the Christie residential school, painted a very different picture of the school from what Brother Cavanaugh had described:

> I went to Christie residential school. This morning I heard a priest talking about his Christie residential school. I want to tell him [about] my Christie residential school. I went there for ten months. Ten months that impacted my life for fifty years. I am just now on my healing journey.... I need to do this, I need to speak out. I need to speak for my mom and dad who went to residential school, for my aunts, my uncles, all that are beyond now.... All the pain of our people, the hurt, the anger....That priest that talked about how loving that Christie residential school was – it was not. That priest was most likely in his office not knowing what was going on down in the dorms or in the lunchroom....There were things that happened at Christie residential school, and like I said, I'm just starting my healing journey. There are doors that I don't even want to open. I don't even want to open those doors because I don't know what it would do to me.[21]

These two, seemingly irreconcilable, truths are a stark reminder that there are no easy shortcuts to reconciliation. The fact that there were few direct exchanges at TRC events between Survivors and former school staff indicates that for many, the time for reconciliation had not yet arrived. Indeed, for some, it may never arrive. At the Manitoba National Event in 2010, Survivor Evelyn Brockwood talked about why it is important to ensure that there is adequate time for healing to occur in the truth and reconciliation process. She said:

> When this came out at the beginning, I believe it was 1990, about residential schools, people coming out with their stories, and ... I thought the term, the words they were using, were truth, healing and reconciliation. But somehow it seems like we are going from truth telling to reconciliation, to reconcile with our white brothers and sisters. My brothers and sisters, we have a lot of work to do in the middle. We should really lift up the word *healing*.... Go slow, we are going too fast, too fast.... We have many tears to shed before we even get to the word *reconciliation*.[22]

To determine the truth and to tell the full and complete story of residential schools in this country, the TRC needed to hear from Survivors and their families, former staff, government and church officials, and all those affected by residential schools. Canada's national history in the future must be based on the truth about what happened in the residential schools. One hundred years from now, our children's children and their children must know and still remember this history, because they will inherit from us the responsibility of ensuring that it never happens again.

What is reconciliation?

During the course of the Commission's work, it has become clear that the concept of reconciliation means different things to different people, communities, institutions, and organizations. The TRC mandate describes "reconciliation" as an ongoing individual and collective process, and will require commitment from all those affected including First Nations, Inuit and Métis former Indian Residential School (IRS) students, their families, communities, religious entities, former school employees, government, and the people of Canada. Reconciliation may occur between any of the above groups.[23]

The Commission defines "reconciliation" as an ongoing process of establishing and maintaining respectful relationships. A critical part of this process involves repairing damaged trust by making apologies, providing individual and collective reparations, and following through with concrete actions that demonstrate real societal change. Establishing respectful relationships also requires the revitalization of Indigenous law and legal traditions. It is important that all Canadians understand how traditional First Nations, Inuit, and Métis approaches to resolving conflict, repairing harm, and restoring relationships can inform the reconciliation process.

Traditional Knowledge Keepers and Elders have long dealt with conflicts and harms using spiritual ceremonies and peacemaking practices, and by retelling oral history stories that reveal how their ancestors restored harmony to families and communities. These traditions and practices are the foundation of Indigenous law; they contain wisdom and practical guidance for moving toward reconciliation across this land.[24]

As First Nations, Inuit, and Métis communities access and revitalize their spirituality, cultures, languages, laws, and governance systems, and as non-Aboriginal Canadians increasingly come to understand Indigenous history within Canada, and to recognize and respect Indigenous approaches to establishing and maintaining respectful relationships, Canadians can work together to forge a new covenant of reconciliation.

Despite the ravages of colonialism, every Indigenous nation across the country, each with its own distinctive culture and language, has kept its legal traditions and peacemaking practices alive in its communities. Although Elders and Knowledge Keepers across the land have told us that there is no specific word for "reconciliation" in their own languages, there are many words, stories, and songs, as well as sacred objects such as wampum belts, peace pipes, eagle down, cedar boughs, drums, and regalia, that are used to establish relationships, repair conflicts, restore harmony, and make peace. The ceremonies and protocols of Indigenous law are still remembered and practised in many Aboriginal communities.

At the TRC Traditional Knowledge Keepers Forum in June 2014, TRC Survivor Committee member and Elder Barney Williams told us that

> from sea to sea, we hear words that allude to ... what is reconciliation? What does healing or forgiveness mean? And how there's parallels to all those words that the Creator gave to all the nations.... When I listen and reflect on the voices of the ancestors, your ancestors, I hear my ancestor alluding to the same thing with a different dialect.... My understanding [of reconciliation] comes from a place and time when there was no English spoken ... from my grandmother who was born in the 1800s.... I really feel privileged to have been chosen by my grandmother to be the keeper of our knowledge.... What do we need to do? ... We need to go back to ceremony and embrace ceremony as part of moving forward. We need to understand the laws of our people.[25]

At the same Forum, Elder Stephen Augustine explained the roles of silence and negotiation in Mi'kmaq law. He said "silence" is a concept, and can be used as a consequence for a wrong action or to teach a lesson. Silence is employed according to proper procedures, and ends at a particular time too. Elder Augustine suggested that there is both a place for talking about reconciliation and a need for quiet reflection. Reconciliation cannot occur without listening, contemplation, meditation, and deeper internal deliberation. Silence in the face of residential school harms is an appropriate response for many Indigenous peoples. We must enlarge the space for respectful silence in journeying toward reconciliation, particularly for Survivors who regard this as key to healing. There is also a place for discussion and negotiation for those who want to move beyond silence. Dialogue and mutual adjustment are significant components of Mi'kmaq law. Elder Augustine suggested that other dimensions of human experience – our relationships with the earth and all living beings – are also relevant in working toward reconciliation. This profound insight is an Indigenous law that could be applied more generally.[26]

Elder Reg Crowshoe told the Commission that Indigenous peoples' worldviews, oral history traditions, and practices have much to teach us about how to establish respectful relationships among peoples and with the land and all living things. Learning how to live together in a good way happens through sharing stories and practising reconciliation in our everyday lives.

> When we talk about the concept of reconciliation, I think about some of the stories that I've heard in our culture and stories are important…. These stories are so important as theories but at the same time stories are important to oral cultures. So when we talk about stories, we talk about defining our environment and how we look at authorities that come from the land and how that land, when we talk about our relationship with the land, how we look at forgiveness and reconciliation is so important when we look at it historically.
>
> We have stories in our culture about our superheroes, how we treat each other, stories about how animals and plants give us authorities and privileges to use plants as healing, but we also have stories about practices. How would we practise reconciliation? How would we practise getting together to talk about reconciliation in an oral perspective? And those practices are so important.[27]

As Elder Crowshoe explained further, reconciliation requires talking, but our conversations must be broader than Canada's conventional approaches. Reconciliation between Aboriginal and non-Aboriginal Canadians, from an Aboriginal perspective, also requires reconciliation with the natural world. If human beings resolve problems between themselves but continue to destroy the natural world, then reconciliation remains incomplete. This is a perspective that we as Commissioners have repeatedly heard: that reconciliation will never occur unless we are also reconciled with the earth. Mi'kmaq and other Indigenous laws stress that humans must journey through life in conversation and negotiation with all creation. Reciprocity and mutual respect help sustain our survival. It is this kind of healing and survival that is needed in moving forward from the residential school experience.

Over the course of its work, the Commission created space for exploring the meanings and concepts of reconciliation. In public Sharing Circles at National Events and Community Hearings, we bore witness to powerful moments of truth sharing and humbling acts of reconciliation. Many Survivors had never been able to tell their own families the whole truth of what happened to them in the schools. At hearings in Regina, Saskatchewan, Elder Kirby Littletent said, "I never told, I just told my children, my grandchildren I went to boarding school, that's all. I never shared my experiences."[28]

Many spoke to honour the memory of relatives who have passed on. Simone, an Inuk Survivor from Chesterfield Inlet, Nunavut, said:

> I'm here for my parents – 'Did you miss me when I went away?' 'Did you cry for me?' – and I'm here for my brother, who was a victim, and my niece at the age of five who suffered a head injury and never came home, and her parents never had closure. To this day, they have not found the grave in Winnipeg. And I'm here for them first, and that's why I'm making a public statement.[29]

Others talked about the importance of reconciling with family members, and cautioned that this process is just beginning. Patrick Etherington, a Survivor from St. Anne's residential school in Fort Albany, Ontario, walked with his son and others from Cochrane, Ontario, to the National Event in Winnipeg. He said that the walk helped him to reconnect with his son, and that he "just wanted to be here because I feel this process that we are starting, we got a long ways to go."[30]

We saw the children and grandchildren of Survivors who, in searching for their own identity and place in the world, found compassion and gained new respect for their relatives who went to the schools, once they heard about and began to understand their experiences. At the Northern National Event in Inuvik, Northwest Territories, Maxine Lacorne said:

> As a youth, a young lady, I talk with people my age because I have a good understanding. I talk to people who are residential school Survivors because I like to hear their stories, you know, and it gives me more understanding of my parents…. It is an honour to be here, to sit here among you guys, Survivors. Wow. You guys are strong people, you guys survived everything. And we're still going to be here. They tried to take us away. They tried to take our language away. You guys are still here, we're still here. I'm still here.[31]

We heard about children whose small acts of everyday resistance in the face of rampant abuse, neglect, and bullying in the schools were quite simply heroic. At the TRC British Columbia National Event, Elder Barney Williams said that "many of us, through our pain and suffering, managed to hold our heads up … we were brave children."[32] We saw old bonds of childhood friendship renewed as people gathered and found each other at TRC-sponsored events. Together, they remembered the horrors they had endured even as they recalled with pride long-forgotten accomplishments in various school sports teams, music, or art activities. We heard from resilient, courageous Survivors who, despite their traumatic childhood experiences, went on to become influential leaders in their communities and in all walks of Canadian life, including politics, government, law, education, medicine, the corporate world, and the arts.

We heard from officials representing the federal government that administered the schools. In a Sharing Circle at the Manitoba National Event, the Honourable Chuck Strahl (then minister of Indian Affairs and Northern Development Canada) said:

> Governments like to write … policy, and they like to write legislation, and they like to codify things and so on. And Aboriginal people want to talk about restoration, reconciliation, forgiveness, about healing … about truth. And those things are all things of the heart and of relationship, and not of government policy. Governments do a bad job of that.[33]

Church representatives spoke about their struggles to right the relationship with Aboriginal peoples. In Inuvik, Anglican Archbishop Fred Hiltz told us that as a church, we are renewing our commitment to work with the Assembly of First Nations in addressing long-standing, Indigenous justice issues. As a church, we are requiring anyone who serves the church at a national level to go through anti-racism training…. We have a lot to do in our church to make sure that racism is eliminated.[34]

Educators told us about their growing awareness of the inadequate role that post-secondary institutions played in training the teachers who taught in the schools. They have pledged to change educational practices and curriculum to be more inclusive of Aboriginal knowledge and history. Artists shared their ideas and feelings about truth and reconciliation through songs, paintings, dance, film, and other media. Corporations provided resources to bring Survivors to events, and, in some cases, some of their own staff and managers.

For non-Aboriginal Canadians who came to bear witness to Survivors' life stories, the experience was powerful. One woman said simply, "By listening to your story, my story can change. By listening to your story, I can change."[35]

Reconciliation as relationship

In its 2012 *Interim Report*, the TRC recommended that federal, provincial, and territorial governments, and all parties to the Settlement Agreement, undertake to meet and explore the *United Nations Declaration on the Rights of Indigenous Peoples*, as a framework for reconciliation in Canada. We remain convinced that the United Nations Declaration provides the necessary principles, norms, and standards for reconciliation to flourish in twenty-first-century Canada.

A reconciliation framework is one in which Canada's political and legal systems, educational and religious institutions, the corporate sector, and civil society function in ways that are consistent with the *United Nations Declaration on the Rights of Indigenous Peoples*, which Canada has endorsed. The Commission believes that the following guiding principles of truth and reconciliation will assist Canadians moving forward:

1. The *United Nations Declaration on the Rights of Indigenous Peoples* is the framework for reconciliation at all levels and across all sectors of Canadian society.
2. First Nations, Inuit, and Métis peoples, as the original peoples of this country and as self-determining peoples, have Treaty, constitutional, and human rights that must be recognized and respected.
3. Reconciliation is a process of healing of relationships that requires public truth sharing, apology, and commemoration that acknowledge and redress past harms.
4. Reconciliation requires constructive action on addressing the ongoing legacies of colonialism that have had destructive impacts on Aboriginal peoples' education, cultures and languages, health, child welfare, the administration of justice, and economic opportunities and prosperity.
5. Reconciliation must create a more equitable and inclusive society by closing the gaps in social, health, and economic outcomes that exist between Aboriginal and non-Aboriginal Canadians.
6. All Canadians, as Treaty peoples, share responsibility for establishing and maintaining mutually respectful relationships.
7. The perspectives and understandings of Aboriginal Elders and Traditional Knowledge Keepers of the ethics, concepts, and practices of reconciliation are vital to long-term reconciliation.

8. Supporting Aboriginal peoples' cultural revitalization and integrating Indigenous knowledge systems, oral histories, laws, protocols, and connections to the land into the reconciliation process are essential.

9. Reconciliation requires political will, joint leadership, trust building, accountability, and transparency, as well as a substantial investment of resources.

10. Reconciliation requires sustained public education and dialogue, including youth engagement, about the history and legacy of residential schools, Treaties, and Aboriginal rights, as well as the historical and contemporary contributions of Aboriginal peoples to Canadian society.

Together, Canadians must do more than just *talk* about reconciliation; we must learn how to *practise* reconciliation in our everyday lives – within ourselves and our families, and in our communities, governments, places of worship, schools, and workplaces. To do so constructively, Canadians must remain committed to the ongoing work of establishing and maintaining respectful relationships.

For many Survivors and their families, this commitment is foremost about healing themselves, their communities, and nations, in ways that revitalize individuals as well as Indigenous cultures, languages, spirituality, laws, and governance systems. For governments, building a respectful relationship involves dismantling a centuries-old political and bureaucratic culture in which, all too often, policies and programs are still based on failed notions of assimilation. For churches, demonstrating long-term commitment requires atoning for actions within the residential schools, respecting Indigenous spirituality, and supporting Indigenous peoples' struggles for justice and equity. Schools must teach history in ways that foster mutual respect, empathy, and engagement. All Canadian children and youth deserve to know Canada's honest history, including what happened in the residential schools, and to appreciate the rich history and knowledge of Indigenous nations who continue to make such a strong contribution to Canada, including our very name and collective identity as a country. For Canadians from all walks of life reconciliation offers a new way of living together.

Notes[8]

[1] TRC, AVS, Alma Mann Scott, Statement to the Truth and Reconciliation Commission of Canada, Winnipeg, Manitoba, June 17, 2010, Statement Number: 02-MB-16JU10-016.

[2] Media coverage on the call for an inquiry on missing and murdered Aboriginal women has been extensive. See, for example: "Women's Memorial March in Vancouver Attracts Hundreds," *CBC News*, February 14, 2015, http://www.cbc.ca/news/canada/british-columbia/womens-memorial- march-in-vancouver-attracts-hundreds-1.2957930; "Murdered and Missing Aboriginal Women Deserve Inquiry, Rights Group Says," *CBC News*, January 12, 2015, http://www.cbc.ca/news/politics/murdered-and-missing-aboriginal-women-deserve-inquiry-rights-group-says-1.2897707; Ken S. Coates, "Aboriginal Women Deserve Much More than an Inquiry," *National Post*, February 16, 2015, http://news.nationalpost.com/2015/02/16/ken-s-coates-aboriginal-women-deservemuch- more-than-an-inquiry/. On economic development issues, see, for example: Jeff Lewis, "TransCanada CEO Says Canada Needs to Resolve Conflicts over Pipelines," *Globe and Mail*, February 4, 2015, http://www.theglobeandmail.com/report-on-

business/economy/transcanadaceo- says-canada-needs-to-resolve-conflicts-over-pipelines/article22798276/; Daniel Schwartz and Mark Gollom, "NB Fracking Protests and the Fight for Aboriginal Rights," *CBC News Canada*, October 19, 2013, http://www.cbc.ca/news/canada/n-b-fracking-protests-and-the-fight-for-aboriginal- rights-1.2126515; Michael MacDonald, "Shale Gas Conflict in New Brunswick Underscores Historical Grievances, Rights of First Nations," *Toronto Star*, December 25, 2013, http://www. thestar.com/news/canada/2013/12/25/shale_gas_conflict_in_new_ brunswick_underscores_historic_grievances_rights_of_first_nations.html.

[3] On the role of the courts in Aboriginal rights and reconciliation, see: Joseph Brean, "'Reconciliation' with First Nations, Not the Charter of Rights & Freedoms, Will Define the Supreme Court in Coming years, Chief Justice Says," *National Post*, March 13, 2014, http://news.nationalpost.com/2014/03/13/reconciliation-with-first-nations-not-the-charter-of-rights-freedoms-will-define-   the-supreme-court-in-coming-years-chief-justice-says/. On Aboriginal rights cases, see, for example: "6 Landmark Rulings on Native Rights," *CBC News*, January 8, 2013, http://www.cbc.ca/news/canada/6-landmark-rulings-on-native-rights-1.1316961. On day schools litigation, see, for example: "Residential School Day Scholars Launch Class-action Lawsuit," *CBC News*, August 16, 2012, http://www. cbc.ca/news/canada/british-columbia/residential-school-day-scholars-launchclass- action-lawsuit-1.1146607; Dene Moore, "Federal Appeal Court Gives Ok on Hearing First Nations' Day-school Suit," *Canadian Press*, March 4, 2014, http://www.ctvnews.ca/canada/federal-appeal-court-gives-ok-on-hearing-first-nations-day-school-suit-1.1713809. On Sixties Scoop legislation, see, for example: "Sixties Scoop Case Moves Forward as Class-action Lawsuit," *CBC News*, December 3, 2014, http://www.cbc.ca/news/canada/thunder-bay/sixties-scoop-case-moves-forward-as-class-action-lawsuit-1.2859332; Diana Mehta, "'Sixties Scoop' Class-action Lawsuit to Proceed," *Canadian Press*, December 4, 2014, http://www. ctvnews.ca/canada/60s-scoop-class-action-lawsuit-to-proceed-1.2132317.

[4] Miller, *Lethal Legacy*, vi.

[5] TRC, AVS, Mary Deleary, Statement to the Truth and Reconciliation Commission of Canada, Winnipeg, Manitoba, June 26, 2014, Statement Number: SE049.

[6] TRC, AVS, Archie Little. Statement to the Truth and Reconciliation Commission of Canada, Victoria, British Columbia, April 13, 2012, Statement Number: SP135.

[7] McKay, "Expanding the Dialogue," 107. McKay was the first Aboriginal moderator of the United Church of Canada (1992 to 1994).

[8] TRC, AVS, Jessica Bolduc, Statement to the Truth and Reconciliation Commission of Canada, Edmonton, Alberta, March 30, 2014, Statement Number: ABNE401.

[9] Truth and Reconciliation Commission of Canada, *Educating our Youth*, video, September 19, 2013, http://www.trc.ca/websites/trcinstitution/index.php?p=3.

[10] TRC, AVS, Patsy George, Statement to the Truth and Reconciliation Commission of Canada, Vancouver, British Columbia, September 21, 2013, Statement Number: BCNE404.

[11] TRC, AVS, Dave Courchene, Statement to the Truth and Reconciliation Commission of Canada, Winnipeg, Manitoba, June 25, 2014, Statement Number: SE048.

[12] The mandate of the Truth and Reconciliation Commission of Canada is listed under Schedule N of the Indian Residential Schools Settlement Agreement,

http://www.residentialschoolsettlement.ca/settlement.html. In accordance with the TRC's mandate, the Commission was required to recognize "the significance of Aboriginal oral and legal traditions in its activities," Schedule N, 4(d); and "witness, support, promote and facilitate truth and reconciliation events at both the national and community levels," Schedule N, 1(c). The term *witness* "refers to the Aboriginal principle of 'witnessing,'" Indian Residential Schools Settlement Agreement, Schedule N, 1(c), n1. Aboriginal oral history, legal traditions, and the principle of witnessing have deep historical roots and contemporary relevance for reconciliation. Indigenous law was used to resolve family and community conflict, to establish Treaties among various Indigenous nations, and to negotiate nation-to-nation treaties with the Crown. For a comprehensive history of Aboriginal–Crown Treaty making from contact to the present, see Miller, *Compact, Contract, Covenant.* The term *witness* is in reference to the Aboriginal principle of witnessing, which varies among First Nations, Métis, and Inuit peoples. Generally speaking, witnesses are called to be the keepers of history when an event of historic significance occurs. Through witnessing, the event or work that is undertaken is validated and provided legitimacy. The work could not take place without honored and respected guests to witness it. Witnesses are asked to store and care for the history they witness and to share it with their own people when they return home. For Aboriginal peoples, the act of witnessing these events comes with a great responsibility to remember all the details and be able to recount them accurately as the foundation of oral histories. See: Thomas, "Honouring the Oral Traditions," 243–244.

[13] TRC, AVS, Jim Dumont, Statement to the Truth and Reconciliation Commission of Canada, Winnipeg, Manitoba, June 26, 2014, Statement Number: SE049.

[14] TRC, AVS, Wilfred Whitehawk, Statement to the Truth and Reconciliation Commission of Canada, Key First Nation, Saskatchewan, January 21, 2012, Statement Number: SP039.

[15] TRC, AVS, Vitaline Elsie Jenner, Statement to the Truth and Reconciliation Commission of Canada, Winnipeg, Manitoba, June 16, 2010, Statement Number: 02-MB-16JU10-131.

[16] TRC, AVS, Daniel Elliot, Statement to the Truth and Reconciliation Commission of Canada, Victoria, British Columbia, April 13, 2012, Statement Number: SP135.

[17] TRC, AVS, Clement Chartier, Statement to the Truth and Reconciliation Commission of Canada, Saskatoon, Saskatchewan, June 22, 2013, Statement Number: SNE202.

[18] TRC, AVS, Steven Point, Statement to the Truth and Reconciliation Commission of Canada, Vancouver, British Columbia, September 20, 2013, Statement Number: BCNE304.

[19] TRC, AVS, Merle Nisley, Statement to the Truth and Reconciliation Commission of Canada, Thunder Bay, Ontario, December 14, 2011, Statement Number: 2011–4199.

[20] TRC, AVS, Tom Cavanaugh, Statement to the Truth and Reconciliation Commission of Canada, Victoria, British Columbia, April 14, 2012, Statement Number: SP137.

[21] TRC, AVS, Ina Seitcher, Statement to the Truth and Reconciliation Commission of Canada, Victoria, British Columbia, April 14, 2012, Statement Number: SP136.

[22] TRC, AVS, Evelyn Brockwood, Statement to the Truth and Reconciliation Commission of Canada, Winnipeg, Manitoba, June 18, 2010, Statement Number: SC110.

[23] Indian Residential Schools Settlement Agreement, Schedule N, Principles, 1, http://www.residentialschoolsettlement.ca/settlement.html.

[24] Johnston, "Aboriginal Traditions," 141–159.

[25] TRC, AVS, Barney Williams, Statement to the Truth and Reconciliation Commission of Canada, Winnipeg, Manitoba, June 26, 2014, Statement Number: SE049.

[26] TRC, AVS, Stephen Augustine, Statement to the Truth and Reconciliation Commission of Canada, Winnipeg, Manitoba, June 25, 2014, Statement Number: SE048.

[27] TRC, AVS, Reg Crowshoe, Statement to the Truth and Reconciliation Commission of Canada, Winnipeg, Manitoba, June 26, 2014, Statement Number: SE049.

[28] TRC, AVS, Kirby Littletent, Statement to the Truth and Reconciliation Commission of Canada, Regina, Saskatchewan, January 16, 2012, Statement Number: SP035.

[29] TRC, AVS, Simone (last name not provided), Statement to the Truth and Reconciliation Commission of Canada, Inuvik, Northwest Territories, July 1, 2011, Statement Number: SC092.

[30] TRC, AVS, Patrick Etherington, Statement to the Truth and Reconciliation Commission of Canada, Winnipeg, Manitoba, June 17, 2010, Statement Number: SC108.

[31] TRC, AVS, Maxine Lacorne, Statement to the Truth and Reconciliation Commission of Canada, Inuvik, Northwest Territories, June 29, 2011, Statement Number: SC090.

[32] TRC, AVS, Barney Williams, Statement to the Truth and Reconciliation Commission of Canada, Vancouver, British Columbia, September 21, 2013, Statement Number: BCNE404.

[33] TRC, AVS, Honourable Chuck Strahl, Statement to the Truth and Reconciliation Commission of Canada, Winnipeg, Manitoba, June 16, 2010, Statement Number: SC093.

[34] TRC, AVS, Archbishop Fred Hiltz, Statement to the Truth and Reconciliation Commission of Canada, Inuvik, Northwest Territories, July 1, 2011, Statement Number: NNE402.

[35] TRC, AVS, Anonymous, Statement to the Truth and Reconciliation Commission of Canada, Regina, Saskatchewan, January 17, 2012, Statement Number: SP036.

Notes

1 The agreements reached between the parties indicate that there is a need to constitute a commission for clarifying the truth, restoring social cohesion, and ensuring that acts associated with the internal armed conflict are not repeated.

2 Colombia's official institutions charged with this task are the Comisión Nacional de Reparación y Reconciliación (CNRR-Grupo de Memoria Histórica) [National Commission for Reparation and Reconciliation (CNRR-Historical Memory Group], created in 2008 within the framework of the Justice and Peace Act (Law 978), and the Centro Nacional de Memoria Histórica (CNMH) [National Center for Historical Memory (CNMH)], created in 2011 with a ten-year mandate within the framework of the Victims and Land Restitution Act (Law 1448).

3   The enforcement framework for the Consulta Previa de la Ley de Víctimas y Restitución de Tierras, Indigenous organizations were able to issue their own regulatory framework (Law-Decree 4633 of 2011), which incorporates their proposals for reparation and memory from their own distinctive perspective.

4   At the beginning of the twentieth century and through a gigantic network of rubber extraction sites, a commercial project expanded throughout the Amazon. Its objective was the intensive and systematic exploitation of Indigenous labor in order to increase rubber production. Numerous documents from the era, as well as modern historical analyses, have given accounts of the various mechanisms and relations of domination imposed on Indigenous peoples by commercial agents: the practice was referred to as "debt peonage" based on inequitable commercial relations, assassinations, whippings, torture, death of local laborers from overwork, as well as the maintenance of sites that damaged the traditional forms of production lead to the near disappearance of the area's Indigenous peoples. As a result of these actions, it is estimated that the rubber extraction project cost the lives of 30,000 Indigenous people, or almost 60% of the region's native population.

5   In 2012, which marked the commemoration of the rubber boom's centenary, representatives of the Colombian, Peruvian, and British governments traveled to the Amazon to apologize for the acts associated with the rubber genocide.

6   See, in particular, the documentary *Nabusimake: Memorias de una Independencia* [Nabusimake: Memories of an Independence], created by the Indigenous communications collective, Zhigoneshi.

7   The printed excerpt is taken from pages 113 to 127 of *What We Have Learned: Principles of Truth and Reconciliation* (Montreal and Kingston: McGill-Queen's University Press. 2015).

8   The notes appear in the original document on page 191 to 193.

9   Appropriate references have been gathered from the TRC Report's larger bibliography. As they are integral to that document, they have not been incorporated in the Common Bibliography.

References[9]

Johnston, D. 2005. "Aboriginal Traditions of Tolerance and Reparation: Introducing Canadian Colonialism." In *Le Devoir de Memoire et les Politiques du Pardon*, ed. M. Labelle, R. Antoinius, and G. Leroux, pp. 141–159. Quebec: Presses de l'Universite de Quebec.

McKay, S. 2008. "Expanding the Dialogue on Truth and Reconciliation—In a Good Way." In *From Truth to Reconciliation: Transforming the Legacy of Residential Schools*, ed. M. Brant Castellano, L. Archibald, and M. DeGagne, pp. 103–115. Ottawa: Aboriginal Healing Foundation.

Miller, J. R. 2004. *Lethal Legacy: Current Native Controversies in Canada*. Toronto: McClelland and Stewart.

Miller, J. R. 2009. *Compact, Contract, Covenant: Aboriginal Treaty Making in Canada*. Toronto: University of Toronto Press.

Thomas, R.A. (Qwul'sih'yah'maht). 2005. "Honouring the Oral Traditions of My Ancestors through Storytelling." In *Research as Resistance: Critical, Indigenous, and Anti-Oppressive Approaches*, ed. L. Brown and S. Strega, pp. 237–254. Toronto: Canadian Scholars Press/ Women's Press.

CHAPTER EIGHTEEN

Sophiatown and the Politics of Commemoration

NATASHA ERLANK

In 1956 in *Naught for Your Comfort*, his polemic on Apartheid South Africa, Bishop Trevor Huddleston wrote the following about Sophiatown:

> It is particularly important to me to try and paint the picture that I know and that is yet so elusive, for in a few years Sophiatown will cease to exist … And in a few years, men will have forgotten that this was a living community and a very unusual one. It will have slipped away into history. (1956: 89)

Little could Huddleston have dreamed of the grip that Sophiatown would come to exercise on people's imaginations, not only in South Africa, but globally. However, while Huddleston might not have imagined the extent to which the suburb, its inhabitants, and their forced removal would come to occupy an iconic space in South Africa's history, his words about community are still recognizable in the suburb today. In mid-2011, participants in a public history project in Sophiatown, Johannesburg, composed a project vision: "The vision of the project is for individuals to share experiences, so as to understand/respect each other in order to create a new sense of community so that they can be active participants in the future" (Sophiatown Project notes 2011). As one of the aims of the project, participants expressed the desire to "Create opportunities for individuals to talk about the things in their pasts that are important to them, what they bring from their pasts to current-day Sophiatown. To get to know and build trust in their neighbours."

Ironically, the language here echoed Bloke Modisane's description of the "know-your-township" campaign instituted by Johannesburg municipal officials in order to figure out who were bona fide residents of the suburb, who would thus qualify for rehousing. Modisane was one of the group of journalists based mostly in Sophiatown and who wrote for the publication, *Drum*. After he had to leave Sophiatown, he wrote a bitter and poignant account of the process, entitled *Blame Me on History*.

A Companion to Public History, First Edition. Edited by David Dean.
© 2018 John Wiley & Sons Ltd. Published 2018 by John Wiley & Sons Ltd.

This set off a vigorous know-your-township campaign, and some of the questions alleged to have been put to applicants were brought to the attention of *Drum* magazine.
Who is the fattest woman in Sophiatown?
Who is Sophiatown's oldest Chinese woman?
Where is the biggest rock in Sophiatown?
Who operates the biggest fah-fee pool in Sophiatown? (Modisane 1986: 110)

While the work that forms the core of this chapter was never intended to evoke the nostalgia that still surrounds Sophiatown, the past is still current in the present suburb in the evocations of multiculturalism and community that residents knowingly invoke. For many of them, a comparison between the cosmopolitanism of Sophiatown then and now provides a framing for community pride and an interest in projects that are about improving the neighborhood. In what follows, I describe the community-based public history project undertaken by myself and colleagues in Sophiatown from 2009 to 2014. While the Sophiatown Project is only one of many community-based public history projects in South Africa, its differences from and similarities to other projects allow a consideration of the current nature of public history work in South Africa, as well as some of the shifts it has undergone in the last 20 years. Further, by including a detailed consideration of how we went about our work, it is possible to reflect upon the methodological challenges that faced the project. This piece is then both reflexive and a theoretical framing of community heritage initiatives in South Africa.

Heritage and the past in contemporary South Africa

History is a fraught subject for many South Africans. In late 2015, democratic South Africa experienced an unprecedented upsurge in concern for its racialized and colonial past, expressed through a series of protests which began around the continued presence of the statue of Cecil John Rhodes at the University of Cape Town, and the lack of transformation that this signified (Hodes 2015). By the end of the year, a wave of protest had broken out among university students across the country, engulfing most of its 23 institutions of higher education, and firmly located in ideas around lack of redress and the continuation of apartheid's wound (Grootes 2015; Lewis 2015).[1] Words like "legacy," "history," "wounds," and "pain" are receiving intellectual airtime, in all senses of the word, in a way not previously encountered. This attention to history is both for the signs of the past – statues and other symbols of commemoration – but also for psychic wounds caused by a lack of transformation and decolonialization that should have occurred – but failed to occur – following the end of apartheid in the early 1990s. Harsh economic disenfranchisement for most black South Africans is refracted through a sense of betrayal at the recent past. South Africa, it is suggested, must return to and resurrect its African ways of knowing and its African intellectuals, its indigenous knowledge systems, and a proper reverence for culture.

The 2015 protests reflect a critically needed reengagement with history for many South Africans, both black and white. Some of the references are to recent history. Students at the University of the Witwatersrand have called for the renaming of one of its buildings after Solomon Mahlangu, an anti-apartheid activist of the June 1976 uprising, who was later hanged for terrorism by the South African state.[2] At the same time, the many and deep conversations and study circles that have formed as a result of the movement often reference a more distant history through ideas about an African philosophical heritage, untainted by colonial and extra-African influences.

While this chapter is not the space for a consideration of the politics of protest in South Africa in 2015, the ways in which ideas about heritage, history, and commemoration have been employed resonate with broader South African public discourse since the early 2000s. In a 2000 paper, Ciraj Rassool commented upon the rise of heritage politics in South Africa in relation to the idea of a rainbow nation:

> In broad outline, these discursive contours – of a society of 'many cultures' and a history of 'great lives of resistance and reconciliation' – have been emerging and taking shape in almost every sphere of heritage construction and public culture in South Africa, from television histories and cultural projects of newspapers to the T[ruth] and R[econciliation] C[ommission] and claims for land, from museums (new and old) and legacy projects to new monuments and cultural tourism. (2000: 1)

However, if the 1990s were the decade of reconciliation, epitomized in the Truth and Reconciliation Commission, then the 2000s reflect state failure, the deepening economic crisis, and continuing racism. These currents are reflected in heritage initiatives in different ways, including a reneging on the democratic promises of the 1990s. Across the country, ordinary people complain about lack of consultation and participation in local-government-run projects, including heritage initiatives. In her work on the Walter Sisulu Square of Dedication in Kliptown, Johannesburg, Christa Kuljian interviewed local residents about the square:

> 'Those JDA [Johannesburg Development Agency] people made so many promises that didn't materialise', says Aunt Eva, who now uses a wheelchair. 'They asked me to be part of their forum. I said I would, but I told them I don't have transport. "Transport is no problem," they said. "We'll come and pick you up." They didn't do it even once. (2009: 456)[3]

Since 1994, the South African state at the local, provincial, and national levels has embarked on a number of historical heritage initiatives, where heritage is understood to include historical sites and objects of importance to the nation. These include Freedom Park in Tshwane/Pretoria, the Robben Island Museum in Cape Town, and a host of others. While legislation around heritage uses a UNESCO-derived understanding to drive policy, most often what has emerged is a series of initiatives that either commemorate the apartheid past, or look to reproduce African culture on the understanding that it represents a proxy, via the notion of intangible or living heritage, of the African past. Much of what is commemorated resides within a canon of events and figures, which reference events like the Sharpeville Massacre in 1960, the Soweto Uprising of 1976; and figures like Nelson Mandela.

Viewed as a whole, these monuments, heritage sites, and museums all contribute toward what has been referred to as a "post-apartheid heritage complex." Minkley (2008) explains this complex as follows: "In essence, this can be characterized as a return to a heritage complex in which its hegemonic discourse is to frame the 'national estate' as comprised of the indigenous and traditional and the root and route of resistance as the basis of inherited 'entitlement'" (2008: 22). The formulation links African intangible heritage from the pre-colonial past to a set of dates which trace the high points of anti-colonial and anti-apartheid protest, including the Defiance Campaign of the early 1950s, the Freedom Charter in 1955, the Sharpeville Massacre in 1960, the Soweto Uprising of

1976, and more recently a memorial to Chris Hani, who was assassinated in 1993. The politics of public heritage reflect a nationalist historical canon (Baines 2007), reflecting principally the achievements of the African National Congress, even if academic historians might question the extent, for instance, to which the ANC was responsible for the Sharpeville Uprising in 1960.

In a context where state funding is directed toward projects that meet the imperatives listed above, in addition to facilitating "the economic empowerment and skills development of a people" (Republic of South Africa 2015), community heritage museums and initiatives either have to follow suit, or struggle to cover their costs (Marschall 2010). The District Six Museum in Cape Town, for example, has continually struggled to raise funding (Rassool 2006a). A current effort under way to build a Women's Living History Museum in Pretoria is caught between the opposing impulses of ANC funding, which seeks to valorize the contribution of ANC female members to the anti-apartheid struggle, and the wish of board members to acknowledge and commemorate all South African women, irrespective of political affiliation.

In Sophiatown, the Trevor Huddleston Memorial Centre (THMC) secured start-up funding for a museum, because the site chosen was the house of former ANC President Albert Bitini Xuma. While the metropolitan council of Johannesburg lacks the capacity to run the initiative, it certainly expressed a desire to have the museum present a narrative which emphasized the role Xuma had played as an anti-apartheid and ANC figure in the 1950s.[4] Across the country, museum curators and boards have had to balance the wishes of their funders with what is often and generally a very sensitive approach to presenting a less partisan history. It should perhaps be noted that few heritage sites in South Africa, be they state driven or private, expect to cover their running costs from income generated.

State-sanctioned heritage production is paralleled by a series of initiatives represented in the privately funded (or funded only in part by the state) community-history museums. These projects challenge and subvert official and (it should be said) academic authority about the past.[5] Some of the better known include the District Six Museum (Rassool 2006a), the Red Location Museum in Port Elizabeth (Baines 2005; Msila 2013), and the Lwandle Migrant Labour Museum in Somerset West (Witz 2011; Witz and Murray 2011). Community heritage initiatives are also present in a range of projects more expressly connected to working with public history, such as those undertaken under the auspices of the Wits History Workshop, a more recent project undertaken by the *Sunday Times* newspaper (Kros 2008; Marschall 2011), and a host of other, smaller community-generated imaginings of the past (Ward 1992), not all of them written about. Work conducted in and on Johannesburg townships, for instance, Alexandra, has also incorporated the idea of a community history written from the bottom up (Bonner 2008).

Characteristic of these projects is a view of collective memory and nostalgia which often romanticizes community as an antidote to the vicissitudes of twenty-first century life. In practical terms, this often translates into heritage initiatives projecting what Svetlana Boym (2001) refers to as restorative nostalgia, where collective memory desires to restore what has passed, rather than reflective nostalgia, where memory is examined for how it can enlighten. Outside the academy and its habitual cynicism, in many South African circles a nostalgic view of the past still prevails, whether it is a shared past as victims of apartheid, or a past which looks to plucky community activism in the face of apartheid. I shall return to the issue of community below.

The Sophiatown project

The idea for this work emerged from a three-month process in 2008, when David Thelen, an American academic working in public history, and the University of Johannesburg Historical Studies Department engaged in a community oral history project in Sophiatown. As part of his work, Thelen connected with the THMC, a non-governmental organization working in Sophiatown, on issues of heritage and development. From our preliminary work, it rapidly became apparent that there was a much greater scope for engagement than we had originally thought.

Some of the initial thinking arose from Thelen and Erlank's own research (Murray, Tshabangu, and Erlank 2010). Indeed, Rosenzweig and Thelen's work on popular understandings of history in the United States gave us a good starting point:

> The hard civic challenges for a participatory culture grounded in history revolve around how people might move outward from their intimate worlds, connect with others, recognize common challenges and settle on common narratives ... In the 1960s it was easy for citizens to find and engage each other. Unprecedented numbers of people mobilized in highly visible social movements through which they spoke collectively and acted to engage everyone in public contests. Over the next generation, as those social movements have receded, new industries have merged to reshape the very meanings of "political participation" and "civic forum". They have tried to change who participates in the civic forum and on what terms. (2000: 202)

This, coupled with engagements with Sophiatown residents about what might interest them, presented something of a way forward. The minister at Christ the King in Sophiatown, significant as the church of Anglican anti-apartheid cleric Trevor Huddleston, expressed his wishes in this way: "We want to marry our ancestors in a way to look into the future together. We want to marry the memory of Sophiatown to the memory of Triomf" (Mongezi Guma, interview, 2008).

Guma's words alerted us to one of the blank pages in the history of the suburb, the history of what Sophiatown became under white suburbanization after the forced removals of its black, Indian, and Coloured inhabitants during the 1950s. During the 1940s and 1950s, Sophiatown was a mixed-race suburb, one of only two spaces in Johannesburg where Africans could own their own houses. Its cheap rents and proximity to the center made it a favored location of black artists, writers, singers, and politicians. Writers like Bloke Modisane and Can Themba, part of a group known as the Drum Writers (after a local newspaper), made the suburb their home. When Sophiatown was destroyed in the mid-1950s in order to make way for white resettlement, these writers made the suburb famous in an outpouring of literary heartbreak and loss. This is the Sophiatown that is most often remembered in the industry that has arisen to commemorate it, and Guma's words reflect an absence that many contemporary Sophiatown (and former Triomf) residents feel.

In the project brief that accompanied one of our first funding proposals, we described what we wanted to do as follows:

> The aim of the project is to develop and apply new ways of engaging the past that can assist in developing South Africans' capacity to participate in the country's continuing transition to a more democratic society, a civil society characterised by a more civically-engaged citizenry. We aim to create an innovative methodology in order to do so: forging oral history

methods with civic engagement and memorialisation strategies so that people's experiences of the past can serve as a conduit to the future. We wish to make individuals and their experiences in a fractured community, Sophiatown, both visible and recognizable to others within the community, which we hope will occur through the uncovering, sharing and presenting of mutual and shared pasts, revisioning the presents and imagining and reaching towards futures. This will serve as a platform from which to foster healing and develop community pride in a community with a deeply conflicted history. (2009)

The work we wanted to undertake in Sophiatown rested on the notion of community history, created and owned as a community resource. Notwithstanding the difficulties associated with using terms like "community," which in South Africa staggers from overuse by well-weaning activists to downright scorn from academics as a Utopian chimera, the term slipped into common usage during the project despite attempts to use alternatives like "public history" or, following the input of Dutch colleagues on the project, "history from the streets." Indeed, it became clear during the five-year term of the project that "community" had tremendous salience for the residents of Sophiatown who co-participated in the project. Returning to the start of this chapter, the idea of community evoked for many a link to Sophiatown's history. This was typically expressed as an awareness that the current suburb bore no relationship to the Sophiatown of the past, except in that both were spaces of community and coming together of diverse people.

In Sophiatown, we wanted to work beyond the suburb's embeddedness in a collective nostalgia for its 1950s avatar (including among residents), so our initial plan was to see what emerged as we engaged people around the history of the suburb. What later emerged was a project-focused initiative, but one that was significantly different from the projects mentioned in the previous section of this chapter. While my project insider status may well have affected by ability to see clearly, along the way the project has encompassed a community history, created by current residents, and in consultation with that community and its diaspora. In its explicitly political aim, the project was concerned with overcoming tensions between communities and promoting reconciliation between them, via a shared history that did not rest in the kind of collective memory which constitutes other South African public histories.

The core of our work began around May 2009, when David Thelen and Thomas Chapman, a project researcher, wore out their shoe leather recruiting residents to an initial series of discussions. Four what we termed "block groups" coalesced out of these initial approaches. They consisted of residents from three separate streets, as well as the vertical monstrosity, the public housing block used by the South African Police Service (SAPS) as a barracks in Sophiatown. During June and July, Thelen and Chapman held four group meetings with residents from two parallel streets, Good and Gold Street, and five house-based interviews with participants. On Bertha Street, they held two group meetings, and had follow-up meetings with six family groups. Toby Street was the site of two meetings, with three follow-up interviews, while the Police Flats managed one general meeting.

The people who initially attended our gatherings were largely middle-class. They tended to be working or retired, and many were already civically involved in some capacity. A large number of our participants were Coloured and self-described as such, including people whose parents had been removed from Sophiatown to a neighboring suburb called Westbury, which had been created to receive former inhabitants of Sophiatown under the Group Areas Act of 1950.

The four groups listed above – Good/Gold Street, Toby Street, Bertha Street, and the Police Flats – all participated in a similar process. In the initial meetings, depending on how the meeting had been initiated, Thelen, Chapman, or one of the residents would introduce the project to the other residents attending the meeting. The emphasis was similar in the first meetings, with Thelen and Chapman raising the issue of getting to know neighbors and sharing experiences and listening with people. Subsequent meetings involved sharing people's memories of how they came to Sophiatown, and what they found distinctive about living in the suburb. Some of the block groups were more enthusiastic about their involvement, some less.

Where people showed real interest in the process, coming to the local park at the bottom of Good and Gold Street for meetings, meeting in a local restaurant in the neighboring suburb of Westdene, or in the hall at the Dutch Reformed Church, we moved into a process we called photo-voice. Similar to techniques used elsewhere, but introduced to us by artists at the University of Johannesburg's Fine Arts Department, photo-voice involved participants using disposable cameras to take pictures of objects, of people, and of spaces in Sophiatown and its surroundings that were important to them. From Good/Gold Street and Bertha Street we had five families participating in taking photographs, four from Toby Street, and two from the Police Flats.

Another initiative of this early stage of the project involved contextualizing what we wanted to achieve in relation to other community-based heritage initiatives, both in South Africa and elsewhere. We examined the work then being conducted around the memory of Fietas, a suburb close to Sophiatown which had also experienced forced removals (Corrigall 2012). Faizel Mamdoo, a community heritage activist who works in Fietas, described the difficulties he faced in attempting to raise community interest in the area. The project group, including the residents, found the work done in the Berlin suburb of Schoneberg on memorializing streets whose Jewish inhabitants had been part of the Holocaust especially relevant, but our project budget made no provision for such an initiative (Wiedmer 1999). Likewise, the work in bringing individuals and their memories into spaces of their own selecting that characterized work in Amsterdam (Polak, pers. comm., January 2010) and Zoetemeer (Koch and Van der Ploeg 2009) resonated with the contemporary ordinariness of Sophiatown. In the Amsterdam neighborhood of De Pijp, Polak had worked with residents to create a book of life histories; while the project hoped to be inclusive, the final product included life stories from fewer than 30 of the neighborhood's 33,000 inhabitants. Issues about who could speak for whom in De Pijp were an early indication that we were likely never to produce stories centered on Sophiatown which would be to the satisfaction of the entire suburb.

By early 2010, and drawing on the best practices examples we had examined, we had on paper the beginnings of a cooking club, an exhibition based on photographs people had taken as part of photo-voice the previous year, and a series of activities centered on mapping memory. Over the next few months, the UJ researchers and residents directed their energies into these activities. Of the 40–50 residents who had involved themselves with us in 2009, about 20–25 continued into these groups, while a few more people also joined.

In most instances, these activities were jointly undertaken by residents and UJ project members including a number of graduate students who worked on the project. Katherina Fink, a doctoral researcher from Germany, worked with a group of youth who called themselves the Sofiretown Crew on the way in which Sophiatown is subject to continued reinvention and reinterpretation (Fink 2014). Yavini Naidoo, another graduate student, worked with residents on a series of exercises around memory maps and family trees to explore "their conflicting and familiar relationships to the past, space, and community through narrative and visual exercises centered around the creation of personal histories" (2015: 99). We also organized various low-key exhibitions to showcase the work of the photo-voice project, and residents contributed to the drafting of a "Power Map" for Sophiatown, a community resource which was then distributed throughout the suburb. These activities constituted the bulk of the work of the project between 2010 and late 2013, together with the book project discussed below.

Representivity, authenticity, and whose history?

Threading through the lifetime of this project were different ideas about community: the project itself set up a particular idea of a community, but this did not necessarily tally with those of former residents, of the tour guides who conduct historic tours through the suburb, of foreign tourists, and also the many and constant numbers of university researchers who want to work in Sophiatown.[6] Many heritage workers (professional and otherwise) know that these are questions without answer. As Witz and Murray wrote about their work around the Lwandle Migrant Workers' Museum:

> We are not denying that there are identifiable formations in Lwandle that speak for and identify themselves as community structures. What we want to assert rather is that these configurations, much like the museum, are themselves continually making and remaking, sustaining and addressing, shifting publics. (2011: 2)

Nevertheless, issues to do with representivity, and also authenticity, were a continual reminder that the production of history is never uncontested. In Sophiatown, these issues tended to surface in two ways.

First, our participant profile was a departure from most community-history projects in South Africa. The kind of dynamic established by the self-selection process that characterized our initial work was very different from what might be detected in other community-history projects in South Africa, many of which have occurred in working-class or township environments. We were told more than once that the class background of residents meant that they had not earned the "moral right" to speak on behalf of Sophiatown, a position articulated among others by the local branch of the ANC Youth League. In part, this position is understandable since many current residents have not been happy with the suburb's renaming, and are not favorably inclined toward the ANC.

A second "community legitimacy" issue arose in relation to the discussions around the commemoration of the Sophiatown of the 1940s and 1950s. From the start of the project, we had been meeting regularly with the staff and director of the THMC, in order to bring our joint energies to bear on heritage work in Sophiatown. Initially we had been involved in discussions around the renovation of Dr. Xuma's old house as a memorial center or museum for Sophiatown. Xuma's house was one of the few buildings left after the forced removals in the 1950s. By 2008, with the THMC as a driving force, the City of Johannesburg had begun the process of buying the house to be run by the THMC as a memorial center or museum. The initial budget from the City covered only the purchase and basic renovation of the house. The acquisition of the house was part of the THMC's heritage vision for the suburb, a vision which at the time was expressed in an exhibition at the THMC premises and their provision of walking tours through the suburb for people interested in Sophiatown before the removals.

The THMC, which had been working in Sophiatown since the late 1990s, had focused its heritage-related efforts on reproducing a sense of old Sophiatown, what it termed "The Spirit of Sophiatown." It had secured funding for and driven an oral history project which collected testimony from prior residents, especially those who had some memory of the forced removals. As part of the oral history initiative (valuable in itself), it had organized the training of young black tour guides on the history of Sophiatown. While extremely valuable work, it did not attempt to integrate current residents into its programs. A tension, therefore, existed between what we wanted to achieve (working with current residents of Sophiatown), and the mission and vision of the THMC, which was located in the framework of a recuperative nostalgia.

The tension between these two visions of the suburb's history became apparent in 2009. One of the first issues that came before our organizing committee of roughly ten residents and ourselves was the wish to put forward commentary on a THMC-proposed heritage route for Sophiatown. While consultation extended to members of our organizing committee and the Sophiatown Residents' Association, it soon became apparent that the route and the markers or sites it envisaged commemorating, responded only to the history of Sophiatown prior to the removals. It did not pick up on sites or places of importance to the residents with whom we had been working, nor did it raise the suburb's link with the famous Afrikaans novelist, Marlene van Niekerk and her novel, *Triomf* (2005).Van Niekerk is internationally renowned, and in 2015 was shortlisted for the Man Booker Fiction Prize.

At issue were questions of both representivity and authenticity: who should speak on behalf of the suburb and its history, and which part of its history was more authentic? At the time, a position which has since changed (see, for instance, www.Sophiatown. net), the THMC maintained that it spoke on behalf of former residents, those removed, and that the moral thing to do was to mark the suburb to represent the pain of the removals. While current residents would not necessarily have disagreed, they resented the inference that they – people active in the local residents' association and a range of other civic activities – were not qualified to contribute to the history of the space in which they lived.

Most recently, at the book launch for *Experiencing Sophiatown* (see below) in early 2014, an irate former resident claimed the book had nothing to do with the history of Sophiatown, and that it was not justified in using the suburb's name in its title. Rather, he suggested, its title should have referenced inter-racial dialogue in South Africa. Even at one of the project's culminating points, issues of who might speak for Sophiatown and its "real history" had circled round to confront the project once more.

In retrospect, it is possible to see other currents at work in the constitution of community, which were not apparent at the time. The majority of foreign visitors to Sophiatown arrive expecting to learn about Trevor Huddleston, the ANC, Congress, the Drum Writers, and the forced removal. It is possible then to see the THMC responding not only to its own commemorative agendas, but also to a need to stage an "authentic" Sophiatown tourism experience in response to the imperatives of the global tourist gaze (Urry 2002). Under these circumstances, Sophiatown is as much constituted – and creates a community to reflect this constitution – as an epiphenomenon of global tourist patterns as it is constituted by local exigencies. A linked phenomenon lay in the fact that non-state funders to the THMC were themselves also more interested in historic Sophiatown. These issues – who may speak for whom, what pasts should be represented, and which heritage should be re-presented – have tremendous traction on the South

African imagination post-1994. They form a significant element of the Rhodesmustfall and Feesmustfall protests of 2015, where black students articulated a dissatisfaction with the ways in which certain histories continue to be represented in South Africa.

Toward the end of the project and subsequently, the community that came into being around the project has shifted and expanded. Social media and smartphones transformed the form of neighborliness in Sophiatown. When the project began in 2009, few participants had smartphones. We used disposable cameras in the photo-voice portion of the project because many of the participants did not have cameras as part of their cellular phones. Initial attempts to set up a Facebook page for the projects were met with little enthusiasm.

By 2013, this had largely shifted. This issue has partially been ironed out through the post-project transition of the "getting to know your neighbors" element of the project into a Facebook page, Faces of Sophiatown. Most participants were using smartphones and connecting through Facebook. The kind of interaction we struggled with face to face was happening more easily, albeit in a different way and to a different extent, via social media. A separate, closed, Facebook page, Experiencing Sophiatown, collates and collects conversations about the launch of the book, and media publicizing the book. At a recent check, the Faces of Sophiatown page had 196 followers. While this figure does not represent active participants, none of our community meetings ever came close to this total.

Modes of participation and the dynamics of power

Once the project had been running for a few months, and we had begun amassing data, we realized that our modus operandi reinforced – however unwittingly – a separation between ourselves as researchers, located within a university, and Sophiatown residents as participants, located at a research site. This was both physical and reflective of a separation of power. Both of these affected participation in the project. It also did not help that the university calendar meant that academics and, especially, students were only available ten months of the year, and that students entered and exited the project before meaningful relationships could be built.

Several of our regular participants found it difficult to make it to meetings at the university, although the university is less than two kilometers from Sophiatown. We also struggled to find venues to meet in Sophiatown, and while people felt comfortable inviting us into their homes as individuals, this was not the case with larger project meetings which involved neighbors from different streets. For anyone familiar with South African history, or with the history of community-based initiatives, it should come as no surprise that the majority of our meetings either took place at Christ the King Anglican Church, or the Dutch Reformed Church. This was to remain the case throughout the project.

The difficulty of finding venues, though, obscured the larger issue of the relationship between the project participants. A frequent comment, too, concerned what residents viewed as the one-sided nature of the project. This would be expressed along the lines of "you come and take from us and expect us to answer your questions, but what do we get in return?" Several residents viewed the project as channeling benefits in only one direction, the university benefiting from the research it conducted but offering nothing to residents in exchange. Other residents were convinced that their participation in the project would channel donor or university funding to Sophiatown, for the building of community centers and other needed infrastructure. While time and care taken in building relationships in the suburb would eventually mitigate some of these feelings, another solution lay in a greater collapsing of the divide between the university and the suburb.

There was little for us to go on in terms of imagining a different mode of operation. The history of Alexandra project had relied on stakeholder committees offering advice and suggestions, but with little ongoing creative agency in the project (Philip Bonner, pers. comm., 2010). As a result, we began to look to models used outside of history, including models of active citizenship and public participation. This led us to the (now disbanded) Institute for Democracy in Africa (Idasa), which had extensive experience in community organization and mobilization around civic projects. We formed an advisory group including both academics and residents, to design and carry the project forward. In August and September 2009, we held the initial meetings of this group. The formation of an advisory group, however, had little initial impact in boosting attendance or participation. While the advisory group had initially shown great enthusiasm for participating in the creation of a heritage trail in Sophiatown (see above), a month later the plans for moving toward a City-funded trail had evaporated. At the same time, residents who had been attending meetings with us began to express frustrations. These centered on meetings which seemed to involve too much talking and not enough planning.

As academics we did not want to impose an agenda on the project, and we were keen that any outputs should arise from discussions within Sophiatown. However, we had under-estimated the amount of effort it would require busy residents to think beyond their daily business and civic concerns, in the small amount of leisure time most of them had available. We were witnessing an example of stakeholder fatigue, where residents – who were active across other forums as well – had neither the time nor inclination to drive the project but preferred to remain as participants (Murray et al. 2010: 47). In the literature on participation, this is described as the need to tailor levels of participation to "situations where participants can make a meaningful contribution and where resources are available to implement outcomes" (Richards and Carter 2007: 8).

By the end of 2010, drawing on our experience of stakeholder fatigue and the desire for concrete outcomes, David Thelen and Karie Morgan (who had recently joined the project) presented a relatively structured proposal, incorporating a specific "deliverable" to Sophiatown residents. At the meeting, residents were asked to comment about the viability of writing a book based on their collective histories. The idea was met with immediate enthusiasm, though few of us at the time had any sense of what this would entail. In subsequent meetings, the book group outlined a series of themes around which to organize material: Meeting Neighbours, Imagining Community; Making a Community Together; Preparing and Eating Meals; How Families Live and What they Value; Making Neighbours and Community; and Experiencing Change. These became chapter titles in the book published as *Experiencing Sophiatown: Conversations Among Residents about the Past, Present and Future of a Community* (Thelen and Morgan 2014).[7] The upsurge in interest generated by the book proposal resulted in a recommitment to some of the broader project ideals, the ideals that emerged in 2011 as a vision for the project and that are present at the start of this chapter.

The collection of material for the book, and its organization into a narrative, took until early 2014. The book constituted itself as an exercise in relatively low-tech but labor-intensive methodologies, which were tailored to the time and inclination of participants. In its final version, the book is a pastiche of interviews and reflections from residents. It is distilled from many hundreds of audio hours, which were transcribed and then presented to participants. In follow-up conversations, which often involved a joint reading of the transcript, book participants indicated what they felt ought to be included in the book.[8] In this way, although the book is very much directed and put together by Thelen and Morgan, the selection of material within it reflects the wishes of residents who had chosen to become involved in the process.

Conclusion

At the beginning of this chapter, I set out to examine to extent to which the Sophiatown project, as a community history project, had achieved its ideals. By and large this has been the case, though project members would likely disagree on how or to what extent they think the different aims had been achieved. Nor would they necessarily agree on which community's history had been written. For some, the active presence of a Facebook page joining Sophiatown residents together would be evidence of a new sense of community; for others, evidence of community spirit lies in the feelings that motivate people to contribute to the page in the first place.

While the project has produced new histories of Sophiatown, including of Triomf, not all of these are readily available to the public, making it difficult to assess the extent to which new history has been made. Most of the project aims, however, are readily visible in the book, *Experiencing Sophiatown* (everyone involved in the project received a free copy, and it is readily available). The book is a reminder that no meeting can ever generate the tactile sensation of achievement that comes through a book with a bright red cover.

The project's successes, though, are qualified, and I have attempted to discuss the challenges it faced in this chapter. The constraints discussed here are not peculiar to the Sophiatown project, and heritage and memory professionals will recognize many of them in their own work. Given the protests and conversations that began in the country in 2015, questions of representivity, authenticity, of the power of academics to drive research projects, and of the extent to which people are able to participate in community activity, seem to have a particular and persistent resonance in contemporary South Africa.

Notes

1 The protest centered on removing a statue of Cecil John Rhodes, infamous for his role in colonial South Africa, from its position on the campus of the University of Cape Town. For the students and others who participated in the project, the statue enacted on a daily basis the historical degradation of black South Africans under colonialism and later apartheid.
2 A call which the university authorities have heeded. https://www.wits.ac.za/news/latest-news/general-news/2016/feesmustfall2016/statements/naming-committee-recommends-senate-house-be-renamed-solomon-mahlangu-house.html.
3 For a more detailed discussion about local government's failure in relation to heritage, including development, see Kulijian (2009).
4 The state in South Africa has three tiers: local, provincial, and national. Each of the nine provinces has its own responsibilities and budgets in terms of which it allocates funds for heritage. In Johannesburg, both provincial and municipal structures of government are involved in projects in Sophiatown.

5   For their cogent comments on the involvement of professional historians in heritage initiatives in South Africa, see Ciraj Rassool (2000) and Cynthia Kros (2008).

6   Either because it fulfills some notion of their own ideas about the suburb's history, or because it is a suburb that is both convenient as a research space, both in terms of its location and also the extent of the academic literature produced on it.

7   In the book, "Sophiatown" acts as a geographical location for bringing memory together. While not a history of Sophiatown, its final chapter, "Experiencing Change," includes sections on Sophiatown's history.

8   A more detailed explanation of this method may be found in the introduction of *Experiencing Sophiatown* (Thelen and Morgan 2014).

CHAPTER NINETEEN

Tourism and Heritage Sites of the Atlantic Slave Trade and Slavery

ANA LUCIA ARAUJO

Since the end of the Cold War in the late 1980s and early 1990s, a growing number of initiatives started highlighting slavery and the Atlantic slave trade in the public spaces of cities in Europe, Africa, and the Americas. Part of a broader interest in all issues related to past human atrocities, which was also visible in the memorialization of the Holocaust, this trend can be associated with the emergence of local identities that became more prominent as a reaction to an era when globalization interconnected societies and populations.

The dialogue between history and memory, which also orients public history initiatives, has shaped the phenomenon of memorialization of slavery and the Atlantic slave trade in former slave societies. On the one hand, collective memory is defined by Maurice Halbwachs (1950) as a mode of memory carried out by social groups and societies who associate their common remembrances with historical events. Conceived within particular social frameworks, this mode of memory becomes public memory when it is transformed into a political instrument to build, assert, and reinforce particular identities of social groups. In this context, public memory can be defined as the common way societies or groups recover, recreate, and represent the past to themselves and to others in the public sphere. On the other hand, in societies marked by traumatic events and human atrocities like the Atlantic slave trade, in which the transmission of past experiences was disrupted, collective memory gives way to historical memory that can take more permanent forms like monuments, memorials, and museums, in processes that have been defined as memorialization. Depending on whether or not these initiatives succeed in obtaining official recognition by governments and institutions, historical memory can become official memory.

The initiatives memorializing slavery and the Atlantic slave trade can be divided into four different categories. The first category includes the promotion of existing heritage sites associated with the Atlantic slave trade and slavery, found along the African coasts and in various parts of the Americas. In West Africa, West Central Africa, and East Africa, among these sites are slave castles and dungeons, fortresses, and the ruins of old slave depots, while in the Americas these sites include slave wharfs, slave markets, and former plantations. The second category comprises newly built memorials and monuments paying homage to the victims of slavery and the Atlantic slave trade that resulted from the efforts of social actors and groups who fought to have their views recognized in the public space in processes that combined collective, public, and official memory. The third category, related to the two previous ones, includes festivals and commemoration activities aimed at promoting intangible heritage associated with slavery and the Atlantic slave trade, such as music, dance, food, and other forms of living traditions. Finally, the fourth category comprises state, private, and community museums that focus on slavery and museum exhibitions on slavery. Like in the previous categories, the existence of these initiatives usually results from the intervention of organized social actors, but in several cases these initiatives can be labeled public history projects. Having educational goals, their development often relied on the contribution of public historians.

This chapter discusses several kinds of ventures aimed at bringing to light slavery and the Atlantic slave trade in the public space, with a particular focus on heritage sites of the Atlantic slave trade. Depending on the geographical area, these sites attract greater or smaller numbers of tourists with various profiles. As an effective way of promoting economic development, slave trade tourism in African countries like Senegal, Ghana, and Republic of Benin has been conceived as a form of roots tourism that, although appealing for local populations, has traditionally attracted well-off tourists from the African diaspora. In Brazil and the United States, recently uncovered slave wharfs and cemeteries have interested a varied, but still limited, number of tourists, mainly composed of local and international black visitors.

Slave trade tourism in West Africa

Although the majority of enslaved Africans who were transported to the New World embarked from West Central African ports like Luanda, Benguela, and Cabinda, most initiatives to memorialize the slave trade were developed in West Africa (Schenck and Candido 2015). The first initiatives to preserve West African Coast slave trade tangible heritage sites started in the 1940s (Araujo 2010a; Araujo 2010b). This process intensified over the next two decades, especially in the 1960s, during the period of African decolonization. The promotion of Atlantic slave trade sites such as European castles and fortresses that served as slave depots was consolidated first with the addition of some of these sites to the national heritage lists and later with their addition to the UNESCO World Heritage List. The promotion of the Atlantic slave trade heritage sites contributed to the development of the West African tourism industry.

In 1972, the government of Ghana added 22 old fortresses and castles to its national heritage list, placing these sites under the protection of the law and under the authority of the Ghana Museums and Monuments Board (Singleton 1999). In 1979, during the third session of the World Heritage Committee, UNESCO approved the addition of Elmina Castle, founded in the Gold Coast by the Portuguese in 1482, to the World Heritage List. Moreover, another 10 castles in the regions of Volta, Accra and its environs, and in central and western Ghana were also included on the list. Therefore, Ghana witnessed the development of African diaspora roots tourism.

Among the most important sites visited by tourists in Ghana are Cape Coast and Elmina castles (Macgonagle 2006). Tourists from around the world, including many

African Americans and Afro-Caribbeans, visit Ghana castles to mourn and to celebrate the memory of their ancestors (Hartman 2008; Richards 2008). In Ghana, as in other slavery sites in West Africa, tourist guides provide accounts of the Atlantic slave trade to satisfy an international audience. Usually, they emphasize "the suffering of Africans at the hands of Europeans," often by omitting African participation in the slave trade enterprise (Macgonagle 2006: 252). The goal of these simplified narratives is twofold. On the one hand, they prevent the emergence of conflict among local communities that still today include descendants of enslaved individuals who were brought from the North and remain in the region (Holsey 2008). On the other hand, they fulfill the specific demands of the tourism industry, offering quick visits to the castles. Since the early 1990s, during the government of Jerry Rawlings, Elmina and Cape Coast castles received prestigious visitors, including the former US presidents Bill Clinton and George W. Bush, President Barack Obama and his family, as well as Michäelle Jean, former Governor General of Canada (Bruner 1996; Macgonagle 2006; Schramm 2010). Moreover, since 1998, August 1, the date of slave emancipation in the British colonies, is officially commemorated in Ghana (Holsey 2008), in a clear attempt to promote and reinforce the connections with the African diaspora.

Since the 1960s, Gorée Island and its Slave House began acquiring notoriety among international visitors, including African American tourists and political and religious authorities. The promotion of Gorée as a slave trade site of remembrance started when Léopold Sedar Senghor was president of Senegal. In 1966, the First World Festival of Black Arts was held in the country. By developing and promoting African arts, Senegal called the public's attention to African heritage and to the importance of Gorée Island in the history of West Africa. The festival had significant effects in Europe and the Americas, contributing to the development and promotion of Gorée Island and its Slave House not only as a site of memory of the Atlantic slave trade, but also as a tourist destination.

In the early 1960s, Senegal created the BAMH (Office of Historical Monuments Architecture). In 1972, the country ratified the Convention Concerning the Protection of the World Cultural and Natural Heritage, adopted by UNESCO during the 17th session of its general conference. Three years later, the country included Gorée Island in its inventory of historical monuments. In 1978, during the second session of the Intergovernmental Committee for the Protection of the World Cultural and Natural Heritage held in Washington, D.C., UNESCO added Gorée Island to the list of World Heritage sites. In the 1980s, Amadou-Mahtar M'Bow, UNESCO's general director, launched an appeal to the international community to help finance and safeguard Gorée Island, by emphasizing its role in the shared imagination of Africa and the Americas. After this initiative, at least eight postal stamps were created to promote Gorée's future. During the 1990s, as part of the same trend already observed in Ghana and The Gambia, the Slave House, as well as other buildings, were rehabilitated.

A contested slave trade heritage site, the Slave House became internationally known thanks to the narrative developed by its curator, the late Boubacar Joseph N'Diaye. His convincing story describing the tragic experience of enslaved men and women during their passage through the slave warehouse touched the hearts of thousands of tourists who visited the island each year. According to N'Diaye, between ten and fifteen million enslaved Africans passed through the Slave House before leaving for the New World, an estimate higher than the volume of slave imports for all the Americas. According to the most recent estimates established by Voyages: The Trans-Atlantic Slave Trade Database about 12,521,000 enslaved Africans crossed the Atlantic Ocean during the Atlantic slave trade. In addition, the latest estimates provided by the database. indicate that between 1514 and 1866 the slave exports from Gorée Island were approximately 33,562. The Slave House remains a major place of memory of the Atlantic slave trade, attracting 200,000 tourists each year.

Although evidence confirms that the owner of the Slave House was not a European slave merchant, but an Afro-European woman slave trader (*signare*), several factors allowed the Slave House to become a successful slave trade tourist site; primarily N'Diaye's ability to transmit the experiences of the victims of the Atlantic slave trade (Araujo 2010a). Regardless of whether N'Diaye's narrative is accurate or not, he was able to bring the slave past to life by describing and narrating in detail the sufferings of those men, women, and children who were deported from West African shores to the Americas.

The popularity of the Slave House on Gorée Island can be explained by other factors as well. Its location, dungeons, and door opening to the sea function as architectural elements that incarnate the memory of the Atlantic slave trade (Singleton 1999). These elements allowed N'Diaye to construct a convincing and moving narrative illustrating the experience of enslaved men, women, and children. This context allowed the controversial Slave House to become not only a slave trade tourist site, but also a site of repentance that attracted important political, religious, and artistic personalities such as Pope John Paul II, US President George W. Bush, and Brazilian President Luiz Inácio Lula da Silva, whose visits to the site received great media coverage.

Like Ghana and Senegal, the Republic of Benin (former Kingdom of Dahomey) also developed a significant tourism industry associated with the Atlantic slave trade. Since the early eighteenth century, Dahomey dominated the slave trade in the Bight of Benin. The high degree of militarization and the introduction of firearms by the Europeans allowed the kingdom to expand its territory. Most of Dahomey's war captives were sold to European slave merchants, while others remained in the kingdom performing several kinds of agricultural and domestic activities, or were sacrificed to honor the ancestors.

Dahomey became a French colony at the end of the nineteenth century. The conservation and promotion of built heritage sites associated with the Atlantic slave trade began during World War II. In 1943, the French administration created the Abomey Historical Museum at the site of the old royal palaces of Abomey. The colored bas-reliefs decorating the walls of the palaces constitute a visual narrative illustrating events that marked the history of the Dahomean dynasties. The representations of Dahomean female and male warriors and decapitated prisoners evoke the military campaigns waged by Dahomey against its neighboring kingdoms.

In 1985, after a tornado damaged the royal palaces, the buildings were placed simultaneously on UNESCO's World Heritage List and the List of World Heritage in Danger. The project of restoration and conservation of the royal palaces, included in the program of PREMA (Prevention in Museums in Africa), started in 1992 and received the support of Benin's government. On June 25, 2007, the palaces were eventually removed from the List of World Heritage in Danger (Araujo 2010a).

The promotion of and investment in the restoration of the palaces in which bas-reliefs celebrate military campaigns convey a complex and sometimes contradictory message because it occurred during the same period that other projects developing the public memory of Atlantic slave trade victims were also in progress in southern Benin. Eventually, the promotion of the royal palaces contributed to highlight Dahomey's slave trade past from the point of view of the perpetrators, instead of the victims. Although the palaces are visited by hundreds of tourists every year, its location, about 82 miles from the coast, prevents it from becoming a major tourist destination in the country.

In the early 1990s, Benin's military dictatorship ended, and an agitated period of redemocratization began. In 1991, Nicéphore Soglo was elected president of the country and claimed a new Marshall Plan for Africa in order to renegotiate or release the external debt of African countries. As the country started requesting financial aid from the World Bank and the IMF, cultural tourism became a viable alternative for promoting the region's economic development.

The end of the dictatorship encouraged public debate regarding Benin's slave past. However, there were sensitive elements involved in this discussion, because even today Benin's population includes descendants of Abomey's royal family, who captured and sold prisoners into slavery; descendants of slave merchants; and descendants of former slaves, who were either sent to the Americas (especially Brazil) and returned to Dahomey, or who remained on Dahomean soil. Moreover, among the Brazilian returnees, several became slave merchants and others, who married Portuguese and Brazilian slave merchants established in the region, became slave owners. Because slavery still carries a heavy stigma in Africa, some descendants of slaves prefer not to claim this ancestry publicly. In this context of plural and conflictive memories of slavery, the government of Benin, UNESCO, and the Embassy of France encouraged the development of official projects focusing on the region's Atlantic slave past, whose main goal was stimulating cultural tourism (Araujo 2010a; Forte 2010). As a result of these efforts, in 1994, UNESCO launched The Slave Route Project during an international scientific conference held in Ouidah.

The Slave Route Project was entrusted to an international scientific committee composed of some twenty members from different disciplines and geographical areas, whose responsibility was to guarantee an objective and consensual approach to the main issues of the Project. National committees were created in order to promote the objectives of the Project in various countries involved in the Atlantic slave trade. The Project relied on a scientific research program; an educational and academic program; a program on the contribution of the African diaspora aimed at promoting the living cultures and artistic and spiritual expression that resulted from the slave trade and slavery; a program aimed at collecting and preserving the written archives and oral traditions related to the slave trade; and a program to identify and preserve the tangible and intangible heritage of the slave trade and slavery, especially through memory tourism. When the Project was initiated, the need to emphasize the importance and the estimated volume of the trans-Saharan and internal slave trades was discussed. However, the Atlantic slave trade became the actual focus of the Project. UNESCO's choice to keep the main focus on the Atlantic slave trade and to neglect the other trades that strongly affected West African populations reinforced the idea that The Slave Route Project was intended for an international audience and not for the local population, which includes descendants of slaves who remained living on African soil.

In the early 1990s, parallel to the debates aimed at developing The Slave Route Project, Beninese government authorities proposed the creation of a Vodun festival in Ouidah. Both the Vodun festival and The Slave Route Project aimed at promoting cultural tourism in Benin and as a result stimulating the local economy. As Dahomey is the cradle of Vodun, a religion characterized by trance, possession, and the belief in a great number of deities (Blier 1995), the choice of a Vodun festival was justified because enslaved Dahomeans brought this West African religion to Brazil, Cuba, and Haiti, contributing to the emergence of religions such as Candomblé, Santeria, and Voodoo in the Americas. Yet, debates about the Vodun festival were surrounded by controversy, because some social actors perceived the festival as an attempt to diminish the importance accorded to The Slave Route Project. In a context of conflicting memories of slavery, the descendants of slaves and slave merchants would better accept celebrating the intangible heritage of the Atlantic slave trade represented by the religions and cultures derived from Vodun. Moreover, as Vodun worshippers were denounced, persecuted, and sent to prison as "sorcerers" who opposed the goals of the "revolution" in the years of military dictatorship, the Vodun festival could underscore the emerging religious freedom (Rush 2013; Tall 1995).

Unlike The Slave Route Project, the Vodun festival, Ouidah 92, was perceived as a project that unified different groups. This initiative was seen as one that could eventually allow the descendants of the Dahomean royal family to obtain political gains without emphasizing debate about the Atlantic slave trade past (Tall 1995). Following these debates, the festival Ouidah 92: Festival mondial des cultures vaudou: retrouvailles Amériques-Afriques (Ouidah 92: World Festival of Vodun Cultures: Reunion Americas-Africas) and The Slave Route Project were finally linked.

The Vodun festival was held in February 1993 in Ouidah, Porto-Novo, and Cotonou, one year before the launching of The Slave Route Project. Among the most visible initiatives of the festival was the creation of The Slaves' Route, a two-mile road that starts at Ouidah's downtown, close to a former slave market, along which enslaved men, women, and children allegedly walked until arriving at the beach, where they boarded pirogues that brought them to the slave ships. Because the coastal lagoon separated the town from the shore, it is likely that captives covered part of the way to the outer shore by canoe as well (Law 2004).

About one hundred monuments and memorials especially created for the occasion mark various stations along the road. Passing through several neighborhoods, The Slaves' Route highlights the existing historical sites and Vodun temples, decorated with paintings during the preparations for the festival. Whereas some of the monuments and memorials mark actual historical sites, other statues do not mark any specific point of reference but were placed along the route just to emphasize the idea of continuity. The number of foreign guests who attended the festival, the financial support of the United States government, and the brochure translated into English show the extent to which the festival was designed to be a meeting place for the African diaspora, especially African Americans and Afro-Caribbeans.

Situated in the western half of the coast of Benin, during the eighteenth century Ouidah became the most important African slave port, second only to Luanda in present-day Angola. After the end of the Atlantic slave trade and the beginning of French colonization, the city's economic life declined dramatically. During the twentieth century, the lack of economic opportunities led the children of elite families to leave Ouidah and move to Cotonou, Benin's economic capital. But after the festival and the launching of The Slave Route Project, Ouidah started attracting more national and international tourists, who came to the city to visit its built heritage attractions such as the former Portuguese fortress that houses the Ouidah Museum of History, as well as the monuments and memorials unveiled during the early 1990s. Moreover, after the launching of the official projects, a number of hotels were opened on Ouidah's beach.

Ultimately, slave trade tourism helped intensify Ouidah's economic activity. At the same time, the city became not only an intriguing example of the impact of UNESCO's influence in the region, but also an interesting case of the commodification of the Atlantic slave trade for tourism purposes. Today, the monuments, memorials, and museums created during the establishment of the Vodun festival and The Slave Route Project share the public space with other projects such as the Gate of Return and the Door of Return Museum, as well as the memorial for the Great Jubilee of the Catholic Church of the Year 2000. These different initiatives provide a revealing image of the national and international political issues associated with the recovery and promotion of the memory and heritage of the Atlantic slave trade.

Slave trade and slavery tourism in Brazil and the United States

Some of the largest slave ports in the Americas were situated in Brazil and the United States, although the volume of the Atlantic slave trade greatly varied in these two countries. According to the latest estimates made available in the Voyages: The Trans-Atlantic Slave Trade Database (2013), between 1601 and 1866, the number of enslaved Africans who disembarked for the United States was 252,653, whereas between 1501 and 1866, the number of slaves who arrived in Brazilian ports was 5,099,816. Unlike West Africa, The Slave Route Project launched by UNESCO in 1994 was not very visible in these two countries. Although neither Brazil nor the United States oriented the memorialization of slavery and the Atlantic slave trade toward the development of tourism initiatives as was done in West Africa, in both countries slave trade heritage sites are receiving growing attention and attracting an important number of tourists.

Despite the importance of slavery and the presence of traces of the slave past in the urban and rural landscapes of Brazil and the United States, the promotion of slavery heritage and the development of projects to memorialize slavery have encountered many obstacles. Starting in the 1990s, a small number of monuments, memorials, and museum exhibitions were gradually unveiled in both countries. This interest in the Atlantic slave past was favored by the new context that emerged at the end of the Cold War, which benefited the assertion of national identities and collective identities of historically oppressed groups. Additionally, the 500th anniversary of the arrival of Columbus in the Americas made visible the crucial role of the Atlantic slave trade in the construction of the American continent. In Brazil, the end of the Cold War coincided with the end of the military dictatorship that ruled the country from 1964 to 1985. The end of military rule allowed Afro-Brazilian activism to resurface in the public sphere, demanding affirmative actions and calling for the official recognition of the role played by black historical actors in the construction of the nation (Araujo 2014).

In the United States, the largest part of the tourism industry associated with slavery is concentrated around former plantations, several of which are officially listed in national heritage registers. These heritage sites, most of which are located in southern states, include the plantations and homes of the founding fathers of the United States, such as George Washington (Mount Vernon), Thomas Jefferson (Monticello), and James Madison (Montpelier), all located in the state of Virginia. Although thousands of local, national, and international tourists visit these sites each year, the motivation of most guests is to learn more about the history and sophisticated lifestyles of these founding fathers. Yet, over the last ten years, public historians have made important efforts to finally highlight the importance of slavery and enslaved populations at these sites.

In Brazil, despite the increasing number of monuments and initiatives highlighting Afro-Brazilian history, the projects aimed at developing cultural tourism on sites related to slavery are still incipient and scattered. In the former coffee industry zone in the Paraíba Valley, some estates were restored and transformed into hotels. In the Fazenda Ponte Alta (Barra do Piraí, Rio de Janeiro), the original slave quarters were preserved. The Fazenda Santa Clara (Valença, Rio de Janeiro), one of the largest coffee producers of the region, once held 2,800 slaves and is visited by hundreds of tourists each year. However, these privately owned initiatives do not aim to emphasize the slave past of the region and are still perceived as rural tourism (Araujo 2010b).

Among the most visible initiatives memorializing slavery in the United States is the African Burial Ground in New York City. The site, which includes the remains of thousands of men, women, and children either African-born or of African descent, was discovered in 1991 during an excavation to construct a new federal building at 290 Broadway. After protests led by African American activists, the work stopped. A report examining the history of the burial ground as well as the recovered remains and artifacts was assigned to scholars based at Howard University in Washington, D.C. Research concluded that the site was a former burial ground containing the remains of about 15,000 enslaved and free African individuals buried during the seventeenth and eighteenth centuries. Located in a port city that imported about 8,500 slaves, the New York African Burial Ground, as it became known in the following years, is the largest of its kind in the United States.

The discovery of the burial ground occurred in a context that favored the promotion of black history in New York City: the mayoralty of David Norman Dinkins, the city's first African American mayor, who took office in 1990. His intervention was crucial to the development of the African Burial Ground. But the controversies among members of the federal government, politicians, scholars, and activists (who identified themselves as descendants of the men and women buried at the site) regarding the future of the site continued in the following years. This context shows how the public memory of slavery is shaped by the disputes of various social groups that attempt to occupy public space.

The unearthing of the burial ground brought to light the importance of slavery in New York City. As a result, debates emerged involving questions of how to make the city's slave past visible as well as how to memorialize African American ancestors in the city's public space. In 1998, the General Service Administration (GSA) launched a design competition for the memorial that would occupy the site, receiving 61 proposals. By the end of September 2003, the Schomburg Center for Research in Black Culture organized a series of ceremonies that began at Howard University, where the remains were examined, and that culminated on October 4, 2003, with the reinternment of 419 bone remains in New York's financial district, the same site where they were discovered.

Since 2003, October 4 has been marked by annual commemorative ceremonies held in the African Burial Ground to pay homage to the men, women, and children who were buried there. Also in 2003, the United States Congress appropriated funds for the construction of the memorial. But the debates regarding how these Africans and African Americans would be memorialized continued and became highly politicized along racial lines. Central to the debate led by African American activists was whether a memorial would be placed on top of the African Burial Ground. The National Park Service (NPS) and the GSA organized a series of public forums to discuss the final decision, but activists contested the initiative. Representatives of the Committee of Descendants of the African Ancestral Burial Ground maintained that no structure should be placed on the sacred site. Another controversial issue was the possible hiring of white architects to design the memorial. The African Burial Ground thus illustrates well the contentious issues surrounding a site of memory of slavery. The unearthing of the burial ground and its interpretation were closely associated with issues of race and identity that were not directly related to the historical past of the site but to the total lack of public visibility of the city's slave past in the present. Although not all the issues raised by African American activists were addressed, eventually, in June 2004, two Haitian American architects, Rodney Leon and Nicole Hollant-Denis (AARIS Architects), won the competition to design the memorial.

After being officially proclaimed a National Monument in 2006, the memorial was dedicated on October 5, 2007. Built with granite, the memorial is divided into two sections, the Circle of the Diaspora and the Ancestral Chamber. Through a ramp, the visitor is led to the interior of a circular wall on which various Akan symbols are depicted. In the interior of the court, a map of the Atlantic world evoking the Middle Passage is depicted on the ground. The Ancestral Chamber, placed next to the ancestral reinternment ground and symbolizing the interior of a slave ship, was conceived as a place for contemplation and prayer. As in other monuments, memorials, and heritage sites of the Atlantic slave trade, the idea of return is evoked by a Sankofa symbol carved on the chamber's external wall, which became the memorial's central element and was dedicated as follows: "For all those who were lost; For all those who were stolen; For all those who were left behind; For all those who were not forgotten." In the various official descriptions of the memorial, the symbol is translated as "learn from the past," but a more accurate translation is "go back to fetch it," referring to a proverb that states: "It is not a taboo to return and fetch it when you forget," evoking the links between the spiritual and material world (Seeman 2010: 109). The symbol's choice was further justified because the coffins recovered during the archaeological excavation displayed a heart-shaped pictogram identified as an Akan symbol associated with present-day Akan mortuary practices (although some scholars contested this interpretation).

In 2010, as part of the development and promotion of the site, a visitor center housing a permanent exhibition was created in the federal building adjacent to the memorial. Unlike the memorial, a site whose sacred dimension was emphasized, the visitor center is a public history initiative, with the goal of celebrating African presence in New York City and disseminating the history of the most important archaeological project ever undertaken in the United States (Kardux 2009). African American tourists, scholars, and members of the African diaspora are the most frequent visitors to the memorial. During the year, especially in October, various ceremonies are held at the memorial to honor African ancestors.

Its location at the heart of New York City's downtown meant that the promotion of the African Burial Ground was affected by the events of September 11, 2001. The two towers of the World Trade Center, destroyed by the terrorist attacks that killed thousands of individuals, were located just over half a mile from the burial ground. This tragedy created another mass grave near the site and imprinted the collective memory of New York City's population with a more recent traumatic event. When visitors to the area, whether they are whites or African Americans, ask where the African Burial Ground is, they will often be redirected toward Ground Zero, where the National September 11 Memorial and Museum, dedicated on September 11, 2011, is located. In spite of these hindrances, the unearthing of the site brought to light the existence of slavery as a central institution in New York until its abolition in 1827. This largely unknown chapter of American history was absent from official narratives presented in textbooks and museum exhibitions, where slavery is usually described as existing only in the southern United States (Berlin and Harris 2005; Wilson 2005). The discovery also led to the development of several other ventures focusing on the existence of slavery in New York City. Among these initiatives was the exhibit Slavery in New York held by the New York Historical Society in 2005, which was followed by a series of other exhibitions problematizing slavery in the United States (Hulser 2012).

Unlike New York City, whose slave past was a forgotten chapter of American history, slavery was a central element in Rio de Janeiro's daily life until the end of the nineteenth century. Between 1758 and 1831, and especially after 1811, about one million Africans came ashore in the Valongo Wharf. But the area of disembarkation of Africans was gradually erased from the urban space after the slave trade was banned in 1831. Following the chaotic process of modernization and urbanization of the early twentieth century, the old port zone of Rio de Janeiro, close to the city's downtown area, remained nearly abandoned. Not only had the underprivileged black populations who were resident in the port zone been totally neglected by public authorities, but also the buildings and heritage sites located in the area were in an advanced state of decay (Cicalo 2015).

Similar to what occurred in New York City in 1991, in 1996 an archaeological excavation on a private property at 36 Pedro Ernesto Street (formerly Cemitério Street) in the Gamboa neighborhood revealed a burial ground containing bone fragments of dozens of enslaved African men, women, and children. The site was identified as being the Cemitério dos Pretos Novos (Cemetery of New Blacks), a common grave where newly arrived Africans who died before being sold in the Valongo market were buried. Scholars estimate that more than 6,000 Africans were buried at the site. But following this important and unprecedented discovery, the cemetery and the port area continued to be neglected for a long period of time. Unlike the African Burial Ground in New York City, the site was private property and not a federal building. As a result, the Brazilian federal government had no jurisdiction over the site, whose preservation was the responsibility of City Hall. Although the couple who owned the property where the cemetery was uncovered embraced the cause of protecting the site with the great support of Rio de Janeiro's black activist movement, they received little public or official assistance (Saillant and Simonard 2012). Yet this situation drastically changed in March 2011 when drainage works started in the Rio de Janeiro port region, as part of the project Rio de Janeiro: Porto Maravilha (Rio de Janeiro: Wonderful Port), which aimed to recuperate the city's old port in anticipation of the 2014 FIFA World Cup and 2016 Olympic Games. During the work, the ruins of Valongo Wharf were eventually rediscovered. The excavations also recovered numerous African artifacts, including ceramic pipes, cowries employed in religious practices, and buttons made of animal bones.

Following this second discovery, black activists, scholars, and politicians intensively debated the project that would be developed on the wharf. If until recently Rio de Janeiro's authorities rarely expressed interest in promoting the slavery heritage of the city's downtown area, there was now an urgent need to find an urban solution to a site associated with the forthcoming Olympic Games. As expected, the discussion about strategies to preserve the site became politically contentious. Politicians, real estate companies, scholars, and black organizations quickly understood its tangible and symbolic importance; both locally and internationally, the wharf embodies the connections between Brazil, Africa, and the African diaspora. With different interests at play, each of these groups attempted to appropriate the site and orient the ways that the history of the Atlantic slave trade would be exposed or concealed. Moreover, the possibility of nominating the newly discovered site for inclusion in the UNESCO World Heritage List raised the interest of various companies and organizations as well.

The initial project of Rio de Janeiro's City Hall was to create a huge memorial with portals that, according to black activists, would divert attention from the archaeological site. Additionally, because the wharf is located next to Morro da Providência, the first Brazilian favela, most of whose residents are Afro-Brazilians, black organizations were concerned about how an architectural intervention on the wharf would affect the neighboring community. Finally, by keeping the simple original structure of the wharf, during this first stage of the process of memorialization black activists rejected the creation of a memorial structure that would compete with the archaeological site.

Gradually, both the Valongo Wharf and the Cemetery of New Blacks are being incorporated into Rio de Janeiro's urban landscape and becoming part of the country's official national narrative that now recognizes the importance of the Atlantic slave trade and Brazil's crucial role in it. Through the municipal decree number 34.803 of November 29, 2011, the Circuito Histórico e Arqueológico da Celebração da Herança Africana (Historical and Archaeological Trail of African Heritage Celebration) was created to highlight several heritage buildings and sites of memory associated with the Atlantic slave trade and African presence in the port area of Rio de Janeiro.

In 2012, the site of the Cemetery of New Blacks was transformed into a memorial. The main exhibition was reshaped, with the inclusion of explanatory panels with text and images reconstituting the history of the site, large photographs of Africans and Afro-Brazilians, and a huge panel wall with the names of enslaved individuals who were brought to Brazil. Moreover, glass pyramids were installed on the memorial's floor, allowing visitors to see the archaeological findings discovered at the site. As a sacred site, the memorial's unveiling ceremony had the participation of Candomblé priests, who paid homage to the African ancestors who died without ever receiving a proper burial. The community of Gamboa and different black organizations are slowly appropriating the Valongo area, organizing black heritage tours, public religious ceremonies, and spectacles of capoeira (an Afro-Brazilian martial art, combining dance and music).

Regardless of this appropriation by local actors, the Valongo area remains negligible in comparison with most other Rio de Janeiro tourist sites, and even many locals are unaware of its historical importance. Its visitors are mainly Afro-Brazilians or international tourists with a particular interest in the history of African diaspora. In addition, because until recently no memorial was constructed on the Valongo Wharf (only the ruins were preserved), the visit to the site becomes meaningful only if oriented by the few Afro-Brazilian guides associated with local black organizations.

Conclusion

This chapter explored how heritage sites of slavery and the Atlantic slave trade in Senegal, Ghana, Republic of Benin, Brazil, and the United States have been memorialized and gradually transformed into sites to attract local, national, and international tourists. Despite the hindrances to make the Atlantic slave trade past visible within public space, especially after the 1990s, these initiatives have been successful in developing cultural tourism and attracting visitors to West African countries. Although tourism in sites of suffering have traditionally been labeled as dark tourism or grief tourism, slave trade tourism in West Africa has other crucial dimensions. For African tourists and white tourists, especially Europeans, visiting slave trade heritage sites may be associated with a process of repentance and also with self-awareness of human atrocities. For black tourists from the Americas, the central dimension of slave trade tourism in West Africa is still associated with the search for their ancestors' roots.

In Brazil and the United States, slavery and the Atlantic slave trade are not central elements of tourism ventures. However, over the last two decades, the recovery of a number of slave trade heritage sites has led to the development of important initiatives, even though they do not yet attract a significant number of tourists. Although the preservation and promotion of these heritage sites face various political and economic obstacles, Brazilian and American black populations are appropriating these sites and transforming them into sacred spaces and public shrines to mourn and celebrate their African ancestors. Gradually, black social actors, often supported by scholars who lend their expertise to the study of the newly uncovered wharfs and burial grounds, are forcing the governments of Brazil and the United States to officially recognize the Atlantic slave trade as a central element of an uncomfortable chapter in the histories of these two countries.

PART V

Preserving Public History

Material Culture as History: Science and the International Ordering of Heritage Preservation

TIM WINTER

Introduction

In the last forty years or so, heritage has emerged as an increasingly expansive, elastic, and at times bland and contrived sphere of public history. Much has been written about the modern heritage phenomena, with analytical explanations couched within theories of late or high modernity, identity politics, or the rise of post-industrial cultural economies (see, for example, Harrison 2013; Hewison 1987; Lowenthal 1998). As the academic dialogue around heritage has evolved in recent decades, numerous valuable studies have also investigated the complex, and often elusive, relations between material culture and the cultural sector institutions that curate the cultural past, and the production of social memory or collective identities at the scale of the nation-state (Guha-Thakurta 2004; MacDonald 2013; Smith 2006). Less attention, however, has been given to understanding the ways in which heritage and the ethos to preserve the past have been an important component of the story of globalization over the last 150 years (Winter 2015). This chapter picks up this latter theme by examining how cultural heritage has formed as an arena of public history at the international level, via the interaction between particular modes of expert knowledge and the wider political economies within which these have formed. As we shall see, such interactions have had a critical influence on the narrative framings of history, and created the drivers by which certain groups and their interests come to be privileged, and others marginalized.

Rather than focusing on one particular heritage site or country, the chapter offers a critique of some prevailing international trends and the forces through which certain structures have solidified to shape heritage as a sector of cultural and spatial governance, as well as public history. In that respect, the chapter builds on and extends the focus of recent studies on UNESCO (Cameron and Rössler 2013; Singh 2011), and the growing literature analyzing its portfolio of international heritage governance. While much of this literature has provided instructive critiques of the highly influential conventions on

A Companion to Public History, First Edition. Edited by David Dean.
© 2018 John Wiley & Sons Ltd. Published 2018 by John Wiley & Sons Ltd.

world heritage, intangible culture, or "memory of the world" projects, my concern here is that this literature has overprivileged one particular organization in what has become a highly complex landscape of institutional networks. Beyond those other agencies in Europe and North America – such as the Cultural Ambassadors Fund, World Monuments Fund, the International Council of Museums (ICOM), or the International Centre for the Study of Preservation and Restoration of Cultural Property (ICCROM) – which, together, led international heritage policy since the end of the Second World War, we also need to attend to those organizations that have shaped regional dialogue and policy outside the West, such as the Islamic Educational, Scientific and Cultural Organization. Largely ignored by Western academics, ISESCO has been in operation for more than three decades, and has a constituency of over fifty member states. Much like its UN "equivalent," the organization works across a number of sectors, through a range of activities that aim to advance national capacities, build knowledge and research, and create productive networks across its member states, with culture and heritage serving as one of its pillars for engagement.

Narrating the material past as heritage

Back in 1984, Bruce Trigger's article "Alternative Archaeologies: Nationalist, Colonialist, Imperialist" created a long-running debate around the political and social dimensions of archaeology's history. Inspired by Immanuel Wallerstein's account of the "Modern World System," Trigger called for greater reflexivity toward the ways in which archaeology, as both academic discipline and profession, had emerged in relation to a variety of wider historical processes, most notably the birth of modern nation-states and the rise of European colonial powers (see Hopkins and Wallerstein 1982). In his discussion of "imperialist archaeology," for example, Trigger focused specifically on the United Kingdom, United States, and the Soviet Union. More detail has been added to this picture since Trigger's initial analysis, and a number of authors – including Shanks and Tilley (1987), Meskell (1998), and Allais (2013) to name a few – have taken great pains to map out a number of reasons why archaeological practice needs to be understood in relation to wider historical events.

Despite such critiques, Meskell maintains archaeology as a field of expertise and knowledge production that continues to suffer from a lack of engagement with its wider sociopolitical contexts. Reflecting on the state of the field in 2002, she contends that "the ethical dimension of our work is often overlooked or rendered mute by force of scientific objectivity and research agendas" (2002: 280). The crucial point that Meskell raises, and one that has been echoed by others (see Smith 2004), is the centrality of science with its claims of objectivity, authority, and rigor within archaeological practice. This chapter pursues similar themes but seeks to extend the analysis further in three key directions. First, it aims to identify more closely the actual mechanisms by which fields like archaeology have delivered universal "truths" of place, landscape, and history at the global level. Second, it seeks to extend such critiques beyond archaeology to show how the field is merely one aspect of a bigger discourse of global heritage governance; a discourse which incorporates a multitude of natural and cultural, historical, and "living," heritage forms. Third, it aims to more closely link heritage to accounts concerning the consequences of global capitalism and the emergence of certain world orders within it. Situating archaeology in these larger contexts also takes us some way in explaining why the persistence of certain positivist, scientistic approaches remains so rigid, and why the reflexivity that Meskell and others call for has yet to occur in ways that lead to sector-wide reforms.

In one of his more recent narrations of the world systems paradigm, Wallerstein (2006) argues that the structures of empire and international capitalism that emerged from the sixteenth century onward were supported and maintained by a number of intellectual binaries. He suggests that the economic, political, and ideological nexus of the world system as it evolved led to the widely adopted idea that those in the dominant position embodied the powers of universalism and that particularism could be attributed to those of marginal strength and influence. This was closely linked to a second idea of associating the universal with modernity (Europe and latterly the West) and, by implication, the particular with the traditional ("rest of world") (Wallerstein 2006). In other words, these geographically construed metanarratives of European supremacy were essential to the maintenance of the region's political and economic control throughout an era of colonialism. Of course, all of this would change with the rise of Fascism and the turmoil of World War II. In a few short years, the certainties of European modernity, and a belief in the universalism of the values that had underpinned it to date, collapsed. The crumbling of Europe's territorial influence and the shift to a postcolonial era also brought about an end to the institutional and discursive structures of Orientalism, and its "certainties of essentialist particulars – [such as] how one is Persian, how one is 'modern'" (Wallerstein 2006: 52). However, for Wallerstein the vacuum left by the undermining of an Orientalist metanarrative was re-filled by science. Even in an era of post-war, post-imperial introspective reflection, Europe continued to draw upon its intellectual and scientific heritage to promote to the world "the certainties of progress, especially in scientific knowledge and its technological applications" (Wallerstein 2006: 52). The formation of the United Nations and the creation of the Bretton Woods institutions, including the International Bank for Reconstruction and Development (IBRD) and the International Monetary Fund (IMF), would be instrumental to the solidification of a highly technocratic language of "development." Indeed, as Escobar (1995) points out, the modern transnational aid industry would be born out of a belief that agricultural societies could be transformed by technological transfer; a situation that would continue to reinforce an occidental worldview.

In the new post-1945 world order, the division between the science and humanities would only increase further. The pursuit of "new, complicated and expensive technology in the operation of the modern world-system," together with the soul searching of humanists created by the collapse of previous Orientalist certainties, ensured that science pulled further ahead (Wallerstein 2006: 78). For those countries around the world engaged by the challenges of post-war reconstruction and/or postcolonial nation building, development, progress, and modernization remained the certainties for which technical solutions were consistently sought. Wallerstein thus argues that by continuing to present itself as value free and politically inert, science succeeded in sidestepping the critiques of a postcolonial era to become the essential "domain for justifying the legitimacy of power in the modern world." He asserts that "scientism has been the most subtle mode of ideological justification of the powerful. For it presented universalism as ideologically neutral ... deriving its justification primarily from the good it can offer humanity through the applications of the theoretical knowledge scientists have been acquiring" (2006: 77). By promoting itself as a value-free field of enquiry, science has been able to shield itself from wider social evaluation, a process that has included the devaluing of moral critiques as less than scientific and therefore supposedly lacking rigor (Wallerstein 2006).

In essence, Wallerstein's argument centers on the deep-rooted connections between the structures of the world system, the capitalist world economy, and an epistemological revolution that consolidated into the so-called two cultures that C.P. Snow identified back in 1955, from which scientific universalism emerged triumphant (Snow 1998). For Wallerstein, it is essential to understand such interconnected processes as a historical system, one that has evolved over the course of 500 years. Crucially here, this historical system was also the context from which heritage emerged as a globally roaming concept over the course of the eighteenth and nineteenth centuries. It is often suggested that the first declaration of the need to respect cultural property rights came in the wake of the Napoleonic Wars in the form of the 1815 Congress of Vienna, which partially succeeded in enforcing restitution orders on the French delegation. More than a century later, though, and with the widespread devastation caused by two world wars, it was plainly evident that major steps still needed to be taken to help ensure that the cultural treasures of the past, both movable and immovable, were safeguarded from the dangers of modern life, including warfare. Given that so much of the destruction occurred across Europe, it was hardly surprising that the UN institution charged with promoting respect for cultural property, cultural diversity, and intercultural harmony came to be headquartered in one of the region's most historic cities, Paris. The formation of UNESCO, together with the international ratification of the Hague Convention for the Protection of Cultural Property in the Event Of Armed Conflict in 1954, and the Venice Charter for the Conservation and Restoration of Monuments and Sites in 1964, would be among the legal and institutional instruments introduced to help globalize such concerns. It can thus be seen that a number of historical developments – the need for conservation and protection in the face of immensely destructive conflicts; Europe's long-maintained dominant position in the world system and global capitalist order; and the division of disciplines with science being held up as an arbiter of truth and force of social emancipation – defined the epistemological foundations of the modern heritage sector and preservation movement. These factors also came to shape how the notion of heritage was globalized in the decades after the Second World War.

If, however, we are to situate the ongoing evolution of the heritage sector in relation to these historical circumstances, interesting analytical challenges arise. Given that heritage as a discourse – and by that I mean a language that is transmitted via particular knowledge/power relations and institutionalized structures – initially formed around the protection of culture, it is not a sector that naturally aligns itself with the "universal truths" of science-based knowledge domains. Indeed, as a professional sector and site of knowledge creation, heritage firmly straddles the cultural divide identified by Snow (1998). Throughout its history, it has sought rigor, objectivity, and truth in science; while at the same time embracing the humanities for understanding the particular, the local, and the contextual. However, crucially, as a set of knowledge practices, the heritage sector has not only been underpinned by a belief in the merits of scientific universalism, and thus by implication devalued humanist methodologies, but has also evolved on the back of Europe's privileged position in the world system. More specifically, heritage exemplifies Wallerstein's (2006) account of how, in a postcolonial era, science was adopted in order to justify the legitimacy of power. It enabled the Allied powers to maintain the political and moral authority they had secured in the aftermath of World War II. As the UN was formed, it was recognized that so much devastation caused by aggressive nationalisms and hostilities had, in part, been created through cultural, religious, or ethnic prejudices. The founding of bodies like UNESCO and UNICEF thus reflected a desire to promote the broad ideals of "collaboration among the nations through education, science and culture" (Constitution of UNESCO 1945). Nevertheless, such organizations were established at a time when it was widely believed that little or no social and cultural progress could be achieved in the absence of a robust economic environment (Kennedy 2007). By implication then, in order to gain traction in an environment that privileged rational, positivist models of security and socioeconomic development, heritage sought its legitimacy in scientific rational enquiry; a language, which as Wallerstein (2006), Escobar (1995), and others have pointed out, also enabled European ideas to maintain their authority at the global level.

Like many arenas of professional conduct, authority in the quest to preserve the cultural past stemmed from the establishment of a highly extensive network of "scientific experts," most of whom have come from the fields of archaeology, architecture, engineering, or material conservation. Crucially here, however, while such experts might well operate within fields typically associated with the humanities, the techniques of technologies of heritage governance and administration have invariably revolved around the delivery of "technical reports" and the assessment of a site's value via "scientific criteria." At the scale of the international and cross-cultural, the establishment of heritage value has thus proceeded through a process that has sought rigor, standards, and objectivity; a process that somewhat paradoxically aligns itself with the scientific principle of value-free neutrality. One of the key instruments for internationalizing the modern heritage movement since the early 1970s, the world heritage system has also given primacy to the principle of Outstanding Universal Value. The need to determine significance across an extremely diverse range of cultural and natural sites demands a framework that proclaims consistency and coherence. As the arbiter of truth and objectivity, scientific knowledge has maintained its dominant position throughout the history of World Heritage by providing criteria that are universally applicable across all contexts. Indeed, the concept of Outstanding Universal Value sits within an institutional and intellectual paradigm that privileges certain kinds of expert knowledge. This is in large part driven by a need to demonstrate authority; a position that is invariably constructed, and subsequently communicated, through a language of "scientific studies," "surveys," and "technical reports." It is also driven by a need to uphold certain standards that are declared to be universally applicable. Guidelines and charters are among the mechanisms by which such standards are maintained.

But if we recall Wallerstein's earlier arguments, we are charged with the task of considering how this privileging of scientifically oriented discourses of heritage has formed part of a modern world order that is maintained by a series of European universalisms. As we have seen, the concept of world heritage emerged at a time when organizations like the UN believed that the betterment and development of societies could only take place on the solid foundations offered by rational economic and political modeling. We can, however, move beyond the claim that heritage has merely been a passive recipient of this wider environment. In fact, I would suggest that as a sphere of professional practice, policy, and knowledge production that straddles Snow's (1998) two-culture divide, the continual invoking of a scientifically oriented discourse over a humanities-based one has served a number of specific purposes. First, a language of universal value, together with the notion of "the property of mankind" and the mechanisms by which such ideas have been measured, legislated, and ratified has proved extremely effective in globalizing certain value regimes that emanated from particular historical circumstances within Europe. Second, emphasizing scientifically verifiable universals has enabled the heritage sector to transcend the critiques of a postcolonial era, most notably the accusations of how Orientalism created its "others." In order to legitimize the claim that traditional cultural forms should be preserved in a postcolonial context, it was essential that they be valorized to a level beyond the particular. Third, elevating heritage to the level of humanity enabled the sector to set itself apart from politics. By transcending the local, cum-national, the universal rendered culture and nature politically benign. Fourth, an infrastructure built around scientific universalism, as Wallerstein (2006) points out, could also insulate a particular value regime from wider social evaluation, and present its goals as morally unquestionable.

It is a situation that has ensured that organizations such as UNESCO have been extremely successful at mobilizing their goals and ideals internationally. Moreover, it is widely recognized that the World Heritage Convention has been one of UNESCO's most successful instruments of international governance and legislation. There is little doubt that a more interpretative, humanities-based discourse would have led to greater introspection and in some cases created a crisis of purpose. Of course, World Heritage has also needed to construct an extremely rigid, unequivocal framework to ensure the protection and management of sites in highly challenging circumstances. Despite often working from very limited resources, its legal and institutional structures have been – in certain instances – effective in preventing the destruction of dozens of sites from the threats posed by real estate developers, urban planners, corrupt bureaucrats, looters, and thieves. The challenge posed by ISIS/IS, and its destruction of cultural heritage in Syria and Iraq in 2015 has, however, raised extremely challenging questions about the effectiveness of this international order of heritage protection.

Colonialism or coloniality?

Today, the world heritage movement garners both extensive praise and sustained criticism. Indeed, a small academic literature has evolved around critiques of UNESCO as an agency imposing a supposedly Eurocentric worldview upon the world. First published in 1991, Denis Byrne's article "Western Hegemony in Archaeological Heritage Management," for example, identifies strong continuities between archaeology conducted in nineteenth-century Europe and "the imperialist underpinnings of the world heritage concept" (274). He suggests that archaeologically informed heritage management too often remains unaware of the complexities of applying Western models to non-Western contexts. According to Byrne:

> what is missing in the consciousness of heritage management practitioners generally [is] an understanding of the values underlying the Western management ethos and an openness to alternatives. If, in the postmodern world there can be alternative histories why can't there be alternative heritages and alternative models of heritage management? (1991: 273)

Clearly, Byrne's argument closely ties into the critiques of archaeology and the associated field of cultural resource management (CRM) offered by Meskell, Smith, and others, as noted earlier. However, among those considering the field of heritage management more generally, there is a common call to consider the degree to which today's global heritage movement remains an imperialist discourse; one that is deployed through highly advanced technologies of governance. To better understand some of the problems created by a scientifically oriented, universalist notion of heritage and the past, the insights offered by various scholars working in the field of Latin American Studies are helpful. The analysis of Castro-Gómez (2002; 2007) is particularly pertinent here as he too considers the intersections between science as a dominant episteme and the global ordering of capitalism, but does so in order to ask whether we are in a postcolonial era or an enduring state of coloniality. To begin answering this question, he revisits the arguments laid out by Hardt and Negri (2001) in their highly influential book, *Empire*. In brief, Hardt and Negri contend that an age of imperialism, an era defined by the strong demarcation of political boundaries, had passed by the end of the twentieth century and that we had entered a phase which has no spaces "outside" the logics of capital. Capitalism is no longer driven by an old regime of Eurocentric colonial states, or confined to the borders of specific territories, and is instead "a decentered and deterritorializing apparatus of rule that progressively incorporates the entire global realm within its open, expanding frontiers" (Hardt and Negri 2001: xii). This last and definitive stage of capitalism was also marked by a departure from those forms of wealth creation that centered around the production of commodities, in favor of an economy that is immaterial and driven by the circulation of symbols, data, and commoditized forms of knowledge. In an age of intellectual labor in high-value-added sectors, their contention was that the manual work and slave economies of colonialism had been relegated to history. By implication then, with the core and peripheries of a colonial era made redundant, the "other" of a European identity also fades away. According to Hardt and Negri, the "dialectic of colonialism," whereby the European self of modernity emerges in opposition to the constructed subjectivity of the colonized, disappears.

While agreeing with much of this analysis, Castro-Gómez takes issue with this final assertion by teasing out the distinction between colonialism and coloniality. Colonialism, as he states, pertains to a historical period in which a series of territorial "domains" were subjugated to a powerful core via a series of knowledge/power relations. Accordingly, Europe's modernity constructed its values of reason, civility, and culture in large part by distinguishing itself from the supposed barbarism, irrationality, and tradition of the pre-modern periphery. In contrast, coloniality refers to "a technology of power that persists until today, founded on the 'knowledge of the other.'" The term resists placing the traditional and modern in chronological order, and instead sees them in synchronic terms, such that "coloniality is not modernity's 'past' but its 'their face'" (Castro-Gómez 2002: 276). To illustrate this, Castro-Gómez considers aspects of the global economy which fall within Hardt and Negri's notion of immaterial production in relation to the politics of development. As he notes, the profound shifts that have occurred in Western developmentalist discourse since the Second World War have realigned how the "traditional" and "modern" are constructed in relation to one another. In the 1960s and 1970s, it was held that modernization occurred only through industrialization. "Traditional" society was equated with underdevelopment, and an inferior phase to full development (2007: 436). Indeed, in pointing out that "in terms of culture, virtually all early modernization theorists were convergence theorists," Wood (1993: 51) highlights how industries like tourism were enthusiastically adopted by the development industry in order to reform or erase localized, traditional cultural practices; the cultural heritage, and thus cultural memory, of communities and groups in economically uneven regions such as South America. Castro-Gómez points toward the role of the state in such processes, suggesting its role was to

> eliminate obstacles to development, that is to say eradicate, or in the best cases discipline, all those whose profiles of subjectivity, cultural traditions and ways of knowing would not adjust to the imperatives of industrialization. (2007: 436)

Clearly, such discourses not only reflected the legacies of colonialism and its Orientalist ideas, but also the chronological ordering of the traditional and modern noted above. However, as numerous observers have suggested, these hierarchical ideas of industrialized development would come to be replaced by attitudes that engaged with ethnic, historical, and cultural diversity in more positive terms; such that culture would eventually come to be celebrated by organizations that promoted alternative forms of development from the early 1990s onward, most notably via the discourse of sustainability (Enders and Remig 2015). Perhaps the best-known commentator on this discursive shift, Arturo Escobar (2004) has argued, however, that sustainable development has effectively reordered the modern developmentalist ideals within a postmodern register. Sustainable development focuses more specifically on "human capital" as the locus of economic growth, rather than the "physical capital" of manufactured products, physical infrastructure, or natural resources. For both Escobar and Castro-Gómez, then, it is a process that upholds an imperialist politics of public goods; a case they make via the issue of biodiversity heritage. Like most observers of this issue, they point to The Agreement on Biological Diversity signed at the United Nations Conference on Environment and Development, held in Rio de Janeiro in 1992, as a landmark agreement which catapulted the "common heritage of mankind" into the global economy of biotechnology and genetic research. The vast industries that have emerged through the capturing, modification, and ownership of genetic material created a need for the recognition of property rights at the international level. As Castro-Gómez and others have pointed out, the introduction of Trade Related Intellectual Property Rights, or TRIPs agreements, would give a small number of multinational companies monopolistic control over much of the planet's genetic heritage. Accounting for such processes then leads Castro-Gómez to disagree with Hardt and Negri's description of Empire as an era which dispenses with alterity and the othering of the traditional by the modern. He thus argues that biodiversity and sustainable development re-solidify the traditional in "new representations of development [which] reinforce the modern/colonial hierarchies in a postmodern register" (2007: 440). Together these authors point to the "indigenous" as a prototypical category that safeguards traditional knowledge forms and cultural practices. No longer seen as an inhibitor to progress and development, the indigenous person now holds new economic value. For Escobar then, the "semiotic conquest" of this new cultural economy of sustainable development thus becomes a form of coloniality:

> Once the semiotic conquest of nature is complete, the sustainable and rational use of the environment becomes imperative. Here is found the underlying logic of the discourses of sustainable development and biodiversity. This new capitalization of nature not only rests on the semiotic conquest of territories (in terms of biodiversity reserves) and communities (as the 'guardians' of nature); it also requires the semiotic conquest of local knowledges, in the sense that 'saving nature' requires the valuation of local wisdom about the sustainability of nature. Modern biology begins to discover that local systems of knowledge are useful complements. (Escobar 2004, cited in Castro-Gómez 2007: 441)

Alternative narratives and knowledge orders

As the analysis of Escobar, Castro-Gómez, and others illustrates, a small number of multinational corporations seek to make vast profits from a language of biodiversity and cultural diversity. To date, the worldview for organizations in the international sector – UNESCO, ICOMOS, ICOM, and IUCN – has been built upon a discourse that seeks to preserve and safeguard heritage for future generations by placing "culture" and "nature" outside networks of capitalism.[1] The examples cited here, however, present a contrary picture. In all its forms, heritage is thoroughly entangled by the tentacles of Empire, as manifest in the political economies of states, the agendas of sustainable development, and industries like tourism. I would also argue that the current orientation toward scientistic discourses within the heritage profession and fields like CRM only serve to advance these interconnections. As the "traditional" is framed through an episteme that privileges measurable criteria, objectivity, scientific rigor, and so on, it is brought into close proximity with other paradigms and discourses infused with similar values. The universal truths that continue to be made in the name of Development, Progress, Diversity, and Democracy each share a common genealogy, that of the hierarchical ordering of different knowledge forms which took place in Europe in the eighteenth and nineteenth centuries. And as we have seen, it was a structuring of knowledge, and in particular the privileging of science, that was essential to the evolution of the capitalist world order from its earliest phases of colonialism into its current form. The issue of biodiversity alone vividly illustrates some of the mechanisms by which such interconnections will only continue to be strengthened in the future. As Castro-Gómez succinctly reminds us, science continues to be "a slave of capitalism" (2007: 444).

The challenge, then, is creating "a world in which non-occidental systems of knowledge can be incorporated ... on equal grounds" (Castro-Gómez 2007: 444; see also Byrne 2014). For Connell (2007), there are a number of benefits that arise from undertaking such an enterprise, most notably the possibility of injecting themes from the periphery that are relatively uncommon in metropolitan thought. Indeed, this is demonstrated by Dove, Sajise, and Doolittle (2005) in their analysis of nature conservation in Southeast Asia. They point out that much of the conservation planning that has taken place in the region over recent decades was oriented around an artificial dichotomization between humans and nature. By implication, communities are treated as separate from the ecosystem, and instead typically regarded as "alien elements responsible only for its destruction" (p. 6). This leads to a misguided approach that attempts to reconcile or 'balance' conservation with development. As an alternative, they argue that it is more productive to move beyond essentialized bipolar positions of natural and unnatural by considering the patterns of social relations that contribute to the preservation of heritage. Only by doing so can researchers and policymakers begin to understand the multiple ways in which communities have managed their environments over a long history in ways that enhance conservation, both cultural and natural. These and other critical analyses of heritage governance illustrate the need to incorporate approaches to conservation which, all too often, continue to be excluded from the orthodoxies of "expert knowledge" (see Frossard 2005; Lye 2005). Crucially, however, for greater parity between alternative epistemologies to emerge, different approaches to research and knowledge creation are required. In particular, this means giving greater attention to those methodologies capable of interpreting social practices, collective knowledges, and the subtle ways in which populations live within, and sustainably manage, their environments. It is also important to harness approaches that recognize how the social relations and political cultures, which shape the contours of value systems and conflicts alike, differ from country to country. As I and others have illustrated elsewhere, tourism often raises similar questions (Shepherd 2006; Winter 2007). Through its particular cultural economies, it aestheticizes history and memory as heritage for consumption. To cite just one example, Robert Shepherd (2006) has examined heritage tourism nexus in the representation of Tibetan history and culture. The long held notion of Tibet as the real-life Shangri-La, the quintessential exotic, mountainous culture, neatly fits into Chinese government programs for tourism development that align minority groups with backwardness and as communities in need of modernization. Crucially, the state uses this vision of Tibet and its people to advance a model of tourism that depoliticizes the region. Stripped of their political and social values, Tibetan cultural traditions are thus transformed into cultural motifs for consumption by both international and domestic tourists. Reduced to a series of aesthetic expressions, traditional Tibetan culture was narrated as a celebration of the nation's cultural diversity. At the same time, a language of sustainable tourism development enabled the state to modernize the region in a way that draws it "closer" to Beijing. As an illustration of this process, Shepherd (2006) highlights how parts of Lhasa were demolished to make way for a museum and a public square modeled on Tiananmen Square. Perhaps more significantly, however, the construction of a rail link connected the region to other cities in China, including Chengdu, Shanghai, Guangzhou, Shanghai, and, of course, Beijing.

Shepherd (2006) suggests that the approach taken by UNESCO contributed to this process, through an approach that principally focused on the technical aspects of physical conservation. Adopting an apolitical stance toward cultural preservation feeds directly into the cultural politics created by the state, such that Tibet's past is reduced to questions of aesthetics and the technicalities of material conservation. Stripped of all its political impetus, Tibetan history is thus absorbed into a wider narrative of Chinese modernization and national progress.

Conclusion

Through examples that straddle the culture/nature divide, we have seen how the arena of heritage preservation can, paradoxically, suppress localized cultural practices and tradition-based value systems. A brief account of some key ways in which heritage governance has been internationalized in the modern era points toward the dominant role that scientific, technocratic discourses have played in this. It has been suggested that, in this regard, heritage preservation shares characteristics with other international discourses such as development. While the emergence of the metanarrative of sustainability has opened this up somewhat, creating space for alternative knowledge practices, we have seen how the ties that have long connected expert knowledge and its institutions with capital remain in place, creating new forms of coloniality. The question thus remains, then, of whether the old epistemological hierarchies of knowledge made rigid by colonialism have disappeared, or whether we are witnessing a reorganization of coloniality? In non-Western contexts, ensuring non-occidental knowledges are effective across multiple layers of decision making and bureaucracy represents a huge, but important, challenge. All of this has significant bearing upon how heritage operates as an arena of memory production and public history. To consider such issues then, the themes explored here suggest the importance of developing critical frameworks that extend the discussion beyond the actual texts of heritage and memory, such as museums, memorials, or historic buildings, into the wider domain of international heritage governance, the cultural politics of expert knowledge, and the relationships these hold with capital.

Note

1   ICOMOS – International Council on Monuments and Sites; ICOM – International Council of Museums; IUCN – International Union for Conservation of Nature.

CHAPTER TWENTY ONE

Preservation and Heritage: The Case of Al-Jazeera Al-Hamra in the United Arab Emirates

HAMAD M. BIN SERAY

Introduction

Given that the United Arab Emirates (UAE) is a relatively new country, established by the Union on December 2, 1971, the role of heritage in shaping public memory is a complex issue. In older nation–states, it is relatively easy to make a case for the historical preservation of a tangible and intangible heritage that speaks to a shared history extending into past decades, or even centuries. In the case of countries such as the UAE, disinterest in history and heritage before the formal establishment of the nation poses a particular challenge to those seeking the preservation and conservation of a vital archaeological and architectural past.

This chapter highlights the importance of the UAE's architectural past in giving younger generations the opportunity to understand the importance of heritage in general and architectural heritage in particular. Equally important is the need to impart understandings of the social, cultural, historical, economic, and commercial conditions and environments that have shaped the architectural heritage of the UAE. This will encourage an awareness of the dangers that globalization, modernization, and uncontrolled development pose to our traditional buildings and architecture. Many heritage sites are under threat from neglect or destruction, and with them we lose something of our identity and our history. Through this case study of Al-Jazeera al-Hamra, one of the oldest and most traditional towns in the UAE, I argue that preserving and protecting heritage towns enhances public memory and national identity, and is an important topic in the field of public history.

At the present time, as a result of modernization and globalization, more value seems to be placed on feats of engineering and construction than on preserving and understanding traditional architecture. There is, however, another impulse in UAE society, namely, a certain nostalgia of the people for the historic buildings and heritage places that have their roots and origins in the hearts of citizens in spite of the presence

A Companion to Public History, First Edition. Edited by David Dean.
© 2018 John Wiley & Sons Ltd. Published 2018 by John Wiley & Sons Ltd.

of beautifully designed modern buildings. Older people in particular remember and look back with nostalgia to the old architecture.

Drawing on personal investigation and field work, this chapter takes the form of a descriptive photo essay. In the first part, I offer a brief discussion of a case where traditional architecture in the old towns and cities in the Gulf region has been preserved successfully, and describe the location and topography of Al-Jazeera al-Hamra. In the second part, I offer a detailed and practical description of the traditional architecture of Al-Jazeera al-Hamra through a descriptive analysis of photographs associated with the heritage project on the site.

Traditional architecture in the Gulf region

We have a significant example of how the desire to conserve architectural heritage can lead to a successful local governmental project in Dubai. The district of al-Bastakiya, whose date of establishment goes back to around the year 1890, represents an important stage in the history of architecture, urban development, and the history of the city in the region. One of the oldest neighborhoods in the city of old Dubai, its architectural heritage, in the form of separate buildings as well as groups of buildings, has survived for two reasons. First, they were maintained in good condition through the continuous inhabitation of wealthy families. Second, with the advent of the oil era, those families chose to leave the area, and so the buildings were occupied by low-income families or members of the city's non-indigenous population, which led to a clear deterioration in its condition, but not its destruction.

This was a neighborhood of more than sixty two-floor units connected by narrow, shaded alleys which do not see the sun for most of the day. These converge in courtyards of varying dimensions, including ones occupied by the mosque. The region is characterized by distinctive "al-brajīl" wind towers, stucco, and carpentry. All of this is a winning combination which attracts visitors to the city, both commanding their attention and leaving a deep impression, as I have witnessed. After saving, cleaning, reconstructing, repairing, preserving, and protecting these properties at considerable cost to the owners, al-Bastakiya has become one of the most popular tourist sites in Dubai.

The preserved buildings of al-Bastakiya in Dubai, which carry traces of those found in Al-Jazeera al-Hamra and many other towns in the UAE, are proof that conservation and preservation can work well as a way of capturing the cultural and historical heritage for contemporary society and future generations. Moreover, it underscores the importance of such sites as a way of introducing the heritage of our grandfathers in the UAE and understanding the conditions in which our ancestors had to live. From these historical architectures, we learn about the materials used for building, methods of construction, and how people lived their everyday lives before the Union and also before the oil era. At the same time, they encourage us to utilize some of these heritage sites for tourism as a way to introduce our heritage, culture, and traditional architecture to others.

The location and topography of Al-Jazeera al-Hamra

Al-Jazeera al-Hamra (the Red Island) lies about 20 km south of Ras al-Khaimah in the UAE (Figure 21.1). About 3 km long, it was originally an island surrounded by water and connected to the mainland by a bridge whose traces are still visible. During the last three decades, however, much construction and dredging have happened along the coast

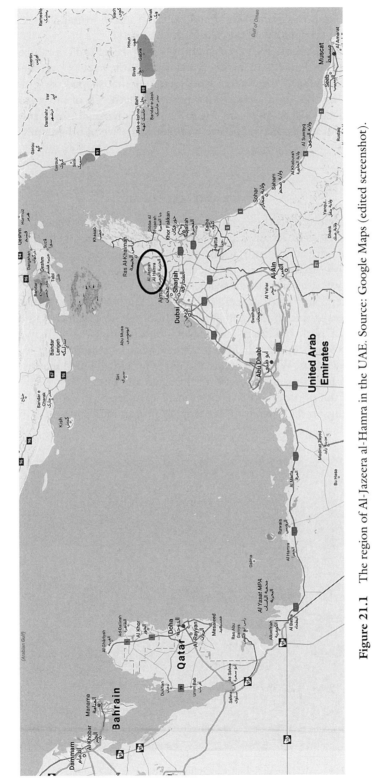

Figure 21.1 The region of Al-Jazeera al-Hamra in the UAE. Source: Google Maps (edited screenshot).

and in the sea around the island. These works have caused several changes in the area, and kept the island completely connected to the mainland.

The traditional mixed material construction of Al-Jazeera al-Hamra produced architectural forms and settlements that offer a snapshot of the society over time. Subjected to conditions of geography, commerce, and sociology that shaped these developments, the site demonstrates the significance of urban society in the life of the region: its people, nations, and civilizations. In this way, it can be said to have all the characteristics of a traditional town, for its distinctive features are representative of other cities and towns in the Gulf region.

Space and settlement

Our first photograph reveals the essential nature of Al-Jazeera al-Hamra. Off the major arteries are narrow streets (locally called al-sīkīk) and the twisting roads that worked well with earlier animal-driven transportation. The roads of the town merged at one of three major sites of daily commercial activity: the port, the sea, or the main market. The sea on the western side was accessible by all roads.

From this general view of Al-Jazeera (Figure 21.2), it is clear that the houses are close to each other. Less visible in this half-tone rendition is the dominant mud brick color. The small sizes of both buildings and spaces indicates that the settlement was over-crowded, but this also brought relief from extreme climatic conditions as well as meeting social and military needs. Winding roads and alleys provided added security and protection, as well as ventilation and protection from wind and dust.

To the left of the photograph is a tower that was part of the ruler's house. One of the largest buildings in the town to judge from the traces indicating its many rooms, the

Figure 21.2 Al-Jazeera al-Hamra General View. Photo: Hamad M. Bin Seray.

house once had an exterior wall. The house had two towers: the round mud brick tower visible here, and another consisting of both square and octagonal elements. All of these components reflect the social and environmental conditions in which people lived.

Exterior structures

Because it was on the coast, most of Al-Jazeera's houses were built in what is known as the winter style, noted for its lack of elaborative baroque decoration. Instead, the architecture is distinguished by flat surfaces, walls with small apertures, internal courtyards, and rooms open to the inside. Although there is general uniformity in terms of the clay color, size, and capacity of houses, there are variations in materials, shapes, and designs, reflecting the situation and social status of the owner. This might materialize in the presence (or absence) of wells or of roofed areas in front of the rooms (usually not exceeding two meters and known locally as "Laywan" for providing more shade), the inclusion of bathrooms inside a bedroom, or the size of the courtyard (usually divided into several bedrooms, a kitchen with an oven, a male sitting room (majlis), and a store).

In this photograph (Figure 21.3), we also see that the exterior wall in front of the house is built almost as a battering ram to protect the buildings against the wind. This traditional method of construction was also intended to ensure privacy for the owners because when the door is opened, strangers would be unable to see directly into the lobby of the house. The exterior fronts of housing units always turned directly toward the outside without surrounding walls. The homogeneity of these fronts made them seem like one integral unit due to the use of local materials such as gypsum and wood in the doors and windows, iron bars on the windows to offer protection from intruders, and, of course, columns, arches, and other decorative features.

Figure 21.3 Al-Jazeera al-Hamra Building Exteriors. Photo: Hamad M. Bin Seray.

Decorative elements

Mud brick, stones, and corals from the sea were the main building materials, although in the 1950s, 1960s, and early 1970s cement was often also used. While high walls afforded protection from the wind, ventilation openings were always placed at the highest points and were open to the outside (Figure 21.4). In this photograph, both the decorative elements of the window frame, window bends, and the rectangular ventilation openings (blocked by stone rubble) can be seen.

The curved window bends were considered to be a decorative feature visible from both the inside and outside, but they also served a structural (load-bearing) purpose. They were often used for councils (majlis) or sitting rooms. They had to be integral to the structure of the building. The exteriors of the houses thus reflect several architectural elements, and as there were no laws or regulations governing their appearance, they reflect each owner's desires, subject to the requirement that other properties or the public road could not be infringed upon. They were expressions of the residents and their responses to social, economic, climatic, and environmental conditions.

Interiors

There were many different peoples living in Al-Jazeera al-Hamra, but the majority belonged to the tribe of Za'āb who worked in professions such as fishing, pearl diving, trading, and crafts. Often living in harsh conditions in the countryside, these people created civil societies characterized by deep conservatism and strong social bonds. The spaces of Al-Jazeera al-Hamra reflected the commercial and social relations of the community.

While neighborhoods may have been divided according to tribal affiliations, they were not distinguished in terms of housing styles or preferences. All houses were built according to climatic and environmental considerations. In general, winter houses were constructed from materials that could be found locally such as stones, marine rocks, corals, mud brick, and the trunks of palm trees. Many of these houses were decorated both inside and outside: walls, doors, windows, columns, and roofs.

Figure 21.4   Al-Jazeera al-Hamra Decorative Elements. Photo: Hamad M. Bin Seray.

Figure 21.5 Al-Jazeera al-Hamra Roof. Photo: Hamad M. Bin Seray.

Mangrove and bamboo wood from East Africa and India were popular in the Gulf region because of their strength (Figure 21.5). Used for roofs and covered by black paint for protection, bamboo was also cut into smaller strips and placed on top of mangroves to produce a very beautiful decorative element. This photograph shows a roof made from mangrove wood. Laid out width-wise side by side on top of this wood are palm tree sticks laid out lengthwise and tied together by ropes made from palm leaves. The length of the mangrove wood usually dictated the width of the room. As protection against rainwater, thick mats made of palm leaves (locally called "manqir" or "bawari") were placed on top, and on top of these a layer of mud (called locally "silbi") was placed followed by ash and then another layer of mud. This method of construction kept the room dry and protected it from rain during the winter season. Craftsmen specializing in the cutting of palm tree planks (locally called "mujaddi") were called in to replace old or damaged wood, and also supplied long pieces from the trunks for summer houses, tents, and roofing, or bridges. This was also the wood used for lintels and frames for doors and windows, and for separating levels of mud bricks, which in modern days are usually made from concrete cement.

The mosque

It is a typical feature of the UAE that each town has one main mosque which is called "al-Masjd al-Jami," and usually it is the largest one in the city (Figure 21.6). Here people gather during Friday prayers, which is an opportunity to meet and exchange news and discuss the last week's events. In the case of Al-Jazeera, there was a famous mosque in the northwest of the town, not far from the coast and close to the main market.

Figure 21.6   Al-Jazeera al-Hamar Mosque. Photo: Hamad M. Bin Seray.

Built from mixed materials (mud brick, coral, and sea stone, and later cement as reinforcement), the mosque is a very good example of the use of cement alongside traditional materials in the same structure. It has ten windows (four in the eastern side, two in the northern, two in the southern, and two in the western). As can be seen clearly in this photograph, the windows are rectangular and long, and each one of them has iron bars. It has clearly been neglected; some of the roof has collapsed, exposing it to the elements.

The mosque has four lines for the faithful to stand during the prayer facing Makka, a covered roof in the front, and there are small holes in the walls for ventilation. It is also clear that the woods of the roof are not from mangroves. This can be explained by the fact that either the mosque was built completely without using mangrove wood or, more likely, that it was later removed and replaced, with different woods being used for the roof and the wood lintel on top of the door of the minaret.

Although it was built in the 1950s, the mosque has a minaret which is unique for its period. The minaret, like so much of the town's buildings, was made from mixed materials including sea stones, mud brick, and cement. It has a stairway inside which takes one to the top for calling to prayer. The door is small and short, and on the top there are five halls that acted as natural sound enhancers and enabled the caller's voice to reach the farthest reaches of the town.

Conclusion

Al-Jazeera al-Hamra contains much that is typical of historic towns in the UAE, but also much that makes it unique. The mosque is an example, and another example is the marketplace, which has two rows of shops (the larger ones used mostly for storing dates, woods, rods, and fishing, diving, and shipping tools and equipment), opposite each other, protected by a roof covered by palm tree sticks. In the case of Al-Jazeera al-Hamra, however, only shops remain, and there are no traces at all to show that there was a roofed market. This suggests that there is much more to be learned about diversity and difference in the architectural heritage of the UAE, but this will only be possible if preservation and conservation become important priorities in the face of modernization and globalization.

Further reading

Al-Abdouli, Kh. J. 1989. *The Evolution of Architectural Direction of the State of the United Arab Emirates*. Abu Dhabi: Al-Ittihad Foundation for Press, Publication and Distribution.

Abd al-Jaleel, M. M. J. 2000. *Traditional Urbanism in the United Arab Emirates*. Abu Dhabi: Zayed Centre for Heritage and History.

Al-Hajjaj, Y. Abu (ed). 1978. *United Arab Emirates: A Comprehensive Survey*. Cairo: ALECSO – Arab League Educational, Cultural and Scientific Organization, Institute of Arab Research and Studies (IARS).

Ali, F. A. 2007. "Traditional Houses in the UAE Society: A Study in Cultural Ecology." In *Folklore in a Changing World: Studies in the Reproduction of Heritage*, ed. M. al-Jawhari, pp. 257–336. Cairo: Ein for Human and Social Studies.

Boussa, J. 2006. A Future to the Past: The Case of Fareej al-Bastakiya in Dubai, *UAE. Proceedings of the Seminar for Arabian Studies*, vol. 36, pp. 125–135.

Goudie, A.S., A.G. Parker, and A. Al-Farraj. 2000. Coastal Change in Ras Al Khaimah (United Arab Emirates): A Cartographic Analysis. *The Geographical Journal*, vol. 166, no. 1, pp. 14–25.

Dostal, W. 1983. *The Traditional Architecture of Ras Al Khaimah (North)*. Wiesbaden: Dr. Ludwig Reichert Verlag.

Hansman, J. 1980. Archaeological Excavations of the Islamic Period in Ras al-Khaimah. *Proceedings of the Seminar for Arabian Studies*, vol. 10, pp. 33–35.

Hawker, R.W. 2006. Tribe, House Style and the Town Layout of Jazirat al-Hamra, Ras al-Khaimah, UAE. *Proceedings of the Seminar for Arabian Studies*, vol. 36, pp. 189–198.

Kennet, D. 1992. Towers of Ras al-Khaimah. *Tribulus*, vol. 2, no. 2, pp. 29–30.

Kennet, D., D. Connoly, and F. Baker. 1993. Towers of Ras al-Khaimah Survey, 1991–2. *Proceedings of the Seminar for Arabian Studies*, vol. 23, pp. 9–47.

Rustumani, A. 1995. Studies of Facials of the Traditional Houses in the UAE. *Proceedings of the Seminar of Preservation of Architectural Heritage of the UAE*, vol. 1, pp. 71–85.

Rashed, A. M. 2010. Traditional Markets in the Ras al-Khaimah. *Nakheel Magazine*, vol. 29, pp. 48–55.

CHAPTER TWENTY TWO

Centennial Dilemmas

JOHN H. SPRINKLE, JR.

Since 1916, the American people have entrusted the National Park Service with the care of their national parks. With the help of volunteers and park partners, we safeguard these more than 400 places and share their stories with more than 275 million visitors every year. But our work doesn't stop there. We are proud that tribes, local governments, non-profit organizations, businesses, and individual citizens ask for our help in revitalizing their communities, preserving local history, celebrating local heritage, and creating close to home opportunities for kids and families to get outside, be active, and have fun. Taking care of the national parks and helping Americans take care of their communities is a job we love, and we need – and welcome – your help and support. Our Mission: The National Park Service preserves unimpaired the natural and cultural resources and values of the National Park System for the enjoyment, education, and inspiration of this and future generations. The Park Service cooperates with partners to extend the benefits of natural and cultural resource conservation and outdoor recreation throughout this country and the world. (National Park Service 2015)

In general, national parks are areas set aside by a federal government that illustrate some distinctive natural or historical element, characteristic, or theme that is best manifested in the unique qualities of an individual place. Large or small, these places are preserved by governments for the benefit and inspiration of present and future generations. Through their identification, selection, and protection, parks convey, in a very pragmatic way, what resources and stories we think are worthy of sharing with the future. Over the last century in the United States, the National Park Service, a bureau within the Department of the Interior, has had the responsibility to create and maintain a system of park units that its citizens, through their political leadership, have chosen for this honor – known as "America's best idea." For public historians, national parks are both a subject of historical inquiry and a classroom within which to elucidate a country's history and heritage.[1]

A Companion to Public History, First Edition. Edited by David Dean.
© 2018 John Wiley & Sons Ltd. Published 2018 by John Wiley & Sons Ltd.

On Founder's Day, August 25, 1966, when the National Park Service celebrated its 50th anniversary, there were 231 units (grouped in 16 distinct categories) in the system that encompassed nearly 27 million acres spread across the United States and its territories.[2] Despite the just-completed billion dollar infrastructure investment program known as Mission 66, the Park Service in 1966 retained the same fundamental mission and character as in 1916: it was a (mostly western) land management agency dedicated to the stewardship of nationally significant historical, natural, and recreational resources. All this was about to change. The "new conservation," as promulgated during the 1960s with the Kennedy and Johnson administrations would transform the mandate of the National Park Service, adding major roles and responsibilities that focused attention beyond the boundaries of its traditional activities. Adjustments within the mandates and missions of the National Park Service over the last 50 years highlight the constellation of administrative dilemmas that continue to challenge the agency, its leadership, and its employees as the institution celebrated its centennial.

The dual goals expressed in the agency's 1916 legislative mandate ("to conserve the scenery and the natural and historic objects and the wild life therein and to provide for the enjoyment of the same in such manner and by such means as will leave them unimpaired for the enjoyment of future generations") established a Janus-like binary conflict (enjoyment of the people vs. impairment of the resources) that has perplexed its leadership over the last century.[3] The National Park Service dilemma was articulated in the aftermath of World War II by Director Newton Drury in 1949.[4] Existing parks were overcrowded and understaffed, with crumbling infrastructure and insufficient funding to address pressing needs. Drury calculated that larger, modern facilities were required to meet the demand of ever-increasing automobile tourists. Addressing the diverse crises became the job, in late 1951, of Conrad Wirth, who designed and implemented Mission 66, a story that was masterfully detailed in Ethan Carr's *Mission 66: Modernism and the National Park Dilemma* (2007). This fundamental conundrum – enjoyment versus impairment – was the foundation of an interconnected series of challenges, ones shared by those who seek to ensure the stewardship of protected areas at all levels, that can be termed "gaps in the system," "maintenance and other backlogs," and "mission creep" (Vincent 2014).

Gaps in the system

One perennial debate swirls around the question of the National Park Service's manifest destiny toward an ever-expanding system. It encompasses not only the idea of the kinds and distribution of protected areas, but also the question of how many of a particular type are necessary: for example, how many Civil War battlefields are required to tell the story of the "Great American Strife?" (Northington et al. 1937). "The whole structure," reflected Ronald Lee regarding the agency's disparate management of natural, historical, and recreational areas during his 30-year career, had "grown like Topsy" (1969). Traditionalists within each generation have decried the addition of what were seen as less than nationally significant units – sometimes called "park-barrel" projects (a sly reference to the pejorative "pork-barrel" projects, applied to federal undertakings that agencies have conducted for no other reason than to cater to political support), where agency guidelines, standards, and analyses were swept away by a deliberate application of political pressure known as "Criterion P." Reflecting this attitude on the agency's 65th anniversary, NPS Director Russell Dickenson exclaimed that the growth of the system "must now be curtailed" (1981). The Park Service, it was frequently argued, could not adequately fulfill its role as steward to an ever-increasing portfolio without substantial reinvestment in stewardship and interpretation, maintenance and operations. Others were more pragmatic in recognizing the reality that Congress and the executive branch rarely tire of creating new units, viewing the park ecosystem as organic and mutable, and embracing the episodic ability to fill gaps in the system so that it reflects a representative panorama of America (Sprinkle 2010).

Shaping the System, the story of how the National Park System has grown over the last century, illustrates the assemblage of forces that have influenced the creation of protected areas within the United States (Mackintosh and McDonnell 2005). Every collection of parklands requires a strong set of criteria that define what should (and should not) be included within the system, with clearly defined goals that shape how political forces decide what properties are selected. This is vital, because once properties are acquired, it is rare for them to be de-accessioned (Mackintosh 1995). Traditionally, the choice of what to include has ultimately been a political decision, somewhat influenced by systems of evaluation to defer, deflect, and delay the acquisition of new properties. The fact remains that some themes in American history are difficult to recognize through park designations.[5] Witness the creation of new types of federal recognition over the last five decades, including National Historic Trails, National Heritage Areas, and the Underground Railroad Network to Freedom. Current thematic work includes undertakings designed to identify nationally significant places associated with various populations (American Latino, Asian American and Pacific Islander, LGBTQ, and women's heritage initiatives), and with the post-Civil War era of Reconstruction. The National Park System was designed to be the head of the pyramid of recognition and stewardship with state, tribal, and local government taking care of places of less than national significance. In the aftermath of World War II, park planners and historians recognized that there were many more nationally significant sites than could be maintained by the federal government; thus, the goal was to develop overlapping systems that identified layers or levels of significance. As Ronald Lee described it to the architectural critic Ada Louise Huxtable soon after the creation of the National Historic Landmark program in 1960, the Park Service would designate nationally significant historic properties as a model of identification, evaluation, and stewardship that state, tribal, and local governments could follow in recognizing and conserving less than nationally significant resources (Lee 1963). When it came to historic preservation, Congressman Craig Hosmer agreed on the limits of federal responsibilities, comically proclaiming in 1966 that "If Jubilation T. Cornpone's birthplace is to be preserved, let Dogpatch do it!" (Congressional Record 1966: 22957).[6]

The National Park Service has long recognized that these philosophical and pragmatic quandaries regarding the shape and content of the system are influenced by a wide variety of forces. In 1972, an immediately controversial National Park System Plan called for the addition of nearly 200 new units in order to acquire sites that presented a comprehensive panorama of American history. From the mid-1930s until the mid-1990s, the agency's approach to gaps in the system was shaped by a thematic framework that presented a consensus view of American history. This chronological and geographic structure was replaced, via a Congressional mandate, with a collection of themes and concepts presented in a complex Venn diagram (Figure 22.1; National Park Service 1994).

The recent work of the National Park System Advisory Board under the leadership of historian John Hope Franklin and the National Parks Second Century Commission illustrated the ongoing debate about the future of the agency and its mission (NPS Advisory

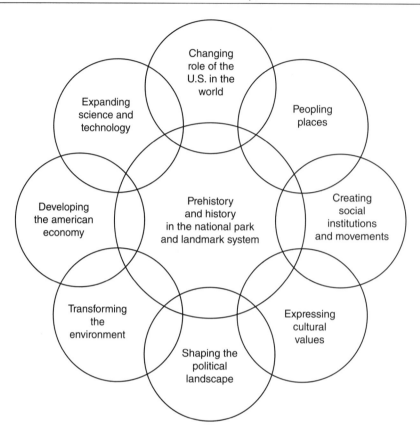

Figure 22.1 Chained Circles. National Park Service Themes and Concepts Venn Diagram (author generated).

Board 2001; National Park & Conservation Association 2009). These studies, and others, recognize that, despite its seemingly unique mission within the federal government, the agency's status within the broader nationwide conservation movement has evolved – some would say declined – over the last five decades. Now serving as stewards for more than 400 units and administering dozens of external programs, the dilemmas facing the National Park Service are not new; they are well worn and familiar. Over the last five decades, filling the gaps in the system had the unintended result of exacerbating extensive backlogs in planning, maintenance, and interpretation (Vincent 2014).[7]

Maintenance and other backlogs

Since 1916, while acknowledging the pragmatically unattainable goal of completing the system, each generation has added fiscal and administrative burdens to the challenge of maintaining an ever-growing collection of protected areas. The NPS maintenance backlog (estimated most recently as totaling $12 billion) is frequently cited by the agency's leadership, park boosters, and politicians as evidence that park facilities are not receiving adequate funding (Repanshek 2015). Because of the size of these figures, parallel concerns about the overall state of American infrastructure, and its potential public relations and political impact, the agency takes its calculations seriously.[8] The Park Faculty

Management Division annually calculates deferred maintenance statistics for almost 76,000 "constructed assets" located within parks. Employees use a Facilities Management Software System to track changes in the Facility Condition Index, and especially Critical Systems Deferred Maintenance. The high status of this issue among bureaucrats is highlighted by the adoption of two standardized maintenance backlog reports within the agency's Project Management Information System (PMIS). Efforts to identify and estimate the infrastructure backlog have withstood Congressional scrutiny, and the figures are considered fairly precise (General Accounting Office 1998).

The concern for calculating an accurate estimate of the maintenance backlog, especially the creation of statistics designed to shock park promoters, the general public, and politicians, illustrates the conversion of "ideological debate into a technical one" that focused on the "problems of data collection" as a means to delay any real action to address the issue at hand (Lehman 1992). How any government institution spends its allocations from the people is an indication of what issues it sees as being relevant to its mission. For the Park Service, as noted by Director Drury in 1949, much of the need to rehabilitate the physical plant comes from the "enjoyment" side of the agency's mandate.

The unease regarding an expanding infrastructure maintenance backlog has a long history within the agency. President Franklin Roosevelt's incorporation of dozens of historic properties into the park system during the 1930s forever shifted the balance of parks within the agency's portfolio (Unrau and Williss 1983). Roosevelt also suspended the designation of new parks during World War II. Since then, historic units, with their maintenance-needy aboveground resources, have dominated the system in terms of numbers of designated units. Newton Drury argued that the "development backlog" totaled almost $500 million in 1949 (Carr 2007). In 1954, Charles Porter thought that it would be difficult to justify the cost of securing properties that would protect the view into Maryland across the Potomac River from George Washington's Mount Vernon when the restoration and maintenance of nearby Fort Washington was so underfunded. A decade later, Ronald Lee (1964) noted that the agency was having "great difficulty keeping up" with needed restoration work, a situation that was only exacerbated with the addition of new stewardship responsibilities each year. Here is the obvious link between the ongoing need to fill in the gaps in the system with the ever-increasing maintenance backlog and why the most important actions taken by Congress and the President each year is not the agency's annual appropriation, but rather the creation of new units.

Hidden within the estimates for the Park Service's maintenance backlog is a calculation for the restoration and rehabilitation of the physical infrastructure that helps interpret the natural, historic, and recreational public spaces, and yet substantially less attention is paid to the revitalization of the overall interpretative program. While some data is available through the PMIS system, the agency's leadership can only extrapolate the overall need for its museum, interpretive, and conservation programs.[9] The Organization of American Historians' Imperiled Promise report recalled recommendations that the Park Service needed to address museum backlogs and archival access to its collections, as well as improve the agency's administrative history program (Whisnant et al. 2011). Under the slogan "Putting Education Front and Center," the Second Century Commission recommended that, as a first step, the agency had to invest in replacing "broken, dilapidated, out-of-date, inaccurate, and irrelevant media, including exhibits, signs, films, and other technology delivered information" (National Parks Conservation Association 2009: 24). Such concerns are magnified where the interpretive device is an entire building, such as the reconstructed McLean House at Appomattox Courthouse National Historical Park seated within a cultural landscape that attempts to replicate a cross-roads village community that existed at the close of the Civil War (National Parks and Conservation Association 2008). The agency has exhaustive esti- mates regarding the life-cycle maintenance for heating, ventilation, and air conditioning systems within its visitor centers, but what about the replacement costs associated with interpretive exhibits and other media?

And what about the stories we tell our visitors: how well can the agency define its "interpretation backlog"? In fact, it appears that the agency spends very little, relative to the robust procedures used to identify and compile the infrastructure maintenance back- log, on identifying and estimating backlogs in its history infrastructure. Established as a separate operation during the mid-1930s, the National Park Service's interpretation pro- gram was challenged by the addition of large numbers of historic units over the last 75 years. Scenic beauty and nature's wonders are easily visible and inspirational at "natural" parks, observed Bureau Historian Barry Mackintosh (1986), while the interpretation at historic sites had to focus on the past, often on features, buildings, and landscapes that did not survive into the present. In addition, there is the administrative gulf between the staff that conducts historical research (or more commonly, manage contractors who con- duct studies) and those who interpret its findings to the public, a divide that was the overarching theme of the Imperiled Promise (2014) study. Dealing with the interpreta- tion backlog has often resulted in charges of revisionism as the focus of commemoration at various parks has changed in the past.[10] And yet, there have been ongoing calls to revisit, revise, and replace old and outdated interpretation within the multiple media through which the Park Service portrays American history. Chief Historian Robert Sutton privately recalled a "back of the envelope estimate" for the comprehensive review and revision of interpretation at the various parks which tell the story of the Civil War at $100 million (2008). As noted by the Organization of American Historians:

> History in the NPS has been under resourced for decades. Chronic underfunding and understaffing have severely undermined the agency's ability to meet basic responsibilities, let alone take on new and bolder initiatives, nurture and sustain public engagement, foster a culture of research and discovery, and facilitate connectivity and professional growth among NPS staff. Reducing inefficiencies and forming productive partnerships can help address these gaps, but after decades of deferred maintenance, the history infrastructure seriously needs repair. (Whisnant et al. 2014: 80)

Mission creep

Prior to the mid-1960s, the mission of the National Park Service was focused almost entirely on the internal management of the units in the system. During the agency's first half-century, most administrative forays into looking at the broader context of land con- servation, historic preservation, or recreation were limited and designed to ensure that the system acquired or retained only a limited number of nationally significant proper- ties.[11] Over the last 50 years, the agency's mandated portfolio has expanded to encom- pass a diversity of external programs that extended "park philosophy and influence beyond park boundaries" (Advisory Board on National Parks, Historic Sites, Buildings and Monuments 1969). Several of the Great Society conservation programs, such as the Land and Water Conservation Fund (1964), the National Historic Preservation Act

(1966), and the National Scenic Trails Act (1968) gave the NPS a substantially enhanced role in conserving areas that would never be national parks. Prior to 1966, for example, the Park Service was legislatively hindered in its ability to assist states, local communities, or other federal agencies in addressing historic preservation issues at sites that were not deemed nationally significant. Efforts to assist federal urban renewal agencies in accommodating historic preservation concerns within redevelopment projects were thwarted during the early 1960s because of this limitation. The expansion of the National Register of Historic Places, the execution of the Section 106 process on federal undertakings, the rehabilitation tax credit program, and the creation of the diverse array of departmental standards and guidelines all represented another layer of administrative responsibility that was external to what some saw as the agency's core mandate.[12] From a benefit/cost aspect alone, the influence of the external programs is comparable to the economic activity generated by traditional park operations (Cullinane, Huber, and Koontz 2015).

Another impact during the second half-century was the transformation of the agency's "conservation" message into an "environmental" focus. In the 1950s, the interpretive program had a "real obligation and opportunity" to advance the preservation and enjoyment aspects of the agency's mission (Wirth 1953). By the early 1970s, it had become imperative that the system serve as "more than a showplace" of natural, historical, or recreational assets; it had become a tool by which to "fashion a deep and permanent public awareness and concern for fundamental environmental issues" (Dennis 1972: 9). In addition, at several points in its history the agency has embraced job training and other social programs that sought to use outdoor experiences to foster the development of engaged and productive citizens (Sirna 2015).

Both Congress and commentators have frequently highlighted concerns that the National Park Service has the potential to stray from its mandated mission, and those debates usually fall along either side of the agency's fundamental dilemma: accommodating a diversity of visitors and their multiple expectations, while ensuring the stewardship of the resources the parks were designated to protect.[13] At the same time there are calls for the creation of a more inclusive National Park System, a goal that, if fulfilled, would only exacerbate well-documented issues of maintenance and interpretive backlogs (Thakar, Moser, and Durso 2015).

NPS exceptionalism

Over the last half-century as "America's best idea," the National Park Service has endured a seemingly unending series of jeremiads that described a declension in the quality of its new properties – thinning the blood of a system of truly exceptional places. Some observers blamed the wholesale addition of historic properties, the incorporation of recreational areas with little claim to national significance, or the creation and expansion of external programs. The end of the agency's culture of exceptionalism appears to have paralleled the decline of a consensus approach to American history after the 1960s, and other social movements.[14] Originally, parks and other protected areas were conceived of as "possessing inherent moral value" that justified an "interventionist role" for their creation, stewardship, and enjoyment by a limited sector of American society (Schmidt 2008). As conservation arguments shifted from consideration of natural beauty in the 1960s to a more scientific ecosystem management approach in the 1970s, traditional claims for the agency's expertise in stewardship were challenged. Separate administrative policies for each type of area (natural, historical, recreational) were merged into one policy to govern every type of park unit. The agency's conservation-focused mandate (and the source of its fundamental dilemma) was the foundation of its uniqueness among other federal land management agencies. For more than 60 years, the Park Service was the federal steward of choice for national monuments designated by the president under the Antiquities Act of 1906. Over the last 30 years, this distinction has changed as other agencies were selected to oversee nationally significant parcels within the federal portfolio. NPS now manages only about 70% of the 129 national monuments (Vincent and Alexander 2010). If the distinctiveness of the traditional NPS mission has been compromised over the last 50 years, its reluctance to fully embrace external programs or its inability to divest less than nationally significant properties has hampered the agency's effectiveness and status. The agency came to recognize its new role as a "catalyst to encourage collaboration" that developed from operation of diverse conservation assistance programs as expressed in the concept of a "seamless network" of parks, historic places, and open spaces (National Park Service 2002). Filling the gaps, revisiting interpretation, and expanding the mission will continue as challenges, and these centennial dilemmas are similar to those faced by local, state, and tribal governments. Some observers have nostalgically suggested that:

> It is not, then, the standoff between conservation on the one hand and use and development on the other that is the most significant problem for national parks. Rather, it is the challenge of communicating the founding ideal of the parks to a wider public, and persuading them to expect their national park experience to be an authentic one. (Lemons et al. 2015)

For public historians who serve as the researchers, interpreters, and administrators of the spaces and places that our predecessors have thought historically significant and worthy of conservation, the elegant dilemma of ensuring the integrity of identification, recognition, and stewardship remains a relevant and worthy goal if our parks are truly a gift from one generation to the next.

Sidebar: Appomattox Courthouse National Historical Park

Few would question the national significance of the "surrender grounds" at Appomattox Courthouse, Virginia, where Robert E. Lee capitulated to Ulysses S. Grant on April 9, 1863, effectively ending the American Civil War. However its acquisition, development, and interpretation as a historic site were fraught with difficulties, some of which illustrate the dilemmas that face park administrators. Efforts to complete a comprehensive system of national parks often lead to controversies between the "inconsequent opportunism" of local park boosters and the long-range view of professional historians within the National Park Service (Kimball n.d.: 32). Seated within a typical mid-nineteenth-century crossroads village, the McLean House, which housed the actual surrender, had been dismantled in the early 1890s with an eye to exhibiting it at the World's Columbian Exposition in Chicago and other venues. Initial proposals in the 1920s to mark the site with an appropriate memorial located on one acre adjacent to a state highway that cut through the village were soon cast aside over criticism regarding design issues; a statue had the potential to symbolically reflect issues of loyalty, patriotism, and disunion that were still controversial some six decades after the event (Janney 2011). Patterning the successful "restoration" of Colonial Williamsburg, local concerns strongly backed plans to extensively reconstruct the historic scene, including the McLean House, based on a detailed set of architectural drawings, in an "attempt to fix forever a static cross-section … as it existed at one given time interval" (Holder 1942: 50). Yet reconstruction was contrary to the ascribed historic preservation policy of the National Park Service; in general, sites that required reconstruction of essential elements were not considered good candidates for inclusion in the National Park System. At Appomattox, despite consistent opposition from NPS historians, local opinions, backed by extensive political power within the Congress, held sway and vanished elements of the community's built environment and landscape were recreated after an extensive program of interdisciplinary historical, architectural, and archaeological research (Happel 1940).

As the terminus of the American Civil War, Appomattox Courthouse might easily be described as the first site of the Reconstruction era, as well as the birthplace of the "lost cause" of the southern Confederacy and, by extension, of Jim Crow segregation.[15] Such multilayered interpretive meanings are found at many park units – a situation reflected in how Civil War parks were managed since their incorporation into the National Park System (Hosmer 1981). For public historians working at a variety of historic properties over the last two decades, shifting the interpretive paradigm at the many sites associated with the American Civil War was fraught with challenges and controversy as the country came to understand changes in our society during the five decades between the war's centennial (1961–1965) and its sesquicentennial (2011 to 2015).[16]

Originally conceived of as a one-acre parcel suitable for the location of a commemorative statue, the park has grown to encompass more than 1700 acres as its interpretive mission has expanded to include not only the McLean House and the mostly reconstructed core of the mid-nineteenth-century village, but also the outlying headquarters camps of the opposing generals. Living history and other interpretive media at the park have broadened its scope to provide a "more comprehensive visitor experience" and a "more complete version of the history" of this rural Virginia community, including the restoration of its agricultural landscape. Moreover, based on a national "policy and responsibility" to "protect all resources within regardless of the impetus behind a park's establishment," the park's environmental program has grown since 2000 to include numerous studies that document existing conditions within the unit (National Parks Conservation Association 2008). This beyond-the-borders vision for the parks is reflective of a continuing twentieth-century paradigm where protected areas provide muchneeded comfort and solace for an increasingly urban population.

Notes

1   On the history of the National Park System, see Denise Meringolo, *Museums, Monuments, and National Parks: Toward a New Genealogy of Public History* (Amherst: University of Massachusetts, 2012); and Richard West Sellars, *Preserving Nature in the National Parks: A History* (New Haven: Yale University Press, 1997).

2   In 2017, as it completed its centenary year, the National Park System contains 417 units, comprising 84 million acres, which supports 330 million annual visits, as managed by 22,000 employees with an annual appropriation of $3 billion.

3   See Lary Dilsaver, ed., *America's National Park System: The Critical Documents* (New York: Rowman & Littlefield, 1994)

4   Drury's recognition of a postwar crisis in the management and use of the parks was echoed in a variety of publications, most notably by Bernard de Voto, "Let's Close the National Parks," *Harper's Magazine*, vol. 207, no. 1241 (October 1953), pp. 49–52.

5   Barry Mackintosh writes: "The System is indeed imbalanced, but this is not necessarily bad.
    The problem lies less with the imbalance than with those who either deny it – pretending the
    Service is telling the whole story – or deplore it and urge expansion into subject areas better
    communicated by other media" (1986, p. 36)

6   Cornpone was a fictional Confederate General from Dogpatch, Kentucky in Al Capp's long
    running comic strip, *Li'l Abner.*

7   There is frequently a backlog of congressionally mandated studies designed to identify poten-
    tial new units of the National Park System. In 2014, there were 27 incomplete studies, which
    generally took three to six years to complete, at an average cost of $500,000 each (Vincent
    2014). Ironically, the establishment of new parks does not substantively add (on a percentage
    basis) to the overall maintenance backlog.

8   In 2009, the NPS Second Century Commission reported: "Today the agency faces a backlog
    of deferred maintenance and construction projects that carries an estimated price tag of more
    than $8 billion."

9   For example, on the basis of estimates from the Intermountain Region, the national Museum
    Management program extrapolated that artifact conservation backlog at $144 million in
    2015. Figures generated from the PMIS system are somewhat biased in that generally only
    projects that have some chance of receiving funding within a tightly competitive fiscal envi-
    ronment are entered into the database.

10 For example, see Avi Kelman's account of the long struggle to identify, acquire, establish, and
    interpret the side of the 1864 massacre of Native Americans by the United States Army at
    Sand Creek, Colorado. *A Misplaced Massacre: Struggling over the Memory of Sand Creek*
    (Cambridge: Harvard University Press), 2015.

11 Part of this pattern harkens back to the 1930s when regional offices were developed to over-
    see Depression era work on state and local parks. Helping state park systems was an effective
    means of reducing pressure on additions to the already overburdened natural and historical
    units of the National Park System.

12 For a short time during the Carter administration, the NPS external programs were merged
    with the Bureau of Outdoor Recreation (the agency that managed the Land and Water
    Conservation Fund) with the creation of the Heritage Conservation and Recreation Service
    (HCRS).

13 For example, see Oversight Hearing on "Examining the Spending, Priorities, and
    Missions of the National Park Service and the President's FY2012 Budget Proposal,"
    Thursday, March 10, 2011, US House of Representatives, Subcommittee on National
    Parks, Forests and Public Lands, Committee on Natural Resources. 10 March 2011.
    Congressman Rob Bishop (R-Utah) stated: "So protecting the core mission of the Park
    Service means that in a time of fiscal constraint, we have to make choices. That means
    we must distinguish between wants and needs, and cannot allow either mission creep or
    a quest for expansive new programs to come at the expense of the irreplaceable and
    existing national treasures."

14 On NPS exceptionalism, see Joseph P. Sánchez and Angélica Sánchez-Clark, "An Enlightened
    Beginning: The National Park Service and the American Latino Heritage," The George
    Wright Forum, vol. 30, no. 3, (2013), pp. 217–224.

15 Caroline Janney, "War over a Shrine of Peace: The Appomattox Peace Monument and
    Retreat from Reconciliation," The Journal of Southern History. vol. 77, no. 1 (February
    2011), pp. 91–120 and Gregory Downs and Kate Masur,"The Era of Reconstruction,"
    1861–1900: A National Historic Landmark Theme Study: National Park Service, 2017.

16 For example, see National Park Service, "America's Civil War: Challenges, Perspectives,
    Opportunities," CRM: Cultural Resource Management, Volume 25, No. 4, Special Issue
    (2002).

CHAPTER TWENTY THREE

Preserving Public History: Historic House Museums

LINDA YOUNG

Houses are the most numerous type of built structure on earth, and the most familiar built form in human experience. In the sense of housing, they range from hut to palace, may be permanent or impermanent in construction and inhabitation, and shelter people in nuclear and extended families, as well as in institutionalized forms. In short, houses frame the lives of most people and can therefore be seen as fundamental psychological, experiential, and material structures in daily life, for the whole of life. The critical element here is the affective shift from a house to a home, with the latter's implication of special insight into true personality. Thus, a home becomes effectively a shorthand for the distinction between public and private life. "Home" is often the rationale for nominating some houses as exemplary specimens, to be preserved in museum format as "heritage." Other rationales are more associated with museum-driven aims, including specimens of historic style and collections of such significance that they merit museumization in situ.

Why particular houses have been transformed into public sites as museums is a problem that can be illuminated by context and comparison. They show that the history of house museumization concerns not only architecture, splendor, or the social conditions of life, but also the construction of sights, and lessons, for the public. The founders of house museums usually intended to enable visitor affiliation with a place, a character, a style, a collection, or a theme in social history – set in the particular house. In conspectus, house museumization occurs nearly always within the frame of national identity. In this vein, some have more enduring public resonance than others. It is unfortunately the case that a considerable fraction of house museums today lack enough significance to visitors or community to keep them viable. Nonetheless, house museums continue to be established every year, indicating a conviction that they are still perceived as positive cultural resources.

By comparison with more comprehensive types of museums, house museums have a highly specialized focus, being museums of themselves. Since the significance of most

A Companion to Public History, First Edition. Edited by David Dean.
© 2018 John Wiley & Sons Ltd. Published 2018 by John Wiley & Sons Ltd.

houses is understood as lying in the fabric of the building and its furnishings, outbuildings and gardens, there is a high degree of expectation that the place will be preserved
against change. The aim of house museumization is therefore to depict a certain historic
period in contrast to the visitor's own day, in order to situate the person, event, style,
or collection ready for imaginative identification by the visitor. Old-style exterior and
interior details may survive or be reinstated or replicated. Inevitably, this frames house
presentations as still lives or, less charitably, as beautiful corpses. The goal of showing
"life" in the house therefore looms large in presentation via museum exhibition technologies such as diorama settings, costumed guides, and elaborate multimedia.
Spectators seem to be able to address the house museum with bifocal attention, as both
a historic object and a stage set for an interpreted meaning – evidence of the sophisticated capacity of contemporary media consumers. At the same time, conventional
reportage of house museums, like much about heritage work, focuses on the "restore
to former glory" trope.

The totalizing environment of many houses often means there is a lot to restore.
Relatively few houses come into public ownership fully furnished, but most contain
some fraction of furnishing or relic of inhabitation. The nature of houses as real estate
means they have footprints that vary from narrow easements to vast gardens, often containing outbuildings which are integral to the house as a system to sustain living. Thus,
not only is the house a complex artifact in itself and the container of many more artifacts,
but it is located on a piece of land that requires management according to civic regulations. Here, the house museum crosses over from pure museumhood, focusing on collection management, conservation, and interpretation, to the category of historic site,
drawing on the more recent concept of cultural resource management. The distinction
is philosophically unnecessary – it is all heritage – but the fact is, museums and sites are
often managed in separate organizational structures. Hence, unless they are in a large
network like the National Trust, house museum staff must be multi-skilled, capable of
wisely employing specialists in heritage building trades, historic garden maintenance,
visitor services, collection management, fund-raising, financial management, and so on.
History and archaeology are common disciplines among house museum staff, but it is a
very interdisciplinary field.

There is little written on house museums as a distinctive species, despite an avalanche
of glossy souvenir and coffee table books, which sometimes contain sound historical
material on the context, construction, and current situation but are essentially descriptive. That said, much of the larger museological and heritage management literature
applies equally to house museums. There is a small professional house management literature, from organizations dealing with house museums and historic sites: the American
Alliance of Museums; the (US) National Park Service; the American Association for State
and Local History; and the National Trust (in England, Scotland, and the United States).
More productively and promisingly, the rise of public history and acceptance of professional historians as integral to heritage management processes have generated a considerable literature of individual site and administrative histories, and critical case studies.
Many of the former constitute part of the gray (unpublished, but sometimes available on
the Web) literature of heritage management; the latter appear readily in the new journals
of public history and heritage.

The following discussion addresses why and how houses have been museumized;
the contemporary consequences of enthusiastic museumization, emerging as the possibility that there are enough house museums already; and some thoughts on the
future of the genre.

Why and how historic houses have become museums

House museums in the English-speaking world are nearly as old as broader-themed public museums. The first handful arose in the 1830s–1850s in both the United Kingdom and the United States; more emerged in the 1880s–1990s; they took off in the inter-war years of the 1920s–1930s; and they reached a crescendo in the museum/heritage surge of the 1970s–1980s, though their history in each nation was stirred by distinctive conditions. Two major paradigms can be said to inform the history and nature of house museums: shrine magic, updated by social history, and public access to heritage resources. It must be noted that these are simply categories of analysis, and are not mutually exclusive.

Shrines for heroes

The oldest tradition is the shrine with its associated relics and habits of pilgrim visitation. Shakespeare's presumed birthplace in Stratford-upon-Avon and George Washington's plantation at Mount Vernon, Virginia, are very early exemplars of this type. Both demonstrate further characteristics in common: long and complex histories of acquisition for the purpose and multiplication of further house museums dedicated to the hero. The rhetoric surrounding both sites in their early years was attuned to veneration of, respectively, the Great Poet and the Father of His Country. In both cases, the frame of this civil religion was the nation, and Shakespeare and Washington became the first of a long line of British writers and American presidents to be celebrated in house museums. Where one house was a success, more seemed like a logical idea. Consequently, there are 5 house museums with Shakespeare associations in Stratford, and 13 with Washington connections, thanks to the "Washington slept here" phenomenon.

Houses dedicated to national (or, in microcosm, local) culture heroes remain one of the largest species of house museums to this day. Writers and presidents continue to be highly represented. There are more than 50 UK writers' house museums and at least 70 in the United States, with distinctive presences in New England and the South. At least 30 of the current 44 US presidents are commemorated, often by more than one house museum. The houses of equivalent UK leaders are less numerous because political and military leadership was frequently the role of aristocrats, who tended to have ancestral houses. Other heroes to have their dwellings converted to museums, on both sides of the Atlantic, might be grouped as inventors, discoverers, founders, and creatives.

The associational magic of place seems to be concentrated in houses, which may be the site of birth, death, character or talent formation, and/or life's work. When understood not merely as *house* but as *home*, a further depth of insight into the private heart and mind has long been invoked to justify enshrinement – or museumization. Some awkward strains develop in practice, such as length of occupation of a house. Henry Thoreau passed just his first eight months in the house that now celebrates him in Concord, Massachusetts (opened in 2012); by contrast, the engineer Matthew Boulton occupied his house in Birmingham for 43 years (museumized in 1995). On the other hand, countless national culture heroes never achieve house-museumhood because either no house has become available, or no advocate has pushed for it long enough. Meanwhile, deliberate campaigns have flourished in recent decades to museumize houses occupied by heroes of newly acknowledged histories, such as great women and people of color. The National Park Service is an especially active agent in this regard, opening the houses of black leaders, such as Martin Luther King Jr. in Atlanta, Georgia (museumized in 1980), and suffragists like Elizabeth Cady Stanton in Seneca Falls, New York (in 1982).

Social history approaches

As society became more democratic and history grew less hero focused, the houses of ordinary people joined the ranks of house museums. The character of social-history-style house museums today crosses over between the heroization, even veneration, of our anonymous ancestors, and academically informed historical representation grounded in contemporary themes. House museums of people or families of little to no heroic importance emerged first in the United States, where even modest colonial houses acquired a mystically American aura in the face of escalating modernization at the turn of the twentieth century. Women's patriotic societies adopted the museumization of colonial period houses as their special mode of maintaining and spreading American values (Howe, K 2003: 17–18). They were extremely active in the 1900s–1930s, but both mission and numbers declined after World War II. Their surviving house museums, often in partnership with other community bodies, have now largely shifted to the modern social history paradigm. Enormously significant for the growth of professional standards of history and conservation was the 1930–40s era of the foundation of great American historical villages such as Colonial Williamsburg. The model of in situ re-creations and relocated houses was picked up in the 1960s–1970s by big state historical societies to represent invented villages of relocated buildings. Many are of high quality, but endure fluctuating fortunes, for it has never been cheap to manage a historic building well, let alone a bundle of them.

The social history that was described as new in the 1960s filtered slowly into museums and even more slowly into house museums. In the United Kingdom, it appeared first as a new stress on the lives of the servant inhabitants of many existing houses. The National Trust led the way with its first historically grounded kitchen presentations in the 1970s at Cotehele, Cornwall, and Erdigg, Wales. Another key input was new histories of the working class, fortified by the growth of industrial archaeology. Both generated a focus on the domestic as well as industrial aspects of workers' lives. Open-air museums, sometimes on historic sites such as Ironbridge Gorge, Shropshire, became important sites of social history approaches to domestic life from the 1970s.

Since then, social history has been put to increasingly sophisticated use in historic houses, via revisionist interpretations and the acquisition and museumization of the kinds of houses that had never been part of the repertoire before. Revisionism based on historical research has brought to public view more house inhabitants than had previously been evident, especially servants and slaves; however, the presence of the old, the ill, and the disabled still rarely make it into house museums. Explicit presentations of slavery in many American heroes' houses have both shocked and heartened visitors since research began at Thomas Jefferson's Monticello archaeology projects in the early 1980s and oral history project in 1993. Re-creations of slave quarters and biographies of the enslaved are increasingly standard in American house museums in the South. Meanwhile, the bicentenary of the abolition of the slave trade in the British Empire in 1807 launched new acknowledgment that many great fortunes behind Britain's stately homes were funded by slave labor in the Caribbean, as depicted at Harewood House, Yorkshire in 2007.

Over the same period, museums of non-elite dwellings multiplied. An early specimen was the Tenement House in Glasgow, an apartment in an 1890s building, occupied for 54 years by a lower-middle-class widow and her daughter, who lived there for the rest of her life. Fully furnished with necessities, decencies, and modest luxuries, it came to the National Trust in 1982, and set a new standard in "authentic history" for house museums.

The problem of finding intact houses inhabited by the poor and dispossessed has since been addressed by re-creating carefully researched settings in increasingly rare working-class residential buildings. Among early examples were the Lower East Side Tenement Museum in New York City, opened in 1992 to interpret the history of urban immigration to America; and the four 1844 row houses of Susannah Place in Sydney, exhibiting re-creations of different eras, as well as leaving one unit as found in 1990. The high level of professional history applied at these sites has proved much less replicable in un-networked, inadequately funded house museums, leaving many in a state of suspended animation and decline after the initial flush of funding has gone.

Access to heritage

Historic houses straddle the divide between museums, considered as collections of material culture detached from context for purposes of exhibitionary edification, and historic sites in situ. It is preferable to see all of these as objects of a social practice of heritage along a spectrum that includes objects, places, and traditions, linked by their status as the past put to use by the present. In this perspective, several more types of house museums can be discerned. The first is the set of "stately homes" which originated in the United Kingdom on the country estates of the aristocracy, and the translation of this idea to the new world, where very different historical conditions shaped the houses of the elite. The second is the very small set of houses of collectors which have been judged sufficiently important to preserve. The third is the group I call "artwork houses," meaning houses conserved for their aesthetic significance. All of these types are activated by the growth of heritage as a public culture to which citizens expect access as they do to the arts, and tourists expect to find cultural experiences that are worth paying admission fees for.

The British country house and its transnational power

The most remarkable transformation in the species of house museums in the twentieth century was the path of the country houses of the British aristocracy from private palaces, to white elephants, to tourism attractions, to national heritage of the United Kingdom. The process has been thoroughly and critically documented (Mandler 1995) and is reviewed here mainly for its effects on other house museums, particularly in the new world. In the United States, Canada, and Australia can be found endless specimens of more or less grand houses, owned by the elite of their communities. Some were museumized as shrines to national heroes, but others belonging to wealthy but otherwise un-exalted local personages drifted into museumization essentially in imitation of the ideal of the British stately home. This is a conflation of multigenerational estates funded by land rents and transferred by right of primogeniture, with the biggest and grandest houses in the (ex)colonies, developed by men who made new fortunes by many means. While multigenerational properties certainly took root in the new world, few with such histories have come into the public domain as house museums. One is the eighteenth-century Codman Estate in Lincoln, Massachusetts, occupied by five generations (with a break) and bequeathed to Historic New England in 1968. Another is Rouse Hill House in New South Wales, built in 1813 and inhabited until 1993 by six generations. Both are modest by comparison with the more prevalent model of the mansions of nineteenth- and twentieth-century millionaires, such as the "summer cottages" – more correctly, magnificent holiday palaces – of Newport R.I., museumized mainly in the 1960s–1970s.

These are spectacular showpieces, but grandeur is so variable according to time and place that the rationale for museumization can be very confused. A fine house in a city, in an industrial center, or in a mining town that survived after a rush, might be argued by a historian to represent the beginning of settlement, the spread of entrepreneurial success, or a boom period in local development. But its interpretation often turns to the founder in his grand home, for example, the son of the first white man to settle, a successful factory owner, or the lucky miner who stayed on. Fueled by local boosterism, the slip occurs by eliding the idea of the finest house in the region with the image of the stately home open to public visitation. After the first bloom of achievement, such houses frequently fade in esteem and interest because their stories are not big enough to sustain local interest or to attract tourism. Some can be revived with a social history interpretation, a wider local history orientation, or social-cultural programs that meet a community need. Others constitute the substance of the dreaded question raised in the US National Trust in 2002: "Are there too many house museums?" (Moe 2002). This question is pursued below.

Collectors' houses

The history of collectors' house museums begins with two outliers in the 1830s: Sir Walter Scott's house, Abbotsford, Scotland (opened by stages after his death in 1833), and Sir John Soane's Museum in London (opened in 1837). They are the houses of middling class antiquarians with strong romantic sensibilities expressed in their collections of, respectively, Scottish medieval relics, and classical and medieval antiquities. Occasional aristocrats also collected antiquities, and more acquired paintings and sculptures by Old Masters and new, variously motivated by prestige, furnishing, or taste. The high end of this kind of collecting produced now-museumized houses such as Chatsworth, Derbyshire, and Burghley, Lincolnshire; indeed, these and eight other privately owned country house museum-businesses today market themselves under the title "the treasure houses of England." Many town and country houses (the former now practically all demolished due to the value of real estate in London) came to be perceived by the aspirational nouveaux riches of the nineteenth and twentieth centuries as the peak of desirable lifestyle. It offered a model for the super-rich, both British and American, to gild their financial fortunes with the cultural prestige of art collecting.

Practically every case of the full-blown form of the collector's house museum around the turn of the twentieth century was inspired to some degree by the Wallace Collection, a unique crossover of multigenerational aristocratic and modern-style individual art collecting, resulting in a fabulous hoard of Old Master paintings, fine French furniture, and other decorative arts. It was bequeathed to the nation by Sir Richard Wallace's widow as a closed collection. Hertford House, London, where they had lived since 1875, was heavily museumized to open in 1900, and it remains a connoisseur's favorite in London. The goal of a magnificent art collection in a historic house thereafter inspired acclaimed gifts to public agencies, such as Kenwood House, London, filled with Old Master works funded by a second-generation Guinness of Irish stout fame; and Waddesdon Manor in Buckinghamshire, with lavish paintings and decorative art, based on a third-generation Rothschild banking fortune. A lesser order example is the Russell-Cotes Art Gallery and Museum in Bournemouth. Founded on hotel profits, it achieved at its opening the accolade of being "a miniature Wallace Collection" (Waterfield 1999: 864).

American millionaires too were roused by the glory of the Wallace Collection. Isabella Stewart Gardner modeled her new Boston town house on a Venetian palazzo specifically designed to exhibit artworks (opened in 1903); she herself occupied a modest apartment on the top floor. Henry Clay Frick dedicated his last years to a new house in New York City, also designed (and later subtly extended) to house an art museum, opened in 1935 after his widow died. The practice continued throughout the twentieth century. Heiress Doris Duke, for example, began to furnish her Hawaiian home with Islamic pieces acquired on her honeymoon, and developed it into a house museum collection that became public in 2002. These examples illustrate the attraction of the grand public gesture: it generates eternal recognition to the memory of the donor, less and less sullied over time by unglamorous or unseemly origins. The trend thrives today, when Western affluence is so widespread that the merely rich can indulge themselves with houses designed to show their collections (usually of contemporary art, given the scarcity of Old Masters), and dream and scheme to open or bequeath them as museums. A typical example in my hometown of Melbourne is the Lyon Housemuseum, which opened in 2012 and is still inhabited by the collector and his family.

Houses as artworks

The preservation of houses as aesthetic specimens is a house museum growth trend of modern times. It began at the turn of the twentieth century with a focus on vernacular houses museumized as stylistic embodiments of nation. In the United Kingdom, the National Trust's first acquisitions of buildings were a handful of late medieval houses, valued for their Old English character: "they look, and are, indigenous," wrote a commentator (Oliver 1945: 78). But the Trust's future was thereafter diverted to saving country houses. At the same time in the United States, the late medieval vernacular houses built by the first colonists on the East Coast were being preserved by the Society for the Preservation of New England Antiquities (SPNEA, today, Historic New England). Like the houses preserved by patriotic societies, their unpretentious and archaic structure was imbued in SPNEA minds with an essence of Americanness that spread from English roots and asserted its cultural primacy in the face of European immigration. It is now an anachronistic lens, and interpretation has shifted to broader historical themes.

Museumizing interest in vernacular houses was more often driven by inchoate veneration of ancestors, especially "pioneers," in whose memory sundry log cabins and slab huts were renamed museums. But as architects became professionally involved in preservation efforts such as those managed by the SPNEA, the informed awareness of design began to shape a self-conscious genre of house museum as artwork (or design work) in itself. A sweeping new chronological presentation of the history of art at the Philadelphia Museum of Art (PMA) in the 1920s (including many period rooms) was accompanied by an innovatory vision of the dozen city-owned historic houses in nearby Fairmount Park as "a chain of fine old houses" (Kimball 1926: 155). Director Kimball practically invented the concept of American architectural history, and though the PMA became responsible for just two of the houses, it advised volunteer groups on the restoration and furnishing of the others, and lent appropriate material. His scholarly attention raised the bar for accurate presentation of house museums.

A similar specialist link between a major museum and historic houses occurred in the United Kingdom in the early 1970s. The Victoria and Albert Museum took responsibility for the National Trust-owned Apsley House, Ham House, and Osterley Park, in and near London, and applied innovative campaigns of archival research into the re-creation of each house to its most stylistically significant period. These pioneering exercises in "authentic decor" shocked some, startled many, and initiated a new approach to the worldwide conservation of historic houses, museums or not. The joint management came to an end in 1976 for cost-cutting reasons (Burton 1999: 209).

The rising interest in design history led to museumizing modernist architecture in the 1980s. The widow of Walter Gropius offered to Historic New England (HNE) the house he designed for his family in 1937–1938, which had become a key source of American modernism. It opened, furnished with original items, in 1985. Today it is the most visited HNE property, attracting design and fashion buffs as well as the historic house visitor constituency. Another Bauhaus refugee, Mies van der Rohe, built the house often called the pinnacle of domestic modernism in America: the Farnsworth house in Plano, Illinois, which was designed in 1947; built in 1951; and museumized in 2003. It was much more difficult to initiate the preservation of modernist design in the United Kingdom, where the style provoked public hostility, underlain by the trauma of post–World War II austerity, urban clearance, and suburban planning. There was resistance among members when the cognoscenti of the National Trust acquired 2 Willow Road, Hampstead, in 1994, complete with furnishings and artwork, in an uncompromising modernist voice. This was so far out of popular favor by 1991, when heirs offered the house to the Trust, that only intellectual determination to preserve "an aspect of the cultural life of Britain between the Wars" carried the day for preservation (Waterson 1994: 246). British interest in modernism picked up in the early 2000s. The second modernist house to come to the National Trust, The Homewood, located in Surrey and designed by Patrick Gwynne, opened in 2008. At both houses, tours, the only way to access them, are now regularly booked out.

The rising interest in architectural style generated a striking "star architect" phenomenon. More than 20 houses designed by Frank Lloyd Wright have been museumized since Fallingwater, Pennsylvania 1963, and now span the United States, east to west. In Scotland, four crucial houses by Charles Rennie Mackintosh have been museumized, introducing two unique museological realizations. The first is the interior design and some furniture of Mackintosh's own Glasgow house. Demolished in the 1960s, two floors of its layout and interior were re-created in the Hunterian Art Gallery in 1981. The second is the Mackintosh competition design, "House for an Art Lover," of 1901; 90 years later, the house was built in a Glasgow park from the presentation drawings, requiring reverse engineering to establish many structural details. Despite the internationalist ideals of modernist design, there is no mistaking the nationalist frame in which museumized specimens are presented as icons of their country's genius.

Are there too many house museums?

How many Wright or Mackintosh houses is the right number? There is no sensible answer to the question ("It depends..."), but it reintroduces what I referred to above as "the dreaded question." The need for house (and other) museum euthanasia has been a wry lament among professionals around the world for a long time, but the issue appears to have first been put publicly in an article in the US National Trust's *Forum Journal*, entitled "Historic House Museums: Struggling for Survival" (Esler 1996). Its significance resonated through a string of well-informed conferences between 1998 and 2007. They are worth reviewing because they express a watershed in professional confidence in house museums, and the spectrum of pessimistic and optimistic views put forward still frames the field. The issues raised were not new, but in articulating them publicly and attempting to address them head-on, the American house museum scene took stock of itself in an unprecedented way. The themes generated are broadly relevant to house museums throughout the English-speaking world.

A symposium, American House Museums, was held in Philadelphia in 1998. The speakers represented the nonprofit sector, the cradle of American house museums, one of a nest of suburban mansions, a state agency, and a for-profit business. All contributors agreed that historic house museums were facing a bleak future, identified in the public perception of house museums as exclusive and backward-looking; a focus on collection and preservation management at the expense of engagement with visitors; and an economic environment of sparse resources getting thinner. Voices of experience concluded that most museums can barely fund their operational costs. At the same time, the speakers asserted a suite of benefits flowing from house museums, vivid to themselves, their staff, and volunteers (if not to visitors): house museums as precious community resources and local amenities; as affirmative visitor experiences via exposure to history; and as important educational resources. These expressions of faith did not blind the speakers to the urgency of change. It was projected to include hard-nosed strategic planning for creative, entrepreneurial, and cost-effective business; partnerships with community organizations to spread the load; more diverse representations and interactive programming, especially to explore difficult histories; and a shift to a marketing orientation based on customer needs and desires. The Philadelphia symposium laid out experiences and ideas representing the modern boom in historic houses, and exposed a disturbingly hollow core, held together by optimistic conviction.

In 2002, the American Association for State and Local History and the National Trust organized a summit on house museums at Kykuit, the Rockefeller mansion in Hudson Valley, New York. It was introduced with a bald statement: "many, if not most, historic sites are struggling for survival, and the quality of preservation and maintenance of many such sites has declined precipitously" (George 2002). Referring to an old study, blunt facts were reiterated: 54% of house museums surveyed attracted less than 5,000 visitors per annum; 65% had no full-time staff; and 80% operated on budgets of less than $50,000. Such statistics explained the storm of expensive maintenance seen to be threatening the central purpose of historic preservation. Some unflattering truths were acknowledged: the sameness of house museums; dubious period room re-creations; endless guided tours; the "don't touch" mentality; and the lack of connection between houses and their local communities. Some were ascribed to problems that emerged out of the very structures established to support house museums, especially the pressure to implement professional standards with few resources. And yet conviction maintained that house museums are worthy objects, with the emotional capacity to move, inspire, connect, and engender pride, empathy, and identity. The lessons of history here shift to perceiving house museums as resources not only for communicating civic values, but also for imaginative fantasy.

A second summit was held at Kykuit in 2007, reviewing the failures and successes of historic house museums in ever more explicit terms. Kykuit II issued findings and recommendations (Vogt 2007: 20–21). Many were expressed in the rising terminology of sustainability and laid out plain directions. Effective stewardship requires financial sustainability, and sustainability begins with community support, as well as a willingness to change in order to address supporters' needs. It was boldly asserted that "[t]he long-accepted tourism business model is not a sustainable business model for most historic sites," and that "[s]erving the needs of the local community (not the tourist audience) is the most valuable and most sustainable goal for most historic sites." This was a radical finding because it rejected the received wisdom that cultural tourism is the route to viable incomes for house museums (other than the most important destination houses such as Mount Vernon). The Kykuit II recommendations projected that meeting local demands for cultural and educational services is the most sustainable way to preserve a historic house, even at the expense of the museum function, and that in some cases the most effective stewardship is to return a house to private ownership.

These and further options are examined in an important study, *New Solutions for House Museums* (Harris 2007). This study identifies a variety of crucial scenarios in house museum decline: aging boards; lack of endowment or financial reserves; dwindling attendance; increased competition; and questionable relevance to local communities. Using eight case studies of failing house museums, it surveys a range of alternative directions, including sharing the load via co-stewardship agreements or mergers; ownership transfers; short- and long-term leases; and sale to a private owner, under covenant. Meanwhile, the AASLH had obtained federal funding to develop the Standards and Excellence Program for History Organizations (StEPS), a self-assessment schedule launched in 2009. The program aims to guide boards or management committees to make improvements in governance, audience awareness, interpretation quality, and long-range planning, without signing up for the demanding standards of accreditation by the American Alliance of Museums. Noone foresaw the global recession that erupted in 2008, with its devastating impact on local government and charitable funds for museums and house museums. Cuts in state and local government services and shattered investment incomes meant that many house museums (in fact, all types of museum) suffered near-death, or even terminal, experiences. The house museum scene is beginning to re-emerge, though whether it has been altered more sustainably remains to be seen.

Some of the same sustainability issues existed in the United Kingdom, modified by two factors. First is the degree of instrumentalist cultural policy adopted by the government after World War II, and again in the 1990s–2000s. In the latter period, government funding was directly tied to agendas of multiculturalism and social cohesion, driving museums, including house museums, to unprecedented strategies to attract socially excluded population segments. The long-range effectiveness of the policy is arguable, but it forced all kinds of museums to analyze their product and its markets, a usefully realistic perspective. The focus on serving society by catering to culturally diverse and socially marginal visitors constitutes an important alternative to the strategy of restitutional representation adopted in the United States. The second difference affecting the recent history of UK house museums is the strength of networked public and private heritage and museum agencies. The National Trust is not the proprietor of *all* British house museums, as is popularly perceived, but it is a model of efficient management, from economies of scale to strategic planning informed by visionary goals; it grasped the nettle of sustainability early, with focuses on family activities, community gardening projects, and local produce in its cafes and stores. House museums owned by local government are largely managed within regional museums services, for similar efficiencies. Individual house museums managed by small trusts are not infrequent in the United Kingdom, but are far from predominant, as in the United States. The global recession had dire effects on national, local, and private funding for museums of all types, and a heart-breaking record of budget slashes, staff retrenchment, collection sales, and museum closures is recorded in the professional journals since 2009. In 2017, there are signs of recovery, but the long-term effects of the global recession remain to be assessed.

The future of house museums

The purposes and desirability of house museums appear to be deeply embedded in the popular mind throughout the English-speaking world. As proof, consider the clockwork response to announcements of the sale or demolition of the birthplace of hero X, or the best specimen of style Y, or the wonderful mansion-and-collection of millionaire Z: make it a house museum! Professionals in the field wince, knowing the costs and risks all too well. Yet it is a significant expression of public support.

However, the corrective of the observed reality of declining visitation must also be acknowledged. The global recession may turn out to have forced some fragile house museums to the wall, or to have induced others toward the routes suggested by Harris (2007). The extreme test of financial fitness may improve the survival of those that remain. Still requiring serious attention is the challenge to articulate the benefits to individuals and society of spending considerable money on preserving and operating house museums. Those who love museums need no persuading, but there are plenty more who are less convinced; for them, the problem is a subset of the bigger issue of justifying public expenditure on culture, the arts, and heritage. Museum advocates now address the challenge in two major directions: culture as an economically productive field (e.g., Arts Council England 2010), and culture as a form of public value, or "planned outcomes which add benefit to the public sphere" (Scott 2013: 2). The route to both appears to lie in engaging much more proactively with visitors and potential visitors via market, education, and/or entertainment perspectives, as championed in a growing literature on visitor relationships with museums in general (Black 2005; Simon 2010).

Assuming more engaging models which make participatory museums sustainable, I observe three new topical focuses emerging in house museums. The magic of the place where a hero lived is increasingly being discovered in the houses of artists, following in the track of writers' houses. It is a swelling group in the United States (examples include the homes of Donald Judd, 2013, Chaim Gross, 2012, and Louise Bourgeois, imminently), though oddly, there are not nearly as many in the United Kingdom. Modernist architectural design is likewise a surging domain of new house museums (and anything by Frank Lloyd Wright). Perhaps this tunes into the voyeuristic pleasures of "inspecting" real estate for sale, or perhaps modernism has made the transition from current life to historic culture and has become an object suitable for museumization, as seen in the example of Philip Johnson's Glass House, museumized in 2007. Meanwhile, many collectors of contemporary art maximize the cachet of art patronage in a trend toward houses designed for translation to gallery function (and also to private galleries). As the experience of museumizing stately homes has shown, these grand gestures – so-called "ego-seums" – will require large endowments to survive (Alberge 2010).

House museums in contemporary history/heritage practice

Much house museum work today is either project driven or specific house driven, deploying the research skills that have come to characterize the heritage sphere: careful searching of local records to establish property ownership, building histories, biographies of residents, and in some cases, administrative histories of heritage agency management. This work has coalesced since the 1970s as a specialty deriving from experience and increasingly from graduate education. Both sources of knowledge tend to focus attention tightly on the particular place and the fabric of its walls and contents; the focus is efficient in terms of the kind of money available to fund it, which tends to be for capital works on particular projects. (Ongoing, operational funding for staff and maintenance is always difficult to secure.) Some works are spectacularly visible, such as the reproduction of historic decorative schemes, but many are practically invisible, such as new plumbing and wiring. Too often, funds for interpretation are eaten up by major works. Hence, what is often missing or belated is the broad social-economic-political context of the house, which tends to introduce problematic aspects to conventional stories of the domestic past. Academic historians sometimes provide it, as do public historians, when they have the time to look up from project work to write reflective, contextual pieces for professional journals.

The same narrow focus characterizes the work of other professions in house museum settings, such as conservators, heritage architects, collection managers, historic garden specialists, interpreters, and the rest. In the multidisciplinary field of heritage management, many of these professions are filled with folk with some historical training, and perhaps it is only from the vantage point of years of work in the trade that it is never *enough* history. But if house museums are to fulfill current expectations of informed and ethical knowledge production via the material culture of historic and re-created houses, then historians need to constantly find ways to raise awareness that the focused stories of a house always exist in larger contexts. Given also that house museum presentations almost always carry strong (if subliminal) national or local messages, the historian's perspective can introduce wider methodological perspectives that qualify the bent to uncritical boosterism.

CHAPTER TWENTY FOUR

Placing the Photograph: Digital Composite Images and the Performance of Place

JAMES OPP

Each photograph is a certificate of presence.

Roland Barthes, *Camera Lucida* (1981: 87)

Picking potatoes was not a highlight of my youth, but the photograph I hold in my hand (Figure 24.1) places me back into those cold fall days on the windy Canadian prairies when our family would harvest potatoes in the corner of a field and deliver them to the root cellar. The photograph exudes the temporal and affective qualities of what Roland Barthes, in his last work, *Camera Lucida*, termed the "that-has-been," the unique characteristic of the photograph as an "emanation of the referent" (1981: 80–81). Like Barthes, I am drawn to the photograph as a kind of "temporal hallucination" (115) produced by the tension between our present-day perception and the photograph's mechanical existence. At the same time, what attracts me to the image is not just the passage of time, but the question of place, a dimension which remains notably unexplored in Barthes' meditation on photography.[1]

In 2015, I went back to the farm to position the photograph and re-fix its traces against the landscape. The laneway lilac bushes are larger and my grandmother's house is shabbier, but enough remains to affirm the topographic connection between this location and the photograph's representation of place. My own personal memories are enwrapped by this place and framed by thousands of images of the farm stretching back four generations. And yet printed photographs are almost always encountered and viewed out of place. Stored in albums, shoeboxes, or framed for the wall, photographs mediate our memories of the past while simultaneously distancing us from the pictured place. As photographs and photographic negatives move from families and heirs into public institutions, such as archives and museums, the gaps and spaces between the picture, the place, and the accompanying memories of place become even more pronounced. Such photographs are, in Martha Langford's (2001) evocative phrasing, "suspended

A Companion to Public History, First Edition. Edited by David Dean.
© 2018 John Wiley & Sons Ltd. Published 2018 by John Wiley & Sons Ltd.

Figure 24.1   The author's hand, holding a 1980 photographic print of his family. "Jimmy" Opp is pictured second from left. Composite digital image, October 2015.

conversations," removed from the oral contexts of sharing, remembering, and recollection that surrounded their material lives.[2]

However, Figure 24.1 is not simply a photograph that has been put back into its place. It is also an image of an image, a version of a digital object created by using a modern digital camera to capture the moment of setting the print within this landscape. By incorporating the historical photograph within a digital composite of two different visual surfaces, we enter into a very different space and relationship with the photograph. Digital imaging technologies, and in particular, the ease with which digital bits can be manipulated, challenge the status of photography as "an inherently truthful pictorial form," which leads photography scholar Geoffrey Batchen to wonder if "many pictures will have meaning anymore, not only as symbols but as evidence" (1997: 206). Indeed, in an age of digital photography, and the corresponding digitization of vast quantities of historical images, how has the "placing" of photographs shifted now that, as William J. Mitchell notes, "the referent has come unstuck" (1992: 31)?

If the surface of the image is less stable than it once was, digital technologies and composited photographs offer different ways to make the referent "stick." Figure 24.1 was taken with a digital camera, but it is also embedded with data from Global Positioning System (GPS) satellites that frame the organization and viewing of the image when I look at it on my phone, tablet, or computer screen. If place is, as Tim Cresswell suggests, space made "meaningful" (2004: 7), what meanings can we draw from the tension between a visual artifact of personal memory and locative datasets? Kept in clouds and servers spread out across a supposedly placeless space, how do digital photographs delivered to screens appeal to or reshape historical sensibility and a corresponding sense of place?

In this chapter, I explore three distinct and somewhat divergent trends in how digitized historical photographs and modern, born digital, photographic images are combined and composited, reconfiguring photography's claims to temporal and spatial representation: "then-and-now" digital montages; digital applications and websites that use photographs to "augment reality"; and DearPhotograph.com, a popular curated tumblr site where contributors hold prints in place, such as my potato-picking photograph in Figure 24.1. All three of these examples are connected to place in very different ways, and all of them use or presume different kinds of analog/digital combinations or mixing that allow us to consider the distinctive properties of both forms of photography. In an essay written just as digital photography was entering the scene in the 1990s, Lev Manovich suggested that the "digital image annihilates photography while solidifying, glorifying and immortalizing the photographic" (1996: 57). While the ease of manipulation attached to digital objects disrupts the indexical qualities usually associated with analog photography,[3] I suggest that space and place have emerged as new ways to secure historical photographs in these digital formats. For Barthes, it was the mechanical suspension of time that drew him to the photograph as a distinctive form of representation. However, when digital and analog photographs are combined, it is place that anchors our understanding of such works as sites of public and private memory.

Retaking the picture in place

In 2013, the *Guardian* newspaper launched an interactive online photography series entitled "Photography Then and Now." Layering two photographs taken from the same vantage point at different times in history, viewers were promised that they could "leap through time as if by magic," by controlling the points of transition as past fades into present (Johnstone 2013; see Figure 24.2). In 2014, *The Atlantic* magazine presented a similar series as a pictorial commemoration of D-Day, positioning wartime scenes of the Normandy invasion against present-day beach activities (Taylor 2014). While these examples are dynamic in that they are constantly in transition, depending on the level of opacity the viewer chooses, others have taken up the challenge of combining old and new images into a single frame. The results range from crude overlays to seamless constructions that require extensive post-production work to produce. As online archives of historical photographs continue to expand at exponential rates, the acts of sharing, reworking, and manipulating these images have become increasingly commonplace.

There are many ways that such projects could be critiqued. One might lament the loss of materiality in the historical photograph and the eclipse of original contexts for the production of both images. Or one might point to the erasure of the histories and memories that lie between the two temporal points and the very politics of such juxtapositions. But what are we to make of this visual form as a popular expression of public history? Why has there been such an explosion of interest in stitching visual representations of past and present together, whether in its dynamic or static mode?

Technology has certainly played a role in popularizing such efforts. As the digital platforms and programs for image manipulation become more accessible, one no longer requires expert knowledge of advanced software like Adobe Photoshop to produce seamless transitions between layered photographs. Social media enterprises have embraced the visual and created new communities for sharing images. On the popular photographic website Flickr, a group called "Looking into the Past" pools these compositions, and more than 3,000 images now populate its gallery.[4]

Figure 24.2   Screenshot showing a then and now photographic overlay of San Francisco, 1941 and 2016. In the historical photograph, sandbags are piled against the Home Telephone Building to protect against possible air raids. A mixture of people mingle on the streets from both 1941 and 2016 when the slider, visible in the upper right hand corner, is in transition between the "then" and the "now." David Levene, photographer; Jim Powell, picture editor, "San Francisco, then and now," from *The Guardian's* Photography then and now online series. Source: https://www. theguardian.com/us-news/2016/feb/04/san-francisco-then-and-now-super-bowl-50

There is certainly an aesthetic appeal to such creative mashups that evoke the past in present-day spaces. These composite images embody a "history effect," reflecting broader trends in retro modes of visuality as seen in the vintage filters popularized by the picture-sharing social media platform Instagram. Drawing on Frederic Jameson, Nathan Jurgenson (2011) argues that these "faux-vintage" photos offer a "nostalgia for the present" whereby "social media increasingly force us to view our present as always a potential documented past." However, there is an important distinction between adding digital filters as a "nostalgia for the present" and constructing digital objects which incorporate actual historical photographs, albeit in digitized form. In the former, it is a visual style that evokes a sense of "pastness," enveloping the present within an exalted historical haze, whereas in the latter, past and present remain discernibly distinct, even when they are combined within a single frame. It is the distance between layers that matters, which is why vintage filters are rarely, if ever, used on the final composite digital image.

I would argue that then-and-now photographs appeal precisely because the viewer is drawn to the very points of transition between the historical photograph and the contemporary view. Our eyes follow where the two images meet, and assess how successfully past and present have merged by looking for both the visual disruptions and visual seamlessness, qualities that endow the image with artistic qualities while simultaneously affirming its indexical status. We contemplate the feat of alignment; we ask what lines, what buildings, what textures are continued or extended across the shifting temporal horizon? How perfectly do the spatial worlds and contexts mesh? Creating a successful transition is a technical achievement, signaling the photographer's skill both behind the camera and in front of the computer.

Acts of compositing, as Manovich notes, point to an aesthetic of "smoothness," whereby "boundaries [are] erased rather than emphasized" (2001: 142). By drawing the viewer into a fictionalized transitional space, these digital objects maintain the temporal distance between what is past and what is present, but they erase the traditional photographic borders that set each image apart. As the historical distance is compressed between the images, the boundaries between the two layers dissolve in order to speak to a simpler, singular narrative, from then to now. Allan Sekula's assessment of coffee table pictorial history books was written long before digital imagery was commonplace, but his critique remains relevant: "In retrieving a loose succession of fragmentary glimpses of the past, the spectator is flung into a condition of imaginary temporal and geographical mobility ... the machine establishes its truth not by logical argument, but by providing an *experience*" (1983: 199 [emphasis original]). Whether dynamic or static, the remixing of photographic fragments is aimed at offering an "experience" of the image, obscuring just how de-contextualized the visual elements have become in the process.

Here is the paradox of such overt digital manipulations of the image – rather than disrupting the representational claims of the photographs, the ability to layer two different images from different times affirms the integrity of the digital object. In an age of anxiety over digital manipulation, overlaying the historical with the contemporary stabilizes the image and reassures the viewer. The historical image retains a semblance of the pre-digital faith in photographic truthfulness, while the contemporary image suggests that the realness of place is confirmed by its locative properties – after all, one can still visit the place depicted, or at least view it on Google Street View. If, as Fred Ritchin suggests, in the age of digital photography we can no longer with any certainty look at a photograph and say, "So that is how it was" (2009: 58), re-picturing the contemporary spot in digital form allows us to ask *where* it really was. The alignment of two images from different points in time into a single digital object might suspend the need for temporal purity, but the ontological claim to represent an objective locative position is reinforced.

The act of retaking photographs in place is not in itself the product of digital technologies. The Rephotographic Survey Project (1977–1979) and a subsequent Third Views Project (1997–2000) sought to reproduce exacting copies of photographs taken by nineteenth-century survey photographers in the American West. Finding the precise location in which to capture the view with comparable equipment was a technical achievement in its own right, but the privileging of place was not intended to obliterate the element of time. Rather than viewing traditional landscapes as timeless, the side-by-side comparisons made the temporal dimension *more* visible. And yet, photographer Mark Klett, a key figure in both projects, has since moved away from discrete, separate images; in collaboration with Byron Wolfe, he has shifted his work toward producing digital montages of landscapes, "embedded panoramas," that integrate historical images within a wide array of contemporary scenes. Postcards, kitsch, tourist brochures, and other photographic materials of certain points are cropped and overlaid onto the vast panorama. As Navjotika Kumar comments, these digital collages offer a dialogue with the landscape, a "perpetual process of reconstructing, re-evaluating and rearranging imagery." Instead of a linear trajectory of change over time, the combined elements within a single frame evoke a "psychic temporality, or the character of memory that can simultaneously accommodate very different spatio-temporal realities" (2014: 159). Unlike the side-by-side comparisons, however, the fleeting depictions of temporal change in these panoramas affirm and project the underlying landscape as a stable place, the clear topographical point of reference upon which the ever-shifting winds of representation are layered.

Augmenting place

The concept of "layering" historical photographs in place is what lies at the heart of a growing number of applications built for the Web, smartphones, and other mobile digital devices. Historypin.org is the largest entity in this field, as it boasts more than 68,000 members and 22,400 different "collections," with a crowd-sourced photographic archive numbering in the hundreds of thousands. Founded by Shift, a United Kingdom–based nonprofit organization, and propelled by a partnership with Google that facilitates an unlimited storage of image files, Historypin allows users to upload historical photographs and "pin" them to Google maps. In some cases, the photograph can even be viewed as integrated within a Google Street View. Historypin bills itself as "connecting communities with local history," but it is a view that is shaped by a sense of decline, a lamentation over the "breakdown in the structure of communities over the last few decades." In the face of a "decrease in local social capital" and with the aim of reducing "isolation," Historypin offers digital tools to facilitate "collaborative archiving, using local heritage to build communities and strengthen local connections" (Historypin 2015: 1–2). Although other media, including movies and audio, are now handled by the site, photographs were at the heart of the project from the beginning, and they continue to form the bulk of its content. The act of recovering, sharing, and pinning photographs at the local level is part of Historypin's vision of a platform for "a growing community of local history lovers building up a global picture of how the world used to be" (Historypin n.d.).

A variety of other applications follow a similar, if less ambitious, path. London's Streetmuseum app focuses less on community engagement and more on integrating historical photographs within the landscape through augmented reality (AR). The user accesses the image through a map interface or by location triggers which prompt the device to overlay the historical image onto the view through the smartphone's camera. The effect is a real-time experience of creating a then-and-now view on the fly (Museum of London n.d.; Zolfagharifard 2014). Historypin's mobile apps allowed for a similar, if more static, view, whereby the user could make changes in the historical photograph's transparency to line it up with the "real-world" camera view.[5] Academic historians have also dipped their toes into the photographic app waters. In 2012, I co-produced, with Anthony Whitehead, the Rideau Timescapes App, an iOS application that presents the user with more than 700 historical photographs of the Rideau Canal Lockstations, a UNESCO heritage site located in eastern Ontario (Rideau Timescapes 2012; Whitehead and Opp 2013). With this app, the user can view the historical image as an overlay in place or, in some cases, move through time by transitioning through a series of images grouped around a single point on the map interface (Figures 24.3 and 24.4).

Figure 24.3 Screenshot from Rideau Timescapes App. Each pin on the map interface represents one or more historical photographs.

Despite their different features and varying scopes, all of these historical photograph projects are built on image databases that are structured by global mapping coordinates. Locative data is privileged as a key organizing principle for both the map-based user interface and the underlying database. In this environment, temporal questions matter far less than place, since the date of the image can vary, be left ambiguous, or be changed without altering the experience of the photograph "in place." One can pin a wrongly dated photograph to a digital map, but without GPS coordinates, the photograph becomes unmappable and is ultimately rendered invisible. Like then-and-now photographs, location anchors the photographic "truth," but for the apps it is the digital infrastructure that privileges geographical fidelity over temporal veracity.

As a historian, the experience of producing an app that was reliant upon GPS raised a whole new set of questions surrounding how locative data and the photograph should relate and interact. After all, what exactly does one pin to the map – the pictured place, or the point at which the place is viewed? If an augmented, real-time view is desired, then which view becomes the GPS location – the perspective produced by a smartphone wide-angle lens (which can vary, depending on the manufacturer), or the actual location that the photographer might have occupied, depending on the field of view produced by their camera and lens combination? How stridently does one hold to finding the exact view, when users of historic sites are restricted to particular pathways and some views

Figure 24.4 Screenshot from Rideau Timescapes App. The layered historical photographs show the change of the landscape over time, or by pressing the camera button, compare the historical image with the present surroundings.

may not be accessible to the average visitor? To add GPS data to the Rideau Timescapes, graduate students field-tested hundreds of photographs to see where to place the view, but while the exactness of the numbered coordinates might evoke the 1970s rephotography projects, the actual experience was far more fluid in accommodating the practical implementation of sites and pins where the app was usable, rather than strictly accurate.

The significance of the map as the interface for accessing historical photographs cannot be overstated. Spatial relationships are key to both accessing individual photographs within the database and interacting with them in place. Manovich's assertion that "database and narrative are natural enemies" (2001: 225) falters somewhat when one realizes that the narrative structure of mobile apps is often driven by mediating application program interfaces (APIs), tools that allow developers to embed, for example, Google Maps, within the app. In producing Rideau Timescapes, the underlying image database was designed to store information arranged by GPS coordinates so that requests for data from the mapping interface would search only a small portion of the database to recover the relevant pins, rather than searching all of it each time – no small issue when trying to maximize efficiency and minimize the load on the user's mobile dataplan. In general, applications such as Historypin, Streetmuseum, and Rideau Timescapes are not set up as walking tours with fixed starting and ending points (although these can be, and are occasionally, added features). Rather, they are designed so that the user may enter or exit at any point. Individual stories or text may be added to specific photographs or even wider geographical locations, but the narrative is spatially driven by the map – where the user is willing to travel and what has been virtually placed there.

As a result of this mobility, combining or overlaying historical photographs with a real-time camera view becomes a performative act by the user. As discussed previously, the interactive then-and-now digital objects offer a particular kind of prescribed visual experience, but the creative act of combining and aligning the analog and digital images was the product of the photographer or designer. In contrast, for photographs deployed through AR, the user's body is mobilized by the map and put in place to activate the recombinant view.[6] This mobile "visual regime of navigation," as Nanna Verhoeff suggests, is simultaneously a process of seeing and capturing: "producing images while viewing them, the user-navigator engages physically with the screen in a temporally dynamic and spatially layered process" (2013: 25–26).[7]

The act of putting photographs into place has a number of artistic antecedents, such as photographer Shimon Attie's *Writing on the Wall* installation. In the early 1990s, Attie projected historical photographs of Berlin's interwar Jewish street life onto the buildings at or near the location of the original image. By making "fragments of the past" part of the "visual field of the present," Attie saw his project as an effort to reassert a historical presence of working-class Jews in what was once the Jewish quarter of Berlin. In this way, "parts of long-destroyed Jewish community life were visually simulated, momentarily recreated" (2003: 75). In 2002, Attie launched a similar installation in Rome, titled *The History of Another*, projecting photographs of early twentieth-century Roman Jews onto sites like the Colosseum. Although the installations were temporary, Attie took large-format photographs of the projections in place, which have been widely exhibited and reprinted. But even if the final artistic work is ultimately a representation of place, the significance of the initial intervention is apparent. Transformed into a projected transparency, the historical photograph evokes the past and memory, but its meaning is shaped by its very being in place. As Attie states, "One can always overlay images in a dark-room or with a computer. But I wanted to touch those spaces" (Young 2000: 70).[8]

Attie's distinction between computer overlays and the desire to "touch those spaces" is important. AR apps offer a similar visual effect, but in their design and function, the impact of the image on the place is contained within the screen of the mobile device. Attie's projections publicly disturbed and disrupted these spaces by evoking memories and histories that were in danger of being erased. Carefully curated, these temporary installations spoke directly to the politics of memory, and sometimes they were resisted. But rather than imprint the photograph onto a wall, photographic AR apps recreate the space in a mobile virtual form to allow for transparency manipulation and layering. Even if the viewer is standing in place, the digital camera mediates the visual experience, shaping where and how the image is aligned. The user might have agency and creativity in interacting with the space, but the general focus is on trying to get the right perspective, the best merger of lines – the achievement or reward is getting the image "just right." The political significance of layering the past in place, even with (or, perhaps, because of) the vast archive of photographs that could be deployed, is obscured. This is not to say that AR apps are inherently apolitical or could not be designed to offer their own disruptive memories of place, but the infrastructure that links historical photographs with database archives and a locative map interface privileges the aesthetics of represented places over the potential politics of place, and place-histories. Through these apps, the public is invited to interact with the surfaces of the image and the contemporary topography, but the dislocations that Attie sought to highlight are rarely made visible.

Placing memory

The website DearPhotograph.com offers a different understanding of photographs, place, and memory. Founded in 2011 by Canadian Taylor Jones, the users of this tumblr-based website are invited to take an existing, printed photograph, hold it in front of the place where it was originally taken, and then re-photograph the scene as a second, digital image that shows the person's hand within the frame in a style similar to Figure 24.1. Dear Photograph encourages performative acts of putting photographs into place, and enwraps them with personal memories. The captions to all of the images open with "Dear Photograph," as the opening salutation. In almost all cases, the borders of the original image are clearly visible. Unlike the seamless aesthetic of the then-and-now photographs and the technologically advanced AR apps, here the lines do not match perfectly, the angles are tilted, and the fullness of the original image – a sense of scale, its format, its thickness, its materiality – is on display, even if it too is embedded within a new digital object.

The images and stories on Dear Photograph are submitted by users, but they are curated by Jones. Of those that are posted to the site, the dominant themes relate to family experiences, such as children growing up and other life milestones: weddings, going to school, riding bikes, family vacations – these are moments of picture taking, both ritualized and spontaneous. The memories and emotions that accompany the photograph range from happiness, to nostalgia, to contemplation, to a profound sense of loss – the death of people or pets pictured, the selling of the family home, divorce, regrets, and a longing to recover what is seen as a more innocent and happy moment in time. In contrast to the then-and-now photographs and the database apps, these images and places stand for deeply personal memories, even if they are publicly shared. Significantly, the majority of then-and-now photographs appear to have been constructed by male photographers, both professional and amateur, while women are clearly in the majority when it comes to sharing memories on Dear Photograph, reminding us that gender shapes the form and process of pictured memory practice.

In 2012, Diane shared the image shown in Figure 24.5. Her hand holds a photograph in place showing a family in a living room; four children and a woman are happily linked together with each other. The words attached to the image are carefully chosen, poignant, and poetic:

> Dear Photograph,
>   Pretty soon we won't be able to afford to live in this house anymore, and you will be all that I have left. I don't know what's harder … letting go of the house or letting go of the little girl that grew up here.
> Diane.

For Diane, there is a continuity in the pictured place between past and present, but it is one that is about to be broken by the loss of a family home, and a loss of the childhood memories within. Indeed, throughout the website, these emotional landscapes of place pull the viewer in two general directions – as a site of restoration, of making whole again (usually performed on trips back to the family home, familiar streets, or special vacation

Dear Photograph,
Pretty soon we won't be able to afford to live in this house anymore, and you will be all that I
have left. I don't know what's harder…letting go of the house or letting go of the little girl that
grew up here.
Diane

Figure 24.5   Detail of screenshot from DearPhotograph.com. Posted January 10, 2012.

spots), and as a site of imminent loss, of longing to recover or hold on to particular
places and the people (and memories) that occupy them. Diane's caption speaks to what
Svetlana Boym calls "reflective nostalgia," which does not seek to restore the past, but
rather dwells on "longing and loss, the imperfect process of remembrance. … Reflective
nostalgia lingers on ruins, the patina of time and history, in the dreams of another place
and another time" (2001: 41).

The reflection on the "process of remembrance" can also be seen in Amber's contribution to Dear Photograph (Figure 24.6): "I can always return to the streets of my
childhood, but only with you can I recall racing my brother around the block, the wind
in my hair, my Dad close at our heels." How we remember, and the dynamics of memory
between the pictured place and the picture itself, is at the core of the site and central to
many of the contributions. It is worth noting that Jones' innovation was not the act of
re-picturing a photograph, which had been done many times previously.[9] Rather, it was
the narrative convention of personally addressing the printed photograph that marked
Dear Photograph as distinctive. Although some users slip into a dialogue with the pictured people, rather than the print, most maintain the act of addressing the photograph
as a material item. Even the original photographer, present for the initial encounter in
making the image, is usually forgotten or obscured in this direct engagement with the
visual object in hand.[10] Thus, for Diane the photograph is the remnant of a place that is
being dispossessed: "you will be all that I have left." In Amber's case, the meanings
attached to the place and the photograph are almost reversed, as it is the photograph
("only with you") rather than the place that recalls the memory.

Dear Photograph,
I can always return to the streets of my childhood, but only with you can I recall racing my brother around the block, the wind in my hair, my Dad close at our heels.
Love, Amber

Figure 24.6 Detail of screenshot from DearPhotograph.com. Posted June 29, 2013.

In mobile locative apps, the ability to assign specific coordinates is important for both mapping the image and viewing the historical photograph in place. For the images in Dear Photograph, however, place names and specific geographical locations are rarely revealed, unless the picture is taken at an obvious landmark. This is a conspicuous absence, a reconfiguring of place as part of a personal, intimate, and deliberately subjective landscape of memory. For Diane, the pictured place is simply "this house," while in Figure 24.6, Amber speaks of "the streets of my childhood." By positioning the narrator in place, with the hand visible in the frame, the accuracy of the location is visually confirmed and therefore does not need to be explained. At the same time, there is a sense that being "in place" also verifies the memory, authenticating both its affective aspects and the veracity of the narrative. Amber's image offers a striking visual contrast between the vibrant fall colors of the analog photograph and the surrounding digital image, taken in winter. There are very few visual cues to connect the two images, but the seasonal and chromatic contrasts heighten the distance between past and present, childhood and adulthood.

The performative act of putting photographs into place on Dear Photograph is not an attempt to merge past and present seamlessly, but is rather a contemplation on the memories we embed within place and within photographs. It is the sharp edges of the photographic borders that heighten the distance between past and present. Keeping the hand within the frame reminds us that the printed photograph has its own history, its own accumulation of memories over time, its own place in photo albums, picture frames, or stored in old shoeboxes. If the production of a new digital object creates more layers of meaning, more layers of text, and more memories, it does so by acknowledging, and arguably, celebrating, the materiality and histories of the original photograph. It is per-haps slightly ironic that fueled by Dear Photograph's popularity, Jones re-materialized some of its content in the form of a book, published by HarperCollins in 2012.

At the same time, there are certain threads of anxiety that underlie the Dear Photograph project. Are the kinds of memories carried in the printed photograph more "authentic" than digital photographs that document childhoods today, which are still shared, but might only ever be viewed on screens? What kinds of nostalgia are being performed here – a longing for childhood, a longing for place, or a longing for analog markers of memory? Perhaps the answer lies in all three aspects; to return to Boym, "nostalgia … like irony, is not a property of the object itself but a result of an interaction between subjects and objects, between actual landscapes and the landscapes of the mind" (2001: 354). Dear Photograph is a personal visual and textual conversation, publicly performed, between a photographer/narrator, a photograph, and a pictured place. While the origi-nal photograph continues to hold on to its referential elements, this new digital object can only be verified and made meaningful by being constructed in place.

Conclusion

Lev Manovich distinguishes between the montage and compositing, arguing that the former, representative of "old" media, aims to "create visual, stylistic, semantic, and emotional dissonance between different elements." The latter, a contrasting form of "new" media, "aims to blend them into a seamless whole, a single gestalt" (2001: 144). The examples I have discussed above do not fit neatly into this binary of old/new media, but the layering of historical photographs within contemporary digital images does expose the aesthetic fault lines of dissonance versus seamlessness. The then-and-now images, in both static and dynamic form, draw the user into the frame to explore the transition zones of the image, hiding the seams even while heightening the temporal divide. In a divergence from this trend, Dear Photograph uses visual dissonance to sepa-rate past from present and the material from the digital. Historypin and other AR web-sites and apps move between these modes, at times integrating seamlessly into the landscape, and at other times requiring the user to actively perform in place, aligning the image in a manner that both separates and merges the distinction between the historical representation and the contemporary surroundings.

Interlaced within all three forms of remixing historical photographs in new digital contexts is a shift in how the photograph's representational authority functions, moving from the temporal to the spatial. As digital objects that seek to maintain the basic integ-rity of the historical photograph embedded within, these images are tethered to topo-graphical surfaces and locational data in a manner that projects truthfulness. All three stake claims to represent place, but the evidential basis for making the connections vary. The internal coherence of the then-and-now photographs assure the viewer that the spectacle of moving from past to present is "real," even if the image is clearly a digital construction. The GPS data of map interfaces pin the picture to a location, which can be accessed from afar as well as performed on site. Dear Photograph rejects geospatial data in favor of a different kind of performance of place, but one that also depends upon the framing digital image adhering to the visual contours of the historical print. But unlike the seamless transitions of the then-and-now images, the hand of the photographer physically separates the historical print from the place, even if it cannot quite escape also being embedded in the new digital object. A mobile piece of place-memory is momentarily reunited at a different point in time, in order to (digitally) capture a present moment of feeling in a text, a phrase, or a story. Barthes suggests we "enter into *flat Death*" (1981: 92) with photographs; perhaps returning the photograph to place and narrating the encounter is an attempt to re-animate it.

Epilogue: Pictured pasts

In October 2015, the auction sale carried off whatever possessions my parents decided not to move to their new house in a nearby city. After 110 years, the family farm site was put up for sale. The act of picturing a photograph within a place in Figure 24.1 is now a doubled history. It marks not only the childhood past of my family engaged in the yearly ritual of picking potatoes, it also tells another story of returning home, of nostalgia before the sale, and of trying to capture a sense of place before the place is seemingly lost. Barthes' invocation that "Each photograph is a certificate of presence" is echoed in such acts, but digitally capturing the print in hand re-asserts the photograph's material connection and mnemonic claim to place. Boym suggests that "each new medium affects the relationship between distance and intimacy that is at the core of nostalgic sentiment" (2001: 346). Digital contexts reshape how we express our attachment to place as we loosen our grip on both the place itself and the analog visual forms that marked it in our minds' eye.[11]

Notes

1   The same can be said for most commentaries on *Camera Lucida*. See, for example, *Photography Degree Zero: Reflections on Roland Barthe's Camera Lucida*, ed. Geoffrey Batchen (Cambridge, MA: The MIT Press, 2009).
2   For more examples of recent scholarship that takes the materiality of photographs seriously, see E. Edwards and J. Hart (eds.), *Photographs Objects Histories* (London: Routledge, 2004); J.M. Schwartz and J. Ryan (eds.), *Picturing Place: Photography and the Geographical Imagination* (London: I.B. Taurus, 2003); A. Kuhn and K.E. McAllister (eds.), *Locating Memory: Photographic Acts* (New York: Berghahn Books, 2006).
3   How scholars use or misuse the concept of "indexicality" in relation to photography continues to be a point of discussion. See for example, M. Lefebvre, "The Art of Pointing: On Peirce, Indexicality, and Photographic Images," in *Photography Theory*, ed. James Elkins (New York: Routledge, 2007), pp. 220–244; and F. Brunet, "'A better example is a photograph': On the Exemplary Value of Photographs in C.S. Peirce's Reflection on Signs," in *The Meaning of Photography*, ed. R. Kelsey and B. Stimson (Williamstown, MA: Sterling and Francine Clark Art Institute, 2008), pp. 34–49.
4   For more on this group, see J. Kalin, "Remembering with Rephotography: A Social Practice for the Inventions of Memories," *Visual Communication Quarterly* 20 (July–September 2013): 168–179. A second group called "Then and Now" has more than 12,000 images, but only a portion of them are "blended" composites.
5   In April 2015, Historypin announced its decision to stop development and maintenance of mobile apps and focus on "designing 'mobile first' experiences and harnessing HTML5 so that historypin.org will work seamlessly on all tablet and mobile browsers" (Abraham 2015).
6   For observations on the kinetic interaction with the environment through AR overlays, see S. Nixon, "The Grimsby Timescapes App: Encountering the Past on Main Street," (unpublished Masters Research Essay, M.A. in Public History, Carleton University, August 2015), pp. 40–45.

7   See also N. Verhoeff, *Mobile Screens: The Visual Regime of Navigation* (Amsterdam: Amsterdam University Press, 2012).

8   See also D. Apel, *Memory Effects: The Holocaust and the Art of Secondary Witnessing* (New Brunswick, NJ: Rutgers University Press, 2002), Chapter 2; B. Lang, "Second-Sight: Shimon Attie's Recollection," in *Image and Remembrance: Representation and the Holocaust*, ed. S. Hornstein and F. Jacobowitz (Bloomington: Indiana University Press); P. Muir, *Shimon Attie's Writing on the Wall: History, Memory Aesthetics* (Ashgate, 2010).

9   See, for example, "Time Travel on the Cheap," NPR blog post, January 21, 2010, http://www.npr.org/sections/pictureshow/2010/01/looking_backwards.html (accessed January 12, 2016). The convention of holding a photograph in place also shows up in 2010 through a crowd-sourced photographic series, "Now and Then," initiated by the Australian Broadcasting Corporation's Open website. https://open.abc.net.au/explore?projectId=8&sortBy=interest&isFeatured=0 (accessed August 1, 2016).

10 My thanks to Carol Payne for drawing my attention to the question of the original photographer, who is rarely acknowledged in the captions.

11 I wish to thank my tremendous colleagues, David Dean, Jennifer Evans, and Carol Payne for their comments on previous versions of this work. John C. Walsh deserves a special commendation for pushing me to "place" myself. My colleague and occasional digital collaborator, Anthony Whitehead, passed away during the writing of this chapter and I regret that he did not get a chance to read it. This research was funded in part by a research grant from the Social Sciences and Humanities Research Council of Canada, and the Rideau Timescapes App received support from the Canada Interactive Fund, Department of Canadian Heritage. Special thanks to my parents, Don and Frankie Opp, for surrounding me with history and photographs, and only making me pick potatoes once a year.

PART VI

Performing Public History

CHAPTER TWENTY FIVE

Reenacting and Reimagining the Past

Amy M. Tyson

A weekend warrior wearing a meticulously researched American Civil War uniform. A professional costumed interpreter at a restored eighteenth-century fortress, trained to engage the public in conversations about Canada's colonial past. "Practicing ethnologists" in Germany, aiming to recreate North American indigenous traditions, dressed in leather outfits hand sewn with animal sinew. A Renaissance festival tavern girl in a décolleté dress serving beer to a soldier boasting a ridiculous codpiece. It's a motley crew, and its inhabitants do not necessarily have much in common with each other, except for one thing: their common passions call them to reimagine and perform the past.

How did these acts of performing the past come to be? Tracing cultural impulses to perform the past is a challenging genealogical project, given that this urge is as old as culture itself. Indeed, while an elaborate family tree of the living history world may extend to ancient times, contemporary living history practices share roots that extend at least as far back as the nineteenth century in the form of open-air museums, world's fairs, ethnic masquerades, and historical pageants.

As performance studies scholar Scott Magelssen has argued, contemporary iterations of living history have "changed at various moments not because of progress, but rather because there were concomitant events that informed what was possible to stage" (Magelssen 2007: 165). Understanding American Civil War reenactments of the 1910s, for example, may not tell us much about the history of that conflict, but may offer insight into how veterans made meaning from it. Present needs or longings might lead individuals or groups to perceive the past through a nostalgic lens, coloring the past as simple and more meaningful for them than the present. Reenacting thus allows participants to commune with an imagined past and, in effect, to apply a momentary salve on the wounds of the present even as such performances contribute to the refashioning of historical memory (Halbwachs 1992 [1950]).

A Companion to Public History, First Edition. Edited by David Dean.
© 2018 John Wiley & Sons Ltd. Published 2018 by John Wiley & Sons Ltd.

Historical memory refers to the ways in which historical narratives are recalled and remembered, refashioned, and performed. As with any memory, historical memories conceal as much as they reveal about the past, and scholars of historical memory are called to trace those silences, to understand which social actors were highlighted and which were diminished or obliterated, and to discern what social meanings are embedded in acts of performing the past (Trouillot 1995: 27).

In that spirit, what follows is an exploration of how the past has been remembered and performed in the Global North since the late nineteenth century, when nations and groups experiencing social changes wrought by rapid industrialization turned toward the history performance to make sense of or legitimate their present. The examples offered (historical pageantry, ethnic masquerades, ethnographic spectacles, open-air museums, living history museums, and reenactments) are representative, rather than comprehensive, with the intent that such a survey will equip the reader to contextualize additional examples of historical enactments that they stumble upon. Why have people chosen to remember the past through performance? What can historical enactments tell us about social power? How are these enactments related to nostalgia? How might we look for historical silences in the shaping of historical memory?

Historical pageantry

During what is known in the United States as the Progressive Era (roughly 1880 through 1920), communities throughout Europe, Australia, and North America staged elaborate pageants, many of them historical in nature – complete with *tableaux vivants* and live action sequences performed by hundreds and sometimes thousands of community participants. The large scale of these historical pageants did not lend itself easily to nuance. Most pageant writers avoided histories that might be controversial. To avoid potential divisiveness, British pageant writer Louis Napoleon Parker urged fellow pageant writers to focus on history prior to the British Civil Wars of the mid seventeenth century (Yoshino n.d.). Thus, particularly in the era before the First World War (1914–1918), we see pageants such as that of 1914 staged in Hertford, England, which focused on canonical episodes in the town's history beginning in 673 AD and culminating in Queen Elizabeth's 1561 visit to Hertford Castle (Sheail n.d.).

Pageant participants often represented a broad cross section of a community. Drawing on census evidence from 1911, local historian Philip Sheail concluded the participants in the Hertford pageant "were drawn primarily from the town's shopkeeper and tradesmen class, and from families where the main breadwinner was a skilled worker, employed in one of the town's flour mills, breweries and printing establishments, [whereas h]ardly any came from the labouring class." Here, art mimicked life, and the most prestigious roles in the Hertford pageant went to the town's elite or local gentry (Sheail n.d.).

Although both men and women participated in historical pageants, women's histories were silenced, as women were seldom depicted as social actors who took place in shaping history (the English queen being a notable exception). Likewise, ethnic minorities tended to be excluded. In the St. Louis "Pageant and Masque" of 1914, historian David Glassberg observes that pageant masters assigned white ethnic groups, much to their chagrin, roles as "some peasant folks' arriving as new immigrants ... on the margins of the community, rather than having them appear in scenes depicting the making of

St. Louis" (1990: 5). Similarly, despite protest, the city's 44,000 black residents were not at all included in pageant plans. Here, and elsewhere in American historical pageants, immigrants, blacks, and women were cast as people without history.

Yet groups seeking to counter such silences in historical pageants also adopted the form. The countercultural Paterson Strike Pageant of 1913 took place in New York's Madison Square Garden to support 26,000 striking silk workers in Paterson, New Jersey. With the support of the radical labor organization Industrial Workers of the World, strikers protested the replacement of skilled laborers by mechanized silk looms. To gain public sympathy for the cause (which it did) and to raise money for it (which it didn't), leftist journalist Jack Reed penned the pageant and staged it with "expressionist sets" and "towering backdrops" produced by Greenwich Village's bohemian artists. Over a thousand actual strikers, many of them Italian immigrants, reenacted the history leading up to and during the strike (Stansell 2009: 184). Later that same year, in 1913, historian W.E.B. DuBois staged "The Star of Ethiopia," a pageant honoring the 50th anniversary of the Emancipation Proclamation. Premiering in New York City with more than a thousand participants, Dubois's production, as historian David Krasner has noted, did not merely trace black history to pre-historic times through to the present, it "challenged the master narrative of U.S. history" by representing slavery as evidence of black resilience (2001: 119). Such historical narratives were a far cry from the nostalgic and whitewashed visions so common in mainstream pageants.

Ultimately, regardless of the history portrayed, pageants were meaningful to participants in a number of ways and for a variety of reasons. Early-twentieth-century pageants enabled communities to define themselves in an era where rapid advances in telecommunications dispersed connections beyond the local sphere; the pageant reestablished the increasingly tenuous bonds of community. Beyond performing shared historical memories, the weeks of rehearsals leading up to a pageant encouraged face-to-face contact between community participants who might otherwise never encounter each other. After the First World War, however, pageants would be overtaken by other popular culture forms (such as film), which in turn fostered generational divides that pageants once sought to bridge (Glassberg 1990: 288).

Ethnic masquerades

Dominant messages conveyed in many pageants' visions of the future often relied on defining who would be excluded as much as who would be included. Indigenous people were present in Progressive Era American pageants because they included scenes with "Indians" in them. Yet the roles of indigenous people were generally played by white townsfolk, thus silencing indigenous history. In "Pageant and Masque," local whites were chosen to "play Indian" despite offers from the Ojibwe's William Hole-in-the-Day that his people be hired (Glassberg 1990: 178–179). Undoubtedly, their presence would contradict the dominant message that "conquered" indigenous peoples had a place in history but had either stepped aside or vanished to make way for the inevitable "progress" of white "civilization." In this manner, such ethnic masquerades enabled participants to rewrite history, reaffirm prevailing racial hierarchies, and deny indigenous people any meaningful agency in history making.

From the American revolutionary Sons of Liberty, who painted their faces red and plunged trunks of tea into the Boston Harbor, to early twenty-first century boy scouts who camp in wigwams, "playing Indian" erases histories of actual indigenous people in favor of providing participants occasion to stage symbolic disorder, as with the anti-tax Boston Tea Party-ers; to imagine themselves as connected to nature, as with the boy scouts; or to feel connected to a noble or fierce heroic past, as with any number of contemporary American sports teams who persist in using American Indians in their names or as their mascots (Deloria 1998). Such performances of "Indianness" appropriate indigenous people and in the process, real, contextualized, and messy histories are conveniently silenced.

Somewhat paradoxically, however, indigenous Americans have also "played Indian." Borrowing heavily from historical pageantry in its grandeur and its staging of canonical and mythic retellings of history, Buffalo Bill's Wild West toured North America and Europe continuously from the 1880s to 1913, employing over a thousand American Indians during its tenure (Warren 2005). These Wild West "show Indians" joined because they provided a venue for using skills (such as horseback riding) that led to jobs that paid meaningful, if still low, wages, and provided opportunities to travel beyond government reservations, even as far as Europe (Moses 1996). Given that these Wild West shows were most popular at a time when government rations were woefully beneath treaty stipulations and violence against American Indians was rampant (culminating in the 1890 massacre of indigenous women and children at Wounded Knee), it is clear that they shaped the historical memory of the west by reinforcing long-held stereotypes of American Indians as alternately noble (and vanished) or savage (and in need of eradication).

During the heyday of Wild West shows, "playing Indian" was but one of a whole menagerie of ethnic masquerades wherein the not-too-distant past was reenacted and reimagined for audiences in ways that tell us more about the times in which those performances happened than about the specific histories they aimed to recall. Though seldom cast as precursors to the contemporary world of living history, blackface minstrel shows were absolutely intended as reenactments of a certain sort. Popular in the urban centers of the northern United States from the start of the1830s and remaining socially acceptable in the white mainstream through much of the 1950s, these shows featured "white" performers who "blacked up" their faces and portrayed racist caricatures. Skits were often set in antebellum slave plantations, thereby perpetuating widely held nostalgic ideas about the simple "darkie" who loved his "Massa" (Bean, Hatch, and McNamara 1996).

Such performances tell us little about antebellum slave culture and much more about their performers' and audience's racial preoccupations. As historian David Roediger has argued, the process of "blacking up served to emphasize that those on stage were really white and that whiteness really mattered" (1995: 3). In short, blackface minstrel shows conformed to audiences' prejudices, performed nostalgic views of antebellum history, and created a new community of self-consciously white watchers, bound together by race, and not class.

Thousands of white Australians also remembered the past by "blacking up" as Aboriginals as late as 1951 during the nation's 50th anniversary celebration of the Australian Federation. Here Aboriginal people were excluded from the reenactment of British Captain Charles Sturt's 1829–1830 river expeditions of Australia's interior. As the reenactors encountered rural communities, they were greeted by thousands of white Australians in Aboriginal blackface, who often staged attacks. Public historian Stephen Gapps argues that these unscripted acts of Aboriginal blackface self-consciously echoed

Hollywood versions of the American Wild West, with participants even dressing in the manner of film Indians before staging a comic attack on the reenactors, and then "raising three cheers for them and offering a 'peace pipe'" (Gapps 2009: 216). Even though donning the ethnic mask of Aboriginal blackface eschewed the "parades and pageantry of previous didactic performances" that had been performed earlier in the century, rural, white Australians reimagined the past to affirm participants' own place of power, symbolized by their actual whiteness, as aligned with the interests of the colonizers (Gapps 2009: 219).

By the 1960s, Australians turned away from such performances, preferring less problematic ones of medieval European history, with a particular focus on the "'far away lands' of medieval damsels and knights" (Gapps 2009: 219). Gapps suggests that staging spectacles about "foundational history" were increasingly difficult to legitimize at a time when increasing Aboriginal activism creatively resisted their silencing and destabilized national attempts to reenact foundational moments in the latter half of the twentieth century. For example, in 1988, bicentenary commemorations of European settlement in Australia were disrupted when "[i]ndigenous Australians and their supporters ensured that a fleet of 'tall ships' tracing the First Fleet's voyage from England to Sydney could not, as initially planned, end in a reenactment of Governor Phillip and his soldiers and sailors stepping ashore" (Gapps 2009: 211). Thus, while performing the past can be an effective way to display what some believe had occurred, performances of the past afford others opportunities to portray desires of what they wish had happened instead.

Ethnographic spectacles

Beyond national commemorations such as the Sturt reenactment, world's fairs and expositions of the nineteenth and twentieth centuries were also spaces that permitted participating nations to rewrite history by staging living spectacles of colonized peoples. These spectacles promoted nationalism that, as historian Robert Rydell has argued, "if accepted by the lower classes, meant acquiescence in the power relations of the status quo as necessary to progress and therefore as legitimate and right" (1984: 236). While spectacles such as the Crystal Palace (1851), the Eiffel Tower (1889), and the Ferris Wheel (1893) promoted the hosting nation's industrial superiority, reconstructed ethnographic villages promoted a colonizing nation's cultural superiority. By putting "exotic" human bodies on display in these villages, organizers ensured that the "naked nature" of racial and ethnic types was represented (Nelson 1998). In the 1889 Paris Exposition, for example, colonial pavilions included carefully selected colonial subjects, whose bodies were displayed alongside goods and other "natural resources" from the French colonies. Such exhibits rationalized French racial superiority to their colonial subjects, and worked to convince visitors that it was crucial to maintain colonial control. American imperialism was justified through similar human displays that suggested the naturalness of racial hierarchies. For example, fairgoers at the 1904 Louisiana Purchase Exposition encountered a thousand scantily clad Filipinos exhibited in an area spanning forty-seven acres. The Philippine–American War had officially ended two years prior, but American occupation of the Philippines continued to meet armed resistance by Philippine revolutionaries committed to independence. The display of "authentic" Philippine "savagery" was anything but neutral.

Such ethnographic displays were not reenactments of historic events per se; they were carefully curated midway entertainments unabashedly intended to portray exotic visions of colonial subjects badly in need of civilizing. These displays had a timeless quality to them, almost as if those on display had no history, but were arrested in an imagined, pre-contact, or pre-colonial past. Although intended to be "mimetic displays" bearing the weight of scientific truth, that "truth" silenced the histories of those displayed.[1] Although fostering a community of spectators among those not on display, these spectacles shaped a historical memory that justified colonialism by constructing scenes that legitimated how colonial powers had steered the course of history, and erased the rational efforts of colonized peoples to resist occupation.

What was not on display? What do we know about those who were made into spectacles? Because the traces here are scant, some have turned to fictional accounts to resist the silencing wrought by ethnographic spectacle, to give voice to the voiceless. One pair of performance artists even created a satiric reenactment of ethnographic displays: artist-activists Coco Fusco and Guillermo Gómez-Peña in 1992. In this series, the caged Fusco and Gómez-Peña were displayed outside spaces such as Smithsonian's National Museum of Natural History and Australian Museum of Natural Science in Sydney, dressed as "primitives," complete with grass skirts, bare midriffs, bows and arrows, and... sunglasses. Declared to be Guatianauis, a fictionalized tribe of Amer-Indians, the couple went about demonstrating "traditional tasks," ranging from sewing voodoo dolls, to dancing to rap music when gawkers put money in the donation jar. In this manner, the performance ran counter to the purported "authenticity" of the ethnographic exhibitions that it parodied, but also, as performance studies scholar Diana Taylor has written, "confronted the viewer with the 'unnatural' and extremely violent history of representation and exhibition of non-Western human beings" (Taylor 1998: 164). In its deliberate attempt to draw our attention to the history of ethnographic spectacles, Fusco and Gómez-Peña's performance reminds us that performing the past may be adopted by the oppressed as much as the oppressor, and can be an effective tool in questioning prevailing historical memories.

Open-air museums

That human displays of ethnic and racial types was so much a part of nineteenth-century culture made it possible to imagine more permanent installations of such spectacles. Indeed, until the open-air museum movement of the 1890s, such living displays tended to be temporary, existing for but a brief time in circuses, fairs, zoos, gardens, or taverns. Amid "natural" settings provided by picturesque paths and curated vistas, early tourists to open-air museums would initially encounter dioramas, and mannequins dressed in folksy costumes. Skansen, outside of Stockholm in Sweden, was one of the first to use traditionally costumed workers performing folk songs dances and demonstrating pre-industrial activities in reconstructed or restored buildings. In the wake of high capitalism and mechanized mass production, which ushered in a new era of class conflict, the folk at these museums, whether depicted through live bodies or wax dummies, were portrayed as idyllic and even idle; their labor did not appear to be too difficult, and they certainly were neither political nor subversive. Like pastoral paintings of the same era, the nostalgic visions presented at the open-air museums romanticized "the folk" even while those visions possessed the (misleading) aura of realism.

Sten Rentzhog argues that open-air museums such as Skansen in Sweden (1891), Nosk Folkemuseum in Norway (1894), and Netherlands Open Air Museum (1912) often served as vehicles to "counteract civil strife and strengthen fellow feeling by showing how all the different peoples making up the country had developed peacefully, side by side and together with each other" (Rentzhog 2007: 38). These curated visions were not merely nostalgic for the pre-industrial past; they also silenced real dissonance between groups in the industrial present. Such was the case with a 1906 proposal in the Ukraine "to have an open air museum showing Ruthenians, Rumanians, Gypsies, Armenians, Lipovanians, Hungarians, Germans and Jews, all living side by side" (Rentzhog 2007: 39).

While the First World War stymied many plans for open-air museums that had been in development prior to 1914, after 1918, newly formed nations in Eastern and Central Europe embraced the concept. Rather than perform the *past*, however, one such museum, the Village Museum in Bucharest, aimed to reconstruct the rural peasant's *present* by "populat[ing] the village with inhabitants [who] would live and work naturally in the museum, in the same way as at home in their real villages" (Rentzhog 2007: 104).

In the United States, a handful of house museums peppered the nineteenth-century landscape (beginning with the "museum-ization" of George Washington's Mount Vernon plantation in 1859), but true open-air museums did not emerge in North America until the early twentieth century when Greenfield Village (Michigan) and Colonial Williamsburg (Virginia) were founded and funded by two of America's favorite billionaire sons: Henry Ford and John D. Rockefeller Jr. For all of their differences, these two projects reproduced historical narratives that complemented the myopic views of their founders, supporting their own versions of history. Ford's Greenfield Village (1929) showcased a menagerie of American buildings in order to support Ford's understanding of an unfolding history – that, in the words of historian Michael Wallace, "life had been better in the old days and it had been getting better ever since" (Wallace 1995: 12).

While Ford featured a progressive-oriented Industrial Museum alongside a nostalgic Early American Museum, Rockefeller's project (1927) reconstructed the city's colonial past at the expense of erasing all histories that came before or after, including regional Confederate history (the city's 1908 monument to the fallen Confederate soldiers was moved from its prominent location on the city's Palace Green), thus privileging a national narrative and silencing the memories of everyday Williamsburg citizens. Whereas Ford's Greenfield Village exalted the "everyman" (in a similar manner to how its European counterparts exalted the "folk"), Colonial Williamsburg privileged an elitist retelling of the town's past by focusing on the history of the governor and his mansion while ignoring the histories of those who labored (as slaves or otherwise) in it. This museum may have been constructed in the spirit of European's open-air museums but, as was also the case with those spaces across the Atlantic, in its depiction of the past, not everything was out in the open (Handler and Gable 1997: 79).

Living history museums

The years following the Second World War set the stage for what would come to be known as a "living museum," so-called because, rather than artifacts and buildings, costumed guides or interpreters were the main draw.[2] The growth of the middle class after the Second World War created a demand for tourist destinations. City squares, districts, and main streets lined up to receive historic facelifts designed to attract modern tourists. Large-scale living history interpretation as a form of playful and educational spectacle was employed in spaces that were large enough and well funded enough to accommodate its concomitant cadre of interpreters.

Thus, while places like Colonial Williamsburg increased their use of costumed guides, in the post-war years many more living history museums appeared, such as Massachusetts' Old Sturbridge Village (1946), Massachusetts' Plimoth Plantation (1947), Iowa's Living History Farms (1970), and New Mexico's El Rancho De Los Golondrinas (1972). The expanding National Park Service (NPS) also took a liking to living history as a method of interpretation at its sites. By the early 1970s, living history programming had been formally established at several NPS military forts including Fort Laramie (Wyoming), Fort Davis (Texas), Fort Pulaski (Georgia), Fort Union (New Mexico), and Fort Vancouver (Washington). Canada also saw a boom in living history museums: Ontario's Doon Pioneer (now Heritage) Village opened in 1957, Black Creek Pioneer Village in 1960, and Upper Canada Village a year later; Fortress of Louisbourg National Historic Site of Canada began its partial reconstruction in 1961; and Heritage Park Historical Village in Calgary opened in 1964. Folklorist Jay Anderson has noted that while "no one knows for certain just how many true living history museums there are in North America. In 1978, I estimated there were about eight hundred" (Anderson 1984: 41).

For tourists, these living museums offered leisure-time opportunities to exchange their wages for immersive, time-traveling experiences providing windows into the every-day lives of people of the past. For public historians, these museums offered a chance to work in their chosen field researching, designing, and planning programming. Given public history's roots in the social history movement, its professionals tended to steer the interpretation of living history museums toward a focus on the lives of everyday people rather than (solely) on history's elites. This historiographical preference helps account for the kind of everyday history (albeit somewhat sanitized) interpreted at many of these sites beginning in the late 1960s.

Significantly, the professional public historians described above were not generally charged with face-to-face content delivery at living history museums. Rather, living historical programming was, and continues to be, performed by a relatively new class of paraprofessionals (costumed tour guides or living history interpreters), whose labor centered on the production of what social theorist Dean MacCannell has called a "work display," that is, the display of someone else's labor for the delight of the tourist. Labor was being transformed "into cultural productions attended by tourists and sightseers who are moved by the universality of work relations.... as it is revealed to them at their leisure through the displayed work of others" (MacCannell 1999: 36). Since their inauguration, living history museums have doubly produced work displays, first through the expected costumed demonstrations of industrial or pre-industrial labor (blacksmithing, musket drills, churning butter), and second, through performances of service encounters: conversations between costumed interpreters and museum guests that are often (though not always) related to the site's history.

A common critique from academics has focused on living history museums' failure to satisfactorily interpret the past, a shortcoming brought on in large part because as tourist spaces, they have tended to favor portraying simplified historical narratives over histories that might be emotionally or intellectually uncomfortable (Schlereth 1978).[3] Despite many progressive changes to living history programming since the 1970s, most living history museums continue to focus predominantly on white people's history from pre-industrial eras, even when they have successfully "integrated" a more diverse complement of non-white history into their offerings (Tyson 2013).

One struggle for these spaces is that while public historians and interpreters might be doing yeomen's work to unearth the silences in historical narratives and bring diverse historical perspectives into the fray, they continue to fight against visitors' expectations about the histories portrayed therein, a testament to the power and persuasiveness of one's own sense of historical memory. Azie Mira Dungey, creator of the "Ask a Slave" Web series, had worked as a first-person interpreter at both the Smithsonian Museum of American History in Washington, D.C., and at Mount Vernon (President George Washington's plantation estate) in Virginia. In her interview for *The Public Historian*, Dungey reflected that visitors to her civil rights history presentations at the Smithsonian were overwhelmingly positive, whereas many visitors she encountered while portraying an enslaved woman at Mount Vernon seemed to want to deny that slavery was all that bad, or that it even existed. Dungey attributed this difference to the degree by which visitors wanted to identify with the histories portrayed:

> the narrative about Civil Rights – for the most part – is embraced by so many as an American narrative to be proud of. And for some people, all of black history is separate history to them, but I think as a general rule, culturally, we see Civil Rights as part of our story. ... But when it comes to slavery, especially slavery in relation to a founding father – George Washington – everybody's got their own interpretation of it or their own projection. Like they project their own story on George Washington's story. I saw a lot of emotion about it and a lot of defensiveness and a lot of resistance and a lot of shame. (Tyson and Dungey 2014: 46)

When confronted with a history of slavery in the home of a founding father, Dungey presumes that some visitors experienced an emotional quagmire because, through their visit to Mount Vernon, they deeply desired to connect not with the enslaved woman Dungey portrayed, but with America's founding father, George Washington.

Drawing on information gleaned from contemporary audience surveys, public historian Cary Carson has observed that "modern museum-goers" yearn "to imagine themselves back in the past, and their expectation that their pretended persona will share history's trials and tribulations with the historical figures they meet there" (Carson 2008: 19). Helping us make sense of these longings to connect with the past, MacCannell has posited that tourist rituals are efforts "to overcome the discontinuity of modernity" (1999 [1976]:13); they overcome the ways in which our modern world makes us feel disconnected from authentic connections with each other and our past. And while MacCannell denies the possibility of actually overcoming that discontinuity through tourism (because tourism is always staged, and so, always already inauthentic), he persuasively argues that behind touristic excursions lie deep desires to connect more intimately with, and to build a "fragile solidarity" in, the present (83).

Anthropologist Cathy Stanton, in her ethnographic study of Lowell National Historic Park, concluded that the park's history professionals, and "especially, but not exclusively, the frontline rangers" were participating in "rituals of reconnection" through their cultural work at the park (Stanton 2006: 179). In these rituals of reconnection, employees valued their own personal connections with the site's history, and emotionally bonded with visitors who were moved by the historical narratives imparted at the site. Stanton maintains that interpreter–visitor interaction at the industrial history site helped both parties "to locate themselves and their work more firmly in the present day" (2006: 179).

Similarly, historian Tammy S. Gordon's work on local history exhibits shows that visitor encounters with non-white curators at historical venues such as Shoshone-Bannock Tribal Museum in Idaho, or Olde Mill House Museum in Florida, have proved personally transformative for many visitors. To take one example, an elderly repeat visitor (presumably white) to the Olde Mill House Museum reported that the African American curator there "helped her overcome a lifetime of prejudiced thinking" (Gordon 2010: 109). Although this example places the burden of responsibility on non-white museum workers to serve as cultural ambassadors for white clientele, anthropologist Laura Peers' ethnography of First Nation and American Indian interpreters at Canadian and American living history museums suggests that many indigenous interpreters seek out this kind of work not only because they value seeing their own history represented, but also for opportunities to teach non-native people about indigenous culture which, as a ritual of reconnection, they find personally fulfilling (Peers 1999; 2007).

My own research at the living history museums of Historic Fort Snelling in Minnesota and at Conner Prairie Interactive History Park in Indiana has also shown that underpinning tourist desires to see a musket fired or participate in a reenactment of a fugitive slave program are complementary desires to have fun, and to connect more deeply with others through engagement with the past (Tyson 2008). Similarly, like others who work in the nonprofit cultural sector of the new economy, the promise of external monetary rewards or benefits is not what inspires people to pursue or perform this interpretive work. Rather, what inspires them is the promise of meaningful work, the promise of connecting with others through the medium of history, and the promise of fun and play at their worksite; promises that are not easily fulfilled at many worksites in today's economy.

Reenactment

Enacting "rituals of reconnection," alongside the promise of fun and play, has also guided those drawn to the hobby of reenactment. Generally, the term "reenactors" refers to those whose living historical performances are recreational and inwardly focused, whereas the term "interpreters" denotes those whose more professionalized living history services are primarily intended to engage the public. And yet distinguishing between a "reenactor" and an "interpreter" is a slippery business given that some "reenactors present themselves as historical interpreters" and greatly value the pedagogical possibilities of living history (Thompson 2004: 108). It might be best to think of these terms as describing individuals on an ever-shifting continuum.

Before considering how contemporary reenactment hobbyists yield insight into the making of modern memory, we should look backward to the first commemorations of the American Civil War. Proto reenactments of this conflict occurred as early as 1866, only one year after the war concluded, when Union veterans formed the highly influential Grand Army of the Republic (GAR). The GAR's purpose – and that of its Confederate counterpart founded in 1888 – was to provide a fraternal space for veterans to ritually reconnect and understand the meanings of the war, and to encourage patriotism among the public. In addition to supporting memorial building and battlefield preservation, from 1866 through the early 1900s GAR members staged massive, nostalgic outdoor military encampments. Of course, the size of these diminished over time and by 1913, for the semi-centennial of the battle of Gettysburg, most veterans were well into their seventies. Still, Union and Confederate veterans participated en masse in commemorations of this watershed battle, with nearly 54,000 attending the reunion, bedecked in their uniforms, at the site itself in Pennsylvania.

Whereas the 1863 conflict pitted Union and Confederate groups against each other, the 1913 reunion staged symbolic meetings between white veteran attendees. Old soldiers, some in Union colors and others in Confederate, posed for photographers, shaking hands across the battle line (one such photograph documents this symbolic gesture as the culminating activity of a reenactment of Picket's Charge, one of the infamous Gettysburg battles). Such acts aimed to reaffirm bonds of fraternal whiteness in the service of healing a nation (Blight 2001). In 1913, with lynchings of blacks on the rise and President Wilson's mandate to segregate federal agencies, the symbolism of such staged rituals of reconnection were not lost on African American activists who rightly saw the Gettysburg reunion as an effort to silence the past and write both blacks and slave emancipation out of American Civil War history.

Although American Civil War reenactments would see a resurgence in 1938 for the 75-year anniversary of its conclusion, for several decades reenactments of war tended to be reserved for the silver screen, rather than for large community events. In the 1960s, however, Civil War reenactment units spread like wildfire as a result of centennial celebrations. In these nationalist commemorations, battle reenactments loomed large. The restaging of First Manassas (the Battle of Bull Run) in July 1961, for example, involved around 3,000 reenactors (half of whom were purportedly National Guardsman and military cadets) who performed "sham battles" for crowds of over 50,000 spectators at Virginia's Manassas National Battlefield Park (Jones 2014).

Following the Civil War Centennial in 1965, we see the founding of scores of reenactment divisions in the United States, the same year that Canada saw the founding of the Service Rifle Shooting Association (SRSA), an organization committed fully to outfitted reenactments of military conflicts. Whereas war reenactment groups founded in the 1960s tended to be dominated by conservative white males, around the same time, in 1963, the hippie-infused American Renaissance fair in the countercultural hub of Laurel Canyon, California, was founded, a performance space which initially emerged in the vacuum left by a shrinking public sphere with closures of bohemian coffeehouses. More than filling a void, however, American Studies scholar Rachel Lee Rubin argues that, in contrast to the kind of patriotic fanfare that often accompanied war reenactments, Renaissance fairs, with their tights-wearing bands of players, were "well situated to marshal a sense of motivated whimsy to serve an antiestablishment agenda" (2012: 10).

Regardless of the type of history portrayed by reenactment groups of the last half-century, whether that history be centered on medieval knights, Renaissance minstrels, soldiers, pirates, cowboys, or Indians (what scholar Vanessa Agnew has called "the perennial favorites of grade-school history"), in reenactment hierarchy, material culture, authenticity, and extremism reign supreme (Agnew 2004). For some, at the top of the hierarchy requires the most authentic impressions: the right shoes, the right hats, the right look. In his book *Confederates in the Attic*, journalist Tony Horwitz (1998) shares a somewhat extreme example from his experience of "going native" and joining Civil War reenactors. Some are so serious in seeking authenticity in their "impressions" of American Civil War soldiers that they praise individuals who are gaunt and thin, and also soak their pewter buttons in urine so the buttons will acquire an authentic-looking sheen. While earning reenactors a stigmatized place in mainstream popular culture, such a focus on authentically representing the past in its minute detail also bespeaks a deep yearning for creative and emotional expression through this performative medium. "Getting it right," it seems, allows reenactors to feel more connected to the past, and to each other.

By the same token, many reenactors are willing to make compromises with regard to the "authenticity" of their impressions. To take an example from European contexts, a group of "practicing ethnologists" known as the Kitoki were founded in Frankfurt, West

Germany, in 1981 with the express aim to reimagine, reenact, and perform North American Indian traditions. Anthropologist Petra Tjitske Kalshoven describes one member of the Kitoki negotiating the authenticity of his "Indian" performance given the German climate and landscape where he practiced his hobby. "Crow clothing," he explained, was made for drier weather than German Indianists generally had to cope with. For winter moccasins, he added a second sole with synthetic glue. As long as such tricking "did not show, he felt it was legitimate" (2012: 152). The meaning of authenticity is not static, and often involves concessions or deliberate performative anachronisms (Rubin 2012).

The willingness to make concessions to what constitutes authenticity supports one of Cathy Stanton's (1997) conclusions about reenactment hobbyists, based on her two years of participant observation in American Civil War units. Despite the hobby being dominated by largely white, conservative males, Stanton found it to be rather accommodating. As a woman in the ranks, Stanton found herself to be the proverbial elephant in the room; someone everyone was aware of, but few mentioned. Though questions about "women in the ranks" had drawn national headlines and no doubt ruffled the feathers of many hardcore reenactors, Stanton's own experiences led her to conclude that "performative space and time" had the potential "to accommodate widely divergent views and practices" and that through these reenactments, hobby participants in this "ever more fragmented culture" found a space where a "kind of coexistence can take place" (1997: 111, 121).

Conclusion

As we have seen from the above examples, performing the past has often been a tool used to respond to needs in the present, rather than an earnest effort to interpret the past in all of its complexity. In times of increasing distance from one's immediate neighbors, historical pageantry was used to reinforce tenuous community bonds; when nations sought to justify colonial exploits, ethnic masquerades and ethnographic spectacles presented timeless visions of indigenous peoples, denying them a history outside of their presumed "primitivism"; when tensions between groups have threatened to unravel the delicate tapestry of national unity, open-air museums erased difference through the performance of pastoral folk scenes; and in the wake of an increasingly fragmented and globalized society, living history museum interpreters and reenactment hobbyists have worked to build a fragile solidarity between participants through the medium of historical performance. Likewise, historical enactment has served as a means by which those whose histories were often silenced have harnessed their creativity to stage critiques of mainstream histories, to perform counter-narratives, and even to rewrite the past.

These examples are offered as but an introduction to the study of reenactments and reimaginings of the past. School plays, theatrical productions, films, digital historical role-playing games, Disneyland, Jane Austen societies, even Holocaust museums (among other spaces) have made use of embodied performance to immerse people in other times, other places, other identities. As we seek to understand what such enactments have to tell us about the times in which they were created, we are called to examine not merely the content of those productions, but also to excavate those productions of historical memory for the silences that surround them. Often, it is in the silences that history resonates most.

Notes

1 On primitivism and display, see Jane C. *Desmond, Staging Tourism: Bodies on Display from Waikiki to Sea World* (Chicago: University of Chicago Press, 1999); Barbara Kirshenblatt-Gimblett, *Destination Culture: Tourism, Museums, and Heritage* (Berkeley: University of California Press, 1998).

2 Some of the material appearing in this section is drawn from my book, Amy M. Tyson, *The Wages of History: Emotional Labor on Public History's Front Lines* (Amherst: University of Massachusetts Press, 2013).

3 Schlereth's criticisms of living history museums were echoed three years later by a fellow historian in Michael Wallace, "Visiting the Past: History Museums in the United States," *Radical History Review* 25 (1981): 63–96.

CHAPTER TWENTY SIX

Reenacting the Stone Age: Journeying Back in Time Through the Uckermark and Western Pomerania

VANESSA AGNEW

Introduction

We are looking for the moment when it all went wrong, that turning point in the human order of things that divided before from thereafter – a time when life was simpler, the body healthier, and social life more transparent. Friends and family find this quest a little unsettling. They are in favor of self-improvement, new diets, and reviving exercise programs; they like history and they have read Rousseau as much as the next person. Yet they find our move to Germany and our current enthusiasms faintly questionable. After all, if ever there were an object lesson in political wrong turns, Germany would be it. The *Stolpersteine* set into the cobblestones on our street – miniature memorials to victims of the Holocaust – give a daily reminder of the very wrongest of turns. Yet, as I try to explain, we are looking for an earlier time, a time before the conflagration, a time less tainted and more primal.

Somehow we get it into our minds that that historical turning point lies due north of Berlin. On a damp, autumnal day, we take the decision to go there, following a bicycle path from Berlin to the Baltic island of Usedom. With a gesture toward conjectural history, we plan to reverse the turn and re-enact the fatal moment in the proverbial yellow wood. Rather than choosing one way, we will take both roads, reflecting from the vantage of the present on a millennia-old past as it might have unfolded. This journey will be a journey from the inside out. Vigorous exercise and a new diet will set us on a course to reverse the ravages of time. We will emerge from that double journey as Stone Age people – more sociable, leaner, longer-lived, hairier.

The way back in time is not immediately apparent. If the signs are there, we miss them. In the fog and the morning chill, one Uckermark meadow rolls into another, as we slip between Brandenburg and Western Pomerania. The harvest is in and the fields stand damp and fallow, quietly awaiting human agency. The hay is baled and trussed for the winter; crows pick over the ground and in the hedgerow, finches are feeding. The last

A Companion to Public History, First Edition. Edited by David Dean.
© 2018 John Wiley & Sons Ltd. Published 2018 by John Wiley & Sons Ltd.

of the cornflowers and Queen Anne's lace is going to seed; a few poppies commemorate the summer. Oaks and beech once covered this place; now just a few stately trees remain, their acorns surprisingly small fodder for the wild boar that turn earth in the night. Each ancient tree is witness to its place, to its own changing corner of wood and field.

What we are looking for lies further back in time, before the Nazi nature enthusiast Hermann Göring reintroduced wisent and aurochs to the Schorfheide in order to re-enact his own primal fantasies (Kolbert 2012). To cycle farther and look closer is, we hope, to find what we are coming for – the vestiges of an ice melt that left chains of lakes from Berlin to the Baltic and glaciers that deposited ground moraines and terminal moraines. Grubbing around in the fields will turn up the material for stone tools – flint and obsidian – with its glossy surfaces and suggestive edges, tools already half made in the finding. And it will turn up dolmen – piles of red sandstones and what geologists term glacial erratics – boulders carried improbably far from their points of origin. In this part of the world, the boulders have been formed into portal tombs that locals refer to as *Hünengräber*, giants' graves. Traveling from one derelict village to another, we are told that there is one of these giants' graves outside Trebenow, a stone's throw from Prenzlau. The megalith is said to have been made by Neolithic *Trichterbecher* (TRB) people, named for what they left behind – crude funnel-necked vessels – some five or six thousand years ago (Witzke n.d.). If there is evidence to be found, perhaps it will be here, somewhere in a foggy field, still fifty miles from the coast.

* * *

Others, looking for evidence of the historical "big mistake," head south rather than north to re-enact the past on a grander scale than ours. The four-part historical reality television series produced in 2007 by Südwestrundfunk, *Steinzeit: Das Experiment* (Woetzel 2007), is one such example. Like other German television productions, including *Abenteuer 1900: Leben im Gutshaus* ("Adventure 1900: Life in the Manor House," Heise 2004), *Abenteuer 1927: Sommerfrische* ("Adventure 1927: Summer Retreat," dir. Rönneburg 2005), *Windstärke 8: Das Auswandererschiff 1855* ("Gale Force 8: The Emigrant Ship," dir. Wesseley 2005), and *Die Bräuteschule 1958* ("Bride School," Abel 2007), *Steinzeit: Das Experiment* adopts a model developed in the late 1990s by British production company Wall to Wall and BBC Channel 4. These series involve historians recreating historical conditions with contemporary participants "going back in time" to try and experience what life was "really like" (Agnew 2004; 2007). The participants in these series are generally confined to a house, although *The Ship: Retracing Cook's Endeavour Voyage* (dir. Terrell 2002), a BBC 2 documentary in which I took part, participants spent six weeks aboard a replica of *HM Bark Endeavour* retracing a leg of James Cook's 1769 voyage – a kind of historical Big-Brother-at-Sea, which gave spatial as well as temporal unity to the exercise of historical re-enactment (Agnew 2010). Besides drawing on these kinds of television series for inspiration, *Steinzeit* belongs to a decades-old documentary tradition of portraying prehistory on television. This, Georg Koch (2014) points out, has always been predicated not on increasingly robust findings within archaeology, but rather on claims to depict Stone Age life as it "actually was."

Steinzeit: Das Experiment adopts the conventional format: a band of seven adults and six children are sent to live in a recreated Stone Age settlement near Lake Constance. Three wattle-and-daub houses have been erected for them to inhabit; animals are corralled nearby, and a wheat field is ready for harvesting. During the opening credits, a voice-over sets up the conceit on behalf of the viewer: the group of participants are to live as people did 5,000 years ago and, in so doing, put the "everyday lives of [their] ancestors to the test" ("*erproben den Alltag unserer Vorfahren*"). This ancestral everyday was, says the narrator in a deliberate collapsing of past and present, "particularly hard in August 2006" when filming took place. While the group struggles through a rainy, frigid summer, two of the participants are dispatched on a 200-mile journey over the Alps to retrace the footsteps of Ötzi, the 5,300-year-old mummified man discovered by hikers in 1991 on an Alpine pass between Austria and Italy. The pair of reenactors is to cross the Alps in the manner of their "ancestor," wearing "Stone Age gear" ("*steinzeitliche Ausrüstung,*" episode 2), foraging for berries, mushrooms, and nettles, and eating jerky and a self-made pemmican of dried fruit, meat, and fat. As the narrator informs us, the two men, following an ancient trading route, may only consume what was really eaten during the Stone Age. The participants are given basic instruction in various aspects of daily living, including fire making and the use of stone axes and bows and arrows, before being turned loose by their anthropologist and archaeologist handlers, who reappear periodically to troubleshoot and provide an expert counterpoint to the bumbling, but ultimately triumphant, efforts of the *Steinzeit* reenactors. If the pretext of the series is to stage life "as it really was," the artifice is disrupted by the scientific pretensions of the undertaking. In contradistinction to many other reenactments, which aim for an educative but entertaining staging of the past, this series claims to intervene in scientific debates, providing answers to apparently unanswered questions. In the first instance, however, the band of settlers demonstrates only an inexpert grasp of ancient technology. As the project's historical advisor notes: "we don't have the experience from back then … don't have the knowledge of generations" ("*Wir haben nicht die Erfahrung von damals… nicht das Wissen von Generationen*"). The Alpine adventurers, in contrast, show where real-world investigation and testing hold apparent advantages over lab and library. They discover a natural shelter where they feel sure Ötzi himself once rested, and they discover the benefits of boots soled with bearskin. Demonstrating the efficacy of their hide clothing testifies to what experts in the lab had only crudely shown using a walking automaton, a machine designed to stress-test different types of leather.

The participants' most significant contribution, however, is provided by the direct, and hence apparently indisputable, testimony provided by their own bodies. Prior to entering the Stone Age compound, they are subjected to a series of physiological tests. For comparative purposes, their physical condition during the reenactment is tracked using wearable health-monitoring devices. The resulting data points yield information about their movement, metabolism, caloric expenditure, and sleep quality. In the absence of artificial light and electronic gadgetry, with limited shelter and warmth, they sleep collectively on a pallet in the long house. Their sleep, we learn, is longer and deeper than that of "modern" humans, distracted by media, relegated to solitary, climate-controlled bedrooms, and disrupted by work stress. It is the defining feature of the Neolithic Revolution – agriculture and the associated changes to the organization of social life – that spawns some of the problems with nutrition, conflict resolution, and social life confronting the brave band. As they struggle to take in the harvest, grind wheat, and insulate their houses against the unseasonably cold and wet summer, these New Age Stone Agers have little time for leisure or for the meaningful social lives they craved when embarking on the project. Their days are spent in a harried scrabble for food that proves unpalatable and insufficiently nutritious. The children cry, women fret, men posture and threaten. The conclusion that participants – and by extension viewers – draw from the series confirms at once the superiority of contemporary life, and, contradictorily, the superiority of a pre-Neolithic, that is to say, Palaeolithic existence. In keeping with other such historical reenactment television series, dramatic tension arises principally from disputes over the division of labor. In historical reality television shows like *Windstärke 8: Das Auswandererschiff*, such labor disputes play into stereotypes of German-German identity – individualistic *Wessis* (West Germans) are contrasted with communally minded *Ossis* (East Germans), who find themselves doing more work aboard the ship than their calculating West German shipmates (Agnew 2007). Here, where all the participants hail from western German states, the conflict over labor serves a different set of interests. Taken out of the intra-national framework and given a more universal cast, the dichotomy is between contemporary society and the lifeways of their putative ancestors. Farming, particularly harvesting grain, is shown to be a time-consuming and essentially futile exercise. The narrator announces:

> Fazit der ersten 10 Tage: Alles dauert länger und ist komplizierter als erwartet. Die Sippe kommt mit der Arbeit kaum hinterher, obwohl alle Erwachsene mitanpacken. Allein 6 Stunden dauert es, das Korn zu enthülsen und [zu] mahlen und Teig für das Fladenbrot zu machen. Sie stellen fest, dass sie ganztägig mit Nahrung zu tun haben. (*Steinzeit*, episode 1)
>
> Findings from the first ten days: everything takes longer and is more complicated than expected. The tribe hardly makes progress with the work, although all the adults pitch in. It takes six hours just to thresh and grind the wheat and make dough for the flatbread. They realize that getting food is an all-day activity. (*Steinzeit*, episode 1)

Only once the participants learn to differentiate poulard wheat (*Triticum turgidum*, Nacktweizen) from the other varieties – tougher einkorn, emmer, and spelt – are the participants able to efficiently thresh the wheat, grind enough flour to mix a glutinous gruel, and bake unleavened bread. In consequence of this new, more satisfying diet, the mood of the children lifts, yet they also subsequently develop dental caries during the course of the "experiment" (Baumgartner 2009). Experts inform viewers that a settled lifestyle and associated changes to the human diet some five to ten thousand years ago resulted in both shorter stature and deteriorating dental health. Neolithic skulls with missing teeth and evidence of dental abscesses are shown to vividly reinforce the point.

Curiously, the one event about which there is well-documented historical evidence – the violent death of Ötzi around 3,300 BCE – is passed over as the subject for reenactment. Decades of scientific research have elucidated the nature of the man's clothing, the manufacture and source of his weaponry and possessions, the nutritional contents of his stomach, and the timing, and location of his last meal. Minute forensic examination has revealed the injuries to his hands, head, and torso, and the flint arrowhead buried in his back. Genetic sequencing now demonstrates that he had brown hair and eyes, ancestral roots in the Middle East, lactose intolerance, exposure to the *Borrelia* bacterium responsible for Lyme disease, and a predisposition to arteriosclerosis (Science Daily 2012).[1] Ample, well-reasoned academic conjecture about his final hours exists, yet, in the *Steinzeit* series, no effort is made to stage his demise: the pair of reenactors do not attempt to embody him, nor do they identify emotionally when, after hard slog through snow to 10,000 feet, they come upon his final resting place in the Alps. With the entire series built around the conceit of following in the Iceman's footsteps, the lack of a denouement is a striking omission.

Contrast this with the US History Channel version of the series, *Digging for the Truth: The Iceman Cometh* (2005; season 1, episode 6), in which television presenter and adventurer Josh Bernstein, along with the same cast of experts used in *Steinzeit: Das Experiment*, investigate Ötzi's life and times. In place of the band of reenactors, the presenter and a professional mountain guide are sent to retrace Ötzi's footsteps through the mountains – also purportedly with the aim of elucidating "one of the most baffling questions in archaeology: what was life really like 5,000 years ago in the Stone Age? Our guide – a Stone Age man." The presenter goes on to pose the leading question: "Did Ötzi freeze to death or was he murdered? To find out," he continues, "I'll be testing his weapons, following in his footsteps and using forensic science to reconstruct his last day on earth" (*Digging for the Truth* 2005). An impending storm later sees the presenter trudging through snow and rescued from a mountaintop by helicopter. This "real-life" drama is interspersed with scenes in which costumed actors portray Ötzi's final chase and murder.

Comparing the German and American versions of the Ötzi story suggests something about the limitations of the genre. In neither *Steinzeit: Das Experiment* nor *Digging for the Truth* does embodying historical subjects appear adequate to the task. Though both television productions insist upon historical fidelity and claim to represent the past "as it really was," they stumble over Ötzi's last hours. The *Steinzeit* reenactors, who until they reach the death site on the mountain, have simultaneously "followed in the footsteps" and attempted to "be" Ötzi, revert at the crucial moment to their contemporary selves. A mumbled exchange has them cursorily reflecting on his manner of death before they shuffle back down the mountain. Whereas reenactment aims to collapse temporalities in order to merge the ontological and the epistemological; in death, the ontological separation between past and present must be upheld. Reenactors cannot act; they must be. Thus, other deaths – for example, that of a deer (shot with a rifle rather than a now illegal bow and arrow) – offer a kind of metonymic catharsis: the reunited reenactors will indulge in an orgy of meat eating before the experimental setting is finally dissolved. For American viewers, in contrast, conditioned perhaps to a theater of identification and to seeing historical drama carried through to its denouement, the lacuna on the mountain needs to be filled. *Digging for the Truth* intersperses the presenter's forays into experimental archaeology with expert testimony and enacted scenes. Ötzi, with his markers of wealth and prestige, will be killed before the viewer's eyes, a sacrifice to capitalist accumulation and civilizational progress.

For Caspar David Friedrich and other Romantics, Neolithic Mecklenburg represented something quintessentially German and, at the same time, universal: these stone relics connected Germans to the landscape and were invested with spiritual meaning that could be mobilized for political ends (Figure 26.1).[2] While interest in these sites has never gone away, this might be a new moment in what archaeologist Cornelius Holtorf (2000) calls the "life histories" of megalith sites.[3] How societies treat their relics says something about the sites' changing uses as well as about the biographies of those who engaged with them. Were megalith tombs used for reburial and worship, he asks? Were they raided? Are they conserved and celebrated? (Holtorf 1998).

On our journey north, such megalith sites have special meaning because they are among the few extant remains of Europe's early farmers. Five thousand years ago, these stone-stackers relinquished the hunter-gathering ways that had hitherto characterized most of human existence. With this shift came larger societies, food surpluses, more sophisticated culture, and dietary changes. It is among the *Trichterbecher* people, for example, that lactase persistence – the ability to express gene allele 13,910*T beyond infancy – is thought to have originated (Itan et al. 2009; Swallow 2003).[4] Common

Figure 26.1   Caspar David Friedrich, *A Walk at Dusk* (c. 1830–1835). Oil on Canvas. Getty Museum.

among northern Europeans, it coevolved with the domestication of cattle, sheep, and goats, and thus emerged in conjunction with a culture of dairying (Krüttli et al. 2014).[5] If agriculture – a precondition for civilization – has historically been regarded in positive terms, the status of the Neolithic Revolution has begun to change. The developmental pyramid that arranged human societies in a progressive sequence – hunter-gathering, pastoralism, agriculture – is subject to revision. Whereas hunter-gathering San peoples and Aborigines were once thought to embody primitive simplicity, and farming Europeans the surplus-accumulating heights of human sophistication, new skepticism greets this model. Hunter-gatherer societies are often now viewed as ecologically friendlier, more egalitarian and sociable, and conducive to a healthier, longer life (Cordain et al. 2000; Cordain et al. 2005). This view suggests nostalgia for "deep history" – human development on a geological scale – and a monistic relation to nature, a nostalgia spawned by anthropogenic global warming, environmental degradation, and social change (Osborne 2014).[6] And so if we are looking for a moment when things started to go wrong, then the Uckermark and Mecklenburg-Lower Pomerania are not bad places to start. This contested region is Germany's crucible, scalded for thousands of years by incursions from the north and east, for centuries by war and plague, feudal inequities, and garrisoned armies. It is a history that has rendered an unstable identity. Surely, to journey back far enough will show a wayside marker. If Paleo enthusiasts are to be believed, that marker will be the Neolithic Revolution – the beginnings of agriculture and the domestication of animals – the moment, science writer Jared Diamond suggests in his 2012 book, *The World Until Yesterday: What Can We Learn From Traditional Societies?*, when human societies adopted less cooperative, more hierarchical, and environmentally destructive forms of social organization.

There are more than a thousand Neolithic megaliths still littering the countryside in Brandenburg and Mecklenburg-Western Pomerania, one of the greatest concentrations of dolmen in the world (Holtorf 2000; Schuldt 1972). None has the majesty of a Stonehenge nor attracts a comparable cultic following; most are just a few clumps of stone in a lonely field – hence our fruitless search that foggy morning. Yet for the trained observer, these rocky outcrops start to take form and an order emerges. They resemble the simplest arrangement of building blocks in an old-fashioned set of children's *Ankerbausteine* – two vertical building blocks connect via a horizontal one to form a heavy-roofed structure. Many, but not all, are oriented north-south. There does not seem to be much astronomical significance in this, no recognition of the winter or summer solstice, no deeper celestial meaning. Too low for huddling in; too small even for sheltering animals, they are just large enough to stretch out a body. The odd skeleton has been recovered there, along with a few artifacts. Now these dolmen stand empty and silent on the question of where their makers went wrong. They are modest structures in fallow fields; not evidence of the monumental history we have learned to doubt (Young 1993). No Ozymandian lessons bespeak a Neolithic hubris. Whatever mistakes the *Trichterbecher* peoples made – the leisure they sacrificed to take in the harvest, the changes they wrought on their bodies, the violence they perpetrated on neighbors – it hardly seems to lie with these modest relics of an earlier time. Starving after a long day in the saddle, it is carbohydrates I have on my mind.

* * *

For those who now believe that agriculture was where human societies took a turn for the worse, the primal Arcadia predates anything we are likely to find roaming around the Uckermark. To return to a more wholesome way of life means looking behind the 10,000 BP-mark, before farming, herding, timber longhouses, clever tools, and sophisticated pottery. There are, however, few testimonials to that time. Stone hand axes and decorated rock shelters, perhaps, but no megaliths and little to seize our fancy as we plough north toward the Baltic.

Given the paucity of evidence, reenactments do not typically thematize the "Old Stone Age." Stefanie Samida and Ruzana Liburkina (2014), investigating reenactors' motivations and choice of historical subject matter, state the obvious: reenactors tend to shy away from the Paleolithic because of a paucity of source material (*"eine dürftige Quellenlage"*) and because of a reluctance to inhabit the "Neanderthal," with its associations of ill-kempt, uninventive brutality. The Neolithic, in contrast, offers more immediate comparisons with contemporary life – similar enough to provide a comparative framework for the division of labor, organization of social life, and mechanics of food procurement, but different enough to offer apparent lessons for the present.

This would all appear to be changing with the enthusiasm for things Paleolithic, that protracted period of hominid and human development from around 2.6 million until 10,000 years ago. Although proponents of the Paleo movement have been around since the 1970s when Loren Cordain, the self-designated founder, proposed a "return" to the Stone Age diet, the past few years have seen an explosion in popular interest (Cordain 2010). This interest is shared in virtual communities, analyzed in the popular press, and, increasingly, addressed by scholars as well. North Americans might be most invested in the Paleo movement, but it has a growing following in countries like Australia, where the foodie culture of the early 2000s rejected agribusiness and the alienation of food from its means and mode of production, embracing the turn to "real" food. Paleo, however, also has a following in Germany, where there is long-standing interest in the lifeways of traditional societies, a strong environmental consciousness, a widespread practice of eating seasonally and locally, and a sizeable middle class with the means to selectively choose what it eats. In Germany, Paleo is known as *Steinzeiternährung* ("Stone Age diet") or *genetischangepasste Ernährung* ("genetically appropriate diet"), with blogs, social networking sites, radio programs, diet books, television specials, restaurants, and fitness studios enjoining enthusiasts to live as *"Steinzeit- und Naturvölker"* ("Stone Age and primitive people") once did (Muth 2006).

Specifically, the Paleo diet emphasizes a high protein and fiber, low carbohydrate approach that is thought to have characterized the hunter-gatherer existence. This is construed in terms of grass-fed meat (the "whole animal"), free-range poultry, wild fish, fresh vegetables and fruit, and natural fats like avocado, coconut, and olive oil. To be avoided are "fake foods" like grains, legumes, dairy products, salt, refined sugar, and processed oils (*Paleo Magazine* 2016). The approach promises to mitigate many of the "lifestyle diseases" that now characterize Westernized societies – obesity, cardiovascular disease, and type II diabetes. Other widely touted benefits of the Paleo approach include improved skin, increased libido, and greater mental clarity (Cordain n.d.).

Such health claims are predicated on the assumption that there is a "mismatch" or discordance between the way humans evolved over millions of years and current ways of life (Abuissa, O'Keefe, and Cordain 2005; Lindeberg 2012). "We get sick," says one blogger, "because our genes didn't get what they were expecting" (Sims 2014). According to this view, the human genome is attuned to the kind of hunter-gathering lifestyle that prevailed through most of human history, not to the dietary innovations wrought by agriculture and the domestication of animals during the most recent fraction of human existence (hence the title of Diamond's 2012 book). By returning to "ancestral" ways, we can, apparently, begin to undo some of the ill effects wrought by what has until recently been government-sanctioned dietary advice – the consumption of complex, low-glycemic-index carbohydrates and the minimization of saturated fats.[7]

While the Paleo movement is based in reforming diet, its claims extend beyond what goes onto the table. In addition to the blogs and podcasts, a welter of cookbooks, magazines, restaurants, and conventions help induct newcomers into the newly constituted "Paleo community," where proponents share information and forge social connections. The health food industry has been quick to capitalize on the trend, marketing products such as ground coconut, whey protein, omega-3 fatty acids, and "green supplements" to consumers looking for newly sanctioned ways to eat (Runyon n.d.). Products like energy bars, which once had a nutritional profile high in carbohydrate calories, now substitute gluten with "nutrient-dense" sources of protein derived from buffalo, venison, and rabbit. Other less commonly eaten animals being marketed to consumers include insects and snakes.

Since Paleo aims for a holistic approach, exercise companies have responded, too. The CrossFit company, for example, aims to replicate forms of exercise thought to be characteristic of indigenous societies. According to enthusiasts, such exercise involves bursts of vigorous physical activity interspersed with inactivity – sprinting, jumping, calisthenics, and weight lifting (sometimes involving heavy rocks) – designed to produce "*Alltagsathleten*" ("everyday athletes").[8] Though CrossFit gyms are franchised, members take part in organized competitions and are linked by a common vocabulary (gyms, for example, are referred to as "boxes") and by a collective workout program ("workout of the day"). This unites a worldwide community in a shared activity at a particular moment in time: collectively cultivating the body is redolent of Benedict Anderson's (1983) notion of the imagined community, which united individuals under a national banner through the medium of a local vernacular and the publication of newspapers. Critics, however, point to CrossFit's dubious physiological claims, its ultra-competitiveness, and potential for physical injury (Robertson 2013).[9]

Paleo is generally construed as a health and fitness trend and discussed in academic terms, often critically, by evolutionary anthropologists, dieticians, biologists, and archaeologists (Zuk 2013). Yet its historical focus prompts us to think in broader terms. The Paleo movement informs, and is informed by, experimental archaeology, living history displays, open-air museums, television documentaries, and "themed walks" to historical sites, all of which attempt to generate and loosely test hypotheses by re-creating historical artifacts and practices.[10] By following the Paleo way, enthusiasts can be thought of as participating in a populist form of history culture when they connect with their ancestors through diet and exercise. Historical reenactment – that diverse set of practices ranging from living history and open air museums, to battle reenactments, pageants, historical reality TV, and experimental archaeology – thus suggests itself as a fruitful analytic framework.[11] Construing the Paleo as a form of reenactment allows us to ask what this particular past does for us.[12] It also inquires into what Paleo does for contemporary forms of historical representation (Koch and Samida 2012).

Paleo bares many of the hallmarks of conventional historical reenactment, including the sense of belonging to a performative community. Including CrossFit exercise within reenactment's ambit shows how such participation is predicated on a quasi-militaristic form of organization – at once individualistic and disciplined, but also subordinate to a larger historical purpose. In this sense, Paleo fitness practitioners are not unlike American Civil War or World War II reenactors: personal camaraderie and collective zeal emerge from simulating battle experiences that commemorate culturally significant historical events.[13] In its civilianized context, CrossFitters perform "Hero Workouts," exercise regimens named for individual soldiers killed in conflicts in Afghanistan and Iraq (CrossFit Hardcore n.d.). The CrossFit "box" constitutes a substitutive battlefield, where "elite fitness is forged" and friendships cultivated through a chastening of the body.[14] The "box" is also the site where living history can be staged. As in other forms of reenactment, the haptic functions here as an authenticating gesture. Indeed, the Paleo body may be the haptic object par excellence, with the individual's interpretation of the past ratified by its own self-evidence. The Paleo body testifies to its own interpretation by being thinner, less disease ridden, more "elite," and hence truer to the past. Central to this evidentiary corpus is the before-and-after shot – selfies that enthusiasts post to mark their physical transformation and corroborate their membership within the (pre)-historical community (Paleo Hacks 2013). This dualistic temporality – simultaneously of the present and the past, the same but better – offers a comparative, emotionally freighted framework characteristic of a wide range of reenactment forms.

Conclusion

Most reenactors understand their practices as pleasurable, theatrical, and educative, but also as investigative. By testing practices like flint-stone fire making and fur cloth tailoring, they hope to contribute meaningfully to historical understanding. Hypotheses, they maintain, can best be tested by putting things into practice in order to produce knowledge that is more reliable and useful than the book learning pursued by academic historians. The comedian Stephen Colbert (2005), invoking a kind of Barthean "reality effect," refers to such rejection of book knowledge as "truthiness," a rhetorical gesture in which authority is conferred by the haptic.

For Jared Diamond, the reenactor's experiment is a fait accompli. "Traditional societies represent thousands of millennia-long natural experiments in organizing human lives," he argues. "We can't repeat those experiments … wait decades and observe the outcomes; we have to learn from the societies that already ran the experiments" (2012: 32–33). "What we can learn and potentially emulate," he continues, "are small-scale societies where no one is a stranger (obviating the need for laws or police); conflict resolution, child-rearing, treatment of the elderly, and 'routine' multilingualism; along with the avoidance of non-communicable diseases associated with a Westernized lifestyle" (Diamond 2012). Diamond's primitivist enthusiasms might look different if one asked, "better for whom?"

The evolutionary biologist, Marlene Zuk (2013), a trenchant critic of what she calls "paleofantasies," refutes many of the movement's key tenets, including the notions that humans have ceased to evolve, that we are "meant" to be any particular way, or that it is possible, other than in the most simplistic terms, to imitate life in a pre-agricultural society. We are subject to cultural forces – medical and agricultural – as well as environmental ones, and these "leave their mark." We would do well, she implies, to appreciate the particularity of our time and place, and to accept change.

Usedom, the final destination for our bicycle journey, proves not to be the island-grail we'd hoped. Not here do we find evidence of a past more ancestral, harmonious, or closer to nature. So late in the season, the berries are over, and the apples already spoiling under the trees. There is little to collect, and the historical sites are few and far between. Yet every once in a while, we do come across a forager. Near the coast we pass through mixed forests of pine, beech, oak, and ash. There is a woman wearing dish gloves picking nettles by the side of the road and an elderly couple, with baskets in hand, going mushrooming. With their gimpy gate, they set off into the gloom to carefully pick out the edible *Mohrenkopf, Krause Glucke,* and *Pfifferling* from the poisonous *Gift-Häubling.* Old names – "Moor's head" (*Lactarius lignyotus*), "ruffled hen" (*Sparassis crispa*), "chanterelle" (*Cantharellus cibarius*), and "deadly skullcap" (*Galerina marginata*) – and old ways are perpetuated in the couple's annual foraging rituals. Perhaps we should pedal on a ways, I suggest, north of the Baltic to Copenhagen. We could go and eat at Noma, rated the best restaurant in the world, where chefs look to the Nordic landscape to "rediscover our history and shape our future" (Redzepi 2010; 2013), where food is regarded as an *objet trouvé* and curated on a bed of moss and stony platter. There, I encourage my cycling companion, the Paleo surely awaits.

Notes

1   According to anthropologist Albert Zink and bioinformatics expert Andreas Keller, "evidence of a genetic predisposition [to arteriosclerosis] in Ötzi … indicates that cardiovascular disease is by no means an illness chiefly associated with modern lifestyles." "Initial genetic analysis

reveals Iceman Ötzi was predisposed to cardiovascular disease," *Science Daily*, February 28, 2012 [Online], available at www.sciencedaily.com/releases/2012/02/120228123847.htm.

2   On the German relation to nature, see David Blackbourn, *The Conquest of Nature: Water, Landscape and the Making of Modern Germany* (London: Random House, 2007).

3   See also T. Grütter, *Melancholie und Abgrund. Die Bedeutung des Gesteins bei Caspar David Friedrich. Ein Beitrag zum Symboldenken der Frühromantik* (Berlin: Reimer, 1986).

4   Some scholars attribute lactose tolerance to their predecessors, the *Linearbandkeramik* (LBK) people, a millennium and a half earlier (Itan et al. 2009; Swallow 2003).

5   The window for the introduction of lactase persistence is a wide one, as Ötzi's own lactose intolerance suggests. In Europe, genetic selection is thought to have occurred between 3000 BCE and CE 1200. This questions current "Paleo" claims about the Neolithic period (Krüttli et al. 2014).

6   On deep history as the study of human origins and development on a geological time frame, see Andrew Shryock and Daniel Lord Smail, *Deep History: The Architecture of Past and Present* (Berkeley: University of California Press, 2011).

7   There is no consensus among scientists that the "Stone Age diet" was dominated by animal protein. See, for example, Dunn (2014). It is also erroneous to speak of a single Stone Age diet, given the temporal span of the Neolithic period and the variability in environmental conditions under which Neolithic peoples lived.

8   CrossFit company was founded in 2000 by Greg Glassman and Lauren Jenai. See https://www.facebook.com/CrossFitWerk/info?ref=page_internal.

9   Eric Robertson (2013), reporting in *The Huffington Post*, referred to CrossFit's "dirty little secret," rhabdomyolysis, a condition in which skeletal muscle under extreme duress breaks down, releasing myoglobin into the bloodstream and causing potentially fatal kidney damage.

10   See, for example, EXARC, the ICOM-affiliated organization that represents open-air museums, experimental archaeology, ancient technology, and interpretation, and which is devoted to "the investigation, contextualisation, presentation and interpretation of archaeological and experimental archaeological heritage." See http://exarc.net/about-us/exarc-vision-2013–2017.

11   Work that comes closest to this looks at present-day pilgrimages and visiting heritage sites, and Alpine tourism that generate particular forms of historical understanding. See Willner (2014).

12   For a discussion over whether Paleo constitutes re-enactment, see Paleo Hacks, available at http://paleohacks.com/paleo-reenactment/paleo-reenactment-4079.

13   For a vivid account of Civil War re-enactors' motivations and experiences, see Tony Horwitz, *Confederates in the Attic: Dispatches from the Unfinished Civil War* (New York: Vintage, 1998).

14   A CrossFit WOD, for example, might include the following: RFT 35, 1 Hang Power Clean,1 Hang Squat Clean, 1 Thruster @60% of 1 RM PC, with all Rounds unbroken. See https://en-gb.facebook.com/CrossFitWerk. On the DYI aspect, see the instructions for constructing one's own workout equipment available at http://www.crossfit.com/cf-info/faq.html#Nutrition0.

CHAPTER TWENTY SEVEN

Performing Continuity, Performing Belonging: Three Cabarets from the Terezín Ghetto[1]

LISA PESCHEL

In the spring of 2005, while interviewing Czech-Jewish survivors of the World War II ghetto at Terezín (in German, Theresienstadt), I made a startling discovery: some survivors still had in their possession theatrical scripts they themselves had written or had received from friends in the ghetto. The project had begun with the goal of preserving and analyzing their memories of the past – more specifically, of Terezín's surprisingly rich cultural life – but was unexpectedly enriched by these artifacts from the present of the ghetto. The scripts, almost all of them comedies, engaged with every aspect of the prisoners' lives, from their experience of the woefully inadequate food supply of the ghetto to their hopes for the postwar future.

Once it became clear that there were still more scripts to be found, I began a systematic search that took me to archives and private collections in the United States, across Europe, and in Israel. The search also included months of additional interviews with the survivors as they explained references to events and people in the ghetto and the jokes sometimes carefully concealed in the text. With their help, I was able to publish an extensively footnoted volume of eleven scripts, including the three discussed in detail in this chapter, first in a bilingual Czech/German anthology, and then in a revised and expanded English language edition.[2]

As soon as the plays began to come to light, I was inspired to restage them, to try to share the Terezín prisoners' humor and creativity and their revelations about daily life in the ghetto with a wider public. The scale of these performance projects slowly grew and eventually led to my role as a co-investigator on a 40-month, £1.8 million project, Performing the Jewish Archive, funded by the UK Arts and Humanities Research Council.[3] The project will feature five international performance festivals in which my colleagues and I will bring forgotten works by Jewish artists back to today's audience. But why engage with these plays as more than historical curiosities? After ten years of work with the scripts as a scholar, translator, producer, and performer, I believe we have

A Companion to Public History, First Edition. Edited by David Dean.
© 2018 John Wiley & Sons Ltd. Published 2018 by John Wiley & Sons Ltd.

much to learn from these texts about the role theatrical performance played in helping a society cope with an unprecedented crisis.

Immediately after the Nazi occupation but long before deportations to the ghettos and concentration camps began, the Czech Jews experienced a sudden assault on their sense of self as fully integrated Czechoslovak citizens.[4] Unlike in Germany, where anti-Jewish legislation had been implemented step by step over several years, a torrent of discriminatory measures followed the invasion of the Czech lands in March 1939. The occupation marked a radical break between the "before" of the tolerant society of the interwar Czechoslovak First Republic and the "after" of life in the "Protectorate of Bohemia and Moravia," and the Nazi-enforced process of legal and social separation from their fellow Czechs soon followed (Figure 27.1). Just two-and-a-half years later, deportations began that led to another drastic break: physical separation from the non-Jewish population. For almost all of the Czech Jews, the first stop in their journey through the Nazi ghettos and camps was Terezín.

More than 70 years after the end of World War II, the Terezín prisoners' cabarets and plays are providing new insight into the ways in which the Czech Jews tried to retain their prewar sense of self. In this chapter, I argue that the Terezín prisoners used theatrical performance to resist the homogeneous and dehumanizing identity of racial inferiority that had been imposed upon them by the Nazis by performing themselves in all their national, political, linguistic, and religious diversity on the stages of the ghetto. More specifically, they maintained their prewar identities by creating narratives for themselves and their spectators that established continuity between their prewar past and their Terezín present, and they countered their enforced separation by performing plays that expressed their identification with larger communities outside the ghetto.

What were the larger communities to which the Czech Jews in Terezín felt they belonged? Before the war, they had belonged to political parties ranging from the Communists to the conservative Agrarian Party, had represented religious viewpoints from Orthodoxy to atheism, and had spoken German or Czech or both. But in this chapter, I structure my analysis around another category of identification that was institutionalized in the Czechoslovak census: nationality. In 1921, the Statistical Bureau decided that nationality was to be understood as ethnic belonging with mother tongue as the main criterion; however, since few of the Czechoslovak Jews spoke Yiddish, they

Figure 27.1 The Partition of Czechoslovakia 1939. Source: Wikipedia.

were allowed to choose Jewish nationality regardless of language spoken.[5] Interestingly, in the interwar period, their sense of national identification was divided almost evenly among three groups: in the 1930 census, of those citizens living in the Czech lands (Bohemia, Moravia, and Silesia) who indicated Judaism as their religion, 36% chose Czechoslovak nationality, 30% chose German nationality, and 31% chose Jewish nationality (Rothkirchen 1984).

The borders distinguishing these three groups, however, were much more flexible and porous than census statistics suggest. Therefore, rather than focusing on mutually exclusive categories of Czech, German, or Jewish nationality, I will discuss their identifications with Czech-language culture, with German-language culture, and with one type of Jewish national identity: Zionism.[6] In my examination of three cabarets, one representing each group, I will demonstrate how these texts enabled the prisoners to perform continuity from past into present, and to create a sense of connection to communities in the world outside the ghetto.

Laugh with Us (The Second Czech Cabaret)[7]

Czech-speaking Terezín prisoners performed and attended a wide range of theatrical works from the prewar period, from *Bouquet* (*Kytice*), a cycle of ballads published in 1853 during the Czech National Revival period, to plays by renowned interwar playwright Karel Čapek (Heřman PT 4304, PT 3883). By far the most prominent influence on original Czech-language scripts written in the ghetto, however, was the tremendously popular Liberated Theater (*Osvobozené divadlo*) of comic duo Jiří Voskovec and Jan Werich. In preserved notes by prisoner Josef Taussig, who apparently planned to write an essay on Terezín cabaret after the war, he mentions three Czech cabarets in the ghetto that "knew and admired the Liberated Theater"; one of them was *Laugh with Us* (Taussig 1994). Survivors who have seen the script have recognized the influence of Voskovec and Werich in everything from the revue form to the specific style of wordplay.[8]

According to documents preserved in the Terezín Memorial, four authors contributed to the cabaret: Dr. Felix Porges, Vítězslav "Pidla" Horpatzky, Pavel Stránský, and Pavel Weisskopf (Heřman PT 3826–31). All four authors arrived in Terezín on the same transport of young working men from Prague in December 1941. Porges, according to his sons, had studied for a career in law but had always been interested in theater. Because he and his wife and fellow performer, Elly Bernstein, remained in Terezín until the end of the war, he was able to preserve an entire small archive of works he had written or collected in the ghetto.[9] Porges and Horpatzky apparently got to know one another shortly after their arrival, and a year later they performed together in a play re-creating the broadcasts of prewar radio station Prague 1 (Peschel 2014). Their collaboration continued and, in the spring and summer of 1944, they wrote and performed together in *Laugh with Us*. Stránský, who wrote the lyrics for some of the songs, was no longer in the ghetto when the cabaret was performed. He was deported to Auschwitz in December 1943. Unfortunately, little is known about Weisskopf other than his date of birth, his date of arrival in Terezín, and that he perished after deportation from the ghetto to Auschwitz in September 1944.

With their script the authors established continuity between the prewar past and their present in the ghetto by importing the style of beloved artists Voskovec and Werich. This style, however, meant more than familiarity and pleasure; it also offered a model for dealing with adversity through humor. Voskovec and Werich did not shy away from commenting on any political event, no matter how gruesome. As Hitler's power grew, they unfortunately had plenty of material. For example, in the summer of 1934, the political executions known as "Night of the Long Knives" took place in Germany. Between June 30 and July 2, the Nazi regime killed at least 85 people, most of whom were members of the Sturmabteilung (SA) – their fellow fascists – to eliminate them as a threat to Hitler's power. In Voskovec and Werich's revue *The Executioner and the Fool* (*Kat a blázen*), which premiered in the fall of 1934, Raduzo the executioner tried to figure out how to execute Mahuleno the fool according to the proper protocols, even though they had been stranded alone on a deserted island for years:

> MAHULENO: Everybody knows I'll get some rum; I have the right to a flask of rum before my execution, a swig to brace myself!
>
> RADUZO: For Christ's sake, he's right, I have to give him rum, where am I going to get that?
>
> MAHULENO: Don't ask me; it's your responsibility. I'll go to jail and wait for my rum. And don't think that I'm going to wait until June 30th – the anniversary of the day when friends put friends to death. (Voskovec and Werich 1980)

In this passage, Voskovec and Werich confronted the ominous events taking place just over the border and defused their audience's anxiety with humor. Porges and Horpatzky, in their roles as the comic duo, used a similar strategy to take on one of the most traumatic events in the history of the ghetto. On November 11, 1943, a census of all the prisoners took place on a field called Bohušovice Hollow, located just outside the ramparts of Terezín. Almost 40,000 people were forced to stand outside the entire cold and damp day, not sure if they were to be counted or killed.[10] Many prisoners subsequently died of exposure-related illnesses. *Laugh with Us* (Figure 27.2) confronts this event during a scene in which Horpatzky notices that Porges is humming the Czech folk song "On the Lord's Meadows."

> P. HORPATZKY.   You're in a good mood. But did you know that we also had a lord's meadow in Terezín?
>
> F. PORGES.   I didn't know about that.
>
> P. HORPATZKY.   It was called Bohušovice Hollow. There was a massive event there, a beautiful public demonstration.
>
> F. PORGES.   Aha, I know, there was that international Sokol rally. (Peschel 2014)

Sokol, the Czech nationalist gymnastics organization, was a point of reference that Czech Jews would have recognized immediately. The huge choreographed performances of calisthenics that took place at international Sokol rallies involved hundreds of members. By comparing the census with a Sokol rally, Porges and Horpatzky assimilated the event into their script in a comic way and placed it firmly within a prewar interpretive framework that, even though entirely fictional, may have offered the prisoners some relief through laughter.

The authors also made continuity an explicit theme of the script, not only by linking their Terezín present with their prewar past but by linking both with their imagined future. All the scenes except for the first and last, in which Porges and Horpatzky address their spectators from the Terezín present, are set in a postwar Prague that is identical in

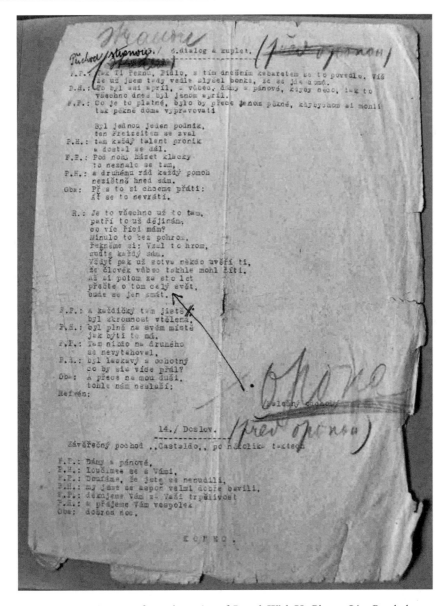

Figure 27.2 Page from the script of *Laugh With Us*. Photo: Lisa Peschel.

every way with the Prague they remembered from the 1930s. During the cabaret, Porges and Horpatzky visit beloved landmarks on Wenceslas Square, the bustling heart of the city, and the continuity extends even to the staffing of their favorite institutions:

P. Horpatzky.   I would go to Juliš's [restaurant, but] there they still have the same headwaiter as before the war.

F. Porges.   You still owe him money, don't you? (Peschel 2014).

They also meet old friends from Terezín who are thriving as performers in some of the most prestigious venues in the city. Horpatzky remarks upon one such encounter:

P. Horpatzky. I've noticed that Terezín always follows you. I run into reminders all the time. There I was in Lucerna[11] and who didn't take the stage but that star from Terezín, that Hanka Ledererová. You remember her, right?

By representing continuity, not only from past to present but from the present into the future, they wove even Terezín itself into a narrative that projected their own survival.

Laugh with Us enabled the actors and spectators to perform their sense of belonging to specific communities within and outside the ghetto, including the community of those who admired the work of Voskovec and Werich. This particular affiliation had not only an aesthetic aspect but also a specific political valence. Many Liberated Theater fans belonged to the generation whose earliest memories were of the Great Depression and who had come of age as the threat of fascism spread across Europe. Voskovec and Werich, both born in 1905, had become standard-bearers for these young Czechs, Jewish and non-Jewish. Although they resolutely refused to join any political party, they espoused leftist principles of social and economic justice in their performances and were committed anti-fascists. As Hitler's power grew, their revues became increasingly politically engaged and their comedy grew fiercer but they remained optimistic, reinforcing audience morale with their faith in the strength of ordinary but united people (Burian 2000). The Terezín prisoners knew that Voskovec and Werich had fled to the United States in 1939, before the Nazi occupation of Bohemia and Moravia, and continued to reach out to the Czech anti-fascist community through their radio broadcasts on Voice of America. By bringing Voskovec and Werich's style into the ghetto, they performed their ongoing belonging to the larger community of anti-fascists outside the walls of the ghetto – and their own opposition to the Nazis.

The Hofer Cabaret

Czech Jews involved in the German-language cultural life in Terezín worked closely with prisoners from Austria and Germany, who brought influences from both countries into the ghetto. For example, a reading of *Faust* organized by Philipp Manes of Berlin included participants from Germany, Austria, and Bohemia, as did perhaps the best-known cabaret in the ghetto, Berlin actor and director Kurt Gerron's *Carousel* (Heřman PT 3981 and PT 3933). Austrian influence is clear, for example, in an original operetta written in Terezín, *Girl of the Ghetto* (Das Ghettomädel), perhaps because at least one of the authors and several members of the cast were from Brno, a Moravian city only 80 miles north of Vienna (Heřman PT 3853).[12] However, the cabaret artist I will examine here experienced Viennese influence more directly: he began his theatrical career there.

Hans Hofer (real name Hans or Hanuš Schulhof), the son of actor Siegfried Schulhof, who also used the stage name Hofer, was born in Prague in 1907. The family moved to Vienna in 1924 when Hofer was 17. He was active in Viennese theater until after the Nazi annexation of Austria, when he returned to Prague with his Austrian-Jewish wife, Lisl (Ehrmann et al. 1965). Hans Hofer performed in a Jewish cabaret until 1941, and in July of 1942 he and Lisl were deported together to Terezín, where they immediately became active in the German-language cultural life of the ghetto (Weiner 1999).[13]

Although no complete scripts have been preserved, a collection of Hofer's song lyrics has been preserved in the Jewish Museum in Prague.

The continuity of prewar cultural forms within Hofer's texts would have been clear immediately to his Terezín spectators who were familiar with Viennese culture, for he set almost all of his songs to Viennese operetta and cabaret melodies. Most of his works feature lyrics about the ghetto itself, and references to events in Terezín often make it possible to date them fairly specifically. For example, one of his works, "The Main Square" (Der Hauptplatz), addressed the so-called *Stadtverschönerung* or "city beautification" that took place in preparation for a visit by a commission of the International Red Cross in June of 1944. The text, probably written in the spring of 1944, was set to the melody of the song "Mein Herr Marquis," otherwise known as "Adele's Laughing Song," from the operetta *Die Fledermaus*:[14]

> There was once a square
> No one set foot there
> Barbed wire blocked everyone's way
> Then they hauled in sand
> The barb-ed wire was banned
> New flower beds brightened our day
> They built in a hurry a pa-vi-lion
> And rushed in the fiddles and sax-o-phones
> And a forty-piece band,
> Was suddenly there on hand ...
> Now concerts echo through the ghetto gloriously
> And when I hear the music, it occurs to me:
> So amusing, hahaha, their little project, hahaha
> Seems so harmless, hahaha, who could object? hahaha ...
> So amusing, hahaha, their little project, hahaha ...
> So very very very funny ... are *they*. (Peschel 2014)

Hofer established one form of continuity by simply bringing a melody from this beloved operetta into the ghetto. He established another with his specific approach to making the song relevant to their own experience in the present. In *Die Fledermaus*, the character of Adele is the maid of Gabriel von Eisenstein, but in Act 2 they both attend a masked ball. She recognizes him, but he does not recognize her in disguise as an actress. With her song she gently mocks him when he notices a "resemblance" to his maid, thus temporarily reversing the power relations between herself and her employer. With his lyrics, Hofer adopts a similar strategy. He temporarily places himself and his audience in a position of power: as critics who evaluated the Nazis' actions as bizarrely comic but not especially threatening. In the last line of the song, Hofer made his only subtle reference to their oppressors, cutting them and their entire elaborate project down to size by making both a source of amusement rather than fear.

Hofer's comic response to the *Stadtverschönerung* bears a resemblance to Porges and Horpatzky's interpretation of the census in that both use humor to create manageable narratives from threatening events. There is a marked difference, however, between Hofer's comic style and the humor in the Czech-language scripts. As one scholar has noted, the mark of the Viennese cabaret was its "mixture of whimsy and genial wit" rather than biting satire (Appignanesi 2004). Hofer's texts bear this out;

his verses are mildly satirical but more bemused than biting. While the humor in the Czech-language cabarets confronted the most traumatic events of the ghetto, such as the census and outgoing transports, Hofer's German-language texts avoided them. His songs portray everyday problems in the ghetto such as an attempt to recover a stolen thermos bottle, corruption in the Terezín kitchens, and the bureaucracy involved in obtaining a ticket to the theater. He traces these daily travails in meticulous and witty detail, but does not attempt to convert the most dangerous aspects of life in the ghetto into comedy.

The German-language texts also differed from the others in that they lacked a clear orientation toward the future. In their cabarets, the Czech-speaking Jews imagined their return to Prague, and the Zionists prepared for life in Palestine; the German-language cabarets did not look beyond the present. Why was this the case? As Hitler's influence grew, German-speaking Czech Jews had witnessed the increase of anti-Semitism among their non-Jewish German-speaking neighbors. They had also experienced the rising anti-German feeling among their Czech-speaking neighbors. Perhaps it was difficult for them to imagine the place of German-language culture in postwar Czechoslovakia and their own place in the postwar Czechoslovak community. Unlike *Laugh with Us*, which connected its Terezín spectators with a specific Czech political community they expected to rejoin after the war, Hofer's texts did not represent an alignment with any particular group. His songs may have created a sense of solidarity among his spectators by performing their shared devotion to German-language and specifically Viennese culture, but they did not perform a relationship with a specific political community outside the walls of the ghetto.

Purimspiel

Zionists in Terezín were not extensively involved in theatrical activities; they tended to focus on other areas of the cultural life such as the lecture series and work with children and youth. Specifically Jewish theater was in the hands of just two groups. Prague director Irena Dodalová, assisted by Evžen Weisz, organized a few programs based on classic Yiddish works.[15] A much more prolific organizer of specifically Jewish-themed performances was young Zionist Walter Freud.

Freud was born in 1917 in Vienna but grew up in Brno. During the Nazi occupation, he was employed by the Jewish congregation of Brno as a *shaliach* and traveled widely in Moravia, delivering lectures on Jewish topics.[16] He frequently visited the town of Strážnice to work with a large Maccabi youth group.[17] There he met Ruth Felixová, and they married in 1941. At the beginning of 1942, Walter was named head of the Jewish orphanage in Brno; just a few months later, the 80 children and all their caretakers were deported to Terezín.

In the ghetto, Walter and Ruth were assigned to work in the girls' youth home L410. As posters preserved at the Terezín Memorial reveal, many of his performances featured young actors from both L410 and Q710, the Zionist youth home. He assembled several programs for specific holidays and authored works such as a German-language revue titled *Wie war Mordechai?* (What was Mordechai Like?) and a Czech-language Hanukkah play called *Menorah* (Heřman PT 8413 and 8420). The only original text written by Freud that has thus far come to light is the German-language *Purimspiel*, which was preserved in the archives of Beit Terezín in Israel.

According to a poster in the archives of the Terezín Memorial, it was performed in March of 1943 (Heřman PT 4041).

The text of the *Purimspiel* established continuity from the prewar past into the present in several ways. For example, its themes and comic style perpetuated the tradition of *Purimspiels*, humorous performances that have been used to mark the holiday of Purim since the sixteenth century (Dalinger 1998). The content of the Purim narrative, although ostensibly about the past, also spoke to their present and future: it represented the victory and survival of the Jews when confronted with the threat of annihilation.[18] By bringing the Purim story into Terezín, Freud implied that their own imprisonment in the ghetto was simply another trial in the series of catastrophic events the Jewish people have overcome.

The text also brought European and German-language cultural traditions into the present of the ghetto. The *Purimspiel* itself was structured as a cabaret, with short sketches and scenes alternating with musical numbers. Freud drew on many of same musical influences as Hofer, basing scenes on popular German-language cabaret songs and using melodies from films and operettas. For example, one entire scene was based on the song "Auf Wiedersehen Herr Fröhlich," which was already a popular cabaret number in the 1920s. It ended with the following verse, in which events of the Purim story are recognizable:

FRAU MÜLLER.	Herr Schön, Herr Schön!
HERR SCHÖN.	What's going on, Frau Müller?
FRAU MÜLLER.	Haven't you heard the news?
HERR SCHÖN.	I know, there's something up in Shushan!
FRAU MÜLLER.	And how, Herr Schön!!
HERR SCHÖN.	Do you know?
FRAU MÜLLER.	Hmph, do I know … that Haman's gotten mixed up in some quarrel at the castle, with the king and the queen, and the king will see him hang.
HERR SCHÖN.	Is it really so?
FRAU MÜLLER.	Of course, and now we'll go free; the fourteenth of Adar has been cancelled!
HERR SCHÖN.	Auf Wiedersehen, Frau Müller.
FRAU MÜLLER.	Auf Wiedersehen, Herr Schön! (Peschel 2014)

There is a fundamental difference, however, in the way that Hofer and Freud used these songs. Hofer's songs linked the beloved cultural forms of his spectators' past with the events of their present in the ghetto. In his case, the medium is the message: his spectators experienced the longed-for continuity of their own German-language culture even in songs about the hardships of life in Terezín. In Freud's play, the German language and the prewar melodies familiar to the young Zionists were simply vehicles for the much more important, specifically Jewish content. In fact, in the verse above based on "Auf Wiedersehen Herr Fröhlich," the rhythm of Freud's text does not fit the melody. The scene may have been spoken rather than sung, using the content as inspiration but revealing no particular attachment to the original song. As later scenes emphasized, the young Zionists' goal was to learn Hebrew, which would then replace German as the medium of transmitting Jewish culture.

Both the text of the *Purimspiel* and the style of performance, as suggested by the stage directions, served to strengthen bonds among the Zionists in Terezín and establish a sense of connection with the larger Zionist community outside the ghetto. Right from the start, the performance established a strong sense of inclusiveness and informality among the actors and the spectators by means of the players' actions:

> (The entire theater troupe, with the Director, enters through the audience and takes the stage, singing a Huha Horra.)[19]

> DIRECTOR.   Now all you players, gather 'round
>   Look what an audience we've found
>   To watch the scenes that you'll perform … (Peschel 2014)

By entering through the audience, the players embodied their status as members of and representatives of the community. The boundaries between the audience and actors remained fluid as the players continued to move among the spectators and to comment overtly on their presence. For example, when the Director tried to get the King to join the rest of the players on stage, the King replied:

> King. I'll tell you why I'm here, to wit:
> I'm looking for a place to sit.
> Director. Whatever has come over you?
> The first two rows, as usual,
> Are set aside for VIPs.
> King. Well, as the king, I'm one of these.
> Director. They're for the Jewish council members
> Not for stateless kings, remember …
> Off-stage, you have no commonweal.
> King. And they – no robes, no crowns – are real? (Peschel 2014)

It is quite likely that some of the members of the Terezín Jewish Council of Elders (Ältestenrat) were actually present at the performance. The deputy head of the ghetto in the spring of 1943, Jacob Edelstein, was a Zionist, and the performance was held in the Magdeburg barracks, where the Jewish Council's administrative offices were located. Rather than treating them solemnly as honored guests, Freud brings them into the community by drawing them inside the circle of humor and inviting them to laugh along.[20] This joke, however, in its own way, is just as biting as Porges and Horpatzky's joke about the census. On one hand, it is quite true that the council members, dressed in civilian clothes, did not bear the trappings of power that the King would expect. On the other hand, as all the prisoners and the Jewish Council members themselves knew, regardless of their titles and their power, any of their decisions could be overturned at any moment by members of the SS. In the *Purimspiel*, Freud did not shy away from the existential threat they faced: they were all ultimately at the mercy of their captors.

* * *

With all three of these cabaret-style texts, the authors created a sense of continuity between their prewar pasts and their present in the ghetto and, in some cases, extended that continuity into an imagined postwar future as well. The plays also allowed actors and spectators to perform a sense of belonging to the communities they felt were their own, both in Terezín and in the world outside the ghetto. But for those prisoners who survived the war, were the hopes embodied in these plays fulfilled in the postwar period?

Did the continuity they performed actually extend into the future, and were they able to rejoin their communities outside the ghetto?

Many of the Czech-speaking Czech Jews, especially those who were relatively young and left-leaning, reintegrated fairly smoothly into postwar Czechoslovak society which, after six years of German fascist occupation, was now much more nationally Czech and politically leftist than before the war. They experienced various degrees of difficulty in encounters with postwar anti-Semitism and struggles to recover their property, and thousands decided to emigrate when the Communists came to power in 1948. However, many of those who believed in the promise of social and economic justice the new government offered stayed in Czechoslovakia. For them, the continuity they had performed in the ghetto translated, to some degree, into continuity in the postwar period, and into membership in a leftist political community. Horpatzky and Weisskopf, however, did not live to see the new order. Both perished after deportation from Terezín to Auschwitz in the fall of 1944. Stránský survived seven months in Auschwitz, hard labor at Schwarzheide, and a death march – back to Terezín. He and the other surviving author of *Laugh with Us*, Felix Porges, both remained in Czechoslovakia. Neither was involved in theater after the war.

The German-speaking Czech Jews returned to a postwar Czechoslovakia in which there was little place for German-language culture. Those who had selected German nationality on the 1930 census were actually faced with the threat of deportation and were required to submit formal applications to retain Czechoslovak citizenship. By the time that, in September 1946, the Ministry of the Interior finally issued an order that clarified the position of "people of Jewish origin," approximately 1,500 Jews applying to retain their citizenship had been investigated based on questions regarding their "national reliability" (Krejčová 1993).

Hans Hofer returned to Prague in July of 1945, after surviving deportation to Auschwitz and several months in a slave labor camp. Bilingual and a committed leftist, he remained in Czechoslovakia and continued in his career as an actor there for 15 years, performing in both Czech and German.[21] In 1960, he moved to the German Democratic Republic and joined the troupe of the Rostock *Volkstheater*, playing various comic roles. He retired in 1973 and died on April 12 of the same year.

For those Zionists who survived, the war had only increased their conviction that emigration to Palestine offered the only secure future. When immigration to Israel was legalized in 1948, thousands of Czechoslovak Jews left the country.[22] Many of the Terezín survivors settled on a kibbutz called Givat Chayim, where the Beit Terezín archives are now located. Although the script of his *Purimspiel* somehow made it to Israel and into the archives, Freud himself did not live to fulfill his dream. He perished after deportation from Terezín to Auschwitz in the fall of 1944.

As we have seen, although all of these Terezín authors were able to establish a sense of continuity from their prewar pasts into the ghetto through their theatrical works, only a few were able to extend that continuity into their postwar reality. For some, there simply was no "postwar." For others, the very worlds they hoped to rejoin – such as the world of German-speaking Prague – were themselves casualties of the war.

But what types of continuity have the members of the Performing the Jewish Archive project been able to establish by bringing such works back to stage? As of this writing, we have completed a one-day pilot festival and one of our five planned international performance festivals in the United States and are in the midst of the second in the United Kingdom. The act of rehearsing and staging plays by the Terezín authors for these three festivals has already effected two types of continuity.

One is the reestablishment of a long-forgotten identity: the Terezín authors' identity as artists. That is, in addition to being members of particular national groups and political movements, these authors were acknowledged by their fellow Terezín prisoners as having something valuable to say and the skill to express it in aesthetically successful ways. Public audiences at our festivals are now encountering them, not just as Hitler's victims, but as individuals with names and faces, with political and social agendas, whose works still have the power to move spectators to tears and to laughter.

Another is continuity of influence. In our most recent festival, colleagues and I worked with a group of students at my university to understand the Marxist principles behind 23-year-old Terezín author Zdeněk Jelínek's script *Comedy about a Trap* (Figure 27.3).[23] The students then staged an adaptation of the play that included their own scenes on collective action, having a voice, and the meaning of labor. During our post-performance discussions with the audience, the students spoke eloquently about how the experience had changed them: the play had enabled them to rethink their automatic response of "Communism is a system that failed" and consider the value of the ideals upon which it was based. Through his play, Jelínek influenced a group of students just a few years younger than he was when he wrote it, more than 70 years after his death.

I am sure that additional types of continuity will become apparent during our final three festivals in the Czech Republic, Australia, and South Africa. One possible type of continuity in our Czech festival is continuity of place. We hope to stage a reconstructed Terezín children's opera, *The Fireflies*, in a restored performance space on the site of the former ghetto with a panel of survivors in attendance. As we continue to prepare these

Figure 27.3   *Comedy about a Trap* Production. Photo: Dan Cashdon.

plays for public performances, I look forward to the insights we will gain, not only through rigorous examination of the texts but through the experience of the actors who will embody them and the response of the spectators who will bear witness to them.

Notes

1 An earlier version of this chapter was published in German under the title *Gegen eine uniforme Definition des Jüdischseins: Drei Kabaretts aus dem Ghetto Theresienstadt* ("Against a Uniform Definition of Jewishness: Three Cabarets from the Theresienstadt Ghetto") in the edited volume *Alltag im Holocaust: Jüdisches Leben im Großdeutschen Reich 1941–1945* (2013), ed. Andrea Löw, Doris L. Bergen and Anna Hájková, Oldenbourg, Munich, 167–179.

2 See Lisa Peschel, ed., *Divadelní texty z terezínského ghetta/Theatertexte aus dem Ghetto Theresienstadt, 1941–1945 (Prague: Akropolis, 2008) and Performing Captivity, Performing Escape: Cabarets and Plays from the Terezin/Theresienstadt Ghetto* (Calcutta: Seagull Books, 2014).

3 For details on the project, please see the website https://jewishmusicandtheatre.org.

4 See, for example, Rabbi Richard Feder's description of the situation of the Czech Jews in his postwar memoirs: "We Jews lived peacefully and safely and therefore contentedly and happily in the First Republic, the republic of Masaryk. We were her citizens with full rights, and not only on paper, but in real life." Richard Feder, *Židovská tragedie: dějství poslední* (Kolín: Lusk, 1947). All translations from the Czech are my own.

5 The Bureau's decision came after a long debate regarding whether nationality should be based on subjective choice or on more objective criteria such as language, especially since the Bohemian and Moravian Jews had "lost their national language." See Tatjana Lichtenstein, "*Making Jews at Home: Jewish Nationalism in the Bohemian Lands, 1918–1938*" (PhD diss., University of Toronto, 2009), 80–81.

6 The choice of Jewish nationality could reflect various stances, ranging from support of a Jewish state to a desire to strengthen Jewish identity in the diaspora to a reluctance to take sides in Czechoslovakia's Czech-German "nationality conflict." Regarding the Czech Jews and the nationality conflict until the end of World War I, see Hillel Kieval, *The Making of Czech Jewry: National Conflict and Jewish Society in Bohemia, 1870–1918* (New York and Oxford: Oxford University Press, 1988).

7 The title on the preserved script is *The Second Czech Cabaret* (II. český kabaret); the title on a souvenir poster and other materials preserved in the Heřman Collection is *Laugh with Us* (Smějte se s námi), which is one of the first lines of the opening song. The close correspondence of the names on the poster with the names of the participants listed in the text confirm that the two titles refer to the same cabaret.

8 The acts of a revue, as opposed to cabaret, are usually linked by a theme or loosely organized plot, but both are defined as popular theatrical entertainment combining music, dance, and sketches, and frequently satirizing contemporary figures, news, or literature.

9 I am grateful to Porges' sons Miroslav, Jan and Zdeněk Prokeš for access to this archive, and to survivor Hana Ledererová-Lojínová for an additional version of the script.

10 For a description of this event, see H. G. Adler, *Theresienstadt: das Antlitz einer Zwangsgemeinschaft* (Göttingen: Wallstein, 2005), 158–161.

11 The Lucerna building, located just off Wenceslas Square, includes a large hall that can seat up to 4,000 spectators, a cinema, coffeehouses, and so on.

12 For an account of the performance, see Philipp Manes, *Als ob's ein Leben wär: Tatsachenbericht Theresienstadt 1942–1944*, eds. Ben Barkow and Klaus Leist (Berlin: Ullstein, 2005), 178.

13 Hofer is featured in several posters preserved in the Heřman collection, including PT 3850, 3911, 3981, 4072–4076, 4045 and 4194–95.

14   See Heřman PT 4045.

15   See, for example, the souvenir poster for a performance of Yitzkhok Leibush Peretz's *The Golden Chain* and Scholem Aleichem's *Tevye the Milkman*, Heřman PT 3918. Weisz came from the Carpatho-Ukrainian region that formed the eastern tip of interwar Czechoslovakia and may have been a native Yiddish speaker.

16   In the Zionist movement, the *shaliach* devoted himself above all to educating youth and preparing them for emigration to Palestine.

17   Maccabi groups were branches of an international Jewish sports organization. The first Czechoslovak chapter was founded in 1919. See Ruth Bondy, *Mezi námi řečeno: Jak mluvili Židé v Čechách a na Moravě* (Prague: Nakladatelství Franze Kafky, 2003), 90.

18   The Book of Esther describes events that took place in Shushan, the capital city of Persia, in the fifth century BCE. The Persian king, Ahasuerus, has been deceived by the villain Haman into agreeing to the murder of the Jews. Haman, the king's minister, begins to plot against the Jews after Mordechai, Ahasuerus's Jewish doorkeeper, refuses to bow to him; as a Jew, Mordechai bows only before God. Haman tells Ahasuerus that the Jews are disobeying the king's laws and requests a decree granting the enemies of the Jews the right to kill them all on the appointed day: the thirteenth of Adar. The king agrees, not knowing that Esther, his second wife, the young and beautiful queen, is a Jewish orphan and Mordechai's niece. When Esther reveals Haman's plot to the king, Ahasuerus sentences Haman to death. Although he cannot annul his own royal decree, he issues a second decree granting the Jews permission to defend themselves, and they triumph over their enemies.

19   Huha Horra: probably the *hora* (also spelled *horah*), a circle dance often performed to the Hebrew folk song "Hava Nagila," which is perhaps the song the actors are singing as they enter. The significance of "Huha" is unclear; perhaps it is just a comic twist on the name of the dance.

20   During Purim, a carnivalesque holiday, it is traditional to overturn hierarchical relationships of power. Although other Czech- and German-language cabarets satirize the Jewish leaders of the ghetto, this is the only script in the collection that satirizes the leaders in their presence.

21   Opportunities to perform in German in postwar Czechoslovakia were not plentiful, but in the 1950s, he was engaged with the German-language traveling troupe of the Czechoslovak Rural Theater. The Rural Theater (*Vesnické divadlo*), later known as the State Traveling Theater (*Státní zájezdové divadlo*), was founded in October 1945 and brought theatrical performances to rural areas of Czechoslovakia. In 1954, a troupe performing in German was adding to the already existing ten Czech-language troupes to serve the few German speakers still living in the border regions of Czechoslovakia. See Jaroslav Pucherna, ed., *Přijelo divadlo: patnáct let putování za divákem* (Prague: Státní zájezdové divadlo, 1961).

22   Estimates vary, but according to the most frequently quoted statistics, of the 43,000 Jews who had returned to Czechoslovakia after the war, 15,000–19,000 left in 1948–1949 for Israel. See Petr Brod, "Židé v poválečném československsku," in *Židé v novodobých dějinách*, ed. V. Veber (Prague: Karolinum, 1997), 151.

23   I am grateful to Dr Eva Šormová, Luděk Eliáš, Miloš Dvorák, Jirí Schmiedt, Vojtěch Kynčl, Edward Einhorn, and Josef Horáček for their help in recovering, interpreting, translating, and developing the script, and to my colleagues Dr Alan Sikes of Louisiana State University and Mark France of the University of York for their help in devising the adaptation and performance.

CHAPTER TWENTY EIGHT

Performing History: *Jongos*, *Quilombos*, and the Memory of Illegal Atlantic Slave Trade in Rio de Janeiro, Brazil[1]

HEBE MATTOS AND MARTHA ABREU

The 1988 Brazilian Constitution opened the door to the development of policies of reparation in relation to African slavery in Brazil. Among them is the possibility of granting collective ownership rights to traditional black communities known as "remaining members of *quilombo*" and of officially recognizing the legacy of enslaved peoples as intangible cultural heritage.

The Southeastern *jongo*, a manifestation of song, verse, dance, and percussion whose origin is attributed to African slaves from the former coffee-growing regions of Southeastern Brazil, was recognized as Brazilian cultural heritage in 2005. In this chapter, we highlight the social background of the *jongo* performers to understand how their struggle against racism and for ownership of traditional lands enables a shift of meanings that transformed their performances into a public counter-narrative about their slave past.

In particular, this chapter discusses the process of identifying three black communities in the state of Rio de Janeiro as remaining members of *quilombo* on the basis of research carried out during our work as specialists in compiling the technical surveys that were part of the legal proceedings for government titling of lands. The communities are the São José da Serra *quilombo* in the municipality of Valença; the Bracuhy *quilombo* in Angra dos Reis; and the Pinheiral *quilombo* in the city by the same name. These groups hold the art of *jongo* as intangible cultural heritage, and today, through public performances, they are making it a symbol of a past that must be honored and made known. To that end, the chapter also reflects upon the new dimensions of the profession of historian in Brazil as interlocutor in the processes of patrimonialization of cultural manifestations and recognition of constitutional rights.[2]

A Companion to Public History, First Edition. Edited by David Dean.
© 2018 John Wiley & Sons Ltd. Published 2018 by John Wiley & Sons Ltd.

Jongos and *Quilombos*: Public policies and politics of the past

Article 68 of the Temporary Constitutional Provisions Act (ADCT) of the 1988 Brazilian Constitution recognized the territorial rights of "remaining members of the *quilombo* communities," ensuring them definitive ownership by the Brazilian State.[3] To understand the wording of Article 68 and its inclusion among the temporary constitutional provisions, we have to first and foremost take into account how Brazil's black movements gained momentum throughout the 1980s, and proposed a revised notion of slavery and abolition in the public mind. The image of the young white Princess Isabel de Orleans e Bragança liberating submissive and well-treated slaves by decree, disseminated for decades in Brazilian textbooks, came to be contrasted with the image of a cruel and violent system in which black slaves resisted, especially by escaping and forming autonomous communities known as *quilombos* (maroon communities), which were very important in the Brazilian abolition process. In a limited interpretation of the constitutional provision, only remaining members of settlements that once belonged to runaway slaves were protected by the constitutional article, which should have facilitated their approval in discussions of temporary constitutional provisions.

However, in the late twentieth century, most of the many rural black communities spread around Brazil that had experienced disputes over recognition of traditional ownership of collective lands, generally identified pejoratively as "negro lands," were not always associated with the historical definition of *quilombo* as a settlement for runaway slaves. Some even boasted origin stories that involved land bequeathed within the context of abolition. These communities, with special support from the Brazilian Anthropological Association, began to claim that Article 68 ought to apply to them as well, since the experience of racism and the stigma attached to collective land ownership of "negro lands" linked them to the memory of slavery and afforded them a new, now positive, meaning for their ethnic identity as remaining members of *quilombo* while demanding reparation for historical injustice. Not without controversy, this combination of public policies, rural activism, and academic research led to an important process of ethnogenesis whereby traditional populations were able to mobilize a memory of ancestral slavery, giving rise to the contemporary *quilombola* social movement. At the same time, in anthropological and juridical spheres, the interpretations that had taken into account the semantic shift regarding the word *quilombo* for purposes of enforcing the constitutional provision began to prevail, adding value to the context of cultural resistance that had enabled the historical establishment of such communities (Mattos 2008).

Decree 4887 of November 20, 2003, approved to regulate Article 68 of the Constitution, more carefully examined this interpretation, emphasizing its nature as reparation for Brazil's historical debt with regard to the experience of slavery. According to the decree, "the characterization of the remaining members of the *quilombo* communities will be attested by the self-definition of the community itself," understanding them as "ethnic-racial groups according to criteria of self-attribution with their own historical trajectory, characterized by specific territorial relationships, with the presumption of black ancestry related to the historical resistance to oppression endured." Since the publication of this decree, the Palmares Cultural Foundation, an agency of the Ministry of Culture that maintains close ties with activists in the Brazilian black movement, has begun the work of certifying the communities that have petitioned for recognition as remaining members of *quilombo*. By 2014, the foundation had certified more than 1,500 communities as remaining members of *quilombo* (Palmares Cultural Foundation 2015).

Palmares certification gives rights to access public policies in the field of health and education that have been drawn specially for the *quilombolas* communities in the last decade. The certification is also necessary for opening an administrative process for receiving the collective ownership of the land that operates in another governmental agency, the National Institute of Agrarian Reform (INCRA). For official recognition and legal entitlement, an anthropological report and many legal issues apply, including expropriation of absentee legal owners by the state, with compensation or not, depending on the case. Even after official recognition, legal contestation is possible, and the final ownership title is, in most of the cases, a question decided by the judicial system. Because of that, the number of communities officially recognized and legally entitled is small up this point. But certification built a legal personality for the *quilombola* communities, with collective rights to land protected by the state, even if the amount of land it should really occupy is in dispute.[4]

The 1988 Constitution further expanded the notion of rights and extended them to cultural practices. In addition to Article 68 of the ADCT, Articles 215 and 216 of the 1988 Constitution also established important potential changes in the understanding of Brazilian cultural heritage, which came to be defined as "assets of a tangible and intangible nature, taken individually or as a whole, which bear reference to the identity, action and memory of the various groups that form the Brazilian society." The image of Brazilian cultural heritage, once identified only by magnificent brick and mortar buildings, began to include the notion of intangible heritage, identified by diversity and expressions of popular culture.

The prospects introduced by the constitutional articles became even brighter following the approval of Decree 3551 in 2000, which regulated the recognition and preservation of intangible cultural heritage and became a favorite theme of the Ministry of Culture with the arrival of the Luiz Inácio Lula da Silva administration in 2002. The decree allowed even international recognition of popular cultural assets of recognized Afro-descendancy, which included such things as the *samba de roda* of the Recôncavo Baiano, the culinary art of the *baianas do acarajé*, Maranhão's *tambor de crioula*, the roots of Rio de Janeiro's samba (*partido alto*, *samba de terreiro* and *samba enredo*), the artistry of the *capoeira* masters and circles, the musical rhythms of the Northeastern *maracatu*, and the Brazilian folk theatrical tradition of *bumba-meu-boi* (IPHAN 2014). By regulating the possibility of recognizing intangible cultural manifestations as national heritage, the 2000 Decree paved the way for those who claimed identity as *quilombolas* (communities of remaining members of *quilombo*) to be granted cultural heritage status for their cultural manifestations. Emergence of the new *quilombo* communities, in a process that has been national in scope although conceived largely within the context of territorial disputes, is today closely associated with the parallel movement of patrimonialization of the intangible culture identified with Afro-Brazilian populations, and the *quilombos* themselves have been recognized as cultural heritage (Mattos and Abreu 2011).

The new ways of thinking about the status of national cultural heritage has enabled several social groups, by using the new laws and with the support of experts, to revise the images and allegories of their past and begin to determine what they wish to remember and define as their identity, through various performative expressions such as festivals, songs, dances, and an oral tradition replete with particular ways of speaking and acting. The possession of cultural heritage related to the experience of slavery and memories of Africa or the slave trade have therefore become symbols of cultural resistance, capable of strengthening the territorial claims for collective land title rights for peasant groups that may potentially be classified as *quilombolas*.

In the old slaveholding Southeast, the region we studied, the association between memories of captivity and the legacy of *jongo* are quite clear. As mentioned at the beginning of this chapter, the Southeastern *jongo* was recognized as Brazilian cultural heritage in 2005. It is a cultural expression that features the Afro-descendants of populations from the slaveholding coffee-growing regions of Southeastern Brazil that received the final waves of enslaved Africans, after independence had been declared in the first half of the nineteenth century. According to historian Robert Slenes (2013), the current reemergence of the *jongo* in several *quilombo* and other communities of the Southeast is one of the greatest indications of the cultural strength exerted by the presence of Central African slaves during the nineteenth century in the former coffee-growing regions. According to Slenes, words we hear in twenty-first century *jongo* circles were already part of the lives of enslaved nineteenth-century *jongueiros* and their Central African ancestors. Sung using African words or encrypted Portuguese, their meanings were not understood by the uninitiated.

The presence of bonfires and, hence, fire in the Southeastern *jongo* harken back to the symbolic elements that were important to African religiosity, such as ancestor worship. All over the Atlantic region and even in inland Central Africa, one could find *puítas* and drums like the *caxambu/angoma* and their smaller companion. The word *ngoma* was used to refer to the largest of the drums, whose single face was tuned with the heat of the fire. Dancing couples moving in a circle, a trademark of present-day Southeastern *jongo*, were described by nineteenth-century travelers in interior Luanda and Southwestern Angola. The lyrics and verses, interactions between soloist and chorus in a call-and-response pattern during work or leisure, in turn represented typical characteristics of Central African songs from the region of the ancient Kingdom of Kongo. Also, according to Robert Slenes (2013), several themes of *jongo* songs that we know today were sung around the region of Congo and Angola in the early twentieth century as challenges between local leaders, master *jongueiros* known as *cumbas*.

The linguistic, musical, and religious proximities to the Bantu peoples certainly created cohesive elements between the experiences of captivity and the art of the Southeastern *jongo*, even after abolition and well into the twentieth century (Monteiro and Stone 2013). The link between the new heritage agenda that valued Afro-Brazilian cultural expressions – raised to the status of icons related to "resistance to historical oppression endured" (as stated in Federal Decree 4887) – and the actions involved in claiming title as remaining members of *quilombo* appears to be growing in the old slaveholding Southeast. In this context, there has been increased interest in historical research into the memory phenomena that exist among the groups in question. At the same time, the *quilombola* movement, increasingly more knowledgeable about its rights, is using the recognition of historiographical knowledge and its academic authority to strengthen and legitimize its demands.

The case of the São José da Serra community, the rural descendants of slaves from the municipality of Valença in the state of Rio de Janeiro, officially recognized today as the São José da Serra *quilombo*, is exemplary (Mattos 2008). Dancing and drumming were everyday practices of the group, but as Manoel Seabra, one of the community's oldest members, stated in an interview given in 2005 such expressions have gained new significance with dissemination of the possibilities afforded by new legislation from the Palmares Foundation technical staff and numerous researchers who began to contact them:

We didn't know the value of the drums...But they have great value, right? For the whole world, right? After we [started] dealing with you, we realized what great value they have! ... And this is why we need to preserve them because they are very important. (Petrobas Cultural Collection 2005)

In 2014, after years of legal process, the São José *quilombo* finally received the title of most of the lands claimed. But since the 1990s, it had been holding a big public festival, which has attracted thousands of people, on May 13, the day Brazil signed the law abolishing slavery. The 2005 celebration is recorded in the video documentary *Memórias do Cativeiro/Memories of Captivity* (2005). Thousands of people took part in the community event. On numerous occasions, the *jongo* group from the São José *quilombo* has been invited to give public performances at theaters in Brazil's major cities (Figure 28.1).

Figure 28.1   The Jongo Circle of the Quilombo São José. Photo LABHOI/UFF (2005).

In the words of Antônio Nascimento Fernandes, political leader of the *quilombo*, in an interview with the Laboratory of Oral History and Image at the Universidade Federal Fluminense (LABHOI/UFF) during the group's trip to the Banco do Brasil Cultural Center in Rio de Janeiro, in 2003:

And the jongo at the São José da Serra community, I'm going to talk a little about the *jongo*. The *jongo* of the São José da Serra *quilombo* is one of the things that we know is a good thing, because that's how the *jongo* was created: during slavery, blacks came all the way from Africa and when they got to Brazil, they did everything they could to be able to change, establish relationships, some degree of kinship. Everyone brought their own language to the place ... they didn't even speak the same dialect ... to compound the situation in the community ... on the plantations. And in the *jongo*, the blacks organized themselves through chants. So they began to sing ... and by singing, they got to know each other through the chants and that led to courtships in the coffee fields. And they began to trust each other. And that's also how the *quilombo* was established. Because *jongo* is an undecipherable chant. The guy would sing, arrange who would run away, how he would run away, when he would run away and who he would run away with. But the foremen who spent all day in the coffee fields had no idea of any of that. And so it was, and as time passed, they started to establish *quilombos.* There was the one from Palmares and then came other *quilombos* like the one in São José da Serra today ...

By establishing the bylaws [of the Quilombo Residents Association] we said that only those who were born in the community, relatives of the community, could stay, but through the association. Someone from outside, to get back to the community, has to go through the association. So if someone moves out of the community, their house stays in the community and goes to the association. The association takes care of it ...

But I also see *jongo* as the salvation for everything. We ... come to Rio, in fact tomorrow we'll be here at the Banco do Brasil, and this type of thing makes the people in our community very optimistic, because over in the district of Santa Isabel no one travels more than the São José da Serra community. And I let them know that, and do you know why? It's because of the *jongo*, it's our calling card. And what is it that *jongo* has to have? Connection. Without connection, it doesn't work. The *jongo* doesn't sing or dance by itself, it needs a group. So this is what we've really been working on with the children ... tomorrow we're going to be there with the children ... six-year-old, five-year-old kids dancing the *jongo* ... there are little kids there, two-year-olds who already know ... put them in and they know what to do. It's something we couldn't have done before, but now we let them [be]cause I think the community's salvation will be the *jongo*. (Petrobas Cultural Collection 2005)

Like the São José da Serra community, other *jongueiro* communities are politically reaffirming their historical trajectory and ethnic and cultural authenticity in the new legal context, gaining visibility and new perspectives for collective survival. Through cultural performances, they are strengthening their ties to the culture of the African diaspora and the group's self-worth in the fight against racism. Their performative practices are producing a counter-narrative of their slave past and of black culture, despite the fact that scholars and folklorists have predicted its disappearance as a result of the death of the Africans and the pressures of modern life since at least the early decades of the twentieth century (Abreu and Mattos 2013).

Performing history: The memory of slavery in the cases of Bracuhy and among the *jongo* performers of Pinheiral

In addition to the São José da Serra *quilombo*, other Afro-descendants of the Southeast, such as the Bracuhy and Pinheiral communities discussed in this second part of the chapter, have associated the memory of slavery with the struggle for land title, beginning with the public performance of *jongo* as inherited and reconstructed cultural heritage. In the forms of dancing and singing, of playing and making special percussion instruments, of narrating the stories heard from the elders, the Southeastern *jongo* performance group evokes memories of former coffee plantations situated in the Paraíba do Sul River Valley, bringing to life the memory of old coastal plantations associated with the illegal slave trade from Africa and redefining the research agenda of the professional historians in contact with them. It is precisely this aspect we wish to emphasize now: how the emergence of the memory of the illegal African slave trade tragedy, through the performative practices of the *jongueiros*, came to strengthen these group's demands for policies of reparation (Mattos 2013).

The history, memory, and trajectory of the Bracuhy *quilombo* near the city of Angra dos Reis in present-day southern Rio de Janeiro State is a prime example of the process described above. Its residents, descendants of former slaves, today present a rich oral tradition from which they build their identity as remaining members of *quilombo*. By accompanying this process, in addition to the *jongo* performances, we are witnessing oral traditions that have directly dialogued with the historical records of the past. These oral traditions have provided us with assistance in revisiting many of the all but forgotten aspects of the history of illegal Atlantic slave trade in the region involving the ancestors of the new *quilombolas*.

A particular repertoire of narratives passed verbally from parent to child encouraged and continue to justify the Bracuhy group's presence in the region, despite several attempts to expel it since the late nineteenth century. These narratives may be referred to cryptically in the *jongo* songs, but they exist in an organized fashion beyond the space of the *jongo* circle. At the heart of the narratives is preservation of the memory of the will written by the former master, Commander José de Souza Breves, great coffee-producing slaveholder and owner of several plantations who in 1878 willed plots of land to a group of freed slaves, ancestors of many of the current residents. The plots of land granted on one of his seaside plantations along the southern coast of present-day Rio de Janeiro State established the community's current territory and its network of kinship and solidarity. The memory of this inheritance in land also ended up turning the freed heirs into guardians of memory and witnesses to the old plantation's use in receiving illegally enslaved Africans (Pessoa 2013).[5]

The oral tradition, transmitted through rich narratives known as "stories" – the term used by the narrators themselves – constitutes one of the most important bases for the group's identity and possession of its territory. The group took up the public narrative of the stories told by elders during the process of *quilombo* identification, and by doing so, reinforced the more systematic return of the *jongo* circles as public performances of encrypted song, percussion, and dance, taught by the elders to the group's younger members. If the *jongo* seems to have been forgotten for a time, telling stories to children, nieces, nephews, and grandchildren about enslaved ancestors freed and made heirs to land from the estate was a continual strategy employed by the elders of an illiterate community so that the past could remain in the present, and that moreover, the right to ownership of the inherited land, which included a small cemetery alongside a Catholic chapel, would never be forgotten. The cemetery, built during the time of captivity, made a distinction between the plantation's slave community and recent arrivals known as "new-blacks," who according to oral tradition often died while recovering from the Atlantic crossing and were taken there to be buried on Cabral's Hill without religious rites (Petrobas Cultural Collection 2006).

The oral tradition, along with the *jongo* songs, refers to stories from the region, on this side and beyond the Bocaína Forest in the coffee-growing Paraíba Valley of Southeastern Brazil. They are presented against the backdrop of former coffee plantations or the buildings that remain out of the sugarcane and rum mills of the Atlantic coast plantations. The protagonists are slaves, generally named among the heirs of Commander José de Souza Breves. The amount of repetition and coincidence in the story narratives as well as form of intonation shared by various residents of Bracuhy are performative practices that confer a special intensity to the statements. They can be seen accompanied by English subtitles, in a sequence of the documentary *Passados Presentes: Memória Negra no Sul Fluminense/A Present Past: Afro-Brazilian Memories in Rio de Janeiro* (2011), which highlights the narrative and physical performance by the tellers of the stories. The complete narratives can be found in the LABHOI/UFF Petrobras Cultural Collection.[6] These audiovisual records, containing over 300 hours of performances and interviews given by black peasants, the descendants of former slaves from Southeastern Brazil, were produced as part of a research project we conducted about the social memory of *jongo* in the region.[7]

The performative nature of the narratives focuses on the oral tradition of the Bracuhy *quilombo*. However, this tradition presents several coincidences with regard to narratives found in other *jongo* communities of the slaveholding Southeast, analyzed in the book *Memories of Captivity* (Rios and Mattos 2005) and the documentary film with the same title.[8] As noted in that project, which brought together 61 different testimonials by descendants of slaves from the coffee-growing regions of Southeast Brazil born in the early decades of the twentieth century, those interviewed rarely used the word "slave" or "slavery," preferring instead to use terms such as "captive" and "captivity," introducing the notion of the "time of captivity" as a more general reference of periodization. The idea of enslavement is that it focuses on the specific use that the interviewee makes of the word *captive*. In the interviews, life in captivity is almost always narrated through incidents and stories passed down from parents and grandparents. Generally speaking, these stories say nothing directly with regard to the experiences of the original storytellers (parents or grandparents), but instead talk of narratives passed down from parent to child because they are known, or known through hearsay. In this respect, it is a generic memory of slavery associated with notions of violence, torture, and mistreatment as well as with the power of the master and his desire to do good or evil. If the stories refer generally to distant characters out of family memories themselves, it is the family relationship or the specific cases of violence that befell them that the narratives emphasize, to the extent that they become more personal and refer directly to memories of experiences by ancestors of the interviewees. The power and significance of primary relationships (father, mother, children) are what are most evident in the narratives, and they define the originality and humanization of the interviewee's ancestors in the face of captivity's generic dehumanization.

The set of narratives of the old Southeastern slaves gathered together in the book *Memories of Captivity* (2005) produced an ethnotext, according to the meaning of the word used by Philippe Joutard (1980) that has a particular style and content in which the narratives from Bracuhy could also be included. Of primary importance in them is the fact that the "time of captivity" seems to be defined largely by a sense of humans reduced to the condition of mere commodity through violence. Their herd status and the association with livestock breeding are recurring themes in the various testimonials, especially in references to the preference for long-legged negroes when buying slaves, and to the act of eating at feed troughs like animals. The physical punishments also essentially define this time in various narratives with all manner of cruelty, often associated with a "magic spell," in other words, punishment of the torturer by the magical powers of the tortured captive – the death of the children in cases of jealous mistresses, suicides, incurable diseases, total loss of harvest, fires, and so on – always defined as foreign and African. Despite this, in most cases and for various reasons, the parents or grandparents of the narrators were not subject to the conditions generally attributed to the time of captivity. As members of the more deep-rooted slave community, they define themselves as exceptions, reaching out for the experience of freedom, and they consider themselves as people, not as things, and as Brazilians, not as foreigners (Memories of Captivity 2005).

Among this collection of testimonials from the Southeast, however, the Bracuhy narratives offer a performative uniqueness, standing out because of their dialogue with the specific history of slaves from the old Bracuhy plantation. One of the stories told about the landing of Africans at the mouth of the river by the same name had a particular impact on our activities as professional historians in the field of slavery and post-abolition research. The story referred directly to the history of the crackdown on illegal slave trade of Africans in Brazil, a topic we had been studying closely by researching nineteenth-century archives (Mattos and Schnoor 1995). Its development in the collective memory of the group came as a complete surprise to us, however. According to the narrative of Mr. Moraes (2007), one of the oldest residents of the Bracuhy *quilombo*:

> This was the point of arrival and departure for Commander Souza Breves when the slaves came and went ... Here was where, aside from the docks, there was also a fattening station, you know? It was hereabouts, although I don't know where exactly, where the newly arrived slaves, when they were at sea, they didn't eat well and lost their value, they got skinny and sick. So they were of no value. So they kept them here. They'd spend some 20 days here.
>
> The story I heard ... is that ... when the last boat came up here full of slaves, it was already illegal to sell them. But I don't know how they did it, they still managed to get the opportunity to round up some slaves to sell here again. They kidnapped some slaves and filled the boat up with them and brought them here. And they got up to here. Around some island ... What was it called? Cunhambebe Island. An island back there ... The boat went in up there ... in order to bring the people up here. And that's when they saw that they had a police escort coming up behind them to arrest them ... So the story goes that they scuttled the boat: the boat had a hole ... they pulled out a plug and let the water in. Some of the slaves fell overboard and many were saved, but a bunch of them died and the boat sank right off the point of that island. Back in the day, people still talked about that boat and folks liked to fish there because it attracted a lot of fish. People were always fishing there. (A Present Past 2011)

In this testimonial by Mr. Manoel Moraes, grandson of the slaves owned by José Breves, we were surprised to again find a story we had come across in previous research, which had led to the 1995 publishing of the book *Resgate – Uma Janela para o oitocentos/Rescue - A Window into the Nineteenth Century*, edited by Hebe Mattos and Eduardo Schnoor. It is a collection of essays by several historians about a large coffee plantation known as the Resgate Plantation in the São Paulo region of the Paraíba Valley, and its owner Manoel de Aguiar Vallim. Among the authors, Martha Abreu (1995) was responsible for the research and writing of a piece about Vallim's involvement in what is known as the "Bracuhy incident," a clandestine landing of African slaves in 1852 on the grounds of the Santa Rita do Bracuhy plantation then owned by José Breves. The crackdown on the landing resulted in the arrest of his brother, Joaquim Breves, his neighbor Pedro Ramos and Vallim himself, owner of the Resgate plantation. More than 15 years later, the case took on new proportions according to the narratives of Mr. Manoel Moraes and other residents of the present-day Bracuhy *quilombo*. In the midst of an oral history interview, in the middle of fieldwork, we discovered a lively tale about the powerful slave traders that made no mention of Vallim (who owned land only in Bananal), but that practically brought José Breves and Pedro Ramos to life. The dialogue between memory and historical research is the recurring theme of the documentary *A Present Past: Afro-Brazilian Memories in Rio de Janeiro* (2011) mentioned here earlier.

The landing that became known as "the Bracuhy incident" was one of the last to take place in the waters of Angra dos Reis, close to the mouth of the Bracuhy River. The narrative of Mr. Moraes processed over time is clearly an oral version of the episode that occurred in 1852 when the imperial government spared no expense to show its intention to eliminate the African slave trade in Brazil. So intent was it that, in order to capture Africans who were illegally enslaved, it would venture into the slave quarters of the powerful owners of coffee plantations in the region of Bananal, on lands owned by Vallim in the São Paulo Paraíba Valley, connected to the mouth of the Bracuhy River by a road through the Serra do Mar. In the version offered by Mr. Moraes, many slaves died

because the boat was sunk so that it would not be found. We have proof that the slave
ship in question – the brig *Camargo* – did in fact sink because its captain had given the
order to set it on fire (Abreu 1995). According to newspaper accounts at the time, however, the Africans would have landed and been sold off among the plantation owners up
the mountain. The deaths reported by Mr. Moraes may have been from other landings
associated with this one in collective memory, or may have been omitted from the discussions that at the time ensued in the Brazilian press. According to these discussions, in
December 1852, 540 Africans from Quelimane and the isle of Mozambique disembarked from the brig *Camargo* on the grounds of the Santa Rita do Bracuhy plantation.[9]

Manoel Moraes, one of the oldest *jongueiros* in the community, has lived on the
grounds of the Santa Rita do Bracuhy plantation for over 80 years. His maternal and
paternal grandparents were slaves owned by Commander José de Souza Breves. "Preto
Forro," as his paternal grandfather was known, and Antônio Joaquim da Silva, his maternal grandfather, lived out the final years of slavery on the plantation. Both were freed in
the 1870s and listed as legatees of the estate in the Commander's will, written in 1877
and opened in 1879 (Museum of Justice of Rio de Janeiro State n.d.). According to him,
it was his parents and grandparents who perpetuated the memories of the stories that he
continued to tell as if he had actually known the plantation owners himself.

From the oral testimony of Mr. Moraes, repeated through similar narrative performances by other residents, we have structured our new research study around the use of
this oral tradition as a source for the history of how plantations in the region were organized to receive illegal slave trade. The dialogue between oral tradition, written sources,
and archeological sites related to the Atlantic slave trade in the area has since then continued to be a source of research (Mattos 2013).

Santa Rita do Bracuhy, purchased in 1829, besides having the infrastructure to
accommodate the landing of Africans, productively organized itself for the Atlantic
enterprise, specializing in the production of sugarcane rum, which it used to trade for
slaves in Africa (Pessoa 2013). Nowadays, the ruins of the old sugarcane mill are still
visible. They are but a few indications of tangible heritage that have withstood the passage of time. Only someone who knows the site is able to pick out the stones that are
partially hidden and scattered among the dense vegetation. We visited the ruins in 2007,
accompanied by Mr. Romão, resident of the region and, according to his own words,
descendant of Africans. His mother, Maria Romão Custódio, talked about how her
ancestors had come from Africa. Enslaved along with many others, they were the ones
who would have built the mill. The performance by Mr. Romão in describing the ruins
and the group's history on the lands of the old plantation may also be seen in the
documentary *A Present Past* (2011).

In the new context, the nature of the crime against humanity embodied in the slave
trade and the role of the group as guardians of the memory of such practices is becoming
increasingly important in the public interpretation of the past through oral tradition and
jongo circles. The heritage built through the stories, memories, *jongos*, and ruins is
becoming a tribute to the African origins of their ancestors and is granting entitlement,
meaning, and shape to the group's new *quilombola* identity. With the support of professional historians and access to public funding for the preservation of intangible heritage,
the group is now beginning to organize in order to achieve economic sustainability
through memory tourism, seeking to make its history visible by organizing historical
tours inside the community along with festivals to honor Saint Rita, the patron saint of
Bracuhy (Mattos and Abreu 2014).

Not far from the Bracuhy *quilombo*, on land also owned by Commander José de Souza Breves, higher up the mountain along the banks of the Paraíba do Sul River, sits the small city of Pinheiral. Living there are those who today claim title as remaining members of *quilombo* based on the cultural heritage of the *jongo* inherited from their ancestors. Most are the descendants of slaves from nearby plantations who migrated to the area near the old Breves mansion (which in the early twentieth century was also a railway station and agricultural school), either in search of better opportunities or because they had been expelled from their small plots of land in successive waves following abolition in 1888. Organized as the Jongo de Pinheiral Reference Center, they perform *jongos* and engage in storytelling on the site of the ruins of the once magnificent Pinheiro plantation, central location and residence of the powerful Commander José de Souza Breves, and its surroundings which include the former garden, coffee fields, and old slave quarters that have been refurbished as residences. During the final minutes of the film *A Present Past* (2011), the group performs in front of the old mansion, now in ruins. At that point, a *jongo* verse refers directly to the history of abolition experienced by the group's ancestors:

> *Eu tava dormindo*/I was sleeping
> *Carimbomba/Angoma me chamou*/When the cangoma drums called me
> *Acorda povo*/They said "rise up people"
> "*Cativeiro acabou*"/Captivity is over.

The group also conducts guided tours of the city, recounting the history of the practice of *jongo* at the site since slavery times. The group is considering filing a claim for identification as "remaining members of *quilombo*" as a way to obtain legal access to ownership of the land alongside the mansion, understood to be a place of remembrance on which to celebrate black festivals and the cultural heritage of the group's ancestors in the fight against discrimination and racism. The group defends its right to hold onto and revive Afro-Brazilian memories and history in the area, marked by *jongo* and slavery. Its goal is to lend visibility to an intangible cultural heritage handed down from their African slave ancestors, using the architectonic and artistic heritage, symbolic of the masters of the coffee-growing valleys. The group considers themselves to be the legitimate heirs to this tangible cultural heritage: the mansion, built by the hands of the illegally enslaved and the sacrifices of their ancestors. They represent this in their performances through singing, dancing, percussion, and storytelling at the site.

We know that preserving cultural heritage carries with it the notion that we must save what is in danger of disappearing or what we do not want to be silenced or forgotten. The performances at the Jongo de Pinheiral Reference Center, the ruins of the mansion, and the *jongo* itself constitute what must be remembered and serve as instruments of reparation to the descendants of the slaves who built the city and its cultural heritage.[10]

Conclusion: public history and the duty of remembrance in Brazil's slaveholding southeast

Negro no cativeiro	/	*Negro in captivity*
Passou tanto trabalho	/	*Worked so hard*
Ganhou sua liberdade	/	*Won his freedom*
No dia 13 de maio	/	*on May 13th*

These are lyrics to a *jongo* still sung today in some of the new *quilombos* of Brazil's Southeast. It is not hard to find among the elderly in these communities those who claim to be grandchildren of a "May thirteen-er" and who can tell stories of the time of captivity, just like their grandparents told them. Our research clearly shows what little significance there is, from a historical perspective, in the time that separates twenty-first-century Brazil from a time when Brazilians were divided between free citizens (from a wide variety of backgrounds and about whom color was rarely mentioned) and slaves (all of them descendants of Africans often with their color of origin recorded in their very names – José Preto, Antônio Pardo, Maria Crioula, etc.). By breaking the silence, the "negro lands" appeared first, followed by the memories of slavery and the slave trade, the *jongos*, and spaces for celebrating and performing the African past. The new cultural heritage that is emerging today and includes such things as *jongos*, *sambas de roda*, *maracatus*, and *folias de reis* (king's processions), even if they do not always go on to become *quilombos*, is also breaking the silence to reveal a new pride about the past in the form of new demands for rights and reparations.[11]

In the three cases we studied, the performative practices of the slave past, through oral tradition, *jongo* performances, celebrations, and guided tours, reinforce the history that the groups wish to tell and make public. They lend visibility to their presence and the political fight, just as they are fed by the fight itself. Every expression strengthens the groups and becomes an essential part of the strategies that may enable political victory, even if only partial, for the groups' demands for reparation. Colonists, squatters and workers fighting for land or for rights to cultural heritage by identifying themselves first as blacks and then as *quilombolas*, have become collective political subjects. The social metamorphoses possible for such actors, however, were firmly anchored in the association between black identity and the memory of captivity, whether as family remembrance, stigma, or commemorative and cultural expression.

We also need to remember that adding a cultural heritage component to the political agenda in demanding collective land rights and *quilombo* identity did not just involve cultural expressions of music, verse, and dance associated with slavery and Afro-descendancy. It also involved the perception of the history, memory, and oral tradition of the group as heritage that must be valued, remembered, and in this way, subject to reparations. The cases of Bracuhy and Pinheiral demonstrate that the *quilombola* groups are also beginning to demand material and symbolic reparations on behalf of a duty of remembrance owed by Brazilian society with regard to the history of slavery and the illegal importation of African slaves who served as the economic basis for the birth of the Brazilian nation.

The legal act of definitive abolition of slavery in Brazil occurred by means of a law that simply declared slavery abolished and revoked provisions to the contrary on May 13, 1888, followed by celebrations that lasted another three weeks. After the law took effect, and over the course of several years, the former masters continued to organize themselves politically to demand compensation for the loss of their slave property. There was very little discussion of ways to provide reparation to the former slaves, but in the final months of the monarchy, abolitionist supporters floated the issue of the rural democracy, and discussed projects that included some type of access to land granted to the recently freed as a necessary complement to the abolition of slavery (dos Santos 2000). With regulation of ADCT Article 68 of the 1988 Constitution, more than 100 years overdue, the possibility of imagining any land for descendants of the last slaves freed in the nineteenth century is finally coming to fruition. And the memory and practice of the *jongo*, now transformed as cultural heritage, has played an important role in this rendering of accounts with the past – opening new doors to the future.

Notes

1 Translated from Portuguese by Kim Frances Olson.
2 Historical-anthropological reports are legal prerequisites for official recognition of communities as remaining members of *quilombo*. The technical survey on the São José da Serra *quilombo* was produced by Hebe Mattos and Lídia Meirelles in 1998 at the initiative of the Palmares Foundation. Reports for the Bracuhy and Pinheiral *quilombos* were prepared by the two authors of this chapter at the request of the federal government agency Instituto de Colonização e Reforma Agrária (Institute of Colonization and Agrarian Reform) in 2009 and 2010, respectively. See E.C. O'Dwyer, 2002, *Quilombos: Identidade étnica e territorialidade*, Rio de Janeiro: Editora FGV; and E.C. O'Dwyer, 2012, *O fazer antopológico e o reconhecimento de direitos constitucionais*: O caso das terras de quilombo no Estado do Rio de Janeiro, Rio de Janeiro: e papers.
3 The full text of Article 68 of the Temporary Constitutional Provisions Act states that "definitive ownership will be recognized, and the respective title will be issued by the State, to those descendants of the *quilombo* communities occupying their lands."
4 See also KOINONIA n.d., Atlas Observatória Quilombola, at http://www.koinonia.org.br/atlasquilombola/.
5 See also the documentary film *A Present Past: Afro-Brazilian Memories in Rio de Janeiro* (2011)
6 The archive catalog is available on the LABHOI/UFF website at http://labhoi.uff.br/jongos/acervo.
7 In addition to the archives, the project resulted in the documentary *Jongos, Calangos and Folias: Black Music, Memory and Poetry* (2007).
8 Memories of Captivity, directed by Hebe Mattos, Martha Abreu, Guilherme Fernandez and Isabel Castro, LABHOI/UFF, 2005 (available online with English subtitles at http://www.labhoi.uff.br/passadospresentes/en/filmes_memorias.php)
9 Among the 540 Africans, only 60 were women.
10 The Pinheiral group now has an established headquarters – the Southern Rio de Janeiro State Reference Center for Afro-Brazilian Studies (CREASF) – where it welcomes groups of visitors interested in hearing its histories and organizes community festivals to strengthen and lend additional visibility to the *jongo*. In the final part of the film *A Present Past* (2011), we recorded one of its leaders showing visitors the small museum at the group's headquarters. On display there are the *jongo* drums and posters that advertise *jongueiro* gatherings since the 1990s.
11 For information about other forms of musical performances present in the area studied, see the video documentary *Jongos, Calangos and Folias: Black Music, Memory and Poetry* (2007).

CHAPTER TWENTY NINE

Video Games as Participatory Public History

JEREMIAH MCCALL

Play with the past. Explore uncharted waters, drive hard bargains, rule the empires, fight the battles. Historical simulation games are a unique manifestation of public history because they are participatory. More than any other medium, they invite the public to play with the past, to enter virtual historical problem spaces and solve problems reflective of those faced by actors in the past. Though there is a distinction between designer and player, the act of gameplay by necessity allows players to take an active role in simulating the past. In the gameplay itself and in the forum dialogues spurred by the game, players are empowered to interact with the past and, as they do so, analyze and critique the game designers' visions of the past.

Video games like *Total War*, *Civilization*, and *Crusader Kings II* can usefully be labeled historical simulation games. They encompass historical settings and have core gameplay that models one or more systems of the past in a plausible way (McCall 2011, 2012). In the *Total War* series, for example, the player takes on the role of a political and military leader, tasked with building an empire in settings ranging from the ancient Mediterranean to feudal and early modern Europe. The player manages the economy and production of cities, researches technologies, engages in trade with other powers, and, most of all, controls the military. The actions the player takes and the choices they make as part of the core gameplay – moving armies, setting taxes, fighting battles, annexing territory, and so on – to an arguable extent simulate some of the historical actions taken by rulers in the periods modeled by the games. In the *Civilization* series, to offer a second example, the player controls the development of a civilization from its origins in the fourth millennium to the twenty-first century. The player determines where cities are founded, what resources are exploited from the terrain, what the civilization researches, constructs, trades, and so on. They also engage in diplomacy and, not uncommonly, war with other civilizations. Again, the core gameplay goes beyond the historical setting to include gameplay that abstractly models the past to some plausible extent. This category of historical simulation games includes the historical grand strategy games of

A Companion to Public History, First Edition. Edited by David Dean.
© 2018 John Wiley & Sons Ltd. Published 2018 by John Wiley & Sons Ltd.

developer Paradox such as *Crusader Kings II*, city builders such as *Children of the Nile*, and the numerous war games made by smaller-scale developers.[1] Public history, of course, can be defined in many different ways. Appreciating games as forms of public history requires us to use an expanded definition, one that includes activities in which amateurs investigate and interact with the past in such ways that academic historians are peripheral, at most influencing amateur investigations through the historical monographs they have created (Jordanova 2000; Tosh 2008). In such history-making opportunities, understanding the dialogue between the public and the past is an important goal, and so it is appropriate to explore how developers of historical simulation games approach the history referenced by their choice of game.

First of all, unlike designers of games set in fictional worlds, those developing historical games have at least some level of obligation to the documented historical record. Consider the claims Paradox Interactive makes for *Crusader Kings II*:

> Crusader Kings II explores one of the defining periods in world history in an experience crafted by the masters of Grand Strategy. Medieval Europe is brought to life in this epic title rife with rich strategic and tactical depth. (Crusader Kings II 2015)

The references this and other historical simulation game designers make to specific historical periods, characters, and concepts tie them to documentable history and create an expectation that there will be some connection between the game and the particular aspects of history that game explores. After all, there is no reason to make a game on a historical topic at all if not to leverage elements of the past to create engaging gameplay.

How do developers go about researching the historical content for such games? Our best evidence comes from developer interviews scattered across the Internet. These interviews suggest that those who design historical video games desire for their games to be historically accurate, or at least not demonstrably inaccurate. To achieve the goal of basic accuracy, developers draw upon historical evidence, but the levels and kinds of historical research they employ can vary greatly. For some developers, like Paradox and the Creative Assembly, it is a matter of conducting independent research, which generally means reading secondary and sometimes primary sources about the historical time and place. Conducting such research is a point of pride for these developers, something brought up in interviews (Gamers Nexus 2013; Mana Pool 2011; Worth Playing 2008).

The developers of the *Civilization* series, however, offer a striking contrast to the emphasis some developers place on research. Rather than conduct detailed research, the designers opt to include what they judge to be commonly known and shared historical ideas and narratives. Sid Meier, creator of the original *Civilization*, comes to this point in an interview:

> *When you were creating Civilization, how much research did you put into world history?*
> Sid: Not a whole lot. I did do a little bit of reading ... But basically, I tried to use fairly well known concepts, well known leaders, and well known technologies. I mean, it wasn't intended to be 'bizarre facts about history.' It's more like, 'Here, we all know a little bit about history, but now you get to take control of it, invent gunpowder, and the wheel, electricity, all sorts of cool stuff.' But you don't have to research to know what it is, you just know. *So you mostly based it off your personal knowledge and education?*
> Sid: Right, it was intended to be something that anybody could play. (Gamasutra 2007)

Soren Johnson (2009), lead designer of *Civilization IV*, follows Meier's lead. In a blog entry, he comments, "While designers should still be careful not to include anything factually incorrect, the value of an interactive experience is in the interplay of simple concepts, not the inclusion of numerous facts and figures."

The historical ideas formed, whether through formal research or not, are intended to serve a successful commercial game, not a monograph or some other form of historical work. This is a critical point for understanding the connection between these games and the documentable past. Though developers of historical simulation games generally seem to want to achieve some level of historical accuracy, their primary goal is to a make a successful game. The medium brings with it special design tensions. Time and again, developers and players alike note that historical detail and engaging gameplay can conflict. But what makes for engaging gameplay? One of the key elements, often cited by Gamasutra (2012), is the player's ability to make interesting choices. Historical simulation games appeal largely because they empower. Players are in a position of importance, able to participate in a model of the past, making decisions that have a lasting effect on the game world. To allow a player to experience this power, a game must present meaningful choices to the player with reasonable clarity. This can lead the designers to create choices where historically there may have been none. So, for example, historical city builders like *Imperium Romanum* allow the player to place personally every building in their fledgling Roman city, though the historical processes that determined where buildings were located were far more complicated. *Civilization* allows players to decide which resources each and every city in their empire will harvest and what each will produce. *Total War* games empower players to try virtually any formation and tactic of their choosing on the battlefield. In addition, these games create quantifiable goals through scoring systems and other metrics, embedding in their model of the past a clarity of purpose rare for historical agents (McCall 2012).

Interesting choices are of little appeal to players if they are not clearly presented along with their potential effects on the game world. One of the hallmarks of successful video games, accordingly, is that they effectively train players to play them, providing necessary information and context in discrete chunks as needed – on-time and in-demand (Gee 2003). Choosing to situate a game in the historical world can go a long way toward providing players with the background knowledge they need to make informed choices in-game. Doing so can create a comforting sense of familiarity with the game world (Destructoid 2012). A game as complex as a historical simulation, however, runs the risk of overwhelming – and thus losing – players. Too much detail and the player can become swamped, familiarity changing to overload (Johnson 2009). So, the trick for developers is to leverage the powerful benefits of a game's historical setting while avoiding the drawbacks of confounding detail. Ultimately, this requires designers to engage in a significant amount of simplification as they model their historical topics in a game. The level of detail retained in a game will vary from designer to designer. The *Civilization* series is well known for taking complicated historical processes like research, economics, diplomacy, and warfare and simplifying them into a manageable form for the player. Other games like those made by Paradox abstract historical processes less, and feature more complicated interfaces and the inclusion of a great deal more historical detail.

Regardless of the level of detail in the game, however, many details from documented history must simply be left out to make the game manageable and engaging.

Jim McNally, lead designer of Longbow Games' *Hegemony: Philip of Macedon*, calls this process "caricature" and notes:

> Why do we use a caricature of history? Because a caricature is easier to manipulate than the raw history. A caricature is a simplification that distorts the history to highlight major concepts or points of interest. Those simplified points of interest can then be manipulated by the game engine rules, much like the points of a digital model can be manipulated by an animator to create an expression or artistic image. For example, our current project, Hegemony Rome: Rise of Caesar, is not intended to be an exhaustive simulation of the Roman Empire, or Roman society, or even the life of Caesar. It focuses on a single extended military campaign, and even with that the simulated elements must be abstracted in such a way to highlight the historical concepts; distortion can illuminate. (2012)

Call it caricature, abstraction, or simplification, it is critical to the game-design process. Certain key features are emphasized while others are ignored altogether.

The process of simplifying is not the only way designers shape the historical content of their games. They convey their understandings of the past in the games' systems. In a very real sense, historical simulation games are rhetorical in that they promote principles accepted by the designers, principles often seen by the designers as common sense. It has been well discussed that the games in the *Civilization* series promote a sense of geographical determinism not unlike that hypothesized by Jared Diamond (1997) in *Guns, Germs, and Steel* (Fogu 2009; McCall 2011). Critics have also noted that despite the seemingly open-ended play in the series, the technology tree, that branching list of technologies and their prerequisite technologies, assumes a Western-style narrative of progress (Poblocki 2002). The assertions embedded in the logic of simulation games need not be so loaded, however. The city builder *CivCity Rome* places the player in the role of a city governor who ultimately must keep the inhabitants of his city happy, implying that maintaining the population's material happiness was an important goal of Roman rule (McCall 2010). The *Total War* series of games includes the effects of morale in battle. Soldiers in their games do not always fight to the death but are routed when their morale drops too low (McCall 2014). The list could go on indefinitely; simulation games operate according to the historical principles accepted by their design teams.

Upon completion, simulation games offer to players historical problem spaces, working models of spaces with environmental features, agents, goals, affordances, and constraints (McCall 2012). The initial state of a game's problem space, to the extent it is fixed, can be thought of as a historical representation. It establishes the starting state of the virtual historical world. As soon as play starts, however, the player is enabled to make important choices in order to overcome obstacles and achieve goals embedded in the problem space. The game reacts to players' choices, updates the problem space according to the logic defined by the designers, and play continues.

Necessarily, however, player interactions take the game from a historically documentable starting point to a counterfactual history. *Crusader Kings II*, for example, allows the player to start his game at various dates in European history. At any given date the map of Europe is divided into territories under the control of nobles according to the historical information the developers have been able to find. As one simple example, starting in late 1066 the player finds William of Normandy as the new king of England; starting in 1337, Edward III is king and the Hundred Years War has just started. Paradox does not stop with historical kings; barons, dukes, and counts generally map to documentable agents when that information is known, and the political boundaries of the map change to match the history of the time and place. Once the player selects a dynasty to control and starts to play, however, the game simulates the actions of all these various rulers as they engage in politics, diplomacy, war, and economics. Each ruler operates according to the rules and priorities established in the game code. In the best of circumstances, those rules and priorities authentically map to some of those that were in play in the documentable past. Even so the player's freedom of choice and the fact that artificial intelligence (AI) agents' choices are coded as probabilities, not certainties, means that the narrative of gameplay will bear similarities to the broader historical context of the period and place but likely not to the specific historical chronology. So one can centralize eleventh-century England under King Harold instead of William the Conqueror, but doing so still requires mastering feudal politics, diplomacy, and military strategy. Indeed, this ability to create an alternate history is one of the appeals of such games. "Can I do better than a historical figure did?" can be a powerful incentive for gameplay. As one player puts it when referring to the game *Civilization*, "I do consider a Civ game to be much more satisfying and engrossing when it feels like I have actively participated in the unfolding of a sweeping epic saga of humankind that spans a whole world and several millennia" (Civilization Fanatics Center Forums 2011).

Since historical simulation games generate experiences that, when played, do not map readily to documented historical chronologies, debates about their historical accuracy require a reconsideration of terms. Uricchio offers a helpful point by distinguishing between a historical representation and a historical simulation (2005). A historical representation is defined by its fixed nature. Representations, most often created in the medium of textual narrative, relay the events and causes of those events in a fixed, linear fashion which, if done according to the standards of the historical discipline, correlates to the documentary evidence for the event or phenomenon in question. Historical accuracy as a standard applied to representations means bearing a narrative or fixed illustration that is faithful to the evidence. A simulation, unsurprisingly, does not behave as a representation. It models systems and processes and requires player input, input that changes the outcome. These systems and processes, in conjunction with player interaction, lead to problems, choices, actions, and outcomes that when narrated quite probably will not correlate well to any evidence-based narrative.

What games have the potential to do, however, is provide a historically authentic simulation by modeling the effects of historically documentable systems and processes in their problem spaces. They can generate understanding of historical context, the factors that were at play in the past that led to certain outcomes over others. In this respect, they share common ground with good counterfactual history (Ferguson 1997). Whether it is a matter of planting a city in a geographically advantageous area, conducting profitable diplomacy, commanding troops, or establishing trade routes, historical simulations can model past systems potentially very well. In this way, they have the potential to be very powerful media for encouraging thought about historical processes and how they have influenced agents in the past.

Once a game is released to the public, the main wave of historical play and interpretation begins. Work on public history talks of shared authority between historians and members of the public. When it comes to simulating the past with a historical game, authority is likewise shared between designers and players. For the game does nothing without a player, and so designer and player are in a sort of active, constructive dialogue about the past through gameplay.

Though we should like to know more about players' experiences with historical simulation games, those of most are beyond our reach. The multitude of Internet forums, however, where players can and do share their thoughts and opinions about games with their peers, offer an untapped resource for investigating how players can interact with the history embedded in games. Of course, using forum posts is not without its problems. Most of all, it is very difficult to know how much the ideas of those posting are representative of the – assuredly – many more who do not post their opinions about a game. Furthermore, the number of different forums and the thousands of posts make it difficult even to guess whether a particular point of view represents the majority of posters. Still, since the forums allow essentially any gamer to participate in them, they publicize players' ideas ranging from support to analysis and criticism of their games. Forum threads, therefore, illustrate the types of experiences and understandings players *can* have interacting with these games. This is a critical point: the forums show us a range of possible interactions with the game available to anyone who wants to share their thoughts. Accordingly, a qualitative study of several forum threads can illustrate some of the ways players interact with historical games.

Before beginning, a couple of notes are in order. The source of each post on a thread is identified by the poster's user ID followed by a number in parentheses indicating the number of the post in the thread. Egregious errors in spelling or punctuation have been corrected for the sake of the reader. The genders of posters are generally not known, and so the text uses gender-neutral pronouns.

Debating the simulation of history in the forums

The topic of the first thread to be considered, Total War Forums (2013), is the portrayal of the Spartan faction in *Total War: Rome 2*, a strategy game set in the third-century-BCE Mediterranean. The original poster (OP), OJSAMPSON, alleges there have been complaints that Creative Assembly made the Spartans too weak in the game. They begin with this provocatively polemical post:

> I've seen so many threads from fans of [the movie] *300* complaining about the Spartan faction. Have you people even read a history book? The Spartans were in a MASSIVE decline at the time of this game (272 B.C.) They had discontinued the Spartan Agoge and had a pretty bad military … The fact that they're even a faction is almost wrong due to them being annihilated a few years after the game's start. *300* fans, get a history book and read some actual facts about the Spartans, not what Hollywood wants you to believe. (2013)

Significantly, the OP proposes an arguable hypothesis to answer a meaningful historical question, and they do so by using the game as the framework for the discussion. In this instance, game discussion becomes a historical debate. Note, too, that the player has actively thought about the game's models, not passively accepted them.

There are various responses to the OP. One type notes that historical accuracy needs at times to give way to gameplay. Zerik (24) has the snappiest articulation of this: "Sometimes when playing a video game, the Rule of Cool must outweigh historical accuracy." Several other posters concur, showing that like designers, players also recognize the tension between historical detail and engaging gameplay. Ethabus (5), who noted that sacrifices sometimes had to be made for gameplay, also commented: "One of the perks of the game is being able to change history." SusaVile (14) concurred: "I really don't want to follow history, I want to recreate history, that's the idea here." These comments reveal players that are firmly aware that through their gameplay they are creating their own narratives that will, by definition, differ from documented historical narratives. Sarog (20), provides an intriguing take on the idea of players changing history:

> The game involves changing history in the sense of exploring military counterfactuals. What if Carthage had won the Punic Wars? What if Gaul was never conquered? etc. This ability to change history really only involves battles won and lost, factions risen and fallen, the way empires become drawn on the map. That is not some kind of broad break with history. The factions, the map, the unit rosters, all continue to remain bound by historical confines. Taking a faction that failed historically, and turning it into a great empire, is your objective in Rome II. Changing that faction, remaking it into your own image, is not .... Things like Sparta's unit limit exist for very good historical reasons, and if you want to triumph as Sparta you must overcome its historical flaws. By all means, change history. But do it credibly, without demanding that the flaws of your chosen faction be conveniently forgotten so that you can have an easier time of it.

This is a particularly interesting post because it touches on the differences between representation and simulation. Sarog's point here is essentially consistent with what Uricchio has written about representations versus simulations. Furthermore, Sarog considers operating within historical limits adds an entertaining challenge to the game.

There are a number of posts arguing against the OP's position. One of the more substantial comes from Banta (27), who writes:

> Lol. Sorry bud, but you're wrong. By 272 BCE, Sparta is still in her 200 year period of DECLINE, where she continually becomes less of a regional power. This collapse comes to a head in 146 BCE when Rome absorbs Greece as a full province ...

The post continues in this vein, then concludes with the following:

> Lastly, I'd like to point two things out. First, ... the player is allowed to manipulate and completely alter history, so to some degree the only historical accuracy that matters is the history before the start of 272 BCE. Second, there are how many footnote nations in this game that can be brought to power. Do I need to name a few? [the poster does] The only notable nation to resist Roman rule, and even to beat Rome on many accounts, are the Parthians. It would be a pretty shallow game if you could only play Rome, Egypt, or the Parthians.

Like Sarog, Banta fully agrees that historical accuracy, if that means matching the documentable past, can only pertain to the very start of the game. This authoritative sounding post not only provides a substantial historical argument against the OP, but it also delves into the connection between history and gameplay, noting that the inclusion of historically weak factions is a desirable concession to gameplay because it broadens the players' options for play. What comes next is something of a rarity in the forums but still worth noting. Poster ThOms (39) quotes Banta (27) and asks: "Your source," to which Banta responds with a demonstrably true statement: "Paul Cartledge: The Spartans, and A History of Sparta: W G Forrest. Both leading experts in Spartan history." Not only does the debate probe a legitimate historical issue, there is even some source criticism at work.

There are a number of other interactions in this thread introducing other, smaller points of historical argument on topics relevant and unrelated to the main thread. A final entry from Kidlegionae (61) will have to suffice here:

> [The Spartans] were excellent soldiers IN THEIR TIME, but apart from good soldiers they were good for nothing else. NEVER achieved an empire or did something great. Some people make fun of Spartans because they were only good to polish their shields and march (most of the time not even going to war); overspecialization is bad, to make an empire you don't need only soldiers.

Kidlegionae offers a different interpretation of Sparta from what has been advanced so far in the thread. It is sophisticated enough in its premise, if not in its wording: Sparta was the supreme power on the battlefield but was structurally unequipped to rule an empire. Their last comment is particularly noteworthy: "Perhaps to please the Spartan fans something fair in the game would be to give them boosts in their hoplites but nerf them a lot in economy." To translate: Kidlegionae suggests that the game could stay historically accurate and deal with the complaints of fans by making Sparta's hoplite soldiers outstanding warriors while drastically reducing ("nerf") the economic power of the faction. In short, Kidlegionae offers both historical interpretation and a way to implement it in the simulation game. They are engaged in participatory play with history.

This thread illustrates some important possibilities for player participation in games about the past. First, it is clear that players do not have to accept passively the models of the past that the developers have embedded into their games. Rather, they can actively critique the models, and even offer suggestions for how to adapt gameplay to better fit their historical understanding. They participate in the representation and simulation of history. Second, the posters are engaged to varying extents in the craft of history as they discuss the game. Discussions of what count as historical facts and how those facts may be interpreted take place. There is even the occasional reference to sources of evidence. Third, the topic itself is one of substance. Antiquarian discussions abound on the forum to be sure; nevertheless, players can develop deeper historical issues. Finally, the forums are their own manifestations of public history in action, but a public history largely independent of both game designers and, it would appear, academic historians. This latter group enters the debate only if their works on the subject have been consulted.

A second thread, Civilization Fanatics Center Forums (2011a), centers on the historical accuracy of the *Civilization IV* modification, *Rhye's and Fall of Civilization*. The OP, SilchasRuin, begins their post by criticizing the starting locations of various civilizations in the game. Then they move to a second point, concerning the implementation of religions in *Civilization* itself:

> I also read a lot about people saying that Judaism should not spread so far or even be a religion in the game. Well, firstly Christianity and Islam originated from Judaism. Secondly, after the diaspora Jewish people spread throughout the known world, and played a major part in the development of European history, especially (and I know this sounds stereotypical, but if you look at the history it is true) in economics. So, I think that it was just as important in world history as say, Zoroastrianism, even if less people followed it.

Essentially, the problem as this poster sees it is that Judaism spreads too easily between cultures and across territories in the game. The game's model makes the religion appear to be more of a missionary religion than it historically was or is. Still, SilchasRuin implies the religion should be kept in the game because of its great significance in world history. In response to this portion of the thread, Kairob (2) responds:

> Name one Civilization that should historically adopt Judaism as its state religion. Now compare that to the civs that shouldn't but often do. (Greece, Rome, Babylonia, Egypt, Carthage, Ethiopia, sometimes Persia). There is a pretty clear clue here about how to improve historical accuracy.

Umarth (4) joins in the discussion:

> Regarding Judaism, I've said before that I think the whole religion system is broken from a historical/sociological point of view. But Judaism is especially broken because
>
> a) it's not a missionary religion, so it doesn't fit Civ's religion spread model at all
> b) it has never been a major "world religion" in terms of numbers, even if it is geographically widespread
> c) you can count the political entities that have had Judaism as their state religion on one hand …
>
> It would be interesting to have a mod that represented the Jewish diaspora in some other way though.

This post essentially ends this part of the thread: the three agree that the model of religion in the game does not simulate Judaism well.

Even more than in the last thread the debate remains ostensibly over game mechanics – the model of world religions in the game. But the posters use the mechanics to discuss a deeper issue of real historical significance, the features of Judaism and other world religions and their impact on world history. The mechanics of the game in short, have led them to reflect, however briefly, on the role of world religions in history.

A third thread, Steam Community Forums (2013), discusses Paradox's *Crusader Kings 2*. In this grand strategy title, the player guides a medieval dynasty through centuries of simulated history and numerous generations, arranging marriages, building family and political ties, intriguing against rivals, fighting wars, and trying to improve the rank of his dynasty through the acquisition of new titles and new lands. Succession laws are an important feature in the game. These differ from region to region and, as in history, have a critical influence on the transition of power and status from one generation to the next. The legal form of inheritance for most areas in Europe at the start of the game is agnatic-cognatic succession, where women can only inherit land and titles if there are no eligible male heirs. The OP seeks a solution to a problem this has caused him:

> So I'm trying to get my girlfriend to play Crusader Kings with me, but she's pretty displeased at the difficulty of maintaining a female ruler. Is there any mod or console command I can use to make gender irrelevant to rulership?

The thread is initiated because a pair of players seek some way to modify the game, either by typing a special code while playing (the console command) or loading a player programmed expansion to the game that modifies existing features (the mod). FrogDog (1) responds with two suggestions for how to play the game as is and have more women inherit positions: "You could have the Basque culture, which allows absolute cognatic [inheritance]. I think the Cathar religion allows it too." This is followed up by Ninthshadow (2):

> FrogDog nailed it, in game wise. Absolute cognatic succession (in the laws tab) sounds like the ingame solution and it's not particularly hard to institute for a lot of rulers. With SoA [note: the *Sons of Abraham* expansion for the game] it seems the Cathar religion allows women in almost all major roles, from leading armies to council spots.

The OP rejects FrogDog's suggestion that his girlfriend play as a Basque: "Absolute Cognatic [succession] however is ONLY available for Basque, and we want to be able to start outside of Portugal." Several posters offer more technical solutions. By editing certain files that are part of the game's data, it is possible to change the game rules so that all cultures allow true cognatic succession; that is, women can inherit titles on an equal footing with men. Another poster shares their own experience:

> Is it difficult to have a female ruler? I had a game where I had three female rulers in a row. This was in Agnatic Cognatic succession. They took all of the places required to form the Roman Empire and all of the land the Karlings had except West Francia and Aquitaine and maintained it. It is possible to have good female rulers however ... it is a historical game set at a time period where woman are generally disrespected by men ... However some of my best rulers have been females.

Like the previous thread on Judaism, this thread shows a conversation operating on multiple levels. Ostensibly the conversation is about game mechanics pure and simple. At the same time, however, it is a discussion about women's historical ability to inherit land and exercise political power in the Middle Ages. The posters use the medium and terminology from the game to address a historical issue. In doing so on a public forum, they have engaged in their own work of public history.

Developing personal rules of play and modding the game

The previous post raises another important point. Not only can players actively critique the games they play, they can make choices regarding how they will play a game. This point also arises in the thread "Does anyone play CIV realistically?" (Civilization Fanatics Center Forums 2011b), which begins:

> When I play a game of Civ I'm playing it to build a civilization and try my best to create a story with it. I'm building my Civ not to win the game, but to stand the test of time. I love history and like to use Civ as a tool to in a way create it, or change it. Beating the AI can be fun, however I've found it more enjoyable to just see how my civilization lasts and builds in time. If it fails, it fails, if it conquers the world ... well, I have a story to tell don't I. To help with this, I've always set house rules for myself.

ScubaSteveWA, the OP, goes on to list a number of rules he imposes on himself while playing. Most involve role-playing, essentially restricting him from taking advantage of flaws in the game's AI. Though not all posters agree with him, several do note that at times they play Civ for the experience of building a civilization rather than simply striving to beat the game's AI.

Another thread showing similar features discusses the role of slavery in *Civilization*. Lynxlynx (OP) begins the thread:

> What [do] you think about slavery in Civilization? Does it fit the game? Some may think that slavery is questionable, but it is not. Slavery is just pure evil just like war. Yet it is part of the past, and quite a lot of early civilizations [were built] on slaves. :-(Just [because] we don't want to think of it doesn't meant it [didn't exist].

Lynxlynx then offers suggestions for how the game might be changed to incorporate slavery mechanics. Essentially they propose that a player can enslave inhabitants of conquered cities. The enslaved become workers who can develop the land around cities, but who also create unhappiness for the enslaving civilization. Lynxlynx also proposes that civilizations can eventually reach the point where slaves can be freed if the player chooses, increasing the happiness of the civilization. They finish by suggesting that incorporating a slavery mechanic in the game would provide more incentive in the ancient portion of the game to go to war, since war would bring slaves as was the case historically. It would also give players more options upon conquering a city than the usual two: incorporate it into one's civilization or raze it.

Several posters essentially agree, and there is a healthy level of debate about whether this proposal would be a good change to make and whether including slavery would hurt the popular appeal of the game. Three posts stand out in this dialogue. First, Tahitian moon (5) comments:

> I think [slavery's] already in the game in a way: you can make raids to capture other empire's and city-state's civilians and make them your workers, I imagine it [as a] kind of slavery. Also you can demand a tribute from city-states that are afraid of you, and one of the option[s] is 'enslave a worker'. Actually that level of slavery in the game is enough for me at least.

Krikkitone (13) adds:

> Basically your empire is made up of "slaves" one way or the other … the actual specific status doesn't affect gameplay.

After this, Cliomancer (14) notes:

> I think the way the game is set up you can assume that you've got slaves if you want. From Slavery to Serfdom to Indentured Servitude to Not Really Having Any Better Options, all flavours of historical human misery are open to your imagination.

This exchange is significant for a number of reasons. First off, we see, yet again, players pushing back against the models in a game, playing with their very gameplay, and offering their own additions and subtractions. Second, discussing those additions and subtractions essentially amounts to a legitimate historical discussion on the effects of slavery, again mediated through a discussion of game mechanics. What stands out most of all, however, is that these final three posts suggest the power that the player has to construct their own historical narrative through gameplay. They are not forced to understand the games' components in a particular way – for example, capturing enemy workers as a form of slavery – but can choose to do so. In short, the player takes an active role constructing their own historical meaning from the game.

The next stage of players actively choosing how to experience their game is the mod-makers. Mods are unofficial additions to a game that in some way modify gameplay. They are made by fans who feel they can improve one or more aspects of the game's play. Some mods add or change game features, others revise the graphics or interface of the game. Then there are those, the minority to be sure, that make changes to the core game in order to make it play more historically accurately. *Rome Total Realism* provides a use-ful example. The official site for this mod to *Rome: Total War* calls the mod "a set of complete modifications for *Rome: Total War* developed by an international team of skilled individuals with a passion for history" (Rome Total Realism). The feature list of the mod is impressive: "hundreds of new historically accurate units," "authentic battle formations and army deployments," and a "totally revamped combat system" are just some of the changes made to the core game. The list of contributors is no less impres-sive. Artists, digital musicians and filmmakers, coders, and even a group called historians. Ultimately, as is appropriate for what is essentially an open-ended dialogue about the past, once the game is modified for historical realism, the mod itself becomes grist for the forums to debate.

From the initial planning and research to the gameplay and public discussions, his-torical simulation games both are and foster important participatory forms of public history. The games themselves offer interpretations of the past in the form of simula-tions. They offer to players historical problem spaces in which players can act and inter-act. There are as many styles of play as players. Many simply play and enjoy. Even then the game is a participatory form of public history, and the player has a great deal of choice in how they choose to play, from the adoption of special rules of play to the instal-lation of game mods. Some go still further and engage in the messy work of history making on the forums as they debate the historical merits of this game feature or that. Many posters raise questions about the historical accuracy of the games they play. In response, others say it is just a game, suggesting that they are highly aware of the mediated nature of history in their games. One of the most striking features of forum discussions is how authentic historical discussions are generated by the game mechanics. In a variety of ways, players are using the historical simulation game as a point of entry to play with the past.

Note

1   For a list of historical video games, see McCall 2011.

PART VII

Contesting Public History

CHAPTER THIRTY

Public Historians and Conflicting Memories in Northern Ireland

THOMAS CAUVIN

Doing history in public implies specific practices. Among them is the capacity to work with various, and sometimes opposite, interpretations of the past. What happens when historians work in conflicting environments where past events remain controversial? This chapter focuses on Northern Ireland where, perhaps more than anywhere else, the role of historians has been linked to ethnic identity and political issues.[1] Since the 1960s, the cultural and ethnic divisions between Nationalists and Unionists led to regular scenes of violence (Connolly 2014; Jackson 2014).[2] In addition to a military struggle among the Nationalists, Unionists, and British forces, the people in Northern Ireland were in opposition over economic, religious, and cultural issues. During the Troubles, spanning three decades from 1968 to 1998, representations and interpretations of the past were used, debated, and challenged according to political stands (Guelke, Cox, and Stephen 2006).[3] For instance, on November 8, 1987, the Provisional I.R.A. set up a bomb near the Enniskillen First World War memorial, leaving 11 people dead. The site was chosen because of its association of Remembrance Day (and the presence of British Army veterans) with Unionism in Northern Ireland.[4] Some Nationalists considered the memorial symbolic of submission to the British rule. Although most public history projects are not doomed to such tragic results, they symbolize the challenges that historians may encounter while working in conflicting societies.

Examining the role of public historians within conflicting societies requires a broader reflection on the relations between history and conflicting memories (Kalela 2012). Through concepts of history and memory, it is important to explore how historians address conflicting narratives. Initially, academic and theoretical discussions on the relations between history and memory tended to oppose the two concepts. However, that changed with the rise of public history, and resulted in memories being reconsidered in historians' quest to understand the past (Glassberg 1996). Public historians cannot simply disregard public memories because interpretations differ. After all, they may be responsible for the conflicting memories. By celebrating only certain

A Companion to Public History, First Edition. Edited by David Dean.
© 2018 John Wiley & Sons Ltd. Published 2018 by John Wiley & Sons Ltd.

aspects of the past, historians establish unilateral interpretations and memories of the past that exclude other historical actors.

This chapter therefore explores the ways in which public historians address memories in conflicting societies when the past is subject to controversial discussions. Should public historians take part or try to remain neutral in conflicting debates over the past? And if so, at what risk do they do so? Should they contribute to appeasing tensions by providing new narratives? This discussion addresses not only the relations between history and memory, but also the links among public history, activism, and civic engagement. Are public historians equipped to address conflicting uses of the past? Highlighted by specific projects in Northern Ireland, this chapter presents some options employed during the peace process in the 1990s and early 2000s.

Historians and public memories: An ambiguous relationship

In the last three decades, memory has become a buzzword in academic circles. Historians such as Jay Winter (2000) even speak of a memory boom due to the multiplication of commemorations in the 1980s and 1990s. The memory boom has been the subject of both worries and subjugation from historians. In the early twentieth century, memory emerged as an object of study. In the 1920s, French sociologist Maurice Halbwachs developed the concept of collective memory. Memory was no longer considered strictly as an individual and personal process, but also as a collective mechanism. As such, scholars could analyze memory to study social interactions and group identity.

Historians became interested in memories, too. However, the relations between historians and memories have been ambiguous, plagued by both curiosity and aversion. Since the 1980s, a huge number of works have been published about the concept of memory and its use for historians (Connerton 1989; Nora 1996). Historians like David Lowenthal have been careful to distinguish between memory and history, though. In his comparison between the two concepts, he opposes historians who "while realizing that the past can never be retrieved unaltered … still strive for impartial, checkable accuracy, minimizing bias as inescapable but deplorable" and those – he does not call them historians – who "see bias and error as normal and necessary" (1997: 32) In other words, the main distinction between history and memory would be historians' quest for objectivity. Carried by groups and individuals, there is a plurality of memories. As such, some historians have used the concept of memory as an object to study the changing representations of events over time. For instance, French historian Henry Rousso (1991) studied how the memories of the Second World War – in particular, the French Collaboration with the Nazis – changed since 1945. According to this approach, historians study but do not take part in the construction of memories.

The rise of public history has also brought about new debates on the relations between history and memory. It is no coincidence that memory studies and public history emerged simultaneously in the 1970s and 1980s. Since the 1980s, increasing anniversaries and commemorations have produced multiple occasions for historians to take part in public debates. Public historians tend not to oppose history and memory; therefore, public history's participatory practices provide a space for individual and collective memories in the production of historical narratives. Public history is an example of how history and memory may influence each other. In 1996, public historian David Glassberg started a discussion in *The Public Historian* about the links between public history and memory. The discussion explored how individual and collective memories can be part of public history projects. For example, it is not rare in historic preservation to see members of the local communities taking part in discussion with public historians about what should be preserved, why, and how. Public memories of sites can help discover new layers of interpretation. The production of public understanding of the past is more complex than the opposition between history and memory.

Audience-based public history practices also highlight the relevance of memories. In his answer to Glassberg's article, public historian Robert Archibald points out that "the new memory research is especially important because it is audience-focused and recognizes that examining how humans receive information and construct memory is critical to our work" (1997: 64). The different public uses and interpretations of the past are crucial for public historians who intend to understand how audiences make "sense of history," or as Glassberg put it, as evidence of the intersection of the intimate and the historical (2001: 6). Public historians are aware that individuals and groups not only interpret the past differently, but they also use it according to their personal needs and experiences. These uses of the past are particularly obvious in conflicting societies where the past is subject to controversies. It is important for public historians addressing the past's conflicting memories and interpretations to provide a space for discussion. The challenge is to avoid the simple juxtaposition of public memories.

The participatory process and the relevance of public memories must not deter historians from critical analysis of the past. Public historians may give voice to personal experiences and memories, but should not limit their involvement to a simple public platform. Public historians are not passive vectors of individual and group memories. This is especially relevant in the context of new media and web technology. It is increasingly possible to express one's views through personal blogs, websites, comments, and social networks. The multiplication of public memories requires public historians to adapt their practices, too. Historians should play a role by providing critical analysis of sources and helping people to set individual and group memories in a broader context of interpretation.

Commemorations, celebrations, and conflicting memories

A large number of commemorations have been organized in both the Republic of Ireland and Northern Ireland (Graff-McRae 2010; Leonard 1996; McBride 2001). Irish historians have been among the scholars who have benefited the most from the "crumbs at the commemorative table" in the form of increased funding and public interest (Dolan 2015). Historians must be aware that historical narratives are used for different purposes during commemorations. Groups understand and use the past for different – and sometimes competing – purposes. The competition is partly due to the relevance of commemorations – and, more broadly, history – for identity issues. One critical challenge for historians involved in commemorations is to address both the celebration and glorification of aspects of the past. Although distinguishing between celebration and commemoration is not always easy, the main difference comes from their dissimilar purposes (Gillis 1994). Celebrations focus exclusively on positive, rewarding, and identity-based aspects of the past, and create pride, glory, martyrs, and heroes. Likewise, neutral definitions of commemorations insist upon educational and critical objectives that do not ignore controversial aspects of the past.

In Northern Ireland, selecting and celebrating certain aspects of the past has played a major role in the opposition between community memories. Some of the most controversial commemorations arose from the interpretations of historical links between Ireland

and Britain. With the partition of the island of Ireland into two distinct entities in 1922, the past has been used to distinguish between two sets of identities. The ethnic divisions between Catholic Nationalists (who were in favor of an independent Ireland) and Protestant Unionists (who supported the political and cultural union with Britain) led to different choices about what part of the past should be remembered. The use and selection of the past according to ethnic identity resulted in the celebration of some events and the oblivion of others. On the one hand, Catholic Nationalists mostly chose to remember historical revolts against the British rule, like the 1798 Rebellion, to exemplify a historical distinction between the two islands. On the other hand, Protestant Unionists largely celebrated the British and Protestant presence and control in Ireland, notably through William of Orange and the 1690 Battle of the Boyne (Cauvin 2011).[5] Likewise, different interpretations of the year 1916 have become symbolic of the ethnic uses of the past. While Nationalists have celebrated the 1916 Easter Rising in which Republicans attempted to break free from Britain, Unionists have instead celebrated their participation within the British Army and their sacrifice during the 1916 Battle of the Somme (McBride 2001).

Historians and historical institutions have not only reflected, but also have participated in conflicting interpretations of the past. The role played by museums in the construction of national identity has been long studied (Fladmark 2000; Kaplan 1994). In the island of Ireland, many historians contributed to the creation and development of national historical narratives in museums. Some community museums have embraced ethnic interpretations of the past. Created in Belfast in 2007, the Eileen Hickey Irish Republican History Museum focuses on the Republican history of prisoners during the Troubles. On the other side, the Apprentice Boys of Derry Museum tells the Unionist interpretations of the 1688–1689 Siege of Londonderry by celebrating its defenders (Apprentice Boys Today n.d.). National institutions have participated in conflicting interpretations as well. For a long time since being created in late nineteenth-century Dublin (now in the Republic of Ireland), the National Museum of Ireland (NMI) has celebrated Nationalist interpretations of the past. Organized by the NMI's history department, the 1916 historical collection has celebrated, at least until the 1990s, Republican heroes and martyrs of the 1916 Easter Rising. On the other side of the border, the Ulster Museum, the national museum of Northern Ireland in Belfast, organized an exhibition for the 50th anniversary of the 1916 Battle of the Somme. In the 1960s, the Ulster Museum had no interest in the Easter Rising at all (Cauvin 2012). While public history projects may contribute to conflicting memories through celebratory narratives, historians should ask if – and how – they should appease controversies.

Public history as peacemaking

Since the 1970s, uses of the past have been at the core of the public history movement. Public historians, for instance, participate in the preservation of sites and districts, including urban revival, legal processes, and public policy. History serves as a powerful tool to analyze contemporary issues and social concerns. However, in doing so, public historians are confronted with the concept of activism. Applied to history, activism assumes that the past can be used to improve present-day issues (Korza and Bacon 2005). In 2008, a conference entitled "Active History: History for the Future" resulted in the creation of Active History, an organization that intends to "make a tangible difference in people's lives" through a "history that makes an intervention and is transformative to both practitioners and communities" (Active History n.d.). Activist historians are interventionists and act to foster social justice, cultural diversity, or peacemaking. Therefore, historians' activism is controversial because it is often based on personal convictions. Public historian Cathy Stanton explains that "most public historians are reluctant to describe themselves as advocates, activists, or political actors per se." One reason is that "deeply-held values within the historical profession still tend to place advocacy in direct opposition to analytical rigor" (2015). The National Council on Public History's Code of Ethics and Professional Status indeed warns that "a public historian should critically examine personal issues of social conscience as distinct from issues of ethical practice" (NCPH 2007). It is therefore interesting to explore the zone where historical practices meet personal convictions. This zone is critical for historians working in conflicting societies.

Since the early 1990s, the number of peacemaking processes all over the world has increased. Institutions like the United States Institute for Peace, the International Center for Transitional Justice, the Institute for Historical Justice and Reconciliation, and Facing History and Ourselves support public history projects as part of peacemaking.[6] In an article about historians and reconciliation, Professor of International and Public Affairs Elazar Barkan explains that "because group identity is shaped by historical perspectives, historical narratives have an explicit and direct impact on national identities" (2009: 900). Likewise, the links among historical narratives, national identity, and ethnic divisions are part of a wider process of mobilizing the past for political purposes in Northern Ireland. Historians could play a role in making peace.

Although various attempts were made during the 1970s and 1980s to stop violence in Northern Ireland, the peace process did not start until the 1990s (Darby 2003). Peacemakers saw ethnic violence as the result of not only economic and political but also cultural issues. Accordingly, in addition to projects dealing with unemployment, discrimination, and power sharing, the peace process also encouraged cultural reconciliation. From 1995 onward, the European Special Support Programme for Peace and Reconciliation in Northern Ireland (EUSSPPR, commonly known as PEACE) supported cultural projects addressing cultural community relations. Cultural institutions received funding under the condition that they contributed to S.S.P 4.5 *Promoting Pathways to Reconciliation: Building Inclusive Communities*. One of its main objectives was to produce new cultural narratives to improve community relations. As part of this agenda, historians were solicited to consider how to represent, interpret, teach, and remember the past in less divisive terms.

Public history and the creation of cultural spaces of dialogue

At a global level, many historians have been involved in reconciliation and human rights campaigns. Historians have been asked to help people to come to terms with difficult pasts. Initially used to enable Germans confront the Nazi past, the expression "come to terms with the past" is now more broadly employed to make peace with the past. Before participating in peacemaking processes, historians need to discuss if – and if so how – new historical narratives could bring peace. According to Barkan, "by playing an adjudicatory role in the creation of such narratives and ensuring adherence to ethical norms, historians can contribute to reconciliation among nations" (2009: 900). In other words, extensive historical research would contribute to reconciliation. But reality is not quite that simple. Barkan acknowledges that historians need to address several questions about contested interpretations of the past, such as "Does constructing a 'shared' narrative mean giving equal time to all sides? How do the goals of delegitimizing the Nationalist historical myths that feed ethnic hatred and conflict converge with the aim to construct, through history, a new national identity?" (2009: 903). Historians must be aware of the uses and consequences of their research and projects on the different communities. One step historians can help to create is a space where members of communities can meet and safely discuss their interpretations of the past. The goal may be first achieved through historical acknowledgment of victims.

History of the difficult past: Acknowledging the victims

In order to make peace with the past, historians can help communities acknowledge past crimes and injustice. Recovering the history of victims has become part of a global process. For instance, in 1999, the International Coalition of Historic Site Museums of Conscience was created to foster public dialogue on pressing contemporary issues in historical perspective. The founding members "believed that remembering sites of both abuse and resistance were critical in the transition to democracy" (Ševčenko and Russell-Ciardi 2008: 9–10). The coalition's website stresses that "erasing the past can prevent new generations from learning critical lessons while forever compromising opportunities to build a peaceful future" (n.d.). According to this statement, the history of crimes could contribute to peacemaking by giving victims a voice, and their descendants a way to mourn. Representing and discussing the history of human rights – and their violation – also has a direct connection with democratic engagement. For instance, through the South African Truth Commission, perpetrators had to confess their past crimes to be officially forgiven by their victims. The argument is that coming to terms with the violent past can help populations overcome past tensions and move toward better democratic systems.

For instance, Memoria Abierta (part of the International Coalition) sheds light on the human rights abuses during the dictatorship in Argentina. Memoria Abierta encourages public discussion "about what should be done with the clandestine detention centers where torture was perpetrated" (Ševčenko and Russell-Ciardi 2008: 12–13). Likewise, in Romania, the Institute for the Investigation of Communist Crimes and the Memory of the Romanian Exile aims at collecting online archives, organizing exhibits, and providing student programs to support public awareness of the history of the atrocities perpetrated in Romania. Historians can also work in commissions like the Latvia's History Commission that studies the Crimes against Humanity Committed in the Territory of Latvia, from 1940 to 1956 during Soviet occupation.

Projects have developed in Northern Ireland about the history of victims. In 1998, British Prime Minister Tony Blair established the Bloody Sunday Inquiry, later known as the Saville Report, to clarify what had happened to the 1972 shooting victims. Other projects acknowledged the victims of the Northern Irish conflict. For its 2006 permanent exhibit about the history of wars and conflicts in Northern Ireland – including the Troubles – the Ulster Museum decided to give voice to victims, too. Historians Jane Leonard (outreach officer) and Trevor Parkhill (curator of the historical collections) asked various groups of victims to select and comment on objects of the collection. Groups of victims included Nationalists and Unionists, as well as prison officers and police forces. The museum staff recorded the comments and stories that served as captions for the display.

Giving voice to the victims of the conflict allowed the museum to acknowledge their sufferings. However, historical research on past crimes does not necessarily lead to reconciliation. For example, no truth commission exists in Northern Ireland (Lundy and McGovern 2006). Unlike other peacemaking processes (for example, South Africa or Chile), it has been difficult to establish a clear-cut distinction between victims and perpetrators in Northern Ireland. While identifying lists of victims of the conflict, the Northern Irish peace process was much less clear in identifying perpetrators and those responsible for violence. The Bloody Sunday Inquiry's report – and the conclusion that the British soldiers were responsible for the shooting – was only made public in 2010, after several failures to identify responsibility. In order to create a safe public space of dialogue about the past, Northern Irish historians and cultural institutions presented victims-based narratives and avoided interpretations of responsibilities.[7]

In some instances, historical narratives about victims can actually add fuel to conflicting memories. In North America, two examples demonstrate how the history of casualties can raise new controversies. In the early 1990s, the Smithsonian National Air and Space Museum in Washington, D.C., prepared an exhibition on the B-29 aircraft Enola Gay and, more largely, on the bombing of Japan in 1945. Instead of a more restricted interpretation on the use of the atomic bomb to end the war and preserve American lives, the museum also wanted to focus on the Japanese victims to open debate about the use of the atomic bomb. However, some US veterans groups considered such action – especially the focus on Japanese victims – as offensive and anti-patriotic. Discussing the appropriateness of the bombing was going against the traditional representation of the US involvement in WWII and against the museum's long-time celebratory focus on aviation and technology (Linenthal and Englehardt 1996). In spite of adjustments, the Enola Gay exhibition was ultimately cancelled.

Similarly, in 2006–2007, the Canadian War Museum (CWM) wanted to arrange an exhibit about the Combined Bomber Offensive, or Bomber Command.[8] Like the Enola Gay project, the exhibit proposed to include historical narratives of the victims of the bombing and asked about "the efficacy and the morality of the … massive bombing of Germany's industrial and civilian targets" (Dean 2009: 1–2). Although the CWM received positive feedback from prominent historians, and had consulted with some veterans groups early in the process, the museum became the target of an intense critical campaign. The campaign resulted in Parliamentary sub-committee hearings that forced the CWM to make major changes to the display (Dean 2009: 1–2). In the Smithsonian and the CWM, the focus on the victims of Allied Bombing created controversies and forced the two museums to withdraw their plans. Historical narratives of victims may create conflicting interpretations when victims are perceived as enemies.

Historical research may also undermine the fragile status quo between communities. Some members of the communities may not want historians to dig up the past. In March 2011, William "Plum" Smith, a former member of the Red Hand Commando (Loyalist paramilitary group in Northern Ireland) explained that "the majority of people have moved on … The world has moved on and life has moved on." He noted: "While recognising the hurt of all victims' relatives, the future cannot be held hostage to the past" (Rowan 2011). According to Smith, history – at least the history of victims of the conflict – could be counterproductive. He thought the work of the Historical Enquiries Team (HET) "is killing the peace."[9] The HET was strictly a criminal process, directly managed by the Police Service in Northern Ireland. However, the reluctance to dig into the past appeared broader. If Smith was concerned about the history of crimes – he, himself, having been involved in paramilitary actions – the reluctance to dig into the past was much broader.

Following the publication of the Saville Report in 2010, other people reacted against historical investigation. On June 6, 2010, the *Belfast Telegraph* published a photograph of a wall graffiti with the message "The Government And Our People Wanted Peace! This Was Delivered! So Don't Disrupt Our Present And Future By Digging Into The Past!" (Rowan 2010). Historians working in conflicting societies should consider the possibility that forgetting controversial aspects of the past – or at least, not proposing new historical interpretation – may also contribute to making peace. Tensions in Northern Ireland did not come from an absence of historical narratives – the annual Unionist parades commemorating the 1688 Siege of Londonderry and 1690 Battle of the Boyne are among the most popular examples – but from highly conflicting interpretations. Northern Ireland did not lack history, but needed safe public space for discussion.

Historians' relations with local communities

One goal for historians working in peacemaking is to facilitate public spaces of discussion for conflicting interpretations of the past. As the International Coalition of Sites of Conscience explains, "Without safe spaces to remember and preserve these memories, the stories of elderly survivors of atrocity can vanish when they pass away" (n.d.). Safe public spaces can serve to disarm conflicting memories. Historians, according to Linenthal, can participate in the construction of "demilitarized zones of public conversation where people can engage various, perhaps even irreconcilable, interpretations of our past" (1997: 45). Different voices and interpretations of the past can be heard without fearing prejudice. In order to create such spaces, the links between historians and communities are critical.

Public history encourages public participation and often helps people understand the multiple meanings and interpretations of the past. The cross-community Healing Through Remembering (HTR) project has provided public spaces to discuss the different interpretations of the Northern Irish conflict. In 2014, for the *Everyday Items Transformed by Conflict* exhibit, HTR asked members of local communities to provide and comment on everyday objects that they thought symbolized the Northern Irish conflict. The multiple voices and interpretations of the past in a common public space symbolized the complexity of the conflict and the multiple perspectives.

In addition to public participation, other peacemaking projects have encouraged the presence of "external" historians – in other words, the participation of historians who do not belong to local communities. Not sharing sociocultural background with local communities may help historians create more neutral spaces of discussion. For instance, a committee of historians from different countries and different cultures led by Charles Ingrao and Thomas Emmert (2012) worked to confront the controversial past in former Yugoslavia. Historians discussed not only subjects such as the dissolution of former Yugoslavia, but also ethnic cleansing. Likewise, regarding the expropriation that took place during the Second World War, the Austrian government created a commission with historians from different countries and invited Jewish representatives (Barkan 2009: 900). The diversity of the profile may help create less passionate and more diverse narratives and representations of the past.

Historians from the United States Institute for Peace published research on how to teach history in Northern Ireland (Cole and Barsalou 2006). Nevertheless, in spite of this example, few international projects took place in the Northern Irish peace process. Public history in Northern Ireland remains largely driven by local actors. Enlarging the process to international practitioners could help foster diversity of representation. Historians who do not belong to local communities may provide some solutions, but they can also meet open reluctance from community members. Throughout his research on a 1919 violent labor confrontation that killed at least six people in Centralia, American public historian Robert Weyeneth (1994) experienced how not being part of local communities can also lead to conflicting relations. Being an outsider did not help Weyeneth to recover the historical narratives of this long-forgotten event. He noticed that "the assumption is that a community or group who were historical participants-authors of the past – enjoy some right of copyright that gives them control over the 'fair use' of the past" (65). As an outsider, it may be difficult for historians to gain the confidence of local community members. As he raised controversial aspects about the past, Weyeneth explained how local actors campaigned to suppress his book and to silence his inconvenient narratives. Some groups may deny historians their authority in narrating the past. In his book on memory and power relations, Steven Dubin points out that "the certainty of lived experience is a powerful credential to invoke and it is virtually impossible for someone else to rebut without seeming arrogant or insensitive" (1999: 5). External historians may more easily design safe spaces of dialogue, but may fail to engage community members due to the lack of confidence. Public historians who do not belong to the local community should not see themselves as agents of catharsis or as missionaries bringing the truth. Public historians work with the public, and conflicting societies are no different.

Common historical narratives

In order to create a public space of discussion and appease conflicting memories, some projects provide historical narratives that different communities can share. The initial objectives of those projects are to avoid being associated with only one community. Projects develop as sites of discussion and do not embrace one particular political agenda. As a national institution, it has been critical for the Ulster Museum to take into consideration the different interpretations of the past. Initially created and managed by the dominating Unionist political tradition, the Ulster Museum attempted to change its policy in the 1990s.[10] As part of the peace process, the museum changed its historical collection and exhibiting strategy.

In 1990, the Ulster Museum arranged an exhibit for the commemoration of the 1690 Battle of the Boyne. The decision to mount a display about an event that the Unionist community celebrated seemed to be in line with the previous museum's strategy. However, in connection with the peace process, the approach changed. The decision to have an exhibit about 1690, according to historian and curator William Maguire, implied another exhibition for the bicentenary of the 1798 Rebellion. The fact that the Battle of the Boyne and the 1798 Rebellion were respectively celebrated by the Unionists and Nationalists would avoid, according to Maguire, any criticism of museum bias. This choice mirrored more broadly how the peace process was conceived and implemented in Northern Ireland. In order to make peace, various organizations such as the Community Relations Council promoted "parity of esteem" through equal representations between the two main traditions. This parity of esteem also affected how specific events from the past were interpreted.

Public projects could highlight aspects of the past that both Nationalists and Unionists could remember. In 1998, the Ulster Museum arranged an exhibit that commemorated the 1798 Rebellion. Funded by the EUSSPPR, the Ulster Museum exhibit focused on aspects that both Nationalists and Unionists could share. For instance, the museum explained that the United Irishmen – the group of Irish radicals who initially organized the rebellion – were mostly Protestants who succeeded in mobilizing Catholic troops to fight for an independent Ireland. In doing so, the museum worked to create links between the two main present-day communities. The commemorative exhibition of the 1798 Rebellion expressed a conception of Ireland defined as a multicultural entity in which Catholics and Protestants could cohabit.

When a Unionist paramilitary group killed a young Catholic in April 1998, the museum decided to invite the victim's family as well as both the Nationalist and Unionist communities of his hometown. Led by their respective Catholic priest and Protestant minister, the two communities met at the Ulster Museum and discussed how they actually shared similar roots in 1798. Instead of solely associating the 1798 Rebellion with the Nationalist community, the Ulster Museum provided a space of mourning as well as a space of discussion. This approach to the past was influenced by present-day politics. To some extent, the present political opposition between Nationalists and Unionists was transposed and reflected in the past.

Another approach more traditional to historical methodology was to broaden the contextualization in which the past was interpreted. The objective was not to reflect but to challenge the current binary opposition between the two political groups. The uses of the past often result in the celebration of a single moment in history, without paying attention to the long-term consequences. In order to provide narratives that different communities could accept, the Ulster Museum challenged traditional celebratory and heroic community representations of the past. The European framework provided broader and safer representations of conflicting issues. While mounting *Kings in Conflict: Ireland the 1690s*, the 1990 exhibit about the 1690 Battle of the Boyne, historian William Maguire aimed to challenge the Unionist community's unilateral celebration to justify their political domination in Northern Ireland. In order to do so, Maguire realized that changing the framework of interpretation allowed the UM to provide new spaces of discussion. While the Battle of the Boyne was an important event, the 1690 issues at stake went beyond local politics. Instead of focusing on the religious opposition between William (Protestant) and his opponent James II (Catholic), the exhibit internationalized the context of the Battle. The main historical tension was no longer between James and William – in other words, between Catholics and Protestants in Ireland, but between William and Louis XIV for supremacy in Europe. The Battle was merely one event of the Nine Years' War (1688–1697) that involved many European countries. In 1690, William of Orange led the Grand Alliance in which not every monarch was Protestant. The display became symbolic by associating Pope Innocent III and Protestant William of Orange.

Unlike the 1798 display that linked the past to the two main political communities, the 1990 exhibit provided a more complex interpretation of the past through a broader European contextualization. By interpreting the 1690 Battle of the Boyne not as a local Irish event but rather as a European conflict, the UM made easier the local discussion over the past. The UM refrained from providing a past that any community could use for group and political identity. The two displays reflected different approaches to how balance could be achieved between public participation, public uses of the past, and the creation of more neutral spaces of discussion.

Conclusion

To conclude, public historians working in conflicting societies can participate in the general reconsideration of the links between history and memory. Although public history is based on public participation – and therefore, public memories – the process is problematic in regions such as Northern Ireland where interpreting the past remains divisive. The Northern Irish examples highlight the difficult task of public historians, who have to facilitate public discussion and encourage critical analysis of the past. Working in communities driven by conflict requires self-reflective practice from historians. How do the communities use historians and historical narratives? Are historians contributing to peaceful relations, or adding fuel to divisive interpretations of the past? Should historians build stronger links with communities, or try to provide new spaces of discussion that go beyond the local framework? However, the ultimate role of historians is not to provide reconciliation on behalf of local community members. Reconciliation can only come from initiatives that originate within those communities. What historians can do is provide a space to interpret and discuss the past where members of the communities can interact with each other. In doing so, historians work as public facilitators. Historians are not simple activists, and therefore need to convey a sense of critical understanding of the past. Through the recovery of historical narratives about victims, through the contextualization of local ethnic tensions in a broader historical framework, and through more complex interpretations of Manichean representations of the past, historians can contribute to transforming the past from a battlefield of political and ethnic memories to a space of interrogation and mutual understanding.

Notes

1   The island of Ireland has been partitioned since 1922. The Republic of Ireland in the South is independent, while Northern Ireland remains part of the United Kingdom of Great Britain and Northern Ireland. Dublin is the capital of the Republic of Ireland, while Belfast is the capital of the province of Northern Ireland.

2   Although various internal currents and divisions exist, Unionists (or Loyalists) in Northern Ireland are mostly Protestant and have supported the Union with Great Britain. Nationalists (or Republicans) are mostly Catholic and have challenged the links with Britain.

3   Although the dates are subject to discussion, the Troubles started in the late 1960s and opposed paramilitary groups such as the Provisional I.R.A. (Irish Republican Army) for the Nationalists and the U.D.F (Ulster Defence Forces) for the Unionists who opposed each other over the status of Northern Ireland and the political rights of the Catholic minority – as well as the British Army. The Northern Irish Troubles produced more than 3,000 casualties. A major step in the peace process was the signature of the Good Friday Agreement in 1998, in which Irish and British governments associated with most of Northern Ireland's political parties, agreed to set the bases for restoring peace.

4   Many Unionists enlisted during the First World War and fought with the British Army.

5   Organized by the United Irishmen in the wake of the French Revolution, the 1798 Irish uprising attempted to break free from the British rule in Ireland (May – September 1798). In spite of a late French landing, the uprising was repressed by the British troops, and resulted in the

1801 Act of Union (the Irish Parliament was suppressed, and Ireland utterly passed under British rule). While twentieth-century Irish Nationalists traditionally interpreted the Rebellion as an early attempt from Irish Republicans to break free from the British colonizers, Protestant Unionists have portrayed the event as a Catholic insurrection that led to atrocities toward Protestants. On the other hand, the 1690 Battle of the Boyne has been celebrated by the Northern Irish Unionist community as the victory of Protestantism – through King William of Orange – over Catholicism. Even today, the Orange Order organizes annual parades every July 12 to celebrate William's victory. The Orange Order has been called after William's color.

6   For instance, created in 1984 by the US Congress, USIP undertook a history initiative that aimed to explore how divided societies recovering from violent conflict have been teaching the conflict's history to participate in a larger process of social reconstruction and reconciliation (Cole and Barsalou 2006).

7   Historical interpretations of perpetrators and responsibilities were limited to community institutions that merely supported one community.

8   It was an Anglo-American offensive between 1943 and 1945 on the European front. Ten thousand Canadian airmen died between 1943 and 1945.

9   The HET was a unit set up in 2005 to investigate the more than 3,000 murders committed during the Troubles between 1968 and 1998.

10 Originally called the Belfast Municipal Museum and Art Gallery, the Ulster Museum was created in 1962. In spite of its national status, the museum initially merely supported dominant Unionist narratives.

CHAPTER THIRTY ONE

Trauma and Memory

JENNY EDKINS

Trauma and memory seem at one and the same time to be both intensely personal and inevitably shared. The memory enshrined in monuments to war dead and the trauma expressed in marches protesting disappearances, to take just two examples of how trauma is marked in public spaces, can be seen as public manifestations of private loss. They also have a political significance. They are part of a struggle over state power and forms of community: a claim to be heard by those who contest existing practices, for example, or an attempt by political authorities to cover over their failings.

The personal and the communal are intertwined in a more profound way too. Though memories may seem to be internal – images stored in the head – those memories are formed in the present moment and in a social context: within a symbolic framework that separates past from present in a particular way and provides ways of thinking that are not purely individual. In that sense, memories are never merely personal. Given the impossibility of distinguishing individual memory from its social context, the idea of collective memory, seen as a coming-together of discrete memories, needs to be reexamined (Halbwachs 1992).

Trauma too is not just something that happens to someone faced with violence or brutality. It is too easy to talk of war or conflict as traumatic events, as if they existed as such outside any particular context. On the contrary, for many thinkers, events are only traumatic in relation to a particular symbolic order. From a psychoanalytic point of view, for example, trauma in the sense of a lack, excess, or gap is inherent both in what we call social order and in forms of subjectivity (Žižek 1989). Normally, that gap is not visible. It is concealed. When an event occurs that reveals or exposes the incompleteness, our notion of who we are, framed by the social or symbolic order, no longer works – it no longer makes sense – and the traumatic core is made visible.

In this chapter, I shall expand on these ideas through a discussion of examples of memorials and protests, and introduce some of the theoretical thinking that provides the basis for this view of trauma and memory. I begin by exploring the way events such

A Companion to Public History, First Edition. Edited by David Dean.
© 2018 John Wiley & Sons Ltd. Published 2018 by John Wiley & Sons Ltd.

as wars and conflicts are followed by periods of contestation over questions of public memory. The nation-state often wishes to impose heroic narratives and forms of commemoration that reinforce national identity. Sometimes, veterans and their families, and the public in general, may share this desire. However, publics who have encountered a traumatic disruption of their assumed social order – and veterans too – can demand something rather different: forms of memorialization that contest state narratives and hold open instead the memory of an encounter with the real. Examples such as the Vietnam Memorial and the London Cenotaph can be read as an encircling of the trauma at the root of the social order and a challenge to heroic narratives (Edkins 2003a). The work of Cathy Caruth (1995; 1996; 2013) on trauma and Slavoj Žižek's (1989) examination of Lacanian notions of subjectivity and the symbolic provide the basis for these reflections.

Jacques Rancière's work on the aesthetic politics of dissensus and disruption is also important in the consideration of how certain forms of political action after events such as state terror and disappearances can contest the return to an order that pretends nothing has happened to challenge that order (1999; 2004). An investigation of how systems of tracing the missing and displaced after war or disaster are similarly a contested terrain gives further insight into what forms of personhood and politics are at stake in contemporary forms of memory and memorialization (Edkins 2011).

Finally, I examine how forms of accounting for the past that rely on linear temporality – a smooth progression from past through present to future and a simple notion of cause preceding effect – are challenged by the disruptive betrayals of what I call "trauma time," and how certain forms of memory and storytelling can reinstate politics and remain faithful to the traumatic event.

Memory and trauma in the aftermath of war

In the aftermath of war, on the victorious side at least, celebrations of the heroism of those who were killed in combat translate into monuments, victory parades, and ceremonies of remembrance that reinstate stories of national pride. Twentieth-century world wars largely involved conscript armies: civilians sent by the nation-state into battle in its name. The state, whose job it is to protect its citizens, did the opposite: it sent them to their deaths. Afterward, a narrative had to be put in place that could authorize what happened, through notions of sacrifice, courage, and selflessness.

Those who fought and survived often see things differently. Their comrades have died, often in horrendous circumstances and often seemingly without purpose. Moreover, the deaths they have witnessed frequently appear to have been avoidable: by better tactics, more equipment, better decisions by commanding officers. The assumed wisdom and good intentions of the authorities that have sent them to fight are thrown into question. There is a sense of betrayal. What has happened does not make sense. The survivors could do nothing to stop the deaths they witnessed, and nothing was done by others either. The supposed expertise of those in charge is revealed as fallible. The futility of war is apparent, as First World War poets and novelists remind us (Owen 1963; Remarque 1929).

For Cathy Caruth, trauma "involves the recognition of realities that most of us have not begun to face" (1995: vii).[1] She notes that although there is a need to attend to and help those who suffer from the impact of trauma, this must be done "without eliminating the force and truth of the reality that trauma survivors face and quite often try to transmit to us" (vii). To do so would be to lose the political potential of trauma, the way in which trauma can "open, in the individual and the community, new possibilities for change, a change that would acknowledge the unthinkable realities to which traumatic experience bears witness" (ix).

Caruth notes that it is not the threat of one's own death that is traumatic, so much as the witnessing of another's death and the fact of survival (Caruth 1995; 2013). What is revealed is not just the incompetence of those in whom we had placed our trust as our protectors, but our own mortality, which is something we prefer to forget. There are parallels here with sexual abuse in the family, where the same logic is found: those supposed to protect us turn into our tormentors (Herman 1992). Such abuse also reveals our inevitable vulnerability (Butler 2004). Caruth (1995) also notes that trauma cannot be defined by the event itself: an event may or may not be an appalling disaster or an instance of extreme brutality, and its impact may not be traumatic for everyone. A trauma occurs when one is confronted with an event that does not correspond with one's previous idea of the world, and those prior understandings will be different for different people. However, in another sense, trauma provides a potential for connection across individuals:

> One's own trauma is tied up with the trauma of another [and] trauma may lead, therefore, to an encounter with another, through the very possibility and surprise of listening to another's wound. (Caruth 1996: 8)

More than that, it can also lead to a connection across cultures, through the "indissoluble, political bond to other histories" that it produces (Caruth 1996: 18). In other words, "history, like trauma, is never simply one's own ... history is precisely the way we are implicated in each other's traumas" (24).

Another way in which trauma is never simply one's own is the effect of trauma on a community as a whole. In an interesting study of several communities that have experienced disasters of different types, Kai Erikson remarks:

> One can speak of traumatized communities as something distinct from assemblies of traumatized persons. Sometimes the tissues of community can be damaged in much the same way as the tissues of mind and body ... but even when that does not happen, traumatic wounds inflicted on individuals can combine to create a mood, and ethos ... that is different from the sum of the private wounds that make it up. Trauma has a social dimension. (1994: 230–231)

For those touched by it, trauma "can mean not only a loss of confidence in the self but a loss of confidence in the scaffolding of family and community, in the structures of human government, in the larger logics by which humankind lives, and in the ways of nature itself" (Erikson 1994: 242).

In Lacanian psychoanalytic thinking, we are told that from the so-called mirror stage on, we are seeking an impossible completeness (Lacan 1977). When we see ourselves as infants in the gaze of a carer, as in a mirror, we appear to ourselves as whole, complete, autonomous beings, separate from the world around us and in charge of ourselves. This is a misrecognition, though it is reinforced by the approving reaction of the caregiver or parent (Fink 1997: 88). The lack or trauma around which we are constituted as subjects – the impossibility of wholeness – is concealed from view. We appear capable of mastery and selfhood. It seems that it is just some external factor that is preventing us from attaining that mastery, and we strive endlessly to overcome whatever we identify as that obstacle.

In a similar way, the social or symbolic order appears to us as complete and whole, there to provide security against the sort of catastrophes that Erikson writes about. Indeed, the symbolic order is there to make sense of things for us. However, what we call social reality is a fantasy: "the symbolic order itself is also ... structured around an impossible/traumatic kernel, around a central lack" (Žižek 1989: 122). The lack or gap around which it is structured is concealed by the operation of what Lacan calls a master signifier. This master signifier can be any signifier – God, reason, the hidden hand of the market, nationalism – that holds together a particular symbolic order and gives the impression of completeness (Žižek 1992: 39). It appears to provide the imaginary wholeness and mastery that we seek, and answers to our troubling questions – or at least allows us to forget those to which we have no answers.

When something happens that we call traumatic, what has happened, in this account, is that the incompleteness of the social or symbolic order has been revealed; the traumatic kernel is no longer hidden. The social reality (or fantasy) that had been carefully put together and sustained is shattered. Nothing makes sense any more. The state, which is supposed to protect us, has sent us into harm's way; ideas of military training and discipline do not protect us either; those that are supposed to know what to do turn out to be wrong. To return to Caruth, we are forced to confront realities "that most of us have not begun to face" (1995: vii). In Lacanian terms, this represents an encounter with the real, from which "social reality" can no longer protect us. We can either maintain a sense of that encounter – encircling the trauma of the real – or hastily return to and reassert the fantasy of social reality.

In the aftermath of wars and conflicts, returning veterans bring back with them this sense that nothing that held together before – the previous common sense – works any longer. The old stories of nation and patriotism are threadbare and unconvincing. The emperor has no clothes. They have come face to face with the realities of death and dismemberment. Their friends have gone missing in action or been blown to pieces. They may have been injured or disfigured themselves. Slotting comfortably back into civilian life is impossible for many. On the other hand, for the government that sent them to war, the nation that was threatened has to be reasserted: ceremonies purportedly to remember the dead and celebrate their sacrifice for crown and country have to be held, monuments to the fallen erected, soldiers demobbed, traumas healed. Some of those ceremonies arguably function more to forget the dead and what they endured rather than to remember them.

What happens then is a period of contestation and struggle over what forms of memorialization are to be considered appropriate. While George Mosse (1990) draws attention to the largely patriotic and nationalist tenor of war memorialization, Jay Winter (1995) points to a much more complex and nuanced picture (Mosse 1990; Winter 1995; Winter and Sivan 1999). Winter notes that after the First World War, "slowly but surely, expressions of patriotism, or inhumanly idealized images of combat, suffering, and death as 'glory', began to fade away" (1995: 8). Instead, he paints a picture of "the powerful, perhaps essential, tendency of ordinary people, of many faiths and of none, to face together the emptiness, the nothingness of loss in war" (53). The war memorials that were erected in towns and cities are reflections of how communities mourned together, but they are also the outcome of a process "in which sculptors, artists, bureaucrats, churchmen and ordinary people had to strike an agreement and carry it out" (86). James

Young (1993) reminds us, in his discussion of memorials to the Nazi genocide, that the process of discussion and deliberation over the form a memorial should take is more important than the final built monument itself. The resulting local war memorials, Winter tells us, generally incorporate both motifs that see war as "noble and uplifting" and those that see it as "tragic and unendurably sad" (1995: 85-86). The memorials were intended to serve the families of the lost – to help them in the mourning process.

On a larger scale, the grand monuments in national capitals or in war cemeteries obeyed a different logic, though they were still, and perhaps even more, the subject of contestation. One memorial in particular, designed by Sir Edwin Lutyens, the London Cenotaph, is very far removed from patriotic forms. The Cenotaph was originally made out of wood and plaster and intended as a temporary marker for a victory parade that would take place down Whitehall, the street that runs past Downing Street, the Foreign and Commonwealth Office, the Treasury, the Ministry of Defence, and other government buildings. Right from the start, people in their hundreds brought flowers to lay at the Cenotaph, petitions were raised by members of parliament, and correspondents to *The Times* voiced their support for a permanent memorial in the same place. Despite later objections from the police that it would cause an obstruction, Cabinet approved the permanent placing of the structure in Whitehall (Edkins 2003a). It had been "transformed by popular demand into a permanent war memorial ... [where] millions could contemplate the timeless, the eternal, the inexorable reality of death in war" (Winter 1995: 104).

The Cenotaph, literally an empty tomb and described by Winter as an "embodiment of nothingness," was placed in the center of a busy metropolitan street, at the heart of government, where traffic flows around it continuously (1995: 105). It is still the center for annual commemorations nearly a hundred years later. It functions as a stand-in for the traumatic gap or lack, the meaninglessness revealed by the betrayal of war. We encircle the trauma, moving carefully around it rather than covering it up. The Cenotaph is a materialization of the traumatic absence of meaning – the lack or the gap – at the very center of the social or symbolic order.

Dominick LaCapra notes that while Pierre Nora (1989) uses the term "memory sites" (*lieux de memoire*), Claude Lanzmann (1995) talks of "*non-lieux de memoire*." LaCapra calls the latter "trauma sites." For him:

> A memory site is generally also a site of trauma, and the extent to which it remains invested with trauma marks the extent to which memory has not been effective in coming to terms with it, notably through modes of mourning. (LaCapra 1998: 10)

Although "trauma is precisely the gap, the open wound, in the past that resists being entirely filled in, healed, or harmonized in the present," and narratives that deny trauma are "objectionable," nevertheless LaCapra remains committed to "the attempt to work through problems, mourn the victims of the past, and reengage life in the interest of bringing about a qualitatively better state of affairs" (1998: 109, 40). However, as I shall discuss further below, there is an incompatibility between any attempt to "work though" trauma, which inevitably brings it within existing frames of political understanding – the state, the nation, and the market, among others – and keeping faith with the encounter with the real that trauma involves. The latter can lead, potentially, to a different politics, or, at the very least, mark that possibility: the possibility of a politics that recognizes the impossibility of closure and no longer seeks mastery and control.

In the case of the events of September 11, 2001, the contestations over memory took place *before* the war that ensued – the so-called "war on terror" (Greenberg 2003; Simpson 2006; Sturken 2007). President George W. Bush called for a moment's silence at a press conference at the Booker Elementary School in Florida at 9:31 a.m. on September 11: before the buildings of the World Trade Center had collapsed, before the plane had been brought down over the fields of Pennsylvania, before the Pentagon had been hit. During the moment's silence, which lasted five seconds, there was anything but silence in New York: people were still frantically phoning the emergency services from the upper floors of the Trade Center buildings, firefighters rushing to their aid. Some three days later, as a day of remembrance was being held and a three minute silence observed, relatives of people still missing were searching for those who had not returned home. It seemed "as if people were already talking of memorials the day after, when the numbers and names of the missing were unknown and the search for survivors still the focus of national attention" (Sturken 2002: 375). The rush to memorialization took place alongside a state-sponsored rhetoric of war and revenge and a Manichean division of the world: "You are either with us or against us." It enabled the United States Federal Government to reassert its authority and to justify its move to a violent response. We were all "set on a strange looking-glass journey into reverse time" (Edkins 2003b: 238). This move was contested, of course, and time experienced in Manhattan very different: a suspension of the incomprehensible *now* into a time where it might be understood, in "the future, looking back" (Taylor 2003: 241). People took to the streets to escape media portrayals that made no sense; students who had gone home after the events returned to New York for the same reason (Martin 2012).

At some distance from the First and Second World Wars, and the events of 9/11, heroic narratives have come to predominate once again, and state authorities have become more adept at pre-empting any contestation. However, other ways of challenging these framings and of imagining differently can perhaps be found (Miller 2014). After a visit to the World Trade Center memorial in May 2014, I concluded that, although the site had been sanitized and the trauma seemingly covered over, it might still be there, hidden but not absent, if we choose to acknowledge it (Edkins 2016b).

Politics of protesting disappearances

When someone goes missing, the normal processes of mourning cannot take place. Healing is not possible. In the context of what Pauline Boss (1999) calls "ambiguous loss," it is impossible for relatives to grieve, since that implies an acceptance of the loss. Families are impelled to maintain the possibility, even when it seems to go against all logic and all probability, that the person who is missing may return one fine day. Furthermore, the relatives insist on processes of tracing to establish where the missing person might be and what has happened. In most cases, the disappearance is incomprehensible; there is no explanation for it. Those left behind cannot go on; time is suspended.

In many cases, the authorities seem unresponsive: the missing person is not a problem unless in some way their disappearance threatens the state's administration of persons. In the case of soldiers missing in action in the Second World War, for example, extensive procedures were in place to determine what had happened in order to prevent desertion and to establish whether death had occurred, so that benefits to dependents would only be authorized in approved cases. Careful reports were compiled drawing on eyewitness accounts from the soldier's comrades of when they were last seen, and what was happening. Factual details were checked and cross-checked for consistency. In the case of civilians missing in the aftermath of the war, however, efforts to trace them and reconnect them with their families were seen as of secondary importance in terms of military and government priorities. There was no recognition that, until families were reunited, reconstruction and rebuilding would not be possible. In the end, it was through the work of voluntary organizations, the Red Cross in particular, acting on behalf of families, that proper procedures and resources were eventually put in place (Edkins 2011).

The missing after the two world wars are memorialized alongside those of the fallen whose names are known. In the Commonwealth War Graves Commission cemeteries throughout the world, headstones marking those "Known unto God," in Rudyard Kipling's famous epitaph, sit alongside the graves of those whose headstones carry their name, age, and a personal inscription from relatives (Summers 2007). The nation-state assumes ownership of the bodies, disallowing repatriation, and insisting on uniformity of memorial headstones, though not without challenge (Edkins 2011; Sledge 2005). There has been no move, as yet, to exhume and attempt to identify these remains through modern techniques of DNA analysis, despite the fact that such methods are now used when new remains are located on former battlefields. A recent example of the latter is the new cemetery at Fromelles in northern France, where the remains of servicemen recovered from a mass grave were painstakingly identified and reburied with full military honors (Summers, Loe, and Steel 2010; Whitford and Pollard 2009). More remarkable than these individual graves, perhaps, are the huge monuments to the fallen built after the First World War: sites like the Thiepval memorial and the Menin Gate in Ypres. On these memorials, the names stand in for missing bodies (Edkins 2016a). Missing civilians from these conflicts have no similar memorials.

When the state itself is responsible for disappearances, matters are, of course, much worse. The authorities deny that anything has happened, or suggest that the missing person has walked out on their family of their own accord. Disappearances are used as a deliberate tactic to create fear and uncertainty, and make opposition to the regime impossible, and those that protest or enquire after relatives are often afraid, with reason, of being targeted themselves. Nevertheless, despite denials and intimidation, relatives do act. One of the most well-known protest movements is the Madres of the Plaza de Mayo in Argentina (Jelin 2003; Robben 2005; Taylor 1997; van Drunen 2010). This movement began when people who had gone to various offices in an attempt to get information about their missing sons and daughters recognized people they had seen in queues at other offices. They realized that there were others in the same position as themselves, and a group of mothers began to meet and eventually to demonstrate. They would arrange to gather in the Plaza de Mayo, a square at the center of government and administrative offices in Buenos Aires, take out their white headscarves, and walk quietly around the monument that stood in the center of the square. Their demand famously was "They took them away alive; we want them back alive!"

Encircling the monument in the Plaza was like an encircling of the trauma: drawing attention to the lack or gap at the heart of the social order. It was what Pedro Orgambide, in a poem quoted by Matilde Mellibovsky in her collection of testimonies, calls "a circle of love over death." The march around the obelisk, a symbol of patriarchal power, was in obedience to a policeman's instructions to "circulate," but what the policeman did not realize was that he was setting up "an endless dance ... a ring around his own neck" (Mellibovsky 1997: 81). The refusal of the Madres to go home quietly and wait, as mothers should do, was politically effective in drawing attention to the disappearances and putting pressure on the military regime. They refused to countenance what had happened, to forget or conceal the trauma, instead encircling and marking it, and insisting that the authorities live up to their claim of respect for human rights. They remained visible, exposing the lack at the heart of the totalitarian social order (Edkins 2011).

When the military dictatorship was overthrown and democratic elections took place, the new authorities began to address the question of the disappearances. However, the trials were limited, and the protests of the Madres continued, challenging the desire of the new regime to move on and to forget. When exhumations and identifications of the disappeared began, the protests of the Madres intensified. There were internal disagreements in the movement. Initially, exhumations had been badly organized and indiscriminate excavations of mass graves were destroying evidence. However, one of the main problems was that the focus seemed to be on gathering information about the disappeared, rather than prosecuting their persecutors. Once the disappeared had been "found," and their bones returned to their families, what had happened could be forgotten. One group of Madres found the idea of exhumations without justice so objectionable that they refused to collaborate. They preferred to continue in a state of uncertainty rather than accept the return of the remains of their missing sons and daughters without justice for the perpetrators of the disappearances and recognition of the political activism of their children (Edkins 2011).

Their demand was a demand that they and their children be heard as "equal speaking beings," not just as mothers or as victims whose lives, and whose political stance, had been disregarded. This demand can be read as politics that, for Rancière, is concerned with "the distribution of the sensible":

> It is a delimitation of spaces and times, of the visible and the invisible, of speech and noise, that simultaneously determines the place and the stakes of politics as a form of experience. Politics revolves around what is seen and what can be said about it, around who has the ability to see and the talent to speak, around the properties of spaces and the possibilities of time. (2004: 13)

In their initial demands to agencies of the state to locate their missing, in their protest marches in Plaza de Mayo, and even more in their refusal to accept the return of the remains of their disappeared children, the Madres refused to act as they were supposed to act within the police order. They refused to remain within the private sphere; they refused to allow the trauma to be forgotten. Instead, they demanded that they be heard and seen as capable beings – that they be seen as counting, and that their children count too. Their intervention was an example of politics in Rancière's terms: by assuming that they were equal speaking beings, they changed the relationship

> between the ways of *doing*, of *being*, and of *saying* that define the perceptible organization of the community, the relationships between the places where one does one thing and those where one does something else, the capacities associated with this particular *doing* and those required for another. (Rancière 1999: 40)

In the actions of the Madres, and of successor groups such as the H.I.J.O.S., the children of the disappeared, memory was refused in favor of continuing activism (Taylor 2003). Those who had been disappeared were joined in the protests, either as faces, carried on placards or printed on huge sheets carried by the living, or as silhouettes, outlined on pavements or standing on street corners.

Years after the events, the struggle continues. There is an increasing institution-alization of memory, in places such as the Parque de la Memoria, a huge memorial park set up in 1998 by the city government, which contains the Monument to the Victims of State Terrorism, inaugurated in 2007. The monument comprises gray walls inscribed with the names of the disappeared, reminiscent of many other memorials elsewhere. Members of the Madres who had opposed exhumation opposed the inclusion of their children's names here, on a monument erected by those who had denied them justice (Friedrich 2011). However, more informal sites of public art and memorials exist throughout Buenos Aires, and are mapped in Memoria Abierta's book, *Memorials of Buenos Aires: Signs of State Terrorism in Argentina* (2013). This book is, again, a political intervention that makes visible the pervasive presence of sites of disappearance, detention, murder, and protest throughout the city: "monuments, sculptures, plaques, paving stones, stencils, and murals" and "locations bearing commemorative names, including classrooms, grandstands, sports facilities, auditoria, public squares, gardens, cultural centers, and clinics" (xix). It reveals "the suppressed history buried in every location where the last military government focused its reign of terror, in order to transform these hidden spaces into outlets for remembrance" (xvii). Others might prefer these sites to fade into invisibility and be forgotten, but they intrude into public space and challenge any attempt to continue as before. As Page suggests in his introduction, the book shows "how crucial the artistic efforts to expand public memory were in creating the conditions for procedural justice in the present" (2013: xv).

A North Dakota Museum of Art traveling exhibition curated by Laurel Reuter, *Los Desaparecidos/The Disappeared*, was shown in El Museo del Barrio, New York, in 2007 (Reuter 2006). It included a wide range of work addressing disappearances, such as Colombian artist Juan Manuel Echavarría's beaten-up mannequins, photographer Marcelo Brodsky's work documenting his classmates and his lost brother, and Fernando Traverso's bicycles (Brodsky 2006; Echavarría 2005; Traverso 2015). All the works shown wrestle in different ways with questions of time and memory in the context of events that would be called traumatic. Colombian artist Oscar Muñoz's portraits are remarkable in the way that they enact bringing back those made faceless. In one series of works, anonymous faces – not of the disappeared, just random faces from newspapers – are etched in grease on mirrors. They only become visible when a visitor looks into the mirror and breathes on the glass: the breath of the living makes the face appear. In his other work, a five-screen video installation *Project for a Memorial*, "the artist endlessly draws the faces of the dead and endlessly they disappear" (Reuter 2006: 104). On each screen, we see a hand swiftly sketching outlines of faces with a brush dipped in water, and the faces fade the minute they are finished. As Reuter notes, we are reminded that "to stop the forces of forgetting" is "an impossible task" (2006: 104). But we are also reminded that the memories can be endlessly redrawn, and we can repeat what has been forgotten. The cycle is never over: there is no beginning and no end, no past and no future, only a present where partial visions appear and disappear, at one and the same time.

Conclusion: Trauma time and linear temporality

In concluding the chapter, I want to return briefly to the question of time and temporality, and the distinction that I argue might usefully be made between trauma time and the linear temporality of the state (Edkins 2003a). The temporality of trauma is well expressed by Caruth. For her, "the event is not assimilated or experienced fully at the time, but only belatedly" (1995: 4). This retrospective temporality is what is central to trauma, not its distortion of reality, nor the way it represses or gives an unconscious meaning to something we want to ignore. The traumatic event is continually revisited, but we cannot make sense of it. There is "an inherent latency within the experience itself":

> The historical power of the trauma is not just that the experience is repeated after its forgetting, but that it is only through its inherent forgetting that it is first experienced at all. And it is this inherent latency of the event that paradoxically explains the peculiar, temporal structure, the belatedness, of historical experience. (Caruth 1995: 8)

Trauma time, then, is a time that cannot be inserted into linear narrative time. The story of the trauma cannot be told, insofar as a story is something with a beginning, a middle, and an end because, once it is put into a framing of that sort, its distinctiveness – its traumatic impact – is forgotten, by definition.

Memorials and commemorations generally work by inserting events that have had a traumatic impact into a linear narrative. For example, a narrative of heroism and sacrifice in the service of the nation-state. The nation-state itself relies on such narratives: of historical origins, belonging, and ancient roots. Some forms of memorial can attempt instead to encircle the trauma and retain its political impact. I have discussed the London Cenotaph as an example here. Sometimes resistance to commemoration or memory is appropriate, as in the case of the protests of the Madres in Argentina, and their refusal to accept the "closure" that identifying their children's remains would bring without the justice they were campaigning for. Memorials that encircle the trauma, rather than covering it over and forgetting it, can hold open the possibility of political challenge, or even of a different form of politics. Other memorials, though erected in the name of memory, enable us to forget, to gentrify the trauma and to carry on as before, as if nothing had happened, and with the fantasy that we call social reality intact.

Note

1   For other discussions of trauma, see Antze and Lambek 1996; Herman 1992; Leys 2000; Tal 1996.

CHAPTER THIRTY TWO

Museums and National History in Conflict: Two Case Studies in Taiwan

CHIA-LI CHEN

Introduction

By interpreting and representing national history, memorial museums not only shape collective memories and identities but also generate controversies. The Taipei 228 Memorial Museum and the Jing-Mei Human Rights Memorial and Cultural Park are two museums that were created to address the most traumatic and authoritarian period in the modern history of Taiwan. The 228 Memorial Museum presents exhibits that relate to the causes and the aftermath of the 228 Incident, a government-led massacre of Taiwanese that occurred in 1947. The Jing-Mei Human Rights Memorial and Cultural Park presents exhibits that relate to the suppression and prosecution of political dissidents during the White Terror Era, which followed the 228 Incident. Both museums are situated on historical sites and are regarded as "difficult heritages," which Macdonald (2009) defined as historical events that are not related to positive national achievements and that promote nation making by shaping shared identities. In her discussion, difficult heritages may "threaten to break through into the present in disruptive ways, opening up social divisions, perhaps by playing into an imagined, even nightmarish future" (2009: 1). Nevertheless, since the 1990s, widespread attempts worldwide have been made to tackle difficult heritages through preservation. However, the formats of many of the memorials to difficult-heritage events have been shaped by current political agendas (Young 1994: 20). Following the end of martial law in 1987, Taiwan began to preserve, consider, and negotiate the meanings of its difficult heritages in the late 1990s. Different political parties and stakeholders played important roles in this movement. This chapter will explore several questions, including: For whom and for what purposes were these historical sites preserved? under what circumstances and social milieu were the Taipei 228 Memorial Museum and the Jing-Mei Human Rights Memorial and Cultural Park established? and what controversies and conflicts have these two museums generated in relation to the cultural politics and the shaping of national history?

A Companion to Public History, First Edition. Edited by David Dean.
© 2018 John Wiley & Sons Ltd. Published 2018 by John Wiley & Sons Ltd.

This chapter first introduces briefly the histories of the 228 Incident and of the White Terror, and then discusses the social context in which the Taipei 228 Memorial Museum and the Jing-Mei Human Rights Memorial and Cultural Park were established. Controversies over selecting the names and defining the roles of these museums and the conflicting interests at play are highlighted. The perspectives and discourses of several major stakeholders, including government officials, victims and their families, artists, and scholars are described in order to show how museums resolved conflicts, reframed their interpretations, and transformed their roles. Lastly, the current challenges faced by the two museums are discussed in the conclusion.

The 228 incident, 1947

The 228 Incident, the most deadly massacre in modern Taiwanese history, began on February 28, 1947. This incident occurred two years after the end of Japanese colonial rule and the reunification of Taiwan with China after 50 years of separation. The reunification, however, did not bring joy to most people in Taiwan. The cultural gap and tensions between the Taiwanese people and Mainlanders (new immigrants from China after 1945) caused many conflicts and disputes, which triggered the 228 Incident.

First, the colonial experience of Taiwanese distinguished them from the new arrivals from Mainland China. For those who came from China after 1945, the recent war against Japan had been a horrible and unforgivable experience. Taiwanese, however, had lived under Japanese colonial rule from 1895 to 1945. Many spoke fluent Japanese, and some had served, whether willingly or under duress, in the Japanese army fighting against China during World War Two. In this respect, Taiwan and China had been enemies during this war. Thus, many Mainlanders, including the island's first post-unification Governor-General Chen-Yi, perceived Taiwanese as essentially Japanese who needed to be reformed and re-educated. In other words, the new arrivals did not treat Taiwanese as fellow citizens and compatriots. Discontent naturally grew as the process of decolonization failed to meet expectations and Taiwanese dreams of equal political participation failed to materialize.

Second, the political monopoly and corruption of Mainland Chinese further exacerbated social conflicts (Huang 2007: 16). Mainland Chinese assumed control of most of the property and positions vacated by the Japanese. Moreover, the rampant corruption and inefficiency of the Nationalist (KMT) government of Taiwan significantly increased problems of unemployment, disease, and social disorder (Chang 1989: 116; Kerr 1966: 243).

The immediate cause of the February 28 Incident was an attempt by government monopoly officials to arrest a woman who was selling untaxed cigarettes that ended with her being beaten unconscious. The brutal behavior of these government officials inflamed the anti-Mainlander sentiment among Taiwanese. After a brief period of social unrest, the government began negotiating with citizen representatives, whose stated primary goal was political reform. These citizen representatives demanded a peaceful resolution with many political reforms that included increased opportunities for Taiwanese to participate in politics. While promising to bring about a peaceful solution, General Chen requested that Chiang Kai-shek send backup troops from China. As soon as the troops arrived in Taiwan, they began a massacre of Taiwanese. Furthermore, they arrested representatives of the Taiwanese opposition, newspaper reporters, doctors, lawyers, and others who had spoken out for political reform. Today, it is widely accepted that 10,000 to 20,000 died as a result of the 228 Incident and that most of Taiwan's intellectuals and members of the elite were either killed or "disappeared" forever.[1]

The White Terror, 1949–1992

Following the military defeat of the Chinese Nationalists (led by the KMT) by the Chinese Communists (led by the CCP), the Nationalist government along with its military and many civilians retreated to Taiwan in 1949. In order to suppress alleged communist activities in Taiwan, the government declared martial law and enacted a series of regulations that banned unauthorized assemblies, associations, petitions, and strikes; controlled the media; and punished all activities that were deemed as "subversive." The experience of the 228 Incident had taught the KMT government the importance of maintaining tight control of the Taiwanese population through the restriction of political rights and the enhancement of pro-Nationalist education. The Temporary Provisions Effective During the Period of Communist Rebellion were promulgated in 1948 and martial law was announced in 1949. Taiwan was governed under martial law for the subsequent 38 years (1949–1987), and it was not until 1992 when the law of rebellion amended that the White Terror Era was truly ended.

The National Security Bureau, established during the 1950s, was in charge of the Taiwan Garrison Command, the Bureau of Investigation, and the Intelligence Bureau. These intelligence agencies were authorized to arrest anyone who criticized government policy. According to a report by Taiwan's Executive Yuan, around 140,000 Taiwanese were arrested, tortured, imprisoned, or executed for their real or perceived opposition to the KMT. An estimated 3,000 to 4,000 people were executed during the White Terror Era. About half of these executions occurred during the first decade (1950–1960). An estimated maximum of 900 of those could have been actual communists, as the last communist underground organization in Taiwan had been eradicated before the mid-1950s (Lee 2004; Ou 2008). Nevertheless, the prosecutions continued in order to strengthen the totalitarian government. In his analysis of the causes of the White Terror, Wu (2008) noted that the KMT regime was a "settler state" or "settler colonialist," a minority group that aimed to enhance its power of governance by dividing and mobilizing ethnic groups. Wu posited that the White Terror Era before the mid-1950s was a continuation of the Chinese Civil War and after the mid-1950s was a tool that used the rhetoric of anti-communism and the Cold War to suppress political dissents, particularly dissents that advocated the independence of Taiwan. Lee (2004) listed eight major targets for prosecution during the White Terror Era: left-wing movements sympathetic to the Chinese Communists, the Taiwan independence movement and its proponents, the indigenous autonomy movement, the democracy movement, political opponents within the KMT government and the military, losers in power struggles within the secret police, dissident authors, and cases that were fabricated by the secret police. In this context, not only political dissidents but many with no relationship to politics were imprisoned because of personal resentments or conflicts of interest with the authorities or intelligence agencies, who would get good rewards for cases they reported and properties they confiscated (Liu 1999).

One example of the victims of this political oppression was Po Yang, a newspaper columnist and translator of the serialized comic strip *Popeye the Sailor Man*. In 1968, the comic strip depicted Popeye and his son buying a small, uninhabited island. Both wanted to be elected president. Po Yang's translation of the English phrase "To my fellow countrymen" was censured as making fun of a phrase commonly used by President Chiang Kai-shek, and he was sentenced to a prison sentence of 12 years. It is worth noticing that whereas most of the victims of the 228 Incident were Taiwanese, Wu (2006) estimated that 40% of the victims of the White Terror were Mainlanders, who comprised only 15% of the total population of Taiwan. Many of these victims were prosecuted at the Jing-Mei Military Detention Centre and then transferred to prisons on Green Island, a small island off the southeast coast of Taiwan. Some of those sent to prison were arrested during the Kaohsiung Incident, which erupted on December 10, 1979. This incident was a demonstration initially launched by political dissidents demanding democracy and freedom, which snowballed into the largest confrontation between the police and the public since the 228 Incident. Several participants in the Kaohsiung Incident such as Hsin-je Huang (Chairman of the DPP from 1988 to 1992), Ming-te Shih (Chairman of the DPP from 1994 to 1996), and Annette Lu (Vice President of Taiwan from 2000 to 2008) became successful politicians and core members of the Democratic Progressive Party (DPP), which was established in 1986.

The establishment of memorial museums in Taiwan

Following the lifting of martial law in 1987 and the process of democratization, the 228 Incident became one of the most fervently discussed issues in Taiwanese society. The populace demanded to know the truth of this Incident and demanded that the government publish all of the available first-hand historical documents. The Committee for the Promotion of the 228 Peace Day was founded in 1987. Furthermore, the DPP made uncovering the truth of the 228 Incident part of its party manifesto, and DPP legislators regularly pressured the government to reveal related information (Tseng 1997: 150). However, it was not until the late 1990s, under the leadership of the first DPP mayor of Taipei (and later president from 2000 to 2008), Chen Shui-bian, that the proposal to build a museum commemorating the incident took shape. At that time, although five monuments in Taiwan commemorated the victims, no museum was responsible for collecting and presenting historical artifacts. After a year of preparation, the former Taiwan Broadcasting Station was chosen as the site for the museum, which was opened to the public in 1997.

The Taipei 228 Memorial Museum is housed in a renovated historical building that was originally built for the Taipei Broadcasting Bureau in 1930 by the Japanese colonial government (Figure 32.1). In 1947, during the 228 Incident, the station became the center for representatives of both sides to broadcast news. Thus, the Bureau building shared a historical connection with the Incident. Meanwhile, demands to preserve former prisons as memorials for the victims of the White Terror increased as well during the late 1990s. In 2002, the Green Island Human Rights Memorial Park was opened. In 2007, only a year before Chen Shui-bian's term of office as president ended, the former Jing-Mei Military Detention Centre in Taipei, which had been used in the prosecution and imprisonment of political prisoners during the White Terror, was proclaimed a historic site and converted into the Taiwan Human Rights Jing-Mei Park. Tsao et al. (2008: 34) hold that the preservation symbolizes the transformation of historical political prisons into human rights museums in a democratic society, providing a place where citizens can experience history and become better informed about this period in history. However, both the Taipei 228

Figure 32.1 The Taipei 228 Memorial Museum is housed in a renovated historical building. Photo: Chia-Li Chen.

Memorial Museum and the Jing-Mei Human Rights Memorial and Cultural Park were under pressure to adhere to the conflicting objectives of different stakeholders. These conflicts were particularly apparent when the museums were under the administrative control of the KMT government, when the distrust and discontent of survivors and of the family members of victims highlighted the conflicts with regard to management ideas, ideas about the naming of museums, and interpretations of exhibit contents.

The management and naming of museums

As the first museum dedicated to the 228 Incident, the Taipei 228 Memorial Museum aims to reveal and represent the historical facts of the 228 Incident as well as to promote harmony among different ethnic groups. The Taiwan Peace Foundation was the first private sector organization contracted to manage the museum. This foundation established the framework and management structure of the museum and ran the museum from 1997 to 2000. With a strong commitment to reveal the historical truth to the public, the foundation also won the trust of the families of victims, who donated the many artifacts and objects that created the basis of the museum's permanent collection. The election of Ying-jeou Ma, a KMT party member, as the mayor of Taipei in 1999 reoriented the attitude of the Taipei City administration toward the management of the Taipei 228 Memorial Museum. In 2000, management responsibilities were rebid, and the Taiwan Peace Foundation was replaced by the pro-KMT Taiwan Regional Development Institute.

The shift in management was not smooth. First, the new team reduced the number of museum staff from 16 to 11. Second, some pieces in the permanent collection were withdrawn by their contributors due to distrust in the new management direction. Furthermore, volunteers, some of whom were relatives of 228 Incident victims, expressed suspicion about the new team. Despite efforts to promote a politically neutral image for the museum, including keeping the permanent exhibition unchanged, it is not hard to find hints of a political agenda in the management shift. Because the 228 Incident was a key agenda in the political reform movement of the late 1980s, it was widely believed that a DPP mayor of Taipei was critical of its creation. In 2003, after the Taiwan Regional Development Institute decided not to renew its contract, the Bureau of Culture of Taipei City assumed responsibilities for museum operations, employing a skeletal staff of four paid employees. Meanwhile, an increasing number of victims' families and scholars were pressing for the creation of a national museum dedicated to the 228 Incident in order to highlight its significance in modern Taiwanese history. The site for the National 228 Memorial Museum was chosen in 2006 during Chen Shui-bian's presidency, and the museum was opened in 2011 during Ying-jeou Ma's presidency.

Similarly, the Jing-Mei Human Rights Memorial and Cultural Park underwent a very turbulent first few years after its opening. One year after the park opened in 2007, Ying-jeou Ma was elected president. He directed the Council of Cultural Affairs (the present Ministry of Culture) to assign a team to run the museum. An objective treatment of the violation of human rights by the KMT government during the White Terror was a discomforting and challenging task for the KMT-led government. In February 2009, the management team decided to change the name of the museum from the Taiwan Human Rights Jing-Mei Park to the Taiwan Jing-Mei Cultural Park. This decision triggered vociferous protests from survivors and victims' families, who believed that the KMT government planned to eliminate the museum's connection to human rights and its own ugly past under the veil of cultural and art activities. However, Wang Shou-lai, Director of the Preparation Office of the Bureau of Cultural Heritage of the Council of Cultural Affairs, explained that: "The connection to human rights has not been diminished ... We would like to use culture to soften the dark gloomy atmosphere of death because culture also contains the meaning of human rights" (Wang, Chao and Chiu 2009). He also said that the focus of the previous DPP-government-assigned museum management team, the Peng Ming-min Cultural Foundation, on only the negative aspects of past KMT government activities would have a divisive impact on the harmony among Taiwan's different ethnic groups (Wang, Chao, and Chiu 2009).

Former Vice President and White Terror victim Annette Lu protested that the name change was "using culture to deceive the human rights":

> If a nation yearns for progress, people must learn their history, regardless of whether it is 'good' or otherwise. But Ma's government was in a hurry to cover up the history just one year into his presidency. If we don't stop this, Ma's government will destroy the memorial buildings including the military court and conceal the historical facts that underlie the persecution of human rights. (Lee 2009)

After a public hearing, the management team decided on the new name of Jing-Mei Human Rights Memorial and Cultural Park in order to retain both human rights and culture in the name (Lin 2014). After that, the museum also organized a new consultant team that included survivors, scholars of human rights and museology, and community representatives in order to ensure decisions had broad-based support and backing. However, the controversy over how to interpret the traumatic past did not end and reached a crescendo when contemporary artwork was displayed in the museum in 2009.

Human rights versus contemporary art? A battle of remembering

To attract more visitors, the Jing-Mei Human Rights Memorial and Cultural Park held several consultative meetings in 2009 to discuss the role and management of the museum as a first step to developing more services and to plan its exhibitions. As a member of the consultant team, I had opportunities to observe how the team managed the difficult issues and this rather large historical site, which included a large cellblock with many small cells that once held political prisoners, several military courtrooms, and several buildings that once housed soldiers. The gray concrete and barbed wire-enclosed prisons exude a lifeless and oppressive atmosphere. The management team believed that the best way to revive this historical site and bring visitors in was through art and cultural events. Thus, several steps were proposed, including introducing art exhibitions and activities along with exhibitions on the White Terror and on other human rights issues. During these consultative meetings, survivors of White Terror expressed the suspicion that art and cultural events would detract from the site's historical atmosphere. Furthermore, they worried that events such as live music would refocus the site as an entertainment venue and cause it to lose its status as a memorial. However, a school principal who was serving as a representative of the community expressed strong support for holding cultural events because this site remained a horrible and daunting place for schoolchildren in the neighborhood. Scholars agreed with the importance of better serving the needs of visitors while stressing the need to strike an equitable balance between representing the history of the White Terror and holding cultural events. These scholars emphasized that the latter should have a direct relationship with human rights issues and education.

To prepare for the opening of several exhibitions on December 10, 2009, the management team proposed to commission an artist to create artworks in and around the building where the former Bureau of Investigation Chief Hsi-ling Wang had been imprisoned. He had been accused of ordering the 1984 assassination of famous Taiwanese writer Yi-liang Liu in the United States. Liu wrote the book *Biography of Chiang Ching-kuo*, which criticized Chiang Ching-kuo, the son of Chiang Kai-shek and Taiwan's president from 1978 to 1988. The assassination made headlines in the United States. Under pressure from the United States government and international human rights organizations, Hsi-ling Wang was sentenced to life imprisonment in 1985. He was "imprisoned" at the Jing-Mei Detention Centre in a specially built building with a private bedroom, study, bathroom, and kitchen and was granted parole in 1991. Compared with the crowded, cramped cells reserved for political dissidents, Wang's prison was luxurious. The holding of a special exhibit on the former Bureau Chief provoked fury among the representatives of survivors, who demanded that the building be torn down rather than be featured as its own exhibit. However, the management team continued forward with this exhibit. They noted that the DPP-affiliated Peng Ming-min Cultural Foundation had also organized an exhibit that highlighted the different treatments received by Wang and political dissidents. Thus, the team argued, it was still important to preserve the building and display the historical facts. As consultants, myself and other scholars on the committee reminded the management team to treat this issue and exhibit with appropriate sensitivity.

Ultimately, Wen-fu Yu was commissioned to execute the artwork for Hsi-ling Wang's prison. He stayed in the building for two nights to experience how Wang experienced life behind bars. He created several sound installations inside the building as well as a landscape installation around it called *Beyond the Wall*, which consisted of a sea of bamboo skewers capped by pigeons that were painted white as symbols of the longing for hope, freedom, and peace (Figure 32.2). The English panel for this exhibit reads:

> This land art work is located on the exterior of the "confinement area" wall. Tens of thousands white bamboo skewers are inserted into clay, resembling a bamboo forest or grassland. This alludes to white clouds, a scenario we can see doves resting or flying away [*sic*]. It also creates a scene that is pure white and symbolizes the eternal spirit of freedom ... The piece *Beyond the Wall* expresses humanity's natural love of freedom.

While an aesthetically beautiful piece of artwork, White Terror victims Ming-te Shih and his wife Chia-chun Chen were irritated by the presentation because they believed that this artwork was "glorifying" a killer and insulted those who suffered during the White Terror. At the opening ceremony, Ms. Chen broke several of the bamboo skewers and pigeons and threw red paint on the piece. The artist broke into tears immediately upon witnessing the destruction. The event made immediate headlines. Over 30 artists protested the incident at the Council of Cultural Affairs (CCA) the next day, demanding that the government protect Taiwanese artists' freedom of artistic expression. On the

Figure 32.2 Wen-fu Yu, *Beyond the Wall*, comprising of bamboo skewers with doves, symbolizes the longing for hope, freedom, and peace. Photo: Chin-jung Tsao.

same day, CCA chairman Chih-jen Sheng proclaimed that artwork and different interpretations of history should be respected and tolerated.

Why did Ms. Chen choose physical destruction over verbal protest? In a letter addressed to President Ma, Chia-chun Chen explained:

> I wanted to make a forthright statement because this despoils the dignity of more than ten thousand victims ... The state may regard us as "rubbish" but it cannot "glorify" a terrible assassin. This is unbearable. (Chen 2009)

She also claimed that freedom of artistic expression does not extend to glorifying dictators. A young artist with little understanding of history, she said, may be forgiven his mistake, but the government that is responsible for spending taxpayers' money should not be allowed to support such an absurd work. However, groups of artists stated their belief that criticism may be expressed and voiced through the media but not through violence. Yu (2010) clarified that he had no intention of glorifying a killer, but rather executed his project within the requirement set by the government that submissions should explore the meaning of the site. He also admitted that he did not have much information or education about the White Terror Era. He expressed his apologies for any harm done to the families of victims but said that he wished that Ms. Chen would have contacted him beforehand to discuss possible alterations. Furthermore, Yeh (2009: 1) pointed out: "We have suffered under political taboos and social apathy for a long time. We don't understand the political truth, so how can we ask artists to create and cure, transcend and sublimate the historical trauma?"

In response to this dispute, Yu agreed to shorten the exhibition and invited survivors of White Terror to disassemble his artwork together (Figure 32.3; Tsao 2011). This is

Figure 32.3 Yu invited survivors of White Terror to disassemble his artwork together. Photo: Chin-jung Tsao.

significant because it demonstrates that the problem arose not from a conflict between human rights and art but rather the lack of expertise in curatorship. Moreover, this controversy shows the wide gap in the interpretation of Taiwan's traumatic past between government officials and the families of White Terror victims. For the latter, showing the historical truth of the White Terror is the paramount mission of the museum. For their part, it is believed that government officials sought to use art to blur historical memories (Huang 2010) while attempting to revive a difficult heritage through art and cultural events – an approach they had used successfully to revive several of Taiwan's industrial heritages. However, difficult heritages differ significantly from commercial or industrial heritages, and their revival and portrayal in museums must be carefully planned. Kavanagh (1996: 5) indicates that "museums can be places where history is both remembered and forgotten, as curators have to decide what to collect and what to let go, what to record and what to ignore." The controversy is thus also a battle of remembering.

The controversy over the new permanent exhibit at the Taipei 228 Memorial Museum

After 10 years in operation, the management team of the Taipei 228 Memorial Museum decided to replace the museum's permanent exhibition. The new permanent exhibition opened in 2011 after four years of planning, and comprised panels, newspapers, paintings, sculptures, photographs, oral histories, and objects once used by 228 Incident victims. Several messages conveyed by the exhibition emerge from an analysis of the historical narrative in these panels.

First, unlike the previous permanent exhibition, which contrasted daily life for Taiwanese under Japanese colonial rule and under early KMT rule, the new permanent exhibit focused on the history of the building and its role in disseminating the news. Second, unlike the old permanent exhibition's message that tragedy was the result of confusion of identity (Chen 2003), the new exhibit focused on describing the political corruption and social upheaval that occurred in the run up to the 228 Incident and used theatrical techniques to present the Incident using video clips and oral history. The exhibit also presented video-based oral histories along the panels, which were more vivid than those presented previously. Third, the new exhibit cut the direct link between the 228 Incident and the White Terror Era and rather linked 228 to the global human rights movement by adding an International Human Rights Forest theme area. This theme area introduced other major memorial museums in the world such as the Hiroshima Peace Memorial Museum and the Jewish Museum Berlin. Tsao (2011) criticized the lack of introduction to the White Terror and the intertwining of the International Human Rights Movement with the 228 Justice Movement, which confused the contexts of Taiwan's own democratization.

When the new exhibition opened in 2011, panels printed with quotes from the official records in 1947 showed how the government dealt with the 228 Incident. The text of panels such as "Recovering the Order/Troops Sent from the Central Government" and "New Election of County and City Mayors/Announcement of Martial Law" and descriptions such as "Every yellow paper showed the use of government authority ... it repressed the fury and re-established the order" quickly evoked severe criticism from some historians and victims' families. It was reported that Te-chen Lin, a grandson of a 228 victim, said that the exhibition confused the historical truth with the panels such as the use of government authority and the establishment of a new order, which was unacceptable. Yen-hsien Chang, a widely respected historian whose research career focused on the collection of oral histories of the 228 Incident, also criticized the display of a panel with an official contemporary government statement that the government would console the people, which he felt would confuse visitors. In response to this criticism, the 228 Memorial Museum director explained that the museum had retained several historians as consultants to examine the content of the new permanent exhibition, and that these panels were intended to show government's dual role of treatment. However, he promised that he would consider their comments and added descriptive titles such as "Dual-Sided Treatment" to explain that the museum compares what the government said with what it actually did (Chen 2011). Later, panels were changed to provide clearer explanations such as "Claimed that the Central Government would not send troops but in reality allowed troops to shoot their way from Keelung to Taipei" in order to show both sides of stories and to display the historical reality.

Kavanagh (1996: 4) has posited the existence of two meanings of history: the actual events of history and the representation of these events by historians. Museums offer the greatest breadth of creativity and challenge for historians due to the wide range of materials and evidence that may be used to reconstruct history. Furthermore, museums may help form a national consensus and shape the collective memory of society. Through the new permanent exhibit, the museum intended to provide a more holistic view of the 228 Incident by paralleling what government said and did. Nevertheless, the protests highlight the dangers that are inherent in offering the public mixed messages or confusing them with ambiguous panel titles.

Beyond commemoration: The museum as a site of countering social amnesia

Young indicates that the relationship between a state and its memorials is never one-sided. He points out: "On the one hand, official agencies are in a position to shape memory explicitly as they see fit, memory that best serves a national interest. On the other hand, once created, memorials take on lives of their own, often stubbornly resistant to the state's original intentions" (1993: 3). It is especially challenging when it came to having the incumbent regime (KMT) reflect on its past crimes against human rights in a memorial museum that was established by its political rival (DPP). Thus, it should be no surprise that the museum management team assigned by the KMT government would try to downplay the role of Taiwan's memorial and human rights museums through the introduction of works of art. However, resistance to diluting the original purpose of these museums as memorials for the victims of autocratic terror is strong in Taiwan, with survivors and the families of victims posing a major challenge to the presentation of narratives and memories that are more favorable to the KMT government.

Since February 28 was declared a national holiday in 1997, ceremonies to memorialize the victims of the 228 Incident have been held every year in the 228 Peace Memorial Park hosted by the Taipei 228 Memorial Museum. However, these ceremonies are attended by all major politicians and have become largely a show of political correctness. Chen (2005) described the cult of 228 ceremonies and exhibitions as "narrative fetishism," with apologies and statements of forgiveness and moving on repeated for the sake of ethnic harmony, which in fact project a collective forgetting. Young (1993: 5) explains this phenomenon: "Once we assign monumental form to memory, we have to some degree divested ourselves of the obligation to remember. In shouldering the memory work, a monument may relieve viewers of their memory burden." Might it apply to these two cases that once the museums were established, the traumatic memories and history have become forgotten? Might Taiwan's difficult heritage threaten the present and create social division?

As with artist Yu, many younger Taiwanese have limited knowledge of the 228 Incident and White Terror. Moreover, high school textbooks give only cursory coverage of this period. Thus, the museum has a significant role to play in countering the social amnesia and shaping the future of Taiwan. More resources must be invested in researching this period. After the *Beyond the Wall* fiasco, a new team was assigned at the urging of human rights scholars and historians, and the Preparation Office of the National Human Rights Museum was established in the Jing-Mei Human Rights Memorial and Cultural Park in 2011. This new team has carefully focused their work on collecting oral histories and documents related to the White Terror, promoting human rights education through workshops, and conserving and reconstructing historical settings based on oral histories (Huang 2011). However, the continued status of this organization as a preparation office at the time this chapter was written shows the reluctance of the current KMT-led government (2008–2016) to establish a national museum with adequate resources to conserve the heritage and research the history of White Terror. In contrast, the National 228 Memorial Museum, which opened in 2011, is largely symbolic due to the small scale of its exhibitions and collections in comparison with those of the Taipei 228 Memorial Museum.

Carter and Orange (2012) proposed a human rights museology that encourages moral reflection on civic duty and links teaching with memorialization. Human rights and memorial museums thus play a pivotal role not only in memorializing the victims but also in shaping the history and in teaching the value of human rights and democracy. However, Chen (2005:vi) argued that the commemoration of the 228 Incident from the mid-1980s to the 1990s "contributed to the discursive formation of contemporary Taiwanese national and cultural identities and subjectivities" in which male victims were "glorified as national forefathers and as national subjects of a new nation" while the role played by females was neglected and hidden. Furthermore, in my research on the Taipei 228 Memorial Museum, I point out that the museum overlooks the experience of Mainlanders during the 228 Incident (Chen 2007).

Therefore, how to represent the long-repressed histories of the 228 Incident and the White Terror while promoting human rights education is the core challenge for both of these museums in the future. This challenge is especially daunting in the context of the history of the White Terror, which has received comparatively less attention than the 228 Incident. In history textbooks, the White Terror Era is always mentioned as a period of booming economic growth, with the contemporary human rights movement and the totalitarian policies of the KMT government largely ignored. The conflicts involved in writing and interpreting museum texts are indeed a struggle of filling in the missing pages of modern Taiwanese history. Historical events cannot be described in a single perspective. Therefore, different accounts and perspectives supported by artifacts and documents should be presented in museum exhibitions for scholars to investigate and for visitors, especially younger visitors, to learn from historical tragedies, reflect on the essence of totalitarianism, and appreciate the value of hard-won democracy. Moreover, those women who suffered and sacrificed during the 228 Incident and the White Terror contributed in a myriad of ways to Taiwan's ultimate democratization and should be given their rightful place in the museum narrative as subjects that shaped modern national history. In addition, the experiences of different ethnic groups such as Mainlanders, Hakka, and Taiwan's indigenous peoples should be further investigated, discussed, and displayed, as all have contributed to the democratization of Taiwan. Introducing multiple perspectives and the experiences of different ethnicities and genders may not only help make amends to those victims and to their relatives but also help heal social divisions by constructing a society of harmony and peace that is based on a shared understanding of a traumatic past.[2]

Notes

1   There was no accurate record of deaths during this massacre because many people were afraid to admit that a family member had died during this incident. In his report on the 228 Massacre, Chang (2007) estimates that approximately 18,000 to 28,000 people were killed in the 228 Incident.
2   The author would like to thank the support of the Jing-Mei Human Rights Memorial and Cultural Park, Taipei 228 Memorial Museum and Mr. Chin-jung Tsao. This chapter is part of the result of a research project entitled "The Roles and Functions of Museum Exhibitions in Human Rights Education" funded by the Preparation Office of the National Human Rights Museum.

CHAPTER THIRTY THREE

Between Public History and History Education

JOANNA WOJDON

Introduction

In the good old days when history had just established itself as an academic discipline, its main goal was to find out what had happened in the past, to use the words of Leopold von Ranke from the 1820s, "how it really was" or "how it essentially was" ('Wie es eigentlich gewesen'). The primary role of history teachers was therefore "to instill knowledge and a certain persuasion within the students" (Bracke et al. 2014). Lecturing was the dominant teaching method both at universities and at schools; history graduates were prepared either for academic or teaching careers.

This situation changed significantly in the course of the twentieth century. The discipline itself was changed with the adoption of postmodernist approaches. History was therefore no longer simply about reconstructing the past, but rather about deconstructing narratives dealing with the past. This posed a dilemma, for if academics claimed to be unable to provide a single "true" story about the past, what should school teachers present to their students? As advocates of postmodern history education continue to argue, what needs to happen is a shift from presenting one "official," "scientifically proven" truth, to discussions about different interpretations of the past (Segall 2006; Seixas 2000). This change has not happened quickly, and in some countries it has barely even started. For example, as I have argued elsewhere, history education in Poland may have changed recently in terms of adopting more active teaching methods, but it has not changed in terms of giving up the idea of transmitting a single, authoritative narrative to students (Wojdon 2017).

Both in Poland and elsewhere, then, it is clear that the methodologies of teaching history did change following the postmodern intervention. Historical education followed more general pedagogical trends, notably the shift from teacher-oriented to student-oriented classrooms, and from lecturing to interactive and inquiry-based learning methods (Cuban 2013). Yet, academics specializing in history education argue that

A Companion to Public History, First Edition. Edited by David Dean.
© 2018 John Wiley & Sons Ltd. Published 2018 by John Wiley & Sons Ltd.

much more needs to happen: not only changes in teaching methods and/or techniques but in the very philosophy of history education in order to make it "a system of knowledge rather than a set of bare important facts" (De Groot 2009: 40). What has emerged from these discussions is a new concept of historical thinking (Andrews, Warren, and Cousins 2016; Wineburg 2009). Indeed, some luminaries of the historical sub-discipline dealing with education – called history didactics in Germany (Geschichtsdidaktik) and Central European countries – began to pay less attention to methodologies. As Karl-Ernst Jeismann pointed out: "the particular way of presenting material, discussion, evaluation – depends on teacher's competencies … and is so dependent on an individual situation that no general guidance can replace the individual teacher's effort and even less so pretend to be the verified solution" (2015: 93). Instead, the researchers focused on the bases and results of history education: on the historical consciousness of society and historical culture (Koster et al. 2014; Seixas 2004; Carretero et al. 2017).

New research on historical consciousness, historical memory, and historical narratives within the field of historical education paralleled similar concerns with another emerging historical sub-discipline: public history. The whole field of public history also opened up new professional career opportunities for history graduates.[1] Now, rather than just being trained for academic and teaching careers, students had opportunities to work in other fields (Gelles 2012).[2]

The purpose of this chapter is to discuss the mutual relations (existing and potential) between various aspects of public history and history education. So far, as Marko Demantowsky (2015) has aptly noticed, while the German researchers of historical consciousness and historical culture tend to ignore the concept of public history,[3] English-speaking public history discourse rarely includes the research and practices of history teaching in school.[4] This is an invitation to explore the differences and similarities between public history and historical education.

Similarities and differences

Both history education and public history share a desire to spread history beyond academia. They both address large non-professional audiences. The audiences differ, however, since public history is "for the public, of the public, by the public and with the public," while history education targets primary and secondary school pupils in the interest of the nation and state (or nation-state) (Elson 1964; Franco 1997: 65). Goals specific to each of these diverse audiences necessitate not only differences in methodologies, but also in the professional profiles of those in charge of delivering content and in academic research areas. Indeed, even the understanding of what constitutes "audience" differs. History educators or "didacticians" in their research on historical consciousness concentrate on the effects of history education: how accurate the historical knowledge among "laymen" is, how they had absorbed historical narratives, and how the narratives could change in order to prevent the distortions noticed (Michalski 2015; Traba and Thunemann 2015). Public historians are interested in society's engagements with the past in order to uncover what issues should be dealt with because they generate public interest, explore ways of representing history that will be attractive to the public, and, at a time of diminishing resources and competing interests, where best to invest money, time, and effort.

As a result, it could be argued that audience counts for much more in the field of public history than in the field of history education. After all, students *must* attend their lessons as a legal obligation (in schools at least), while the public needs *encouragement* to come to a museum, buy a historical magazine, or to watch a historical feature film. As Ann Clark (2008) has shown for Australia, governments or individual politicians have a say in the content of the history curriculum in a way that they cannot shape the forms of history presented to and for the public. In Australia's case, there was little concern among policy makers if students disliked school history because they received little of what they were really interested in (for example, American or world history). And yet, while public historians certainly cannot ignore their audience in this way, it is also true that despite this difference there are definite advantages when the interests and preferences of students are taken into consideration. Indeed, educators seem to be becoming more and more aware of this fact. As Terry Haydn (2011) has argued, giving up the master narrative of building national pride in the imperial past in England may have upset conservative politicians, but decisions instead to promote critical inquiry, encourage classroom discussion on controversial topics, and explore the everyday life of ordinary people resulted in the growing popularity of history as a school subject (Crawford 1995).

As some researchers have pointed out, education in general is highly politicized (Apple 1995). History in particular can be used as a propaganda tool by the state (Wojdon 2012; 2013). Although public history is subject to less overt politicization, public historians are not necessarily independent from pressure groups (including politicians and corporations) wishing to promote certain narratives, perspectives, or even particular policies and strategies, especially if they offer financial support (Jordanova 2006). Cathy Stanton (2006), for example, notes that local businesses were concerned about representing working-class inequality as something that was firmly in the past in a public history project in Lowell, Massachusetts, in the United States. Ludmila Jordanova (2006) draws attention to the possibility that historians writing commissioned histories of associations or political organizations can find themselves facing limited access to materials and influence on interpretation. It is not surprising then to find examples where "historical politics" or the "politics of history" promoted by the state shape both public history and history education. Thus, sites of public history, such as historical monuments, commemorations, exhibitions, and publications can be as much a focus for dispute as history textbooks, curricula, and pedagogy.

Luigi Cajani (2009) has argued at the conference of the International Society for History Didactics that textbooks have to be approved by state authorities in a number of European countries, including the former Soviet Bloc. In Poland, there is no limit to the number of approved books that are available for adoption in the classroom, and teachers are free to choose which ones they will use. While formal approval of a text is the prerogative of the Ministry of Education, decisions are based on the opinions of selected academics and teachers. By contrast, in Greece, only one textbook is approved per subject and grade. As a result, the textbook wars in Greece, which involved state authorities, political parties, and the Orthodox Church, had considerable media coverage. The authors of one textbook were accused of deconstructing national history and identity, were condemned by the archbishop, and their book was withdrawn from schools (Liakos 2008). While Russia may be notorious for undue political influence in historical education,[5] scholars such as Terry Haydn (2014) have found much to write about in regard to Britain.

Whereas public history aims to attract as many people as possible to its various representations of the past, not just encouraging people to "use" public history, but also to invest their money in it (whether buying tickets, souvenirs, or books), history education has the narrower goal of enhancing students' historical knowledge. This is usually measured by examinations, sometimes obsessively so to the detriment of the discipline. In England, according to Harris and Haydn, as a result of the exam pressure, some "lower attaining pupils ... were being pressurised, or in some cases, prevented from taking the subject, and being directed to take other subjects which were felt to be 'less challenging' or 'more appropriate'" (2012: 1). Examination techniques also reflect concerns about historical consciousness. For example, too often, multiple-choice tests focused on facts or specific fact-centered "historical skills" (such as map reading, analysis of statistical data, finding data in primary sources, etc.) leave little or no room for evaluating critical reflections about the past (Grant and Gradwell 2010). Teachers' freedom of setting goals and choosing material and interpretations can be severely limited by authorities responsible for curricula, textbooks, or examinations. School history education has to comply with large volumes of official regulations, requirements, and recommendations issued by state and local authorities, including ministries of education, school boards, and examination boards. Teachers themselves complain that they have to concentrate more on bureaucracy and discipline in the classroom than on teaching itself.

The professional profiles of public historians and teachers reflect the priorities set and instruments available for each profession. Public history educators should be, according to Faye Sayer (2015), enthusiastic, creative, flexible, communicative, and patient; competency in the discipline came only sixth in their list of criteria. It is quite the reverse in case of teachers, who, at least in Poland, are expected to first be competent in the discipline and only after that to have the skill to evoke interest, and to be kind or openminded (Chorąży, Konieczka-Śliwińska, and Roszak 2008). These criteria are important because employers (school heads, education boards) pay particular attention to examination results when measuring the competence and ability of teachers (Grant and Gradwell 2010). By contrast, research shows that for students the most important factors in successful learning are teachers' fairness and ability to maintain discipline in the classroom, as well as to explain complicated subjects (Chorąży, Konieczka-Śliwińska, and Roszak 2008; Chańko 2015). While public historians also face regulations and restrictions, management, and controls over their work, particularly those in institutions such as museums, others face less politically controlled structures of supervision and evaluation.

Pre-service and in-service teacher training plays an important role in forming teachers' attitudes. About a fifth of a recent academic textbook for history teacher trainees published in Poland is devoted to administrative procedures and documents (Chorąży, Konieczka-Śliwińska, and Roszak 2008). The teachers' meetings that I attended in 2015 in Wrocław were dominated by laments about the poor exam performance of students at various grades. No wonder then that a recent report on history education in Poland, based on observations of history lessons in schools, states that secondary school teachers mostly lecture to enable their students to "acquire knowledge" and that textbooks are the most important teaching tool (Choińska-Mika 2014). Similar observations have recently been made in Canada, where 68% of high school students reported that they received history lessons through "listening to teacher and taking notes" and 60% on "reading textbooks and answering questions." None of the other activities surveyed reached higher than 30% (Lévesque and Zanazanian 2015).

History teachers' attitudes towards the subject "history and society," introduced in Polish upper secondary schools in 2012 for those students who were not going to take final exams in history, illustrates this phenomenon. The national curriculum gave teachers a lot of freedom in shaping the subject. They were supposed to choose four modules out of eight proposed (such as media history, family history, history of science, and history of wars) or four historical periods (Antiquity, Middle Ages, modern times, nineteenth century, and twentieth century) and work on them using whatever methods they choose. The guidelines were very general. Teachers could also propose their own module (for example, local history) (Podstawa programowa kształcenia ogólnego dla gimnazjów i szkół ponadgimnazjalnych 2011). Both teachers and conservative politicians complained from the very beginning that teaching without the goal of a final exam would diminish the position importance of the subject since students would not want to learn without the pressure of external assessment, even though at the same time many teachers complained that exams killed their passion for teaching. Informal talks I had with some teachers and students indicated that many teachers kept teaching "regular" history classes on "history and society," and students saw no difference between the two subjects.

Nevertheless, there are "ambitious teachers" who know how to create the space necessary for themselves and their students to explore the past in innovative ways despite a general environment that is unsupportive (Grant and Gradwell 2010). Asked what they liked most during their history lessons, British students pointed to interactive methods such as role-playing, drama, and debates, as well as watching videos, drawing, and "making things" (Harris and Haydn 2006). In many ways, these activities are similar to what public history institutions propose and practice, and in such cases the distinctions between history education and public history are blurred. Indeed, teachers sometimes devote some time to include public history endeavors in their teaching process: taking their students to a museum, watching a video, or taking part in games. Research shows that although making lessons enjoyable and meaningful does not necessarily produce higher performances in exams, it also does not produce poorer results, and the benefits of increasing student motivation and satisfaction, and enhancing the pleasure and desire for learning history are clear (Grant and Gradwell 2010).

Recent reflections by theorists and practitioners of history education more and more often include the concept of "attractiveness." Harris and Haydn argue that "how pupils are taught appears to matter more than what they are taught" and that not only curricula but also teaching methods should be debated (2006: 315) Teachers ask students for feedback on the lessons. Historical "edutainment" has become a topic of a professional conference where most papers concentrated on pedagogical advantages of certain public history products, from museum exhibits through computer and board games and mobile-phone applications to films, television shows, and popular history magazines (International Society for History Didactics 2014). Although some argue that "it is impermissible to learn history pleasurably," (Kondo and Tanaka 2016) many others feel that it is quite possible and, indeed, valuable, as the next section will show.

Interactions

This section presents some examples of interactions between public history and history education under thematic headings. Most of the case studies and references relate to Poland due to my own personal experience, but are considered using knowledge gained from discussions with colleagues at conferences and international project meetings, making them relevant to other countries as well. Suggestions for further research are also offered.

Teachers use strategies and methods developed by public history. Teachers engage students in projects such as gathering oral history interviews, preserving family memorabilia, and organizing school exhibitions and events related to the past. James Wolfinger

(2008) discusses how oral history material can serve as a starting point for the lessons on wider issues, such as immigration or the Holocaust (see also Llewellyn and Ng-A-Fook 2017). Polish school textbooks sometimes encourage students to undertake such activities, especially in relation to the recent past, and to contested pasts. For example, Dariusz Stola (2012) proposes that students ask their relatives about what they remember from the martial law of 1981–1982 and to compare those testimonies with the three that he cites in his textbook. Thanks to the opportunities offered by the Internet, students can present the results of their work not only to their teacher and classmates, but also to the general public. They publish their papers and posters or engage in online discussions on historical topics. While completing these tasks, students become public historians themselves. They become familiar with the potentials of historical research and representation and learn the historians' craft, experiences that can be shared and discussed in the classroom. Reflections on methods and not just on content is one element of the "new history" in schools.

Teachers use public history facilities to teach. History lessons are taught not only at schools but also in the public sphere: in the streets, in museums, in cinemas, or during historical events, reenactments, fairs, and shows. Students are asked by their teachers to attend such events, as well as to participate in or attend public debates about the past and history book club meetings. Teachers thus bring an important part of public history to their student audience, and public history institutions usually respond favorably to these initiatives. Most museums in Poland, for example, have special "educational sections," administrative units that specifically deal with schoolchildren. They train special guides and offer lessons and other activities that correspond with school curricula. Polin, the Museum of the History of Polish Jews, organizes special two-hour thematic workshops for various age groups, from early primary to upper secondary school, in addition to special guided tours on the museum's exhibits. They deal with Jewish history and culture, religion and tradition, alphabet, childhood, and also with the Holocaust and human rights.[6] Museums may design or redesign part of their exhibitions in order to adjust them to the needs of young visitors, as was the case in the Museum of the Warsaw Uprising, which found an engaging way to tell the tragic story of the uprising to primary school children. Cards from the calendar of August and September 1944 are collected, and there is enough room to run around the exhibition. In institutions where educators are not consulted over core exhibition design, it is much harder to organize educational activities.

Other public institutions participate in classroom activities. Cinemas might organize special screenings during school time addressed to the young audience, sometimes with accompanying commentary by a professional public historian. Teachers request lessons from public history institutions, thus enriching the pedagogical experience of students who learn from new people in new surroundings and benefit from focused materials prepared by well-resourced public institutions specializing in the area of interest.

Museums, on the other hand, may ask teachers to prepare students in anticipation of their visit. Preparing students beforehand, and discussing their memories and outcomes after the visit, is a condition of participation in the project "Education in Memorial Sites," sponsored by the local authorities and attended by schoolchildren from the city of Wrocław (Municipality of Wroclaw 2016). Primary schoolchildren visit local sites within the city, such as the "neighborhood of four confessions," while lower secondary schools leave Wrocław for a one-day trip to Lower Silesia, for example, to a former concentration camp of Gross Rosen or Łambinowice. Upper secondary students stay overnight in Warsaw or Cracow and visit historically significant places on their way to and from destinations such as the former German concentration camp in Auschwitz.

Public history institutions instruct teachers. Some museums offer special workshops for teachers where they instruct them on how to prepare students. The Museum in Auschwitz publishes preparation tips for teachers online. They also have online lesson plans in the form of narratives illustrated with pictures and primary sources from the archives of the concentration camp. Even if the narrative itself may be too complicated for schoolchildren, it may be useful for teachers or people who have a special interest in the period. The museum also organizes teachers' conferences devoted to various aspects of teaching about the Holocaust, visits of Polish educators in foreign institutions dealing with Holocaust education, and many other projects designed for teachers.[7]

Polin organized an international conference on "Interculturalism in Historical Education" in April 2015 where the discussion focused around topics such as "Educational Comics in the Classroom – Teaching Diversity," "The Beit Project: Using the City for Educational Purposes," "A Meeting with a Person, Culture, and Nation – Elements of Drama in Building Intercultural Competencies," and "The Role of History Education in the Prevention of Hate Speech and Discrimination."[8] It also offered workshops on teaching with oral testimonies and demonstrated the educational potential of material culture collections in museums dealing with the Jewish history. These workshops were prepared in consultation with teachers involved in the activities of Polin who hold the title "Ambassador of Polin." This is an example of good practice where public historians and teachers are partners working together to enhance historical understanding among children.

Teachers organize public history events for their students. Teaching history at school does not only take place during formal lessons. In Poland, for example, history teachers are usually responsible each year for preparing celebrations of national holidays related to historical events such as Independence Day on November 11 and Constitution Day on May 3. These events may take the form of an official meeting with poems recited and songs sung, but may also be a sort of edutainment with role-playing activities, historical contests, and so on, open not only to the students of a particular school but also parents and other members of the public. In Wrocław, for example, an in-service teacher-training center annually organizes The Joyful Parade of Independence for primary and secondary school students on the occasion of November 11. Students and their teachers march in the city center. They wear and carry paraphernalia such as balloons or banners in Poland's national colors. Historical contests, whose topics change annually, accompany the event.[9]

Similar events take place elsewhere. I had the pleasure to observe a public history event, organized by history teacher trainees from Bristol, England, under the supervision of Dr Dean Smart for the schoolchildren of the area. It took the form of a medieval picnic at Chepstow Castle. Trainees prepared food following medieval recipes and sewed historical costumes for themselves and for the young participants. Archery competitions were arranged along with a trebuchet demonstration, coin minting, and building castles from wooden blocks according to specific historical designs. Schoolchildren were given certain tasks to complete while exploring the castle, and teacher trainees served as their advisers. In this way, these history-teaching graduates were well prepared to incorporate public history projects and learning strategies, whether they went on to become teachers or to find work as public historians.

Teachers build on the public history experiences of their students. Some public history educational proposals are simply too time consuming or too expensive to be used in school. However, teachers can incorporate them into the teaching-learning process if they are aware that their students use them in their leisure time. History-related computer games are one example. The reason why many teachers refrain from using such games in the school practice is simply the fact that it often takes a lot of time to familiarize players with a particular game's mechanics. Still, as game enthusiasts claim, students may, and do, play at home, and teachers can offer guidelines and instructions although this has led to concerns that they might "spoil" the game, or can refer to the gameplay that they know students are performing anyway (McCall 2011). The literature on history-related computer games has mushroomed recently and is a sign of their growing role in historical education.[10] Not only are video games an important forum of public history (since they present certain imaginings and interpretations of the past, usually done by non-professional historians for non-professional audiences), but many have significant educational value. Overviews of history-based computer games are available, for example, on the YouTube channel "History respawned," where recorded gaming sessions are commented on by professional historians.[11] In these cases, deconstructing the historical narratives of a particular game is similar to deconstructing any other historical narrative and can be an exciting and challenging task for secondary school history students.

Similar strategies can be used in relation to history-related television shows or popular history magazines. Such interactions should not only be about recommending one product and advising against another or, in other words, about deciding what is "correct" and what is "wrong." Rather, teachers can encourage their students to deconstruct historical narratives presented in these media, thus educating them to become critical consumers of public history, although further research is needed in this area.

Dealing with controversial historical topics and bringing public history debates into the classroom has also become a common practice in history education in many countries. Teaching in the multicultural milieu encourages openness, particularly when some of the students' families do not share common interpretations of historical events and processes due to cultural differences (for example, topics such as the Ottoman Empire or the Holocaust), and history teachers cannot ignore these differences (Grever 2012). In many, if not most, countries, controversial historical topics are publicly debated, and both public historians and history teachers build programs around them. Students are therefore engaged in discussions and debates, in the hope that it will set patterns and standards for public debates in their adult lives. This has become a topic of great interest to researchers from various countries (Lässig, Repoussi and Cajani, forthcoming).

Public history institutions address activities to teachers and students. Public history institutions involve both teachers and students in their programs. For example, the Memory and Future Center in Wrocław used to organize an oral history contest for secondary schools. Students, assisted by their teachers, held interviews with people from a given group (one year, local sportsmen and another year, representatives of disappearing professions). Schoolteachers served as tutors. The Institute of National Remembrance in Poland organizes an Oxford-style debate contest for upper secondary schools, intended to focus attention on controversial issues from the post-1939 history. The thesis of the nationwide final debate in 2015 was "The history of Poland in the twentieth century was mostly the history of martyrdom" (Institute of National Remembrance 2015). In local debates in the 2015/2016 edition, students discussed the events of 1956 as a step toward the end of the Communist regime in Poland (it was the sixtieth anniversary), the reasons behind the introduction of martial law in Poland in 1981, the effects of the border changes in Poland in 1945, the nature of the Solidarity movement, and the role of the Catholic Church in abolishing Communism. Teachers prepare the teams that represent schools and assist them during the debates.

Public history educators challenge teachers. Public historians work on the same topics as teachers, but are able to explore interactive and engaging ways of representing the past. DUCH (the Polish Dziecięcy Uniwersytet Ciekawej Historii, or the Children's University of Interesting History) in Warsaw offers paid weekend classes for schoolchildren of various ages. The educators use interactive methods such as role-playing or drama, they prepare costumes, and encourage students to perform history, often focusing on themes absent from the regular school curriculum such as everyday life. Similarly perhaps, in England the book series "Terrible Histories" challenges formal history education by its irreverent take on history designed to enhance empathy with people from the past (De Groot 2009). Once again, further research is needed to enable us to see if participating in public history projects raises the overall interest of young people in history, including school and academic history, or whether this simply reflects the fact that participants are already fond of history at school.

History educators evaluate public history projects. Individual history teachers choose public history products to incorporate into their teaching practice. There are also international research projects that analyze the pedagogical potential (and drawbacks) of various public history endeavors. EHISTO (European History Crossroads as Pathways to Intercultural and Media Education) concentrates on popular history magazines. The most recent publication offers general observations and case studies from Germany, Sweden, Denmark, and the United Kingdom. In the final chapter, Terry Haydn (2015) discusses both the advantages and the difficulties of using popular history magazines in history education, on the basis of his experience of using them in his university-level teacher education course. EMEE (EuroVision – Museum Exhibiting Europe) is an attempt to develop strategies to be used in the museums "to re-interpret their objects in a broader context of European and transnational history" (EuroVision n.d.).

Conclusion

All of the interactions discussed in this chapter are encouraging, but there are also concerns. Both public history and history didactics have established themselves as sub-disciplines of history. Both have founded their professional organizations, conferences, and journals. Sometimes, however, they are still looked down upon by "real" academic historians, and they also regard each other suspiciously. Their research areas overlap at times, but it seems that conclusions found in one field are ignored by the other. They share audiences, but their core publics are different, and the goals of their work and their methods of reaching them are also different. All of these factors do not necessarily make cooperation impossible, but it might be said that more often they work in parallel rather than together, and they perceive each other with suspicion rather than appreciation.

It is important, in my opinion, that they cooperate. Terry Haydn (2015) notices that the teachers are not so eager to use popular history magazines in their school practice, but also that not all the texts from those magazines are engaging or even understandable to the pupils. I could observe positive and encouraging examples of students' participation in public history events, but also instances of "boring" or "wasted" excursions or museum lessons, either because public historians did not take into account pedagogical factors such as, for example, the short attention span of younger audiences, or because the audience came unprepared. If public history is applied to history education in the "wrong" way, the effect may be quite opposite to the initial goal: students would be discouraged both from learning history and from public history materials, institutions, and endeavors.

How do and how can teachers choose public history elements to be used in the teaching-learning process? What factors do and should they take into consideration? What influence has using public history in the teaching-learning process had on students, on their school achievements, attitudes, or career choices? Does it help public historians to have been trained as teachers? How similar or different are the perspectives, concepts, and attitudes of teachers and public historians working with a museum or with another public history institution? These are only some questions arising from this discussion of the relationship between history education and public history that need further research. It seems then that the dialogue between the two sub-disciplines has only just started and will be continued.

Notes

1   On the history of public history, see Sayer (2015).
2   At the Polish universities, new "specializations" of historical studies opened. Before, all students had been trained to become history teachers. Since the early 1970s, they could choose archivist training instead.
3   As Demantowsky writes: "The term [public history] makes German-language purists sweat, for sure."
4   *Public History Weekly* is an effort to overcome this situation.
5   Russia is notorious in this regard. See, for example, Repoussi (2009), J. and R. Zajda (2003), and Khodnev (2015).
6   Visit the educational section of the museum's website at http://www.polin.pl/pl/program/strefa-dla-nauczyciela.
7   For the educational offerings at the Museum in Auschwitz, visit http://www.auschwitz.org/edukacja/.
8   You can view the conference program online at http://www.polin.pl/en/education-conference-interculturalism-in-historical-education/conference-program.
9   For the details, see the brochure *Radosne obchody Święta Niepodległości* (Wrocław: Ośrodek Pamięć i Przyszłość, 2012).
10 For example, see Whalen and Taylor (2008), Kee (2014), and Winnerling and Kerschbaumer (2014).
11 As of January 2016, it had over 2,700 subscribers, and some individual videos could have over 10,000 views. The channel was presented by Robert D. Whitaker, editor, on the session *Historia Ludens: Games and Play in the Practice of History* during the 130th meeting of the American Historical Association in Atlanta, GA, on January 8, 2016.

CHAPTER THIRTY FOUR

Labeling History: Localizing Olives and Negotiating the Greek Past in Turkey

Helin Burkay

This chapter examines the historical narratives mobilized in the branding and labeling of olive oil in Turkey. Local olives emerged as a product of economic value and cultural heritage in recent years due to the expanding market for artisanal and locally produced Mediterranean culinary items. The growing market for storied foods revealed multiple and competing claims and histories that speak to the politics of authenticity and belonging. This chapter interrogates the tensions and negotiations involved in the making of a coherent narrative of the olive's origins in Turkey. It shows that these narratives operate without disrupting the overarching narrative of harmony, diversity, and authenticity that blanket the contentious ethnic history of the region, including the systematic eradication of Greek presence. Focusing on the artisanal, organic olive oil from Gökçeada, an island in Northwest Mediterranean between Greece and Turkey, I argue that how olives are localized is an ongoing political process sustained by historical narratives of belonging, not only of olives but also of peoples.

As local food has become associated with healthier, more natural, and more sustainable consumption, the proximity of food items to their place of origin has become a crucial requirement. Proximity to origin, however, does not only entail closeness to geographical origins of food production as in North American understandings of local food. In the European context, origin also entails a historical component where proximity takes a temporal turn denoting the closeness of food's production to its original forms and techniques of production. The claims to originality and authenticity thus usually overlap with a historical narrative that frame the food's historical closeness to origin.

Like every attempt to claim authenticity and originality, the adoption of historical origin stories by local food movements manufactures narratives and fixes the local to a certain place and time, usually ignoring the diversity of different origins and ongoing changes. Additionally, these historical narratives and origin stories testify to the different attempts to negotiate and consolidate contestations and claims between different actors, perspectives, and political agendas. Thus, while adding value to the food item through claims of proximity to origin that would provide the consumer with a sense of authenticity and naturalness,

A Companion to Public History, First Edition. Edited by David Dean.

these narratives are also a channel through which history becomes a powerful tool used to forge and craft new stories about the meaning and the value of a place.

In this chapter, as I examine how the claims to proximity to origin play out in the origin stories of olives in Turkey, I pay particular attention to how the ethnically contentious history of the Greek past is incorporated into the history of the olives. I argue that a brand's origin stories and visual narratives presented on the labels sustain insidious ways in which the displacement and cultural appropriation of Greek presence in Turkey is still an active and unfinished project. From a broader lens, these narratives demonstrate how understanding the "local" as historically constructed is critical to unpacking the politics of belonging, authenticity, and memory.

More specifically, I suggest that the olive has been culturally appropriated and reinvented as a symbol. Olives were already implicated in the discourse of nationalism as a trope of strength and rootedness because of the longevity and endurance of olive trees. With their connections to Greek antiquity, olives also represented what the Turkish nation aspired to in terms of Westernization and modernization, as well as permanence and civilization. As Herzfeld (2014) points to the nation-state's desire to claim its permanence and eternity within an origin story, even modernization and narratives of social change are accompanied by what he calls "the semiotic illusion of cultural fixity" and "construction of timelessness" (21–22). The olive tree, as a symbol, thus also speaks to the nation-state's "structural nostalgia," based on "a longing for an age before the state, for the primordial and self-regulating birthright that the state continually invokes" (2014: 22), which shapes its national narrative.

Olives have drawn global attention to the industrialized food producers as well. It has become an artisanal consumption item in Western markets appealing to the more affluent consumers. As eating and consumption tastes reflect cosmopolitan aspirations and emerging sensitivities of sustainability and authenticity, olive oil has become a staple in supermarkets, often featuring more than a dozen varieties. Meneley (2007) aptly traces the dynamics of the global circulation of olive oil and demonstrates how the imaginary of the Mediterranean, both as a diet and a geographical boundary, occupies the frontier of the industrial and the real, the technological and the natural.

In order to follow the historical narratives of olives in Turkey, this chapter is organized in four sections. In the first section, I briefly describe how local historical narratives gained importance as markers of food quality based on the Quality Turn in agro-food relations, and locate the particular role of stories in the more connected and industrialized foodscape. The second section focuses on how the meaning and value of the olives on Gökçeada are negotiated under the shadow of the Quality Turn and the history of the appropriation of Greek heritage under the banner of sustainable rural development. The third section takes a closer look at the particular components of the making of "tradition" in Gökçeada and addresses prominent tensions that disrupt and shift what constitutes "traditional" on an everyday basis. Following the disruptions and contestations around narratives of the past, the fourth section looks at how branding and labeling incorporates these tensions not only in Gökçeada, but also in other regional contexts with similar pasts.

The Quality Turn and origin stories

The local food literature broadly uses the "Quality Turn" to refer to the emerging moral and economic sphere of consumer groups' orientation toward supporting or consuming foods with particular quality attributes (Allen et al. 2003; Goodman et al. 2012; Ilbery and Kneafsey 2000; Morris and Young 2000). The Quality Turn is often identified by such labels as organic, alternative, sustainable, fairly traded, locally resourced, and artisanal food production. These terms refer not only to food as produce, but to all the places, people, and relations that are invested in making food. The scope of the Quality Turn extends to processes of production in ways that transform the values and meanings associated with spaces and relations of food production (Goodman 2004; Goodman et al. 2012; Ilberry and Kneafsky 2000; Morris and Young 2000).

As an alternative to models that glorify the modernization and industrialization of agriculture, the Quality Turn encapsulates movements that perceive the quality of a consumer food product to be proportional to its proximity to the source, be it through geographical closeness to the place of origin or proximity as enacted through materials or standards that represent, perform, or guarantee the closeness to the source (Trentmann 2007).[1]

Parallel to the ethos of alternative food movements, including slow-food, sustainable rural development, and local food, organic food does not only perceive organic as a farming technique, but in certain contexts constructs the concept of sustainability in reference to supposed traditional knowledge of the land. These movements revive an idea of time and place in which the connection between land, people, and food developed through the preservation of ancient knowledge and technique. Thus, in contrast to mass-produced, standardized, fast food that relies heavily on the detachment of production and consumption processes and that reduces food to a product and eating simply to a need, these movements value slowing down production and consumption at every step of the food production process. This usually involves reviving older techniques, recovering traditional knowledge, or re-localizing products with the idea that it will create a much more harmonious and sustainable relationship between people, land, and produce (DuPuis and Vandergeest 1996; Guthman 2008; Harris 2010).

Critics argue that the focus on traditional production creates another level of standardization related to idealized notions of the connection between land and people in farming and social conditions that are typically diverse and historically situated. Moreover, by fixing tradition as an aesthetic marker of authenticity, it caters only to a group of consumers that seek meaning along with food in a market environment that sometimes prioritizes market imperatives over producers' sustainability (Harris 2010; Hinrichs 2003).

Changing agro-food relations under the broader banner of the Quality Turn brings together different and contradictory understandings of power, authenticity, belonging, and the inclusivity and exclusivity demarcated by (national, cultural, and geographical) borders around what constitutes the authentic rural, natural, and healthier. Recent literature offers significant insights into how to critically interpret these concepts.[2] Both the rural and the local have spatial connotations, but their complex social and material connections cannot be confined to a physical space. Rather, the rural and the local are collectively made, agreed upon, or contested and are thus inherently social. At the same time, they manifest themselves through various materialities: agricultural economies, cultural artifacts, the built environment, and socio-ecological change and technologies.

Quality Turn also refers to increasing and concerted efforts for defining rural development in alignment with consumer demand. Historically, as a tool for intervening in spatial relations, rural development invokes the foundational binaries of the national imaginary, such as inside/outside, modern/traditional, and progress/stagnation. Within the nationalist economic lexicon, rural development describes the simultaneous processes of modernizing the nation's peasantry, food production, and agriculture, and of safeguarding and promoting the nation's idealized authentic identity (Herzfeld 2014).

As such, rural development is laden with the tensions of nation building even in the context of neoliberal market-oriented food production and consumption.

Turkey experiences the same tensions imposed on other rural places and communities by nation-building projects. Especially along the Aegean coast of Turkey, local olive groves have been both praised for being part of the national heritage due to their natural beauty and maligned as backward rural areas in need of modernization and improvement. In addition, for Gökçeada especially, its borderland status with Greece produces other tensions that intensify and alter the scope of how rural development is used as a policy tool for nation building. Greek history, villages, and culinary culture are being revived and rediscovered for their value to marketing. Similarly, in this revival, olives, especially local varieties, have been rediscovered as symbols of the longevity and purity of the agro-food culture.

The local, as a place, as an imaginary connection, and as a practice, has become an important factor in the valuation of marketable items, especially in Alternative Food Networks (AFNs). The aestheticization of rural and local agro-food landscapes for marketing purposes has been extensively debated (DuPuis and Vandergeest 1996; Finney 2014; Woods 2010). Tidy, aesthetic representations of rural life, along with idealized, romantic depictions of the model local producer working in harmony with nature, have been the simple and unifying tropes with which products have been inscribed. At the same time, scholars argue that the tourist gaze has transformed unruly, messy, fragmented rural spaces into neat, organized, clean, and consumable spaces (Darling 2005; Little and Austin 1996; Urry 1995; Van der Ploeg, Jingzhong, and Schneider 2012).

Imbros to Gökçeada: The making of a settler island

In this section, I focus on the olive oil of Gökçeada (Imbros) and the historical narratives mobilized by the rural development programs on the island. The unique history of nation building and the complex social and cultural landscape of the island positions it very well to highlight the ongoing negotiations of incorporating the Greek past in an orderly manner into current local agriculture efforts. These efforts go beyond being marketing tools and actively generate narratives of belonging and cultural appropriation, as they are adopted by public and local authorities.

The scale and consequences of nation building on Gökçeada[3] have often been interrogated within the framework of the Turkish Republic's social and demographic engineering, which is geared toward the homogenization of its population as Turkish and Muslim (Babül 2004; Erginsoy 1998; Tansuğ 2012). Literature on nation building sheds light on different aspects of the nationalization of the citizen body through genocide, population exchange, and forced migrations, combined with land and property appropriations. These practices illustrate the crafting of an imaginary Muslim Turkish national community (Aktar 2003; Bali 2006). To understand how nation building operates at the margins, in liminal spaces like Imbros, attention must be given to how these borderlands are continuously defined as part of the nation, yet their distance from the center and proximity to borders elude inclusion in the central national imaginary. Approaching these places as "frontiers" that illustrate the politics of reordering relations between land, people, and things enables a deeper understanding of how places are made by the state, people, and space (Tsing 2005). As a frontier territory with an ethnic minority population, Imbros has experienced several attempts at governance, all of which have been tinged with a settler-colonial logic.[4] That is to say, the technologies of nation building on Imbros have operated through the disruption of the Greek population's relation to the land, and by shifting the epistemic foundations of this relation.

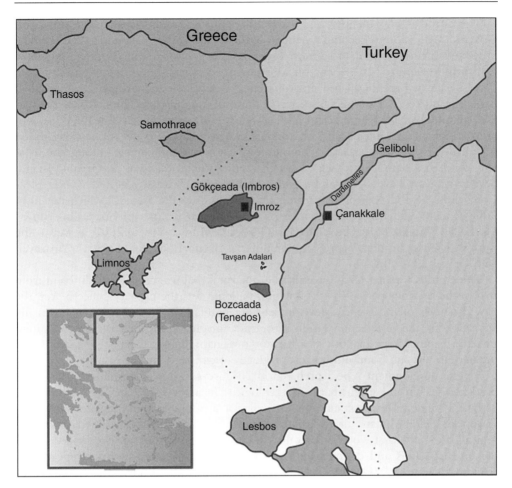

Figure 34.1 Map of Imbros. Source: http://www.gunubirlikgeziler.com/wp-content/uploads/2016/06/gokceada-harita.jpg

Persistent and orchestrated attempts at land appropriation from the local Greek population, displacement, institutionalized linguistic and religious discrimination and its consequences lasted until the European Council's resolution in 2008 (No: 1625), aimed at "preserving the bicultural character of the two Turkish islands as a model for co-operation between Turkey and Greece in the interest of the people concerned" (Gross 2008: 1).

The resolution came at a time when Turkey's EU candidacy was on the agenda and when the country's agricultural policy was taking a neoliberal turn. No longer considered a national security zone, complementary developments were under way in Gökçeada that helped it gain its reputation as the Organic Island rather than as a settler project. Among these developments was the designation of the island as a heritage zone, which prohibited any construction or change to the landscape in critical areas including the Greek villages, coastal lines, and some of the former military areas. This designation was a way for the state to maintain its control and governance of the island space, while at the same time preventing further deterioration of the area. At around the same time, following the recommendations of the EC resolution, Greeks were given the right to reclaim their properties in case they wanted to return to the island (Figure 34.1).[5]

The island's new identity and rural development ethos harmonized well with Gökçeada's decision to become a member of the Citta Slow Consortium in 2011, which raised its touristic potential to a more organized, institutional level. On the Citta Slow Consortium website (2014), the island is described as having unique potential of "its own specific geographical and environmental conditions and protected, untouched natural resources."[6] The site's historical account of the island presents Gökçeada's past as a continuous path from ancient civilization extending to the Turkish Republic with no mention of its long decades of conflict or the unlawful eradication of livelihood potential for the island's Greek communities. Despite conflicting opinions, the Slow City status has significantly helped the marketing of the island as an Organic Island. Several projects have been supported by Çanakkale University and the Citta Slow Convivium: an EU project, "Learning Organic Life on the Island," which ran from 2008 to 2009 and was complemented by "Traditional Recipes in Gökçeada" run by Çanakkale Onsekiz Mart University and Gökçeada Municipality in 2007, as well as the Turkish Sciences Academy's project, "Traditional Occupations in Gökçeada" (Yurtseven and Karakaş 2013: 96).

These projects relied on an imaginary of the rural that was completely different from that of the previous period in which nation building was the primary concern. Yet, the new dynamics of the island's development are built on its historical foundations. By appropriating the Greek countryside as the rural imaginary, the local is being re-crafted not as a national territory but as a harmonious, natural, and sustainable space where organic farmers and bountiful organic produce enrich island life.

A rural development report prepared in 2012 reveals how the politics of historical narratives sustain and articulate the market logic of local food. Prepared by the Southern Marmara Region Development Agency, a regional public planning agency under the European Union Ministry of Turkey, the Report comes up with a plan based on a sociological data – one that would, ironically, "focus on negative and positive aspects of the life on the islands and definitely not mention anything related to the ethnic origin, religion or language" (GMKA 2012: 42). In other words, the study would ignore major aspects of social life. The report's statement is a good illustration of how the state is invested in reordering the island, as a place, without acknowledging its history.

The 2012 Report suggests tackling the issue of development in less political and historically controversial terms. Thus, to "focus on [p]ositive and negative aspects of the life on the island" essentially refers to telling a narrative of the island that does not threaten the status quo with regard to settler presence and the politics of land. That way, not only would the history of ethnic violence, appropriations, and militarization be erased, but the historical continuities, leaks, and overlaps in actors' positions and the island's landscape would be made invisible. This position is not only voiced by policy makers in official narratives, but it is shared by civil society actors, land owners, business owners, and academics.

Traditional tensions: Locating the olive in history

The olive occupies a crucial place within these narratives, both as a potentially lucrative commodity to be developed and as a product that is used to embody the characteristics of a place. Whereas olive trees were once used to encourage settlement or were neglected, they recently became attractive for local resource development. Organic farming projects began to claim olives as a local natural resource belonging to the cultural and historical landscape of the island. This association re-localized the olive as part of the island identity and brought forward different imaginaries of space. Among these different imaginaries, historical narratives of cultural and ethnic diversity are dominant. The very same 2012 report summarizes the island's cultural landscape thus:

> Gökçeada offers a very rich social structure where diverse cultures coexist and citizens with different ethnic backgrounds live together ... In addition to citizens with Greek origins, there are people from Bulgaria and different corners of mainland Anatolia living there. Co-existence of different peoples from different regions has enriched the island socially and culturally. (GMKA 2012: 4–5)

The planners' vision of Gökçeada, which is such a seemingly obvious statement about the demographic structure of the island, takes on a wholly different meaning when it is read against the island's history of settlement, appropriation, and ethnic violence. Not only does it ignore the fact that the Greek population of the island has been reduced to a miniscule number, but by simplifying the presence of Bulgarian and other communities as a sign of coexistence and diversity the report hides the forced and top-down aspect of the developmental history that brought these communities to the island in the first place. It also brings these communities together in a level-field cultural diversity narrative, locating them side by side, without any attention to the different landscapes and spatial politics that form the basis of their presence on the island (Ahmed and Swan 2006). By erasing their different histories of settlement and migration, the statement becomes part of a depoliticized history of diversity on Imbros.

Another report from 2007, prepared by Industrial Research and Development Directorate identifies the "[u]nique historical and architectural fabric, coexistence of different cultures, being an island, virgin nature, clean air and sea, olive groves and cuisine of Gökçeada have been important for development" (Erginöz 2007: 18). This statement, like the previous one, conflates natural landscape and social life elements. It replaces conflicts between different groups and contestation of development and settlement policies with permanence, harmony, and naturalness in its description of the island. Not only does it invoke an imperial cosmopolitan nostalgia (Türeli 2010), but it also presents harmonious social life as a permanent natural feature of the island life. Thus, the statement is crucial in highlighting how a superficial diversity discourse is not only a depoliticizing strategy, but is also partially connected to turning the island into an administrable resource for the planners. For example, the 2007 Report also suggests that Greek citizens, who used to constitute the majority of the island's population, migrated from the island due to economic factors, whereas there has been continuous immigration to the island from other parts of the country (Erginöz 2007: 20). Again, by ironing out some of the unpleasant details of how the island space has become a multi-ethnic and multicultural place, the eradication of the Greek presence is omitted, simplified, and sterilized as a marketable feature of the island. According to the report, the island's long history of demographic landscape changes and the corresponding reassignment of functions to spaces are simply the result of voluntary and smooth economic choices, implying that Gökçeada's current ethnic composition was a natural evolution, sans conflict, harm, or opposition.

This vision of its cultural and social identity, of course, supports the effort to transform Gökçeada into a tourist destination, and the island's naturally existing resources are given a similar role. In this context, olives, as local produce, become markers of place, adding to the island's touristic potential and economic development. Not only are olives important because they are a natural resource, but the olive's relation to Greek culture and its significance to the island's history represent anxieties and concerns with which developers and entrepreneurs must grapple. The manufactured cosmopolitanism and invented imperial diversity on the island blankets a reactionary localism shaped under market pressure.

The planners' and entrepreneurs' perspectives on strengthening the olive's presence in Gökçeada are informed by examples set by other Greek islands; the 2012 Report describes how the Greek islands have built a successful model by tapping into the connection between land, resources, and quality food products. Suggesting that this model is necessary for drawing a higher-income tourist crowd, planners are invested in the olive's place on the island (GMKA 2012: 14). Consequently, they have constructed narratives about how olives are crucially embedded in the local landscape – narratives that are neither complete, coherent, nor stable. In crafting the relations between the space, the product, and the producer, along with the cultural skills that are tied to a place, these narratives illustrate a multiplicity of cracks and concerns encapsulated in the discourse of development. On the one hand, developers see a lucrative business opportunity in the market potential of the local olive variety and understand that the marketing strategy has to include its connection to the land and the people. On the other hand, the history of development and settlement policies of nation building that sought the ethnic Turkification of the island gives them little room to maneuver. While Gökçeada's symbolic fault lines remain, the discourse and the practice of development have reordered the island's space, reconfiguring its historical narrative and rendering the space legible within the framework of the market imperatives of the current development ethos.

One of the first dimensions that can be closely studied to help unpack producers' positions is the tension generated by the Organic Project's claims about traditional olive farming.[7] In addition to promoting adherence to the organic regulations, the discursive framework of organic farming refers to the island's traditional olive farming as an important temporal asset for organic agriculture. Here, the Project's discourse locates the production of olive oil and olive farming within Gökçeada's history and local culture; it imbues organic olive farming with authenticity by reinvigorating those values that come to be associated with more traditional ways of producing, preparing, distributing, and consuming food. However, most of the producers and participants of the Project are settlers who have not engaged in the type of traditional olive farming described by the Project. The methods of production have changed. If anything, the social and economic landscape of the island are examples of how the state manufactures a new local by severing ties with old local and traditional elements. As such, resorting to an ideal of "tradition," as a discursive justification, comes with its own tensions.

How is the traditional olive farmer ideal constructed on Gökçeada, where the communities of olive farmers were destroyed? How do different actors recover and reinvent sources of knowledge about the material and cultural aspects of this tradition? What are the narratives that sustain this reinvention? What is lost and what is recovered? In the case of Gökçeada's small-scale organic producers, the connection between land and people through tradition is problematic, if not ironic, because it was the state itself that deliberately eradicated traditional olive farming through rural development plans. Within the Organic Project, the meaning associated with the olive's place on the island is highly idealized and rests on the imagination of an idyllic Greek past. Thus, Gökçeada's olive producers experience the tensions that arise from the temporal location of their practices of production, which have changed over time due to modernization and changing techniques of olive picking and pressing, as well as the particular history of resettlement and ethnic cleansing that destroyed most of the island's traditional olive- growing knowledge. Although some producers aspire to uncover and implement what they consider to be more traditional olive growing and olive oil making practices, most do not share the Project's vision of the temporal meaning of olive production. For them, there is a sense of the present moment in Gökçeada that defies the imposed association of olives with tradition that exists in the minds of some consumers, researchers, or other actors implicated in the island's olive production.

Accordingly, the symbolism of the olive has been infused into current narratives about the value of local olives in Gökçeada; it has been used to reinforce claims of cultural longevity and belonging, and to romantically depict the island's idyllic cultural landscape. Appearing on product labels, in brochures, booklets, and tourist pamphlets, as well as in reports and in official discourse, olives have functioned as a symbol of the island.

This appropriation of the olive is characteristic of what Tuck and Yang refer to as "enclosure" and to the "domesticating colonization" of a cultural symbol as inclusion (2012: 3). Furthermore, ownership (and the economic value) of olives on Gökçeada is claimed by the state through its promotion of particular organic olive growing and maintenance procedures, which are aligned with the Quality Turn. In this sense, while olive trees have been claimed as resources for economic development due to their valuable produce, they have also occupied a symbolic place within the imaginary of the local.

Hart (2011), in her ethnographic account of a small weaver's cooperative in rural Turkey, talks about a memory paradox that is experienced by the community when the commercial value of the rugs they produce is tied to the proximity of their crafting to traditional weaving practices. She shows vividly that the weaver cooperative has a very strong connection to their craft, but refuses to identify what they do as traditional. Instead of being categorized as relics of the past, the weavers position themselves as full members of contemporary modern society. For those researchers and tourists who look to tradition as the main indicator of how a community relates to its past, the cooperative's insistence on disassociating themselves from a particular past while at the same time commercializing traditional weaving practices seems like a paradox.

The reconstruction of a connection between past and current olive production is, understandably, full of paradoxes. Producers on Gökçeada face a similar "memory paradox" caused by the friction between their identities as olive producers and the history of olive production on the island. The olive's links to Greek culture and livelihood are very well (though superficially) known, and are constantly drawn upon to connect olive growing to the island. This association of local olives with Greek traditions and culture also works as a romantic motif that aims to invoke feelings of connection and permanence in the relations between the producers, the land, and the olives (Herzfeld 2014).

The history of that connection is, however, marred by the eradication of the Greek community from the island. In most of project documents and rural development booklets about the island, the emphasis is on how the olive is part of Gökçeada's historical and natural landscapes. Although the demographic transition and ethnic-religious homogenization process of Gökçeada is mostly described as a voluntary economic migration, the Greek presence is not completely removed from the narratives of these documents. In Gökçeada, narratives about the Greek population leaving the island echo the trope of vanishing indigenous people by continuously referring to the island's impossibly harsh economic conditions and the underdevelopment of rural space as push factors leading to their mass migration. It fails to mention the bureaucratic harassment, land appropriations in the name of infrastructural development, random break-ins, and continuous assaults on Greek property, as well as the prohibitions on fishing, quotas on meat prices, and banning of all sorts of educational and religious activities of the community under the blanket of economic underdevelopment to make Greek migration seem voluntary rather than forced.

The rhetoric of economic migration is accompanied by the promotion of histories of the island that are exclusively focused on the early classical period and on archeological findings and that seek to establish a Turkish presence on Gökçeada that pre-dates that of the Greeks (Akdemir et al. 2008; Saygi 2010). These studies recall the island's imperial importance for the Ottoman sultans and present themselves as valuable narratives of the island's Turkish culture. Consequently, the history of the Greek population is further dislocated from its recent political predicament, and despite the physical and demographic remnants of the Greek community, which are visible in the living environment, new narratives that emphasize the island's Turkish past attempt to erase the Greek population's contribution to Gökçeada's culture. These dynamics contribute to the emergence of different and competing narratives of the local in Gökçeada. Thus, the inclusion of this incomplete and altered historical narrative does not constitute a complete denial and rewriting of history. Nevertheless, most of the official narratives recount the legacy of the Greek community and olives as nostalgic elements of a romantic, pastoral island past.

The particular history of the island is significant for understanding one of the many ways that the reconstruction of traditional practices and tapping into producers' existing relations to the land are part of a political process of invention that creates tension, contestation, and negotiation. Its documents and plans rarely refer to the fact that the very traditions the Organic Project is attempting to recreate were destroyed by previous development plans. Instead, repeated references to the tradition and history of olive farming on the island prompt present producers to mobilize the invented image of the ideal, traditional, Greek producer for marketing leverage. Thus, the ghost of the historical Greek farmer haunts the planners, and yet, his reinvention to make organic olive production more marketable does not resonate fully with how small-scale producers see themselves.

Branding and labeling: Marketing the producer

The traditional producer ideal not only creates a temporal tension between the past and present by attempting to impose a romanticized historical identity on contemporary producer-owners, but it also positions the ideal producer as an entrepreneur. This drive becomes more apparent in the contentious debates about the roles of labeling and branding as manifestations of entrepreneurialism. In keeping with their belief that branding is important for marketing, especially for accessing niche markets, some development project officers voiced their concerns about the ineptitude of current producers in utilizing the history of olive production on the island to their advantage. From the officials' perspective, missing or poor branding and labeling are a symptom to be cured through a value-adding strategy that relies on the imaginary of the island's olive production traditions. According to the officials, it is not only that current producers do not properly embody the traditional olive producer ideal that prevents the officials' vision from being fulfilled, but rather that they lack the market-orientation skills that would maximize the value of their produce.

Economically speaking, labeling and branding are necessary both for identification purposes and to represent the product, which is an especially important aspect of the marketing strategy for artisanal and niche consumption items. Labels and brands function as the aestheticization of the connection between the produce and the producer, who is always positioned as the subject embodying this connection through practice, ethics, and knowledge of the land. With local foods, the producer's connection to the product is critical in appealing to consumers' preferences (Bowen and De Master 2011; Bruwer and Johnson 2010; Guthman 2007; Warner 2007).

In a comparative regional context, the branding of olive oil produced in the small village of Adatepe, located in the Ida Mountains on the mainland, around the Dardanelles region, is a significant example of how branding and labeling show that the producer is constructed through the aestheticization of tradition. The label of Adatepe brand olive oil features the face of a young female relic (Figure 34.2). The colors and details of the figure are reminiscent of females portrayed in Greek mosaics and material culture recovered in the area, associating the brand's origins with the Greek history and tradition of olive oil production. Adatepe's label includes the story of the young woman, supposedly a Greek woman who lived in Adatepe until she was forced to move to Greece. The story goes as follows:

> She used to sing at the weddings and she used to dance. Making a name for herself with her talent, she was very well known in surrounding villages, as well. Especially during harvest season, farmers around the groves where she used to work would pick the olives as they listened to her songs. (Adatepe 2015)

Figure 34.2 Adatepe Olive Oil Label (detail). Source: https://www.adatepe.com/.

The narrative provides customers with the comfort of an origin story that successfully connects the local Greek producer to the land and the tradition of the village by drawing on the gendered trope of the dancing, singing woman. The end of her story in Adatepe is recounted as a source of great sadness for the village community as they lost track of the woman after she left; it is a rendition of a forced migration story that neatly glosses over the history of ethnic conflict in the area. Overall, Adatepe's branding is a very good example of how Greek tradition and the ideal Greek producer figure are invoked as part of a marketing strategy that makes a claim about the producer rather than about the product itself.

The producers in Gökçeada, however, see things differently. Not only do they consider labeling and branding to be unnecessary for their producer identity, but they also feel that they do not have sufficient cultural or social resources to undertake proper branding and labeling for their produce. Labeling has a primarily functional purpose for them: to show the product itself. Aesthetics and packaging style, in their experience, do not change the outcome of what and to whom they can sell. As long as the produce and the product are visible and there is trust between the consumer and the producer, they say, labeling is seen as unnecessary.

Mostly along the sides of the streets and at the entry of the villages, some producers set up modest stands where they choose to sell their product in transparent plastic bottles. Although some of the producers also have a stand at the weekly farmers' market in the central part of the island, the main connection to customers for the majority of small-scale olive producers is made through these small roadside stands (see Figure 34.3). Sold

Figure 34.3   Olives and olive oil at a sidewalk stand. Photo: Helin Burkay.

at around 8 lira (about 3 USD) per liter by 2014, the bottles, which are recycled soda or water bottles without any markings that identify either the producer or the product, are the main packaging used by most of the small producers for selling locally available organic olive oil in Gökçeada. Despite concerns about the quality of the olive oil stored in transparent plastic bottles in the hot sun, producers operate on the basis of functionality and simplicity, choosing not to aestheticize their produce with labeling and branding. Furthermore, by being present themselves at the stands, producers establish a direct link with consumers, cutting out the need for the representative aesthetic of the label. The transparency of the bottle is complemented by the transparency of a direct interaction with the producer. In addition, transparency exists in how consumers make the decision to purchase: by tasting and smelling the oil on site.

The lack of labeling and branding, on the one hand, makes identification of a product impossible when the item is transferred from its original production site to another setting. On the other hand, as is the case in Gökçeada, it also creates a more spontaneous, direct, and unmediated sensory interaction with the producer and the product, replacing the need and function of a narrative on a label. In other words, the experience of buying olive oil from clear, unmarked bottles facilitates a one-time, non-transferable, performative knowledge about the oil and the producer, in contrast to the replicable, legible information provided on a label.

Conclusion

As a contested activity at the intersection of cultural politics and market orientation, branding and labeling is an important interface between the producers and the customers. As with the appropriation of tradition, producers' attitudes vary in embracing or rejecting this aspect of marketing olive oil on Gökçeada. The standardization and commodification of agricultural practices due to market pressure generate a reactionary localism that is paradoxically based on a nostalgia for imperial cosmopolitanism that blankets competing settler narratives. In this chapter, I trace these competing historical narratives of the local through the representing, branding, and labeling of local organic olives. I suggest that the discursive replacement of Greek producers with narratives of the economic value of the olive is critical to understanding the unevenness of the local. The symbolism of the olive (permanence, longevity, and civilization) has been infused into current narratives about the value of local olives in Gökçeada. It has been used to reinforce claims of cultural longevity and belonging, and to romantically depict the island's idyllic cultural landscape. This nostalgic narrative is adopted differently by different actors on the island. It serves as a strategy that actors might use with different purposes in different contexts. This is relevant not only for settings that are imbued with a contentious history of ethnic conflict but also for any place where land and its symbols are colonized resources.

I suggest that the history of local olives is invoked by the territorial and militarized logic of nation building and by the market-oriented, aestheticized constructions of the Quality Turn. These are two different and key imaginaries of the local that help us understand the socio-cultural morphology on Gökçeada. I regard the efforts of both as unfinished, incomplete, and mutable series of negotiations and contestations between these two imaginaries that take place on a daily basis and involve different actors. The ongoing efforts to fix the historical narrative demonstrate that the local organic olive on Gökçeada, as an object of rural development, is deeply embedded in the history of settlement and an ethnically contentious politics of land. Its current value and meaning in the Organic Project are configured through a series of attempts that normalize and naturalize this history, and generate uneven and heterogeneous consequences for the producers. What the local means and how it is enacted and promoted as a value in agro-food relations should therefore be carefully considered to avoid perpetuating assumptions about inherent value and positivity.

Notes

1   This corresponds to different meanings of the "local" in local food in different contexts. In the European context, local food implies proximity to the source of production, whereas in the North American context, when a food is qualified as "local," it usually refers to a known place that is not necessarily physically close.
2   See DuPuis and Vandergeest (1996), R. Feagan (2007), Halfacree (2006), Hinrichs (2003), Ilbery and Kneafsey (2000), Morris and Young (2000), and Woods (2010).
3   In this section, I use both Imbros and Gökçeada as the island's name. Until it was changed to Gökçeada as its Turkish name in 1970, the island was known as Imbros (Ἴμβρος). The local Greek population still uses Imbros (or Imvros). For the period before the name change, I use Imbros as the island's name.
4   I suggest approaching Imbros as a settler-colonial project for three reasons. First, as border land with a Greek rural population, Imbros has been gradually occupied and settled by the Turkish state through appropriations of land, the elimination of livelihood resources, and the purposeful settlement of mainlanders. Its mechanics of social and economic change, similar to those of settler-colonial projects, has been based from the beginning on asymmetrical power relations between settlers and natives. Second, a settler-colonial approach complicates a nation-building perspective by exposing the cracks, frictions, and contingencies of the nationalist imaginary and allowing place-based relations to be interpreted as unfinished, continuing colonial projects with present-day consequences. Lastly, I suggest that Imbros can be understood through a settler-colonial lens because, as an occupied land to which autonomous status was granted by international treaties but denied by the settler state, the politics of the island still revolve around the management and governance of land and resources, and seek to appropriate the meanings attached to the island itself (Babül 2004).
5   Although this has created a climate of optimism in terms of the relaxation of national security measures and the rectification of systematic errors in the Land Registry, the restrictions and bureaucratic hurdles associated with acquiring property on the island or claiming a former property have recently taken a turn for the worse. That is why most of the elderly Greeks who have been living abroad for over 30 years decide to sell their property even after they gained ownership (personal communication with owners and Erhan Pekçe).
6   The website contains brief snippets of information on the Slow City activities on the island (Citta Slow 2014).
7   Although the formal name of the project is much longer, officials and the producers on the island use "Organic Project" to refer to the ongoing rural development project on the island since 2002. The Project is operated by the District Directorate of Agriculture on the island under the supervision of Ministry of Agriculture and Livestock. The project provides direct monetary support to participating producers, assistance with pest and fertilizer management, as well as training. The Organic Project also covers costs for organic certification by private agencies for each farmer.

Epilogue: To Put Your Signature: Tanzania's Graffiti Movement

SETH M. MARKLE

The hip-hop art of graffiti dates back to the 1970s in the United States, but it was not until 2007 when the art form in Tanzania really took hold of the imagination of urban youth. During the nation's late socialist period in the early 1980s, youth found ways to leave their mark by using charcoal and writing their names on walls. Once state-led socialism ended and gave way to a neoliberal capitalist economy, access to hip-hop culture and commodities increased, giving birth to rap and breakdancing in the late 1980s. However, graffiti was nowhere to be found. In fact, the first graffiti pieces to emerge in Dar es Salaam, the country's largest city, was from a South African artist whose "CURE" mural was meant to be a message about the HIV/AIDS epidemic in Africa. But it was the presence of Sela (Kiswahili for "homeboy"), a German expatriate student at the University of Dar es Salaam, who contributed to the spread of graffiti among Tanzanian urban youth. While Sela was covering Dar es Salaam's public and private walls with his trademark "Sela" tags and murals in 2005 and 2006, Tanzanian artist Mejah Mbuya was tagging the political statement "Mkapanization" at dala dala (bus) stops. It was a tag meant to express his opposition to President Mkapa's economic globalization policy, largely for how it disenfranchised youth. When the two finally met, Sela taught Mejah some basic graffiti techniques that led him to graduate from "tagging" to large-scale murals with two-dimensional lettering.

Mejah's encounter with other skilled graffiti writers did not stop with Sela. The movement's growth also owes a great deal to the African American graffiti pioneer Kool Koor of New York City. In 2007 and 2009, he traveled to Dar es Salaam and facilitated a series of graffiti workshops. "I met him there," remembered Mbuya. "He was being sponsored by Montana-Cans so he decided to do a graffiti workshop and I happened to be there. From that time, Koor shared with us techniques and the basics of graffiti, which we did not know. From there everything came into place." Koor's mentorship marked a turning

A Companion to Public History, First Edition. Edited by David Dean.

point, as it led Mejah to form the country's first graffiti crew called Wachata (WCT), Kiswahili for "To put your signature," which also consisted of Local Ism, Kala Singa, Medy, and Edot.

For the past seven years, WCT's goal has been to promote graffiti as a credible form of visual artistic expression, to combat the stigma associated with graffiti as an act of criminality, and to develop and nurture an indigenous aerosol movement in the country's major cities such as Dar es Salaam, Arusha, Bagamoyo, and Mwanza. With a motto that reads "Respect the Art form," WCT has sought to earn that respect with work that tackles sociopolitical and economic themes that speak to the Tanzanian lived experience. Much of their large-scale murals, replete with characters and classical graffiti lettering styles, from bubble letters to Wild Style, has taken on themes such as education, government corruption, animal and nature preservation, electoral violence, unemployment, and the criminalization of youth and Islam.

The featured graffiti murals, until last year, were showcased on the exterior walls of the British Consul in Dar es Salaam, which is located on Samora Avenue and Ohio Street in the downtown section of the city. Both of these "pieces," a graffiti term meaning masterpieces, use bright colors and the majority of the wall space to grab the audience's attention. The pieces are also produced in what is known as "Widstyle," which is an advanced two-dimensional graffiti style whereby the letters are modified and disguised in complex and intricate ways such as the incorporation of similar colors and other small flourishes, intentionally making it difficult for the audience to decipher without some effort. While Image 1 is accompanied by a "tag," a personal signature of one of the WCT members in order to clarify primary authorship of the design structure, Image 2 contains images of books in the background to drive home the piece's key political message.

By exhibiting at art festivals at home and abroad, participating in hip-hop performance showcases and global exchanges, doing commissioned work for NGOs, corporations and sports teams, and teaching weekly graffiti classes to youth at the primary and secondary school levels, WCT has enhanced the visibility and credibility of graffiti art in a very short period of time. When WCT secured a studio at the Nafasi Art Space in 2014, it illustrated the entrepreneurial approach that the crew employs in showing young people how graffiti can serve as a source of economic collective and self-empowerment. Through education, social media, collaboration with foreign graffiti artists, commissioned work, and the sale of WCT-designed t-shirts and sneakers, WCT has managed to inspire a new generation of graffiti artists spearheaded by Sheepskin, Bonny Sangijo, D-Man, Beatrice, and Stanfox Def. Without question, what was once a non-existent and, at times, peripheral element in the hip-hop movement is steadily being embraced by the government, public, and media and gradually permeating and beautifying the post-socialist landscapes of Tanzania's most populous cities.

Hali Mbaya (Hard Times), Dar es Salaam, Tanzania. WaPi, British Consul, 2009. Photo with permission from the Wachata Crew.

Elimu (Education), Dar es Salaam, Tanzania. WaPi, British Consul, 2009. Photo with permission from the Wachata Crew.

Bibliography

1877. Wi Parata v. The Bishop of Wellington. (1877) 3 New Zealand Jurist Reports (New Series) 72 (SC).

21st International Congress of the Historical Sciences, Amsterdam. 2010. Panels on "Who Owns History?" and "The Rights of the Dead." At http://www.ichs2010.org/home.asp.

AAM. 1978. Minimum Standards for Professional Museum Training Programs. *Museum News*, vol. 57, pp. 23–24.

AAM. 1983. Criteria for Examining Professional Museum Studies Programs. *Museum News*, vol. 61, pp. 70–71, 99.

AASLH. 1956. Attracting Competent Personnel in the Field of Local History. AASLH Committee Report. December 29, 1956. Records of the American Association for State and Local History. Box 11. Nashville: Tennessee State Library and Archives.

AASLH. 1960–1986. Annual Report of the Director. Records of the American Association for State and Local History. Box 53. Nashville: Tennessee State Library and Archives.

AASLH. 1961. Minutes. AASLH Meeting of the Council. August 29, 1961. Records of the American Association for State and Local History. Box 12. Nashville: Tennessee State Library and Archives.

AASLH. 1980. Subcommittee on Historical Agency Training Programs Final Report, July 15, 1980. Records of the American Association for State and Local History, Box 66. Nashville: Tennessee State Library and Archives.

AASLH. 1981. Standards for Historical Agency Training programs. *History News* vol. 36, July 1981, n.p.

Abraham, R. 2015. Making the Tough Decision to Pull our Mobile Apps. Historypin. Blog post. April 22, 2015. At http://blog.historypin.org/2015/04/22/tough-decision-to-pull-mobile-apps/.

Abreu, M. 1995. O Caso do Bracuí. In *Resgate: Uma Janela para o Oitocentos*, eds. H. Mattos and E. Schnoor, pp. 165–197. Rio de Janeiro: Top Books.

Abuissa, H., J.H. O'Keefe, and L. Cordain, 2005. Realigning our 21st-Century Diet and Lifestyle with Our Hunter-Gatherer Genetic Identity. *Directions in Psychiatry*, vol. 25, pp. 1–10.

Abungu, G.O. 2008, "Universal Museums": New Contestations, New Controversies. In *UTIMUT: Past Heritage – Future Partnerships: Discussions on Repatriation in the 21st Century*, eds. M. Gabriel and J. Dahl. pp. 32–42. Copenhagen: The Greenland National Museum and Archives and International Work Group for Indigenous Affairs.

Acervo Petrobras Cultural Memória e Música Negra. N.d. Petrobras Cultural Collection of Black Music and Memory. Audiovisual Archives of the Laboratory of Oral History and Image of the Graduate History Program at the Universidade Federal Fluminense. LABHOI/UFF. Niterói, Brazil (APCMMN/LABHOI/UFF, 01.0064).

Active History. n.d. At https://activehistory.wordpress.com/

Adair, B., B. Filene, and L. Koloski. (eds.) 2011. *Letting Go: Sharing Historical Authority in a User-Generated World*. Philadelphia: The Pew Centre for Arts and Heritage.

Adatepe. 2015. At www.adatepe.com.tr.

Advisory Board on National Parks, Historic Sites, Buildings and Monuments. 1969. Papers. 60th Meeting. April 21–24, 1969. National Park Service, National Historic Landmark Program, Washington, D.C.

Agnew, V. 2004. Introduction: What is reenactment? *Criticism*, vol. 46, no. 3, pp. 327–329.

Agnew, V. 2007. History's Affective Turn: Historical Reenactment and Its Work in the Present. *Rethinking History*, vol. 11, no. 3, pp. 299–312.

Agnew, V. 2010. History's Pure Serene: On Reenacting Cook's First Voyage. In *Staging the Past: Themed Environments in Transcultural Perspectives*, eds. J. Schlehe, M. Uike, C. Oesterle, and W. Hochbruck, pp. 205–218. Bielefeld: Transcript.

Ahmed, S. and E. Swan. "Doing Diversity." *Policy Futures in Education*, vol. 4, no. 2, 2006, pp. 96–100.

Akdemir, A., O. Demircan, S. Yılmaz, T. Takaoğlu, and C. Akbulak. (eds.) 2008. *Gökçeada Değerleri Sempozyumu*. Çanakkale: Çanakkale Onsekiz Mart Üniversitesi Yayınları.

Aktar, A. 2003. Homogenising the Nation, Turkifying the Economy. In *Crossing the Aegean*, ed. R. Hirschon, pp. 79–96. Oxford: Berghan Books.

Alberge, D. 2010. Art Collectors Build Museums to Let Public See Private Hoards. *The Observer*. July 11, 2010. At http://www.theguardian.com/artanddesign/2010/jul/11/modern-art-collectors-private-museum.

Alderson, W.T. 1980. Letter to D.J. Reed and L.E. Tise. January 14, 1980. Records of the American Association for State and Local History. Box 66. Nashville: Tennessee State Library and Archives.

Alexander, E.P. 1957a. Letter to R.P. McCormick. May 6, 1957. Colonial Williamsburg Archives. Williamsburg, Virginia.

Alexander, E.P. 1957b. Memorandum re: Historical Preservation Seminar. February 4, 1957. Colonial Williamsburg Archives. Williamsburg, Virginia.

Alexander, E.P. 1957c. Memorandum re: Sample Study Program for a Historical Preservation Seminar. January 11, 1957. Colonial Williamsburg Archives. Williamsburg, Virginia.

Alexander, E.P. 1957d. Training Interpreters of America's Heritage. Colonial Williamsburg Archives. Williamsburg, Virginia.

Alexander, E.P. 1981. Interview by Charles B. Hosmer, August 12, 1981. Hosmer Papers, Hornbake Library. College Park: University of Maryland.

Alexander, E.P. 1985. Interview by P.M. Butler. June 18, 1985. Colonial Williamsburg Archives. Williamsburg, Virginia.

Allais, L. 2013. Integrities: The Salvage of Abu Simbel. *Grey Room*, no. 50, pp. 6–45.

Allen, P., M. FitzSimmons, M. Goodman, and K. Warner. 2003. Shifting Plates in the Agrifood Landscape: The Tectonics of Alternative Agrifood Initiatives in California. *Journal of Rural Studies*, vol. 19, no. 1, pp. 61–75.

Almeida, J.R. and M.F.O. Roval. 2011. *Introdução à História Pública*. São Paulo: Letra e Voz.

Alves, C. F. 2008. The Agency of Gell in the Anthropology of Art. *Trans. Bruno Reinhardt*. *Horizontes Antropológicos*, vol. 14, no. 29, pp. 315–338.

Amato, J. 2008. *Jacob's Well: A Case for Rethinking Family History*. Minnesota: Minnesota Historical Press.

American Association for State and Local History. 2015. StEPS. At http://tools.aaslh.org/steps/.

Ames, M. 1992. *Cannibal Tours and Glass Boxes: The Anthropology of Museums*. 2nd edition. Vancouver: University of British Columbia Press.

Amos, D. n.d. Framework Knitters. At http://www.nottsheritagegateway.org.uk/people/frameworkknitters.htm.

Anderson, B. 1983. (Rev. ed. 1991 and 2006). *Imagined Communities: Reflections on the Origin and Spread of Nationalism*. London: Verso.

Anderson, J. 1984. *Time Machines: The World of Living History*. The American Association for State and Local History.

Anderson, J. 2004. Talking whilst Walking: A Geographical Archaeology of Knowledge. *Area*, vol. 36, no. 3, pp. 254–261.

Anderson, M. 2002. Oh, What a Tangled Web … Politics, History and Museums. *Australian Historical Studies*, vol. 119, pp. 179–185.

Anderson, M. and A. Reeves. 1994. Contested Identities: Museums and the Nation in Australia. In *Museums and the Making of Ourselves: The Role of Objects in National Identity*, ed. F. Kaplan, pp. 79–124. London and New York: Leicester University Press.

Andrews, G., W. J. Warren, and J. Cousins. 2016. *Collaboration and the Future of Education: Preserving the Right to Think and Teach Historically*. New York: Routledge.

Anonymous. 1979a. First National Symposium on Public History: A Report. *The Public Historian*, vol. 2, no. 1, pp. 73–81.

Anonymous. 1979b. Public History in the Academy: An Overview of the University and College Offerings. *The Public Historian*, vol. 2, no. 1, pp. 84–116.

Antze, P. and M. Lambek. (eds.) 1996. *Tense Past: Cultural Essays in Trauma and Memory*. New York: Routledge.

Appadurai, A. (ed.) 1986. *The Social Life of Things: Commodities in Cultural Perspective*. Cambridge: Cambridge University Press.

Appignanesi, L. 2004. *The Cabaret*. New Haven: Yale University Press.

Apple, M. 1995. *Education and Power*. Hove: Psychology Press.

Araujo, A.L. 2010a. Welcome the Diaspora: Slavery Heritage Tourism and the Public Memory of the Atlantic Slave Trade. *Ethnologies*, vol. 32, no. 2, pp. 145–178.

Araujo, A.L. 2010b. *Public Memory of Slavery: Victims and Perpetrators in the South Atlantic*. Amherst, New York: Cambria Press.

Araujo, A.L. 2014. *Shadows of the Slave Past: Memory, Heritage, and Slavery*. New York: Routledge.

Archibald, R.R. 1997. Memory and the Process of Public History. *The Public Historian*, vol. 19, no. 2, pp. 61–64.

Aronsson, P. and G. Elgenius. (eds.) 2014. *National Museums and Nation-building in Europe 1750–2010: Mobilization and Legitimacy, Continuity and Change*. New York: Routledge.

Arts Council England. 2010. Cultural Capital: A Manifesto for the Future. At http://www.artscouncil.org.uk/publication_archive/cultural-capital-manifesto-future/.

Ashbery, J. 1994. The Ridiculous Translator's Hopes. In *And the Stars Were Shining*, p. 16. Manchester: Cancarnet.

Ashton, P. and H. Kean. 2009. *People and their Pasts: Public History Today*. Basingstoke: Palgrave Macmillan.

Ashton, P. and P. Hamilton. 2010. *History at the Crossroads: Australians and the Past*. Sydney: Halstead Press.

Athenaeum of Philadelphia. 1998. American House Museums Symposium. December 4–5, 1998. At http://www.philaathenaeum.org/hmuseum.

Atherton, J. 1979. The Origins of the Public Archives Record Centre, 1897–1956. *Archivaria*, vol. 8, pp. 49–54.

Attie, S. 2003. The Writing on the Wall, Berlin, 1992–93: Projection in Berlin's Jewish Quarter. *Art Journal*, vol. 62, no. 3, pp. 74–83.

Attwood, B. and F. Magowan. (eds.) 2001. *Telling Stories: Indigenous History and Memory in Australia and New Zealand*. Crows Nest: Allen & Unwin.

Attwood, B. and S. Foster. (eds.) 2003. *Frontier Conflict: The Australian Experience*. Canberra: National Museum of Australia.

Auslander, L. 2010. Archiving a Life: Post Shoah Paradoxes of Memory Legacies. In *Unsettling History: Archiving and Narrating in Historiography*, ed. S. Jobs and A. Lüdtke, pp. 127–148. New York: Campus Verlag.

Australasian Federation of Family History Organisations Inc. 2004. About. At http://www.affho.org/affho/about.php.

Australian Broadcasting Corporation. Now and Then. At https://open.abc.net.au/explore?proje ctId=8&sortBy=interest&isFeatured=0.

Autosport-Forums. n.d. Motorcycle Racing Nostalgia. At http://forums.autosport.com/forum/27-motorcycle-racing-nostalgia/.

Babül, E. 2004. Belonging to Imbros: Citizenship and Sovereignty in the Turkish Republic. Nationalism, Society and Culture in Post-Ottoman South East Europe. May 29–30, 2004. St. Peter's College, Oxford.

Bailey, M. and S. Popple. 2011. The 1984/5 Miners' Strike; Re-Claiming Cultural Heritage. In *Heritage, Labour and the Working Classes*, eds. L. Smith, P. Shackel and G. Campbell, pp. 19–33. Abingdon: Routledge.

Baines, G. 2005. Narratives of New Brighton: Representations of the Port Elizabeth Township in Official Discourse, Cultural Memory, and Public History. *African Studies*, vol. 64, no. 2, pp. 243–261.

Baines, G. 2007. The Politics of Public History in Post-Apartheid South Africa. In *History Making and Present Day Politics: The Meaning of Collective Memory in South Africa*, ed. H. E. Stolten, pp. 167–182. Uppsala: Nordiska Afrikainstitutet.

Bali, R.N. 2006. The Politics of Turkification during the Single Party Period. In *Turkey beyond Nationalism: Towards Post-Nationalist Identities*, ed. H.L. Kieser, pp. 43–49. New York: I.B. Tauris.

Ballara, A. 1998. *Iwi: The Dynamics of Maori Tribal Organisation from c.1769 to c.1945*. Wellington: Victoria University Press.

Balogh, T. 1959. The Apotheosis of the Dilettante: The Establishment of Mandarins. In *The Establishment: a symposium*, ed. H. Thomas, pp. 83–126. London: Anthony Blond.

Banner, J.M. 2012. *Being a Historian: An Introduction to the Professional World of History*. Cambridge: Cambridge University Press.

Barabash, E. 2003. Mission Sokurov. Film.ru. April 23, 2003. At http://www.film.ru/articles/missiya-sokurova.

Barkan, E. 2009. AHR Forum: Truth and Reconciliation in History. Introduction: Historians and Historical Reconciliation. *The American Historical Review*, vol. 114, no. 4, pp. 899–913.

Barratt, N. 2004. *The Family History Project*. London: National Archives.

Barthes, R. 1981. *Camera Lucida: Reflections on Photography*. Trans. R. Howard. New York: Hill and Wang.

Bashforth, M. 2012. Absent Fathers. Present Histories. In *People and their Pasts: Public History and Heritage Today*, eds. P. Ashton and H. Kean, pp. 203–222. Basingstoke: Palgrave Macmillan.

Bashforth, M. n.d. Radical History, Radical Theory. Martin Bashforth. At http://bashforth.wordpress.com/politics/.

Basu, P. 2007. *Highland Homecomings: Genealogy and Heritage Tourism in the Scottish Diaspora*. London: Routledge.

Batchen, G. 1997. *Burning with Desire: The Conception of Photography*. Cambridge, MA: MIT Press.

Baumgartner, S. 2009. The Impact of the Stone Age Diet on Gingival Conditions in the Absence of Oral Hygiene. *Journal of Periodontology*, vol. 80, no. 5, pp. 759–68.

Beaglehole, J. C. 1936. *New Zealand: A Short History.* London: G. Allen & Unwin.

Bean, A., J.V. Hatch, and B. McNamara. 1996. *Inside the Minstrel Mask Readings in Nineteenth-Century Blackface Minstrelsy.* Hanover, NH: Wesleyan University Press.

Beck, P. 2006a. The Lessons of Abadan and Suez for British Foreign Policymakers in the 1960s. *The Historical Journal*, vol. 49, pp. 525–547.

Beck, P. 2006b. *Using History, Making British Policy: The Treasury and the Foreign Office, 1950–76.* Basingstoke: Palgrave Macmillan.

Becker, C. 1932. Everyman His Own Historian. *The American Historical Review*, vol. 37, no. 2, pp. 221–236.

Belgrave, M. 2005. *Historical Frictions: Maori Claims and Reinvented Histories.* Auckland: Auckland University Press.

Belgrave, M. 2006. Looking Forward: Historians and the Waitangi Tribunal. *New Zealand Journal of History*, vol. 40, pp. 230–250.

Belgrave, M. 2014. Beyond the Treaty of Waitangi: Māori Tribal Aspirations in an Era of Reform, 1984–2014. *Journal of Pacific History (Online), Journal of Pacific History*, vol. 49, pp. 193–213.

Bell, D. 2009. *The Idea of Greater Britain: Empire and the Future of World Order, 1860–1900.* Princeton: Princeton University Press.

Bell, J. 2000, July 1. NCC Opens Roadway Celebrating Heritage: Unfinished Confederation Boulevard to be a "Living Symbol." *Ottawa Citizen*, p. C7.

Bemis, S. 1939. The Training of Archivists in the United States. *American Archivist*, vol. 2, no. 3, pp. 154–161.

Bendorf, O. 2013. Do You Suffer From Archive Fever? October 29, 2013. At http://Oliverbendorf.Com/Comics/Archivefever/.

Benjamin, W. 1977. Über den Begriff der Geschichte. In *Illuminationen. Ausgewählte Schriften I*, ed. S. Unseld, pp. 251–261. Frankfurt am Main: Suhrkam.

Benjamin, W. 1992. Theses on the Philosophy of History. In *Illuminations*, ed. H. Arendt, pp. 245–255. London: Fontana.

Benmayor, R. 2008. Digital Storytelling as a Signature Pedagogy for the New Humanities. *Arts and Higher Education*, vol. 7, pp. 188–204.

Bennett, G. 2013. *Six Moments of Crisis: Inside British Foreign Policy.* Oxford: Oxford University Press.

Bennett, T. 1995. *The Birth of the Museum: History, Theory, Politics.* London: Routledge.

Bennett, T. 1996. The Museum and the Citizen. In *Museums and Citizenship: A Resource Book, Memoirs of the Queensland Museum*, eds. T. Bennett, R. Trotter, and D. McAlear, pp. 1–15. South Brisbane: Queensland Museum.

Bennett, T. 2013. *Making Culture, Changing Society.* London: Routledge.

Benson, S.P. et al. (eds.) 1981. "Presenting the Past: History and the Public," *Radical History Review*, 25, special issue.

Benson, S.P., S. Brier, and R. Rosenzweig. 1986. *Presenting the Past: Essays on History and the Public.* Philadelphia: Temple University Press.

Berlin, I. and L. Harris. 2005. Uncovering, Discovering, and Recovering: Digging in New York's Slave Past Before the African Burial Ground. *New York Journal of American History*, vol. 66, no. 2, pp. 23–33.

Berridge, V. 2000. History in Public Health: Who Needs It? *The Lancet*, vol. 356, pp. 1923–1925.

Berridge, V. 2008. History Matters? History's Role in Health Policy Making. *Medical History*, vol. 52, pp. 311–326.

Berridge, V. and P. Strong. 1991. AIDS and the Relevance of History. *Social History of Medicine*, vol. 4, pp. 129–138.

Bevir, M. and R.A.W. Rhodes. 2010. *The State as Cultural Practice.* Oxford: Oxford University Press.

Bigelow, M. 1979. Letter to W.T. Anderson. October 4, 1979. Records of the American Association for State and Local History. Box 66. Nashville: Tennessee State Library and Archives.

Binfield, K. 2004. *The Writings of the Luddites*. Baltimore: Johns Hopkins University Press.

Binnie, J. 2013. *Perception and Wellbeing: A Cross-Disciplinary Approach to Experiencing Art in the Museum*. PhD dissertation. University of Leicester.

Black, G. 2005. *The Engaging Museum: Developing Museums for Visitor Involvement*. London: Routledge.

Blackbourn, D. 2007. *The Conquest of Nature: Water, Landscape and the Making of Modern Germany*. London: Random House.

Blackburn, S. 1996. *Inside the Drama House: Rama Stories and Shadow Puppets in South India*. Berkeley: University of California Press.

Blair, T. 2003. Speech to Congress. At http://www.britishpoliticalspeech.org/speech-archive. htm?speech=285.

Blick, A. 2004. *People Who Live in the Dark*. London: Politicos.

Blier, S.P. 1995. *African Vodun: Art, Psychology, and Power*. Chicago: University of Chicago Press.

Blight, D. 2001. *Race and Reunion: The Civil War in American Memory*. Cambridge: The Belknap Press of Harvard University Press.

Boast, R. 2013. *The Native Land Court 1862–1887: A Historical Study, Cases, and Commentary*. Wellington: Brookers.

Boast, R. and R.S. Hill. (eds.) 2009. *Raupatu: The Confiscation of Māori Land*. Wellington, N.Z.: Victoria University Press.

Bobrow, D.B. 2006. Social and Cultural Factors: Constraining and Enabling. In *The Oxford Handbook of Public Policy*, eds. M. Moran, M. Rein, and R.E. Goodin, pp. 572–586. Oxford: Oxford University Press.

Bohstedt, J. 2010. *The Politics of Provisions: Food Riots, Moral Economy, and Market Transition in England, c.1550–1850*. Farnham: Ashgate.

Bonner, P. L. 2008. *Alexandra: A History*. Johannesburg: Wits University Press.

Boon, T. 2011. Co-Curation and the Public History of Science and Technology. *Curator: The Museum Journal*, vol. 54, pp. 383–387.

Bordwell, D. 2002. Intensified Continuity: Visual Style in Contemporary American Film. *Film Quarterly*, vol. 55, no. 3, pp. 16–28.

Bordwell, D. and K. Thompson. 2003. *Film Art*. New York: McGraw-Hill Higher Education.

Borges, J.L. 1971. *Ficciones*. Madrid: Alianza.

Boss, P. 1999. *Ambiguous Loss: Learning to Live with Unresolved Grief*. Cambridge, MA: Harvard University Press.

Boswell, D. and J. Evans. (eds.) 1999. *Representing the Nation: A Reader: History, Heritage and Museums*. London: Routledge.

Bourknight, Ashley N. 2016. *Black Museology: Reevaluating African American Material Culture*. PhD dissertation, Middle Tennessee State University.

Bourdieu, P. 1993. *The Field of Cultural Production*. Ed. R. Johnson. New York: Columbia University Press.

Bowden, R. 2004. A Critique of Alfred Gell on Art and Agency. *Oceania*, vol. 74, no. 4, pp. 309–324.

Bowen, S. and K. De Master. 2011. New Rural Livelihoods or Museums of Production? Quality Food Initiatives in Practice. *Journal of Rural Studies*, vol. 27, no. 1, pp. 73–82.

Boym, S. 2001. *The Future of Nostalgia*. New York: Basic Books.

Bracke, S. et al. 2014. History Education Research in Germany: Empirical Attempts at Mapping Historical Thinking and Learning. In *Researching History Education: International Perspectives and Disciplinary Tradition*, eds. M. Koster, H. Thunemann, and M. Zulsdorf-Kersting, pp. 9–55. Schwalbach/Wochenschau Geschichte.

Bradshaw, P. 2003. Review: Russian Ark. *Guardian*. April 4, 2003. At http://www.theguardian. com/culture/2003/apr/04/artsfeatures9.

Brandis, S. 2013. Apprentice Life at Quarry Bank. Quarry Bank Mill. August 1, 2013. At http:// quarrybankmill.wordpress.com/2013/07/29/apprenticelifeatquarrybank/#comment-499/.

Brennan, T. 2000. History, Family, History. In *Seeing History: Public History in Britain*, eds. H. Kean, P. Martin, and S. Morgan, pp. 37–50. London: Francis Bootle.

Brint, S. 1990. Rethinking the Policy Influence of Experts: From General Characterizations to Analysis of Variation. *Sociological Forum*, vol. 5, pp. 361–385.

Brittlebank, K. 1997. *Tipu Sultan's Search for Legitimacy: Islam and Kingship in a Hindu Domain.* Delhi: Oxford University Press.

Brodie, N. 2015. *Kin: A Real People's History of our Nation.* Melbourne: Hardie Grant Books.

Brodsky, M. 2006. *Buena Memoria/Good Memory.* 4th edition. Buenos Aires: La Marca Editora.

Brown, B. 2001. Thing Theory. *Critical Inquiry*, vol. 28, no. 1, pp. 1–22.

Brown, G. 2010. *Beyond the Crash: Overcoming the First Crisis of Globalisation.* London: Simon and Schuster.

Brownlie, R. and R. Crowe. 2013. 'So You Want to Hear Our Ghetto Stories?' Oral History at Ndinawa Youth Resource Centre. In *Remembering Mass Violence: Oral History, New Media and Performance*, eds. S. High, E. Little, and T.R. Duong, pp. 203–218. Toronto: University of Toronto Press.

Bruner, E.M. 1996. Tourism in Ghana: The Representation of Slavery and the Return of the Black Diaspora. *American Anthropologist*, vol. 98, no. 2, pp. 290–304.

Bruwer, J. and R. Johnson. 2010. Place-Based Marketing and Regional Branding Strategy Perspectives in the California Wine Industry. *Journal of Consumer Marketing*, vol. 27, no. 1, pp. 5–16.

Bryant, L.R. 2011. *The Democracy of Objects.* Ann Arbor (MI): Open Humanities Press.

Bryant, L.R., N. Srnicek, and G. Harman (eds.) 2011. *The Speculative Turn: Continental Materialism and Realism.* Melbourne: re.press.

Brymner, D. 1884. *Report on Canadian Archives 1883.* Ottawa: Maclean, Roger, and Co.

Brymner, D. 1887. *Report on Canadian Archives 1886.* Ottawa: Maclean, Roger, and Co.

Brymner, D. 1892. *Report on Canadian Archives 1891.* Ottawa: S.E. Dawson.

Brymner, D. 1898. *Report on Canadian Archives 1897.* Ottawa: Maclean, Roger, and Co.

Bulmer, M, E. Coates, and L. Dominian. 2007. Evidence-Based Policy Making. In *Making Policy in Theory and Practice*, eds. H.M. Bochel and S. Duncan, pp. 87–103. Bristol: Policy.

Burian, J. 2000. *Modern Czech Theatre: Reflector and Conscience of a Nation.* Iowa City: University of Iowa Press.

Burke, P. 1992. *New Perspectives in Historical Writing.* University Park, PA: The Penn State University Press. (2nd edition, 2001.)

Burns, P. 1989. *Fatal Success: A History of the New Zealand Company.* Auckland: Heinemann Reed.

Burrow, J.W. 1983. *A Liberal Descent: Victorian Historians and the English Past.* Cambridge: Cambridge University Press.

Burton, A. 1999. *Vision & Accident: The Story of the Victoria & Albert Museum.* London: V&A Publications.

Burton, A. (ed.) 2005. *Archive Stories: Facts, Fictions, and the Writing of History.* Durham, SC: Duke University Press.

Butler, J. 2004. *Precarious Life: The Powers of Mourning and Violence.* London: Verso.

Butler, S.R. 2007. *Contested Representations: Revisiting Into the Heart of Africa.* Toronto: University of Toronto Press.

Butler, T. 2005. Drifting and Dockers: Voices from the Hidden History of the Thames. London: Museum of London, 2005. At www.memoryscape.or.uk.

Butler, T. 2007. Memoryscape: How Audio Walks Can Deepen Our Sense of Place by Integrating Art, Oral History, and Cultural Geography. *Geography Compass*, vol. 1, no. 3, pp. 360–372.

Butler, T. 2008a. Memoryscape: Integrating Oral History, Memory and Landscape on the River Thames. In *People and their Pasts: Public History Today*, eds. P. Ashton and H. Kean, pp. 223–239. New York: Palgrave Macmillan.

Butler, T. 2008b. *Ports of Call: Walks of Art at the Royal Docks.* London: University of East London. At www.portsofcall.org.uk.

Butler, T. and G. Miller. 2005. Linked: A Landmark in Sound, a Public Walk of Art. *Cultural Geographies*, vol. 12, no. 1, pp. 77–88.

Byrne, D. 1991. Western Hegemony in Archaeological Heritage Management. *History and Anthropology*, vol. 5, no. 2, pp. 269–76.

Byrne, D. 2014. *Counterheritage: Critical Perspectives on Heritage Conservation in Asia*. New York: Routledge.

Byrnes, G. 2004. *The Waitangi Tribunal and New Zealand history*. Auckland: Oxford University Press.

Byrnes, G. 2006. By Which Standards?: History and the Waitangi Tribunal: A Reply. *New Zealand Journal of History*, vol. 40, pp. 214–229.

Cajani, L. 2009. History Textbooks between Teachers' Freedom and State Control. Paper presented during the Annual Conference of the International Society for History Didactics, September 2009. Braunschweig, Germany.

Cajani, L. 2012. History Education and Citizenship Education in Europe and in the USA since the Enlightenment. Paper presented during the first conference of the International Research Association for History and Social Studies Education, September 3–5, 2012. Rome: La Sapienza.

Cajani, L., S. Lässig and M. Repoussi (eds.) (forthcoming). *History Education under Fire. An International Handbook*. Göttingen: Vandenhoeck & Ruprecht.

Caleb, F.A., and Caleb, F. 2008. The Agency of Gell in the Anthropology of Art. Trans. B. Reinhardt. *Horizontes Antropológicos*, vol. 15, no. 29, pp. 315–338.

Cameron, C. and M. Rössler. 2013. *Many Voices, One Vision: the Early Years of the World Heritage Convention*. Farnham: Ashgate.

Caron, C. 2006. *Se creer des Ancetres: Un Parcours Genealogique Nord-American XIX-XX seicles*. Quebec: Septentrion.

Carr, E. 2007. *Mission 66: Modernism and the National Park Dilemma*. Amherst: University of Massachusetts Press.

Carr, E.S. 2010. Enactments of Expertise. *Annual Review of Anthropology*, vol. 39, pp. 17–32.

Carretero, M., Berger, S. and Grever, M. 2017. *Palgrave Handbook of Research in Historical Culture and Eduction*. London: Palgrave Macmillan.

Carson, C. 2008. The End of History Museums: What's Plan B? *The Public Historian*, vol. 30, no. 4, pp. 9–27.

Carter, J., and Orange, J. 2012. Contentious Terrain: Defining a Human Rights Museology. *Museum Management and Curatorship*, vol. 27, no. 2, pp. 111–127.

Cartwright, N. and J. Hardie. 2012. *Evidence-Based Policy: A Practical Guide to Doing It Better*. Oxford: Oxford University Press.

Caruth, C. (ed.) 1995. *Trauma: Explorations in Memory*. Baltimore: Johns Hopkins University Press.

Caruth, C. 1996. *Unclaimed Experience: Trauma, Narrative, and History*. Baltimore: Johns Hopkins University Press.

Caruth, C. 2013. *Literature in the Ashes of History*. Baltimore: Johns Hopkins University Press.

Casey, D. 2001. The National Museum of Australia: Exploring the past, illuminating the present and imagining the future. In *National Museums Negotiating Histories – Conference Proceedings*, eds. D. McIntyre and K. Wehner, pp. 3–11. Canberra: National Museum of Australia.

Cassidy, T.J. Jr., B. Pahl, S. Williamson, E. Merritt, and T.D. Jarvis. 2013. *Historic Leasing in the National Park System Preserving History Through Effective Partnerships*. National Trust for Historic Preservation, September 2013.

Castro-Gómez, S. 2002. The Social Sciences, Epistemic Violence, and the Problem of the "Invention of the Other." *Nepantla: Views from the South*, vol. 3, no. 2, pp. 269–285.

Castro-Gómez, S. 2007. The Missing Chapter of Empire. *Cultural Studies*, vol. 21, no. 2, pp. 428–448.

Cauvin, T. 2011. Quando è in gioco la Public History: musei, storici e riconciliazione politica nella Repubblica d'Irlanda. *Memoria e Ricerca*, vol. 37, pp. 53–71. English translation available at http://www.fondazionecasadioriani.it/modules.php?name=MR&op=body&id=550.

Cauvin, T. 2016. *Public History: A Textbook of Practice*. London: Routledge.

Cauvin, T. and S. Noiret. 2017. Internationalizing Public History. In *Handbook for Public History*, eds. J.B. Gardner and P. Hamilton, pp. 10–25. Oxford: Oxford University Press.

Cauvin, T. 2012. National Museums and the Mobilization of the Past in Ireland and Northern Ireland: Commemorative Exhibitions of Anglo-Irish Conflicts, 1921–2006. PhD dissertation. Florence, Italy: European University Institute.

Cenker, I.C. and L. Thys-Senocak. 2008. Moving Beyond the Walls: The Oral History of the Ottoman Fortress Villages of Seddulbahir and Kumkale. In *Public History and Public Memories*, eds. P. Hamilton and L. Shopes, pp. 65–86. Philadelphia: Temple University Press.

Chang, X. 1989. The Political Background of the 228 Incident and Its Influence. In *The Research Papers on the 228 Incident*, ed. F.M. Chen, pp. 111–130. Taipei: Avant-Garde Publisher.

Chang, Y. 2007. Conclusion. In *Research Report on Responsibility for 228 Massacre: A Brief Introduction*, ed. C-H. Chen, pp. 46–69. Taipei: Memorial Foundation of 228.

Chańko, J. 2015. Akademickie kształcenie nauczycieli historii i wiedzy o społeczeństwie w Uniwersytecie Łódzkim. Paper presented during the conference XI Toruńskie Spotkania Dydaktyczne, Toruń.

Chatterjee, P. 2012. *The Black Hole of Empire: History of a Global Practice of Power.* Ranikhet: Permanent Black.

Chaturvedi, V. (ed.) 2012 (2000). *Mapping Subaltern Studies and the Postcolonial.* London and New York: Verso.

Chen, C-C. 2009. An Open Letter to President Ma. *China Times.* December 12, 2009. At http://www.coolloud.org.tw/node/49102.

Chen, C-L. 2003. Interpreting History: Adults' Learning in the Taipei 228 Memorial Museum. *Museological Review*, vol. 9, pp. 16–29.

Chen, C-L. 2007. *Wound on Exhibition: Notes on Memory and Trauma of Museums.* Taipei: Artco Publisher.

Chen, H. 2005. Beyond Commemoration: The 2-28 Incident, the Aesthetics of Trauma and Sexual Difference. PhD dissertation. School of Fine Art, History of Art and Cultural Studies, University of Leeds.

Chen, J-M. 2011. The Taipei Memorial Museum Change the Permanent Exhibition, Scholars Criticised It Is against the Historical Truth. *Liberty Times Net.* February 20, 2011. At http://news.ltn.com.tw/news/focus/paper/470040.

Chenier, E. 2014. Oral History and Open Access: Fulfilling the Promise of Democratizing Knowledge. New American Notes Online, vol. 5. At www.nanocrit.com.

Choińska-Mika, J. 2014. Nauczyciele historii. In *Liczą się nauczyciele: Raport o stanie edukacji 2013*, eds. M. Federowicz et al., pp. 227–229. Warsaw: IBE.

Chorąży, E., D. Konieczka-Śliwińska, and S. Roszak. 2008. *Edukacja historyczna w szkole: Teoria i praktyka.* Warsaw: Wydawnictwo Naukowe PWN.

Christen, K. 2011. Opening Archives: Respectful Repatriation. *The American Archivist*, vol. 74, pp. 185–210.

Christen, K. 2012. Does Information Really Want to Be Free? Indigenous Knowledge Systems and the Question of Openness. *International Journal of Communication*, vol. 6, pp. 2870–2893.

Christian, D. 2010. The Return of Universal History. *History and Theory*, vol. 49, pp. 691–716.

Cicalo, A. 2015. From Public Amnesia to Public Memory: Re-Discovering Slavery Heritage in Rio de Janeiro. In *African Heritage and Memories of Slavery in Brazil and the South Atlantic World*, ed. A.L. Araujo, pp. 171–202. Amherst, New York: Cambria Press.

Cittaslow. 2014. At www.cittaslow_/network/location/295 (accessed August 20, 2016).

Civil Service Commission and Baron J.S. Fulton of Fulmer. 1968. *The Civil Service. Vol. 1 Report of the Committee 1966–68.* London.

Civilization Fanatics Center Forums. 2011a. Historical Accuracy Issues. At http://forums.civfanatics.com/

Civilization Fanatics Center Forums. 2011b. Does Anyone Play Civ Realistically. At http://forums.civfanatics.com/

Clark, A. 2008. *History's Children: History Wars in the Classroom.* Sydney: University of New South Wales Press.

Clark, C. 2011. Power. In *A Concise Companion to History*, ed. U. Rublack, pp. 131–154. Oxford: Oxford University Press.

Clavert, F. and S. Noiret. (eds.) 2013. *L'histoire contemporaine à l'ère numérique – Contemporary History in the Digital Age*. Brussels: Peter Lang.

Clifford, J. 1985. Objects and Selves – an Afterword. In *Objects and Others: Essays on Museums and Material Culture*, ed. G.W. Stocking, pp. 236–246. Madison, WI: University of Wisconsin Press.

Clifford, J. 1997. *Routes: Travel and Translation in the Late Twentieth Century*. Cambridge: Harvard University Press.

Cocciolo, A. 2014. Mobile Technology, Oral History and the 9/11 Memorial: A Study of Digitally Augmented Remembrance. *Preservation, Digital Technology & Culture*, vol. 43, no. 3, 86–99.

Cohen, D. 2005. The future of preserving the past. *CRM: The Journal of Heritage Stewardship*, vol. 21, no.2, pp. 6–19.

Cohen, D.J. and R. Rosenzweig. 2005. *Digital History: A Guide to Gathering, Preserving, and Presenting the Past on the Web*. Philadelphia: University of Pennsylvania Press.

Cohen, D.J. and R. Rosenzweig. 2011. *Clio Wired. The Future of the Past in the Digital Age*. New York: Columbia University Press.

Cohen, D.J., M. Frisch, P. Gallagher, S. Mintz, K. Sword, A.M. Taylor, W.G. Thomas III, and W.J. Turkel, 2008. Interchange: The Promise of Digital History. *Journal of American History, no. 2*, pp. 452–491.

Cohen, D.W. 2010. Memories of Things Future: Future Effects in `The Production of History.' In *Unsettling History: Archiving and Narrating in Historiography*, eds. S. Jobs and A. Lüdtke, pp. 29–49. Frankfurt and New York: Campus Verlag.

Colbert, C.C. 2010. *Booth*. Ill. Tanitoc. New York: First Second Books.

Colbert, S. 2005. *The Colbert Report*. October 17, 2005. New York: Busboy Productions.

Cole, E.A. and J. Barsalou. 2006. United or Divided? The Challenges of Teaching History in Societies Emerging from Violent Conflict. A Special Report from the U.S. Institute of Peace, #163, pp. 1–16. Washington, D.C.

Coleman, L.V. 1939. *The Museum in America: A Critical Study*. Washington, DC: American Association of Museums.

Colley, L. 2003. The Past is a Foreign Country. *The Guardian*. July 29, 2003. At http://www.theguardian.com/politics/2003/jul/29/labour.tonyblair.

Collins, H. and R. Evans. 2007. *Rethinking Expertise*. Chicago: University of Chicago Press.

Colonial Williamsburg. 1958a. Minutes. Seminar for Historical Interpretation Seminar. September 4, 1958. Colonial Williamsburg Archives. Williamsburg, Virginia.

Colonial Williamsburg. 1958b. Revised Minutes. Historical Interpretation Seminar. March 13, 1958. Colonial Williamsburg Archives. Williamsburg, Virginia.

Colonial Williamsburg. 1959a. Eight CWers Participate on Faculty at Historical Administrators' Meet. *Colonial Williamsburg News,* vol. 13, no. 1. Colonial Williamsburg Archives. Williamsburg, Virginia.

Colonial Williamsburg. 1959b. Press Release. Seminar for Historical Administrators. May 27, 1959. Colonial Williamsburg Archives. Williamsburg, Virginia.

Colonial Williamsburg. 1959c. Tentative Schedule. Seminar for Historical Administrators. Colonial Williamsburg Archives. Williamsburg, Virginia.

Colonial Williamsburg. c. 1980. Seminar for Historical Administration. Colonial Williamsburg Archives. Williamsburg, Virginia.

Committee on Standards in Public Life. 2003. Defining the Boundaries within the Executive: Ministers, Special Advisers and the Permanent Civil Service. London: HMSO.

Commonwealth of Australia. 1975. *Museums in Australia: Report of the Committee of Inquiry on Museums and National Collections including the Report of the Planning Committee on the Gallery of Aboriginal Australia*. Canberra: AGPS.

Commonwealth of Australia. 1983. *The Plan for the Development of the Museum of Australia: Report of the Interim Council.* Canberra: AGPS.

Commonwealth of Australia. 2003. *Review of the National Museum of Australia: Its exhibitions and Public Programs.* Canberra: Department of Communications, Information Technology and the Arts.

Confino, A. 2012. Miracles and Snow in Palestine and Israel: Tantura, A History of 1948. *Israel Studies,* vol. 17, no. 2, pp. 25–61.

Congressional Record. September 19, 1966.

Connell, R. 2007. *Southern Theory: The Global Dynamics of Knowledge in Social Science.* Cambridge: Polity.

Connerton, P. 1989. *How Societies Remember.* Cambridge: Cambridge University Press.

Connolly, S. 2014. Patriotism and Nationalism. In *The Oxford Handbook of Modern Irish History,* ed. A. Jackson, pp. 27–44. Oxford: Oxford University Press.

Conrad, M., K. Ercikan, G. Friesen, J. Létourneau, D. Muise, D. Northrup, and P. Seixas. 2013. *Canadians and Their Pasts.* Toronto: University of Toronto Press.

Cook, T. 2005. An Archival Revolution: W. Kaye Lamb and the Transformation of the Archival Profession. *Archivaria,* vol. 60, pp. 185–234.

Coope, U. 2009. Change and its Relation to Actuality and Potentiality. In *A Companion to Aristotle,* ed. G. Anagnostopoulos, pp. 277–291. Oxford: Blackwell.

Cooper, C.L. and S. Anderson. 2012. The Case for a Chief Social Scientist. *The Guardian.* March 19, 2012. At http://www.theguardian.com/higher-education-network/blog/2012/mar/19/the-case-for-a-chief-social-scientist.

Cordain, L. n.d. About the Paleo Diet. At http://thepaleodiet.com/about-the-paleo-diet/.

Cordain, L. 2010. *The Paleo Diet,* rev. ed. New York: Houghton Mifflin Harcourt.

Cordain, L., J. Brand Miller, S.B. Eaton, and N. Mann. 2000. Hunter-Gatherer Diets – A Shore Based Perspective (Letter). *American Journal of Clinical Nutrition,* vol. 72, pp. 1585–1586.

Cordain, L., S.B. Eaton, A. Sebastian, N. Mann, S. Lindeberg, B.A. Watkins, J.H. O'Keefe, and J. Brand-Miller. 2005. Origins and Evolution of the Western Diet: Health Implications for the 21st Century. *American Journal of Clinical Nutrition,* vol. 81, pp. 341–354.

Corrigall, M. 2012. Material: Tearing the Fabric of Society Apart. Corrigall on Culture. At http://corrigallculture.blogspot.co.za/2012/02/material-tearing-fabric-of-society.html (accessed February 9, 2016).

Cox, P. 2013. The Future Uses of History. *History Workshop Journal,* vol. 75, pp. 125–145.

Craig, D. 1990. *On the Crofters Trail: In Search of the Clearance Highlanders.* London: Pimlico.

Cramer, L. 2017. Keeping Up Appearances: Genteel Women, Dress and Refurbishing in Gold-Rush Victoria, Australia, 1851–1870. *Textile: Cloth and Culture,* vol. 15, no. 1, pp. 48–67.

Crawford, K. 1995. A History of the Right: The Battle for Control of National Curriculum History 1989–1994. *British Journal of Educational Studies,* vol. 43, no. 4, pp. 433–456.

Cresswell, T. 2004. *Place: A Short Introduction.* Oxford: Blackwell.

Criscione, A., S. Noiret, C. Spagnolo, and S. Vitali. (eds.) 2004. *La Storia a(l) tempo di Internet: indagine sui siti italiani di storia contemporanea (2001–2003).* Bologna: Pàtron Editore.

Croick Church. n.d. The Clearances. At http://www.croickchurch.com/clearances.htm.

Cronon, W. 1992. A Place for Stories: Nature, History, and Narrative. *Journal of American History,* vol. 78, no. 4, pp. 1347–1376.

CrossFit Hardcore. n.d. CrossFit "Hero" WODS. At http://www.crossfithardcore.com/extras/hero-wods.html.

Cruikshank, J. 1990. *Life Lived Like a Story: Life Stories of Three Yukon Native Elders.* Lincoln: University of Nebraska Press.

Cruikshank, J. 1998. *The Social Life of Stories: Narrative and Knowledge in the Yukon Territory.* Lincoln: University of Nebraska Press.

Cruikshank, J. 2005. *Do Glaciers Listen? Local Knowledge, Colonial Encounters, and Social Imagination*. Vancouver: University of British Columbia Press.

Crusader Kings. 2013. Crusader Kings 2. At http://www.crusaderkings.com/.

Cuban, L. 2013. The Myth of Teachers Not Changing. Larry Cuban on School Reform and Classroom Practice. November 11, 2013. At https://larrycuban.wordpress.com/2013/11/11/the-myth-of-teachers-not-changing/.

Cullinane, T., C. Huber, and L. Koontz. 2015. *2014 National Park visitor spending effects: Economic contributions to local communities, states, and the Nation*. National Park Service.

Dale, L. 1997. Mainstreaming Australia. *Journal of Australian Studies*, vol. 53, pp. 9–19.

Dalinger, B. 1998. *Verloschene Sterne: Geschichte des jüdischen Theaters in Wien*. Wien: Picus Verlag.

Dalley, B. 2009. Shades of Grey: Public History and Government in New Zealand. In *People and Their Pasts: Public History Today*, eds. P. Ashton, and H. Kean, pp. 74–90. Basingstoke: Palgrave Macmillan.

Dalley, B. and J. Phillips. (eds.) 2001. *Going Public: The Changing Face of New Zealand History*. Auckland: Auckland University Press.

Danniau, F. 2013. Public History in a Digital Context. Back to the Future or Back to Basics? *BMGN – Low Countries Historical Review*, vol. 128, no. 4, pp. 118–144. At http://www.bmgn-lchr.nl/index.php/bmgn/article/view/9355.

Dant, T. 1999. *Material Culture in the Social World: Values, Activities, Lifestyles*. Buckingham: Open University Press.

Darby, J. 2003. *Northern Ireland: The Background to the Peace Process*. CAIN Web Service. At http://cain.ulst.ac.uk/events/peace/darby03.htm

Darling, E. 2005. The City in the Country: Wilderness Gentrification and the Rent Gap. *Environment and Planning A*, vol. 37, no. 6, pp. 1015–1032.

Davis, R.H. 1999. *Lives of Indian Images*. Princeton, NJ: University Press.

Davison, D. 2004. *The Use and Abuse of Australian History*. New South Wales: Allen and Unwin.

Davison, G. 2001. Submission to Committee of Review on Exhibitions and Public Programs at the National Museum of Australia. http://www.nma.gov.au/__data/assets/pdf_file/0011/2414/Prof_Davison_r.pdf

Davison, G. 2009. Speed Relating: Family History in a Digital Age. *History Australia*, vol. 9, no. 2, pp. 43.1–43.10.

de Certeau, M. 1984. *The Practice of Everyday Life*. Berkeley: University of California Press.

de Certeau, M., L. Giard, and P. Mayol. 1998. *The Practice of Everyday Life: Living and Cooking*. Minneapolis: University of Minnesota Press.

De Gaulejac, Vincent and André Lévy, eds. 2000. *Récits de vie et histoire social: Quelle historicité*. Paris: Édition Eska.

De Groot, J. 2016 (2009). *Consuming History: Historians and Heritage in Contemporary Popular Culture*. London: Routledge.

De Groot, J. 2015. On Genealogy. *The Public Historian*, vol. 37, no. 3, pp. 102–127.

Dean, D. 2009. Museums as conflict zones: the Canadian War Museum and Bomber Command. *Museum and Society*, vol. 7, no. 1, pp. 1–15.

Dean, D. and P. Rider. 2005. Museums, Nation and Political History in the Australian National Museum and the Canadian Museum of Civilization. *Museum and Society*, vol. 3, no. 1, pp. 35–50.

Dean, D., Meerzon, Y, and Prince, K. (eds.) 2015. *History, Memory, Performance*. London: Palgrave Macmillan.

Dear Photograph. 2012. At http://dearphotograph.com/.

Delap, L., S. Szreter, and F. Holland. 2014. *History as a Resource for the Future: Building Civil Service Skills*. London: History and Policy.

Deller, J. 1999. *The English Civil War Part II: Personal Accounts of the 1984–85 Miners' Strike*. London: Artangel.

Deloria, P. 1998. *Playing Indian*. New Haven: Yale University Press.

Demantowsky, M. 2015. 'Public History' – Sublation of a German Debate? *Public History Weekly. Multilingual Blogspot for History and Civic Education*, vol. 3, no. 2. At http://public-history-weekly.oldenbourg-verlag.de/3-2015-2/public-history-sublation-german-debate/.

Dening, G. 2002. Performing History on the Beaches of the Mind: An Essay. *History and Theory*, vol. 41, no. 1, pp. 1–24.

Denison, T., S. McKemmish, A. Waugh, and J. Eades. 2012. The Koorie Archival System: Reconciling the Official Record with Community Knowledge. Prato CIRN Community Informatics Conference.

Dennis, R.T. 1972. *National Parks for the Future*. The Conservation Foundation, Washington, D.C.

Derrida, J. 1976 (1967). *Grammatology*. Baltimore and London: Johns Hopkins University Press.

Derrida, J. 1995a. *Archive Fever. A Freudian Impression. Diacritics*, vol. 25, no. 2, pp. 9–63.

Derrida, J. 1995b. *Mal d'archive. Une impression freudienne*. Paris: Editions Galilée.

Derrida, J. 1996. *Archive Fever: A Freudian Impression*. Chicago: University of Chicago Press.

Destructoid. 2012. Paradox: Past, Present, and Future. At http://www.destructoid.com/paradox-past-present-and-future-232917.phtml.

Devine, M. 2001. A Nation Trivialized. *Daily Telegraph*. March 12, 2001. Page 3.

Diamond, J. 2012. *The World Until Yesterday: What Can We Learn From Traditional Societies?* New York: Viking.

Dickenson, R. 1981. Our Challenge Today. *National Park Service: 65th Anniversary*. National Park Service.

Digging for the Truth: The Iceman Cometh. 2005. Season 1, episode 6. At https://www.youtube.com/watch?v=PKqT3LqTBps.

Dobrescu, L.I., M. Luca, and A. Motta. 2012. What makes a Critic Tick? Connected Authors and the Determinants of Book reviews. Harvard Business School Working Papers. At http://hbswk.hbs.edu/item/6823.html.

Docker, J. 2001. *1492: The Poetics of Diaspora*. London: Continuum.

Dolan, A. 2015. Commemorating 1916: How Much Does the Integrity of the Past Count? *The Irish Times*. January 2, 2015. At http://www.irishtimes.com/opinion/commemorating-1916-how-much-does-the-integrity-of-the-past-count-1.2052868.

dos Santos, C.A. 2000. Projetos Sociais Abolicionistas: Rupturas ou Continuismo? In *Intelectuais, História e Política (séculos XIX. XX.*, ed. D. Aarão Reis Filho, pp. 54–74. Rio de Janeiro: 7 Letras.

Doueihi, M. 2011a. *Digital Cultures*. Cambridge, MA: Harvard University Press.

Doueihi, M. 2011b. *Pour un humanisme numérique*. Paris: Editions du Seuil.

Doueihi, M. 2013. *Qu'est ce que le numérique*. Paris: Presses universitaires de France.

Doueihi, M. 2015. Quelles Humanités Numériques? *Des Chiffres et des Lettres, special issue of Critique, no.* 819–820, pp. 704–711.

Dove, M., P.E. Sajise, and A.A. Doolittle. 2005. *Conserving Nature in Culture: Case Studies from Southeast Asia*. New Haven: Yale University.

Dowling, D.B. 1900. A Condensed Summary of the Field-Work Annually Accomplished by the Officers of the Geological Survey of Canada from its Commencement to 1865. *Ottawa Naturalist*, vol. 14, no. 6, pp. 107–118.

Downs, G. and Masur, K. 2017. The Era of Reconstruction, 1861–1900: A National Historic Landmark Theme Study. National Park Service.

Doyle, H. 2001. Royal Australian Historical Society. In *The Oxford Companion to Australian History*, eds. G. Davison, J. Hirst, and S. Macintyre, pp. 569. Oxford: Oxford University Press.

Dresser, M. 2007. Set in Stone? Statues and Slavery in London. *History Workshop Journal*, vol. 64, pp. 175–86.

Drury, N. 1949. The Dilemma of Our Parks. *American Forests*, vol. 55, no. 6, pp. 6–11, 38–39.

Dubin, S.C. 1999. *Displays of Power. Memory and Amnesia in the American Museum*. New York: New York University Press.

Dudley, S. (ed.) 2010. *Museum Materialities: Objects, Engagements, Interpretations.* London: Routledge.

Dudley, S. (ed.) 2012. *Museum Objects: Experiencing the Properties of Things.* London: Routledge.

Dudley, S.H. 2014a. Enlightening British ideas of Burma: Richard Carnac Temple's and James Henry Green's Collections in the Pitt Rivers Museum. Unpublished paper presented at the Association of Social Anthropologists decennial Conference, University of Edinburgh, June 2014.

Dudley, S.H. 2014b. What's in the Drawer? Surprise and Proprioceptivity in the Pitt Rivers Museum. *The Senses and Society,* vol. 9, no. 3, pp. 296–309.

Dudley, S.H. 2015. What, or Where, is the (Museum) Object? Colonial Encounters in Displayed Worlds of Things. In *Theory,* eds. A. Witcomb and K. Message, volume III of *The International Handbooks of Museum Studies,* eds. S. Macdonald and H. Rees Leahy, pp. 41–62. New York: John Wiley & Sons.

Duncan, C. 1995. *Civilizing Rituals. Inside Public Art Museums.* Abingdon: Routledge.

Dunn, R. 2014. Ancient Humans Mostly Vegetarian, "Paleolithic Diet" Critic Says. *Scientific American,* July 3, 2014.

DuPuis, E.M. and P. Vandergeest. (eds.) 1996. *Creating the Countryside: The Politics of Rural and Environmental Discourse.* Philadelphia: Temple University Press.

Ebert, R. 2003. Russian Ark. Roger Ebert. January 31, 2003. At http://www.rogerebert.com/reviews/russian-ark-2003.

Echavarria, J.M. 2005. *Mouths of Ash/Bocas De Ceniza.* Milan: Charta.

Edgerton, D. 2005. C.P. Snow as Anti-historian of British Science: Revisiting the Technocractic Moment, 1959–1964. *History of science,* vol. 43, pp. 187–208.

Editorial Collective. 1976. Editorial. *History Workshop Journal,* vol. 1, pp. 1–3.

Edkins, J. 2003a. *Trauma and the Memory of Politics.* Cambridge: Cambridge University Press.

Edkins, J. 2003b. The Rush to Memory and the Rhetoric of War. *Journal of Political and Military Sociology,* vol. 31, no. 2, pp. 231–251.

Edkins, J. 2011. *Missing: Persons and Politics.* Ithaca, NY: Cornell University Press.

Edkins, J. 2016a. Missing Migrants and the Politics of Naming: Names without Bodies, Bodies without Names. *Social Research: An International Quarterly,* vol. 83, no. 2, pp. 359–389.

Edkins, J. 2016b. Loss of a Loss: Ground Zero, Spring 2014. In *Narrative Global Politics,* eds. E. Dauphinee and N. Inayatullah. London: Routledge.

Edwards, G. 2005. *Moota – Camp 103: The Story of a Cumbrian Prisoner of War Camp.* Cockermouth: Little Bird Publications.

Ehrmann, F., O. Heitlinger and R. Iltis (eds.) 1965. *Terezín.* Prague: Council of Jewish Communities in the Czech Lands.

Eichbaum, C. and R. Shaw. 2010. *Partisan Appointees and Public Servants: An International Analysis of the Role of the Political Adviser.* Cheltenham: Edward Elgar.

Eley, G. 2005. *A Crooked Line. From Cultural History to the History of Society.* Ann Arbor: University of Michigan Press.

Elson, R.M. 1964. *Guardians of Tradition: American Schoolbooks of the Nineteenth Century.* Lincoln: University of Nebraska Press.

Enders, J.C., and M. Remig. (eds.) 2015. *Theories of Sustainable Development.* New York: Routledge.

Erginöz, A.S. 2007. *Gökçeada İlçesi Gelişme Stratejisi.* Ankara: Sanayi Araştirma ve Geliştirme Genel Müdürlüğü.

Erginsoy, F.G. 1998. Sweet as an Almond: From Gliki to "Bademli" Full Time and Part Time Citizenship. At http://openarchive.icomos.org/1241/ (accessed December 16, 2015).

Erikson, K. 1994. *A New Species of Trouble: The Human Experience of Modern Disasters.* New York: W.W. Norton.

Erlank, Natasha. 2011. Sophiatown Project Field Notes, November.

Ernaux, A. 1993. *La place.* Paris: Gallimard.

Erskine-Loftus, P., M. Ibrahim Al-Mulla, and V. Hightower. (eds.) 2016. *Representing the Nation: Heritage, Museums, National Narratives, and Identity in the Arab Gulf States*. London: Routledge.

Escobar, A. 2004. (1995). *Encountering Development: The Making and Unmaking of the Third World*. Princeton: Princeton University Press.

Eskildsen, K.R. 2008. Leopold Ranke's Archival Turn: Location and Evidence in Modern Historiography. *Modern Intellectual History*, vol. 5, no. 3, pp. 425–453.

Eskildsen, K. R. 2013. Inventing the Archive. Testimony and Virtue in Modern Historiography. *History of the Human Sciences*, vol. 26, no. 4, pp. 8–26.

Esler, J. 1996. Historic House Museums: Struggling for Survival. *Historic preservation forum: the journal of the National Trust for Historic Preservation*, vol. 10, no. 4, pp. 42–50.

Esposito, K.G. 2015. Confederate Immigration to Brazil: a Cross-Cultural Approach to Reconstruction and Public History. *Public History Review* 22, pp. 23–37.

EuroVision. n.d. One Object – Many Visions – Eurovisions. At http://www.museums-exhibiting-europe.de/.

Evans, R. 2008. Review of *Who Do You Think You Are? History Australia*, vol. 5, no. 3.

Evans, T. 2011. Secrets and Lies: The Radical Potential of Family History. *History Workshop Journal*, vol. 71, pp. 49–73.

Evans, T. 2012. The Use of Memory and Material Culture in the History of the Family in Colonial Australia. *Journal of Australian Studies*, vol. 36, no. 2, pp. 207–228.

Evans, T. 2015. *Fractured Families: Life on the Margins in Colonial New South Wales*. Sydney: NewSouth Publishing.

Evans, T. 2015. Who Do You Think You Are? Historical Television Consultancy. *Australian Historical Studies*, vol. 46, no. 3, pp. 454–467.

Fabian Society. 1964. *The Administrators: The Reform of the Civil Service*. London: Fabian Society.

Facebook. n.d. Russian Ark. At https://www.facebook.com/pages/Russian-Ark/111990828816698?ref=br_tf#.

Feagan, R. 2007. The Place of Food: Mapping out the 'local' in Local Food Systems. *Progress in Human Geography*, vol. 31, no. 1, pp. 23–42.

Federation of Family History Societies. n.d. What is the Federation? At http://www.ffhs.org.uk/about/whatwedo.php.

Feely, C. 2013. Will the Real Esther Price Please Stand Up? Archival Fiction and The Mill. *Journal of Victorian Culture Online*. August 6, 2013. At http://blogs.tandf.co.uk/jvc/2013/08/06/will-the-real-esther-price-please-stand-up/.

Feldman, D. and J. Lawrence. (eds.) 2011. *Structures and Transformations in Modern British History*. Cambridge: Cambridge University Press.

Ferguson, N. 1997. *Virtual History*. New York: Perseus Books.

Fernando, S. and O. Lloyd. 2009. Jeremy Deller Procession. Video. At http://www.theguardian.com/culture/video/2009/jul/08/manchester-international-festival-jeremy-deller.

Fickers, A. 2012. Towards a New Digital Historicism? Doing History in the Age of Abundance. *Journal of European History and Culture*, vol. 1, no. 1, pp. 12–18. At http://journal.euscreen.eu/index.php/view/article/view/jethc004/4.

Fincham, R. and T. Clark. 2009. Introduction: Can We Bridge the Rigour–Relevance Gap? *Journal of Management Studies*, vol. 46, pp. 510–515.

Fink, B. 1997. *A Clinical Introduction to Lacanian Psychoanalysis: Theory and Technique*. Cambridge: Harvard.

Fink, K. 2014. [Un/doing Sophiatown] Contemporary Reverberations of a Myth and in a Suburb. University of Bayreuth, Bayreuth, Germany. At http://www.bigsas.uni-bayreuth.de/en/Alumni_c_research_p/un_doing_fink/index.html.

Finlayson, C. n.d. Letter to Mathieu Rei. At http://www.nz01.2day.terabyte.co.nz/ots/DocumentLibrary%5CNgatiToaofferletter.pdf

Finney, C. 2014. *Black Faces, White Spaces: Reimagining the Relationship of African Americans to the Great Outdoors*. Chapel Hill: University of North Carolina Press.

Fladmark, J.M. (ed.) 2000. *Heritage and Museums: Shaping National Identity.* Shaftesbury: Donhead Publishing.

Flickr. n.d. Looking into the Past. At https://www.flickr.com/groups/lookingintothepast/pool/.

Fogu, C. 2009. Digitalizing Historical Consciousness. *History and Theory,* vol. 47, pp. 103–121.

Forrest, D.M. 1970. *Tiger of Mysore: The Life and Death of Tipu Sultan.* London: Chatto & Windus.

Forte, J.R. 2010. Vodun Ancestry, Diaspora Homecoming, and the Ambiguities of Transnational Belongings in the Republic of Benin. In *Global Circuits of Blackness: Race, Space, Citizenship and Modern Subjectivities,* eds. J.M. Rahier, P. Hintzen, and F. Smith, pp. 174–200. Champaign: University of Illinois Press.

Foster, F. 2014. Writing Across Generations. Conference paper. Alan Atkinson's Festschrift, ANU, February 8, 2014.

Franco, B. 1997. Public History and Memory: A Museum Perspective. *The Public Historian,* vol. 19, no. 2, pp. 65–67.

Frank, R. 1992. Préface. In Institut d'Histoire du Temps Présent. *Ecrire l'histoire du temps present: En homage à François Bédarida.* Paris: CNRS.

Freeman, R. 2006. Learning in Public Policy. In *The Oxford Handbook of Public Policy,* eds. M. Moran, M. Rein, and R.E. Goodin, pp. 367–388. Oxford: Oxford University Press.

Freire, P. 2009 (1970). *Pedagogy of the Oppressed.* New York: Continuum.

French, P. 2003. Take a chance on a long shot. *Observer.* April 6, 2003. At http://www.theguardian.com/film/2003/apr/06/philipfrench.

Friedrich, D. 2011. The Memoryscape in Buenos Aires: Representation, Memory, and Pedagogy. *Journal of Curriculum Theorizing,* vol.27, no. 3, pp.171–189.

Frisch, M. 1990. *A Shared Authority: Essays on the Craft and Meaning of Oral and Public History.* Albany, NY: Suny Press.

Frisch, M. and Pitcaithley, D. 1990. Audience Expectations as Resource and Challenge: Ellis Island as a Case Study. In *A Shared Authority: Essays on the Craft and Meaning of Oral History and Public History,* ed. M. Frisch, pp. 215–224. Albany, NY: Suny Press.

Frossard, D. 2005. Conserving Nature in Culture: Case studies from Southeast Asia. In *In Field or Freezer? Some Thoughts on Genetic Diversity Maintenance in Rice,* eds. M. Dove, P.E. Sajise, and A.A. Doolittle, pp. 144–168. New Haven: Yale University.

Gaddis, J.L. 2002 *The Landscape of History: How Historians Map the Past.* Oxford: Oxford University Press.

Gamasutra. 2007. The History of Civilization. At http://www.gamasutra.com/view/feature/129947/the_history_of_civilization.php.

Gamasutra. 2012. GDC 2012: Sid Meier on How to See Games as Sets of Interesting Decisions. At http://www.gamasutra.com/view/news/164869/.

Gamers Nexus. 2013. Total War: Rome II Interview: Historic Research, Modding & AI. At http://www.gamersnexus.net/pax/1168-total-war-rome-2-interview-pax-prime.

Gander, P. 2011. Go Faster. At http://www.go-faster.com/SS100.html.

Gapps, S. 2009. "Blacking Up" For the Explorers of 1951. In *Settler and Creole Reenactment,* eds. V. Agnew and J. Lamb, pp. 208–220. New York: Palgrave MacMillan.

Garde-Hansen, J., A. Hoskins, and A. Reading. (eds.) 2009. *Save As... Digital Memories.* Basingstoke: Palgrave Macmillan.

Garden, M.E. 2006. The Heritagescape: Looking at Landscapes of the Past. *International Journal of Heritage Studies,* vol. 12, no. 5, pp. 394–411.

Gardiner, W. 1996. *Return to Sender: What Really Happened at the Fiscal Envelope Hui.* Auckland: Reed.

Gardner, J. (ed.) 1999. *Public History: Essays from the Field.* Malabar: Kreiger Publishing Company.

Gardner, J.B. 2010. Trust, Risk and Public History: A View from the United States. *Public History Review,* vol. 17, pp. 52–61.

Gardner, J.B. and P. Hamilton (eds.) 2017. *The Oxford Handbook of Public History.* Oxford: Oxford University Press.

Gathercole, P. 1989. The Fetishism of Artefacts. In *Museums Studies in Material Culture*, ed. S.M. Pearce, pp. 73–81. Leicester: Leicester University Press.

Gavin, F.J. 2007. History and Policy. *International Journal*, vol. 63, pp. 162–177.

Gee, J.P. 2003. *What Video Games Have to Teach Us about Learning and Literacy*. New York: Palgrave MacMillan.

Gell, A. 1998. *Art and Agency: An Anthropological Theory*. Oxford: Oxford University Press.

Gelles, R. 2012. Wspomnienia z dziejów Zakładu Dydaktyki Historii i Wiedzy o Społeczeństwie Instytutu Historycznego Uniwersytetu Wrocławskiego. *Wokół problemów edukacji*, eds. J. Wojdon and B. Techmańska, pp. 9–14. Wrocław: Chronicon.

Gender, Theory and the Archive: A Symposium. 2013. Newcastle University. December 6, 2013. At http://research.ncl.ac.uk/mems/gendertheoryandthearchive/.

General Accounting Office, *National Park Service: Efforts to Identify and Manage the Maintenance Backlog*. May 1998.

George, G. 1986. "The American Association for State and Local History: The Public Historian's Home?," In *Public History: An Introduction*. eds. B.J. Howe and E.L. Kemp, pp. 251–263. Malabar, FL: Krieger Publishing Co.

George, G. 2002. Historic House Museum Malaise: A Conference Considers What's Wrong. *History News*, vol. 57, no. 4, pp. 21–25.

Gibson, J. 2009. *Managing Indigenous Digital Data: An Exploration of the Our Story Database in Indigenous Libraries and Knowledge Centres of the Northern Territory*. Sydney: University of Technology Sydney Press.

Gibson, R. 1996. *Toppling the Duke – Outrage on Ben Bhraggie?* Evanton: Highland Heritage Books.

Gilding, B. 1971. *The Journeymen Coopers of East London*. Ruskin College, Oxford: History Workshop Pamphlets no 4.

Gillis, J.R. 1994. *Commemorations: The Politics of National Identity*. Princeton: Princeton University Press.

Gillis, J.R. 2009. Detours. In *Becoming Historians*, ed. J.M. Banner and J.R. Gillis, pp. 152–173. Chicago: University of Chicago Press.

Gillot, L., I. Maffi, and A. Trémon. 2013. "Heritage-Scape" or "Heritage-Scapes"? Critical Considerations on a Concept. *Ethnologies*, vol. 35, no. 2, pp. 3–15.

Glassberg, D. 1990. *American Historical Pageantry: The Uses of Tradition in the Early Twentieth Century*. Chapel Hill: University of North Carolina Press.

Glassberg, D. 1996. Public History and the Study of Memory. *The Public Historian*, vol. 18, pp. 7–23.

Glassberg, D. 2001. *Sense of History: The Place of the Past in American Life*. Amherst: University of Massachusetts Press.

Glassie, H. 1995 (1982). *Passing the Time in Ballymenone: Culture and History of an Ulster Community*. Bloomington: Indiana University Press.

GMKA. 2012. Bozcaada & Gökçeada Değerlendirme Raporu. Çanakkale. At http://www.gmka.org.tr/bolgesel_raporlar (accessed January 11, 2013).

Gold, M.K. 2012. *Debates in the Digital Humanities*. Minneapolis: University of Minnesota Press.

Golding, V. 2010. Dreams and Wishes: The Multi-Sensory Museum Space. In *Museum Materialities: Objects, Interpretations, Engagements*, ed. S.H. Dudley, pp. 224–240. London: Routledge.

Goodman, D. 2004. Rural Europe Redux? Reflections on Alternative Agro-Food Networks and Paradigm Change. *Sociologia Ruralis*, vol. 44, no. 1, pp. 3–16.

Goodman, D. and E.M. DuPuis. 2002. Knowing Food and Growing Food: Beyond the Production–Consumption Debate in the Sociology of Agriculture. *Sociologia Ruralis*, vol. 42, no. 1, pp. 5–22.

Goodman, D., E.M. DuPuis, and M.K. Goodman. 2012. *Alternative Food Networks: Knowledge, Practice, and Politics*. London: Routledge.

Gordon, A.F. 2008 (1997). *Ghostly Matters: Haunting and the Sociological Imagination*. Minneapolis MN: University of Minnesota Press.

Gordon, D.A.L. 2015. *Town and Crown: An Illustrated History of Canada's Capital*. Ottawa: Invenere Press.

Gordon, T.S. 2010. *Private History in Public: Exhibition and the Settings of Everyday Life*. Lanham, MD: Alta Mira Press.

Gore, J. 2002. Representations of History and Nation in Museums in Australia and Aotearoa New Zealand – The National Museum of Australia and the Museum of New Zealand Te Papa Tongarewa. PhD thesis, University of Melbourne.

Gosden, C. 2005. What do Objects Want? *Journal of Archaeological Method and Theory*, vol. 12, pp. 193–211.

Grabek, A. 2012. Z prezydentem o historii. *Rzeczpospolita*. April 13, 2012.

Graff-McRae, R. 2010. *Remembering and Forgetting 1916*. Dublin: Irish Academic Press.

Grafton, A. 2014. The Future of History Books. YouTube. January 3, 2014. At http://youtu.be/FCGm2mGz9p0.

Graham, D. 1997. *Trick or Treaty?* Wellington: Institute of Policy Studies Victoria University of Wellington.

Graham, O.L., Jr. 1983, The Uses and Misuses of History: Roles in Policymaking. *The Public Historian*, vol. 5, pp. 5–19.

Grant, S.G. and J.M. Gradwell. 2010. *Teaching History with Big Ideas: Cases of Ambitious Teachers*. Lanham, Maryland: R&L Education.

Great Britain. House of Commons. Public Records. 1837-38 V.653. A Bill for Safely Keeping the Public Records.

Great Britain. House of Commons. Public Records. 1840 XXIX.597. Copy of Rules and Regulations made by the Master of the Rolls for the Management of the Public Record Office.

Green, A. 2014. History as Expertise and the Influence of Political Culture on Advice for Policy Since Fulton. *Contemporary British History*, vol. 29, pp. 27–50.

Green, J. 2000. *Taking History to Heart: The Power of the Past in Building Social Movements*. Amherst: University of Massachusetts Press.

Green, J. 2013. Taking History to Heart The Power of the Past in Building Social Movements. In *The Public History Reader*, eds. Kean and Martin, pp. 83–103. London: Routledge.

Greenberg, J. (ed.) 2003. *Trauma at Home: After 9/11*. Lincoln: University of Nebraska Press.

Greenspan, H. 2013. Voices, Places, and Spaces. In *Mass Violence: Oral History, New Media and Performance*, eds. S. High, E. Little, and T.R. Duong, pp. 35–48. Toronto: University of Toronto Press.

Grek-Martin, J. 2007. Vanishing the Haida: George Dawson's Ethnographic Vision and the Making of Settler Space on the Queen Charlotte Islands in the Late Nineteenth Century. *The Canadian Geographer / La Géographe canadien*, vol. 51, no. 3, pp. 373–398.

Grele, R.J. 1981. Whose Public? Whose History? What is the Goal of a Public Historian? *The Public Historian*, vol. 3, no. 1, pp. 40–48.

Grever, M. 2012. Dilemmas of Common and Plural History: Reflections on History Education and Heritage in a Globalizing World. In *History Education and the Construction of National Identities*, eds. M. Carretero, M. Asensio, M. Rodríquez Moneo. Charlotte, NC: Information Age Publishing.

Grootes, S. 2015. Op-Ed: Say It Aloud - Rhodes Must Fall. *Daily Maverick*, April 6, 2015. At http://www.dailymaverick.co.za/article/2015-04-06-op-ed-say-it-aloud-rhodes-must-fall/#.Vss33-bGrgs.

Gross, A. 2008. *Gökçeada (Imbros) and Bozcaada (Tenedos): Preserving the Bicultural Character of the Two Turkish Islands as a Model for Cooperation between Turkey and Greece in the Interest of the People Concerned*. Report. Doc. 11629. June 6, 2008. Parliamentary Assembly of the Council of Europe Committee on Legal Affairs and Human Rights.

Grütter, T. 1986. *Melancholie und Abgrund. Die Bedeutung des Gesteins bei Caspar David Friedrich. Ein Beitrag zum Symboldenken der Frühromantik*. Berlin: Reimer.

Guelke, A., M. Cox, and F. Stephen. 2006. *A Farewell to Arms?: Beyond the Good Friday Agreement.* Manchester: Manchester University Press.

Guha-Thakurta, T. 2004. *Monuments, Objects, Histories: Institutions of Art in Colonial and Postcolonial India.* New York: Columbia University Press.

Guldi, J. and D. Armitage. 2014. *The History Manifesto.* Cambridge: Cambridge University Press.

Gunew, S. 2004. *Haunted Nation: The Colonial Dimensions of Multiculturalisms.* London: Routledge.

Gunter Demnig Official Website. n.d. Home. At http://www.stolpersteine.eu/en/home/ (accessed May 22, 2014).

Guthman, J. 2007. The Polanyian Way? Voluntary Food Labels as Neoliberal Governance. *Antipode*, vol. 39, no. 3, pp. 456–78.

Guthman, J. 2008. Thinking inside the Neoliberal Box: The Micro-Politics of Agro-Food Philanthropy. *Geoforum*, vol. 39, no. 3, pp. 1241–53.

Haber, P. 2011. *Digital past: Geschichtswissenschaft im digitalen Zeitalter.* Munich: Oldenbourg Verlag.

Habib, I. (ed.) 2001a. *Confronting Colonialism: Resistance and Modernization Under Haidar Ali & Tipu Sultan.* New Delhi: Tulika.

Habib, I. (ed.) 2001b. *State and Diplomacy under Tipu Sultan: Documents and Essays.* New Delhi: Tullika.

Hage, G. 2000. *White Nation: Fantasies of White Supremacy in a Multicultural Society.* Sydney: Pluto Press.

Haggis, J. 2012. What an "Archive Rat" Reveals to Us About Storying Theory and the Nature of History. *Australian Feminist Studies*, vol. 27, no. 73, pp. 289–295.

Halbwachs, M. 1992. (1925). *On Collective Memory.* Trans. L.A. Coser. Chicago: University of Chicago Press.

Haley, A. 1976. *Roots: The Saga of an American Family.* New York: Doubleday.

Halfacree, K. 2006. Rural Space: Constructing a Three-Fold Architecture. In *Handbook of Rural Studies*, eds. T. Marsden, P. Cloke, and P. Mooney, pp. 44–62. New York: Sage Publications.

Hall, S. 2005. Whose Heritage? Un-Settling 'The Heritage', Re-Imagining the Post-Nation. In *The Politics of Heritage: The Legacies of "Race,"* eds. J. Littler and R. Naidoo. Abingdon: Routledge.

Hamilton, P. and L. Shopes. (eds.) 2008. *Oral History and Public Memories.* Philadelphia: Temple University Press.

Hammersley, M. and P. Atkinson. 1995. *Ethnography: Principles in Practice.* Abingdon: Routledge.

Handler, R. and E. Gable. 1997. *The New History in an Old Museum: Constructing the Past at Colonial Williamsburg.* Durham, NC: Durham University Press.

Handler, R. 2015. Cultural Heritage, Patrimony, and Repatriation. *Emerging Trends in the Social and Behavioral Sciences: An Interdisciplinary, Searchable, and Linkable Resource*, Wiley Online Library, pp. 1–16.

Hansen, G. 2005a. Telling the Australian Story at the National Museum of Australia: "Once upon a Time." *History Australia*, vol. 2, no. 3, pp. 90.1–90.9. At http://search.informit.com.au/documentSummary;dn=200602298;res=IELAPA, ISSN: 1449-0854.

Hansen, G. 2005b. Collecting for a nation. *Captivating and Curious: Celebrating the Collections of the National Museum of Australia.* Canberra: National Museum of Australia Press.

Happel, R. 1940. *The McLean (or Surrender) House at the Village of Old Appomattox CH*, VA: A Study for the Reconstruction thereof. National Park Service.

Hardt, M. and A. Negri. 2000. *Empire.* Cambridge: Harvard University Press.

Harman, G. 2002. *Tool-Being: Heidegger and the Metaphysics of Objects.* Chicago: Open Court.

Harman, G. 2011. On the Undermining of Objects: Grant, Bruno, and Radical Philosophy. In *The Speculative Turn: Continental Materialism and Realism*, eds. L.R. Bryant, N. Srnicek and G. Harman, pp. 21–40. Melbourne: re.press.

Harris, A. 2004. *Hikoi: Forty Years of Maori Protest.* Wellington: Huia Publishers.

Harris, D.A. 2007. *New Solutions for House Museums.* Lanham, Altamira Press.

Harris, E.M. 2010. Eat Local? Constructions of Place in Alternative Food Politics. *Geography Compass*, vol. 4, no. 4, pp. 355–69.

Harris, R. and T. Haydn. 2006. Pupils' Enjoyment of History: What Lessons Can Teachers Learn from Their Pupils? *Curriculum Journal*, vol. 17, no. 4, pp. 315–333.

Harris, R. and T. Haydn. 2012. What Happens to a Subject in a "Free Market" Curriculum? A Study of Secondary School History in the UK. *Research Papers in Education*, vol. 27, no. 1, pp. 81–101.

Harrison, J. 1993. An Institution in Transition: An Ethnography of the Bishop Museum. PhD thesis, Oxford University.

Harrison, R. 2013. *Heritage: Critical Approaches*. London: Routledge.

Harrison, R., S. Byrne and A. Clarke (eds.) 2013. *Reassembling the Collection: Ethnographic Museums and Indigenous Agency*. Sante Fe (NM): School for Advanced Research Press.

Hart, K. 2011. *Modernliği Dokumak: Bir Batı Anadolu Köyünde Hayat Aşk Emek*. Istanbul: Koc Universitesi Yayinlari.

Hartman, S. 2008. *Lose Your Mother: A Journey Along the Slave Route*. New York: Farrar, Straus and Giroux.

Hartog, F. 2015. *Regimes of Historicity: Presentism and Experiences of Time*. New York: Columbia University Press.

Hasan, M. 1951. *History of Tipu Sultan*. Calcutta: Bibliophile.

Haskins, V. 1998. Skeletons in Our Closet: Family Histories, Personal Narratives and Race Relations History in Australia. *The Olive Pink Society*, pp. 15–20.

Haskins, V. 2005. *One Bright Spot*. Houndmills: Palgrave Macmillan.

Hay, C. 2002. *Political Analysis*. Basingstoke: Palgrave Macmillan.

Hayday, M. 2010. Fireworks, Folk-Dancing, and Fostering a National Identity: The Politics of Canada Day. *Canadian Historical Review*, vol. 91, no. 2, pp. 287–314.

Haydn, T. 2011. United Kingdom: Politicians', Academic Historians' and History Didactics' Ideas about School History: A View from England. Paper presented during the annual conference of the International Society for History Didactics, September 2011. Basel.

Haydn, T. 2014. How and What Should We Teach about the British Empire in English Schools? *Yearbook – Jahrbuch – Annales. International Society for History Didactics*, vol. 35, pp. 23–40.

Hayden, T., A. Stephen, J. Arthur, and M. Hunt. 2015. *Learning to Teach History in the Secondary School. A Companion to School Experience*. 4th edition. London and New York: Routledge.

Hays, H.R. 1976 (1947) *Bertolt Brecht: Selected Poems*. New York: Harcourt Brace Jovanovich.

Hayward, J. and N.R. Wheen. (eds.) 2004. *The Waitangi Tribunal:Te Roopu Whakamana i te Tiriti o Waitangi*. Wellington: Bridget Williams Books.

Heřman Collection. Collections Department of the Terezín Memorial.

Herman, J.L. 1992. *Trauma and Recovery: From Domestic Abuse to Political Terror*. London: Pandora.

Hermann, M.A. 2013. Then and Now. At http://www.marchermann.com/then-and-now (accessed June 16, 2016).

Herstories. n.d. At http://herstoryarchive.org/about-us/.

Herzfeld, M. 2014. *Cultural Intimacy: Social Poetics in the Nation-State*. London: Routledge.

Hewison, R. 1987. *The Heritage Industry: Britain in a Climate of Decline*. London: Methuen.

Hickey, M. 2006. Negotiating History: Crown Apologies in New Zealand's Historical Treaty of Waitangi Settlements. *Public History Review*, vol. 13, pp. 108–124.

Hickford, M. 2011. *Lords of the Land: Indigenous Property Rights and the Jurisprudence of Empire*. Oxford: Oxford University Press.

Higginbotham, P. n.d. The Workhouse. At http://www.workhouses.org.uk/.

Higgins, R. 2010. *Transforming 1916: Meaning, Memory and the Fiftieth Anniversary of the Easter Rising*. Cork: Cork University Press.

Higgitt, R. and J. Wilsdon. 2013. The Benefits of Hindsight: How History can Contribute to Science Policy. In *Future Directions for Scientific Advice in Whitehall*, eds. R. Higgit and J. Wilsdon, pp. 79–85. New York: Doubleday.

High, S. 2009. Sharing Authority: An Introduction. *Journal of Canadian Studies*, vol. 43, no. 1, pp. 2–23.

High, S. 2014. *Oral History at the Crossroads. Sharing Life Stories of Survival and Displacement.* Vancouver: UBC Press.

High, S., and the Centre for Oral History and Digital Storytelling. 2013. Canal. Audio Walk and Booklet. At www.postindustrialmontreal.ca.

High, S., J. Mills, and S. Zembrzycki. 2012. Telling Our Stories/Animating Our Past: A Status Report on Oral History and New Media. *Canadian Journal of Communications*, vol. 37, no. 3, pp. 383–403.

High, S., L. Ndejuru, and P. Lichti. n.d. Une Fleur dans le Fleuve. Audio Walk. At http://storytelling.concordia.ca.

High, Steven. 2014. *Oral History at the Crossroads: Sharing Life Stories of Survival and Displacement.* Vancouver: University of British Columbia Press.

Higson, A. 2003. *English Heritage, English Cinema.* Oxford: Oxford University Press.

Hill, M.J. 1993. *New Agendas in the Study of the Policy Process.* London: Harvester Wheatsheaf.

Hill, R. S. 2009. *Maori and the State: Crown-Maori Relations in New Zealand/Aotearoa, 1950–2000.* Wellington: Victoria University Press.

Hilton, M., J. Mckay, N. Crowson, and J.F. Mouhot. 2013. *The Politics of Expertise: How NGOs Shaped Modern Britain.* Oxford: Oxford University Press.

Hinrichs, C.C. 2003. The Practice and Politics of Food System Localization. *Journal of Rural Studies*, vol. 19, no. 1, pp. 33–45.

History and Policy. 2007. Call for Government to Appoint a Chief Historical Adviser. At http://www.historyandpolicy.org/docs/chief_historical_adviser_release.pdf.

History and Policy. n.d. At http://www.historyandpolicy.org/.

History as Game Mechanics. PlayThePast. At http://www.playthepast.org/?p=2694.

Historypin. 2015. Historypin in the Community: 2013/14. At http://www.shiftdesign.org.uk/content/uploads/2015/03/Historypin_in_the_community.pdf.

Historypin. n.d. About. At http://about.historypin.org/.

H-net discussion networks. 2013. Looking for Car That Matches 1909 Description. At http://h-net.msu.edu/cgi-bin/logbrowse.pl?trx=vx&list=H-Public&month=1307&week=a&msg=Vcg3Wry9HBrI7%2bdpDjhwxA&user=&pw.

Hodes, R. 2015. "The Rhodes Statue Must Fall": UCT's Radical Rebirth. Daily Maverick, 3 March 2015. At http://www.dailymaverick.co.za/article/2015-03-13-the-rhodes-statue-must-fall-ucts-radical-rebirth/#.VssxkubGrgs.

Hodgkins, J. 1998. *Broken Ground.* Toronto: Emblem Editions.

Holden, S. 2002. All of Russian History, in One Unbroken Take. *New York Times*. December 13, 2002. At http://www.nytimes.com/2002/12/13/movies/13RUSS.html.

Holder, P. 1942. Archeological Excavations at the McLean Site, Appomattox Court House National Historical Monument, Virginia, 1941.

Holsey, B. 2008. *Routes of Remembrance: Refashioning the Slave Trade in Ghana.* Chicago: University of Chicago Press.

Holtorf, C. n.d. *Casper David Friedrich.* At https://tspace.library.utoronto.ca/citd/holtorf/5.2.1.html.

Holtorf, C. 1998. The Life-Histories of the Megaliths of Mecklenburg-Vorpommern (Germany). *World Archaeology*, vol. 30, no. 1, pp. 23–38.

Holtorf, C. 2000. *Monumental Past. The Life-Histories of Megalithic Monuments in Mecklenburg-Vorpommern (Germany).* Electronic monograph. University of Toronto. Centre for Instructional Technology Development. At http://hdl.handle.net/1807/245.

Hood, C. 1995. 'Deprivileging' the UK Civil Service in the 1980s: Dream or Reality? In *Bureaucracy in the Modern State: An Introduction to Comparative Public Administration*, ed. J. Pierre, pp. 92–117. Cheltenham: Edward Elgar.

Hooks, B. 1990. Marginality as site of resistance. In *Out There: Marginalization and Contemporary Culture*, eds. R. Ferguson, M. Geves, T.T. Minh-ho, and C. West, pp. 341–345. New York: New Museum of Contemporary Art.

Hooper-Greenhill, E. 2000. *Museums and the Interpretation of Visual Culture*. London: Routledge.

Hopkins, T., and I. Wallerstein. 1982. *World-Systems Analysis: Theory and Methodology*. London: Sage.

Hoppe, R. 1999. Policy Analysis, Science and Politics: from "Speaking Truth to Power" to "Making Sense Together." *Science and Public Policy*, vol. 26, pp. 201–210.

Hoppe, R. 2011. *The Governance of Problems: Puzzling, Powering and Participation*. Bristol: Policy Press.

Horwitz, T. 1998. *Confederates in the Attic: Dispatches from the Unfinished Civil War*. New York: Pantheon Books.

Hoskins, J. 1998. *Biographical Objects: How Things Tell the Stories of People's Lives*. London: Routledge.

Hosmer, C. 1981. *Preservation Comes of Age: From Williamsburg to the National Trust, 1926–1949*. Charlottesville: University Press of Virginia.

Howe, B.J. 2003. Women in the Nineteenth-Century Preservation Movement., In *Restoring Women's History Through Historic Preservation*, eds. G. L. Dubrow and J. Goodman, pp. 17–36. Baltimore: Johns Hopkins University Press.

Howe, K. 2003. Two worlds? *New Zealand Journal of History*, vol. 37, pp. 50–61.

Huang, C. 2010. Human Rights Trash Work in front of Taiwanese People: The Regime Undergo the Industry of Cultural Amnesia through Human Rights. *Artco*, vol. 208, pp. 77–78.

Huang, H. 2007. Causes of the Massacre and its Damages to Taiwan. In Chin-Huang Chen, ed., *Research Report on Responsibility for 228 Massacre: A Brief Introduction*, pp. 16–20. Taipei: Memorial Foundation of 228.

Huang, L. 2011. The Reconstruction of Traumatic Memories from a Negative Heritage: From Auschwitz to Jing-Mei Human Rights Memorial & Cultural Park. *Journal of Cultural Property Conservation*, vol. 17, pp. 73–88.

Huddleston, T. 1956. *Naught for Your Comfort*. Johannesburg: Hardingham and Donaldson.

Hughes, L.M. 2012. (ed.) *Evaluating and Measuring the Value, Use and Impact of Digital Collections*. London: Facet Publishing.

Hulser, K. 2012. Exhibiting Slavery at the New-York Historical Society. In *Politics of Memory: Making Slavery Visible in the Public Space*, ed. A.L. Araujo, pp. 232–251. New York: Routledge.

Hunt, S.J. 2004. Acting the Part: "Living History" as a Serious Leisure Pursuit. *Leisure Studies*, vol. 23, no. 4, pp. 387–403.

Hurley, A. 2010. *Beyond Preservation: Using Public History to Revitalize Inner Cities*. Philadelphia: Temple University Press.

Ilbery, B. and M. Kneafsey. 2000. Producer Constructions of Quality in Regional Speciality Food Production: A Case Study from South West England. *Journal of Rural Studies*, vol. 16, no. 2, pp. 217–230.

Ingold, T. 2010. Ways of Mind-Walking: Reading, Writing, Painting. *Visual Studies*, vol. 25, no. 1, pp. 15–23.

Ingold, T. 2011. *Being Alive: Essays on Movement, Knowledge and Description*. London: Routledge.

Ingrao, C. and T. Emmert (eds.) 2012. *Confronting the Yugoslav Controversies: A Scholars' Initiative*, 2nd edition. West Lafayette: Purdue University Press.

Institute of National Remembrance. 2015. Debaty oksfordzkie. At http://pamiec.pl/pa/edukacja/projekty-edukacyjne/ogolnopolskie/debaty-oksfordzkie/14945, Debata-oksfordzka-o-Puchar-Prezesa-Instytutu-Pamieci-Narodowej-dr-Lukasza-Kamins.html.

International Coalition of Sites of Conscience. n.d. About Us. At http://sitesofconscience.org/about-us/.

International Coalition of Sites of Conscience. n.d. At http://www.sitesofconscience.org/.

International Slavery Museum. n.d. At http://www.liverpoolmuseums.org.uk/ism/about/index.aspx.

International Society for History Didactics. 2014. History and Edutainment. Annual conference. Wrocław, September 2014. At http://ishd.co/conferences/.

Internet Movie Database. n.d. Reviews & Ratings for Russian Ark. At http://www.imdb.com/title/tt0318034/reviews?filter=chrono.

IPHAN. 2014. Publicações. Instituto do Patrimônio Histórico e Artístico Nacional. At http://portal.iphan.gov.br/publicacoes/lista?categoria=22andbusca=andpagina=2.

Itan, Y., A. Powell, M.A. Beaumont, J. Burger, and M. Thomas. 2009. The Origins of Lactase Persistence in Europe. *PLOS Computational Biology*, vol. 5, no. 8.

Jackson, A. 2014. Loyalists and Unionists. In *The Oxford Handbook of Modern Irish History*, ed. A. Jackson, pp. 45–64. Oxford: Oxford University Press.

Jacobs, J. 2012. Theory, Practice, and Specialization: The Case for the Humanities. *Arts and Humanities in Higher Education*, vol. 11, pp. 206–223.

James, D. 2000. *Dona Maria's Story: Life History, Memory, and Political Identity*. Durham: University of North Carolina Press.

Janes, R. 2009. *Museums in a Troubled World: Renewal, Irrelevance or Collapse?* London: Routledge.

Janney, C. 2011. War over a Shrine of Peace: The Appomattox Peace Monument and Retreat from Reconciliation. *The Journal of Southern History*, vol. 77, no. 1 (February 2011), pp. 91–120.

Jeismann, K. 2015 (2000). Rem tene - verba sequentur! Grundfragen historischen Lehrens. *Myślenie historyczne. Część II. Świadomość i kultura historyczna*, eds. R. Traba and H. Thunemann, pp. 72–94. Poznań: Wydawnictwo Nauka i Innowacje.

Jelin, E. 2003. *State Repression and the Labors of Memory*. Trans. J. Rein and M. Godoy-Anativia. Minneapolis: Minnesota University Press.

Jensen, B.E. 2012. Usable Pasts. Comparing Approaches to Public and Popular History. In *Public and Heritage Today: People and Their Pasts*, eds. P. Ashton and H. Kean, pp. 42–56. Basingstoke: Palgrave Macmillan.

Jessee, E., S. Zembrzycki, and S. High. 2010. Stories Matter: Conceptual Challenges in the Development of Oral History Database Building Software. FQS: Forum Qualitative Social Research. At http://www.qualitative-research.net/index.php/fqs.

Jewsiewicki, B. 1987. *Récits de vie et Mémoires: vers une anthropologie historique du souvenir*. Paris: L'Harmattan.

Jobs, S. and A. Lüdtke. (eds.) 2010. *Unsettling History: Archiving and Narrating in Historiography*. New York: Campus Verlag.

Jochen Gerz Official Website. 1993. 2146 Stones – Monument against Racism. At http://www.gerz.fr/html/main.html?res_ident=5a9df42460494a34beea361e835953d8&art_ident=e796072e25c4df21a6a3a262857e6d3f.

Johnson, G.W. 2015. Interview by P. Scarpino, B. Howe, and R. Conard. April 17, 2015. NCPH Archives. Indianapolis: Purdue University.

Johnson, S. 2009. GD Column 5: Sid's Rules. At http://www.designer-notes.com/?p=119.

Johnstone, R. 2013. Then and Now, Now and Then. Inside Story. November 14, 2013. At http://insidestory.org.au/then-and-now-now-and-then.

Jones, A.A. 1979. Clio Confronts Adam Smith: A Survey of National Trends in the Adjustment of Training Programs for Historians. *OAH Newsletter*, vol. 6, supplement.

Jones, G.L. 2014. Civil War Reenacting. New Georgia Encyclopedia. January 10, 2014. At http://www.georgiaencyclopedia.org/articles/history-archaeology/civil-war-reenacting.

Jones, H.G. 1968. Archival Training in American Universities, 1938–1968. *American Archivist*, vol. 31, no.2, pp. 135–153.

Jones, T. 2012. *Dear Photograph*. Toronto: HarperCollins.

Jordanova, L. 2000. Public History. *History Today*, vol. 50, pp. 20–21.

Jordanova, L. 2006. *History in Practice*. 2nd edition. London: Hodder Arnold Publication.

Jordanova, L. (forthcoming). *History in Practice*. Third edition. London: Hodder Arnold.

Joutard, P. 1980. Un projet regional de recherché sur les ethnotextes. *Annales E.S.C*, vol. 35, no. 1, pp. 176–182.

Joutard, P. 2013. Révolution numérique et rapport au passé. *Le Débat*, no. 177, pp. 145–152.

Jullier, L. and J. Leveratto. 2012. Cinephilia in the Digital Age. In *Audiences*, ed. I. Christie, pp. 143–155. Amsterdam: Amsterdam University Press.

Jurgenson, N. 2011. The Faux Vintage Photo. *The Society Pages*. May 14, 2011. At http://thesocietypages.org/cyborgology/2011/05/14/the-faux-vintage-photo-full-essay-parts-i-ii-and-iii/.

Kalela, J. 2012. *Making History: The Historian and Uses of the Past*. Basingstoke: Palgrave Macmillan.

Kalshoven, P.T. 2012. *Crafting "The Indian": Knowledge, Desire, and Play in Indianist Reenactment*. New York: Berghahn Books.

Kant, I. 2005 (1781). *A Critique of Pure Reason*. Adelaide: eBooks@Adelaide, University of Adelaide. https://ebooks.adelaide.edu.au/k/kant/immanuel/k16p/.

Kaplan, F.E.S. 1994. *Museums and the Making of "Ourselves": The Role of Objects in National Identity*. Leicester: Leicester University Press.

Kardux, J.C. 2009. Slavery, Memory, and Citizenship in Transatlantic Perspective. In *American Multiculturalism After 9/11: Transatlantic Perspectives*, eds. D. Rubin and J. Verheul, pp. 165–180. Amsterdam: Amsterdam University Press.

Karp, I. and S. Lavine. (eds.) 1991. *Exhibiting Cultures: The Poetics and Politics of Museum Display*. Washington, D.C.: Smithsonian Institution Press.

Karp, I., C. Kreamer, and S. Lavine. (eds.) 1992. *Museums and Communities: The Politics of Public Culture*. Washington: Smithsonian Institution Press.

Kavanagh, G. 1996. Making Histories, Making Memories. In *Making Histories in Museums*, ed. G. Kavanagh, pp. 1–14. London: Leicester University Press.

Kavanagh, G. 1999. *Making Histories in Museums*. Leicester: Leicester University Press.

Kawharu, I. H. 1989. *Waitangi: Maori and Pakeha Perspectives of the Treaty of Waitangi*. Auckland: Oxford University Press.

Kean, H. 2000. *Animal Rights. Political and Social Change in Britain since 1800*. London: Reaktion Books.

Kean, H. 2004. Public History and Raphael Samuel: A Forgotten Radical Pedagogy? *Public History Review*, vol. 11, pp. 51–62.

Kean, H. 2005. Public History & Popular Memory: Issues in the commemoration of the British militant suffrage movement. *Women's History Review*, vol. 14, no. 3–4, pp. 581–604.

Kean, H. 2010. People, Historians and Public History: Demystifying the Process of History Making. *The Public Historian*, vol. 32, no. 3, pp. 25–38.

Kean, H. 2011. Editorial Introduction. *Public History Review* vol. 18, pp. 1–11.

Kean, H. and P. Ashton. (eds.) 2009. *People and Their Pasts: Public History Today*. London: Palgrave Macmillan.

Kean, H. and P. Martin. (eds.) 2013. *The Public History Reader*. London: Routledge.

Kean, H., P. Martin, and S.J. Morgan. (eds.) 2000. *Seeing History: Public History in Britain Now*. London: Francis Boutle.

Kee, K. (ed.) 2014. *Pastplay Teaching and Learning History with Technology*. Ann Arbor: University of Michigan Press.

Keenan, D. 2009. *Wars without End: The Land Wars in Nineteenth-Century New Zealand*. Auckland: Penguin.

Keillor, E. 2004. Marius Barbeau and Musical Performers. *Musicultures: Journal of the Canadian Society for Traditional Music*, vol. 31.

Kelley, R. 1978. Public History: Its Origins, Nature, and Prospects. *The Public Historian*, vol. 1, no. 1, pp. 16–28.

Kelley, R. 1988. The Idea of Policy History. *The Public Historian*, vol. 10, no. 1, pp. 35–39.

Kelly, M., A. Morgan, S. Ellis, T. Younger, J. Huntley, and C. Swann. 2010. Evidence based Public Health: A Review of the Experience of the National Institute of Health and Clinical Excellence of Developing Public Health Guidance in England. *Social Science & Medicine*, vol. 71, pp. 1056–1062.

Kenneally, C. 2014. *The Invisible History of the Human Race: How DNA and History Shape Our Identities and Our Futures*. Melbourne: Black Inc.

Kennedy, P. 2007. *The Parliament of Man: The Past, Present, and Future of the United Nations.* New York: Vintage.

Kerr, G.H. 1966. *Formosa Betrayed.* London: Eyre & Spottiswoode.

Kerr, P. and S. Kettell. 2006. In Defence of British Politics: The Past, Present and Future of the Discipline. *British Politics,* vol. 1, pp. 3–25.

Khodnev, A. 2015. War in Russian History Is More than Just a War. *Public History Weekly,* vol. 3 (2015). At http://public-history-weekly.oldenbourg-verlag.de/3-2015-9/3647/.

Kimball, F. n.d. Historic Monuments. Philadelphia Museum of Art, Archives, Fiske Kimball papers, Box 159.

Kimball, S.F. 1926. Philadelphia's "Colonial Chain," *Art and Archaeology,* vol. 21, no. 4, pp. 198–199.

Kingsford, W. 1886. *Canadian Archaeology: An Essay.* Montreal: W.M. Drysdale & Co.

Kirshenblatt-Gimblett, B. 1998. *Destination Culture: Tourism, Museums and Heritage.* Berkeley: University of California Press.

Kiser, E. 1996. The Revival of Narrative in Historical Sociology: What Rational Choice Theory can Contribute. *Politics & Society,* vol. 24, pp. 249–271.

Knell, S, P. Aronsson, A. Bugge Amundsen, J. Barnes, S. Burch, J. Carter, V. Gosselin, S.A. Hughes and A. Kirwan (eds.) 2011. *National Museums: New Studies from Around the World.* London: Routledge.

Knell, S.J. 2012. The Intangibility of Things. In *Museum Objects. Experiencing the Properties of Things,* ed. S.H. Dudley, pp. 324–335. London: Routledge.

Koch, A. and J. Van der Ploeg. 2009. *De Wonderkamer van Zoetermeer. Verslag van Een Geslaagd Museaal Experiment.* Zoetermeer, Nederland: Stadsmuseum Zoetermeer.

Koch, G. 2014. Vom Fund zur Figur. Urgeschichte im Dokumentarformat seit 1970. *Geschichte als Erlebnis: Performative Praktiken in der Geschichtskultur Conference.* July 3–5, 2014. Zentrum für Zeithistorische Forschung, Potsdam.

Koch, G. and S. Samida. 2012. *Theater als Zeitmaschine. Zur performativen Praxis des Reenactments. Theater- und kulturwissenschaftliche Perspektiven,* eds. J. Roselt and U. Otto. Bielefeld: Transcript.

KOINONIA. n.d. Atlas Observatória Quilombola. At http://www.koinonia.org.br/atlasquilombola/.

Kolbert, E. 2012. Recall of the Wild. The Quest to Engineer a World before Humans. *The New Yorker,* December 24–31, 2012. At http://www.newyorker.com/magazine/2012/12/24/recall-of-the-wild.

Kondo, T. and S. Tanaka. 2016. Why Is it Impermissible to Learn History Pleasurably? In *E-Teaching History,* ed. J. Wojdon, pp. 173–188. Newcastle: Cambridge Scholars.

Kopytoff, I. 1986. The Cultural Biography of Things: Commoditization as Process. In *The Social Life of Things: Commodities in Cultural Perspective,* ed. A. Appadurai, pp. 64–92. Cambridge: Cambridge University Press.

Korza, P. and B. Schaffer Bacon. 2005. *History as a Catalyst for Civic Dialogue: Case Studies from Animating Democracy.* Washington, D.C.: Americans for the Arts.

Kosman, Λ. 1969. Aristotle's Definition of Motion. *Phronesis,* vol. 14, no. 1, pp. 40–62.

Koster, M., H. Thunemann, and M. Zulsdorf-Kersting. (eds.) 2014. *Researching History Education: International Perspectives and Disciplinary Tradition.* Schwalbach/Wochenschau Geschichte.

Kraemer, S.K. 2004. Policy Advisors: Historians and Making Policy. In *Public History: Essays from the Field,* eds. J.B. Gardner and P.S. Lapaglia, pp. 217–228. Malabar: Krieger.

Kramer, A.M. 2011. Kinship, Affinity and Connectedness: Exploring the Role of Genealogy in Personal Lives. *Sociology,* vol. 45, pp. 379–395.

Krasner, D. 2001. "The Pageant Is the Thing": Black Nationalism and *The Star of Ethiopia.* In *Performing America: Cultural Nationalism in American Theater,* eds. J.D. Mason and J.E. Gainor, pp. 106–122. Ann Arbor: University of Michigan Press.

Krejčová, H. 1993. Český a slovenský antisemitismus, 1945–1948. In *Stránkami soudobých dějin: Sborník statí k pětašedesátinám historika Karla Kaplana*, eds. K. Kaplan and K. Jech. Prague: Ústav pro soudobé dějiny AV ČR.

Kreps, C. 2003. Curatorship as Social Practice. *Curator*, vol. 46, no. 3, pp. 311–324.

Kros, C. 2008. Prompting Reflections: An Account of the "Sunday Times" Heritage Project from the Perspective of an Insider Historian. *Kronos*, vol. 34, pp. 159–80.

Krüttli, A., A. Bouwman, G. Akgül, P. Della Casa, and F. Rühli. 2014. Ancient DNA Analysis Reveals High Frequency of European Lactase Persistence Allele (T-13910) in Medieval Central Europe. *PLoS ONE*, vol. 9, no. 1, e86251, p. 3.

Kuljian, C. 2009. The Congress of the People and the Walter Sisulu Square of Dedication: From Public Deliberation to Bureaucratic Imposition in Kliptown. *Social Dynamics*, vol. 35, no. 2, pp. 450–64.

Kumar, N. 2014. Repetition and Remembrance: The Rephotographic Survey Project. *History and Photography*, vol. 38, no. 2, pp. 137–160.

Kyle, N. 2001 (1998). "Genealogy." In *The Oxford Companion to Australian History*, eds. G. Davison, J. Hirst, and S. Macintyre, pp. 280. Oxford: Oxford University Press.

Lacan, J. 1997. The Mirror Stage as Formative of the Function of the I. In *Ecrits*, ed. J. Lacan, pp. 1–7. London: Routledge.

LaCapra, D. 1998. *History and Memory after Auschwitz*. Ithaca: Cornell University Press.

LaCapra, D. 2001. *Writing History, Writing Trauma*. Baltimore: Johns Hopkins University Press.

Lagrou, P. 2013. De l'histoire du temps présent à l'histoire des autres. Comment une discipline critique devint complaisante. *Vingtième Siècle*, no. 118, pp. 101–119.

Lambert, R. 1998. A Study of Genealogists and Family Historians. Global Genealogy. At http://globalgenealogy.com/globalgazette/gazrr/gazrr19.htm.

Langford, M. 2001. *Suspended Conversations: The Afterlife of Memory in Photographic Albums*. Montreal and Kingston: McGill-Queen's University Press.

Lanni, A. 2006. *Law and Justice in the Courts of Classical Athens*. New York: Cambridge University Press.

Lanzmann, C. 1995. The Obscenity of Understanding: An Evening with Claude Lanzmann. In *Trauma: Explorations in Memory*, ed. C. Caruth, pp. 200–220. Baltimore: Johns Hopkins University Press.

Lascarides, M. and B. Vershbow. What's on the Menu? Crowdsourcing at the New York Public Library. In *Crowdsourcing Our Cultural Heritage*, ed. M. Ridge, pp. 113–138. Farnham: Ashgate.

Latour, B. 2007. *Reassembling the Social: An Introduction to Actor Network Theory*. Oxford: Oxford University Press.

Law, J. and J. Hassard. 1999. *Actor Network Theory and After*. Oxford: Wiley.

Law, R. 2004. *The Slave Coast of West Africa 1550–1750: The Impact of the Atlantic Slave Trade on an African Society*. Oxford: Clarendon Press.

Layton, R.H. 2003. Art and Agency: A Reassessment. *Journal of the Royal Anthropological Institute*, vol. 9, no. 3, pp. 447–463.

Le Goff, J. 1997 (1992). *History and Memory*. New York: Columbia University Press.

Lee, C-F. 2009. Lu, Hsiu-Lien: Changing the name of the Taiwan Human Rights Jing-Mei Park Would Be a Step Backward. Taiwan News. April 22, 2009. At http://www.etaiwannews.com/etn/news_content.php?id=926933&lang=tc_news.

Lee, J. 1993. *The Old Land Claims in New Zealand*. Kerikeri: Northland Historical Publications Society.

Lee, R. 1963. Letter to Ada Louise Huxtable. 11 October 1963. NPS Park History Program.

Lee, R. 1964. Statement on Historic Preservation Opportunities and Problems for the National Park Service. Regional Directors' Meeting, Philadelphia, PA, 16 July 1964. National Park Service, Harpers Ferry Center, Ronald Lee Collection, Box 1.

Lee, R. 1969. Letter to Roy Appleman. 11 July 1969. National Park Service, Harpers Ferry Center, Ronald Lee Collection.

Lee, S. 2004. The Soul's Long Night. In *The Road to Freedom: Taiwan's Postwar Human Rights Movement*, ed. C-H. Lee, pp. 8–11. Taipei: Dr. Chen Wen-chen Memorial Foundation.

Lefebvre, H. 1991 (1974). *The Production of Space*. Trans. D. Nicholson-Smith. London: Blackwell.

Lehman, T. (Spring 1992). Public Values, Private Lands: Origins & Ironies of Farmland Preservation in Congress, *Agricultural History*, vol. 66, no. 2, pp. 257–272.

Lemons, J., O. Hoffman, L. Meikle, R. Smith, and R. Mackie. 2015. Op-Ed: The Importance of Railroads in the Evolution of National Parks. National Parks Traveler, October 14, 2015. http://www.nationalparkstraveler.com/2015/10/op-ed-importance-railroads-evolution-national-parks.

Leon, S.M. n.d. User-Centered Digital History. At http://digitalpublichistory.org/.

Leonard, J. 1996. *The Culture of Commemoration: The Culture of War Commemoration*. Dublin: Cultures of Ireland.

Lévesque, S. and Zanazanian, P. 2015. Developing Historical Consciousness and a Community of History Practitioners: A Survey of Prospective History Teachers across Canada. *McGill Journal of Education*, vol. 50, no. 2/3, pp. 389–412.

Levine, P. 1986. *The Amateur and the Professional. Antiquaries, Historians and Archaeologists in Victorian Britain, 1838–1886*. Cambridge: Cambridge University Press.

Levitt, P. 2015. *Artifacts and Allegiances: How Museums Put the Nation and the World on Display*. Berkeley: University of California Press.

Lewis, R. 2015. South Africa Student Protests Reveal Deep Discontent with Zuma Government. Al Jazeera. 23 October 2015. At http://america.aljazeera.com/articles/2015/10/23/south-africa-protests-reveal-discontent-with-zuma.html (accessed February 15, 2016).

Lewis, Ralph H. 1941. A Survey of National Park Museums. *Museum News*. October 1, 1941.

Leys, R. 2000. *Trauma: A Genealogy*. Chicago: University of Chicago Press.

Liakos, A. 2008. History Wars: Notes from the Field. *Yearbook of the International Society for the Didactics of History* 2008/2009, pp. 57–74.

Liddington, J. 2002. What is Public History? Publics and their Pasts, Meanings and Practices. *Oral History Journal*, vol. 30, no. 1, pp. 83–93.

Light, A. 2014. *Common People: The History of an English Family*. London: Fig Tree Press.

Lin, C. 2014. Initial Challenges and Missions of the Preparatory Office of the National Human Rights Museum. *Museology Quarterly*, vol. 28, no. 3, pp. 111–126.

Linde, C. 1993. *Life Stories: The Creation of Coherence*. New York: Oxford University Press.

Lindeberg, S. 2012. Paleolithic Diets as a Model for the Prevention and Treatment of Western Disease. *American Journal of Human Biology*, vol. 24, pp. 110–115.

Linenthal, E.T. 1997. Problems and Promise in Public History. *The Public Historian*, vol. 19, no. 2, pp. 45–47.

Linenthal, E.T. and T. Englehardt. 1996. *History Wars: The Enola Gay and Other Battles for the American Past*. New York: Metropolitan Books.

Lipsky, M. 1983. *Street-Level Bureaucracy: The Dilemmas of the Individual in Public Service*. New York: Russell Sage Foundation.

Little, H. 2010. Genealogy as a Theatre of Self-Identity: A Study of Genealogy as a Cultural Practice within Britain since c. *1850*. PhD thesis, University of Glasgow.

Little, J. and P. Austin. 1996. Women and the Rural Idyll. *Journal of Rural Studies*, vol. 12, no. 2, pp. 101–111.

Littler, J. and R. Naidoo. 2004. *The Politics of Heritage: The Legacies of Race*. Abingdon: Taylor & Francis.

Liu, S. 1999. The Role of Chiang Kai-shek and Chiang Chin-kuo during the Period of White Terror. *Taiwan Historical Research*, vol. 6, no. 2, pp. 139–187.

Llewellyn, K. L. and N. Ng-A-Fook (eds). 2017. *Oral History and Education: Theories, Dilemmas and Practices*. New York: Palgrave Macmillan.

Locke, John. 1979 (1690). *An Essay Concerning Human Understanding*. Oxford: Oxford University Press.

Lovell, M. 2005. *Art in a Season of Revolution: Artisans and Patrons in Early America*. Philadelphia: University of Pennsylvania Press.

Lowenthal, D. 1997. History and Memory. *The Public Historian*, vol. 19, no. 2, pp. 31–39.

Lowenthal, D. 1998. *The Heritage Crusade and the Spoils of History*. Cambridge: Cambridge University Press.

Lucchesi, A. 2014. Conversas na antessala da Academia: o presente, a oralidade e a História Pública Digital. História oral e História do Tempo Presente, special issue of the journal História Oral, no. 17/1, pp. 39–69. At http://revista.historiaoral.org.br/index.php.

Ludden, D. (ed.) 2002. *Reading Subaltern Studies: Critical History, Contested Meaning and the Globalization of South Asia*. London: Anthem Press.

Luddite Bicentenary. n.d. At ludditebicentenary.blogspot.com.

Lundy, P. and M. McGovern. 2006. A Truth Commission for Northern Ireland? ARK Northern Ireland, Research Updates, vol. 46, October 2006. At http://www.ark.ac.uk/publications/updates/update46.pdf.

Lye, T.P. 2005. Conserving Nature in Culture: Case Studies from Southeast Asia. In *Uneasy Bedfellows? Contrasting Models of Conservation in Peninsular Malaysia*, eds. M. Dove, P.E. Sajise, and A.A. Doolittle, pp. 83–117. New Haven: Yale University.

Lyon, C.A., E.M. Nix, and R.K. Shrum. 2017. *An Introduction to Public History: Interpreting the Past, Engaging Audiences*. Rowman & Littlefield Publishers: Lanham, MD.

MacCannell, D. 1999 (1976). *The Tourist: A New Theory of the Leisure Class*. Berkeley: University of California Press.

Macdonald, S. 2002. *Behind the Scenes at the Science Museum*. New York: Berg.

Macdonald, S. 2003. Museums, National, Postnational and Transcultural Identities. *Museum and Society*, vol. 1, no. 1, pp. 1–16.

Macdonald, S. 2009. *Difficult Heritage: Negotiating the Nazi Past in Nuremberg and Beyond*. London: Routledge.

Macdonald, S. 2013. *Memorylands: Heritage and Identity in Europe Today*. London: Routledge.

Macdonald, S. and G. Fyfe. (eds.) 1996. *Theorizing Museums: Representing Identity and Diversity in a Changing World*. Oxford: Blackwell.

MacGonagle, E. 2006. From Dungeons to Dance Parties: Contested Histories of Ghana's Slave Forts. *Journal of Contemporary African Studies*, vol. 24, no. 2, pp. 249–260.

Macintyre, S. and A. Clark. 2003. *The History Wars*. Melbourne: Melbourne University Press.

Mackenzie, R. 1793. A Sketch of the War with Tipoo Sultaun: Or, a Detail of Military Operations from the Commencement of Hostilities at the Lines of Tranvancore in December 1789 until the Peace Concluded before Srirangapatnam in February 1792, Calcutta.

Mackintosh, B. 1986. *Interpretation in the National Park Service: A Historical Perspective*. National Park Service.

Mackintosh, B. 1995. *Former National Park System Unites: An Analysis*. National Park Service.

Mackintosh, B., and J. McDonnell. 2005. *The National Parks: Shaping the System*. National Park Service.

Macmillan, M. 2009. *The Uses and Abuses of History*. London: Profile.

MacTotem: Reviewing the Duke of Sutherland Monument: 30 Artists, Amendments, Interferences, Interventions, Ideas. 1998. Stornoway: Gaelic Arts Agency & Lanntair Gallery.

Magelssen, S. 2007. *Living History Museums: Undoing History Through Performance*. Maryland: Scarecrow Press, Inc.

Maiwald, T. 2003. Russian Art – Kritik. Filmhai.de. May 1, 2003. At http://www.filmhai.de/kinofilm/articles,id1287,0,russian_ark.html.

Mana Pool. 2011. Interview with Paradox Interactive on Sengoku. At http://www.manapool.co.uk/interview-with-paradox-interactive-on-sengoku/.

Mandelson, P. and R. Liddle. 1996. *The Blair Revolution: Can New Labour Deliver?* London: Faber & Faber.

Mandler, P. 1997. *The Fall and Rise of the Stately Home*. New Haven: Yale University Press.

Manning, P. 2013. *Big Data in History*. Basingstoke: Palgrave Macmillan.

Manoff, M. 2004. Theories of the Archive from Across the Disciplines. *Libraries and the Academy*, vol. 4, no. 1, pp. 9–25.

Manovich, L. 1996. The Paradoxes of Digital Photography. In *Photography After Photography: Memory and Representation in the Digital Age*, eds. H.V. Amelunxen et al. Amsterdam: G+B Arts.

Manovich, L. 2001. *The Language of New Media*. Cambridge, MA: MIT Press.

Mapping Memories: Participatory Media, Place-Based Stories and Refugee Youth. 2011. Montreal: Concordia University. At http://mappingmemories.ca.

Marschall, S. 2010. Private Sector Involvement in Public History Production in South Africa: The Sunday Times Heritage Project. *African Studies Review*, vol. 53, no. 3, pp. 35–59.

Marschall, S. 2011. The Sunday Times Heritage Project: Heritage, the Media and the Formation of National Consciousness. *Social Dynamics*, vol. 37, no. 3, pp. 409–423.

Marshall, C.C. 2011. Challenges and Opportunities for Personal Digital Archiving. In *I, Digital: Personal Collections in the Digital Era*, ed. C.A. Lee, pp. 90–114. Chicago: Society of American Archivists.

Martin, C. 2012. *Theatre of the Real*. New York: Palgrave Macmillan.

Martin, P. 2002. *The Trade Union Badge: Material Culture in Action*. Aldershot: Ashgate.

Martin, P. 2011. A "Social Form of Knowledge" in Practice: Unofficial Compiling of 1960s Pop Music on CD-R. *Public History Review*, vol. 18, pp. 129–150.

Martinez, M.E. 2008. *Genealogical Fictions: Limpieza de Sangre, Religion, and Gender in Colonial Mexico*. Stanford: Stanford University Press.

Mason, R. 2007. *Museums, Nations, Identities: Wales and Its National Museums*. Cardiff: University of Wales Press.

Mason, R. 2008. Cultural Theory and Museum Studies. In *The Ashgate Research Companion to Heritage and Identity*, eds. B. Graham and P. Howard, pp. 16–32. Aldershot: Ashgate Publishing Limited.

Massey, D. 1995. Places and Their Pasts. *History Workshop Journal*, vol. 39, pp. 182–192.

Mattos, H. (ed.) 2013. *Diáspora Negra e Lugares de Memória: A história oculta das propriedades voltadas para o tráfico clandestino de escravos no Brasil Imperial*. Niterói: EDUFF.

Mattos, H. 2008. Terras de Quilombo: Land Rights, Memory of Slavery, and Ethnic Identification in Contemporary Brazil. In *Africa, Brazil, and the Construction of Trans-Atlantic Black Identities*, eds. L. Sansone, E. Soumoni, and B. Barry, pp. 293–295. Asmara/Trenton: Africa World Press.

Mattos, H. and E. Schnoor. 1995. *Resgate: Uma janela para o Oitocentos*. Rio de Janeiro: Top Books.

Mattos, H. and M. Abreu. 2005. Memórias do Cativeiro/Memories of Captivity. Documentary film. LABHOI/UFF. At http://www.labhoi.uff.br/passadospresentes/en/filmes_memorias. php.

Mattos, H. and M. Abreu. 2007. Jongos, Calangos and Folias: Black Music, Memory and Poetry. Documentary film. LABHOI/UFF. At http://www.labhoi.uff.br/passadospresentes/en/ filmes_jongos.php.

Mattos, H. and M. Abreu. 2011. A Present Past – Afro-Brazilian memories in Rio de Janeiro. Documentary film. LABHOI/UFF, 2011. At http://www.labhoi.uff.br/passadospresentes/ en/filmes_passados.php.

Mattos, H. and M. Abreu. 2011. Remanescentes das Comunidades dos Quilombos: Memória do cativeiro, patrimônio cultural e direito à reparação. *Iberoamericana*, vol. 42, pp. 147–160.

Mattos, H. and M. Abreu. 2013. *Jongo*, Recalling History. In *Cangoma Calling Spirits and Rhythms of Freedom in Brazilian Jongo Slavery Songs*, eds. P. Monteiro and M. Stone, pp. 77–88. Dartmouth: University of Massachusetts.

Mattos, H. and M. Abreu. 2014. Passados Presentes. September 8, 2014. Conversa de Historiadoras. Blog. At http://conversadehistoriadoras.com/2014/09/08/passados-presentes/.

Mauad, A.M., J.R. de Almeida, and R. Santhiago. 2016. *História, Pública No Brasil. Sentidos e Itinerários*. Sao Paulo: Letra e Voz.

Mauss, M. 1967 (1925). *The Gift: Forms and Functions of Exchange in Archaic Societies*. Trans. Ian Cunnison. New York: Norton.

Mayer-Schönberger, V. and K. Cukier. 2013. *Big Data: A Revolution That Will Transform How We Live, Work, and Think*. Boston: Houghton Mifflin Harcourt.

Maynes, M.J. et al. 2008. *Telling Stories: The Use of Personal Narratives in the Social Sciences and History*. Ithaca: Cornell University Press.

McAloon, J. 2006. By Which Standards?: History and the Waitangi Tribunal. *New Zealand Journal of History*, vol. 40, pp. 194–213.

McBride, I. (ed.) 2001. *History and Memory in Modern Ireland*. Cambridge: Cambridge University Press.

McCall, J. 2010. The Happiness Metric in CivCity: Rome and the Critique of Simulation Games. PlayThePast. At http://www.playthepast.org/?p=94.

McCall, J. 2011. *Gaming the Past: Using Video Games to Teach Secondary History*. New York: Routledge.

McCall, J. 2012 Navigating the Problem Space: The Medium of Simulation Games and the Teaching of History. *The History Teacher*, vol. 46, pp. 9–28.

McCall, J. (2014). Simulation Games and the Study of the Past: Classroom Guidelines. In *Pastplay: Teaching and Learning History with Technology*, ed. K. Kee, pp. 228–253. Ann Arbor, MI: University of Michigan.

McCan, D. 2001. *Whatiwhatihoe: The Waikato Raupatu Claim*. Wellington: Huia Publishers.

McCarthy, G. 2004. Postmodern Discontent and the National Museum of Australia. Borderlands, vol. 3, no. 3. At http://www.borderlands.net.au/vol3no3_2004/mccarthy_discontent.htm.

McHugh, P.G. 2004. *Aboriginal Societies and the Common Law: A History of Sovereignty, Status, and Self-Determination*. New York: Oxford University Press.

McIntyre, D. and K. Wehner. (eds.) 2001. *National Museums Negotiating Histories – Conference Proceedings*. Canberra: National Museum of Australia.

McLean, F. 2005. Guest Editorial: Museums and National Identity. *Museum and Society*, vol. 3, no. 1, pp. 1–4.

McNally, J. 2012. The Concept of Caricature as a General Philosophy for Implementing History as Game Mechanics. PlayThePast. At http://www.playthepast.org/?p=2694.

McShane, I. 2001. Challenging or Conventional? Migration History in Australian Museums. In *National Museums Negotiating Histories – Conference Proceedings*, eds. D. McIntyre and K. Wehner, pp. 122–133. Canberra: National Museum of Australia.

Megahey, N. 2003. Russian Ark – DVD Video Review. Digital Fix. October 20, 2003. At http://film.thedigitalfix.com/content.php?contentid=5857.

Mellibovsky, M. 1997. *Circle of Love over Death: Testimonies of the Mothers of the Plaza De Mayo*. Trans. M. and M. Prosser. Willimantic, CT: Curbstone Press.

Mellor, M. and C. Stephenson, Carol. 2005. The Durham Miners' Gala and the Spirit of Community. *Community Development Journal*, vol. 40 no. 3, pp. 343–351.

Memories of Captivity Collection. 2003. Interview with Antônio Nascimento. Fernandes. LABHOI/UFF.

Mendelson, E. (ed.) 1979 (1938). *W.H. Auden. Selected Poems*. London: Cox & Wyman.

Meneley, A. 2007. Like an Extra Virgin. *American Anthropologist*, vol. 109, no. 4, pp. 678–687.

Meringolo, D.D. 2012. *Museums, Monuments, and National Parks: Toward a New Genealogy of Public History*. Amherst: University of Massachusetts Press.

Merleau-Ponty, M. 1962. *Phenomenology of Perception*. London: Routledge.

Meskell, L. 1998. *Archaeology Under Fire: Nationalism, Politics and Heritage in the Eastern Mediterranean and Middle East*. London: Routledge.

Meskell, L. 2002. The Intersections of Identity and Politics in Archaeology. *Annual Review Anthropology*, vol. 31, no. 1, pp. 279–301.

Message, K. 2006. *New Museums and the Making of Culture*. Oxford: Berg.

Message, K. 2009. Culture, Citizenship and Australian Multiculturalism: The Contest over Identity Formation at the National Museum of Australia. *Humanities Research*, vol. 15, no. 2, pp. 23–48.

Message, K. and C. Healy. 2004. A Symptomatic Museum: The New, the NMA and the Culture Wars. *Borderlands*, vol. 3, no. 3. At http://www.borderlands.net.au/vol3no3_2004/messagehealy_symptom.htm.

Metacritic. n.d. Russian Ark. User Reviews. At http://www.metacritic.com/movie/russian-ark/user-reviews.

Metapedia Mission Statement, n.d. in *Metapedia. The Alternative Encyclopedia*. At http://www.metapedia.org/mission.php

Miccoli, D. 2013a. Oltre l'archivio? Storie e memorie degli ebrei egiziani in Internet. *Memoria e Ricerca*, no. 42, pp. 189.

Miccoli, D. 2013b. Digital Museums: Narrating and Preserving the History of Egyptian Jews on the Internet. In *Memory and Ethnicity. Ethnic Museums in Israel and the Diaspora*, eds. E. Trevisan Semi, D. Miccoli, and T. Parfitt, pp. 195–222. Newcastle: Cambridge Scholars.

Michalski, Ł. 2015. *Świadomość historyczna młodzieży szkół ponadpodstawowych aglomeracji warszawskiej*. Warsaw: IPN.

Michalski, S. 1998. *Public Monuments: Art in Political Bondage 1870-1997*. London: Reaktion Books.

Middleton, J. 2011. Walking the City: The Geographies of Everyday Pedestrian Practices. *Geography Compass*, vol. 5, no. 2, pp. 90–105.

Miller, B.G. 2011. *Oral History on Trial: Recognizing Aboriginal Narratives in the Courts*. Vancouver: University of British Columbia Press.

Miller, E. 2013. All I Remember. Short Film. Montreal. At http://mappingmemories.ca.

Miller, J. 2014. Performing Collective Trauma: 9/11 and the Reconstruction of American Identity. In *History, Memory, Performance*, eds. D. Dean, Y. Meerzon, and K. Prince, pp. 187–202. New York: Palgrave Macmillan.

Miller, T. 1993. *The Well-Tempered Self: Citizenship, Culture and the Postmodern Subject*. Baltimore: Johns Hopkins Press.

Milligan, J.S. 2005. `What Is an Archive?' in the History of Modern France. In *Archive Stories: Facts, Fictions, and the Writing of History*, ed. A. Burton, pp. 159–183. Durham, SC: Duke University Press.

Milloy, J. 2013. Doing Public History in Canada's Truth and Reconciliation Commission. *The Public Historian*, vol. 35, pp. 10–19.

Ministerstwo Edukacji Narodowej [Ministry of National Education]. 2011. Podstawa programowa kształcenia ogólnego dla gimnazjów i szkół ponadgimnazjalnych, których ukończenie umożliwia uzyskanie świadectwa dojrzałości po zdaniu egzaminu maturalnego. At http://men.gov.pl/wp-content/uploads/2011/02/zalaczniknr4.pdf.

Minkley, G. 2008. "A Fragile Inheritor": The Post-Apartheid Memorial Complex, AC Jordan and the Re-Imagining of Cultural Heritage in the Eastern Cape. *Kronos*, vol. 34, no. 1, pp. 16–40.

Minuti, R. 2002. *Internet et le métier d'historien: Réflexions sur les incertitudes d'une mutation*. Paris: PUF.

Mitchell, W.J. 1992. *The Reconfigured Eye: Visual Truth in the Post-Photographic Era*. Cambridge, MA: MIT Press.

Modisane, B. 1986. *Blame Me on History*. Parklands: AD Donker.

Moe, R. 2012. Are There Too Many House Museums? *Forum Journal*, vol. 27, no. 1, pp. 55–61.

Monroe, A. 1995. *Open Secrets: Stories*, Toronto: Vintage.

Monteiro, P. and M. Stone. (eds.) 2013. *Cangoma Calling Spirits and Rhythms of Freedom in Brazilian Jongo Slavery Songs*. Dartmouth: University of Massachusetts.

Moore, D., B. Rigby, and M. Russell. 1997. *Old Land Claims*. Wellington: Waitangi Tribunal.

Moretti, F. 2013. *Distant Reading*. London, Verso.

Morphy, H. 2009. Art as a Mode of Action: Some Problems with Gell's *Art and Agency. Journal of Material Culture*, vol. 14, no. 1, pp. 5–27.

Morris, C. and C. Young. 2000. "Seed to Shelf," "Teat to Table," "Barley to Beer" and "Womb to Tomb": Discourses of Food Quality and Quality Assurance Schemes in the UK. *Journal of Rural Studies*, vol. 16, no. 1, pp. 103–115.

Morrison, D. and L. LeBlanc. 2016. Presentation to the *Decolonizing Curatorial Pedagogies: Thinking Through the Museum Workshop*. Canadian Museum of History. April 15, 2016.

Moses, L.G. 1996. Wild West Shows and the Images of American Indians, 1883–1933 Albuquerque: University of New Mexico Press.

Mosse, G.L. 1990. *Fallen Soldiers: Reshaping the Memory of the World Wars*. Oxford: Oxford University Press.

Msila, V. 2013. The Liberatory Function of a Museum: The Case of New Brighton's Red Location Museum. *Anthropologist*, vol. 15, no. 2, pp. 209–18.

Muise, D. 2011. Why Start in Family History. Genealogy in Canada. November 17, 2011. At http://genealogyincanada.blogspot.ca/search/label/WHAT%20MAKES%20A%20GENEALOGIST%20START.

Mulgan, G. 2005. Government, Knowledge and the Business of Policy Making: The Potential and Limits of Evidence-Based Policy. *Evidence & Policy: A Journal of Research, Debate and Practice*, vol. 1, pp. 215–226.

Muller, B. 2006. Archives orales et entretiens ethnographiques: Un débat entre Florence Descamps et Florence Weber. *Genèses*, vol. 62, no. 1, pp. 93–109.

Müller, M. 2015. Assemblages and Actor-Networks: Rethinking Socio-material Power, Politics, and Space. *Geography Compass*, vol. 9, no. 1, pp. 27–41.

Müller, P. 2010. Ranke in the Lobby of the Archive: Metaphors and Conditions of Historical Research. In *Unsettling History: Archiving and Narrating in Historiography*, eds. S. Jobs and A. Lüdtke, pp. 109–126. New York: Campus Verlag.

Municipality of Wrocław. 2016. Education in Memorial Sites. February 24, 2016. At http://www.wroclaw.pl/edukacja-w-miejscach-pamieci-01.

Munroe, A. 1991. *The Beggar Maid: The Story of Flo and Rose*. Toronto: Vintage.

Munroe, A. 1999. *Queenie: A Story*. London: Profile Books.

Murray, J., B. Tshabangu, and N. Erlank. 2010. Enhancing Participatory Governance and Fostering Active Citizenship: An Overview of Local and International Best Practices. *Politikon*, vol. 37, no. 1, pp. 45–66.

Museum of Australia Act 1980 No 115, 1980. At https://www.legislation.gov.au/Details/C2004A02316.

Museum of Justice of Rio de Janeiro State. Inventory of José de Souza Breves, 1879, vol. 1. Rio de Janeiro, Brazil.

Museum of London. n.d. Streetmuseum. At http://www.museumoflondon.org.uk/Resources/app/you-are-here-app/home.html

Muth, J. 2006. Märchenhafte Urkost: Steinzeitdiät. At http://www.deutschlandradiokultur.de/maerchenhafte-urkost.993.de.html?dram:article_id=154319.

Myers, M., H.T. Reedy, and A.M. Samuel. 1948. Report of Royal Commission to Inquire into and Report on Claims Preferred by Members of the Maori Race Touching Certain Lands Known as Surplus Lands of the Crown. Wellington: Appendix to the Journals of the House of Representatives (AJHR).

Nagel, T. 1986. *The View from Nowhere*. New York: Oxford University Press.

Naidoo, Y. 2015. Sophiatown Reimagined: Residents' Reconstructions of Place and Memory. *African Studies*, vol. 74, no. 1, pp. 98–122.

Nair, J. 2005. *The Promise of the Metropolis: Bangalore's Twentieth Century*. Delhi: Oxford University Press.

Nair, J. 2011. *Mysore Modern: Rethinking the Region Under Princely Rule*. Minneapolis: University of Minnesota Press.

Nash, C. 2002. Genealogical Identities. *Environment and Planning D: Society and Space*, vol. 20, pp. 27–52.

Nash, C. 2015. *Genetic Geographies: The Trouble with Ancestry*. Minnesota: Minnesota University Press.

Natale, E., C. Sibille, N. Chacherau, P. Kammerer, and M. Hiestand (eds.) 2015. *La visualisation des données en histoire – Visualisierung von daten in der Geschichtswissenschaft.*, Zürich: Chronos.

National Capital Commission. n.d. Confederation Boulevard. National Capital Commission. At http://www.ncc-ccn.gc.ca/places-to-visit/confederation-boulevard.

National Council for Historic Sites and Buildings. 1949. *NCHSB Quarterly Report*, vol. 1, no. 1, March 1949. Frederick Rath, Jr. Papers, Hornbake Library. College Park: University of Maryland.

National Council for Historic Sites and Buildings. 1949. *NCHSB Quarterly Report*, vol. 1, no. 4, December 1949. Frederick Rath, Jr. Papers, Hornbake Library. College Park: University of Maryland.

National Council for Historic Sites and Buildings. 1950. *NCHSB Quarterly Report*, vol. 2, no. 1, March 1950. Frederick Rath, Jr. Papers, Hornbake Library. College Park: University of Maryland.

National Council for Historic Sites and Buildings. 1950. *NCHSB Quarterly Report*, vol. 2, no. 4, December 1950. Frederick Rath, Jr. Papers, Hornbake Library. College Park: University of Maryland.

National Council for Historic Sites and Buildings. c. 1948. Preserving America's Heritage. Washington, D.C. Frederick Rath, Jr. Papers, Hornbake Library. College Park: University of Maryland.

National Council on Public History. Guide to Public History Programs. At http://ncph.org/program-guide/.

National Council on Public History. 2007. Code of Ethics and Professional Conduct. At http://ncph.org/cms/about/bylaws-and-ethics/.

National Council on Public History. n.d. What is Public History? At http://ncph.org/cms/what-is-public-history/.

National Museum of Australia. 2004. Australian Journeys and Creating a Country. Unpublished exhibition brief. Canberra: National Museum of Australia.

National Park Service. 1972. *Part One of the National Park System Plan: History*. Washington, D.C.

National Park Service. 2000 [1994]. *History in the National Park Service: Themes and Concepts*. Washington, D.C.

National Park Service. 2002. Case Statement: A Seamless National Network of Parks, Historic Places, and Open Spaces. Approved by the NPS National Leadership Council, 6 September 2002.

National Park Service. n.d. About Us. National Park Service. At http://www.nps.gov/aboutus/index.htm.

National Park System Advisory Board 2001. *Rethinking the National Parks for the 21st Century*, National Park Service.

National Parks Conservation Association. 2008. *Appomattox Court House National Historical Park: A Resource Assessment*. Washington, D.C.

National Parks Conservation Association. 2009. *Advancing the National Park Idea*. Washington, D.C.

National September 11 Memorial & Museum. n.d. At http://www.911memorial.org.

NCPE Committee on Promotion and Tenure. 1984. Toward Promotion and Tenure: Guidelines for Assessing the Achievement of a Preservation Educator. National Council for Preservation Education. October 27, 1984. At http://ncpe.us.

Neatby, N. and P. Hodgkins. 2012. *Settling and Unsettling Memories: Essays in Canadian Public History*. Toronto: University of Toronto Press.

Nelson, D. 1998. *National Manhood: Capitalist Citizenship and the Imagined Fraternity of White Men*. Durham: Duke University Press.

Neustadt, R.E. and E.R. May. 1986. *Thinking in Time: The Uses of History for Decision-Makers*. New York: Free Press.

New Zealand Institute of Advanced Legal Studies, and G.P. McLay. 1995. *Treaty Settlements: the Unfinished Business*. Wellington: published by N.Z. Institute of Advanced Legal Studies and Victoria University of Wellington Law Review.

Ngata, A. T. 1963. *The Treaty of Waitangi, an Explanation: Te Tiriti o Waitangi, he whakamarama*. Christchurch: published for the Maori Purposes Fund Board.

Nightingale, P. and A. Scott. 2007. Peer Review and the Relevance Gap: Ten Suggestions for Policy-Makers. *Science and Public Policy*, vol. 34, pp. 543–553.

Noakes, L. 2009. The BBC "People's War" Website. In *War Memory and Popular Culture: Essays on Modes of Remembrance and Commemoration*, eds. M. Keren and H.R. Hewig, pp. 135–149. North Carolina: McFarland.

Noiret, S. 2009. Public History e storia pubblica nella rete. *Ricerche storiche, no.* 2–3, pp. 275–327.

Noiret, S. 2012. La digital history: histoire et mémoire à la portée de tous. In Read/Write Book 2: Une introduction aux humanités numériques, ed. P. Mounier, pp. 151–177. Marseilles: Open Edition Press. At http://press.openedition.org/258.

Noiret, S. 2014a. Internationalizing Public History. *Public History Weekly*, vol. 2, no. 34.

Noiret, S. 2014b. Public History as "Useful History" before Voting for Europe, May 22–25, 2014. *Digital & Public History*. May 19, 2014. At http://dph.hypotheses.org/380.

Noiret, S. 2015. Digital Public History: Bringing the Public Back In. *Public History Weekly*, vol. 3, no. 13. At https://public-history-weekly.degruyter.com/3-2015-13/digital-public-history-bringing-the-public-back-in/

Noiret, S. 2016. La *Public History*: una disciplina fantasma? *Memoria e Ricerca, no.* 37, pp. 10–35.

Noiret, S. and M. Tebeau. Forthcoming 2019. *The Handbook of Digital Public History*. Munich: De Gruyter.

Nora, P. 1989. Between Memory and History: *Les Lieux de Mémoire*. *Representations*, vol. 26, pp. 7–25.

Nora, P. 1992. De l'histoire contemporains au present historique. In Institut d'Histoire du Temps Présent. *Ecrire l'histoire du temps present: En homage à François Bédarida*. Paris: CNRS.

Nora, P. 1996. *Realms of Memory: Rethinking the French Past*. Volumes I–III. New York: Columbia University Press.

Nora, P. 2011. *Historien Public*. Paris: Gallimard.

Northington, O.F., S. Barnette, C. Porter, and R. Poeppel. 1937. *Study of the McLean House and Other Sites at Appomattox Courthouse*. National Park Service, July 1937.

Nottinghamshire Archives. DD 311/16, Diaries of Joseph Woolley, framework knitter, for 1801, 1803, 1804, 1809, 1813, 1815.

Nottinghamshire Archives. M8050 (1772–1812), M8051 (1805–1810), Notebooks of Sir Gervase Clifton JP.

Nowak, A. 2008. Prawdziwy koniec historii. *Rzeczpospolita*. December 18, 2008.

Nowak, A. 2009a. O historii bez końca. *Rzeczpospolita*. January 2, 2009.

Nowak, A. 2009b. Ratujmy historię, ratujmy polski kanon. *Rzeczpospolita*. January 26, 2009.

Nurse, A. 1997. Tradition and Modernity: The Cultural Work of Marius Barbeau. PhD thesis, Queen's University.

O'Malley, V. 2016. *The Great War for New Zealand: Waikato 1800–2000*. Bridget Williams Books, Wellington.

O'Neill, C. 2010. Time Travel on the Cheap. NPR Blog Post. January 21, 2010. At http://www.npr.org/sections/pictureshow/2010/01/looking_backwards.html (accessed January 12, 2016).

O'Toole, Dennis A. 2004. The Seminar for Historical Administration: Déjà vu All Over Again. *History News* 59 (Winter 2004), pp. 21–25.

Oakman, D. 2010. Student sojourners: Museums and the Transnational Lives of International Students. *National Identities*, vol. 12, no. 4, pp. 397–412.

Oakman, D., M. Sear, and K. Wehner. (eds.) 2013. *Landmarks: A History of Australia in 33 Places*. Canberra: National Museum of Australia.

Office of Treaty Settlements. 2016. *What is a Treaty Settlement?* At https://www.govt.nz/browse/history-culture-and-heritage/treaty-of-waitangi-claims/settling-historical-treaty-of-waitangi-claims/.

Oliver, B. 1945. Country Buildings. In *The National Trust: A Record of Fifty Years' Achievement*, ed. J. Lees-Milne, pp. 78–96. London: Batsford.

Oliver, W.H. 1991. *Claims to the Waitangi Tribunal*. Wellington: Waitangi Tribunal Division Dept. of Justice.

Oliver, W.H. 2001. The Future Behind Us: The Waitangi Tribunal's retrospective utopia. In *Histories, Power and Loss: The Uses of the Past*, eds. A. Sharp and P. McHugh, pp. 9–29. Wellington: Bridget Williams Books.

Oliver, W.H. 2002. *Looking for the Phoenix: A Memoir*. Wellington: Bridget Williams Books.

Olsen, B. 2010. *In Defense of Things: Archaeology and the Ontology of Objects*. Lanham: Altamira Press.

Olssen, E. 1997. Mr. Wakefield and New Zealand as an Experiment in post-Enlightenment Experimental Practice. *New Zealand Journal of History*, vol. 31, pp. 197–218.

Orange, C. 1987. *The Treaty of Waitangi*. Wellington: Allen & Unwin Port Nicholson Press with assistance from the Historical Publications Branch Dept. of Internal Affairs.

Oresko, R. 1996. Obituary: Rohan Butler. *Independent*. November 5, 1996. At http://www.independent.co.uk/news/people/obituary-rohan-butler-1350838.html.

Osborne, B.S. and G.B. Osborne. 2004. The Cast[e]ing of Heroic Landscapes of Power: Constructing Canada's Pantheon on Parliament Hill. *Material Culture Review*, vol. 60, pp. 35–47.

Osborne, G. 2014. Stone-Age Nostalgia. *The New Inquiry*, July 2, 2014. At http://thenewinquiry.com/essays/stone-age-nostalgia/.

Ostow, R. (ed.) 2008. *(Re)Visualizing National History. Museums and National Identities in Europe in the New Millennium*. Toronto: University of Toronto Press.

Ou, S. 2008. From 228 to White Terror – A Case Study of Ma-dow Lee. *Taiwan Historical Research*, vol. 15, no. 2, pp. 135–172.

Owen, W. 1963. Futility. In *The Collected Poems of Wilfred Owen*, ed. C. Day Lewis. London: Chatto and Windus.

Owens, T. 2014. Making Crowdsourcing Compatible with the Missions and Values of Cultural Heritage Organizations. In *Crowdsourcing Our Cultural Heritage*, ed. M. Ridge, pp. 269–280. Farnham: Ashgate.

Page, M. (ed.) 2013. *Memorials of Buenos Aires: Signs of State Terrorism in Argentina*. Boston: University of Massachusetts Press.

Paleo Hacks. 2013. Share Your Before and After. At http://paleohacks.com/before-and-after/share-your-paleo-before-and-after-1004.

Paleo Magazine. 2016. Paleo 101. *Paleo Magazine: Modern Day Primal Living*, vol. 6, no. 4 (August 2016), pp. 94–97.

Palmares Cultural Foundation. 2015. Quilombo Communities. At http://www.palmares.gov.br/?page_id=88.

Palmowski, J. and K.S. Readman. 2011. Speaking Truth to Power: Contemporary History in the Twenty-first Century. *Journal of Contemporary History*, vol. 46, pp. 485–505.

Parker, R. 1984. *The Subversive Stitch*. London: The Women's Library.

Parker, R. and G. Pollock. 1981. *Old Mistresses: Women, Art and Ideology*. London: Pandora.

Passerini, L. 1987 (1984). *Fascism in Popular Memory: The Cultural Experience of the Turin Working Class*. Cambridge: Cambridge University Press.

Peccatte, P. and M. Le Querrec. PhotosNormandie. Flickr. At http://www.flickr.com/people/photosnormandie.

Peers, L. 1999. "Playing Ourselves": First Nations and Native American Interpreters at Living History Sites. *The Public Historian*, vol. 21, no.4, pp. 39–59.

Peers, L. 2007. *Playing Ourselves: Interpreting Native Histories at Historic Reconstructions*. Lanham, MD: Alta Mira Press.

Peers, L. and A.K. Brown. (eds.) 2003. *Museums and Source Communities*. London: Routledge.

Peschel, L. (ed.) 2014. *Performing Captivity, Performing Escape: Cabarets and Plays from the Terezin/Theresienstadt Ghetto*. Calcutta: Seagull Books.

Pessoa, T.C. 2013. O comércio negreiro na clandestinidade: as fazendas de recepção de africanos da família Souza Breves e seus cativos. *Afro-Ásia*, vol. 47, pp. 43–78. At http://www.scielo.br/scielo.php?pid=S0002-05912013000100002andscript=sci_arttext.

Pessoa, T.C. 2013. Os Souza Breves e o Tráfico Ilegal de Africanos no Sul Fluminense. In *Diáspora Negra e Lugares de Memória: A história oculta das propriedades voltadas para o tráfico clandestino de escravos no Brasil Imperial*, ed. H. Mattos, pp. 9–36. Niterói: EDUFF.

Peterson, C.E. Interview by C.B. Hosmer. June 17, 1982. Hosmer Papers, Series 4, Box 5, Hornbake Library. College Park: University of Maryland.

Peterson, T.H., P.M. Quinn, and H.A. Taylor. 1977. Professional Archival Training. *American Archivist*, vol. 40, no. 1, pp. 315–320.

Phillipson, G. 2004. Talking and Writing History: Evidence to the Waitangi Tribunal. In *The Waitangi Tribunal:Te Roopu Whakamana i te Tiriti o Waitangi*, eds. J. Hayward and N.R. Wheen, pp. 41–52. Wellington: Bridget Williams Books.

Phillipson, G. 2012 [2001]. A Waitangi Tribunal Odyssey: the Tribunal's Response to the "Presentism" Critique. *Melbourne Historical Journal*, vol. 40, pp. 21–48.

Pilling, J. and B. Hamilton. 2011. *Review of the Government's Official History Programme*. London: Cabinet Office.

Plaster, J. 2010. Polk Street: Lives in Transition. http://campuspress.yale.edu/jplaster/2015/05/14/polk-street/.

Poblocki, K. 2002. Becoming State: The Bio-Cultural Imperialism of Sid Meier's Civilization. *Focaal: European Journal of Anthropology*, vol. 39, pp. 163–177.

Pomian, K. 1992. Les archives. In *Les Lieux de mémoire, sous la direction de Pierre Nora, Volume III, Les France. 3. De l'archive à l'emblème*, ed. P. Nora, pp. 163–233. Paris: Gallimard.

Pons, A. 2013. *El desorden digital: guía para historiadores y humanistas*. Madrid: Siglo XXI.

Portelli, A. 1991. *The Death of Luigi Trastulli and Other Stories*. Ithaca: State University of New York.

Portelli, A. 1997. *The Battle of Valle Giulia: Oral History and the Art of Dialogue*. Madison: University of Wisconsin Press.

Portelli, A. 2010. *They Say in Harlan County*. New York: Oxford University Press.

Porter, C. 1954. Letter to Ronald Lee. Mockley Point, near Fort Washington, Maryland. 11 March 1954. National Park Service, Park History Program, Piscataway National Park, Washington, D.C.

Porter, R. 1986. History Says No to the Policeman's Response to AIDS. *British Medical Journal*, vol. 293, p. 1589.

Preserve the Baltimore Uprising, n.d. At http://baltimoreuprising2015.org/.

Prisons Memory Archive. 2014. At http://prisonsmemoryarchive.com.

Public Administration Select Committee 2001. Special advisers: boon or bane? London: House of Commons.

Public Services Quality Group of the Archives and Records Association (UK & Ireland). 2011. Survey of Visitors to U.K. Archives 2011.

Pye, D. 2007 (1968). *The Nature and Art of Workmanship*. Edinburgh: A. & C. Black Ltd.

Quennell, M. and C.H. Bourne Quennell. 1920. *A History of Everyday Things in England, Part II: 1500–1799*. London: B. T. Batsford Ltd.

Quian Quiroga, R., S.H. Dudley, and J. Binnie. 2011. Looking at Ophelia: A Comparison of Viewing Art in the Gallery and in the Lab. *ACNR*, vol. 11, no. 3, pp. 15–18.

Rancière, J. 1994 (1992). *The Names of History: On the Poetics of Knowledge*. Minneapolis: University of Minnesota Press.

Rancière, J. 1999. *Disagreement: Politics and Philosophy*. Trans. J. Rose. Minneapolis: University of Minnesota Press.

Rancière, J. 2004. *The Politics of Aesthetics: The Distribution of the Sensible*. Trans. G. Rockhill. London: Continuum.

Rancière, J. 2010. *Dissensus: On Politics and Aesthetics*. Trans. S. Corcoran. London: Continuum.

Rassool, C. 2000. The Rise of Heritage and the Reconstitution of History in South Africa. *Kronos: Journal of Cape History*, vol. 26, pp. 1–21.

Rassool, C. 2006a. Community Museums, Memory Politics, and Social Transformation in South Africa: Histories, Possibilities and Limits. In *Museum Frictions: Public Cultures/Global Transformations*, eds. I. Karp, C.A. Kratz, L. Szwaja, and T. Ybarra-Frausto, pp. 286–321. Durham: Duke University Press.

Rassool, C. 2006b. Making the District Six Museum in Cape Town. *Museum International*, vol. 58, no.1/2, pp. 9–18.

Rath, F., Jr. 1975. The Great Adventure: Louis C. Jones and the New York State Historical Association. *New York Folklore*, vol. 1, nos. 1–2, pp. 1–6. Frederick Rath, Jr. Papers, Hornbake Library. College Park: University of Maryland.

Rath, F., Jr. 1982. Interview by C.B. Hosmer. October 19, 1982. Frederick Rath, Jr. Papers, Hornbake Library. College Park: University of Maryland.

Rath, F., Jr. 1987. Cornelius O'Brien Lecture. Nineteenth Annual Indiana Conference on Historic Preservation. September 18, 1987. Frederick Rath, Jr. Papers, Hornbake Library. College Park: University of Maryland.

Rath, F., Jr. 1988. The Founding of the National Trust: Turning Point for American Heritage. *Courier: Newsmagazine of the National Park Service*, vol. 33, no. 11, pp. 4–5.

Rath, F., Jr. 1996. En Route to CGP: A Talk to the Cooperstown Graduate Association. October 5, 1996. Frederick Rath, Jr. Papers, Hornbake Library. College Park: University of Maryland.

Read, B. 1983. *Victorian Sculpture*. Paul Mellon Centre for Studies in British Art, New Haven: Yale University Press.

Redzepi, R. 2010. *Noma: Time and Place in Nordic Cuisine*. New York: Phaidon.

Redzepi, R. 2013. *A Work in Progress*. New York: Phaidon.

Rees, L.A. 2011. Paternalism and Rural Protest: the Rebecca Riots and the Landed Interest of Southwest Wales. *Agricultural History Review*, vol. 59, no. 1, pp. 36–60.

Remarque, E.M. 1929. *All Quiet on the Western Front*. Trans. A.W. Wheen. London: G.P. Putnam's Sons.

Rentzhog, S. 2007. *Open Air Museums: The History and Future of a Visionary Idea*. Trans. S.V. Airey. Nashville: Association for Living History, Farm and Agricultural Museums.

Repanshek, K. 2011. Is the National Park Service Experiencing Mission Creep? The Smokey Mountain Hiking Blog. June 27, 2011.

Repanshek, K. 2015. National Park Service Maintenance Backlog Approaching $11.5 Billion. *National Parks Traveler*. March 23, 2015.

Repoussi, M. 2009. Common Trends in Contemporary Debates on History Education. *Yearbook. International Society for History Didactics*, vol. 29/30 (2008/2009), pp. 75–90.

Republic of South Africa. 2015. Draft: Revised White Paper on Arts, Culture and Heritage | Department Of Arts and Culture. http://www.dac.gov.za/content/draft-revised-white-paper-arts-culture-and-heritage.

Reuter, L. 2006. *Los Desaparecidos/the Disappeared*. Milan: Charta.

Rice, A. 2003. *Radical Narratives of the Black Atlantic*. London: Continuum Books.

Rice, A. 2010. *Creating Memorials, Building Identities: The Politics of Memory in the Black Atlantic*. Liverpool: Liverpool University Press.

Richards, C. and C. Carter. 2007. *Practical Approaches to Participation*. Macaulay Institute.

Richards, S. 2005. What Is to Be Remembered?: Tourism to Ghana's Slave Castle Dungeons. *Theatre Journal*, vol. 57, no. 4, pp. 617–637.

Richmond, R.W. and G. George. 1982. Hard Times for America's Heritage: State Budget Cuts Threaten History Work. Nashville, Tennessee: AASLH.

Rideau Timescapes. 2012. At http://rideau.timescapes.ca.

Riley, M. and D. Harvey. 2007. Talking Geography: On Oral History and the Practice of Geography. *Social and Cultural Geography*, vol.8, no. 3, pp.1–4.

Rios, A.L. and H. Mattos. 2005. *Memórias do Cativeiro: Família, Trabalho e Cidadania no Pós-Abolição*. Rio de Janeiro: Civilização Brasileira.

Ritchin, F. 2009. *After Photography*. New York: W. W. Norton.

Robben, A.C.G.M. 2005. *Political Violence and Trauma in Argentina*. Philadelphia: University of Pennsylvania Press.

Robertson, E. 2013. CrossFit's Dirty Little Secret. *The Huffington Post*, September 24, 2013. At http://www.huffingtonpost.com/eric-robertson/crossfit-rhabdomyolysis_b_3977598.html (accessed August 7, 2016).

Robertson, R. 1995. Glocalization: Time-space and homogeneity-heterogeneity. In *Global Modernities*, eds. M. Featherstone, S. Lash, and R. Robertson, pp. 25–44. London: Sage.

Robertson, S. 2014. The Differences between Digital History and Digital Humanities. May 23, 2014. At http://drstephenrobertson.com/blog-post/the-differences-between-digital-history-and-digital-humanities/.

Roediger, D.R. 1995. *The Wages of Whiteness*. New York: Oxford University Press.

Rome Total Realism. 2005. At www.rometotalrealism.org (accessed January, 1 2014)

Rosenthal, H. D. 1990. *Their Day in Court: A History of the Indian Claims Commission*. New York: Garland Pub.

Rosenzweig, R. and D. Thelen. 1998. *The Presence of the Past: Popular Uses of History in American Life*. New York: Columbia University Press.

Rosenzweig, R. n.d. Afterthoughts: Everyone a Historian. The Presence of the Past. At http://chnm.gmu.edu/survey/afterroy.html#32.

Ross, M. 2002. Interview: Achieving the Cinematic Impossible. IndieWire. November 26, 2002. At http://www.indiewire.com/article/interview_achieving_the_cinematic_impossible_russian_ark_dp_tilman_buttner.

Ross, R.M. 1972. Te Tiriti o Waitangi: Texts and Translations. *New Zealand Journal of History*, vol. 6, pp. 129–157.

Rothkirchen, L. 1984. The Jews of Bohemia and Moravia: 1938–1945. In *The Jews of Czechoslovakia: Historical Studies and Surveys, Volume III*, eds. A. Dagan, G. Hirschler, and L. Weiner. Philadelphia: Jewish Publication Society of American.

Rothman, D.J. 2003. Serving Clio and Client: The Historian as Expert Witness. *Bulletin of the History of Medicine*, vol. 77, pp. 25–44.

Rotten Tomatoes. n.d. Reviews of Russian Ark. At http://www.rottentomatoes.com/m/russian_ark/reviews/#type=user.

Rousso, H. 1984. Applied History, or the Historian as Miracle-Worker. *The Public Historian*, vol. 6, no. 4, pp. 65–85.

Rousso, H. 1991. *The Vichy Syndrome: History and Memory in France since 1944.* Cambridge: Harvard University Press.

Rousso, H. 2011. L'historien du temps présent dans l'espace public. Paper presented at Le passé et nous: de la conscience historique au xxi.e siècle / The Past Around Us: Historical Consciousness in the XXIst Century. Quebec, September 29 to October 1, 2011 (video available online at http://vimeo.com/29896137).

Rowan, B. 2010. Eames-Bradley: Saville Report "Has Revived The Will To Deal With The Past." Belfast Telegraph. June 25, 2010. At http://Www.Belfasttelegraph.Co.Uk/News/Eamesbradley-Saville-Report-Has-Revived-The-Will-To-Deal-With-The-Past-28543444.Html.

Rowan, B. 2011. Digging Up the Past Is Undermining Our Future. *Belfast Telegraph.* March 5, 2011. At http://www.belfasttelegraph.co.uk/opinion/news-analysis/digging-up-the-past-is-undermining-our-future-28594525.html.

Rowbotham, S. 1973. *Hidden from History. Three Hundred Years of Women's Oppression and the Fight against It.* London: Pluto Press.

Roy Rosenzweig Center for History and New Media. 2014. 20th Anniversary Conference, http://chnm.gmu.edu/20th/.

Roy Rosenzweig Center for History and New Media. n.d. Histories of the National Mall. At http://mallhistory.org/.

Roy, S. 2010. *These Mysterious People: Shaping History and Archaeology in a Northwest Coast Community.* McGill-Queen's University Press.

Rubin, R.L. 2012. *Well Met: Renaissance Faires and the American Counterculture.* New York: NYU Press.

Runyon, J. n.d. *Ultimate Paleo Guide.* At http://ultimatepaleoguide.com/paleo-diet-supplements/ (accessed August 7, 2016).

Rush, D. 2013. *Vodun in Coastal Bénin: Unfinished, Open-Ended, Global.* Nashville: Vanderbilt University Press.

Russell, R. 2014. Travelling Steerage: Class, Commerce, Religion and Family in Colonial Sydney. *Journal of Australian Studies,* vol. 38, no. 4, pp. 383–395.

Rutner, J. and R.C. Schonfeld. 2012. Supporting the Changing Research Practices of Historians: Final Report from Ithaka S + R. December 10, 2012. At http://www.sr.ithaka.org/news/understanding-historians-today-%E2%80%94-new-ithaka-sr-report.

Rydell, R.W. 1984. *All the World's a Fair.* Chicago: University of Chicago Press.

SAA. 1988. SAA Guidelines for Graduate Archival Education Programs. *American Archivist,* vol. 51, no. 1, pp. 380–389.

SAA. 2002-present. SAA Guidelines for a Graduate Program in Archival Studies. At http://www2.archivists.org/gpas.

Said, Edward. 1994. *Orientalism.* New York: Vintage.

Saillant, F. and P. Simonard. 2012. Afro-Brazilian Heritage and Slavery in Rio de Janeiro Community Museums. In *Politics of Memory: Making Slavery Visible in the Public Space,* edited by A.L. Araujo, pp. 223–225. New York: Routledge.

Salverson, J. 1996. Performing Emergency: Witnessing, Popular Theatre, and the Lie of the Literal. *Theatre Topics,* vol. 6, no. 2, pp. 181–191.

Samida, S. and R. Liburkina. 2014. Living History and Reenactment: Erste Ergebnisse einer Umfrage. *Archäologische Informationen,* vol. 37, pp. 191–197.

Samuel, R. (ed.) 1975. *Village Life and Labour.* London: Routledge.

Samuel, R. (ed.) 1991. *History Workshop: A Collectanea 1967-1991.* Ruskin College, Oxford: History Workshop.

Samuel, R. 1991. Reading the Signs. *History Workshop Journal,* vol. 32, pp. 88–109.

Samuel, R. 1994. *Theatres of Memory. Volume 1: Past and Present in Contemporary Culture* London: Verso.

Samuel, R. 1998. *Theatres of Memory. Vol. 2: Island Stories. Unravelling Britain.* London: Verso.

Santhiago, R. 2016. Duas Palavras, Mutitos Significados. Alguns comentários sobre a história pública no Brasil. In *História, Pública No Brasil. Sentidos e Itinerários,* eds. A.M. Mauad, J.R. de Almeida, and R. Santhiago, pp. 23–35. Sao Paulo: Letra e Voz.

Santos, L.R. and B.M. Hood. 2009. Object Representation as a Central Issue in Cognitive Science. In *The Origins of Object Knowledge,* eds. B.M. Hood and L.R. Santos, pp. 1–24. Oxford: Oxford University Press.

Sassower, R. 2014. *The Price of Public Intellectuals.* Basingstoke: Palgrave Macmillan.

Savage, K. 2009. *Monument Wars: Washington, D.C., the National Mall, and the Transformation of the Memorial Landscape.* Berkeley: University of California Press.

Sayer, F. 2015. *Public History: A Practical Guide.* London: Bloomsbury.

Sayer, F. 2015. *Public History: A Practical Guide*. Kindle edition. London: Bloomsbury Academic.

Saygi, E. 2010. *Gökçeada Imbros*. Izmir: Gulermat.

Schaffer, K. and S. Smith. 2004. Venues of Storytelling: The Circulation of Testimony in Human Rights Campaigns. *Life Writing*, vol. 1, no. 2, pp. 3–26.

Scheffer, I. 2008. Contemporary Monuments Concepts in Germany. Goethe Institute. At http://www.goethe.de/kue/arc/dos/dos/zdk/en78940.htm.

Schenck, M.C. and M.P. Candido. 2015. Uncomfortable Pasts: Talking About Slavery in Angola. In *African Heritage and Memories of Slavery in Brazil and the South Atlantic World*, ed. A.L. Araujo, pp. 203–242. Amherst, New York: Cambria Press.

Schlereth, T.J. 1978. It Wasn't That Simple. *Museum News*, vol. 56, no.1, pp. 39–40.

Schmidt, S. 2008 (May). The Evolving Relationship between Open Space Preservation and Local Planning Practice, *Journal of Planning History*, vol. 7. no. 2, pp. 9–112.

Schön, D. 1983. *The Reflective Practitioner: How Professionals Think in Action*. New York: Basic Books.

Schorch, P. 2013. Contact Zones, Third Spaces, and the Act of Interpretation. *Museum and Society*, vol. 11, no. 1, pp. 68–81.

Schramm, K. 2010. *African Homecoming: Pan-African Ideology and Contested Heritage*. Walnut Creek, CA: Left Coast Press.

Schreibman, S. (ed.) 2015. *A New Companion to Digital Humanities*. Chichester: John Wiley & Sons.

Schreibman, S., R. Siemens, and J. Unsworth. (eds.) 2004. *A Companion to Digital Humanities*. Oxford: Blackwell, 2004.

Schuldt, E. 1972. Die mecklenburgischen Megalithgräber. Untersuchungen zu ihrer Architektur und Funktion. *Beiträge zur Ur- und Frühgeschichte der Bezirke Rostock, Schwerin und Neubrandenburg*, vol. 6. Berlin: Deutscher Verlag der Wissenschaften.

Schultz, C.B. 1999. Becoming a Public Historian. In *Public History: Essays from the Field*, eds. J.B. Gardner and P.S. LaPaglia, pp. 23–40. Malabar: Krieger.

Schwenger, P. 2006. *The Tears of Things: Melancholy and Physical Objects*. Minneapolis: University of Minnesota press.

Science Daily. 2012. Initial Genetic Analysis Reveals Iceman Ötzi Predisposed to Cardiovascular Disease. *Science Daily*, February 28, 2012. At www.sciencedaily.com/releases/2012/02/120228123847.htm.

Scott, C.A. 2013. *Museums and Public Value: Creating Sustainable Futures*. Farnham: Ashgate.

Sear, M. 2013. History in Communities. In *Australian History Now*, eds. A. Clark and P. Ashton, pp. 198–214. Sydney: NewSouth Publishing.

Seeley, J.R. 1895. *The Expansion of England: Two Courses of Lectures*. London: Macmillan.

Seeman, E. S. 2010. Sources and Interpretations: Reassessing the "*Sankofa* Symbol" in New York's African Burial Ground. *William and Mary Quarterly*, vol. 67, pp. 101–122.

Segall, A. 2006. What's the Purpose of Teaching a Discipline, Anyway? The Case of History. In *Social Studies – The Next Generation: Re-searching in the Postmodern*, eds. A. Segall, C.H. Cherryholmes, and E.E. Heilman, pp. 125–139. Bern: Peter Lang.

Seixas, P. 2000. Schweigen! die kinder! or, Does Postmodern History have a Place in the Schools? In *Knowing, Teaching, and Learning History: National and International Perspectives*, eds. P. Stearns, P. Seixas, and S. Wineburg, pp. 19–37. New York: New York University Press.

Seixas, P. 2004. *Theorizing Historical Consciousness*. Toronto: University of Toronto Press.

Sekula, A. 1983. Photography Between Labour and Capital. In *Mining Photographs and Other Pictures, 1948–68: A selection from the Negative Archives of Shedden Studio, Glace Bay, Cape Breton*, eds. B.H.D. Buchloh and R. Wilkie, pp. 193–268. Halifax and Sydney, NS: Press of the Nova Scotia College of Art and Design and the University College of Cape Breton Press.

Selwyn, A.R. 1887. *Geological and Natural History Survey of Canada: Annual Report. Volume II.* Montreal: Dawson Brothers.

September 11 Digital Archive. n.d. http://911digitalarchive.org.

Ševčenko, L. and M. Russell-Ciardi. 2008. Sites of Conscience: Opening Historic Sites for Civic Dialogue. *The Public Historian*, vol. 30, pp. 9–15.

Shanahan, A. 2001. More Edification, Less of the Gee-Whiz Factor. *The Australian*. March 12, 2001. Page 11.

Shanks, M., and C. Tilley. 1987. *Social Theory and Archaeology*. Cambridge: Polity Press.

Shannon, J. 2014. *Our Lives: Collaboration, Native Voice, and the Making of the National Museum of the American Indian*. Santa Fe, NM: School for Advanced Research Press.

Sheail, P. n.d. The Hertford Pageant of 1914. The Redress of the Past: Historical Pageants in Britain. At http://www.historicalpageants.ac.uk/featured-pageants/hertford-pageant-1914/.

Shepherd, E. 2009. *Archives and Archivists in Twentieth-Century England*. Farnham: Ashgate.

Shepherd, R. 2006. UNESCO and the Politics of Cultural Heritage in Tibet. *Journal of Contemporary Asia*, vol. 36, no. 2, pp. 243–257.

Sherman, D.J. 1995. Objects of Memory: History and Narrative in French War Museums. *French Historical Studies*, vol. 19, pp. 49–74.

Shipley, B. 2007. From Field to Fact: William E. Logan and the Geological Survey of Canada. PhD thesis, Dalhousie University.

Shopes, L. 2016. The Evolving Relationship between Oral History and Public History. *Ricerche Storiche*, vol. 46, no. 1, pp. 105–118.

Shryock, A. and D.L. Smail. 2011. *Deep History: The Architecture of Past and Present*. Berkeley: University of California Press.

Siblon, J. 2012. Monument Mania? Public Space and the Black and Asian Presence in the London Landscape. In *People and Their Pasts: Public History and Heritage Today*, eds. P. Ashton and H. Kean, pp. 146–162. Basingstoke: Palgrave Macmillan.

Sim, W. A., V. Reed, and W. Cooper. 1928. Confiscated Native Lands and other Grievances. Royal Commission to Into Confiscations of Native Lands and other Grievances Alleged by Natives (Report Of).

Simon, H.A. 1972. Theories of Bounded Rationality. In *Decision and Organization*, eds. C.B. Mcguire and R. Radner, pp. 161–176. Amsterdam: North-Holland, Amsterdam.

Simon, N. 2010. The Participatory Museum. Santa Cruz, California: Museum 2.0. At www.participatorymuseum.org.

Simpson, D. 2006. *9/11: The Culture of Commemoration*. Chicago: University of Chicago Press.

Simpson, M.G. 2001. *Making Representations: Museums in the Post-Colonial Era*. Revised edition. Hove: Psychology Press.

Sims, A. 2014. Primalcon Tulum: The Power of Choice. *Paleo Foodies*. March 6, 2014. At http://paleofoodies.com.au/2014/03/primalcon-tulum-the-power-of-choice/.

Singh, J.P. 2011. *United Nations Educational, Scientific, and Cultural Organization (UNESCO): Creating Norms for a Complex World*. New York: Routledge.

Singleton, T.A. 1999. The Slave Trade Remembered on the Former Gold and Slave Coasts. *Slavery & Abolition*, vol. 20, pp. 150–169.

Sirna, A. 2015. Recreating Appalachia: Cumberland Gap National Historical Park, 1922–1972. PhD dissertation. Murfreesboro: Middle Tennessee State University.

Skelcher, C. 2000. Changing images of the State: Overloaded, Hollowed–Out, Congested. *Public Policy and Administration*, vol. 15, pp. 3–19.

Sledge, M. 2005. *Soldier Dead: How We Recover, Identify, Bury and Honour Our Military Fallen*. New York: Columbia University Press.

Slenes, R.W. 2013. Like Forest Hardwoods: Jongueiros Cumba in the Central-African Slave Quarters; and I Come from Afar, I Come Digging: Kongo and Near-Kongo Metaphors in *Jongo* Lyrics. In *Cangoma Calling Spirits and Rhythms of Freedom in Brazilian Jongo Slavery Songs*, eds. P. Monteiro and M. Stone, pp. 49–76, Dartmouth: University of Massachusetts.

Smith, B. 1998. *The Gender of History: Men, Women and Historical Practice*. New Haven: Harvard University Press.

Smith, G. 2007 (1987). From Mickey to Maus: Recalling The Genocide through Cartoon. In *Art Spiegelman Conversations*, ed. J. Witek, pp. 84–94. Jackson: University of Mississippi Press.

Smith, H.I. 1913. Museum Work at the Capital of Canada. *Proceedings of the American Association of Museums*, vol. 7.

Smith, L. 2004. *Archaeological Theory and the Politics of Cultural Heritage*. London: Routledge.

Smith, L. 2006. *Uses of Heritage*. London: Routledge.

Smith, L. 2011. Affect and Registers of Engagement. In *Representing Enslavement and Abolition in Museums: Ambiguous Engagements*, eds. L. Smith, G. Cubitt, R. Wilson, and K. Fouseki, pp. 260–303. New York: Routledge.

Smith, L.T. 2012 (1999). *Decolonizing Methodologies: Research and Indigenous Peoples*. New York: Zed Books.

Smith, S. and J. Watson. 2010. *Reading Autobiography: A Guide for Interpreting Life Narratives*. Minneapolis: University of Minnesota Press.

Snow, C.P. 1998. *The Two Cultures*. Cambridge: Cambridge University Press.

Sorrenson, M.P.K. 2014. *Ko te whenua te utu = Land is the price: Essays on Maori History, Land and Politics*. Auckland: Auckland University Press.

Sparrow, J.T. 2006. *Public History on the Web: The September 11 Digital Archive*. In *Public History: Essays From The Field*, eds. J.B. Gardner and P.S. Lapaglia, pp. 397–416. Malabar: Krieger.

Spongberg, M. 2002. *Writing Women's History Since the Renaissance*. Houndsmills: Palgrave Macmillan.

Sprinkle, J.H. Jr. 2010. "An Orderly, Balanced and Comprehensive Panorama…of American History": Filling Thematic Gaps within the National Park System. *The George Wright Forum*, vol. 27, no. 3, pp. 269–279.

Spurway, J. 1989. The Growth of Family History. *Push*, vol. 27, pp. 53–112.

Stabile, S. 2004. *Memory's Daughters: The Material Culture of Remembrance in Eighteenth-Century America*. Ithaca: Cornell University Press.

Staley, D.J. 2006. *History and Future: Using Historical Thinking to Imagine the Future*. Lanham: Lexington Books.

Stam, D.C. 2005. The Informed Muse: The Implications of "The New Museology" for Museum Practice. In *Heritage, Museums and Galleries: An Introductory Reader*, ed. G. Corsane, pp. 54–70. London: Routledge.

Stanley, P. 2014. *The Lost Boys of Anzac*. Sydney: NewSouth Publishing.

Stansell, C. 2009. *American Moderns: Bohemian New York and the Creation of New Century*. Princeton: Princeton University Press.

Stanton, C. 1997. *Being the Elephant: The American Civil War Reenacted*. Masters Thesis, Vermont College of Norwich University.

Stanton, C. 2006. *The Lowell Experiment. Public History in a Postindustrial City*. Amherst: University of Massachusetts Press.

Stanton, C. 2015. Hardball History: On the Edge of Politics, Advocacy, and Activism. Public History Commons, 25 March, 2015. At http://publichistorycommons.org/hardball-history-stanton/#sthash.T18EK3jY.dpuf.

Steam Community Forums. 2013. Mod for Removing Male Ruler Preference. At http://steamcommunity.com/app/203770/discussions/0/648812917204193097/.

Stearns, P.N. 1982. History and Policy Analysis: Toward Maturity. *The Public Historian*, vol. 4, pp. 5–29.

Steedman, C. 2001. *Dust*. Manchester: Manchester University Press.

Steedman, C. 2011. After the Archive. *Comparative Critical Studies*, vol. 8, no. 2–3, pp. 321–340.

Steedman, C. 2013. *An Everyday Life of the English Working Class. Work, Self and Sociability in the Early Nineteenth Century*. Cambridge: Cambridge University Press.

Stevens, M. 2010. Public Policy and the Public Historian: The Changing Place of Historians in Public Life in France and the UK. *The Public Historian*, vol. 32, pp. 120–138.

Stola, D. 2012. *Historia: Wiek XX: Szkoły ponadgimnazjalne: Zakres podstawowy*. Warsaw: Wydawnictwo Szkolne PWN.

Stolpersteine Gelsenkirchen. 2011. Stumbling Stones – Stolpersteine. At http://www.stolpersteine-gelsenkirchen.de/stumbling_stones_demnig.htm.

Storey, R. 2015. Pessimism of the Intellect, Optimism of the Will: Engaging with the "Testimony" of Injured Workers. In *Beyond Testimony and Trauma: Oral History in the Aftermath of Mass Violence*, ed. S. High, pp. 56–87. Vancouver: University of British Columbia Press.

Stronge, S. 2009. *Tipu's Tigers.* London: Victoria & Albert Museum.

Sturken, M. 2002. Memorialising Absence. In *Understanding September 11*, eds. C. Calhoun, P. Price, and A. Timmer, pp. 374–431. New York: The New Press.

Sturken, M. 2007. *Tourists of History: Memory, Kitsch, and Consumerism from Oklahoma City to Ground Zero.* Durham: Duke University Press.

Subrahmanyam, S. 2001. *Penumbral Visions: Making Politics in Early Modern South India.* Delhi: Oxford University Press.

Summers, J. 2007. *Remembered: The History of the Commonwealth War Graves Commission.* London: Merrell.

Summers, J., L. Loe, and N. Steel. 2010. *Remembering Fromelles: A New Cemetery for a New Century.* Maidenhead: CWGC Publishing.

Sutton, I., R.L. Beals, and American Council of Learned Socieites. 1985. Irredeemable America: The Indians' Estate and Land Claims. *History series no. 1.* Albuquerque: University of New Mexico Press: Published in cooperation with the Instituto for Native American Studies, University of New Mexico.

Swain, S., L. Sheedy, and C. O'Neill. 2012. Responding to "Forgotten Australians": Historians and the Legacy of Out-Of-Home "Care." *Journal of Australian Studies*, vol. 36, no. 1, pp. 17–28.

Swallow, D.M. 2003. Genetics of Lactase Persistence and Lactose Intolerance. *Annual Review of Genetics*, vol. 37, pp. 197–219.

Szonyi, M. 2002. *Practicing Kinship: Lineage and Descent in Late-Imperial China.* Stanford: Stanford University Press.

Szreter, S. 2011. History and Public Policy. In *The Public Value of the Humanities*, ed. J. Bate, pp. 219–231, London: Bloomsbury Academic.

Tabachnich, S.E. (ed.) 2009. *Teaching the Graphic Novel.* New York: Modern Language Association of America.

Taipei 228 Memorial Museum. 2000. *Taipei 228 Memorial Museum 2000 Yearbook.* Taipei: Taipei 228 Memorial Museum.

Tal, K. 1996. *Worlds of Hurt: Reading the Literature of Trauma.* Cambridge: Cambridge University Press.

Tall, E.K. 1995. De la démocratie et des cultes voduns au Bénin. *Cahiers d'études africaines*, vol. 137, pp. 195–208.

Tansuğ, F. 2012. *İmroz Rumları: Gökçeada Üzerine.* Istanbul: Heyamola Yayınları.

Taussig, J. 1994. Über Theresienstädter Kabarette. In *Theresienstädter Studien und Dokumente 1994*, eds. R. Kemper, M. Kárná, and M. Kárný. Praha: Academia.

Taylor, A. 2014. Scenes from D-Day, Then and Now. *The Atlantic.* June 5, 2014. At http://www.theatlantic.com/infocus/2014/06/scenes-from-d-day-then-and-now/100752/.

Taylor, D. 1997. *Disappearing Acts: Spectacles of Gender and Nationalism in Argentina's "Dirty War."* Durham: Duke University Press.

Taylor, D. 1998. A Savage Performance: Guillermo Gómez-Peña and Coco Fusco's "Couple in the Cage." *TDR*, vol. 42, no. 2, pp. 160–175.

Taylor, D. 2003. *The Archive and the Repertoire: Performing Cultural Memory in the Americas.* Durham: Duke University Press.

Teather, J.L. 1991. Museum Studies: Reflecting on Reflective Practice. *Museum Management and Curatorship*, vol. 10, pp. 403–417.

Terras, M. 2010. Crowdsourcing Manuscript Material. Blog post. March 2, 2010, At http://melissaterras.blogspot.it/2010/03/crowdsourcing-manuscript-material.html.

Terras, M. J. Nyhan, and E. Vanhouette. (eds.) 2013. *Defining Digital Humanities: A Reader.* Farnham: Ashgate.

Thakar, N., C. Moser, and L.E. Durso. 2015. Building a More Inclusive National Park System for all Americans. Center for American Progress, June 24, 2015.

Thane, P. 2009. History and Policy. *History Workshop Journal*, vol. 67, pp. 140–145.

Thane, P. 2011. *Happy Families?: History and Family Policy*. London: British Academy.

The Apprentice Boys of Derry Association. n.d. Apprentice Boys Today. At http://apprenticeboysofderry.org/about/4590560772.

The Guardian. n.d. Photography Then and Now. At http://www.theguardian.com/artanddesign/series/photography-then-and-now.

The National Archives (TNA). n.d. Key Sector Statistics. At http://www.nationalarchives.gov.uk/archives-sector/key-sector-statistics.htm.

The National Museum. 1893. [Editorial]. *The Canadian Mining and Mechanical Review*, vol. 12, no. 2, pp. 11–12.

The Scottish Government. 2007. Highland Clearances Memorial. At http://www.scotland.gov.uk/News/Releases/2007/07/23103045.

Thelen, D. and K.L. Morgan. 2014. *Experiencing Sophiatown: Conversations among Residents about the Past, Present and Future of a Community*. Auckland Park: Jacana Media.

Thirsk, J. 2008 (1996). Women Local and Family Historians. In *The Oxford Companion to Local and Family History*, ed. D. Hey, pp. 100–111. Oxford: Oxford University Press.

Thomas, N. 2001. Ethnographic History. In *The Oxford Companion to Australian History*, eds. G. Davison, J. Hirst, and S. Macintyre. Oxford: Oxford University Press. (Published online 2003). At http://www.oxfordreference.com/view/10.1093/acref/9780195515039.001.0001/acref-9780195515039-e-516.

Thomis, M.I. 1972. *Luddism in Nottinghamshire. Thoroton Society Record Series*, vol. 26.

Thompson, A. 2013. Healing Histories. The Age. November 10, 2013. At http://www.theage.com.au/victoria/healing-histories-20131109-2x8wo.html.

Thompson, E.P. 1963. *The Making of the English Working Class*. Harmondsworth: Penguin.

Thompson, E.P. 1971. The Moral Economy of the English Crowd in the Eighteenth Century. *Past and Present*, vol. 50, pp. 76–136.

Thompson, J. 2004. *War Games: Inside the World of Twentieth-century War Reenactors*. Washington, D.C.: Smithsonian Books.

Thomson, A. 1998. Anzac Memories: Putting Popular Memory Theory into Practice in Australia. In *The Oral History Reader*, eds. R. Perks and A. Thomson, pp. 300–310. London: Routledge.

Thrift, N. 2008. *Non-Representational Theory: Space, Politics, Affect*. London: Routledge.

Tilley, C. 2004. *The Materiality of Stone*. Oxford: Berg.

Time Magazine. Cover. 2006. December 25, 2006 – January 1, 2007, vol. 168, no. 26. At http://content.time.com/time/covers/0,16641,20061225,00.html.

Todd, F.G. 1904. *Preliminary Report to The Ottawa Improvement Commission*. n.p.

Tosh, J. 2008. *Why History Matters*. New York: Palgrave Macmillan.

Tosh, J. 2014. Public History, Civic Engagement and the Historical Profession in Britain. *History*, vol. 99, pp. 191–212.

Total War Forums. 2013. A Message to "300" Fans. At http://forums.totalwar.com/showthread.php/97623-A-message-to-quot-300-quot-fans.

Traba, R. and H. Thunemann. 2015. *Myślenie historyczne. Część II. Świadomość i kultura historyczna*. Poznań: Wydawnictwo Nauka i Innowacje.

Trask, D.F. 1978. A Reflection on Historians and Policymakers. *The History Teacher*, vol. 11, pp. 219–226.

Traverso, F. 2015. Documentacion y produccion artistca. http://www.00350.com.ar/

Trentmann, F. 2007. Before "Fair Trade": Empire, Free Trade, and the Moral Economies of Food in the Modern World. *Environment and Planning D: Society and Space*, vol. 25, no. 6, pp. 1079–1102.

Trigger, B. 1984. Alternative Archaeologies: Colonialist, Nationalist, Imperialist. *Man*, vol. 19, no. 3, pp. 355–370.

Trinca, M. and K. Wehner. 2006. Pluralism and Exhibition Practice at the National Museum of Australia. In *South Pacific Museums: Experiments in Culture*, eds. C. Healy and A. Witcomb, pp. 6.1–6.14. Melbourne: Monash University ePress. Web. January11, 2016.

Trouillot, M. 1995. *Silencing the Past: Power and the Production of History*. Boston: Beacon Press Books.

Tsao, C. 2011. Memorial Museum, Memory Study and Transitional Justice: From International Experiences to Green Island Human Rights Cultural Park. Master's Thesis, Graduate Institute of Museum Studies, Taipei National University of the Arts.

Tsao, C., H. Tsai, and S. Lin. 2008. *Green Island Human Rights Memorial Park: Guide Book*. Taipei: Preparation Office of Bureau of Cultural Heritage of Council of Cultural Affairs.

Tseng, M. 1997. The Formation of the Movement of the Reparation of Feb.28 Incident Victims. *Correspondence of Taiwan History & Relics*, vol. 30 & 31, no. 12, pp. 143–167.

Tsing, A.L. 2005. *Friction: An Ethnography of Global Connection*. Princeton: Princeton University Press.

Tuck, E. and K.W. Yang. 2012. Decolonization Is Not a Metaphor. *Decolonization: Indigeneity, Education & Society*, vol. 1, no. 1, pp. 1–40.

Türeli, İ. 2010. Ara Güler's Photography of 'Old Istanbul' and Cosmopolitan Nostalgia. *History of Photography*, vol. 34, no. 3, pp. 300–313.

Turgeon, L. 2010. Towards a Museology of the Intangible. *Musées*, vol. 29, pp. 8–25.

Turner, G. (ed.) 1993. *Nation, Culture, Text: Australian Cultural and Media Studies*. London: Routledge.

Tyson, A.M. 2008. Crafting Emotional Comfort: Interpreting the Painful Past at Living History Museums in the New Economy. *Museum and Society*, vol. 6, no. 3, pp. 246–261.

Tyson, A.M. and A.M. Dungey. 2014. "Ask a Slave" and Interpreting Race on Public History's Front Line: Interview with Azie Mira Dungey. *Public Historian*, vol. 36, no. 1, pp. 36–60.

Tyson, A.M. 2013. *The Wages of History: Emotional Labor on Public History's Front Lines*. Amherst: University of Massachusetts Press.

UNESCO 2017. "Constitution of the United Nations Educational, Scientific and Cultural Organisation." UNESCO. At http://portal.unesco.org/en/ev.php-URL_ID=15244&URL_DO= DO_TOPIC&URL_SECTION=201.html.

Unrau, H.D. and G.F. Williss, *Administrative History: Expansion of the National Park Service in the 1930s*. National Park Service, September 1983.

Uricchio, W. 2005. Simulation, History, and Computer Games. In *Handbook of Computer Game Studies*, eds. J. Raessens and J. Goldstein, pp. 327–340, Cambridge, MA: MIT Press.

Urry, J. 1995. A Middle-Class Countryside. In *Social Change and the Middle Classes*, ed. T. Butler and M. Savage, pp. 205–219. London: Routledge.

Urry, J. 2002. *The Tourist Gaze. London*; Thousand Oaks, California: Sage.

Van der Ploeg, J.D., Y. Jingzhong, and S. Schneider. 2012. Rural Development through the Construction of New, Nested, Markets: Comparative Perspectives from China, Brazil and the European Union. *Journal of Peasant Studies*, vol. 39, no. 1, pp. 133–173.

Van Dijck, J. 2007. *Mediated Memories in the Digital Age*. Stanford: Stanford University Press.

van Drunen, S.P.C. 2010. *Struggling with the Past: The Human Rights Movement and the Politics of Memory in Post-Dictatorship Argentina (1983–2006)*. Amsterdam: Rozenberg Publishers.

Vergo, P. (ed.) 1989. *The New Museology*. London: Reaktion Books.

Verhoeff, N. 2013. The Medium is the Method: Locative Media for Digital Archives. In *Disorienting Media and Narrative Mazes*, eds. Julia Eckel et al., pp. 17–30. Bielefeld, Germany: Transcript-Verlag.

Vernon, K. 2004. *Universities and the State in England, 1850–1939*. London: Routledge Falmer.

Vincent, C.H. 2014. *National Park System: Establishing New Units*. Congressional Research Service. March 26, 2014.

Vincent, C.H. and K. Alexander. 2010. National Monuments and the Antiquities Act. Congressional Research Service. July 20, 2010.

Vogt, J.D. 2007. Kykuit II Summit: The Sustainability of Historic Sites. *History News* (Autumn 2007), pp. 17–21.

Voskovec, J. and J. Werich. 1980. Kat a blázen. In *Jiří Voskovec a Jan Werich: Hry.* Prague: Československý spisovatel.

Voyages: The Trans-Atlantic Slave Trade Database. 2013. At http://www.slavevoyages.org/.

Waiser, W.A. 1989. *The Field Naturalist: John Macoun, the Geological Survey, and Natural Science.* Toronto: University of Toronto Press.

Waitangi Tribunal. 1988. *Report of the Waitangi Tribunal on the Muriwhenua Fishing Claim, Wai 22.* Wellington: The Tribunal.

Waitangi Tribunal. 1991. *The Ngai Tahu Report 1991 (Wai 27).* Wellington: Brooker and Friend.

Waitangi Tribunal. 1993. *Preliminary Report on the Te Arawa Representative Geothermal Resource Claims (Wai 153).* Wellington: Brooker & Friend.

Waitangi Tribunal. 2004. *Te Raupatu o Tauranga Moana: Report on the Tauranga Confiscation Claims (Wai 215).* Wellington: Legislation Direct.

Waitangi Tribunal. 2006. *The Hauraki Report.* Wellington: Legislation Direct.

Waitangi Tribunal. 2007. *The Tamaki Makaurau Settlement Process Report.* Wellington: Legislation Direct.

Waitangi Tribunal. 2014. He Whakaputanga me te Tiriti / The Declaration and the Treaty: The Report on Stage 1 of the Te Paparahi o Te Raki Inquiry [volume 2]. Wellington: Waitangi Tribunal.

Waitangi Tribunal. n.d. A New Approach. At http://www.justice.govt.nz/tribunals/waitangi-tribunal/the-claims-process/the-new-approach#a-discussion-paper-on.

Waitangi Tribunal.1987. *Report of the Waitangi Tribunal on the Orakei Claim (Wai-9).* Wellington: The Tribunal.

Waitangi Tribunal.2009. *Te Urewera Pre-Publication. Part 1 (online).* Wellington: Waitangi Tribunal.

Walker, R. 1992. Maori People Since 1950. In *The Oxford History of New Zealand.* 2nd edition, ed. G.W. Rice. Auckland: Oxford University Press.

Wallace, M. 1995. *Mickey Mouse History and Other Essays.* Philadelphia: Temple University Press.

Wallerstein, I. 2006. *European Universalism: The Rhetoric of Power.* New York: New Press.

Walley, C. 2013. *Exit 0: Family and Class in Postindustrial Chicago.* Chicago: University of Chicago Press.

Walsh, K. 1992. *The Representation of the Past: Museums and Heritage in the Post-Modern World.* London: Routledge.

Wang, Y-C., J-Y. Chao, and Y-L. Chiu. 2009. Taiwan Human Rights Jing-Mei Park Changes its Name, President Ma Pressed the Brake. Liberty Times Net. April 18, 2009. At http://news.ltn.com.tw/news/focus/paper/296469.

Wanhalla, A. 2009. *In/visible Sight: The Mixed-Descent Families of Southern New Zealand.* Wellington: Bridget Williams Books.

Wanhalla, A. 2013. *Matters of the Heart: A History of Interracial Marriage in New Zealand,* Auckland: Auckland University Press.

Ward, A. 1993. Historical Claims under the Treaty of Waitangi: Avenue of Reconciliation or Source of New Divisions? *Journal of Pacific History,* vol. 28, pp. 181–203.

Ward, A. 1999. *An Unsettled History: Treaty Claims in New Zealand Today.* Wellington: Bridget Williams.

Ward, A. n.d. Personal communication to M. Belgrave.

Ward, K. 1992. Making History in Mamre: Community Participation and Response in the Mamre History Society Project. At http://wiredspace.wits.ac.za/handle/10539/8121.

Wards, I. 1968. *The Shadow of the Land: A Study of British Policy and Racial Conflict in New Zealand 1832–1852,* Wellington: Historical Publications Branch Dept. of Internal Affairs.

Warner, K.D. 2007. The Quality of Sustainability: Agroecological Partnerships and the Geographic Branding of California Winegrapes. *Journal of Rural Studies,* vol. 23, no. 2, pp. 142–155.

Warren, L.S. 2005. *Buffalo Bill's America: William Cody and the Wild West Show.* New York: Alfred A. Knopf.

Warwick, C. 2012. *Digital Humanities in Practice*. London: Facet Publishing.

Waterfield, G. 1999. Paintings from the Russell-Cotes Art Gallery and Museum, Bournemouth. *The Magazine Antiques*, vol. 155, no. 6, pp. 858–865.

Waterson, M. 1994. *The National Trust: The First Hundred Years*. London: National Trust & BBC Books.

Weber, M. 1978 (1968). Bureaucracy. In *Economy and Society: An Outline of Interpretive Sociology*, eds. G. Roth and C. Wittich, pp. 956–1005. Berkeley: University of California Press.

Wehner, K. 2007. Exhibiting Australia: Developing the National Museum of Australia, 1997–2001. PhD thesis, New York University.

Wehner, K. 2012. Collection Stories. In *Collection Stories*, pp. 4–9. Canberra: National Museum of Australia Press.

Wehner, K. 2017. Placing the Nation: Curating Landmarks at the National Museum of Australia. In *Humanities for the Environment (HfE): Integrating Knowledges, Forging New Constellations of Practice*, eds. J. Adamson and M. Davis. London: Routledge.

Wehner, K. and M. Sear. 2010. Engaging the Material World: Object Knowledge and *Australian Journeys*. In *Museum Materialities: Objects, Engagements, Interpretations*, ed. S.H. Dudley, pp. 143–161. London: Routledge.

Weil, F. 2013. *Family Trees: A History of Genealogy in America*. New Haven: Harvard University Press.

Weil, S. 1990. *Re-Thinking the Museum and Other Meditations*. Washington, D.C.: Smithsonian University Press.

Weiner, E. 1999. "*Freizeitgestaltung* in Theresienstadt," in *Theatrical Performance during the Holocaust: Texts, Documents, Memoirs*, eds. R. Rovit and A. Goldfarb. Baltimore: Johns Hopkins University Press.

Weir, C. 1998. The Nottinghamshire Luddites: "Men Meagre with Famine, Sullen with Despair." *The Local Historian*, vol. 28, no. 1, pp. 24–35.

Weiser, J. 2012. The National Park Service's Mission Creep. American Enterprise Institute. August 20, 2012.

Weiss, C.H. and M.J. Bucuvalas. 1980. *Social Science Research and Decision-Making*. New York: Columbia University Press.

Weller, T. 2012. *History in the Digital Age*. London: Routledge.

Wells, P. 2007. New Labour and Evidence Based Policy Making: 1997–2007. *People, Place & Policy Online*, vol. 1, pp. 22–29.

Wells, R. 1988. *Wretched Faces. Famine in Wartime England, 1793–1801*. Gloucester: Sutton.

West, P. 1999. *Domesticating History: The Political Origins of America's House Museums*. Washington, D.C.: Smithsonian Institution Press.

Westerman, W. 1998. Central American Refugee Testimony and Performed Life Histories in the Sanctuary Movement. In *The Oral History Reader*, eds. R. Perks and A. Thomson, pp. 224–234. London: Routledge.

Weyeneth, R.R. 1994. History, He Wrote: Murder, Politics, and the Challenges of Public History in a Community with a Secret. *The Public Historian*, vol. 16, pp. 51–73.

Whalen, Z. and L.N. Taylor. (eds.) 2008. *Playing the Past: History and Nostalgia in Video Games*. Nashville: Vanderbilt University Press.

What We Have Learned: Principles of Truth and Reconciliation. Montreal and Kingston: McGill-Queen's University Press. 2015.

What Works Network. 2014. *What Works? Evidence for Decision Makers*. London: Cabinet Office.

Wheen, N.R. and J. Hayward. (eds.) 2012. *Treaty of Waitangi Settlements*. Wellington: Bridget Williams Books with the New Zealand Law Foundation.

Whisnant, A.M., M. Miller, G. Nash, and D. Thelen. 2011. *Imperiled Promise: The State of History in the National Park Service*. Bloomington: Organization of American Historians.

White, H. 2014. *The Practical Past*. Evanston, Illinois: Northwestern University Press.

White, H. 1973. *Metahistory: The Historical Imagination in Nineteenth-Century Europe*. Baltimore: Johns Hopkins University Press.

Whitehead, A. and J. Opp. 2013. Timescapes: Putting History in Your Hip Pocket. In *Proceedings of Computers and Their Applications Conference (CATA)*. March 2013. Hawaii, USA.

Whitford, T. and T. Pollard. 2009. For Duty Done: A WWI Military Medallion Recovered from the Mass Grave Site at Fromelles, Northern France. *Journal of Conflict Archaeology*, vol. 5, no. 1, pp. 201–229.

Wiedmer, C.A. 1999. *The Claims of Memory: Representations of the Holocaust in Contemporary Germany and France*. Ithaca, New York: Cornell University Press.

Wieviorka, M. 2013. *L'impératif numérique*. París: Éditions CNRS.

Willett, J. and R. Manheim. (eds). 1976. *Bertolt Brecht. Poems 1913–1956*. London: Methuen.

Williams, D.V. 2011. *A Simple Nullity? the Wi Parata Case in New Zealand Law and History*. Auckland: Auckland University Press.

Williams, M.M. 2015. *Panguru and the City: ka?inga tahi, ka?inga rua: An Urban Migration History*. Auckland: Auckland University Press.

Williams, P. 2012. *Collaboration in Public Policy and Practice: Perspectives on Boundary Spanners*. Bristol: Policy Press.

Willner, S. 2014. Fühlen mit Ötzi. Emotionale Stile des alpinen Wanderns und Konstruktionen prähistorischer Lebensrealitäten. *Geschichte als Erlebnis: Performative Praktiken in der Geschichtskultur Conference*. July 3–5, 2014. Zentrum für Zeithistorische Forschung, Potsdam.

Wilson, J. n.d. Review. Urban Cinefile. At http://www.urbancinefile.com.au/home/view.asp?a=7341&s=Reviews.

Wilson, S.D. 2005. Rediscovery: The African Burial Ground. *New York Journal of American History*, vol. 66, no. 2, pp. 58–61.

Windschuttle, K. 2001. How Not To Run a Museum. *Quadrant* (September), pp. 11–19.

Wineburg, S. 2001. *Historical Thinking and Other Unnatural Acts: Charting the Future of Teaching the Past*. Philadelphia: Temple University Press.

Winnerling, T. and F. Kerschbaumer, eds. 2014. *Early Modernity and Video Games*. Cambridge: Cambridge Publishers.

Winship, C. 2006. Policy Analysis as Puzzle Solving. In *The Oxford Handbook of Public Policy*, eds. M. Moran, M. Rein, and R.E. Goodin, pp. 109–123. Oxford: Oxford University Press.

Winter, J. 1995. *Sites of Memory, Sites of Mourning: The Great War in European Cultural History*. Cambridge: Cambridge University Press.

Winter, J. 2000. The Generation of Memory: Reflections on the "Memory Boom" in Contemporary Historical Studies. Bulletin of the GHI, vol. 27, pp. 3–33. At http://www.perspectivia.net/publikationen/bulletin-washington/2000-27-2/winter_generation.

Winter, J., and E. Sivan. 1999. *War and Remembrance in the Twentieth Century*. Cambridge: Cambridge University Press.

Winter, T. 2007. *Post-Conflict Heritage, Postcolonial Tourism: Culture, Politics and Development at Angkor*. London: Routledge.

Winter, T. 2015. Heritage Diplomacy. *International Journal of Heritage Studies*, vol. 21, no. 10, pp. 997–1015.

Wirth, C. National Park Service to All Field Offices. 1953. Securing Protection and Conservation Objectives through Interpretation. April 23, 1953.

Wirtz, L. 2012. Meetings of World History and Public History. In *A Companion to World History*, ed. D.T. Northrop, pp. 97–110. Chichester, West Sussex: Wiley-Blackwell.

Witcomb, A. 2003. *Reimagining the Museum: Beyond the Mausoleum*. London: Routledge.

Witcomb, A. 2006. How Style Came to Matter: Do We Need to Move Beyond the Politics of Representation? In *South Pacific Museums: Experiments in Culture*, eds. C. Healy and A. Witcomb, pp. 21.1–21.16. Melbourne: Monash University e-press.

Witcomb, A. 2009. Migration, Social Cohesion and Cultural Diversity: Can Museums Move Beyond Pluralism? *Humanities Research*, vol. 15, no. 2, pp. 49–66.

Witz, L. 2011. Revisualising Township Tourism in the Western Cape: The Migrant Labour Museum and the Re-Construction of Lwandle. *Journal of Contemporary African Studies*, vol. 29, no. 4, pp. 371–388.

Witz, L. and N. Murray. 2011. Writing Museum Biography: Displacing Development and Community in Lwandle. Politics of Heritage Conference, July 8–9, 2011. Johannesburg.

Witzke, T. n.d. *Megalithgräber und Menhire in Brandenburg.* At http://tw.strahlen.org/praehistorie/brandenburg.html.

Woetzel, H. 2007. *Steinzeit: Das Experiment. Germany.* Südwestrundfunk.

Wojdon, J. 2017. How to Make School History More Controversial. In *Teaching Rival Histories: Pedagogical Responses to the History and Culture Wars*, eds. R. Parkes, A. Clark, H. Åström Elmersjö, and M. Vinterek. Basingstoke: Palgrave Macmillan.

Wojdon, J. 2012. The Impact of Communist Rule on History Education in Poland. *Journal of Education, Media, Memory and Society*, vol. 4, no. 1, pp. 61–77.

Wojdon, J. 2013. When History Education Outruns Historical Research. *2013 Yearbook – Jahrbuch – Annales, Internation Society for History Didactics*, pp. 225–237. Wochenschau Verlag: Schwalbach/Ts.

Wolfinger, J. 2008. Historians and History Teachers. An Academic's Approach to Training High School Teachers. In *History Education One Zero One*, eds. W.J. Warren and D. Antonio Cantu, pp. 139–140. Charlotte: Information Age Publishing.

Wood, M. 2014. Bridging the Relevance Gap in Political Science. *Politics*, vol. 34, pp. 275–286.

Wood, R. 1993. Tourism in Southeast Asia. In *Tourism, Culture and the Sociology of Development*, eds. M. Hitchcock, V. King, and M. Parnwell, pp. 49–70. London: Routledge.

Woods, M. 2010. *Rural.* London: Routledge.

Woodward, W. and R. Smithers. 2003. Clarke Dismisses Medieval Historians. *The Guardian.* May 9, 2003. At http://www.theguardian.com/uk/2003/may/09/highereducation.politics.

Wormell, D. 1980. *Sir John Seeley and the Uses of History.* Cambridge: Cambridge University Press.

Worth Playing. 2008. Empire: Total War Developer Interview. At http://worthplaying.com/article/2008/12/1/interviews/57018/.

Wu, N. 2006. Transitional Justice and Historical Memories: Unfinished Project of Democratization of Taiwan. *Reflexion*, vol. 2, pp. 1–34.

Wu, R. 2008. Nation Building, Internal Colonialism and Cold War: The Historical Context of State Violence in Postwar Taiwan. In *The Road to Freedom: Taiwan's Postwar Human Rights Movement*, eds. Editorial Board of the Road to Freedom, pp. 168–174. Taipei: Dr. Chen Wen-chen Memorial Foundation.

Yad Vashem. n.d. The Central Database of Shoah Victims' Names. At http://db.yadvashem.org/names/search.html?language=en.

Yakel, E. 2004. Seeking Information, Seeking Connections, Seeking Meaning: Genealogists and Family Historians. *Information Research*, vol. 10.4, no. 1, pp. 10–11.

Yeats, C. 2008. The Impact of *Who Do You Think You Are?* On Archives Services in Australia. Conference paper. Annual Conference of the Australian Society of Archivists. August 6–9, 2008. Perth: Western Australia.

Yeh, H. 2009. The Artist's Tears. *Liberty Times Net.* December 14, 2009. At http://taiwantrc.org/images/images_read_article/read_article57_1.pdf (accessed March 15, 2015).

Yerushalmi, J.H. 1991. *Freud's Moses. Judaism Terminable and Interminable.* New Haven: Yale University Press.

Yoshino, A. n.d. The Bradford Pageant of 1931. "The Redress of the Past: Historical Pageants in Britain." At http://www.historicalpageants.ac.uk/featured-pageants/bradford-pageant-1931/.

Young, J.E. 1993. *The Texture of Memory: Holocaust Memorials and Meaning.* New Haven: Yale University Press.

Young, J.E. 1994. The Art of Memory: Holocaust Memorials in History. In *The Art of Memory: Holocaust Memorials in History*, ed. J.E. Young, pp. 19–38. New York: The Jewish Museum.

Young, J.E. 2002 (2000). *At Memory's Edge: After-Images of the Holocaust in Contemporary Art and Architecture*. New Haven: Yale University Press.

Yu, W-F. 2010. Statements to the Destruction of the Display of Contemporary Artwork "The Wall" at the Jing-Mei Human Rights Memorial Memorial and Cultural Parks by Wen Fu Yu's Studio. http://jingmei-contemporary.blogspot.tw/2010/02/blog-post.html.

Yurtseven, H.R. and N. Karakaş. 2013. Creating a Sustainable Gastronomic Destination: The Case of Cittaslow Gökçeada-Turkey. *American International Journal of Contemporary Research*, vol. 3, no. 3, pp. 91–100.

Zainaldin, J. 2013. Public Works: NEH, Congress, and the State Humanities Councils. *The Public Historian*, vol. 35, no. 1, pp. 28–50.

Zajda, J. and R. Zajda. 2003. The Politics of Rewriting History: New History Textbooks and Curriculum Materials in Russia. *International Review of Education*, vol. 49, no. 3/4, pp. 363–384.

Zeller, S. 1987. *Inventing Canada: Early Victorian Science and the Idea of a Transcontinental Nation*. Toronto: University of Toronto Press.

Zeller, S. 1996. *Land of Promise, Promised Land: The Culture of Victorian Science in Canada*. Ottawa: Canadian Historical Association.

Žižek, S. 1989. *The Sublime Object of Ideology*. London: Verso.

Žižek, S. 1992. *Enjoy Your Symptom: Jacques Lacan in Hollywood and Out*. New York: Routledge.

Zolfagharifard, E. 2014. Streets of London Now … and Then: Stand Still and Picture Yourself in History with App that Creates Hybrid Images of Present and Past. MailOnline. February 26, 2014. At http://www.dailymail.co.uk/sciencetech/article-2567739/Streetmuseum-app-creates-hybrid-images-London.html

Zubrzycki, J. 1992. *Ethnic Heritage: An Essay in Museology*. Canberra: National Museum of Australia.

Zuk, M. 2013. *Paleofantasy: What Evolution Really Tells Us about Sex, Diet, and How We Live*. New York: W. W. Norton.

Index

Note: page numbers in *italics* refer to illustrations and figures